AUSTRALIA

The Profit of the State

The Afflicted State

Uneasy City

Building the Trireme

First Blood

The Companion Guide to the Lake District

A History of Hong Kong

Dangerous Deceits

A History of South Africa

The Four Nations

AUSTRALIA

A NEW HISTORY OF THE GREAT SOUTHERN LAND

FRANK WELSH

THE OVERLOOK PRESS
Woodstock & New York

First published in the United States in 2006 by
The Overlook Press, Peter Mayer Publishers, Inc.
Woodstock & New York

Woodstock:
One Overlook Drive
Woodstock, NY 12498
www.overlookpress.com
[for individual orders, bulk and special sales, contact our Woodstock office]

New York:
141 Wooster Street
New York, NY 10012

Cataloging-in-Publication Data is available from the Library of Congress

Printed in the United States of America
ISBN 1-58567-692-6
1 3 5 7 9 8 6 4 2

For Lotte and Harry

Contents

4 Occupied Notices

5 Representative Government

6 The Capacity to Govern Themselves

7 The Transition to Responsible Government

8 Exploration and Expansion

9 Federation

10 The Commonwealth Feels its Way

11 War and Peace

List of Illustrations

Photographic acknowledgements are given in parentheses.

Acknowledgements

Where to begin? In the last six years or so of writing, generous help has been proffered by many people and organizations. Much of my research has been done in Sydney's State and Mitchell Libraries, whose staff have for long been patiently helpful, and whose library, shop and tea room are patterns of their kind. Thanks are also due to the staff of the La Trobe Collection in the Victoria State Library, the Battye Library in Perth, the John Oxley Library in Brisbane, the National Library and the National War Memorial in Canberra, the New South Wales Records Office, the Mortlock Library and the Art Gallery in Adelaide and the Darwin Museum and Library, the British Library, the Public Records Office and the Institute of Commonwealth Studies in London, the Cambridge and Durham University Libraries and Rhodes House Oxford. In the USA thanks are due to Hugh Howard of the State Department Archives, the staff of the Library of Congress and the National Archives in Washington and the George Bush Library in College Station, Texas. Robert Maxtone Graham provided one essential reference and Dick Brown an equally essential illustration.

Advice and guidance was welcomed from Robert Lawrie, Roger Bell, Elizabeth Warburton, Angus Trumble, Gerard Henderson and Bob MacIllrae. Henry Reynolds' and Carl Bridge's suggestions, corrections and emendations were invaluable: any errors remaining are due entirely to my own carelessness or perversity (or, as Dr Johnson was not ashamed to admit 'ignorance Madam, pure ignorance').

Hospitality from family and friends was essential, and greatly appreciated; to all the Eltringhams in Horsham, Fishers in Melbourne, Gaskells and Welshes in Sydney and Hoods in Brisbane, many thanks for sheltering and feeding Agnes and me, for indeed without them this book could not have been attempted. Getting to and from Australia was rendered slightly less painful by Jill Weston of Thomas Cook.

Both Stuart Proffitt and Liz Friend-Smith at Penguin Press have done far more than any reasonable person could expect in reading drafts and providing support and encouragement: Elizabeth Stratford performed the appalling task of copy-editing an idiosyncratic typescript, which she bore with admirable fortitude, and Richard Duguid faced the author's quibbles with calm forbearance. But when all is said and done, without the patient industry of Agnes, ably seconded by Kirsten, this book would never have been finished.

Maps

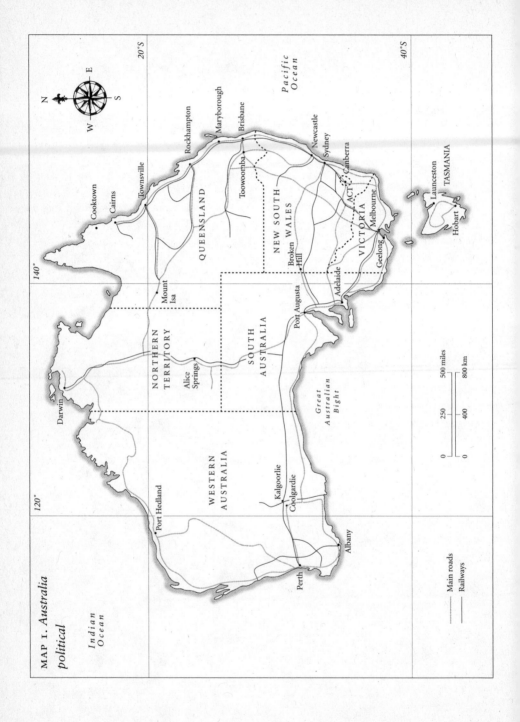

MAP 1. Australia political

N E S W (compass rose)

120° 140° 20'S 40'S

Indian Ocean

Pacific Ocean

Darwin

NORTHERN TERRITORY

Alice Springs

WESTERN AUSTRALIA

Port Hedland

Kalgoorlie
Coolgardie

Perth

Albany

Great Australian Bight

SOUTH AUSTRALIA

Mount Isa

QUEENSLAND

Cooktown
Cairns
Townsville

Rockhampton
Maryborough
Brisbane
Toowoomba

NEW SOUTH WALES

Broken Hill

Port Augusta
Adelaide

Newcastle
Sydney
Canberra
ACT
VICTORIA
Melbourne
Geelong

TASMANIA
Launceston
Hobart

0   250   500 miles
0   400   800 km

———— Main roads
———— Railways

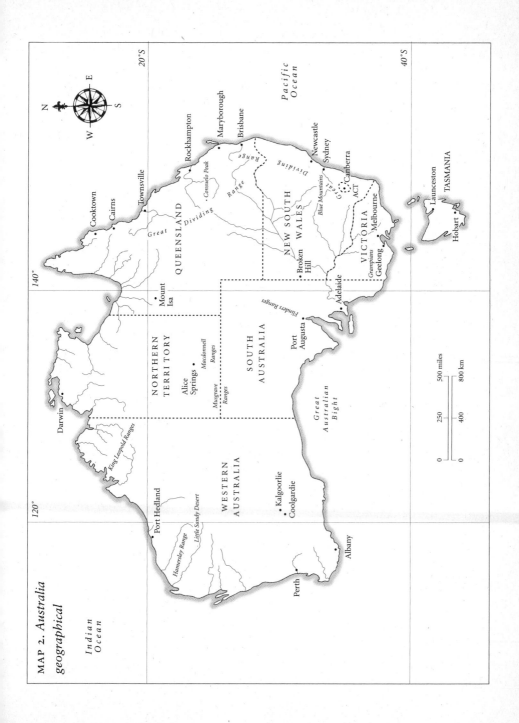

MAP 2. *Australia geographical*

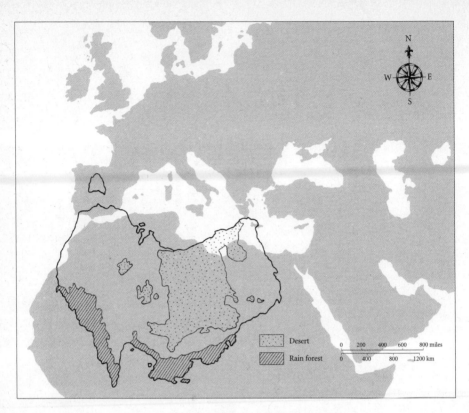

MAP 3. *Australia in the northern hemisphere*

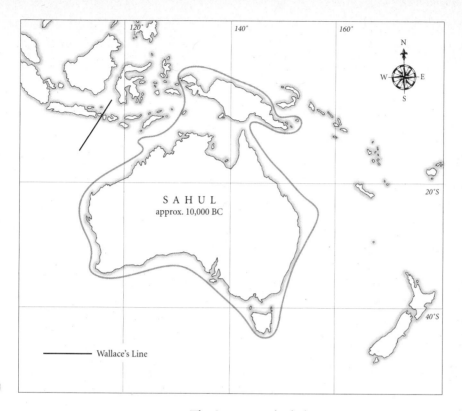

MAP 4. *The Continent of Sahul*
Wallace's Line commemorates the work of the nineteenth-century naturalist
Alfred Wallace, defining the division between Asian and Australasian flora and
fauna; but many Australasian species do not penetrate beyond the continental
shelf indicated here.

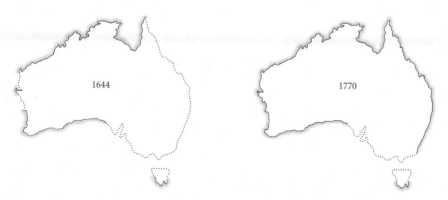

MAP 5. *Charting the coasts*
The dotted line represents uncharted coastline.

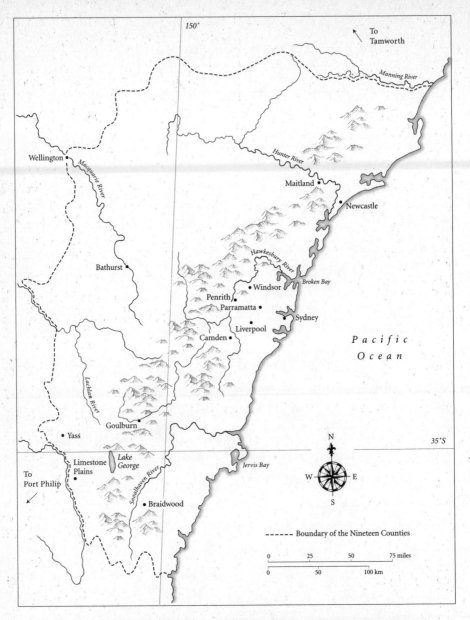

MAP 6. *The 'Nineteen Counties' – the settlement of New South Wales*
The Nineteen Counties comprise only about one-tenth of the present area of
New South Wales (500,000 square miles) but two-thirds of the state's
population live there.

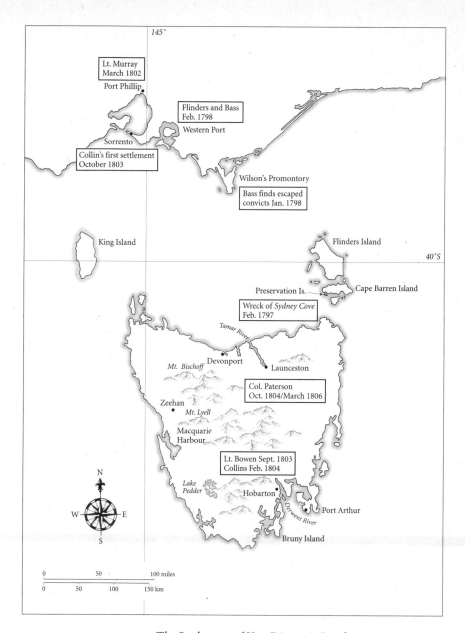

MAP 7. *The Settlement of Van Diemen's Land*
Geography dictates the pattern of settlement in Tasmania. A third of the total
area of 38,500 square miles is taken up by the rugged Western Tiers, which
include an extensive National Park. Hobart and Launceston, with populations
of some 200,000 and 100,000 respectively, are the only two large towns, some
100 miles apart. The most substantial of the other communities are strung along
the pleasant north coast.

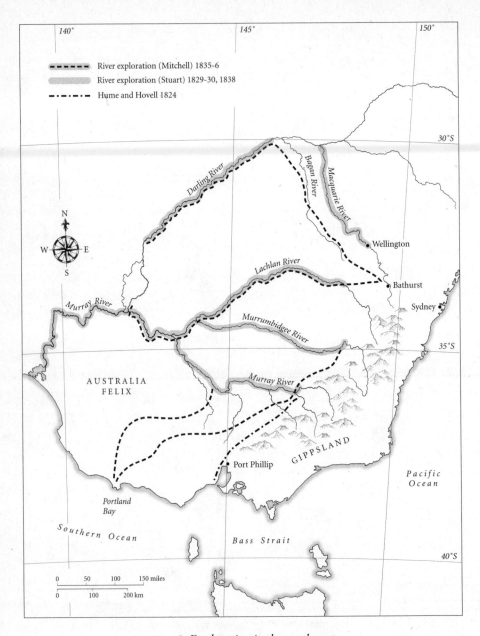

MAP 8. *Exploration in the south-east*

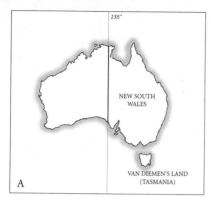

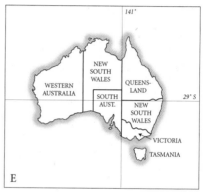

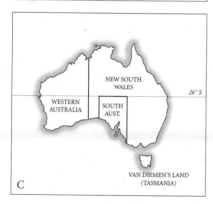

MAP 9. *One colony to six in seventy-five years*

A. *1786*: New South Wales, as annexed in 1770: the mother colony. At the time Van Diemen's Land was not known to be an island.

B. *1827*: The boundary of Western Australia fixed at 129 degrees east. From 1825 Van Diemen's Land government separated from New South Wales.

C. *1836*: South Australia carved out of the enlarged New South Wales: the dog-leg appears.

D. *1851*: Followed by the little state of Victoria, soon to be richer than the mother colony.

E. *1859*: New South Wales split by the new colony of Queensland, north of 29 degrees south.

F. *1861*: The problem solved by extending South Australia north and west to the Western Australian border, eliminating the dog-leg and providing an uncomfortable problem for South Australia in the north. Queensland is allowed an extension westwards, which includes Mount Isa.

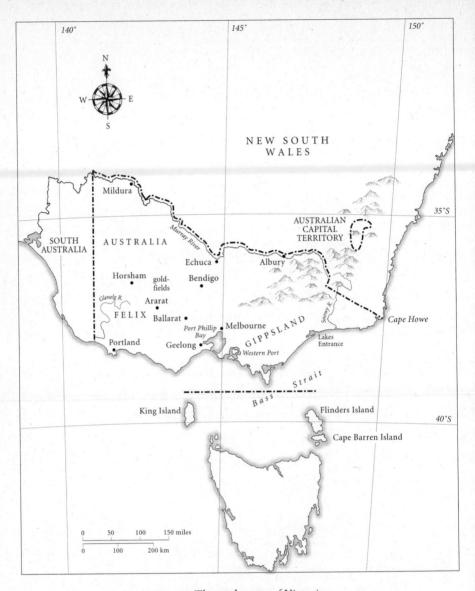

MAP 10. *The settlement of Victoria*

The only Australian state, apart from little Tasmania, to be on a European
geographic scale, about the same size as Great Britain. The population density,
at 19.2 inhabitants per square kilometre, is by some way the highest of any
Australian state, although the total population at some 4.2 million is very much
less than that of Great Britain (approx. 57 million). Like all other Australian
states, most people live in the capital – nearly 3 million in Melbourne, and
another quarter of a million in the nearby cities of Geelong and Ballarat, the
largest towns in the state after Melbourne (the other goldfields town of Bendigo,
population 60,000, is the fourth biggest).

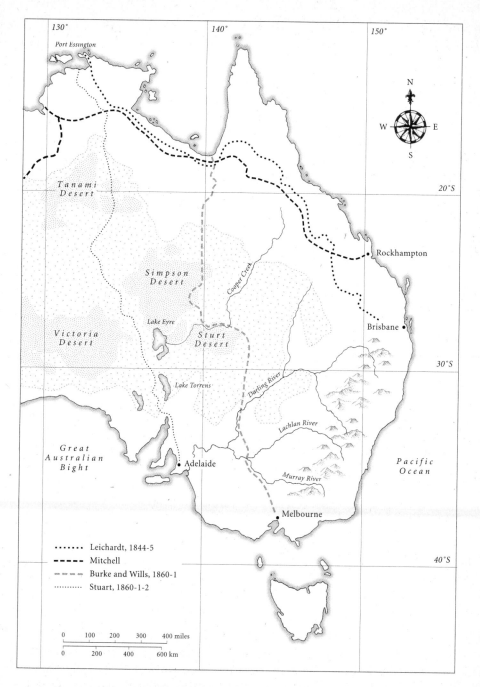

MAP II. *Transcontinental expeditions*

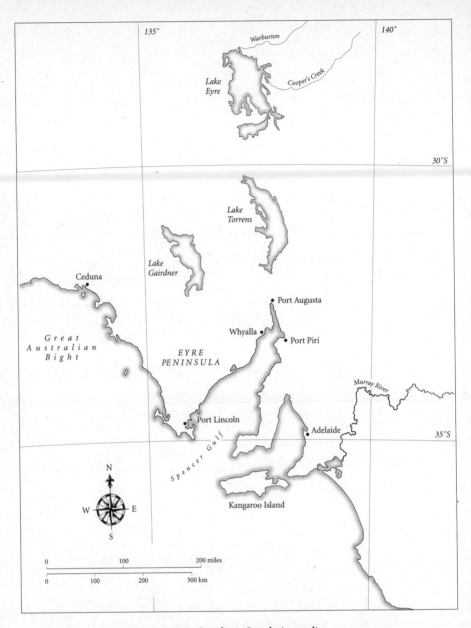

MAP 12. *Southern South Australia*

Perhaps three-quarters of South Australia's million and a half people live in the capital Adelaide and in the towns around the Spencer Gulf. To a great extent this concentration is dictated by the rainfall. By far the greatest part of the state is desert or semi-desert; Adelaide is the dryest of all Australian capitals. Only three indifferent roads lead north past the great salt lakes Eyre and Torrens across the near-1,000-mile border with the Northern Territory and Queensland.

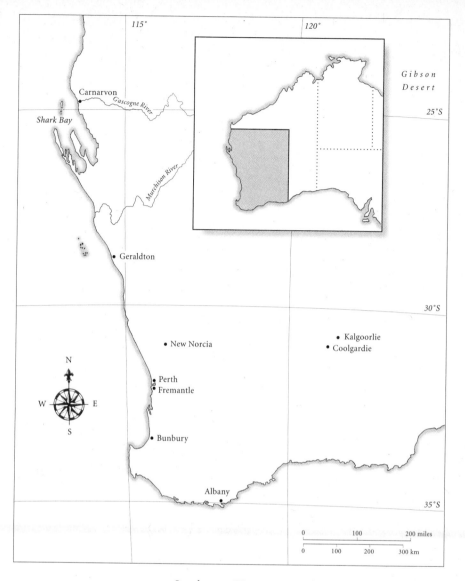

MAP 13. *South-west Western Australia*
Western Australia's population is overwhelmingly concentrated around the
capital, Perth – some 1.3 million of a total of 1.8 million. Geraldton, 350 miles
to the north, is the only sizeable town between Perth and the Timor Sea coast at
Cape Londonderry – and Geraldton has fewer than 30,000 inhabitants. In the
nearly 2,000 miles as the crow flies between Geraldton and the most northerly
settlement at Wyndham the only centre of population is at Port Hedland. With
an area of one and a half million square miles (India's 2 million square miles
shelters more than a thousand millions), Western Australia is one of the world's
most sparsely populated states.

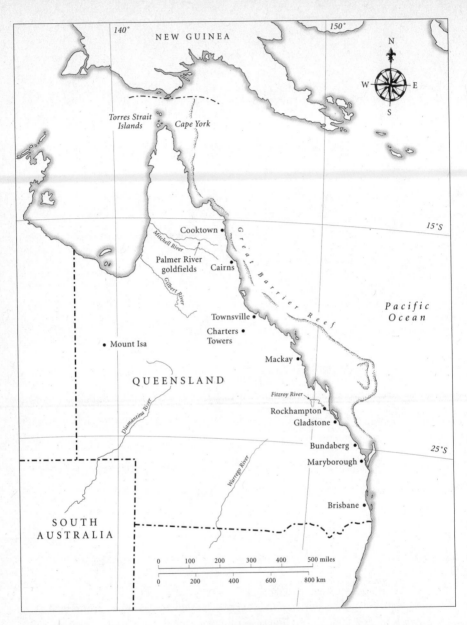

MAP 14. *Queensland*

The towns of Australia's second largest state (1,070,000 square miles) follow the east coast, more than 1,000 miles of settlement from Cooktown, where Captain Cook careened the *Endeavour*, to the Gold Coast, which straddles the border with New South Wales. The only inland settlement of any consequence is Mount Isa, 500 miles west of Townsville. The state's northern boundary is formed by the islands of Badu and Saibi, only 10 miles from the New Guinea mainland.

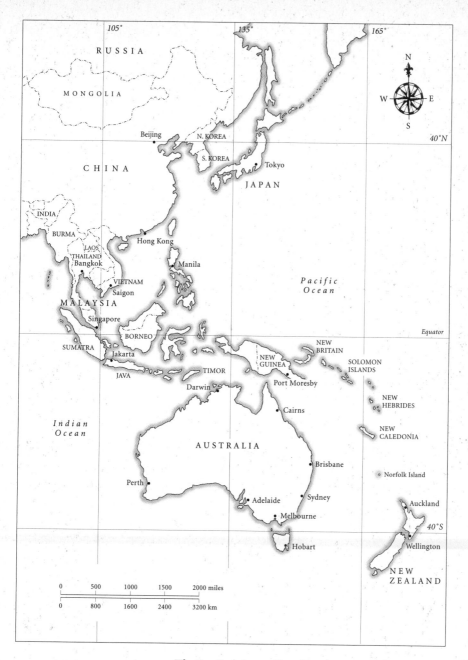

MAP 15. *The Far East is our Near North*
Darwin is equidistant from Hobart and Saigon (and notably nearer to Vietnam
by sea); Perth is closer to Jakarta than to Sydney; Melbourne is as near to the
Antarctic pack ice as to northern Queensland. Sydney is the only state capital
within easy reach of Canberra; from Perth, Darwin, Hobart and Brisbane air
travel is essential.

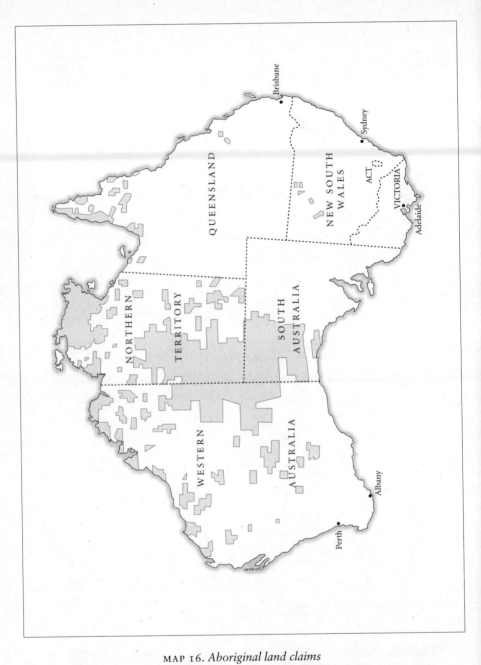

MAP 16. *Aboriginal land claims*
After the 1992 Mabo case, Aboriginal title was widely recognized; but as a
comparison with the extent of hardened roads illustrates, this was in the least
accessible and inhabited parts of the country.

Introduction

THE BEST COUNTRY IN THE WORLD?

In the course of writing this book some polite surprise has been expressed that an English writer should be attempting a history of Australia. Only very occasionally was there a hint of a subtext – what does this Pommie think he knows about our country? I could, defensively, reply that I have known Australia for more than thirty years, travelled over thousands of miles of it and am part of an extended Australian family, established for many generations, which now includes two of our own grandchildren; and perhaps hint that I have read not a little on the subject. In fact, I would use none of these excuses, but say straight out that I have spent five years on the task because I love the place and the people and that it is a privilege to write about them. Australia is probably the most successful society in the world and the most agreeable to live in.

This personal view has official support. With commendable assiduity the United Nations compiles, each year, a sort of international merit table, the Human Development Index. Countries are awarded points for their achievements in education and health care, weighting the cruder measurement of prosperity, measured by GDP (Gross Domestic Product). At the head of the list there are a few surprises; the United States never quite makes it to the top – its education indexes are a little less good than that of New Zealand, at number 19, and its life-expectancy is only marginally ahead of Cuba's, at number 55. Similarly Ireland, with a GDP equal to that of Norway at number 1, appears only at number 18, pulled down by lower health and educational statistics. Positions change from year to year, affected primarily by swings in GDP, but one reliable constant is that the former British colonies, Canada and Australia, are among the top five, often as number 2 and 3 respectively.[1]

Quite why this should be so provokes some interesting questions. Both countries outperform France, Germany and Britain. Together with the

United States, Japan and New Zealand, they are the only non-European countries in the top twenty. If one were to throw in a few other comparative statistics – on crime, violence, individual freedoms, a humane code of justice – Canada and Australia would be even more firmly entrenched in leading places, and the United States, currently at number 6, relegated somewhat lower. What is more, Australia's upward movement has been steady. Since 1975 it has overtaken eight other countries that then ranked higher (and one of these was New Zealand!). Statistics afford amusement to statisticians, but are uncertain guides to making decisions. Who, for example would prefer to live in Iceland (number 7) than Greece (number 24)? With Australia's range of climate, its excellent wines and food (pity about the beer), it would not be too difficult to dislodge Canada and Norway and to place a triumphant Australia as the most desirable country in the world in which to live; and one would not be very wrong in so doing.

One of the aims of this book is to trace the process and explain the reasons for Australia's success and its emergence as an exemplar of what might be called Western, or liberal democratic values. (I own to some reservations as to the specificity of this description; I have observed, in the course of writing their histories, that such things as a rule of law, free media, personal security, the ability to express peaceful dissent and to participate in the processes of government are quite as much valued in Hong Kong or South Africa as in any Western democracy. It is usually unpleasantly authoritarian governments who appeal to 'Asian' or 'African' values to excuse their denial of freedoms.) One particularly striking characteristic of Australian history is the speed of development. French and British societies in North America can trace their origins to the sixteenth century, but the British occupation of Australia took place two centuries later. For the first generation the settlements in New South Wales and Van Diemen's Land were unequivocal penal colonies, with representative civil institutions dating only from the 1820s, yet a mere thirty years later those colonies were self-governing societies where democratic constitutions were well in advance of those in Britain. Transported convicts, their sentences served, sat in the new Legislative Assemblies, elected by manhood suffrage, including those of two more colonies, Victoria and South Australia which in 1820 had barely been glanced at and where no settlement had been attempted – and two more, Western Australia and Queensland, waited in the wings.

By the end of the century colonial statesmen, many of them Australian-born, were designing a constitution for a continental nation, which was duly inaugurated in January 1901, under the beneficent, if by then somewhat bewildered aegis of old Queen Victoria, who had been born in those earliest days, when New South Wales and Van Diemen's Land were still penal colonies controlled by Governors with autocratic powers.

Moreover, the famous fight at the Eureka stockade aside, all had been done by argument, election and compromise. There had been no liberation struggle, no revolutionary dissenters, no painful wrench from the mother country, and government had succeeded government, often with alarming rapidity, but always following the results of elections which were free, fair and unprecedentedly democratic.

Although it would be extremely difficult to find a parallel for such success, one group of Australians had little reason to celebrate the foundation of a new nation and a new century. The original inhabitants, the Aborigines, had been allowed only limited participation in political life. Indeed, at the time, it was widely assumed that they represented nothing more than the dying remnants of a race and of a culture, of little value in the brisk modern world of 1901.

More recently, heated debate has erupted over the extent to which blame should be allocated for what might be described as attempted genocide, as historians dispute the statistics of frontier violence and dispossession.[2] Impatience, insensibility, greed and cruelty certainly went hand in hand with some restrained goodwill and acceptance of responsibility, but the outcome was probably inevitable. The British had for long been distinguished global expansionists, establishing both informal and official influence in and over a substantial part of the world's people. For quite a brief period – to attempt a definition between the end of the Napoleonic wars in 1815 and the upsurge of American imperialism with the assault on the Spanish empire in 1898 – Britain also occupied a unique position. Not only was it an intellectual and technological powerhouse, but it was the only country capable of insisting on fulfilling a world role.

The words have to be chosen carefully, for Victorian Britain, with a relatively small army, and that more than fully occupied with India and its neighbours, was by no means a world power, or even less *the* world power, as is twenty-first-century America. It was rather that control of the seas and of a good deal of the world's resources, with the City of London its unquestioned financial centre, gave the British the habit of thinking and acting on a world stage which the United States has still to develop. In the process, the British developed an uncommonly good conceit of themselves, which subsequent encounters with reality have still not entirely dispelled.

The first Australians were poorly equipped to face the intrusion of so confident and well-equipped a people. Aboriginal societies were fragmented, lacking the numbers and cohesion to mount a sustained resistance, as did the Maori in neighbouring New Zealand, or indeed the offshore islanders in the Timor Sea. During their long near-isolation – 10,000–12,000 years since the inundation of the land bridges which joined the land mass to the neighbouring islands, and much longer since the original migration perhaps 50,000 years ago – Australians, other than those living on the north coast, had little or no contact with other societies' ideas or technologies. Other groups – Inuit, South African Bushmen, Amazonian Indians among many – had developed a similar understanding of their environment, and were able to exercise a degree of control over the most unpromising circumstances, but few had done it in such isolation. A fully developed belief system sanctified Aboriginal Australian relationships and satisfied emotional needs, but was wholly unequipped to cope with intrusion and innovation. The arrival of even a small number of representatives of the most advanced and active of societies, accompanied as they were by rum, tobacco and all manner of new diseases, was, with the best will in the world, certain gravely to damage Aboriginal societies; and good will was relatively quickly expended. But the most serious criticism is that during more than a century of Australian self-government most Aborigines were simply not acknowledged as members of society, equal partners in the nation, and suffered accordingly.

In the absence of written records, and given the disparate opinions of archaeologists, so often contentious and variable as new evidence emerges, Aboriginal history before the British occupation must be largely conjectural. The task is made more difficult by modish theorists who claim that any descriptions of autochthonous Australians should only be attempted by their descendants – a rapidly increasing group, if official statistics can be trusted. Some attempt has even been made to restrict the circulation of researches on Aboriginal cultures, although such obscurantism is usually deplored by librarians.[3] Since the process by which Aboriginal societies have been shattered, or absorbed, or survived, forms an important part of Australian history and remains a subject of often indignant dispute such sensibilities are here discounted.

If the first colonial century had seen rapid movement, political and social development in the second, following Federation, was more measured. The social compact that accompanied Federation, and which in some measure still survives, continued well into the second half of the twentieth century; during most of this period both Australia and New Zealand shared British values without much question. The King Emperor Edward VII and his successors were accepted as heads of an Australian state, and in each war or international crisis Australia hurried to support Britain. All this changed as for the first time, in 1941, world war came to the Pacific, which for so long had deserved its name. Australia became a front-line combatant, with the assumed protection of an Imperial Britain snatched away by a successful Japanese initiative, to be replaced by a worried and one-sided alliance with the United States. Any future conflict was as likely to take place in the Pacific area as in any other part of the globe, and Australia's participation would be almost certain, as wars in Korea and Vietnam both proved.

Post-war Australians reacted to changed circumstances as new realism forced painful alterations to the old Federation concordat. Immigrants, who (except for those from Britain) had been severely restricted, were encouraged, at first as long as they were suitably pigmented, but later with increasing tolerance shown for Asians, if qualified and prosperous. Government control over labour, ensured by wage controls and arbitration, was relaxed, and the Australian dollar exposed to foreign exchange markets. With the British unilateral declaration of independence symbolized by its entry into the European Community, new markets had to be sought in Asia for Australian products: and it was to be on agriculture and minerals rather than a developed manufacturing industry that Australian prosperity depended.

One aspect of Australia's success evidently lies in the great expanse of rich agricultural land producing an astonishing range of food and drink, from Queensland's mangoes and coffee to Tasmanian cheese and apples, and some of the world's best wines; while wool, the foundation of nineteenth-century prosperity, remains a major export, Australia being by far the world's largest producer. Mineral resources seem inexhaustible, Australia ranking among the world's most prolific producers of iron ore, coal, copper, gold, silver, lead, zinc, nickel, aluminium, magnesium and uranium, with access to the potentially rich Timor Sea oilfields and Western Australian natural gas.

But, as the example of such countries as Brazil indicates, bountiful natural resources do not alone ensure stable prosperity. Australian fidelity to parliamentary democracy has been an essential factor; for a century and a half statues of Queen Victoria have looked down benignly on a succession of state and Federal governments, brought to power by democratic election. Indeed, it might be thought that the country is surfeited with democracy, with compulsory voting, often of fiendish complexity, in a proliferation of state and commonwealth elections at unsettlingly frequent intervals, combined with a popular conception, by no means unfounded, that many politicians have their own welfare primarily at heart.

If Australia has made an outstandingly successful adjustment to post-war problems, another question is presented. Do Australians themselves fully appreciate the magnitude of their achievements? Given the ebullient self-confidence of a test match crowd this may sound absurd, but self-doubt is evident in many aspects of society. The magnificent new Melbourne Museum, a monument to fashionable socio-political concepts, provides no indication of the Colony of Victoria's progress from 1834, when a police magistrate, a file of soldiers and a few convicts were sent from Sydney to keep an eye on the handful of Tasmanians who had brought their families and sheep to the south coast, to 1857, when the first democratically elected Victorian Legislative Assembly met in the thriving city of Melbourne.[4] It is true that there are less pleasant aspects of Australian society: one of the world's highest rates on clinical depression; the highest expenditure on gambling; the highest proportion of serious assaults; persistent examples of petty corruption; the harsh treatment of illegal immigrants and the miserable condition of some Aborigines. No country is without reproach, many much more serious, but it seems that Australian opinion-formers are reluctant to accept that they live in what is indeed a lucky country with an exceptional record of achievement.[5]

Part of Australian unease is due to a sense of isolation. Among Australia's neighbours stable democracy is an exotic plant. At best, relations have been mutually wary, and at worst openly hostile; since the end of the Second World War Australian troops have been engaged in Korea, Vietnam, Indonesia, Malaya, Timor, Kuwait and Iraq, often indeed in defence of established governments, and as part of an alliance with Britain or the United States. Such interventions have often been opposed, sometimes vigorously, and to many Asians Australia appears as an integral part of American imperialism, an impression recently reinforced by the government's enthusiasm for a conflict with Iraq, a country totally outside any Australian sphere of interest. On the other hand, the aftermath of the terrorist bombing in Bali in October 2002 has brought Australia and Indonesia closer together, and relations with China have developed smoothly.

To a very great extent this impression reflects reality. Australian values – a passion for fair play, plain speaking, equal opportunities – are those of both Britain and the United States; a total lack of deference and a happy hedonism respectively differentiate Australia from the other two. Australia is, too, more homogenous than the United States, still predominantly Anglo-Celtic in spite of European and Asian post-war immigration; and Americans do not take much interest in those antipodean passions, cricket and the three forms of rugby football.[6] Half a world away from its natural friends, and allies, with only New Zealand in support, Australia is uncomfortably placed geographically. With New Zealand, Japan and the United States, perhaps to be joined by Russia and the western Latin American states, Australia is best defined as a Pacific rather than an Asian power.

The sense of isolation, albeit now diminishing as communications have improved, has driven Australians abroad in an influential diaspora. Rupert Murdoch's position as the most powerful figure in the world's media owes something to his very Australian ability to operate in both America and Britain, to say nothing of such countries as China. Australians, particularly young Australians, are internationalists, finding it much easier than Americans or even Britons to become citizens of the world, self-confident, sure of making themselves comfortable wherever they are. And doing so especially in the arts, with a specifically Australasian style, spontaneous and relaxed, more ironic and tangential than the American model, expressed with the help of a vigorous vocabulary and exemplified by outstanding talents such as those of Cate Blanchett, Nicole Kidman, Sam Neill, Geoffrey Rush, Russell Crowe, Naomi Watts, Peter Weir, Peter Jackson and the incomparable Barry Humphries.

Thirty years and more ago, on my first flight to Australia, I talked to a Queen's Messenger, one of that very select band of former officers, wearing a silver greyhound badge, charged to carry the most sensitive documents to foreign parts. He defined himself as an Australian Briton, from a family living in Australia for a number of generations, but firmly British. Today, I suspect, this would not be so. After Britain's entry into the European Community, the old Imperial ties have been loosened, although Britain still contributes the largest proportion of immigrants, and many Britons have Australian kin. Americans, on the other hand, rarely visit and almost never emigrate; awareness of Australia is, apart from that engendered by Crocodile Dundee, unusual. Bill Bryson revealed the paucity of reporting in Australia in the *New York Times*, compared, for example, with that of Peru – 20 Australian articles in 1997 as opposed to 120 – 'about level with Belarus and Burundi'.[7]

Available histories are not too helpful in explaining Australia to the world: although Australian history is a thriving subject in Australia, with many excellent works published each year (to which this book owes much), they are almost all written from an Australian point of view by resident historians, and rarely place Australia clearly in the world context; such critical events as the 1850 British Whig government's decision to allow the colonies to devise their own forms of government, or the American expansion in the Pacific, are not allotted their real importance. The one widely read work, Robert Hughes's *The Fatal Shore*, brilliantly written and well documented, concerns itself only with the convict story and therefore presents a partial view of true developments; and the frequent popular returns to the Ned Kelly story, which invariably present that murderous horse-thief as an exemplar of romantic heroism, do little to illuminate the truth of Australian history.

This book is therefore primarily an attempt to explain to the rest of the world how this remarkable society has evolved, a continental nation.

AUSTRALIA

I

Terra Australis Nondum Cognita

Terra Nullius?

The future of the world should have been decided at a meeting on 7 June 1494 between representatives of King João II of Portugal and King Ferdinand of Aragon and Castile. Alternately bribed by Ferdinand – the Borgia pope was a devoted family man, and his children Lucrezia and Cesare had expensive tastes – and threatened by João, Pope Alexander VI had decided that those parts of the world still to be discovered were to be shared between the two Iberian kingdoms. By the Treaty of Tordesillas, confirmed by a papal Bull, all lands as yet unknown west of a line drawn 370 leagues (about 1,175 miles) from the Cape Verde islands were to be Spanish, those to the east Portuguese.[1]

It was Cristoforo Colombo's accidental encounter with the American continent that precipitated the argument. Before Colombo's expedition, financed by Spain, the Portuguese had been the leaders in exploration. Initially encouraged by Dom Henrique, Iffante of Portugal (grandson of King Edward III of England and known to the English as Prince Henry the Navigator), Portuguese sailors had been nosing their way down the west coast of Africa and out into the Atlantic since the early years of the century. The Canary Islands and the Azores had already been discovered – in the sense of being shown on charts, although Arab geographers had earlier at least known of their existence – by about 1350, but the first Portuguese expedition was to Madeira, in 1420. Five years later the port of Ceuta, on the African coast opposite Gibraltar, was captured by the Portuguese. Gibraltar remained in Muslim hands, but the Moorish hold on southern Spain was slipping, and by the end of the century the passage from the Mediterranean to the Atlantic would be in Christian control. This was of particular importance, since the rapid expansion of Turkish power threatened to interrupt land communications with the East. Only Constantinople itself was holding out, and that precariously. Even if the Turkish empire allowed the precious spices and silks from India and China to pass through to Western Europe, high duties were likely to be added to the already expensive costs of caravan transport. Since a small Portuguese caravel with a twenty-man crew could carry the loads of a thousand camels, a sea route to Asia was an objective worth much effort.

Bartolomeu Dias was able to report the first stage towards this goal in 1488, after he had rounded the Cape of Good Hope and thereby proved the existence of a possible passage to India. He was followed by Vasco da Gama, who in May 1498 sailed past the Cape into the Indian Ocean to land on the coast of India, thus succeeding where Colombo had failed and opening up the Orient to Portuguese commerce.

Spain and Portugal were at that time the only maritime powers to have demonstrated a persistent interest in exploration. King Henry VII of England had defied the papal edict, but the English voyages to Newfoundland between 1498 and 1506 were not followed up by King Henry VIII, who had pressing concerns of a different nature. The Treaty of Tordesillas was therefore reasonable enough, and its effects have, in part, endured. Brazil, undiscovered at the time of the treaty, remains Portuguese-speaking, the rest of South America Hispanophone (and much of North America as well); relics of the Portuguese empire persisted until recently in Angola, Mozambique, Macao and Timor. One substantial part of the regions allotted by the Pope however, remained, undiscovered and unclaimed.

For many hundreds of years the existence of a great southern continent was acknowledged by European geographers to be at least possible, even if nothing whatsoever was known of it. It was only reasonable, they argued, that the great land masses of the northern hemisphere (medieval scholars were rarely flat-earthers) should be balanced by a southern equivalent. Indeed, argued the great sixteenth-century cartographer Mercator, were there to be no compensating southern land mass, the world would surely fall to destruction among the stars.[2] 'Terra Australis Incognita' or 'Nondum cognita' – the unknown southern land – therefore appeared on European maps as an amorphous mass on the edge of the southern seas. Imperial China, convinced that its own land was the centre of the world, evinced only modest interest in distant regions, but accepted a regular supply of dried sea slugs (Holothurius edulis, the constituent of a glutinous soup much esteemed – by Chinese) from the northern coasts of Terra Australis. Professor Joseph Needham, the great authority on Chinese history, believes that Chinese visitors came there in the fifteenth century, when the last of great Chinese voyages of exploration, under the eunuch admiral Cheng Ho, quartered the Indian Ocean; the evidence, however, is fragmentary.[3] The fact that Marco Polo[4] refers to a 'Great Java' lying just to the south of 'Lytil Java' may suggest that medieval Chinese were aware of the existence of a southern continent, but if so they ignored it.

Authorized by the Treaty of Tordesillas, and with a foothold established by da Gama, Portuguese adventurers and missionaries streamed across the Indian Ocean; Goa fell to Alonso d'Albuquerque in 1510, Malacca, the key to the South China Sea, and the Moluccas, the Spice Islands (whence came such immensely valuable culinary spices as peppers and nutmegs), were discovered in the following year by Francisco Señao. By 1515 a Portuguese fort protected the settlement at Colombo in Ceylon. St Francis Xavier landed in Japan in 1547, and in 1557 the port of Macao was granted by the Chinese emperor as a Portuguese trading post. In this way a chain of safe havens was available to Portuguese sailors, from the coast of Brazil to the furthest Indies.

Another agreement with Spain was needed to settle the line of demarcation in the east to match that in the west agreed at Tordesillas, and a conference was accordingly held on the border of the two countries between Badajoz and Elvas, this time without papal assistance, and with the geographical facts still imperfectly understood. It was left to both sides to agree on a boundary, which was fixed by Portugal considerably further to the west, at 51 degrees, marked by the mouth of the Waipoco River. If this line were to be extended round the globe to 129 degrees east, all the interesting regions, including China, India and the Spice Islands would go to Portugal, leaving Spain with most of New Guinea, a deeply unattractive spot, and a scatter of Pacific islands as yet unknown. Such an outcome was totally unacceptable to the ambitious young emperor, Charles V, who had inherited, along with his imperial title, a good deal of Germany, Spain, Burgundy, Flanders, Naples and all Spanish America. The ensuing conflict left Portugal with all her eastern rights intact, with the exception of the Philippines, acknowledged to be Spanish.

That unknown continent south of Java, divided as it is by 129 degrees east, would, when anyone chanced upon it, therefore be claimed both by Portugal and by Spain. For the moment, however, that was unlikely. Both Spaniards and Portuguese were operating around the Equator, and all Portuguese seamen followed the same route, from Lisbon to the Brazilian coast, then slanting across the South Atlantic and the Indian Ocean to their trading posts on the west coast of India (the Portuguese steered clear of the Cape of Good Hope after one viceroy on his way to the Indies was killed by the inhabitants). Once the Spanish were established on the western coast of South America, communications with the Philippines led to the first explorations of the Pacific, and in 1528 Alvaro de Saavedra sailed along the north coast of the great island later named Nueva Guinea by Inigo Ortez. This had, however, already been sighted by the Portuguese Jorge de Meneses and named Os Papuas, 'frizzle-haired', apparently a term used by the Moluccan traders to describe the inhabitants. If Portuguese or Spanish explorers went far enough south to encounter Terra Australis,[5] they left no record of their landings, other than information which found its way on to a number of sixteenth-century French maps; the argument on the subject continues.

The Pope's original adjudication did not survive unchallenged, as the newly independent and fiercely Protestant United Provinces of the Netherlands paid it no attention. The Dutch had been fighting for freedom from Spanish rule since the 1570s and considered that the world's trade belonged to those powers strong enough to take it. From the end of the sixteenth century Dutch adventurers started to displace the Portuguese who were already settled in Asia. Portugal was in no position to offer too much resistance, since it had been annexed to the Spanish crown in 1580, and Spain was fully occupied in trying to protect its extensive interests in the Americas. The Dutch effort, originally incoherent and economically uncompetitive – no fewer than sixty-five ships left Holland for the Indies in 1601 – was organized the next year by the formation of a chartered monopoly, the Vereenigde Oost-Indische Compagnie, commonly known as the VOC – the United East India Company – tightly controlled by a board of directors, the Heeren XVII in Amsterdam. The next few years saw VOC trading posts established over nearly 1,500 miles of the Java Sea, from Bantam on the island of Java to the islands of Amboina and Banda off the western coast of New Guinea, which marked the most southerly point of European exploration. By the end of the century descriptions of the undiscovered continent began filtering through. 'The south land', the Dutch geographer Cornelius Wytfliet reported, 'extends immediately towards the Polar circle, but also towards the countries of the East – separated by a narrow strait it lies in front of New Guinea, but has been explored only at a few coastal places.' That was published in 1597, presumably from accounts of previous voyages.[6]

The VOC wasted no time in exploring their newly acquired territory. In 1605 the Governor of Amboina, Cornelis de Houtman, despatched a small ship, the *Duyfken*, under the command of Willem Janszoon, to have a closer look at the south coast of New Guinea. What he found was hardly encouraging, since half his crew were murdered by 'the very barbarous' natives, and he found white people, presumably Portuguese, established on the southern shores. Steering away to the south, Janszoon encountered hitherto uncharted land, which he assumed to be part of New Guinea. It was in fact the western shore of the Cape York peninsula on the Australian mainland, which Janzsoon then followed for some 200 miles (his furthest point is still known as Cape Keerweer – 'Turnabout'). The first encounter between Europeans and Australians was not propitious. One of the *Duyfken*'s crew was killed, and Janszoon returned to port, having found 'no good to be done there'. An interesting example of the international nature of the eastern trade was the fact that Janszoon's return was related by the Tamil master of a Banda ship to the English East India Company's agent at Bantam, John Saris.[7]

The *Duyfken*'s voyage, otherwise fruitless, at least enabled the VOC to fend off the incursions of a prospective competitor, the Dutch Australia Company, by citing Janszoon's journals as proof of their own efforts at exploration, but subsequent attempts to find something useful in Terra Australis were no more encouraging. The ruthless expansionism of Jan Pieterszoon Coen, from 1619 the first Governor General of the VOC's eastern possessions, with his headquarters at the new port of Batavia, led to another expedition in 1623, hoping to discover a passage between Cape York and New Guinea that would lead into the Pacific, thus avoiding the Spanish in the Philippines (the fact that Luis Vaez de Torres had actually found a passage – the Torres Strait – at the same time that Janszoon was 'discovering' Australia had prudently been kept secret by the Spaniards). Captain Jan Carstenszoon, commanding the *Arnhem* and *Pera*, failed to find the straits, but did succeed in charting more of the coastline, extending Janszoon's exploration of the Cape York peninsula and cutting north-west across the Gulf of Carpentaria to the tip of what is now called, in recognition of his discovery, Arnhem Land. Foiled by shallows and strong easterly winds from penetrating the straits, Carstenszoon presumed that the land he sighted intermittently was all a continuation of the New Guinea coastline, but he noticed a striking difference between the inhabitants of New Guinea itself and the Torres Strait Islands and those of what was in fact the Australian mainland. The former were bold and aggressive, cannibals wearing strings of human teeth around their necks, with fearsome swordfish teeth thrust through their noses, manning large canoes, whilst the Cape York men were 'less cunning, bold and evil natured', carrying 'weapons less deadly than those we have seen used by other blacks', mingling unconcernedly with the sailors, and having one of their number kidnapped as a result. Once more the reports sent to headquarters were gloomy. There was no sign of spices or gold, indeed 'We have not seen one fruit-bearing tree, nor anything that man could make use of; there are no mountains or even hills . . . this is the most arid and barren region that could be found anywhere on the earth; the inhabitants, too, are the most wretched and poorest creatures that I have seen.' The best that could be said was that Cape York possessed some land 'with good soils for planting and sowing but, so far as we could observe, utterly destitute of fresh water'.[8]

There seemed to be no justification for fitting out more expensive voyages of exploration to this unpromising region, and the most extensive Dutch discoveries were accidental. Their earliest voyages had followed the Portuguese routes, but in 1613 it was discovered that a better course was to sail south from the Cape of Good Hope, which the VOC, on better terms with the Africans than the Portuguese had been, was using as a provisioning stop, to pick up the 'Roaring Forties', the powerful winds that circle the globe from west to east in the latitudes between 35 and 45 degrees south. Then, having reached the appropriate longitude, about 105 degrees east, an alteration of course north would bring the ships to the Sunda archipelago and the VOC's principal station at Amboina. If, however, mariners delayed their turn to the north too long they were bound to run into Terra Australis; and this they duly did, for finding longitude – the position from east to west – was a tricky business. Latitude – the position from north to south – could easily be calculated by measuring the angle of the sun or selected stars, with a simple cross-staff (or even one's extended hand), but before the mid-eighteenth century, when the simultaneous perfection of astronomical calculations and the arrival of a reliable chronometer was achieved, estimates of longitude were unreliable, being usually nothing more than an estimate of distance run by log.

The first accidental visitor was Captain Dirck Hartog of the *Eendracht*, out of Cape Town, who, having overshot his turning point by nearly 400 miles, sighted the offshore islands of western Terra Australis in 1616. From his landfall near Shark Bay Hartog sailed some 300 miles north up the coast, leaving an inscribed pewter plate to mark his stay. (The plate is now in the Amsterdam Rijksmuseum; the Fremantle Maritime Museum has a second plate, placed in 1687 by Willem de Vlamingh.) Subsequent Dutch seamen – and one English ship, the *Tryal* – proved the unreliability of their navigation in similar fashion, but added to the Dutch fund of knowledge of the western and northern coasts. The most notably inaccurate of these captains was François Thijssen of the *Gulden Zeepard*, who in 1627 apparently turned to port 1,500 miles too late, a seemingly impossible error, but was therefore able to chart 1,000 miles of the southern coast, from the present Nuyts Archipelago to Cape Leeuwin.

Thijssen added another unfavourable report on the sterile desert coast, but it was the wreck in 1626 of the *Batavia*, the VOC's new flagship, that warned the directors to avoid the shores of Terra Australis. Caught out by the same navigational error, the *Batavia* foundered on a reef 30 miles from the western shore. Under the command of the senior merchant François Pelsaert, some of the survivors completed the voyage back to Java in a small boat, an amazing feat of seamanship. Returning to the remaining castaways, Pelsaert found that a bloody mutiny had broken out, with more than a hundred deaths; worse, much of the *Batavia*'s gold had been lost. For well over three centuries the *Batavia*'s wreck remained undiscovered, until researchers in 1965 found considerable portions of the wreck and its contents, enabling the Lelystadt shipyard to construct an impressive replica, which revisited Australia in 2000 without such disastrous consequences.[9]

The year 1641 saw a new expansion of Dutch foreign adventure. After a peace treaty had been signed with Portugal, now once more independent, Prince Maurice of Nassau felt free to attempt to take on the Spanish by attacking their South American colonies. It eventually proved to be an expensive failure, and the Dutch West Indies Company had a short and unprofitable life, but Governor General Antonio van Diemen was stimulated to explore the seas between his area of control and the now-open Pacific. Pilot Frans Jacobszoon Visscher was accordingly instructed to prepare a plan, in which he suggested four routes for exploration, which included a westerly passage from South America to the Solomon Islands. Only the first of these was authorized; Captain Abel Janszoon Tasman, with Visscher as his pilot, was instructed to equip an exploratory voyage but to steer well clear of that inhospitable land mass, keeping well to the south of Terra Australis. Van Diemen was not averse to expansion – he wrote 'We are taught by daily experience that the company's trade in Asia cannot subsist without territorial conquests' – but forty years of experience had made it clear that there was no profit to be found in the extensive territory of the great Southern Land.

The Governor General had a very different object, which was to find a passage, and a suitable way station, in the Pacific Ocean. The Dutch West India Company had already taken over half of Brazil from the Portuguese, and were constantly mounting attacks on Spanish possessions, including an expedition to Chile. If the VOC could find a route to South America which would avoid running the gauntlet of the Spanish Philippines, the possibility of a Dutch America sparkled. The Company would be enabled 'to do great things with the Chilese and have opportunities, owing to the said route, to snatch rich booty from the Castilians in the West Indies, who will never dream of such a thing'. Tasman was therefore instructed to sail first for Mauritius, a Dutch possession in the Indian Ocean, then to head as far south as possible before turning east, thus passing clear of Terra Australis. When he reached the longitude where the Solomon Islands were thought to lie, he was to sail north for 2,000 miles in search of that archipelago, discovered by the Spanish seventy years previously, but since mislaid. The islands, van Diemen considered, might make a suitable way station, as the Cape of Good Hope was proving to be, and where Tasman might well find 'divers strange things' before sailing home via New Guinea. In this way a circumnavigation of Terra Australis would have been effected, but Tasman did both more and less. He was unable to keep as far south as planned, and on 24 November 1642 land was sighted in around 42 degrees south which Tasman named after the Governor General as 'Van Diemenslandt'. It was not clear whether this was part of Terra Australis, which had last been recorded by Thijssen 600 miles to the north, but Tasman wasted little time on exploration, sailing on to the east as he had been instructed. Quite by accident, on his turn north, towards, he hoped, the Solomon Islands (which he never reached), Tasman's ships brushed the eastern shore of New Zealand, which he called Staten Land, honouring the States General of the Netherlands. It was now established that land existed between 115 and 175 degrees east, but not whether this was a continuous mass or a number of islands.[10]

Once again, the Dutch encounter with Australia had proved negative. Tasman reported of Van Diemen's Land that the vegetation was abundant but hardly appetizing, landing was dangerous, water could be obtained only with difficulty and no fish had been found. In ten days no inhabitants were met, but he reported that there must be 'men here of extraordinary stature'. Van Diemen persisted, sending Tasman off in 1644 to attempt to find that elusive passage between New Guinea and Terra Australis. He was to start at Cape York and sail westwards, to ensure that there was indeed a continuous coastline, with no prospect of a channel between the North and South coasts of Terra Australis. When the reliable Captain Tasman had completed this, following the coast from Cape York right round to the site of Port Hedland, and landing a number of shore parties, the VOC had charted more than half the Australian coastline, without finding anything to warrant further exploration, with the possible exception of some sandalwood. Tasman's men had little contact with any of the Australians, reported to be 'poor, naked people walking along the beaches, without rice or many fruits, very poor and bad-tempered'. The Heeren XVII were not impressed with van Diemen's efforts: 'We cannot anticipate any great results from the continuation of such discoveries, which besides entail further expenditure for the Company ... These plans of Your Worships somewhat aim beyond our mark.' By 1646, however, the VOC's official cartographer, Joan Blaeu, was able to publish a map of what Tasman had named Nieuw Nederlands, but which was always referred to as New Holland by the British, and which showed, with a fair degree of accuracy, the coast from the present-day Cape York peninsula to near the site of Ceduna, plus the southern part of Van Diemen's Land. Strictly speaking, and relying on a 1663 chart derived from 'the inlaid work upon the pavement of the new Stadt-House in Amsterdam', the British took New Holland to refer only to the western part of the continent, the rest remaining Terra Australis.

After van Diemen's death in 1645, subsequent Governors General stuck more firmly to the Company's brief of maximizing profits. A voyage towards the end of the century by Willem de Vlamingh filled in some gaps, including the area of the Swan River, on which Perth now stands (some of the curious black native fowls were sent back to Holland), but Dutch interest in the region expired, to be taken over by the British and French. Modern empires have not lasted long, and that of the Dutch was no exception. The seventeenth century was the Golden Age of Holland, when Amsterdam was the centre of European finance, but closely pressed by half-a-dozen other Dutch cities, epitomized by Rembrandt and Frans Hals in their group paintings of swashbuckling burgher guards. Dutch commercial hegemony was, however, threatened from the other side of the North Sea. English sea-power, allowed to decline by the first Stuart kings, was revived under Cromwell's Protectorate, its new strength signalled by victory in a bruising three-year war with the Netherlands and by the destruction of the Spanish West Indies fleet in 1657. The Dutch colony in Brazil collapsed in 1654 and ten years later the sparsely settled American New Netherlands accepted English rule without a shot being fired, and became the colonies of New York and New Jersey.

William Dampier, a disreputable but observant navigator, who touched Australia twice – in 1688 as a buccaneer and in 1699 more respectably as a Royal Navy Captain in command of HMS *Roebuck* – gave an even more unflattering report of the country than had the Dutch navigators, comparing the Australians to the Hottentots of South Africa who 'though a nasty people, yet for wealth are Gentlemen to these, who have no Houses and Skin Garments, Sheep, Poultry; and fruits of the Earth, Ostrich Eggs, &c. and setting aside their humane shape, they differ but little from Brutes'. Accurately enough, he described their physique as 'Tall, straight-bodied, and thin, with small long limbs'. Dampier's intolerance of the 'other' was perhaps not purely European, since the first recorded Maori impressions were not much more favourable, the New Zealanders particularly despising the Aborigines' reluctance to kill a defeated enemy.[11]

Lying on no trade route, offering no valuable commodity, the bad-tempered inhabitants of Terra Australis seemed best left to their own impoverished devices; much better prospects for amassing wealth were offered in India, China and Japan. John Welbe, one of Dampier's crew, attempted to raise money for a new company, the London Adventurers, to 'carry on a Trade to Terra Australis', but this, along with many other schemes, evaporated with the bursting of the South Sea Bubble, a venture in which British investors lost millions of pounds in 1720. Dean Swift, in his great satire of *Gulliver's Travels*, situated Lilliput 'to the North-West of Van Diemen's Land . . . in the Latitude of 30 Degrees 2 Minutes South', which might just have put the kingdom in the Great Australian Bight; but for the best part of two centuries after Captain Hartog made his unexpected landfall, the continent remained an object of only literary attention, as undisturbed by Europeans as it had by the Chinese: sea slugs apart, there seemed little in that continent to occupy the civilized world.

After Prince William of Orange, the Dutch head of state, became King William III of England in 1688 the two countries were closely allied. Colonial rivalries abated as the most threatening foe of both was once more the old enemy of France. Seventy years of intermittent warfare – it was to continue for another two generations – came to a temporary conclusion in 1763 with Great Britain (England and Scotland having been united in 1707) established as the leading power in North America and India. If any expansion into the southern oceans was to be attempted it could only be by Britain or France: Portugal, Spain and Holland, although still controlling widespread commercial empires, were out of the competition. Powerful navies were still retained by both Spain and Holland, but the expansionist urge had evaporated.

Academic commentators now revived public interest in the southern hemisphere. Charles de Brosses, whose travels had taken him no further than Italy, and James Callander, who had never left Scotland, published compendia of southern voyages in 1756 and 1766. A rather better informed writer, Alexander Dalrymple, who had worked for the English East India Company, discovered evidence of Torres' passage through the eponymous straits, which had been kept secret in the Spanish archives since 1607. The fact that New Guinea and New Holland were indeed separate was therefore known, but the vast area between Cape York and Staten Land was still unexplored. Dalrymple, a difficult and demanding young Scotsman on the make, published his *Account of the Discoveries Made in the South Pacifick Ocean* (1786), in which he argued:

although the remote parts of the southern hemisphere remain undiscovered, we have traces from ancient times, warranted by latter experience, of rich and valuable countries in it; no subject can be more interesting, to a commercial state, than the discovery of new countries and people, to invigorate the hand of industry, by opening new vents for manufactures, and by introducing, from new quarters the comforts and conveniences of life.[12]

Anxious to pre-empt the French, the British Admiralty sent one sloop, the *Dolphin*, on two successive circumnavigations. The first, commanded by John Byron between 1764 and 1766, was unrewarding; the second, that of 1766–8 under Captain Samuel Wallis, accompanied by Philip Carteret in the *Swallow*, succeeded in discovering many of the hitherto uncharted Pacific archipelagos, but did not add to the knowledge of Terra Australis. It was instead the French who got there first. The remarkable Louis Antoine de Bougainville, soldier, sailor and mathematician – a member of the Royal Society, indeed – left France in 1766 for an extended voyage. After founding a French colony in the Falkland Islands, which he was subsequently ordered to hand over to Spain, Bougainville crossed the Pacific in an attempt to find the eastern coast of New Holland. Steering along 15 degrees south, the known position of the Cape York peninsula, he came within sight of the Great Barrier Reef, but was still 100 miles from the invisible coast. The configuration of the continent continued undefined.

Bougainville only returned to France in March 1769, by which time the next British expedition had already set sail. Its ostensible purpose was to observe the predicted passage of the planet Venus across the sun's face, which could best be seen, on 3 June 1769, in the southern hemisphere. Dr Nevil Maskelyne, the Astronomer Royal, had perfected tables which would at last enable mariners to determine longitude and published these in the *Nautical Almanac* (John Harrison was also developing his chronometer at the same time and for the same purpose). A careful observation of the transit would, he assured the Admiralty, be of inestimable value. The Royal Society was convinced, and successfully petitioned the king for funds estimated at £4,000; but the British expedition was given a second and more important task. The chief architect of the victory over France sealed in the 1763 Peace of Paris was William Pitt. Pitt was convinced that France remained a threat, and that the terms of the peace, too generous in his view, had 'delivered the nation defenceless to a foreign enemy'. By July 1766 Pitt, now Lord Chatham, was back in power and, although frequently ill, was determined to thwart the French. The Admiralty therefore gladly agreed to provide a ship and crew for the Royal Society's expedition which would also settle, once and for all, the mystery of that 'Continent or Land of great extent' that Alexander Dalrymple was convinced must exist, and ensure that it became British. It was not in fact Australia that Dalrymple conjectured – the extent of that was tolerably well known, with only the east coast remaining to be defined – but an entirely undiscovered (and non-existent) land mass which surely must exist between New Zealand and South America, and which must, he insisted, house a population of 50 millions waiting to be incorporated into the British Empire; 'the scraps from this table would be sufficient to maintain the power, dominion, and sovereignty of Britain . . .' Dalrymple, supported by a Scottish clique, which included the President of the Royal Society, Lord Moreton, and the famous economist Adam Smith, pressed for his own appointment as commander, but was too exigent.[13] He had no previous service experience, and when he demanded a captain's commission in the Royal Navy, the Lords of the Admiralty chose a much more suitable candidate, Lieutenant James Cook. Given Dalrymple's exaggerated opinion of his own abilities, an expedition led by him would almost certainly have failed, and the future of Australia might well have been very different. But James Cook was a sailor, a navigator and a man of towering ability, his genius acknowledged two centuries later when NASA named their space shuttle *Endeavour* after Cook's ship – emphasizing their intention by choosing the English rather than the American spelling. The small hull of HMS *Endeavour*, a former Whitby collier, selected by Cook as the best possible vessel for so long an exploration, was crammed with provisions and scientific equipment, with a complement of learned men. These included the rich and influential young amateur naturalist Joseph Banks, the botanist Dr Emmanuel Solander, pupil of the famous Linnaeus and a Fellow of the Royal Society, the astronomer Charles Green and a talented artist, Sydney Parkinson. King George III's Island, better known as Tahiti, discovered by Captain Wallis in 1767, had been selected as the best point for observation, and in April 1769 the *Endeavour* anchored in Port Royal. After a voyage halfway round the world Cook had arrived at precisely the point selected, which indicates the amazing accuracy of both his and Wallis's navigation – using, incidentally, Maskelyne's tables rather than a chronometer.[14]

Having duly fulfilled the Royal Society's instructions, Cook proceeded to follow those of the British Admiralty, which were to sail south from Tahiti to find the eastern shore of New Holland – the Lords of the Admiralty being sceptical of the existence of Dalrymple's great continent. Tahiti lies well to the east of Tasman's Staten Land, so by sailing due south Cook could establish that there was no land mass between that sketchily described coast and South America. Having reached 40 degrees south, he was to run westwards until he either 'encountered the continent above mentioned' or should 'fall in with the Eastern side of the Land discovered by Tasman and now called New Zealand'. The Admiralty instructions were clearly drafted and obeyed to the letter.

On 7 October Cook sighted the east coast of New Zealand, and spent the next six months preparing a detailed hydrographic survey of the two islands. Lord Chatham could be satisfied that New Zealand was saved from the French (who were not lucky in the Antipodes – two years later Captain N. T. Marion-Dufresne landed in New Zealand, and, together with sixteen of his men, was killed and eaten). Only the east coast of New Holland remained to be found, and this was encountered on 20 April 1770. Cook intended to strike Van Diemen's Land, but actually fell in with the mainland, near the south-east extremity of the continent at Point Hicks, about four degrees north of that point on the Van Diemen's Land coast which marked the end of Tasman's survey. It was therefore assumed that Van Diemen's Land was not an island, but a peninsula. Apart from that single misconception, Cook's subsequent four-month voyage north along the coast, culminating in his exploration of that fantastic structure, the Great Barrier Reef, and the rediscovery of a passage through the Torres Strait, finally set the bounds of a new continent.

As a formality, and as the Dutch had done in the preceding century, Cook claimed the land in the name of his sovereign, and called the eastern part of the continent New South Wales. The established doctrine at that time remained that of Van Diemen: if a region was uninhabited, or not under the control of a recognizable sovereign, it was *terra nullius*, and could be appropriated by any civilized nation – or, at any rate, any such country with the will and power to enforce such a claim. Neither the Dutch nor the French showed any inclination to dispute the issue with Great Britain and it was not until the question of indigenous rights was raised two hundred years later that the decision was seriously questioned.[15]

The Land and the People

After Cook's careful delineation of the eastern coast of New South Wales, only the outline of the continent was known, and virtually nothing of the extraordinary people, plants and animals that inhabited it. No creature in the great southern land resembled anything the newcomers had encountered. Even the men were different from the many new races that Europeans had met in the neighbouring islands and the animals seemed almost perversely strange. That area now defined as the continent of Sahul, the Australian mainland plus New Guinea and the adjacent islands, formed a single land mass some 40 million years ago, after the shift in the earth's plates. Since that time the flora and fauna of Sahul have evolved independently, giving rise to an ecology unlike any other in the world. Only comparatively recently, about 10,000 years ago, did the end of the last ice age lead to flooding and the separation of New Guinea and Tasmania from the main Australian land mass, known after Cook's voyage as New South Wales and New Holland. Within the boundaries of those lands lay just under 3 million square miles, a little less than the area of the United States excluding Alaska, stretching from 10 to 44 degrees south: in the northern hemisphere this would be equivalent to the distance between Bordeaux and Sierra Leone, or between Toronto and Caracas. Between Brisbane on the east and Geraldton on the west coast lies approximately the same distance as between Cork and the Caspian Sea, or between Los Angeles and the North Carolina coast.

Present-day Australia is bound together by the ocean. All the state capitals – Sydney, Melbourne, Adelaide, Perth, Darwin, Brisbane and Hobart, and all the larger towns, with the exception of the twentieth-century national capital, Canberra, lie near the coast. Internal communications over these distances remain difficult today and are largely dependent on the road network. Until the advent of air travel the sea remained a channel of domestic trade, as well as the connection to the rest of the world.

Over this great area the single vital factor is water, and the determinator of precipitation is El Niño ('the Christ Child'), a current of warm water flowing intermittently down the coast of South America. In normal years this situation is stabilized, with the warmer water held in the western Pacific by the prevailing westerlies; when these fail the warm water is displaced to the east, where the resultant precipitation leads to violent floods in South America. Conversely, the colder water left around the coasts of Australia reduces precipitation and leads to serious droughts. The frequency of El Niño's anomaly varies from two to eight years, and is unpredictable; it was, moreover, a phenomenon quite unknown to the first British settlers, accustomed to regular seasonal variations. A British stockfarmer would think himself very unlucky to have two bad seasons in succession; his troubles were more likely to be caused by sickness than by gross climatic variations, and the severity and persistence of Australian droughts came as an unpleasant surprise to the first settlers.[16]

The Great Dividing Range, running down almost the whole of the east coast from the Cape York peninsula into Tasmania forms the continental watershed. All that coast is wet, sometimes very wet, with many rivers and frequent floods. In the more northerly areas, over all the continent, a tropical monsoon system prevails; Darwin, capital and only city of the Northern Territory, has two seasons, the wet and the dry. The rainfall caused by easterly winds' passage over the Great Dividing Range, combined with the monsoonal rains feeding the northern tributaries, gives rise to the continent's only large river system, the Murray–Darling, which waters an extensive area for 1,600 miles to its mouth on the southern coast. In the most general terms, a belt some 400 miles inland from the east and south-east coasts is suitable – mountainous areas apart – for cultivation or grazing. The Great Dividing Range's notable peaks are on the south, over 6,000 feet, with Mount Kosciusko at 7,310 feet the highest, and the range eventually declining in the north to the sea near Cairns. In the summer months the continent, apart from the far north, is influenced by the south-east trade winds.

On the other side of the continent only the south-west tip – admittedly a tip not much smaller than France – experiences a consistent winter rainfall provided by westerly winds. Between the tropical north and the two fertile coastal areas, over half the total land area of Australia is occupied by deserts and semi-deserts – the Simpson, the Gibson, the Great Sandy Desert and the arid Nullarbor plain – where rainfall is quickly countered by evaporation. Australia's climate is, however, famously unreliable. Prolonged droughts (seven years ending in 1903 is the record), characterized by great heat and accompanied by devastating fires, may be followed by drastic flooding. During the last two centuries attempts have been made to adjust this irregularity by extensive storage and irrigation works, so energetically carried out as to result in grave damage, reducing the flow of the Murray River by three-quarters, and causing the silting up of the mouths, almost to the point of closure.

But the white settlers were not the first to alter Australia's geography. At some time in the distant past – 40,000 or 60,000 years ago, or even longer, have been suggested – the ancestors of modern Australians must have crossed one of the straits that separated Sahul from the Asian land mass. A word of warning is needed here: every statement made about prehistory is conjectural to a greater or lesser extent, and fresh archaeological discoveries and improved techniques make caution even more necessary (and the recent unhelpful custom of demanding the return of human evidence from museums is robbing a people of much knowledge of their own past and has made clarity even more difficult). Australia's human history seems as distinctively individual as that of its flora and fauna. Arguments continue about the exact age of remains found near Lake Mungo, one of the Willandra lakes in New South Wales, but the consensus indicates a date of around

25,000 BC, with a strong possibility that they may be considerably older. The fact that the bodies were formally interred, ritually arranged and prepared for burial, indicates the existence of a coherent society at a very early date indeed. The Mungos were tall, lightly built individuals, quite different from their neighbours found in Kow Swamp, in northern Victoria, who were heavier and more rugged, with sloping foreheads, more 'primitive' features, big boned and quite possibly not *homo sapiens* at all, a theory reinforced by recent DNA analysis. What is quite extraordinary is that the swamp people are considerably more recent than the Mungos, a date of *c*. 15,000 BC being accepted. It seems therefore that two quite distinct races co-existed, the physical difference between the two being considerably greater than those between any existing population – very much as with Neanderthal man in Europe, but with the difference that it is impossible that the present aboriginal population resulted from hybridization of the two types of people, given the wide difference in dates. Future research has been jeopardized by the Victorian government's unconscionable decision to re-inter the Kow Swamp remains, but the search for knowledge of man's history generally triumphs over the forces of obscurantism. How the first men crossed from the Asian continent, and whether the drift south took place over 30,000 years or a much longer period is to some extent irrelevant. Aboriginal Australians are probably the oldest pure population, possessing the most continuous culture in the world, one that evolved apart from any other.[17]

What might be called the Lake Mungo culture indicates a level of technology and culture similar to that found elsewhere at the same time – ritual cremations and inhumations were paralleled by similar contemporary practices in Spain at about the same time. But when Willem Janszoon made his first landing in Terra Australis, Europeans were quartering the world's oceans, Shakespeare was writing his greatest plays, and William Harvey (the discoverer of the circulatory system) had graduated in medicine from the already ancient University of Cambridge; yet Australians were still living, it seemed, as they had done thirty millennia or so previously. What explanation, other than that of cultural stagnation, or the idea of racial inferiority (still – amazingly – advanced in the Cambridge History of the British Empire's volume on Australia, reissued in 1988), can be offered for this astonishing differential development? Isolation is surely the major factor. Immigrants bring with them new technologies. Taking only the last four millennia of British history as an example, metal-working, pottery, the plough, drainage, glass, central heating, writing, paper, the theatre, most of the existing food crops and all the inventions that enabled blue-water navigation – the stern rudder, the compass, charts – have all been introduced from other countries. Any society not so nourished has to rely on its own resources: Inuit hunter-gatherers and some Amazonian communities have until recently been so isolated, and with similar results. Even when intercourse with other forms of economic activity and more advanced technologies has been available, innate conservatism has led other cultures, such as that of the African Bushmen, to continue with their traditional habits and customs. Nor was change forced upon Australians. The first arrivals found a country metaphorically teeming with milk and honey. Large herbivorous marsupials, kangaroo and wombats were overshadowed by the Diprotodontids, huge creatures that could weigh up to two tons, 500 pound turtles and giant birds roaming ready for the killing. Dangerous carnivores were rare, and easily avoided. The larger animals were comparatively quickly killed off, but the kangaroo population alone was sufficient to support human life for continuous generations. Where food supplies were abundant, little incentive existed to develop new technologies; such cultivation as existed was of the most basic type and no staple food source was encouraged. On the coasts, molluscs could be had for the gathering, but some innovations, such as the use of nets drawn by a kite (surely a remarkable initiative) and multi-pronged spears, helped the fishermen. Inland communities developed different techniques of food collection. River fish were also trapped by weirs, killed by poisonous plants, speared or caught in nets which could be up to 1,000 feet long, buoyed and weighted. Nothing displays the skill and creativity of Aborigines more than their weapons used in hunting large animals. Spear-launchers – 'woomeras' – are known in other societies, as were boomerangs, which can be thrown in such a way as to return to the thrower, but the Australian mastery of these marvels of ballistic technology is unmatched elsewhere. Stasis had not been absolute or continuous: developments had taken place, although many of these were comparatively recent – the use of fish-hooks from early in the second millennium AD being an example. Some new techniques had been introduced and discarded; edged stone axes had been manufactured for many centuries before disappearing from the archaeological record.

At some time about 10,000 BC the Sahulian societies were internally divided as the last ice age ended, flooding the lower-lying areas and separating the three most prominent regions. The only subsequent contact until modern times was that caused by the seaborne explosion of the Lapita, forebears of the Polynesians who populated the Pacific islands, eventually reaching New Zealand about AD 1000. Remarkable navigators, the Lapita voyaged as far as South America, and probably visited Australia frequently, but, like the first Europeans, found nothing to warrant their remaining, although they settled in coastal New Guinea. One Lapita import, however, brought about fundamental changes. In the two thousand or so generations of human life in Australia no animals had been domesticated, but at about the same time that the Minoans were developing the palace complex at Knossos, the dog arrived in Australia and was at least partly domesticated. Perhaps the most remarkable of Australian technologies was the use of fire. Visitors to Tasmania had observed the unusual number of fires to be seen, and had later remarked the custom – universal in Tasmania, and common elsewhere – of carrying a smouldering fire stick; the bush fires seen from the *Endeavour*'s decks had led Cook to write of 'This continent of Smoke'. Sir Thomas Mitchell, the nineteenth-century surveyor and explorer, had offered an explanation:

Fire, grass and kangaroos, and human inhabitants, seem all dependent on each other for existence in Australia; for any one of these being wanting, the others could no longer continue. Fire is necessary to burn the grass, and form those open forests, in which we find the large forest kangaroo; the native applies that fire to the grass at certain seasons, in order that a young green crop may subsequently spring up, and so attract and enable him to kill or take the kangaroo with nets. In summer, the burning of the long grass also discloses vermin, bird's nests, &c. on which the females and children, who chiefly burn the grass, feed. But for this simple process, the Australian wood had probably contained as thick a jungle as those of New Zealand or America, instead of the open forests in which the white men now find grass for their cattle, to the exclusion of the kangaroo.[18]

Whether or not this widespread use of fire can be termed 'fire stick farming' is open to debate, but its effect over thousands of years on the Australian ecology must have been marked, and might well explain the predominance of fire-resistant vegetation.

A population such as that of Australia, which has remained undisturbed, except very sporadically, and that on the extreme fringes, for many thousands of years, is a constant source of interest for anthropologists. At least three races classified as Australids are recognized: the Torres Strait Islanders, Tasmanians, now extinct in the pure line, and Australians, by far the largest grouping. Their provenance and relationship with other populations have been researched, their physical characteristics – the limbs, longer than those of Europids, their blood pressure and metabolic rate, usually lower, their variety of hair colour and type – measured and analysed. One result of these investigations is never mentioned, but it remains embedded in Australian consciousness: Australids have more 'primitive' characteristics than almost any other race; that is, they share many characteristics with the earlier hominids (such as straight hair, a peculiarity they share with Europids, and a smaller cranial capacity). While it is abundantly self-evident that such physical characteristics have no connection with wisdom, intelligence, the capacity to live peaceably in society or any other perceived virtue (abundantly proven this century by the more 'advanced' Europids), the assumption of some such inferiority has never been effaced.[19]

Any remarks about aboriginal cultures have to be taken with considerable reservations. European curiosity concentrated on the more interesting and more picturesque South Sea Islanders and the magnificent Maori. Tahitians were incorporated in decorative motifs, became the object of literary attention from Melville and Stevenson to Rodgers and Hammerstein, were celebrated in Gauguin's canvases and worked over by persistent missionary endeavour; but no author considered an Aboriginal *Omoo*, *Typee* or *South Pacific*. The Islanders of the Torres Strait, who, as the Dutch navigators had found to their cost, reacted in a very different way to the intruders compared with the mainlanders, were a race apart. Matthew Flinders, midshipman on Captain Bligh's sloop *Providence*, charting the straits in 1792, witnessed an attack made on the ship's tender, the brig *Assistant*. Bligh recorded the incident in his log:

I knew that mischief was done to our poor little companion by these wretches, and arrows were fired at us. It was not a time to trifle. My ship might be on shore in a few minutes without being carefully handled, and it was a serious point who were to be masters of the situation. I settled it by discharging two of the quarterdeck guns with round and grape. The contents of one carried destruction and brought horrible consternation to them, and they fled from their canoes and into the sea and swam to windward like porpoises.

Bligh took possession of the islands in the king's name as 'Clarence's Archipelago'. Subsequent relations 'with this fierce and inhospitable race' were decidedly ambivalent, the forty-two skulls of shipwrecked sailors on Darnley Island serving as a reminder that the Islanders were not to be tampered with lightly.[20] Although Australians could mount a determined resistance to intruders, they never displayed the bellicose determined ferocity of the Islanders: much to their own disadvantage, the Australian Aborigines, as their Maori critics observed, were an unaggressive people.

For the first decades after 1788, Aborigines were low down on any colonial worry list; they presented few threats and were generally treated with mild curiosity, generosity and occasional brutality, introduced to new sources of nourishment and exposed to threatening new diseases. The ready availability of rum began that pattern of alcohol abuse which still characterizes many aboriginal communities. When the shepherds and settlers made extensive inroads into Aboriginal territories, resistance was countered by sporadic violence, poorly controlled; some Aborigines were admitted into the lower ranks of European society as shepherds or mounted policemen, but there was little attempt at integration. Only at the start of the twentieth century were systematic and sympathetic researches begun, by which time Aboriginal cultures had been drastically deformed. Those left comparatively undisturbed, in the tropical north, therefore formed the main area of study; how far the conclusions drawn from twentieth-century Arnhem Land were applicable to the natives of eighteenth-century New South Wales is to some degree conjectural.

All Australian Aboriginal societies tended towards polygamy, the number of wives available to a man being anything from one – the most common – to twenty or thirty, in exceptional cases, but as late as the 1930s, 34 per cent of Walibri men had more than one wife. Wives were usually younger, sometimes by a whole generation, and all females were considered inferior in status, to be beaten or even killed with impunity. The resultant kinship group was the basis of society, with families co-operating as occasion offered or convention demanded. Numbers were controlled to match the availability of food by continuing lactation, infanticide and abandoning those incapacitated by age or wounds. Depending on the need to co-operate in food gathering or for defence (or aggression), family groups were recognized as belonging to a larger tribal unit, which might number anything between 100 and 2,000. There may have been some five hundred tribes in a total Australian population, estimates of which vary widely, even wildly, from 300,000 to 3 million. A total of perhaps 300–500 thousand may be an acceptable figure but whatever assumption is made, pre-European Australia was sparsely and unevenly populated.[21]

The earliest scientific investigators revealed some surprising variations. George Grey in the Journal of his expeditions in the 1830s found semi-permanent dwellings and rock paintings quite different in style from those in other regions.

Languages and vocabularies differed, but some mutual understanding must have been possible to permit the large gatherings which sometimes occurred. It has been conjectured that all mainland Australians spoke a related language, which has been divided into 26 categories, one of which, Pama-Nyungan, is believed spoken over nearly 90 per cent of the continent leaving the other 25 confined to a relatively small area along the north coast.[22]

Inter-tribal warfare was not uncommon – in one example a quarter of the community's adult males had been killed – but conventions were recognized as governing all intercourse. All hunter-gatherer cultures are obsessively territorial, as anyone who has attempted to gather fungi in a strange French commune can testify. A group's survival depended on its ability to defend its own food sources and to discover – or if need be to take over – new territories when their own supplies declined. Strangers were therefore always objects of suspicion, to be avoided or rejected until proved harmless, when discussions might begin. 'The first law of Aboriginal morality', one sympathetic anthropologist noted, was 'Always Ask'. In a society without written records, custom took the place of formal law, but it was custom evolved through more than a thousand generations and its observance was literally vital. The only predator Australians had to fear was man, and the mutual observance of tradition could ensure that conflicts were limited, and did not threaten the survival of the group. Traditions were transmitted and customs enforced by complex social and religious rituals, celebrating and confirming man's relations with the physical and spiritual world, relations between individuals and the passage of human life.[23]

Inhabiting as they did an entire continent, with a climate ranging from tropical monsoon bush of the north through savannas to arid desert, and the cool quasi-Mediterranean climate of the south, indigenous Australians adapted to each. A strong preference was shown for coastal and riverine areas, where fish and shellfish, a staple article of diet, could be collected. In northern Australia, for example, the Anbarra community collected an entirely adequate protein intake of fish, shellfish, turtles and aquatic lizards; the thirty-five-strong community consumed more than 22 cwt. of these in one month, and only 180 pounds of birds and eggs, plus about two pounds of mangrove worms. Although fish and shellfish were preferred, the Anbarra could adapt their diet to include more land animals and vegetables – yams, nuts, with a variety of fruit and wild honey. With such a varied, and, apart from perhaps the worms, probably delicious diet available it is not surprising that a well-situated Aboriginal community had plentiful free time. Adults needed to spend only four to five hours a day in hunting or collecting food, leaving time for daytime sleep, artistic work, discussion and ritual.

In desert areas, the only protein source was large animals caught by the men, or such small creatures as lizards and 'wichetty grubs' gathered by the women. Such a life was closely related to that of the southern African Khoisan, with the same reliance on watering holes, and the prevalence of small family units traversing the same well-known region. More generous sources of food enabled larger communities to establish what might even be described as a regional centres of trade. The annual migration of the bogong moth to the Snowy Mountains caused

a seasonal movement of the tribes in the neighbouring areas resulting in large gatherings of people at campsites near the main concentration of moths. Women collected the vegetable foods around the camps while men hunted the moths, either suffocating them with smoke, knocking them down with sticks on to sheets of bark, or catching them with nets in rock shelters. The moths were cooked by placing them in heated sand from which the fire had been removed, and were either eaten at once or ground into a paste and made into cakes.

The moth feasts lasted for several weeks and not only added a valuable supplement to the diet of the local population, but also provided an opportunity for social communication between larger groups of people and opportunities for trade between tribes. Articles such as possum-skin rugs, baskets, and bags were exchanged for spears, shields, and stone implements, and thus contributed not only to the exchange of ideas, but also to a wider base for the local economy.[24]

European reactions to the Australians differed according to the character of the observer and the conventions of the time. James Cook was not only a fine navigator, but a humane and tolerant man; his descriptions of the Australians he met reveal a sensibility far removed from that of Dampier, remarking on their poverty in a very different fashion:

From what I have said of the Natives of New Holland they may appear to some to be the most wretched people upon the earth: but in reality they are far more happier than we Europeans; being wholly unacquainted not only with the superfluous but the necessary Conveniences so much sought after in Europe, they are happy in not knowing the use of them. They live in a Tranquillity which is not disturbed by the Inequality of Condition: the Earth and sea of their own accord furnishes them with all things necessary for life.

. . . In short they seem'd to set no value upon anything we gave them nor would they ever part with any thing of their own for any one article we could offer them this in my opinion argues that they think themselves provided with all the necessarys of Life and that they have no superfluities.[25]

But Cook (born 1728) was two generations younger than Dampier (born 1658) and, brought up in a humane and liberal tradition, was more ready to accept the worth of different cultures. Indeed, given the modern evidence of Aboriginal diet Cook's description hardly seems exaggerated. Bennelong, one of the people the British called 'Eora' (there were some thirty different bands, each with their own name, living near the shores of Port Jackson, when the first British arrived), was an interested observer of the newcomers, but no admirer of their food. When required to exist upon the colonial ration scale – applied to all, convicts and free – Bennelong was horrified. Even when specially supplemented, the weekly ration scarcely sufficed Bennelong for a single day.

To describe the Aboriginal cultures as 'primitive' is unfashionable, and its use demands some caveats. The mere passage of time does not guarantee improvement, an English labourer was perhaps better off in 1420 than in 1820, or a Welsh farmer in 800 rather than five hundred years later. Nor does technical advance necessarily imply benefits; apart from such striking examples as the use and misuse of atomic energy, the decline in the British railway system over the last half century is notable. But when all such reservations are made, the fact remains that Australian cultures in 1750 were at much the same material stage as those in Europe ten thousand years previously, and some such word as primitive becomes essential, especially when comparing Australian with British society. The oldest culture in the world was brought face to face with the most enterprisingly modern.

Observers of primitive cultures often bring to their work their own prejudices, hopes and deficiencies: a yearning (generally misplaced) for a state of nature; admiration, usually equally justified, for artistic achievements and often a desperate hope that contemporary dilemmas can be resolved by embracing ancient religious and philosophical systems, famously exemplified by Prince Charles's devotion to 'Colonel' Laurens van der Post and his tales of life with the Kalahari Bushmen. The attitudes of the New towards the Old Australians (the Aborigines, as they have become irreversibly known) underwent many similar changes as European ideas altered. Cook's sympathetic, idealized view was eroded by the difficulties the first British intruders experienced in coming to terms with the established communities: the blacks were not routinely admitted to full rights of citizenship until after the Second World War, and for many years it was complacently assumed by white Australians that they would simply die off. Only in comparatively recent times has any serious study been made of the different Aboriginal cultures, by which time much damage has been done, and bitter feeling has distorted perceptions. These have gone so far as to advance, in recognized, if not quite reputable, academic circles, the thesis that Aboriginal history should be written only by Aborigines.[26] While discounting such absurdities, one nevertheless treads delicately.

The fact that the first European settlement in Australia was not as a regular colony had profound effects. Not only were the first arrivals, convicts and their gaolers, subject to military discipline, but, less obviously, the

23

existing inhabitants were treated differently from those in lands where occupation and settlement were the principal objectives.

It has been the custom of colonizers from the Emperor Claudius through Peter Stuyvesant, to the Soviet Union in Afghanistan, to single out a prominent native ruler who might be persuaded, coerced or purchased as an ally. After a war or two, necessary to establish relative negotiating strengths, the new ally might be expected to maintain order among the other natives, and to bolster the values of the occupants (it might be observed that the inhabitants of Roman Britannia were a good deal better served than those of Manhattan or Afghanistan). In such a fashion the British Empire proceeded, often successfully. The Sikhs of India, after a hard-fought series of wars, policed not only India, but many other parts of the British Empire on behalf of their conquerors. In South Africa, the Basuto and the Tswana were reliable allies of the British, while almost the whole of the black population joined with the British in suppressing the Boers. Sometimes, and this facilitated matters considerably, it was possible to reach agreement with a single ruler, the terms of which might vary greatly. In Hong Kong this was a complex and carefully negotiated series of treaties, necessitated by the native ruler in question being the emperor of China. In New Zealand it was a less formal but equally binding arrangement with the Maori chiefs. Such agreements were particularly important to the British, since in the Colonial Office and Treasury there was rarely any support for holding down a colonial population against their will, always an expensive and often an unpopular exercise. Even the defence of colonies was a sore subject with the British taxpayer, and the expenditure only conceded, if ever, with much reluctance.

But this well-tried policy could not be employed in Terra Australis. Governor General van Diemen had attempted to impose it in his instructions to Captain Tasman: 'in populated regions or in such as have undoubted lords, the consent of the people with the king would be required ... to which you should attempt to obtain by friendly persuasions.' But New Holland, Tasman was obliged to decide, was a country which 'had no sovereign', one where it would be only necessary to erect some sign that 'such lands fully belong to the discoverers and first occupiers', a convenient doctrine, and one to be adopted by the British.

The insuperable difficulty in negotiating with the Australians was that there were so few of them and they were so widely scattered. Over an area similar to that of Europe or the United States lived hundreds of tribes, none of which owed obedience to a single leader. All were subject to complex societal regulations, and were prepared to adhere closely to custom, to

spend much time in reflection and discussion and to respect the views of the senior men. Not only was there no British intention, initially, to do much more than utilize a tiny fraction of the continent as an open prison, with any incidental advantages that might accrue, but there were no identifiable native powers with whom to negotiate. In the circumstances, nothing much more than a policy of mutual neglect and indifference was likely, and this was duly adopted.

No political organization existed to unite local groups into a polity. Again, the parallel is that with those of the Khoisan rather than the much larger black communities in South Africa; in the first years of their occupation Dutch officers had to invest native 'princes' with imaginary powers in order to seal some formal treaty with them. Some such device would have been necessary had the British been equally punctilious in Australia, and indeed brass gorgets, similar to those worn by subaltern officers, were handed out to the more prominent Aborigines in an equally meaningless gesture. To seventeenth- and eighteenth-century Europeans, nudging aside a sparse population with no coherent structure was accepted as necessary and inevitable, with the proviso that such displacement should be made if possible with the consent of the inhabitants and without unnecessary violence.

James Cook was a man of his times. As an indifferent scholar (his spelling and punctuation are adventurous rather than methodical), Cook had not read Rousseau, who had developed the idea of the 'noble savage', but opinions were formed of common north-country decency and the sentiment then very popular, expressed by Alexander Pope in his *Essay on Man*:

> Lo, the poor Indian! whose untutored mind
> Sees God in clouds, or hears him in the wind!
> His soul, proud science never taught to stray
> Far as the solar walk, or milky-way;
> Yet simple nature to his hope has given,
> Behind the cloud-topped hill, an humbler heaven;
> Some safer world in depth of woods embraced,
> Some happier island in the watery waste,
> Where slaves once more their native land behold,
> No fiends torment, no Christians thirst for gold.
> To be, contents his natural desire,
> He asks no angel's wing, no seraph's fire;
> But thinks, admitted to that equal sky,
> His faithful dog shall bear him company.

Cook, Banks and all eighteenth-century Europeans shared a similar under-standing of human history. Archbishop Ussher of Armagh had calculated that the world and all that was in it was created in it on a Monday morning in March 4004 BC. From that date the years of the world followed as described in the Bible until more reliable historical sources became available. The quite revolutionary change that followed occurred during the lifetime of Charles Lyell (1797–1874), and can be traced in the editions of the *Encyclopaedia Britannica* published in the year of his birth (the third) and that which was in preparation when his life ended. In 1797 Ussher's dates were accepted without question; by 1875 the ninth edition was able to dismiss 'these chronologies, inasmuch as new evidence has changed the aspect of the subject that the quasi-historical schemes of the last century would now hardly be maintained by any competent authority' (although this truth has yet to be recognized by some educationalists in the United States). Much more evidence has been accumulated since – the ninth edition estimated human antiquity at only 120,000 years – but by the mid-nineteenth century educated European thought had undergone a revolution, in large part due to Lyell's own geological researches.

It was easy for eighteenth-century men to accept that God had chosen to populate his world with an interesting diversity of peoples, each with its own character and equalities. The 'noble savage' described by Chateaubriand (in his romance *Atala*, published in 1801, which followed Rousseau's earlier ramblings) was accepted as superior in many respects to the degraded 'civilized' man. Half a century later, steam-powered technology had given Westerners (given the explosive growth of the United States, 'Europeans' is no longer appropriate) a new conceit of themselves. If humanity was 100,000 years old, what had the Australians and other savages, no longer noble, been doing? Their failure to achieve similar standards to those of Queen Victoria's white subjects – or those of the emperor of China, for the matter – could only be attributed to innate inferiority, stupidity and idleness. A muddled interpretation of Darwin's theories led to 'Social Darwinism', in which the races of mankind were classified in order of advancement – with European Caucasians invariably at the top, and Australian Aborigines usually at the bottom. Somewhat reluctantly, it was admitted that individual members of the inferior races might, over the years – and very many years were posited – climb a branch or two up the tree of human dignity, but the commonest attitude of Australian whites, which has only very recently altered, was that the Aborigines, should any survive, would be absorbed into the white population by interbreeding.

Cook died in 1779, killed – and partly eaten – by the Sandwich Islanders,

an ironic end for one who had so earnestly striven for good relations with the native communities. His death was received as an international tragedy: William Hickey, of the East India Company, wrote in his diary: 'The universally lamented death of that great man and intrepid navigator . . . was considered by all Europe to be an irreparable misfortune.'[27] Less than half a century after Cook's death, William Charles Wentworth, son of a convict mother, born on the voyage out, but later a barrister and member of Peterhouse, Cambridge, published a poem, 'Australasia'. Wentworth echoed Cook's ideal view of the Aborigines:

> Ye primal tribes, lords of this old domain,
> Swift footed hunters of the pathless plain,
> Unshackled wanderers, enthusiasts free,
> Pure native sons of savage liberty . . .

and described his own vision of a future when Britain may be reborn:

> May this, thy last born infant, then arise,
> To glad thy heart and greet thy parent eyes
> And Australasia float, thy flag unfur'ld
> A new Britannia in another world.

In 1779 that would have seemed an improbable fantasy.[28]

On his return from the first voyage Cook had been fêted for his skill as a commander, his exploration of the Pacific Ocean and his circumnavigation of New Zealand, rather than for having filled in the missing parts of the Australian map. The picturesque and handsome Tahitians and the fearsome Maori attracted much more attention than the disagreeably reclusive Australians; and the British government had more pressing concerns. By 1775 the thirteen American colonies were in arms; six years later, due largely to the support given by a French fleet, General Cornwallis's army surrendered, and negotiations for peace began. Government after government fell in Britain as her continental rivals, French, Dutch and Spanish, made threatening moves. In 1782 a Franco-Spanish fleet, much superior to anything that could be mustered against it, cruised in the Channel menacing an invasion. Only by February 1783, with the Treaty of Paris settling the issues with France and Spain and guaranteeing peace in North America, could Britain feel secure. But by then a new problem had arisen, to which the neglected spaces of New Holland might afford a solution.

'Matter of advantageous Return'

Social conditions in Georgian London have their parallel today. Conspicuous consumption by the very rich was followed at a respectful distance by a comfortable middle class of traders and shopkeepers. Artisans could, health permitting, enjoy a tolerable standard of living and form part of a literate and informed property-owning society. All were forced to live in close proximity to an impoverished, illiterate, alcohol-addicted and often violent underclass, who lived in squalid conditions and spread disease. Anxious concern with law enforcement and the protection of property and person were therefore widespread.

Pressures for reform were felt from mid-century, when the efforts of the magistrate brothers John and Henry Fielding (the latter the famous and fashionable author of *Tom Jones*) were reinforced by their friend William Hogarth's moralizing engravings of *Gin Lane*. John Fielding's Bow Street Runners were the prototypes of the Metropolitan Police, but a more effective force – which would have made a dramatic difference to crime figures – was strenuously resisted as endangering personal freedom. In the absence of an enforcement agency, the alternative was to increase the severity of punishments. On the Continent, horrifying methods of execution and judicial torture were commonplace (Robert Damiens, the attempted assassin of King Louis XV of France in 1757, was literally torn apart after extensive torture), but in Britain the worst penalty levied was death by hanging, and corporal punishment was in practice limited to whipping or the pillory. (Those convicted of treason were still sentenced to be hanged, drawn and quartered, but the actual capital punishment was limited to the hanging: and as late as 1849 William Smith O'Brien, MP, was so convicted and sentenced; but his punishment was a few years' tolerably comfortable exile.) In 1790 burning women alive for high and petty treason, which could include such offences as coining, was formally abolished; but it had been inflicted within living memory. Imprisonment was only possible where places in prisons were available, and in many parts of the country these were so scarce that minor offenders were often discharged: prisons were therefore generally viewed as places of temporary detention or as encouragements for debtors to discharge their liabilities and fixed sentences of imprisonment were not part of the penal code. Fines were useless as punishments for the propertyless.

Enforced exile, extensively used in Russia, was debated in Britain as early as 1615 as an alternative to execution, but its use as a considered measure of penal policy began, as did so many other reforms, under the Protectorate of Oliver Cromwell, in 1655. Suitable convicts, already conditionally pardoned, could be sent to the American colonies, to serve a term of indenture as servants of an established colonist, usually for seven years. They could then, if they had the means, purchase their liberty – the price for a skilled man was commonly £25 – and both free men and women could voluntarily emigrate under similar conditions. Daniel Defoe pointed out some of the advantages: 'the meanest and most despicable creature, after his time of servitude is expired, if he will but apply himself to the business of the country, is sure (life and health supposed) both of living well and growing rich.' Since such serious offences as murder, rape and witchcraft and buggery did not qualify for such conditional pardons, few of the transportees had committed grave crimes – being a Quaker, or choosing the wrong side in a civil war was enough. Within limits, transportation was generally popular, the colonies got cheap labour, humanitarians could congratulate themselves on the reforming virtues of compulsory work, and all acknowledged that it was much less expensive than having to keep the culprits in prison. The most damaging effect was to allow English legislators to proliferate the number of 'capital' crimes, punishable in theory only by death, but in practice often commuted to transportation. Under the Protectorate there were fewer than 40 such offences; between the Stuart Restoration in 1660 and 1819, 187 more were added. Although this did not result in more executions – perhaps about 1,200 a year in England – it made even-handed administration of justice impossible. Matters were made worse by ancient laws, which littered the statute books with absurd crimes and punishments that were never inflicted. 'Owling' – smuggling sheep out of the country – was punishable by amputation; trial by battle continued legal until the nineteenth century. In the face of such confusion magistrates were reluctant to charge, juries to convict, and judges to sentence the less serious malefactors; punishment was a lottery. Continental critics believed that English courts provided the accused with too many safeguards and so 'sustained a high degree of criminality' (Henri Decremps in 1789); society would surely be better protected by laws more rigorously enforced.[29]

As soon as the outbreak of war made transportation to America impossible, agitated discussion of possible alternatives ensued. The subject of crime and punishment was topical. The Marchese de Beccaria had published his book *Dei delitti e delle pene* in 1764 in which he argued against capital punishment. It was translated into English a few years later, and his theories found many supporters. 'Those dayly Executions so shocking to humanity' could hardly be increased. Could offenders, as William Eden (later Lord Auckland, who happened to own a large part of the Durham coalfield) suggested, be sent to work in the mines? Should these new-fangled 'Penitentiaries', advocated by idealistic Pennsylvanians and by the young Jeremy Bentham, or Jonas Hanway's 'Reformatories', be built? Excellent solutions, but attended by very high expenses.[30]

The great lawyer, Lord Blackstone, and the prison reformer, John Howard (who had the rare qualification for a penologist of having actually been imprisoned), joined forces to obtain the authorization to build two penitentiaries. The Act (19 Geo. III, c. 74) which resulted in 1779 could be regarded as the beginning of the British prison system, but it was a long time before prisons could cope with more than a small proportion of convicts. Bentham's first prison, on Millbank, was opened only in 1816. An immediate solution was to house convicts in obsolete men-of-war 'hulks', cheap enough but lacking any aspect of reform that might be offered by either transportation or properly administered penitentiaries. Recognizing that this should be only a temporary measure, the Act authorized use of the hulks for seven years only.[31]

Alternative sites for transported convicts were canvassed – Madagascar, Tristan da Cunha – and even far distant New South Wales. Joseph Banks, Cook's friend and fellow-voyager, suggested that their first landing place, which had been named 'Botany Bay', might be a suitable spot. It was very thinly peopled, had a climate similar to that of Toulouse, good grass, plentiful fish, and, most important, the region was so 'far distant from any Part of the Globe inhabited by *Europeans . . .*' as to render escape very difficult. Asked by a distrustful committee 'Whether he conceived the Mother Country was likely to Benefit from a Colony established in *Botany Bay?*', Banks could only, rather desperately, suggest that *something* would turn up: surely 'a tract of land such as *New Holland*, which was larger than the whole of *Europe*, would furnish Matter of advantageous Return'. Although Banks was by then famous, very wealthy and the new President of the Royal Society, the Committee was not convinced; the hulks would have to suffice for the time being.

The question was pressed with greater vigour when the next war came to an end in 1783. That fight with France, Spain and, later, Holland, which developed from the rebellion of the American colonies ended with the more southerly colonies independent, English naval reputation damaged, and the usual post-war crime wave as discharged soldiers and sailors struggled to keep alive. Fears of widespread disorder had been kindled by the famous Gordon Riots of 1780, which ended with nearly five hundred dead and wounded in London and carnage on a scale unknown in England since the Civil Wars a century or more earlier. Pressure on prison accommodation grew inexorably as the deadline imposed by the 1779 Hulks Act approached.

From December 1784 a new force entered British politics when Lord Chatham's son, William Pitt the younger, came to power at the age of 24, heading the fourth government to be formed within twenty months. Many more urgent matters occupied the new Prime Minister – mending fences in Europe and America, giving Ireland its first independent parliament and emancipating the Irish Catholics, reorganizing the East India Company and consolidating his own political power base – so that when potential solutions were offered to the convict problem they were eagerly accepted and quickly implemented without too much investigation. Lord Auckland proved the advantages and otherwise of banishment with both classic and modern examples in a pamphlet. The effect was 'often beneficial to the criminal' who was 'merely transferred to a new country; distant indeed, but as fertile, as happy, as civilized, and in general as healthy' – indeed, the prospect of such a sentence might become an inducement to offend.

Transportation was therefore authorized in 1784, but, since a convenient destination was still lacking, there was no possibility of carrying out such sentences, and legal processes became even more discredited. A House of Commons Committee was established in 1785 to consider the future of the thousands of prisoners now miserably confined in the hulks. The members were enthusiastic about transportation – not that they expected that 'the outcasts of an old society [could] serve as the foundation for a new one', but convict labour might be used to build a new settlement that would serve for decent folk to occupy. Where this might be situated was a thornier problem. 'It was immediately necessary to clear the prisons,' the government insisted, and the desperate experiment of sending convicts to the Gambia was attempted in 1785; two hundred were despatched; a year later thirty survived. This was not necessarily a disadvantage, for the Committee considered accepting Lord Auckland's suggestion that especially uncomfortable provision be made for the 'more enormous offenders', and 'atrocious criminals' might be well served by despatch to places where their lives could be 'hazarded in the place of better persons', while younger persons could be accommodated in 'some distant part of the globe' possessing a healthy climate where they might survive to learn better ways. Other 'Parts of *Africa*, which already belong to the Crown of *Great Britain*, or which probably may be acquired for the Purpose in Question' were the first choice. HMS *Nautilus* was sent to investigate. Looked at on maps in Whitehall, Angra das Voltas on the western coast of South Africa, apparently the estuary of a large river, seemed hopeful, but when the *Nautilus* investigated the river was found to be that unreliable stream, the Orange, which falters to the sea in the parched and bleak Namibian desert and on a notably inhospitable coast.

Joseph Banks's suggestion of New South Wales as a penal settlement was revived. 'Heads of the Plan for Botany Bay in New South Wales' suggested:

country which by the fertility and the salubrity of the climate, connected with the remoteness of its situation (from whence it was hardly possible for persons to return without permission) seems peculiarly adapted to answer the views of the government with respect to providing the remedy for the evils likely to result from the late alarming and numerous increase of felons in this country, and more particularly in the Metropolis.[32]

Little was to be feared from the natives, who although 'treacherous and armed with lances', were 'extremely cowardly', and there were no beasts of prey.[33]

The Cabinet was, rightly, suspicious; even after nearly two centuries of desultory voyaging, European knowledge of Terra Australis, New Holland, Botany Bay or what you will was minimal. No sailor had penetrated more than a mile or so from the coast; even Cook, that pertinacious observer, had made only four landings during his first voyage – at Botany Bay, Bustard Bay (where Richard Orton, lying insensibly drunk, had his ears trimmed by a malevolent shipmate), the site of present-day Cooktown, after nearly foundering on the Great Barrier Reef, and Possession Island, when New South Wales was claimed for King George. Seven years later the *Resolution* and the *Discovery* made a short stay in Adventure Bay, Van Diemen's Land. The one indisputable fact, that it was a very long way distant, however agreeable, was certain to prove costly. The Duke of Richmond, anxious to spend whatever cash might be available on the fortification of dockyards, described the plan as 'so very undigested', likely to be 'very expensive' and best abandoned. Evan Nepean, the young under-secretary in the Home department, who had been a purser in the Royal Navy, had anticipated this issue, however, and used his creative accountancy skills to invent figures indicating that the cost of sending convicts and guards to Sir Joseph's recommended site of Botany Bay would turn out to be lower that that of keeping convicts in the hulks let alone building penitentiaries. Having screwed themselves up to the painful recommendation to spend public money, ministers looked for any possible reason that might help to bolster their case, but as those familiar with the immutable ways of government departments can recognize, these were mostly flummery and window dressing; the essential was to get rid of the convicts.

Pitt announced the decision on 23 January 1787, to subdued parliamentary approval – only one member commented – but to much public satisfaction. Might it not be that at Botany Bay 'the perfection of the present race of men appeared on the most enlarged view destined to be consummated', peopled with beings who 'would be an ornament to human nature', and where soon 'broad streets, their stately walls extend'? A new opera, *Botany Bay*, opened in London at the Royal Circus Theatre, but suspicious Scots fretted that the venture would prove fearfully expensive, and Sir Nathaniel Wraxall, MP, was frankly horrified. The huge spaces of New Holland may, 'in the year five thousand from Christ, be peopled by the descendants of British malefactors' but it was

far more probable that, like the Buccaneers, so famous, and so dreaded by Spain in the last century, they will soon emancipate themselves from the feeble restraint impos'd upon them; that they may, in succeeding times, fill the Chinese and Indian seas, with slaughter and depredation, notwithstanding the prodigious distance, at which even these parts of the earth are removed from New Holland.

The responsibility for implementing the decision became that of Thomas Townshend, Lord Sydney, an undistinguished ('although respectable, his abilities scarcely rose above the mediocre') member of a rich and powerful family, who had been rewarded for his consistent support of Pitt the elder and his successor Lord Shelburne by being given the Secretaryship of Home Affairs, which included responsibility for the remaining colonies, in the younger Pitt's administration. 'I am therefore commanded', Sydney wrote to the Treasury, 'to signify to your Lordships his Majesty's pleasure that you do forthwith take such measures as may be necessary for providing a proper number of vessels for the conveyance of 750 convicts to Botany Bay, together with such provisions, necessaries, and implements for agriculture as may be necessary for their use after their arrival.' They were to be accompanied by some 180 marines, which number should include some skilled tradesmen with the necessary tools and provisions, and 'perhaps two hundred females'. Honest work would perhaps achieve the purpose so earnestly desired by the House:

That the enterprizing Disposition which many of them have shewn, would, under a strict Controul, peculiarly fit them for the Defence of a new Settlement – that an Aversion to Labour, and the Inequality of Fortunes, which stimulate Men at Home to the Commission of Crime, could, in such a State of Things, have no Operation – that the ordinary Seductions would be beyond their Reach, and consequently they would remain honest, for Want of a Temptation to be otherwise – That having no Hope of returning, they would consider their own Happiness as involved in the Prosperity of the Settlement, and act accordingly.

And casting about for something that would placate the cheese-paring Treasury, Sydney concluded

that the difference of expense (whatever method of carrying the convicts thither may be adopted) that this mode of disposing of them and that of the usual ineffectual one is too trivial to be a consideration with Government, at least in comparison with the great object to be obtained by it, especially now the evil is increased to such an alarming degree, from the inadequacy of all other expedients that have thitherto been tried or suggested.[34]

As an example, Lord Sydney suggested that New Zealand hemp might be cultivated for rope-making, and that masts and spars might be made available for Indian-built shipping. These proposals were made by Admiral Sir George Young, who saw potential profit to himself in acquiring the rights to exploit Norfolk Island, an isolated spot 1,000 miles from the coast of New Holland; an equally unrealistic idea of the admiral's was that Botany Bay might be used as a port of call for the China trade, in spite of its being 3,000 miles off the usual route. He also suggested the importation of Chinese labourers (as Jan van Riebeeck had so earnestly begged for in South Africa) and of Polynesian women, both ideas that would have been anathema to nineteenth-century Australians. Moreover, should a war with Spain break out – and Spain was being very defensive of her Pacific interests – 'cruisers from Botany Bay might much interrupt, if not destroy, their lucrative commerce from the Philippine islands to Aquapulco, besides alarming and distressing their settlements on the west coast of South America'.[35]

To establish a convict settlement in New Holland was either an extremely bold – and Lord Sydney was never bold – or a desperate enterprise. Previous transportations had been to already established societies, easily accessible, where the convicts could be absorbed, controlled and supplied. To take a thousand people across the world, on a voyage of at least six months, to a region superficially visited and quite unsurveyed, believed to be to all intents and purposes uninhabited, many weeks' sail from the nearest support, was a desperate expedient, to be justified as the only possible 'remedy for the evils likely to result from the late alarming and numerous increase of felons in this country, and more particularly in the metropolis'. Nevertheless, preparations for the selection of suitable convicts, and their despatch under escort to an uncertain future in Botany Bay, were put in hand.

2

The New Australians

'The finest harbour in the universe'

The voyage of the First Fleet, which began from an anchorage off the Isle of Wight on 13 May 1787, was the eighteenth-century equivalent of an interplanetary expedition. A thousand people were setting off on a journey of unknown duration that might take anything from six months to a year, to an unexplored and almost unvisited continent, peopled by men speaking no known language and of doubtful temperament. Except for water and timber, the travellers would be entirely dependent on what they had brought with them, and, in due course, whatever they could grow in a strange climate on untried soil. The voyage itself was full of perils: the fleet's largest vessel was lost within two years, and the best-equipped relief ship sank on the way out. In emergencies, the nearest help was likely to be that of the Dutch in Batavia, although when assistance was urgently needed it was found that the appeal had to be sent halfway around the southern hemisphere, to the Cape of Good Hope.

A prudent and resourceful leader was essential, and it was provided by Captain Arthur Phillip RN. Three things were needed to assure success in the Georgian Royal Navy: talent, luck and patronage, and of these the greatest was patronage. Like Cook, Phillip began his sea service in the merchant marine, and from the start of his career had the backing of the Duke of Grafton. During the early years of Grafton's success – he was Prime Minister at the age of 31 – Phillip's career advanced, but as Grafton's reputation declined, Phillip's popularity waned: he had to wait nineteen years before moving from the rank of lieutenant to that of captain, and his brief career in command (1781–4) had been uneventful. Lord Howe, First Lord of the Admiralty, was surprised when Phillip was suggested for the Botany Bay command. 'I cannot say', wrote Howe, 'that the little knowledge I have of Captain Phillip would have led me to select him for service of this complicated nature.' It is probable, however, that Phillip had the support of his neighbour and MP, Sir George Rose, who had also served in the Royal Navy and was a close friend of Prime Minister William Pitt.[1]

In fact, it would have been difficult to select a better commander than Phillip. During one of his prolonged periods of unemployment he had served with the Portuguese navy, when he conveyed 400 convicts across the Atlantic without losing a man, thus making him probably the only Royal Navy officer with experience relevant to the project; he had farmed his own land at Lyndhurst in Hampshire and it is possible that his German pedagogic breeding – his father was a teacher from Frankfurt – may have contributed to his strong sense of order and organization, not to mention his missing sense of humour. Lord Howe, unsure of Phillip, appointed one of his own favourites, John Hunter, as captain of the frigate *Sirius*, the expedition's flagship. Another excellent officer, Hunter was eventually, after an unfortunate interregnum, to succeed Phillip as Governor in 1796. Phillip himself was able to select one of the officers with whom he had previously served, Lieutenant Philip Gidley King, in due course also to become a Governor of New South Wales. Phillip, Hunter and King were all officers from modest backgrounds who had been obliged to work their way slowly up the naval hierarchy: Hunter was 42, with twenty-six years service, before he even received his first royal commission.

Phillip exerted himself – and exertions were very necessary to ensure that Georgian dockyards performed adequately – in order to have the expedition properly prepared. His campaign began on 24 October 1786, when he made his headquarters in the Deptford dockyard. By the following March, when the convicts were beginning to board, Phillip was growing almost desperate. The ships still needed to be thoroughly cleaned; proper anti-scorbutics had to be provided; one of the transports must be designated as a hospital ship; he had to order clothes for the convicts on his own account. 'These complaints', he told Evan Nepean, 'do not come unexpected, nor were they unavoidable. I foresaw them from the beginning, and repeatedly pointed them out.' He had nothing but contempt for the civil authorities. 'The situation in which the magistrates sent the women on board the *Lady Penrhyn*, stamps them with infamy – tho' almost naked, and so very filthy, that nothing but clothing them could have prevented them from perishing.'[2]

It was not details only, but the tenor of his instructions, which left Phillip concerned. Botany Bay might not prove satisfactory; he might then, Lord Sydney conceded, find somewhere else, but he was not to waste time 'under the pretence of searching for a more eligible place'. It was far too late to do anything about another wise proposal of Phillip's, that an advance party should be sent with a group of artisans in order to build huts 'ready to receive the Convicts who were sick', and to ensure that 'the Stores would be properly lodged and defended from the Convicts'.

Captain Phillip's command consisted of the *Sirius*, the brig *Supply*, 175 tons, acting as tender, three store ships and six transports. The total tonnage of the store ships was 981, that of the transports, 2,164. Overcrowding was inevitable, and the need to replenish water could only be met by calls at Tenerife, Rio de Janeiro and Cape Town, where the fleet lay for a month. The opportunity was taken by Phillip to provide his charges with fresh food (many convicts were to fare much better, in spite of the difficult conditions, than they ever had as free men: 'extreme indulgence', Surgeon Arthur Bowes Smythe called it). When the fleet anchored in Botany Bay on 20 January 1788 after a passage of some 8,000 miles, there had been forty-eight deaths, a remarkably low figure and proof of Phillip's careful planning.

The travellers were now on their own, half a world away from home, dependent on the supplies they had brought with them and their own abilities. Before the expedition left, English publishers had staked their claim to a share of any potential profits by commissioning books from some of the officers. Governor Phillip and his second in command John Hunter had contracted with John Stockdale of Piccadilly, Captain David Collins with Cadell & Davies, and Captain Watkins Tench of the Marines with a house that has survived rather better, that of John Debrett; the enterprise was to be unusually well documented. It was quickly apparent that the attractions of Botany Bay had been greatly overstated by Banks; the ground appeared (wrongly as it subsequently proved) unsuitable for cultivation and the harbour was not as well protected as Phillip could have wished. A much better site was quickly located a few miles to the north, in Port Jackson, which had been noted but not investigated by Cook and named after Sir George Jackson, Cook's patron (who – fortunately later – changed his name to Duckett, which would doubtless have led to countless dubious jokes being made about the inhabitants had it occurred earlier). On 26 January the fleet accordingly shifted the anchorage to Port Jackson.

By fortunate chance Captain Phillip had discovered one of the world's best natural harbours; 'the finest and most extensive harbour in the Universe', enthused Chief Surgeon John White. With sheltered deep water extending several miles inland, it could easily afford 'a sufficient and safe anchorage for all the navies of Europe'. Surgeon George Worgan, an admirer of the picturesque, who had brought a piano in his luggage, described 'a variety of Romantic views, all thrown together into sweet confusion . . . Here a romantic, rocky, craggy Precipice over which a little swirling stream makes a cascade. There a soft vivid-green shady Lawn attracts your eye.'

Master's-mate Daniel Southwell imagined a future harbour ornamented with 'charming seats, superb buildings and grand ruins of stately edifices'. The site selected, named Sydney Cove, allowed moorings close to the shore, and had an excellent water supply from the Tank Stream. But in spite of the fact that, with the change of harbour, no convict was ever sent there, the happy alliteration continued to make 'Botany Bay' synonomous with the convict settlement.[3]

The first exchanges between the visitors and the Old Australians were amiable enough. After refusing to obey the shouts of 'Worra, Worra', later discovered to mean 'go away', the landing party under Philip King's command distributed presents and began to attempt conversation. It was striking how quickly the Old Australians adapted themselves to the astonishing newcomers. Arriving in huge, alien, incomprehensible vessels, in scarlet and blue uniforms (the convicts were kept on board) the Englishmen appeared quite un-human to those to whom any sort of covering was unknown. Better understanding was achieved when an embarrassed marine was ordered to exhibit his essential masculinity, and King had tied a white handkerchief to one girl 'Where Eve did the fig leaf'. Such limited intercourse was not difficult to control, but could not last. The new arrivals were not God-fearing religious men, like the Massachusetts Puritans, or the decent patient Quakers and Mennonites, all anxious to make a new life, who founded Pennsylvania with due (although hardly exaggerated) concern for the rights of the inhabitants. They were instead the convicts and guards of a penal colony, most of whom fervently wished to be at home, all of whom were subject to military discipline.[4]

That discipline ensured a brisk beginning. Within a week, rocks and trees had been cleared, the Governor's tiny prefabricated cottage erected, seeds sown and the astronomical instruments, which provided one reason for the settlement, safely installed. By May, houses, huts and a hospital had been put together, and an elegant three-roomed Government House begun where the Museum of Sydney now stands.

In spite of its advantages, Sydney Cove was not an ideal place for settlement, since the terrain made agriculture impracticable. A better spot was found 15 miles inland at Parramatta (at first named Rose Hill) where a house for the Governor was built in 1789 and a township was begun the following year. Governor Phillip's great plans for a Sydney of 'Imperial grandeur' to be renamed 'Albion' were reluctantly abandoned. 'Sydney', according to Captain Tench, '. . . exhibits nothing but a few old scattered huts and some sterile gardens, and all our strength is transferred to Rose Hill'; by 1792, Parramatta had 1,970 inhabitants to Sydney's 1,170, but thereafter the figures reversed as Sydney became established as the seat of government and the centre of commerce.[5]

Phillip had been given responsibility as Captain General and Governor in Chief for all New South Wales, described as extending to 135 degrees east (a reflection of the old division between New Holland and Terra Australis which runs near present-day Coober Pedy) thus nearly bisecting the land mass; in fact, his effective authority was exercised only within a few miles of Sydney Cove (with the exception of the later settlement on Norfolk Island). The dynamics of newcomers as a group were complex. All of them had been removed from their normal habitat; the marines to become convict guards on shore, and the convicts themselves, uprooted from country villages or the warrens of great towns, left to survive as best they could in a frightening new environment. All were now under sentence of at least temporary exile, all living under miserable conditions, eating similar food, and with further privation, if not actual starvation, a real possibility. The military were constrained by discipline, the convicts by the threat of force, but the civilians continued to be bound by the codes of eighteenth-century England. Dinners, most usually of salt pork, accompanied by rum or a little precious wine, were the common social entertainment of the officers, with guests seated in tents according to their accepted status: they were asked to bring their own bread, the rarest of foods. Disputes and offences naturally continued; the most common and generally abominated crime was the theft of food. Within days of disembarkation, floggings were ordered and one convict executed. On 27 February, a month after the landing, a marine, Thomas Barrit, 'an old and desperate offender', was hanged for stealing food, followed the next day by two more. Phillip's justice was stern, but even-handed. With such unreliable elements among the guards, control was fraught with difficulties. Regular policing began with the Night Watch of 1789, established at the suggestion of a convict, and staffed mainly by convicts 'whose conduct and character has been unexceptionable'. Super-intendents of convicts did not arrive until 1790, and then only five of them; for the rest, convicts elected their own gang leaders. One of the superintendents, Philip Schaeffer, had fought in the American War, as one of the 'Hessian' officers, and in 1791 he was established as one of the first three free settlers, on a Parramatta farm.[6]

The new arrivals were not only criminals (in so far as the word has much moral meaning given the petty offences then classed as crimes), but incompetent criminals, having been caught – often repeatedly – and unlucky, having been charged and sentenced. Like any twenty-first-century prison population, a considerable percentage, perhaps the majority, were guilty only of being unable to adapt to the customs of their society. Of those whose charges have been identified, more than half came from Middlesex, Kent and Sussex – London and the suburbs. About a tenth of the total were sentenced for agricultural offences – sheep and cattle-stealing; Devon was the most criminal county, and Wales the most law-abiding region. Most were thieves, over half with previous convictions, and usually from the cities. Two enterprising villains, William Mariner and Thomas Gearing, were sentenced to death, commuted to transportation, for 'sacrilege' – stealing the silver from the chapel of Magdalen College, Oxford. Contrary to popular belief, very few indeed – about 57 – had any record of violence, and 'political' prisoners represented only a tiny percentage. Nor were there many poachers, the usual penalty for simple poaching being a £5 fine. Many came without proper documentation; some, indeed, without names – 'Black Jack', 'Bone', 'Gash' and 'Major' among them. Of the two hundred women, many, although sentenced for theft, must also have been prostitutes – again acknowledging that the word has little moral significance in a society such as that of eighteenth-century London. Little effort had been made to select convicts or marines who might be useful; few tradesmen were numbered among them, although fortunately a single bricklayer was 'discovered' among the convicts, and was set to constructing the first permanent buildings. Jewish 'white collar' criminals were among the most useful convicts, and included Ikey Solomon, the possible model for Charles Dickens's Fagin, who ended up in Van Diemen's Land demanding the services of a convict domestic. All in all, it was not the ideal material with which to populate a new country.[7]

While it was true that convicts sent to Australia must have included many who were but poorly equipped to cope with the stresses and challenges of life either there or in Britain, once landed a brutally swift process of Darwinian natural selection was set in motion. All had been subjected to a series of ordeals – trial, sentence, confinement, separation from home and family, a long voyage culminating in being landed in the strangest of lands, with no familiar trees or birds, bizarre creatures, and the crushing restriction of infinite space. The older and weaker died; the idle, brutal and resentful crashed head to head with authority, and paid the price with their skin in floggings and in the chain gang; the better educated, the skilled and the adaptable young effected their own compromises and survived – and found partners. Marriage, even of the most unofficial type, conferred a degree of respectability, thereby gaining official protection and access to better assignments and opportunities. Any children of convicts could claim that they descended, not from the dregs of British society, but those who had survived, and had demonstrated remarkable qualities in so doing. It is therefore hardly necessary to claim, as many historians used to do, that the convicts were victims of cruel punishments – which they were – harshly inflicted – which they were not; many judges and juries went to great pains to ensure that charges were reduced and verdicts mollified.

Phillip's first optimistic accounts were received with great enthusiasm in England. Josiah Wedgwood produced a medallion, made of white Sydney clay, which depicted Hope encouraging Art and Labour under the direction of Peace, which figured as the frontispiece to the Governor's book, along with a poem by Erasmus Darwin, grandfather of Charles, entitled 'The Visit of Hope to Sydney-Cove, near Botany-Bay':

> Where Sydney Cove her lucid bosom swells,
> Courts her young navies, and the storm repels;
> High on a rack amid the troubled air
> HOPE stood sublime, and wav'd her golden hair,
>
> .   .   .   .   .   .
>
> 'Hear me,' she cried, 'ye rising Realms! Record
> Time's opening scenes, and Truth's unerring word. –
> There shall broad streets their stately walls extend,
> The circus widen, and the crescent bend;
> There, ray'd from cities o'er the cultur'd land,
> Shall bright canals, and solid road expand. –
> There the proud arch, Colossus-like, bestride
> Yon glittering streams, and bound the chasing tide;
> Embellish'd villas crown the landscape-scene,
> Farms wave with gold, and orchards blush between. –
> There shall tall spires, and dome-capt towers ascend,
> And piers and quays their massy structures blend;
> While with each breeze approaching vessels glide,
> And northern treasures dance on every tide! –'
> Then ceased the nymph – tumultuous echoes roar,
> And JOY's loud voice was heard from shore to shore –
> Her graceful steps descending press'd the plain,
> And PEACE and ART, and LABOUR join'd her train.

Erasmus's optimism took some time to be justified, but fifty years later Charles was able to report: 'This is really a wonderful Colony . . . When my Grandfather wrote the lines of "Hope's visit to Sydney Cove" on Mr Wedgwood's medallion he prophesied most truly.'[8]

The first guards were not much better qualified than the convicts, but they were not, after all, intended to become permanent residents. The three companies of Marines sent with the First Fleet made difficulties about assuming any but the most strictly military duties. They were resentful of the fact that they were treated on a level with the convicts, given the same rations and punished with even greater severity. Their commanding officer, Major Robert Ross, was an aggressive Scot ('the most disagreeable man I ever knew', according to one of his subordinates) who thought little of Port Jackson – 'in the whole world there is not a worse country' – and that Sydney would 'never answer'. In December 1791 the Marines left, to be replaced in the following year by the New South Wales Regiment, formed for the purpose in England, in part from offenders offered the option of Botany Bay or a military prison. The 'Rum Corps', as it became known, has been given a poor press, but their first commanding officer, Major Francis Grose, was a considerable improvement on Ross.

Phillip's firm and fair rule answered extremely well. Tench reported in October: 'All descriptions of men enjoy the highest state of health and the convicts continue to behave extremely well.' In spite of the vagaries of the Sydney climate, 'all is as quiet and stupid as could be wished.' Phillip's clemency was also extended to the 'Indians', in whom the Governor and others found much to admire. Manly Cove was so named by the Governor. 'from the manly, undaunted behaviour of a party of natives seen there'. Undaunted the Old Australians certainly were, disdaining the invaders' firearms and furious at this interference with the environment on which their lives depended. Isolated parties of convicts were speared and clubbed until Phillip ordered some of the natives to be captured, which would either provoke an outburst, or 'induce an intercourse, by the report of which our prisoners would make of the mildness and indulgence' with which they were treated. The first reluctant guest was one Arabanoo, who spent nine months living with the British, certainly treated with 'indulgence', although at first under some form of constraint.[9]

Captain Tench's perceptive account of Arabanoo illustrates how far racial prejudices could be set aside by men of goodwill:

The character of Arabanoo, as far as we had developed it, was distinguished by a portion of gravity and steadiness which our subsequent acquaintance with his countrymen by no means led us to conclude a national characteristic. In that daring, enterprising frame of mind which, when combined with genius, constitutes the leader of a horde of savages, or the ruler of a people boasting the power of discrimination and the resistance of ambition, he was certainly surpassed by some of his successors who afterwards lived among us. His countenance was thoughtful but not animated. His fidelity and gratitude particularly to his friend the governor, were constant and undeviating and deserve to be recorded. Although of a gentle and placable temper, we early discovered that he was impatient of indignity and allowed of no superiority on our part. He knew that he was in our power but the independence of his mind never forsook him. If the slightest insult were offered to him he would return it with interest. At retaliation of merriment he was often happy, and frequently turned the laugh against his antagonist. He did not want docility, but either from the difficulty of acquiring our language, from the unskilfulness of his teachers, or from some natural defect, his progress in learning was not equal to what we had expected. For the last three or four weeks of his life, hardly any restraint was laid upon his inclinations, so that had he meditated escape, he might easily have effected it. He was, perhaps, the only native who was ever attached to us from choice, and who did not prefer a precarious subsistance among wilds and precipices to the comforts of a civilised system.

It was to be many years before any other European could assist the 'Indians' with such decent simplicity.[10]

Arabanoo died from the effects of smallpox. This disease, previously unknown, must have been introduced into Australia by voyagers. Tench pondered possible explanations. Had it been brought with Laperouse? By Dampier or Cook? 'Did we give it birth here? No person among us had been afflicted with the disorder since we had quitted the Cape of Good Hope, seventeen months before. It is true that our surgeons had brought out variolous matter in bottles, but to infer that it was produced from this cause were a supposition so wild as to be unworthy of consideration.' Wild and unworthy the supposition may have been, but it has recently been revived, and the suggestion made that smallpox was deliberately introduced to kill off the Aborigines, a theory for which little evidence can be advanced, and which is contradicted by the attitude of Tench and his colleagues.[11]

At first the Aborigines were the objects of much interested concern, and Governor Phillip set standards of benevolence. Bennelong, commemorated by his name being given to the eastern tip of Sydney Cove, Bennelong Point, regarded himself as a particular friend of the Governor, and was so treated; his wife Barangaroo, whose 'feminine innocence, softness and modesty' so impressed young Tench, was invited to dine at Government House, and Bennelong himself was taken by Phillip on a visit to England. It was to be another two centuries, after familiarity had bred contempt, tinged with fear, before such cordial relationships would be resumed.

Goodwill and efforts at mutual understanding could do little to soften the catastrophic effects of the Europeans' arrival. The new plagues, smallpox, venereal disease and tuberculosis being the first, were followed by influenza and cholera. Adult men usually recovered from smallpox, which could be a death sentence to pregnant women and to children. Twenty years after the first settlement there were probably still as many warriors in the region who had by now experienced the inroads on their own resources being made by the settlers and were more ready to resist them; it was the decline in the female population, smallpox deaths being combined with reproductive damage – 'I fear our people have to answer for that', Collins regretted – that caused the later catastrophic drop in the Aboriginal population around the area of original settlement. As this expanded into areas where Aborigines were comparatively unaffected, the British diseases were reinforced by violence.

'The dread of perishing by famine'

One long, costly and unnecessary burden was added to the new settlement by Phillip's instructions for Norfolk Island to be occupied. Cook, impressed by its magnificent pines, had reported favourably on this unprepossessing piece of rock, isolated in the ocean 1,000 miles to the east of Sydney. One Whitehall map-scanner, Sir John Call, MP, formerly of the Honourable East India Company's army, had pointed out that the island had 'an Advantage not common to New Caledonia, New Holland and New Zealand, by not being inhabited' and should serve at least as a 'useful subsidiary' to any mainland settlement, if not indeed as the proposed colony itself. As well as believing that the magnificent pines native to the island would serve admirably for spars, the Admiralty feared that the French might decide to make it a naval base. This was an unreasonable apprehension; the island had no natural harbour, or even good offshore holding ground (as the unhappy *Sirius* was to find). Had the French been interested in such expansion, which subsequent events showed to be unlikely, they had many better opportunities in the Pacific archipelagos and, even had they taken possession, could not have held on in face of the Royal Navy's command of the seas, then just about to be re-established.

But, obedient to orders, Lieutenant King was sent off to Norfolk Island to do whatever he could, with the assistance of a surgeon, eleven convicts and six marines, and a month's rations. His convicts were carefully selected, none having been sentenced for violent crimes; and the women among them being volunteers. Landing on 4 March, the energetic King set about cultivating the land and attempting, without great success, to grow the flax which had attracted so much interest in London, subsisting meanwhile on rations and the migrating 'mutton birds'. These ground-nesting petrels were found in great abundance, and had saved the lives of many shipwrecked sailors; they were to become a staple food of the Norfolk Island garrison.

Back on the mainland, cultivation was disappointingly slow, and supplies became worryingly short. One tragedy was the loss of the herd of two bulls and five cows which had been carefully brought from Cape Town, and which wandered off – competent countrymen were sadly lacking among the convicts – soon after the disembarkation. By October 1788, with no news of any relief from England, Phillip cut the rations and despatched the little brig *Supply* to Cape Town to obtain food. Captain John Hunter decided on the bold course of sailing westward, round Cape Horn, rather than the much shorter eastward route, on which he would be hampered by contrary winds. His judgement was good, and Cape Town was reached in the fast time of three months. By May 1789 *Supply* had returned, after having circumnavigated the globe – a dramatic indication of the isolation of the new settlement. But her provisions would not last long. By April 1790 rations had been halved, to the basic minimum necessary for survival. One marine officer wrote on 14 April:

By the time this reaches you, the fate of this settlement, and all it contains will be decided. It is now more than two years since we landed here . . . So cut off from all intercourse with the rest of mankind are we, that, subsequent to the month of August 1788, we know not [more] of any transaction that has happened in Europe . . . than of what passes in the moon. It is by those only who have felt the anguish and distress of such a state that its miseries can be conceived . . . the dread of perishing by famine stares us in the face . . . As to parade duties and show, we have long laid them aside . . . Our soldiers have not a shoe, and mount guard barefoot.

In an effort to disperse the burden, *Sirius* and *Supply* were despatched in March 1790 to Norfolk Island, where the energetic King had been tolerably successful in raising food crops. Wheat, maize, potatoes, cabbages, pears, peaches, guavas and lemons were beginning to flourish, all much more successfully than at Sydney, although the flax never came to much. *Supply* would land a third of Port Jackson's convicts, with the necessary guards, before *Sirius* sailed off to Canton to see what help might be had from the East India Company's factories. The results were disastrous. The fine frigate *Sirius* was wrecked on the reef, although all her crew was saved (Hunter, although a prime seaman, was unlucky with ships – *Sirius* was his second total wreck, and he was to have one more before his career ended). Norfolk

Island was left with an unsustainably large population and Phillip with only one small vessel at his disposal and near famine, with the consequent breakdown in discipline, among his colony.[12]

It was not that London had entirely forgotten about its distant responsibility. The Second Fleet had sailed between July 1789 and January 1790. Unlike Phillip's command, this venture had been subcontracted to a commercial firm of slavers, Camden, Calvert and King, who had undertaken to convey convicts for a fee of £17. 7s. 6d. per head, whether they survived the passage or not. As might have been expected, 267 of the 1,000 convicts died at sea, and many more were landed in a dying state. Chaplain Richard Johnson visited the ships and reported:

The misery I saw amongst them is unexpressible; many were not able to turn, or even to stir themselves, and in this situation were covered over almost with their own nastiness; their heads, bodies, cloths, blanket all full of filth and lice . . . one man I visited this morning, I think, I may safely say had 10,000 lice upon his body and bed . . . The usage they met with on board, according to their own story, was truly shocking . . . they have been to the middle in water, chained together, hand and leg, even the sick not exempted.[13]

Philip had proved that transportation could be humanely effected; after the Second Fleet trickled in between June and July 1790, the sentence looked very much like a ticket in a lottery for death.

Conditions were made much worse in that these new mouths to feed were unaccompanied by the anticipated stores. The *Guardian*, a 44-gun frigate, had accompanied the convoy, well equipped with provisions and tools, but attempting to take on water from an iceberg was wrecked, although again (she was commanded by Captain Edward Riou, one of the navy's best officers) all her people were saved. Phillip was horrified by the condition of the convicts, and furious at this aggravation of his responsibilities; he wrote indignantly to William Wyndham Grenville, Sydney's successor from June 1789: 'sending out the disordered and helpless clears the gaols . . . but . . . it is obvious that the settlement instead of being a colony which will supply itself, will, if this practice is continued, remain for years a burthen on the mother country.' A shocked outcry arose in London when the facts were known, and it was discovered that many convicts had not been given their full rations, which were sold on arrival for the company's profit. One captain, Traill of the *Neptune*, was charged with wilful murder but never stood trial.[14]

The 'disordered and helpless'

Were the Botany Bay experience to be repeated two hundred years later it is likely that an even higher percentage of the 'disordered and helpless' would be included, since these form so large a proportion of today's prisoners. New South Wales was fortunate in that a proportion of its first arrivals were people of talent, who had been unlucky enough to be caught offending against one of the great many laws that might result in transportation. Otherwise respectable middle-class convicts were given immediate 'tickets of leave' on arrival at Sydney which enabled them to work in government service. The first convict to be pardoned and given an official function was appointed to the very necessary post of public executioner. Those with a trade were assured of decent terms of employment, especially since there were so few of them – eventually only six carpenters, two bricklayers, one baker and one fisherman. Unskilled labourers had to work for the government for nine hours a day, but were free to do what they could to keep themselves for the rest of the time, with minimal supervision. However harsh the circumstances, hope of a better future could be discerned.

Even the women, with some skill and much fortitude, could make a haven for themselves. Take the career of Elizabeth Needham, a seamstress, sentenced to seven years' transportation in 1786, who arrived in 1788 with the First Fleet. Within a few days of disembarkation, she was married to another convict (she was already married in England, but such administrative inconveniences were often overlooked). Both she and her husband received grants of land when their sentences expired; Elizabeth also took up, after her husband's death, the licence of the Wheatsheaf Inn and worked as a seamstress. In 1797 she married again, her husband being another emancipated convict, John Driver. The Drivers flourished, setting up a shop and licensed store, Elizabeth retaining control of her own money and making substantial investments in shipping. In 1810 she married for the last time, her final husband being Henry Marr; he had been transported in 1800 and by 1810 had also amassed a substantial fortune in property, including the Black Horse Inn in Pitt Street. Before her death in 1825 Elizabeth had returned three times to England: clearly able, had she wished, to re-establish herself there, she instead elected to make her life in the new country.

Elizabeth's career exemplifies the dilemma of New South Wales. As a convict settlement, under the arbitrary control of the Governor, the normal processes of common law did not apply there. Once a convict had served his sentence he was again, overnight, a free English subject, entitled to the full protection of the law and often very willing to exploit those who had not yet achieved that station. Under the humane and egalitarian governorship of Phillip, who pulled the unhappy and hungry community through three years of near-starvation, the anomalies could be contained, but the tension between sentence-expired or pardoned convicts – emancipists – and the slowly growing number of free settlers, many of whom were faring much less well, was to remain a problem for many years.[15]

The colony had to make do with an informal, ad hoc system of administration, concentrating on solving immediate problems. The senior law officer was Deputy Judge Advocate David Collins, a serving soldier commanded by the Royal Instructions to 'observe and follow such orders and directions from time to time as you shall receive from our Governor . . . or any other superior officer . . .', but at the same time to discharge his legal duties and apply English law, although this should be done in a 'more summary way' than in England. It was asking a lot from a marine captain who had left school at the age of 14 to cope with what the Lord Chief Justice himself had described as a 'novelty in our constitution', designed for 'the present state of that embryo (for I can't call it either settlement or colony)', but Collins coped to Governor Phillip's great satisfaction. Criminal cases were dealt with by Collins, presiding over a panel of six service officers; civil jurisdiction was entrusted to the Deputy Judge Advocate together with one or two other 'fit and proper persons' appointed by the Governor.[16]

Civil law in the 'embryo' has been well described as 'informal, accessible and amateur'. It was also speedy and as a result popular. The very first case was brought in May 1788 by two convicts, Henry and Susannah Kable, against the captain of the ship on which they had been transported. Kable won, and went on to become a modestly prosperous businessman, dying at the age of 84. Under English law the Kables, as convicted felons, were 'legally dead' and would have been unable to sue in a court of law, but in New South Wales, a convict colony, the regulation would have been absurd; from the first it was clear that Australia would evolve its own peculiar institutions, which often proved to be well in advance of those in the home country.[17]

After the arrival of the Third Fleet, between July and October 1791, contacts with Britain were never interrupted for so long, but the uncertainty of the voyage and the time involved meant that any useful communication was very difficult. The Third Fleet's people had arrived in little better case than those of the Second; Camden, Calvert and King had again obtained the contract. From 222 convicts landed from the *Queen*, only 50 were still alive nine months later. Once again Phillip raged, regretting that he had not 'the power of inflicting a punishment adequate to the crime'. London promised to try harder, and indeed future transports were usually somewhat better managed; contractors were given a bonus for every convict that was landed, but the fine record of the First Fleet was never repeated. Phillip, granted much-needed leave, left in December 1792, but ill-health prevented his return just as 'the colony is approaching to that state which I have so longed and anxiously wish to see it'. By that time the attention of Pitt's government, never very firmly fixed on colonial matters, was beginning to be occupied elsewhere, notably by the effects of the French Revolution.

The outbreak in February 1793 of a war which was to last, with two brief intermissions, for the next twenty-two years swept Australia to the very bottom of the political agenda. The settlement's isolation became more pronounced – and also indicated how fallacious the arguments for a strategic station in Sydney Cove had been. At the same time, the convict problem was simplified: any of those sentenced in Britain, and even the unsuspecting innocent, could be swept up into the army and navy, while increased employment helped discourage crime, especially in the countryside. And the nature of crime itself was changing under the pressure of revolutionary ideas, as representatives of a different class of convict, those sentenced for 'political offences', the definition of which was sometimes fluid, began to arrive in Australia.

Charles James Fox and his Whig supporters retained their sympathy for the French even after war had begun; others were horrified by republican ideas, and none more so than the Scottish and Irish establishments. Although Scotland was a ferment of intellectual activity – David Hume and Adam Smith had helped in making Edinburgh the modern Athens, with a university better regarded than Oxford and Cambridge (two nineteenth-century British Prime Ministers were educated there) – that country had retained her own laws, in many respects less liberal than those of England (Scottish coal miners, for example, were still held in a state approaching that of slavery). The appalling Scottish judge Lord Braxfield, characterized as 'coarse and illiterate', was of a breed not seen in England since Judge Jeffreys a century before. When the inoffensive lawyer and church elder Thomas Muir was accused in August 1793 of sedition, on the flimsiest of grounds, Braxfield sentenced him to fourteen years' transportation, growling that since the British constitution was perfect, anyone suggesting alteration was, *ipso facto*, an enemy of the state. Faced with a similar charge in May of that year in London, John Frost, another lawyer, had got away with six months (but he *was* a Wykehamist and a former friend of Pitt's). Muir, and the Reverend Thomas Palmer, a Cambridge graduate and Unitarian minister, together with three others, the 'Scottish Martyrs', were well treated on their arrival, allotted land and convict servants, but two died of illness within a short time. It was their acceptance as educated middle-class men that determined their status in New South Wales; middle-class solidarity guaranteeing that they would not be treated with the violence routinely accorded to those lower in the social scale.[18]

One early arrival to benefit from his social status was D'Arcy Wentworth, an Irish gentleman connected with the great family of Earl Fitzwilliam, who arrived, not as a convict, but having left 'his country for his country's good', after surviving two trials for highway robbery. Wentworth progressed to become the colony's chief surgeon, superintendent of police, and the master of an extensive estate; his – very respectable – co-habitation with a convict girl was to found the most ancient of Australian dynasties.[19] Much less respectable was the ex-sheriff of Cork, Sir Henry Brown Hayes, sentenced in 1801 for abducting an heiress. Constantly in trouble with the authorities, Hayes was eventually pardoned but before his return to Ireland had constructed an elegant pavilion on Vaucluse Bay that was subsequently bought and extended by Wentworth's son, William, and is now a national monument. Other Irishmen of all social strata found their way to New South Wales as their country flared into rebellion.[20]

Led by Henry Grattan and Henry Flood, the Irish Parliament, in a disquieting echo of the American colonists, had agitated for freedom from British-imposed restrictions. After the fall of Lord North's government, his successor Lord Rockingham agreed in 1782 that the Irish Parliament should be independent and there should be no right of appeal from Irish courts to Britain; but the executive power in Ireland remained with the resident chief officers appointed by the British government. Grattan continued to press for more independence, and for the removal of the remaining constitutional restrictions on Catholics, declaring: 'The Irish Protestant can never be free until the Irish Catholic has ceased to be a slave.' Pitt agreed, and a Relief Act giving Catholics votes on an equal basis with Protestants was passed in 1793, but further reform was halted by his right wing, and a wide range of Irish opinion moved from discontent to incipient rebellion.

After the outbreak of war with France in 1793 the expression of revolutionary sentiments was more dangerous and government repression more severe. The 'United Scotsmen' were never more than a local difficulty, and a French landing in Wales was quickly suppressed by neighbourhood volunteers, but the 'United Irishmen' saw a potential ally in republican France. Inspired and led by Protestant gentry such as Wolfe Tone and Lord Edward Fitzgerald, the United Irishmen were enthusiastically supported by the Roman Catholic rural population. The brutal Irish rebellion of 1798 was met with an even more brutal Irish suppression ('Murder appears to be the favourite pastime of the Irish militia', Lord Cornwallis sardonically commented, and a regular cavalry regiment, the 5th Royal Irish Dragoon Guards, was disbanded as a consequence of its particularly atrocious conduct). These Irish disturbances resulted in an influx of convicts to Australia who were notably different in character from those who had gone before. Cornwallis had ended the rebellion with a general amnesty; only a handful of those found guilty of 'cold-blooded murder' were executed, the great majority of the leaders were allowed to emigrate, and some were sentenced to transportation: the Irish Protestant Lord Roden bitterly regretted that it had not been possible to 'annihilate one or two million of inhabitants who are a disgrace to humanity'.

An Irish Parenthesis

Two topics in particular have bedevilled and confused Australian history: relationships with the Aborigines and the participation of the Irish immigrants. Although Ireland was formally united with Great Britain in 1801, its laws and governance remained quite separate. Indeed, as the nineteenth century progressed, successive British responses to Irish pressure resulted in dramatic changes, as the Protestant Church of Ireland was disestablished and largely dispossessed and new land laws created a nation of peasant proprietors in place of often absentee landlords. Emigration and famine reduced the population dramatically, and although more Irish emigrants chose the United States or Britain, enough undertook the long voyage to Australia to constitute a significant minority of the population; but from the first beginnings of Australian political society all white inhabitants were subject to all the same laws. Irish, Scots and English, who in the United Kingdom formed distinct societies, in Australia could congratulate themselves on the same freedoms and complain in unison about any perceived infringement of these. In matters of religion, to be sure, the Australian Roman Catholic Church, very largely Irish until recent years, adopted individual political attitudes, and sectarian squabbles were not uncommon, but the instinctive anglophobia that prevailed in Ireland was only sporadically engendered in Australia.[21]

Eventually, around a quarter of transportees were from Ireland, but the first Irish did not arrive until September 1791, 155 of them, aged from 11 to 64. The Irish convicts have been sometimes depicted as 'honorable victims of great injustice, social oppression and national persecution', or as heroic rebels. Except to the extent that all of the earlier convicts, or indeed prisoners at any period, are victims of social oppression, this was not true. Most were either straightforward criminals or simple-minded, like the Irish men and women who attempted to escape by walking to China (equally simple South African Boers, rather better prepared, made the same attempt with similar results).

Although the convict population in New South Wales was not disproportionately Irish (Ireland at that time had a population of 5.2 million, Scotland had 1.6 million and England and Wales 8.9 million; Dublin was the second city of the British Empire), a disproportionate number of Irish convicts had a bitter grudge against the British. Most of the Irish convicts – 50,000 during the whole period of transportation – had been sentenced for ordinary common law crimes, but of these 1,500 were in some sense 'political prisoners', often able and well educated. From the outset, many Irish politicals merged into Sydney society. James Meehan, one of the 1798 rebels, pardoned in 1803, went on to become colonial Deputy Surveyor and an enterprising explorer; another, the Church of Ireland priest Henry Fulton, was immediately pardoned to act as assistant colonial chaplain; 'General' Joseph Holt developed a prosperous farm; even the undefeated Wicklow fighter, Michael Dwyer, a voluntary exile, was appointed chief constable of the new town of Liverpool. Other politicians formed undercover debating circles with British radicals – Henry Hayes provided hospitality – which gave rise to official suspicion, but trouble was more likely to come from resentful Irish 'common criminals'. Some may well have been guilty of violent acts, but others were certainly innocent victims of the authorities' revenge; all had been with good cause resentful of what appeared an alien rule. The Catholic Relief Acts had improved the condition of middle-class Irish Catholics, but had done little for the impoverished labourers. When the first of these 'turbulent and worthless creatures' began to land in New South Wales, the administration was nervous of the consequences, but the first challenges to authority came from annoyed British settlers.

Mr Boston's Sow

The first emancipists – convicts whose sentences had expired, and who elected to stay in New South Wales, or who had no opportunity to return – began to appear from 1793, when those serving seven-year stretches had completed their terms, but for many years these were in a minority, and

New South Wales continued essentially a penal settlement, under military rule. Much therefore depended on the character of the Governor, whose office was left vacant for nearly three years after Phillip's departure. During this time the Acting Governor was the officer in charge of troops, first Major Francis Grose, followed in 1794 by William Paterson. The troops concerned were the newly raised 102nd Regiment, the New South Wales Corps, otherwise the 'Rum Corps' or the 'Botany Bay Rangers', who arrived in Sydney in February 1792. Since Grose was given authority to form a new regiment as early as June 1789, he had been able to select officers with some care. Peacetime opportunities being rare, there was more than adequate interest in even so distant a post, and many of the first officers of the New South Wales Corps went on to have distinguished careers. Grose himself ended as a Lieutenant General, as did Joseph Foveaux; William Paterson had distinguished himself as an explorer and was a Fellow of the Royal Society; Edward Abbott became a member of the Van Diemen's Land Legislative Council, while John Macarthur, the most talented and difficult of all, remained the central figure in New South Wales life for two decades. Men of such abilities were essential, both to the administration and to building the infrastructure of the colony which many of them chose to make their home.[22]

Before the reforms begun by the Duke of York in 1795 the British army, unlike the Royal Navy, was not a professional organization, with only rudimentary training given to often reluctant soldiery. The other ranks in the New South Wales Corps were probably no better or worse than their comrades in other regiments, including as they did soldiers released from military prisons. It was Admiral Bligh, who suffered at their hands, who described the Corps as including 'other characters who have been considered as disgraceful to every other regiment in His Majesty's Service . . .' Although well fitted to act as prison guards, lacking as they did regimental history, traditions or experience of war, they would have been doubtfully effective in the front line, but the New South Wales Corps helped to give the colony both continuity and order. That this was often done in a military style angered civilians, whose resistance contributed to constitutional advances.

Grose, the son of an eccentric and amiable antiquary, badly wounded in the American wars, took the initiative immediately after his appointment. Within two days of Phillip's departure, the civil magistrate, Richard Atkins, admittedly not the most reliable of characters, was dismissed, replaced by Captain Foveaux, quite contrary to the Royal Instructions. 'The whole concerns of the colony were taken into the hands of the military' (that was, however, the opinion of his successor, a naval officer, John Hunter, not free from prejudice).

Whatever their military disqualifications, the New South Wales officers did not lack an entrepreneurial spirit. In the Indian service it was commonplace for army officers to engage in trading on their own behalf. Although no longer possible to make the great fortunes that had characterized the eighteenth-century Indian nabobs, opportunities in New South Wales, if limited, did exist. With the innate difficulties of the passage to New South Wales rendered more perilous by the war, few ships carried much in the way of consumer goods for private sale, most cargoes being destined for the government commissariat stores. Since a penal settlement was not supposed to need a means of exchange, Phillip had not been issued with a store of coins. All business, it was supposed, would be through the government commissary; but the emergence of emancipists, the enterprise of the Kables and Needhams, and the arrival of India-based merchant houses, transformed Sydney commerce. When the Indiaman *Shah Hormuzear* arrived in February 1793, she unloaded a cargo which included meat, flour, sugar, cognac, Madeira, grindstones and writing paper, all much in demand. In the absence of bullion, transactions had to be carried out in some other medium, and this the New South Wales officers were well placed to supply; a guaranteed source of income, in the shape of their pay, could be arbitraged through the commissariat, giving them access to that rare commodity, capital. Allowed to trade on their own account, the New South Wales Corps officers bought goods from visiting captains for resale at very considerable profits. Retail trade was frequently carried out in the common currency of the settlement, rum, at the generally accepted rate of ten shillings a gallon; it was from this that the regiment became commonly known as the 'Rum Corps'. Inevitably, the officer best placed to take advantage of the opportunity was the Paymaster, Lieutenant John Macarthur. Rather than taking a quick profit by buying newly landed stores, Macarthur took a longer view.

In Phillip's instructions Lord Sydney had mentioned that marines and 'others who might resort thither upon their private occupations' should be encouraged by grants of land and (by amended instructions in 1789) having convicts 'assigned' to them as labourers. Land, which had to be cleared, fenced and prepared was of little use without labour, of which convicts furnished a steady supply. Together with the land grants, a number of convicts were therefore 'assigned' to potential settlers, as had been the practice with indentured labour in America. The equation land + convicts + some capital = prosperity was usually reliable; and the convicts themselves might be expected to benefit from the reforming effects of security and hard work; depending on the characters of master and servant, this was not infrequently so. Grose has often been accused of granting land too freely to his own officers, but in fact, once this permission had been given by London, land grants were not excessive – 315 acres to Foveaux being the largest – and Hunter himself, when Governor, gave Foveaux 1,895 acres. Emancipists and free settlers were also granted lands if not on so generous a scale. One Dorset farmer, Thomas Rose, was allotted 120 acres, and industrious emancipists could expect upwards of 30 acres. Convicts were allotted to grantees on a scale ranging from 13 for an officer to 3 for free settlers and 1 for an emancipist. Anyone fortunate enough to be given a grant of good land and supplied with the services of some industrious convicts was almost assured of a prosperous future. John Piper, who came out as an 18-year-old ensign in the New South Wales Corps in 1792, was twenty years later able to buy Vaucluse House from Hayes, and to spend £10,000 on building another residence, Henrietta Villa, as well as owning extensive tracts in Rose Bay and Neutral Bay, farms in Bathurst and Van Diemen's Land, and a large site in central Sydney. It was thoroughly unprincipled (although Grose himself was personally honest) but it worked, and nowhere better than on the new estates of the rapidly rising Captain Macarthur, who was also given the post of Inspector of Public Works.

Emancipists, and those still comparatively few free settlers who had come on their own bold initiative, resented the loss of what they saw as their liberties as Englishmen under military rule. One such was John Boston, an enterprising English radical, a surgeon and apothecary, who had accompanied Thomas Palmer in 1794. In October the following year 'a very fine sow, considerably advanced in Pig' belonging to Boston was shot by Private William Faithfull of the New South Wales Corps after having, in company with other delinquent animals, wandered on to some land owned by Captain Foveaux. An altercation ensued, of which Boston got much the best, but which was eventually settled by the formidable Mrs Boston. Subsequently, Boston sued everyone connected with the incident; the court ruled in Boston's favour with even the military member, Captain George Johnston, insisting that 'it is the duty and province of Courts of Justice to protect from personal outrage all those who are in the King's peace', but Boston got only £1 damages for his dead pig. He was thereafter in persistently bad odour with the authorities, but his business ventures – some in partnership with Palmer – were nevertheless tolerably prosperous.[23]

Such vigorous private enterprise negated many of Captain Phillip's efforts at controlled expansion, but did secure an encouraging advance in agricultural production. The first venture was the development of farms along the

Hawkesbury River system, which flows northwards, parallel to the coast to form a large sea loch in Broken Bay, only 20 miles from Sydney Heads, the entrance to Port Jackson. Phillip himself and Captain Tench had explored the river valley in 1789 and five years later Grose founded a village, later known as Windsor, with some twenty farms. Apart from periodic flooding, the land was fertile and agriculture quickly productive. By 1799 emancipist farmers and Rum Corps officers – who by 1799 owned more than half the colony's horses and three-quarters of its sheep – had enabled the colony to be self-supporting in food.

John Hunter, *Sirius*'s old captain, took up his appointment in September 1795, restoring a more regular government. Hunter, a good and reliable sea officer, ardent naturalist and draughtsman, was out of his depth as Governor. His efforts to reduce the hold the Rum Corps had established on the colony's economy were for the most part ineffective. Even had Hunter been younger – he reached the age of 60 in 1797, a generation older than any of his staff – he would have found it difficult to govern effectively with so little support; Richard Atkins, although acknowledged to be ignorant, corrupt and untrustworthy, leading a life 'worse than a Dogs . . . in a perfect Pigstye', had to be appointed as Judge Advocate, the senior law officer in succession to Collins, because no one else could be found. His work was done mainly by a pardoned convict, Oxford graduate Michael Robinson. In spite of being sentenced again for perjury, Robinson continued in government service for more than twenty years, acting as the Governor's chief clerk and writing bad official verse.

Annoyances inflicted by corrupt and incompetent subordinates in Sydney were paralleled by interference from distant London (the voyage could take over a year, as Hunter himself had discovered in 1792). The unhappy Governor had to report to the Home Secretary, the army officers to the Secretary at War, while the Treasury controlled the purse strings. All these, plus the Ordnance Department, the Mint and the Admiralty, prodded the governor of New South Wales. Of these antagonists – and they were often so perceived by harassed Governors – the most aggressive was the Treasury. Money was the single incontrovertible measure of a Governor's ability; reports were confused and often contradictory, but the final arbitration was the cost of the colony in pounds, shillings and pence. Hunter at least began one important initiative, although some of the credit should also go to the re-sentenced convicts who burnt down their gaol in 1799. A public subscription having petered out, the governor imposed shipping dues – fees for entry, anchorage, wharfing, clearing and landing spirits – subsumed under the soon-misleading title of the 'Gaol Fund'. Extended and formalized by Hunter's successors, the Gaol Fund and its companion Orphan Fund, intended to pay for convicts' children's subsistence and education, formed convenient ledger entries for other fees – public house and auctioneers' licences, export duties, land grant duties and charges – all strictly illegal, and eventually, when British governments resumed a more effective control, the cause of much botheration.[24]

Local control was, at best, intermittent. The officer appointed as commissary, from 1791 to 1811 'Little Jack' Palmer, responsible for the issue of all government stores and for official purchases, kept his own accounts without any proper scrutiny, to the bafflement of British officials when, eventually, these found their way to Whitehall. Hunter found himself quite unable to cope with the unscrupulous and aggressive John Macarthur. The Baughan case in 1796 was one example of the lengths to which Macarthur and the Rum Corps officers were prepared to go. Attempting to investigate the attack by soldiers on the house of the millwright John Baughan, the magistrate and Chief Surgeon William Balmain accused Macarthur of being the instigator. The Governor was in no doubt that 'the turbulent and refractory conduct of the military' was to blame and complained to London of the 'harried depravity and wickedness of this man's [Macarthur's] heart'. Balmain was challenged to a duel, but the pugnacious Macarthur continued to exercise a commanding influence in colonial affairs.[25]

Hunter's real strengths, however, lay in his enthusiasm for exploration – it was one of his expeditions that first described the koala, the platypus and the wombat. He had a stroke of luck soon after his arrival when in November 1795, leading a party to survey the southern parts of the settlement, he came upon the survivors of the lost herd of cows. Thriving, but now completely wild, the beasts had proved the excellence of the grazing in what became the region of Camden. Further southwards still, a party of Irish prisoners, convinced that a new world was to be found some 200 miles away, where they 'would be assured of finding all the comforts of life without the necessity of labouring for them', were allowed to pursue their quest by Governor Hunter (which is indicative of Hunter's tolerant regime). The Irishmen returned, safe and disillusioned, but their escort pressed on towards the present site of Goulburn, reached by a second party two months later.[26] As might be expected of a seaman, the Governor especially encouraged exploration by sea, sponsoring the voyages undertaken by the young naval officers Matthew Flinders and George Bass. Many discoveries were indeed accidental, by enterprising convicts who absconded or by the survivors of shipwrecks. William Bryant, a Cornish smuggler, made a courageous escape in 1791 in Governor Phillip's own cutter, sailing to Timor, some 3,250 miles in 69 days, during which voyage he and his companions landed near the mouth of the Hunter River and discovered coal. Bryant died shortly after reaching Timor, but his wife Mary survived, was pardoned, returned to England and was befriended by the diarist James Boswell. Forty years later another escapee, George Clarke, reported that he had found 'a great river in the north', which the Surveyor General, Thomas Mitchell, found to be the MacIntyre. Perhaps the most dramatic episode was the experience of the survivors of the Indiaman, *Sydney Cove*, making from Calcutta towards Sydney. Rounding Van Diemen's Land in February 1797 the ship was forced to beach on Preservation Island, just off the north-east tip of Van Diemen's Land. Seventeen of the crew set off in the longboat to seek help, but after the boat capsized the survivors were left to make their way north up the coast of the mainland. Of these, only three were able to reach the vicinity of Botany Bay after a 300-mile journey of incredible hardship, but one which added greatly to the colonists' knowledge of southern New South Wales. After sending two ships to rescue those crew left on Preservation Island, Governor Hunter asked the young navy surgeon George Bass to investigate further.[27]

Bass, and another remarkable Lincolnshire man, his friend Lieutenant Matthew Flinders RN, are the two great names in early colonial exploration. Their first voyages along the coast around Sydney were made together in two dinghies, both aptly named *Tom Thumb*, but Bass was despatched in December 1797 by Governor Hunter in a rather larger vessel, a 28-foot whaler, with six seamen. Working their way south and east, they rounded the southernmost point of the continent, Wilson's Promontory, where they found seven unhappy convicts, the survivors of fourteen who had stolen a boat in Sydney, attempting to reach the wreck of the *Sydney Cove*. Making his way a little further to the west, Bass discovered an extensive inlet, which he named Westernport, where the setting of the tides – the northern coast of Tasmania not being visible – indicated that a passage between Tasmania and the mainland existed.

After a few months in Sydney, Bass was off again, this time with Flinders in command, to complete the first circumnavigation of Van Diemen's Land, proving, more than a hundred and fifty years after Tasman first landed, that his soon-to-be-eponymous discovery was indeed an island. Their careful charting of what was immediately called the Bass Strait was a particularly important achievement, since ships using the Strait were able to reduce the voyage to Sydney by up to two weeks, and made possible the rise of the first Australian industry, that of whaling. Had Bass sailed a little further westwards he would have come across the narrow and difficult entrance to an even finer harbour than that of Westernport. It was left to Lieutenant John Murray RN, in command of the extraordinary centre-board brig *Lady Nelson*, to explore this 'most noble sheet of waters' in February and March 1802, named by Governor King 'Port Phillip', forming the approach to what is now the city of Melbourne.[28]

When the first discussions about the prospective colony were held in the early 1780s, with so many possible New South Wales products being canvassed, whaling was barely mentioned. Although 'train oil', derived from the whale, was vital for many purposes, including wool and leather processing, but especially for machinery oils (the Industrial Revolution was lubricated by the unfortunate 'Right whale'), the omission was hardly surprising since whaling was then confined to the Arctic seas; only in 1788 did the first British whalers enter the Pacific. Three years later two whaling ships – which happened to be carrying convicts to Port Jackson – killed the first Australian whales. Officially, all trade and navigation in eastern waters was a monopoly of the Honourable East India Company, but the frequent breaches of this were regularized by an 1801 Act. Deep sea whaling, by British, American and, from 1805, Australian ships (the 185-ton *King George* was built that year) flourished. Less capital-intensive 'bay whaling', in which whales were hunted by shore-based boats, became common all around the southern Australian coasts from 1806. Whale-chasing was a risky business, but sealing was as profitable and much easier, the creatures being quite tame and allowing themselves to be clubbed to death without objection. The beaches, it was reported in 1806, were 'encumbered with quantities . . . and killing the seals was easier than killing captive pigs with a mallet'. Both sealskins and seal oil were sought after and when, for example, the little schooner *Martha* (30 tons) reached Sydney harbour from the Bass Strait in 1799 with 1,300 skins and 30 barrels of oil, she held a valuable cargo. The rich harvest was soon exhausted as the seals were killed off or moved to the southern coasts of Van Diemen's Land, but until the development of the wool industry, marine products continued to be the major Australian exports. One interesting aspect of the Bass Strait sealing was the collaboration engendered between Europeans and the Tasmanians, who were accustomed to make regular crossings to the nearest islands. When their visits coincided agreements were reached between sealers and Aborigines:

After their appearance, usually in a whaleboat containing four to six men, a dance would be held, a conference would take place, and an arrangement would be made for a number of women to accompany the sealers for the season. Some women came from the host band, while others were abducted from other bands and sold to the sealers for dogs, mutton birds, and flour. On other occasions sealers made arrangements to take women for short periods for specific tasks. Sometimes Aboriginal men accompanied sealing parties; one Aboriginal man, Mannalagenna, may have made more than one voyage with the sealers.[29]

The women were not only home-makers, but used their traditional skills in seal-catching, swimming up to the basking seals, lying among them and wriggling their way to their chosen prey, unremarked by the bull seals. After the sealing expeditions stopped a mixed islander population remained – Tasmanian and Australian Aborigines, one with Maori blood, and twelve European men – from whom the present-day Tasmanians identifying themselves as aboriginal claim descent.

Expanding the settlements had profound consequences. Governor Phillip had been able to keep a firm hand on the community in and around Sydney and Parramatta, and enforce his standards of equal justice – and rations – for all. Once convicts were employed further afield, responsibility and power had to be devolved, and Grose took every opportunity of doing so. The military were given virtually unlimited authority: no soldier could be tried by a civil judge, or arrested by a constable, who must 'understand that they are not on any pretence whatsoever to stop or seize a soldier, although he should be detected in an unlawful act'. Such a view was eventually disowned by London, but London was a long way off, and Hunter was obliged to rely on the Rum Corps as his only instrument of control. He was unable to cut back on the number of convicts assigned to officers in spite of the clearest instructions from London, and a dissatisfied Colonial Office recalled him in November 1799.

Philip King, who was promoted from his exile on Norfolk Island to succeed Hunter as Governor in September 1800, was in this respect more effective. His instructions from the Secretary of State, Lord Hobart, reflected London's acceptance that Port Jackson was beginning to be something more complex than a simple penal colony. Emancipists should, Hobart ordained, be given land at the rate of 30 acres plus 20 if married, and another 10 for each child, and provided with stock, provisions and equipment. The grant was to be free for ten years, thereafter subject to a nominal rent. With his long experience of colonial administration, King was able to restrain the dealing-profits of the Rum Corps, some of whose officers were now well on the way to establishing their fortunes. As early as 1793 John Macarthur had been able to exult that his 250-acre Parramatta farm had produced £400 in that year, as well as yielding a substantial surplus of corn. By 1800

Macarthur was, along with his neighbour, the chaplain Samuel Marsden, the richest and most influential of the colonists, their prosperity rapidly increasing with the success of their new importations of sheep.

Pure Bred Merinos

In the world of sheep, one animal was king. The fine-woolled sheep of Spain had been famous as long ago as the second century BC; its modern name had an Arabic root – in 1307 German merchants were buying 'lana quae apellatur merinus' on the Tunis market.[30] The long-legged, long-haired merino, the 'travelling sheep of Spain', was a fussy animal, which had to be moved four times a year to different pastures, but was recognized as producing the finest of wools; one pound could produce 92 miles of yarn. Wool was a subject of much importance to the economy of eighteenth-century England, as it had been for five hundred years, accounting for more than a quarter of the national exports, and a profit of perhaps £14 million. But British sheep produced none of the fine wool needed for the best fabrics, which had to be imported either from Spain or Saxony. Sir Joseph Banks had taken an interest in the subject, and in 1788 had been successful in importing a flock via France: he sent, in grateful token, a kangaroo, the first to be seen in France. By 1792 the British merino stud, originally owned by King George III – Farmer George – had formed the foundation of a number of private flocks, in which the aristocratic Spaniards were cross-bred with sturdier natives. In 1796 some Spanish sheep found their way to New South Wales, imported by Captain Henry Waterhouse RN, who had come with the First Fleet as midshipman on the *Sirius*. Calling at Cape Town in order to acquire some stock for the colony, Waterhouse (now captain of the *Reliance*) recognized the possibility that the animals might do well in Australia and purchased some of the flock of the late Dutch commander, Colonel Robert Gordon; some of these survived a stormy passage to Sydney, where they were taken up by Macarthur, Marsden and others and crossed with less demanding breeds.

Governor King had noted the development, and sent samples of the Australian wool to London. Banks was not impressed:

I have no reason to believe from any facts that have come to my knowledge, either when I was in that country or since, that the climate and soil of New South Wales is at all better for the production of fine wools than that of other temperate climates and am confident that the natural growth of the grass of the country is tall, coarse, reedy and very different from the short and sweet mountain grass of Europe upon which sheep thrive to the best advantage.

I have never heard of any luxuriant pastures of the natural growth of New South Wales at all fitted for the pasturage of sheep till I read of them in Captain Macarthur's statement, nor did I ever see such in that country.[31]

Nor was Sir Joseph taken with Captain Macarthur when he turned up, in disgrace. That quarrelsome character – he had fought a duel with the captain of the ship that had taken him to New South Wales, and quarrelled with a senior officer, Nicholas Nepean, on the voyage – had been out again, with his own commanding officer, Colonel William Paterson, a friend of Banks and a Fellow of the Royal Society. Governor King had given Macarthur a poor character as 'sowing discord and strife', 'a perturbator' whose 'art, cunning, impudence and a pair of baselisk [sic] eyes' enabled him 'to obtain any point he undertakes', and he packed him off back to England for court martial in November 1801. A plausible character, Macarthur wriggled out of the charges by playing the sheep card, which attracted the attention of the Committee on Trade and Foreign Plantations. Although the court martial found Macarthur's conduct 'exremely incorrect', he was allowed to return to New South Wales fortified with the approbation of Lord Camden, who was briefly responsible for the colonies in 1804–5 (having been earlier largely responsible for the Irish Rebellion of 1798, and later described as 'useless lumber'). Despite Banks's opposition, and the reservations of the Trade Committee, Lord Camden agreed that Macarthur should have 5,000 acres for his sheep. In view of the central position that the wool industry subsequently achieved in the Australian economy, this was certainly the best decision made by that undistinguished politician.[32]

Macarthur's triumphal return to Australia in June 1805, accompanied by some of King George's own tups, was greeted by Governor King with wry resignation; Macarthur's intentions were 'laudable', and King should not doubt his assurances that every expected benefit might be derived from his exertions; but King believed, as did Joseph Banks, that Samuel Marsden 'was the best practical farmer in the colony', and Marsden was occupied with breeding sheep for meat rather than for wool. Ambrose Serle, an official in the Transport Department, had written to his friend Marsden in February 1803 telling him that Macarthur's project 'does not appear to have been well-digested, or sufficiently prepared'. Banks, however, seems to have changed his earlier opinion, and by 1804 was recommending the grant of a million acres in order to expand production of fine wool; somewhat cavalierly, Sir Joseph suggested that even if the enterprise failed 'much benefit must rise to the Infant Colony by the Money that will be sent there'.[33]

The time was not, however, ripe for that explosive growth which later made the fine wool industry the first foundation of Australian prosperity. Too few pure-bred merinos – probably fewer than thirty animals before 1820 – had been imported to transform the scrawny Bengal and fat-tailed Cape sheep, which, together with some rather superior British and Irish beasts, constituted the early Australian stock; indeed, the industry's historian judged that 'the period between 1816 and 1817 seems to have been the nadir of the pioneering phase of Australian sheep and wool'.[34]

As had his predecessor, King concerned himself with exploration. In 1801 Matthew Flinders had been commissioned at the suggestion of Sir Joseph Banks to complete the survey of Australian waters, with the co-operation of the Honourable East India Company. Given a former collier, very much like Cook's *Endeavour* and renamed *Investigator*, Flinders finished his survey by 1803, producing charts worthy of the great navigator himself. Others, however, were also showing some interest in the unexplored coast of New South Wales and of Van Diemen's Land, hitherto both neglected and, Governor King worried, possible objects of French attention. In 1800 Napoleon, as First Consul, had despatched a well-equipped expedition, ostensibly to complete that part of the Australian coastline still unsurveyed, but in fact intended, as the English believed – and political advantage was always a prominent factor in Napoleonic schemes – as a *voyage d'espionage*. The truth, in view of the latest research, seems to have been that members of the French expedition had varying views. The commander, Nicolas Baudin, although a competent naturalist, was an indifferent leader, and the history of the voyage was written by his deputy captain François Péron, who succeeded in writing two volumes without ever mentioning Baudin's name. Péron claimed that plans for an invasion of Australia did in fact exist, to be backed by a rising of the Irish convicts, along the lines of the joint attempt in 1798. In practice he was sceptical and 'convinced of their bad character ... To hear them [the Irish] they have all served under General Humbert at Kilala and none of them was guilty ... We took the wise precaution of having nothing to do with these wretches.'[35]

'A long era of opulence and peace'

The decision to settle Van Diemen's Land had been taken in London, as Ambrose Serle at the Transport Office, writing to Marsden, indicated on 9 November 1801: 'A new settlement is now to be made to the South West of you, in or near the Bass's Straits, with Lieutenant Colonel Collins as the head ... It does not appear to have been well-digested, or sufficiently prepared.'[36] But when Governor King, a seaman himself, heard that the French might intend to claim Van Diemen's Land he was sufficiently alarmed to send a man-of-war to warn Baudin off the turf without waiting for further authority. When the French were discovered on King Island in the Bass Strait an agitated Captain Robbins of the *Cumberland* quickly hoisted the Union flag (upside down, as it happened) over the French tents. It then seemed prudent to establish a permanent British presence somewhere on the shore of the Strait. Colonel David Collins of the Marines, former Deputy Judge Advocate, the first volume of whose two-volume *Account of the English Colony in New South Wales*, published in May 1798, was well received in England, was selected. Writing in the *Edinburgh Review*, Sydney Smith, although questioning the utility of 'erecting penitentiary-houses and prisons at a distance of half the diameter of the globe', concluded that Collins's book provided no 'common enjoyment' to reflect that the 'very horrors and crimes' of the Old World may have 'prepared a long era of opulence and peace for a people yet involved in the womb of time'.

Thus established as an expert, Collins was given command of an expedition, including the usual muster of convicts, to found a station at Port Phillip, the enormous bay discovered by Lieutenant Murray. Provided with minimal resources, landing in an unsurveyed region, at the approach of summer, and finding inadequate fresh water, Lieutenant Governor Collins took the sensible decision to transfer his charges to Van Diemen's Land – minus one convict, William Buckley, who absconded to take his chance with the Aborigines. Thirty-two years later, when John Batman's party arrived to make a success of a settlement at Port Phillip, they found Buckley, in good health at 55, having almost forgotten the use of English.

In Van Diemen's Land, Collins chose, in February 1804, to build his settlement at Sullivan Cove on the island's south coast, at the mouth of a reliable river, previously named the Derwent by John Hayes, a visiting Cumbrian Bombay Marine officer. Lieutenant John Bowen RN had already been despatched the previous September with a mixed party of free settlers, soldiers and twenty-four convicts, and established them on the left bank of the Derwent at Risdon Cove as a precaution, 'preventing the French gaining a foothold'. Numbering together some six hundred, and only intermittently supplied from Sydney, Collins's party were saved from starvation by the abundance of game – particularly the kangaroo. It was a miserable place for Collins, either ignored or pestered by Sydney and London, deserted by his wife – though the latter may not have bothered him unduly: he left two illegitimate children in Sydney and another pair in the new settlement of Hobarton, named after the Secretary of State, Lord Hobart. When Captain William Bligh visited Hobart in March 1806 he was shocked to find the Lieutenant Governor 'walking with his kept Woman (a poor low creature) arm-in-arm about the Town, and bringing her almost daily to his Office adjoining the House, directly in View of my Daughter', but in the confined, fluid and relaxed society of Van Diemen's Land, Collins's liaisons were unremarkable.[37]

Typically, in the confusion engendered by poor communications, London had already decided that a settlement should be founded on the north shore of Van Diemen's Land, to secure the Bass Strait, where American whalers and sealers had been making a nuisance of themselves, and Colonel Paterson was sent there in October 1804 with a file of soldiers and seventy-five convicts. The first post, at the mouth of the River Tamar, was later moved up stream to Launceston, thus creating two separate Van Diemen's Land colonies, a state of affairs which continued for the next eight years.

When Governor King left for England in 1806, the British possessions in New Holland were limited to the New South Wales settlement, the two infant communities on Van Diemen's Land and Norfolk Island. New South Wales straggled, by no means uninterruptedly, for 100 miles or so along the coast, and inland only as far as the Blue Mountain foothills. In the north, Lieutenant Charles Menzies had been sent to establish a penal colony at 'Coal Harbour' on the Hunter River, some 70 miles north of Sydney in order to 'separate the worst of the Irish sent here for sedition from the others'. To the south, the Macarthur estate at Camden was to become positively ducal in splendour. In all, there were 8,593 inhabitants, 1,114 of whom, women and children included, were on the government strength, together with some 1,000 'settlers and landholders' and 4,000 other 'free persons'; the convict population was about 2,500, including over 600 women.[38]

Such a community was something more complex than a straightforward penal colony, reflecting the confusion that had surrounded its beginnings. Those unfortunates who were doubly sentenced, first to transportation, thereafter for some other offence to the chain gang, shuffled through a settlement many of whose inhabitants, formerly convicts like themselves, led lives as normal as any that might be expected in so isolated a spot. As well as public houses, there were two churches, a newspaper – George Howe, a ticket-of-leave convict, published the *Sydney Gazette and New South Wales Advertiser* in 1803 – and a theatre, where the first performance, of George Farquhar's *The Recruiting Officer*, was given in 1796, with a prologue spoken by the convict George Barrington:

> From distant climes, o'er widespread seas we come
> (tho' not with much eclat or beat of drum);
> True patriots all, for be it understood,
> We left our country for our country's good.[39]

The Dubliner George Barrington, by turns actor, confidence trickster and pickpocket, previously transported to America, arrived in September 1791. Just over a year later he was pardoned, and in 1796 appointed chief constable of Parramatta at the age of 20. Working with James Underwood, a Kentish convict, he founded an extensive shipbuilding and sealing business, as well as working as a farmer and brewer. Simeon Lord, a Yorkshire thief, was without doubt the most prominent businessman, diversifying from his original partnership with Henry Kable, a burglar, and Underwood to become a China merchant, competing with the Honourable East India Company and a pioneer manufacturer of hats, shoes, textiles and glassware, founding a dynasty of politicians and officials. Even convicts who made a bad start could recover and prosper. Samuel Lyons, a Jewish tailor transported for theft, made two attempts to escape, for which he was flogged, and he earned another flogging and four years in the Newcastle penal settlement for theft, before marrying a Irish girl and settling down. Although it took him, therefore, seventeen years to earn his pardon, by 1834, nineteen years after his arrival, Lyons was one of the richest men in Sydney, earning at one time over £5,000 in a day and having founded something of an Australian dynasty. By the end of the century two important industries were developing – shipbuilding, together with the whale- and seal-hunting in the Bass Strait. The government shipyard on the west shore of Sydney Cove, established in 1798, was being outstripped by Underwood's neighbouring private enterprise where the ship-rigged *King George* was built.

The problem of how to deal with those, already convicted, who re-offended was a constant source of difficulty. The twin carrots of freedom under ticket of leave and of a pint of Sunday grog to every convict who had 'conducted himself in a regular and proper manner during the week . . . and who shall appear clean . . . on the Sabbath day' were not enough to control some of the more hardened criminals. Minor, and not so minor, misdemeanours were dealt with by flogging, which could be ordered by a magistrate, by forced labour in a chain gang, or by exile to a penal settlement where conditions were harsh, even by the standards of the day. Apart from Coal Harbour, soon unsurprisingly renamed Newcastle, sentence to a penal colony meant exile to Norfolk Island, where conditions deteriorated badly after King left in 1796 to be replaced by New South Wales Corps officers. From July 1800 this was Joseph Foveaux, promoted to Lieutenant Colonel two years later.

It was on Norfolk Island that the first signs of the Irish prisoners' unequalled spirit of rebellion broke out. Some Irish convicts had been sent to Norfolk Island after being accused of planning an uprising on the mainland. At first, Foveaux allowed unimpeded association between convicts and settlers, but when a stock of pikes was discovered on the island, in December 1800, an actual attempt at mutiny was exposed, and the two ringleaders summarily hanged. The next rebellion, in March 1804 on the mainland, was more serious, and may well have been related to that described by Péron. His assessment proved correct, for the attempt proved ineffective. Without any clear objectives, and little organization, nearly 300 convicts seized what weapons they could, and marched on Parramatta; none of the original leaders of 1798 took part, one, Father Dixon, doing his best to persuade them to surrender. Father Harrold had earlier bluntly warned discontented Irish: 'you damnation fools, had you not better be content with the government you have than set up one of yourselves which would soon turn out to be one of tyranny and oppression?' The rebels were easily, and brutally, suppressed in the 'battle' of Vinegar Hill by the New South Wales Corps, commanded by George Johnston, and eight of the ringleaders were hanged. It was the only armed action by discontented Irish, but the legacy of distrust which remained in Ireland spluttered on in this society where so many of the Roman Catholic Irish had come as convicts.[40]

Given this sparsely populated and scattered collection of settlements, separated from the home country by 12,000 miles of ocean, the British government continued to rely on naval officers to supply their senior administrators, and King's successor was a very famous one indeed. Captain William Bligh's reputation as a navigator and courageous commander had never been questioned, but after the disastrous mutiny on HMS *Bounty* and a number of subsequent scrapes, including a court martial which resulted in a reprimand, his lack of diplomatic and administrative skills might have militated against his appointment to the governorship of New South Wales, at the suggestion of Sir Joseph Banks. He arrived in August

1806, instructed to suppress the Rum Corps' monopoly of trade, to prevent the widespread alcoholism – the 'source of most calamitous evils' – and to reform the unsatisfactory administration.

From the colony's inception, rum had not only been the common currency, but an instrument of social control. Lieutenant Fyans, when his part in suppressing a convict revolt on Norfolk Island was to be recognized, asked for 5,000 gallons of rum. Bligh was well acquainted with the dangers of drunkenness, and Sydney in 1806 was awash with alcohol. The Reverend Samuel Marsden wrote to Banks:

When Governor Bligh took the Command many serious evils existed, and which had been gradually maturing for the whole thirteen years I lived in the Settlement. The greatest of these, was the barter of Spirits; all others were only Branches that sprung from, and were connected with this. Governor Bligh soon saw the unhappy Situation in which he was placed. He was convinced that if he allowed the Barter of Spirits, the Labouring Class would continue in Ruin and distress, and the general welfare of the Colony would be sacrificed: and to attempt to prohibit this Barter would be dangerous.

Governor Bligh's attempt to restrict the trade did indeed prove dangerous for him. Tactless and overbearing, having learnt nothing about man-management in the last fifteen years, Bligh proceeded to alienate that handful of powerful men, headed by the restored Macarthur, 'sharp as a razor and rapacious as a shark', who had made their fortunes with the aid of Rum Corps generosity. There was a good deal of the sociopath about Bligh. He could be admired, but it was near-impossible to have normal friendly relations with the man. Dr Joseph Arnold, a naval surgeon who visited Sydney in 1809, described the Governor as 'overpowering and affrighting every person that might have dealings with him, expecting from all a deference and submission that the proudest despot would covet'. Difficult though Bligh most certainly was, a much more emollient governor would still have fallen foul of Macarthur.

The incompetent and corrupt Judge Advocate Atkins provided the occasion for Macarthur to draw up a petition, alleging that 'every man's property, liberty and life was endangered', urging Colonel Johnston, defender of Boston's pig, now in charge of troops, to arrest Governor Bligh; this Johnston promptly did, on 26 January 1808. Attempting to justify himself, Johnston – one of the largest landowners, having been given another 2,000 acres for his 'heroism' in suppressing the Vinegar Hill rebellion – accused the Governor of attempting to 'subvert the Laws of his Country, to terrify and influence the Courts of Justice, and to bereave those persons who had the misfortune to be obnoxious to him of their fortunes, their liberty and their lives'.[41]

The colony was divided. Bligh's supporters included those settlers who were offended by the officers' arrogance and corruption and who claimed the Governor was 'doing all that public virtue and private worth' could to 'correct abuses, re-establish discipline, protect and encourage sobriety and industry', while Johnston was backed by the Macarthur power and his own officer corps. For a year Johnston, succeeded first by Colonel Foveaux, then by Colonel Paterson, took over the government with Macarthur as colonial secretary. Bligh was kept a prisoner until February 1809, thereafter winning control of a naval ship, HMS *Porpoise*, declaring New South Wales to be in a state of mutiny, but able to do very little other than take himself off to Hobart. The whole episode had been disgraceful, and proved to the British government the urgent need for a strong but tactful Governor exercising control on the colony.

On the arrival of his successor, Lieutenant Colonel Lachlan Macquarie, Bligh sailed for London, whither the chief culprits in his deposition, Johnston and Macarthur, had already gone to make their excuses. In this they were for the most part unsuccessful: Bligh was exonerated, and resumed his naval career, rising in rank, although he was given few further responsibilities; Johnston's defence was not accepted by the Colonial Secretary Lord Castle-reagh, no friend to insubordination, and Johnston was cashiered, but allowed to return to his Australian estates. Macarthur was advised that he could not be tried for treason in Britain but that if he returned to New South Wales he must be brought to trial. For eight years, between 1809 and 1817, Macarthur had to remain in London, discontented, impoverished and tortured by gout, devolving the whole business of running the extensive Macarthur estates on his talented wife, Elizabeth. She did not lack for advice: her husband wrote on 8 December 1814 proposing she attempt to bribe Governor Macquarie by suggesting to Mrs Macquarie that 'an arrangement' could be made which would secure 'a splendid future for both our families'; if the Governor's wife displayed 'any advance or relaxation . . . your own good sense would suggest what more it would be proper to add'. Elizabeth seems to have had the good sense not to pursue this infamous and, given Macquarie's Scottish incorruptibility, foolish attempt.[42]

Lachlan Macquarie was the first Governor appointed not from the Royal Navy but from the army, which was to become the more usual recruiting ground for colonial Governors. Only the special circumstances of Australian colonies had called for sailors: a post-captain in command of a man-of-war had, like the Governors, almost absolute powers over a small community held under strict discipline; an army officer of equivalent rank would be in charge of a regiment functioning as only one unit in a larger mass, never operating independently, always under the eye of a superior officer. In peacetime, an army commander had to live with civil officials in a garrison town, whether at home or abroad, relying on conciliation and persuasion rather than authority, whereas at sea a captain was, as Lloyds had it 'Master under God'. Under his second royal commission (2 April 1787), Phillip had been given authority to 'proceed in a more summary way than is used in this realm'. He was, as a parliamentary Select Committee reported in 1812, 'made Governor and Captain General, with the most enlarged powers, uncontrolled by any Council, with the authority to pardon all offences (treason and murder excepted) to impose duties, to grant lands and to issue colonial regulations'. In the hands of an authoritarian, self-willed commander such powers could be dangerous indeed, and it is a tribute to the fairmindedness of Phillip, Hunter and King that their periods of administration were as prosperous and relatively untroubled as they were: Bligh was the exception that proved the rule.[43]

The Duke of Wellington's army was a fertile nursery for governors: all the British rulers at the Cape of Good Hope from 1819 to 1848 and those in New South Wales from 1809 to 1846 were Peninsular War veterans. As guardians of penal settlements, soldiers could be effective, but as colonies developed self-governing institutions a military training became less relevant.

'Kind ruler, husband, father, friend – What more can human nature blend?'

If there was one period when New South Wales reached critical mass, in its transition from penal settlement to colony, it was during Governor Macquarie's tenure of office, over a period of twelve years from December 1809 to February 1822, the longest service of any Australian Governor. Lachlan Macquarie had served in India under Wellington, and had administrative experience in London, and both of these were relevant to the challenge of New South Wales. His appointment as Governor there came about by accident. Originally summoned to embark for New South Wales in command of his own regiment, the 73rd, which could be relied upon not to repeat the performance of the Rum Corps, Macquarie was therefore conveniently to hand when the nominated Governor, Sir Miles Nightingall, another of Wellington's officers, fell ill.

When Macquarie arrived on 1 January 1810 with the blessing of Joseph Banks (which provided a sort of apostolic succession from the first landing at Botany Bay twenty-two years previously), his instructions emphasized his responsibilities as prison governor: 'The Great Objects of attention are to improve the Morals of the Colonists, to encourage Marriage, to provide for Education, to prohibit the Use of Spiritous Liquors, to increase the Agriculture and Stock, so as to ensure the Certainty of a full supply to the Inhabitants, under all Circumstances.' Macquarie appreciated, but did not abuse, his wide powers, exercised according to his announced intentions, which were 'to reward merit, encourage virtue and punish vice . . . without regard to rank, class or description of persons, be they free or convicts'. Once a sentence had been served, without re-offending, Macquarie believed that the slate should be wiped clean. 'Emancipation', he wrote, 'should lead a man back to that Rank in Society which he had forfeited and do away with . . . all Retrospect of former bad Conduct.' Such a policy was not likely to appeal to the free immigrants, the 'exclusives' who tended to believe that 'once a convict, always a convict'. The Colonial Office agreed with the Governor, but warned that tolerance could be overdone: 'Nothing could be more unjust to the individuals, nor more impolitic . . . than to lay down a general rule of exclusion against one class of the community . . . but the principle may be carried too far.' In particular, it would not be 'judicious, unless under very peculiar circumstances, to select convicts [Lord Bathurst clearly meant former convicts] for the office of magistrates'. Nevertheless, Macquarie went ahead and appointed to the bench Henry Fulton, an Irish clergyman implicated in the 1798 rebellion (and who was given a full pardon within two years) and a surgeon, William Redfern, sentenced to death for his part in the naval mutiny of the same year, and who – again quickly pardoned – had become the most popular doctor in the colony.[44]

Fortunately the chief nuisance, John Macarthur, remained in exile, but other exclusives protested and continued to treat emancipists 'with rudeness, contumely and even oppression'. The Governor's task was made very much harder by the rapid increase in the number of convicts after the long war came to a staggered halt in 1814–15. In 1815, 909 convicts arrived: by 1818 this had nearly trebled to 2,376 and until 1825 the average annual intake was 2,600. Not all could be assigned, and many were put to work on useful government projects, of which many were initiated by the Governor. The physical evidences of Macquarie's government are still to be seen in Sydney, the most evident being the 'Rum Hospital', designed by the talented convict architect, Francis Greenway (and funded by a consortium headed by D'Arcy Wentworth in return for a near-monopoly on rum imports), together with St James's church and the convict barracks – an interesting example of the nature of Sydney penal practices being that it was thirty years before convicts were properly housed at government expense. Those not on chain gangs, assigned to masters or confined in prisoner boxes had previously been left to find their own accommodation: 'to provide a lodging for themselves by their Crimes and Depredations'.' Greenway's other works, especially St Matthew's in Windsor, are eloquent testimonies to the extent that New South Wales was ceasing to be primarily a penal settlement.

Sydney had begun to look something like a European town, although the French writer Jacques Arago was perhaps exaggerating when he wrote in November 1819:

I will give you a description of the town, which I have just gone through. I am enchanted and I had rather give my admiration some respite. Magnificent hotels, majestic mansions, houses of extraordinary taste and elegance, fountains orna- mented with sculptures worthy of the chisel of our best artists, spacious and airy apartments, rich furniture, horses, carriages, and one-horse chaises of the greatest elegance, immense storehouses – would you expect to find all these four thousand leagues from Europe? I assure you, my friend, I fancied myself transported into one of our handsomest cities.[45]

Macquarie also attempted to implement the ancient system of reforming morals by legislation, a particular temptation to Scots, but one to which Australians subsequently proved highly resistant. 'In view therefore, to check these evils, as well as in the hope of its awaking sentiments of morality, and a spirit of industry amongst the lower orders of the people', the number of inns and licensed premises was reduced, the 'most licentious and dis- orderly houses' closed and 'the most unwarrantable and dangerous practice [which] hath existed for some time past, and appears to be daily increasing, of certain persons carrying guns and shooting in the immediate neighbour- hood of the town of Sydney, and close upon His Excellency the Governor's Domain' must cease forthwith. Warned by Lord Castlereagh that 'unfortu- nately females have been given into the possession of such of the inhabitants free settlers and convicts indiscriminately as made a demand for them from the governor', Macquarie was instructed to ensure that so 'extraordinary and disgraceful a practice must immediately be terminated' – and for good measure he also banned nude bathing.[46] More effective and permanent was Macquarie's ordinance giving Sydney streets their present names, by which, for example, Sergeant Major's Row became George Street. In order to finance the extended programme of public works Macquarie put the finances of the colony on a new basis. The only income generated so far was the modest sum of about £1,000 p.a. raised from customs and excise duties, which had been paid into the self-administered Gaol and Orphan Fund. Macquarie increased the duties and appropriated the greater part to a Police Fund, which was also responsible for building and repairing quays, roads and bridges and was now placed under the efficient rule of the indispensable D'Arcy Wentworth.

Soon after his arrival, Macquarie had to cope with a trade depression which brought about the failure of the colony's most solid merchant, Robert Campbell, an offshoot of a great Calcutta house. Wartime disruption to communications and trade had left the colony without a commonly accepted currency: silver English coins officially circulated at higher value – the shilling at one-eighth of a pound – but rupees, ducats, mohurs and a variety of exotic coins were supplemented by tradesmen's tokens and promissory notes. James Wilshire, a tanner, had formed the Commercial Society of New South Wales in 1813, which attempted to fix the value of members' notes by agreeing to accept them at a premium of 50 per cent – which immediately drove down the value of all other tradesmen's notes.

The Governor was fortunate to have acquired the services of a secretary, John Campbell, with some banking experience, and the even more welcome supply of 40,000 silver dollars – Maria Theresa dollars, the common currency throughout the East. This limited supply was extended by the innovation of punching out the middle of the coin, the 'Dump' valued at 1s. 3d., with the larger external fraction, the 'Holey Dollar', worth 5s. Bringing some order into the situation, Macquarie took the initiative of chartering the Bank of New South Wales, with authority to issue its own notes (legally doubtful, but it worked), an action which he considered 'to be the saving of the colony from ruin, and consequently the greatest benefit that could be conferred upon it at the time the measure was adopted'. Macquarie's Bank still exists, seemingly disguised as a frozen food store under the absurd name of Westpac.[47]

One minor embarrassment of Macquarie's was the presence of his predecessor Admiral Bligh's daughter, Mary, who had married Colonel Maurice O'Connell, the Commanding Officer and Lieutenant Governor, a kinsman of the 'Liberator', Daniel O'Connell. Mary had previously shocked the colonists by her revealing dresses, and in her new position hounded all those 'who were in the least inimical to her Father's Government', to such an extent that Macquarie had to ask for O'Connell to be transferred. That was done in 1814 but Mary, now Lady O'Connell, was back in 1838 to persecute Governor George Gipps, placing him in a position of 'extreme delicacy' by demanding a large slice of the flourishing town of Parramatta, which she claimed as her inheritance. Partly successful in this, Mary left the colony once governed by her father and (temporarily) her husband, to live in Paris.

Macquarie's interpretation of his own powers clashed with that of the first judge of the new Supreme Court of Civil Judicature, established under the 1814 Charter of Justice, a halfway-house between the original authoritarian system and contemporary British law. Under the traditions of the British courts, solicitors who had been struck off the rolls were not allowed to practise, but emancipist solicitors were the only ones the colony possessed, and according to his liberal views the Governor was quite prepared to allow them to work. Not so Judge Jeffrey Bent. The dispute raged for some years before a second Act, 'For the Better Administration of Justice in New South Wales and Van Diemen's Land', was issued in London in 1823, an Act which still forms the foundation of the Australian legal system. What it did not make clear was whether solicitors would be allowed to plead in court alongside barristers. The first Australian barristers to qualify at the English bar, D'Arcy Wentworth's son William and Robert Wardell, 'haughtily rejected such pretensions' of the local solicitors; that argument continued.

The fact that such disputes had to be settled in London obliged the Colonial Office to pay more attention to Australian affairs. The Bligh mutiny had not only led to the replacement of the New South Wales Corps by Macquarie's regiment but had provoked lively debate in London, which, after a good deal of persistence by the reformer Sir Samuel Romilly, resulted in the establishment in 1812 of a Select Committee of the House of Commons to consider the whole question of transportation. Evidence was received by a wide range of witnesses, including Hunter and Bligh, and one of the 'Scottish Martyrs' Maurice Margarot, whose martyrdom had been much allayed by his wife and family joining him in a comfortable house; Margarot's allegations of brutality seem to have been contradicted not only by his own experience but by the testimony of other convicts. Transportation, the Committee concluded, was serving its purpose, but both the right to trial by jury in Australia and the formation of an Executive Council were recommended, the first proposal being that of Bligh, who had observed that the colonists were 'anxious not to be so much in the power of the military' and to have some kind of 'justice that might bring them nearer to their brethren in Great Britain'. Neither of these recommendations was implemented, but with the appointment of Lord Bathurst to the new post of Secretary for War and the Colonies in the same year, usually referred to as the Colonial Secretary, New South Wales was never to suffer from so long a period of neglect. With the relaxed and humorous Bathurst backed by the industrious young Henry Goulburn, the British government began to conduct its colonial affairs with greater method. Even before the end of the Napoleonic wars in 1815, which established the second British Empire and left Britain as the only world power, colonial responsibilities had much increased. The Cape of Good Hope, with its extensive hinterland, and Ceylon had been taken from the Dutch; together with Mauritius, Malta and a number of Caribbean islands, this brought the total of British overseas possessions to over thirty. In this context, the future of New South Wales as a colony rather than a penal settlement had to be considered.

In 1806 Governor King had been forced to conclude that the extension of agriculture beyond the first range of mountains 'is an idea that must be given up' in view of the desolate aspect of the Blue Mountains' western slopes. The 1812 Committee had concurred: the settlement was not capable of extension beyond the existing limits, being as it was 'bounded on the north, west and south by a ridge of hills . . . beyond which no one has yet been able to penetrate the country'. Their conclusion was premature.

One of the great moments of Australian history was the May day in 1813 when Gregory Blaxland, William Lawson and young William Wentworth, who had struggled through the Blue Mountains, beheld what seemed to be the promised land. The event was commemorated by Wentworth:

> The boundless champaign burst upon our sight.
> Till nearer seen the beauteous landscape grew,
> Op'ning like Canaan on rapt Israel's view.

To be sure, they had not *quite* crossed the mountains, but had proved that it could be done. More prosaically, Blaxland claimed that their pioneering 'had changed the aspect of the colony from a confined, insulated tract of land to a rich and extensive continent'. Governor Macquarie was vastly impressed, as it appeared that this barrier, for twenty-five years regarded as impassable, was so no longer. He quickly ordered a carriage road to be constructed over the mountains. It was to be at least 12 feet wide, with all necessary bridges, and just over 100 miles long, with some dramatic descents, on one of which carts had to be braked by dragging a 40-foot tree with three men sitting in its branches. Under the direction of William Cox, a former New South Wales Corps officer, now a prosperous Windsor magistrate, thirty convicts completed the task in six months, over rugged country; it was by any standards an amazing achievement. On 7 May 1815 the Governor, with Mrs Macquarie and a numerous party, having driven over Cox's Road, was able to inaugurate the new township of Bathurst, 125 miles from Sydney, though it was to be some years before more development there was officially permitted, since both Colonial Office instructions and Macquarie's own inclinations prevented any expansion of the settled areas.[48]

Two factors made Australian post-war success possible. After the initial shock of the peacetime slump, world trade expanded, encouraging the British government to drop the protective policies which had for centuries sheltered Britain's woollen industry by such devices as making burial in woollen shrouds obligatory, declaring 'owling' – wool smuggling – a capital crime, and in an unblushing piece of economic imperialism, prohibiting woollen manufacture in Ireland. In 1825 duties on colonial imports, which had been as high as 6d. a pound, were abolished. Australian wool began to trickle into England, nearly 2 million pounds of it in 1830, but still a small proportion of the whole – 26 million pounds came from the major producer of fine wool, Saxony. Secondly, the expansion of New South Wales opened up new grazing areas; in spite of Governor Macquarie's attempts to restrict them, sheep- and cattle-ranchers infiltrated the Bathurst region and moved south from Camden. Taking advantage of the revival in demand were such enterprising pioneers as the Forlong sisters, Eliza and Janet. Together with her sons, Eliza spent three years investigating European merino studs, with gold sovereigns sewn into her stays, and drove ninety-seven of her carefully selected purchases from Silesia to Hamburg. When these animals arrived at Hobart in November 1829 the Tasmanian woollen industry began. Eliza was followed by her widowed sister, Janet Templeton, who chartered a ship, the *Czar*, to bring some more of Eliza's German sheep, which she established near the town of Goulburn. Forlongs and Templetons both flourished and dispersed over three colonies, with Eliza's son William becoming a doggedly extreme spokesman for the Port Phillip – later to be Victorian – pastoralists.[49]

In most societies, 'squatters' are taken to be disreputable persons illegally inhabiting someone else's property, but in Australia a squatter is – potentially and sometimes actually – a rich possessor of extensive land, measured in square miles rather than acres, a self-confident member of the gentry, exemplified in the well-known painting *The Squatter's Daughter* by G. W. T. Lambert in the Australian National Gallery. Squatting was the most basic form of farming and took very similar forms in contemporary South Africa and the United States. A family's possessions were loaded on to a bullock dray and the stock driven off until a suitable homestead site was found, near a dependable water source. The animals were entrusted to the care of convict shepherds, who followed their wanderings, bringing them together for lambing and shearing. Prior to proper surveys being made, boundaries were often merely geographical reference points, and permission to use the land was usually sought later. In the absence of predators, and as long as none of Australia's meteorological catastrophes intervened, squatters could be transmuted from adventurous pioneers to landed gentry in a relatively short time. Legitimizing their position, protecting their interests and monitoring their conduct were to become sources of major concern to colonial government.

Only after the peace of 1815 did British governments settle down to begin the reorganization of society, at home and abroad – now urgently needed – under the affable superintendence of Prime Minister Lord Liverpool, who had been present at the taking of the Bastille and who was learning that simple repression was no longer practicable. After the scandal of the 'Peterloo massacre' of 1819 it was appreciated that such reactionaries as Lord Sidmouth, the Home Secretary, must be replaced, and young reformers were accordingly appointed. The old friends of Fox, led by Charles Grey, still refused to be associated with a Tory government, but such talented younger men as Robert Peel, William Huskisson and George Canning were prepared to rethink ancient Tory doctrine. In the face of stubborn opposition – even the abolition of trial by battle had its opponents, who forced a division in the House of Commons before that venerable judicial institution was abolished in 1819 – the way was prepared for the great reconstruction for which the succeeding Whig government took most of the credit. The culminating achievement of the Tory reformers was the great deck-clearing reform of 1829, the Catholic Emancipation Act, carried in the face of fierce resistance from the King, the House of Lords and the established Church.

Reform affected even the cramped and evil-smelling quarters of the Colonial Office at Number 13 Downing Street, which were slowly sinking into the Thames, and which doubled in size with the acquisition of Number 14 in 1827. Lord Bathurst had recruited a staff of industrious and competent officials, beginning with the appointment of James Stephen in 1813 as legal counsel. Stephen, who retired only in 1847 and continued to exercise considerable influence thereafter, imbued colonial policy with an evangelical earnestness that lasted until the closing years of the century. The talents and industry of Henry Taylor, a much-admired tragedian, James Spedding, author of the classic edition of Francis Bacon's works, and Herman Merivale, Professor of Political Economy at Oxford, all contributed to enable the Colonial Office to administer the British Empire, with a staff, including filing clerks, doormen, messengers and 'necessary women' of some seventy individuals.[50]

Well down the list of their priorities was the 'distant colony of the convicts', that 'rascally community' of New South Wales, still, in Lord

Bathurst's opinion in 1822, 'a place of Punishment and Reform' rather than a colony in any accepted sense. Nevertheless, he accepted that 'such advances as a colony' had been made that some alteration in gubernatorial rule must be contemplated – but certainly nothing like such institutions as a Legislative Assembly and trial by jury, regarded as the prerogatives of established British colonies.

Bathurst, who remained in charge of the Colonial Office until 1827 and may be regarded as one of principal founders of that remarkable institution, which evolved to administer a scattered empire and to transform its largest constituents into self-governing states, was harassed both by his Cabinet colleagues and by the parliamentary opposition. The Home Office complained that transportation was both losing its terrors as convicts were so quickly absorbed into the community, and failing in its reforming aspects owing to the lack of supervision and provision for secondary punishments. Worse, the Treasury was agitating for drastic reductions in colonial expenditure. Both departments were having to cope with post-war conditions, with popular unrest being exacerbated rather than crushed by the oppressive measures of the reactionary Tory government. The Treasury had just cause for complaint, since the annual New South Wales expenditure had increased to nearly £250,000 by 1815, with every indication that this would rise further. For a population, convict and free, of under 12,000, this was a frightening sum.

During Bathurst's term of office the Colonial Secretary's responsibilities grew formidably. In 1806, 2,555 letters were received; by 1824 this had risen to 12,450. These communications came, not quite from all corners of the globe, for the affairs of India and the East were handled by the Board of Control and the Honourable East India Company, but from places as distant as Newfoundland and Tasmania. Delays were accordingly frequent, even when colonial officials and Colonial Office staff produced timely reports and speedy replies, which at first rarely happened. Macquarie complained that 'a great number of very interesting and important points . . . raised in a three year period have never been noticed at all by his Lordship'. Bathurst, sitting as he did in the House of Lords, relied upon his parliamentary under-secretaries to fend off criticism in the House of Commons which Goulburn and his successor Robert Wilmot Horton did with considerable competence. After 1819, when Lord Liverpool's government abandoned its attempt to suppress reformist ideas, parliamentary pressure increased, and a group of usually young and often radical members began to demand a new status for New South Wales. The great reformer William Wilberforce grieved that 'undoubtedly it must be confessed that for some time this colony has attracted too little attention', but produced few remedies. His colleague James Mackintosh, pressing for New South Wales 'aliens' to have the same constitutional rights as the British, was satirized by Foreign Secretary George Canning as 'standing on the pier at Sheerness during the loading of a shipful of convicts' and seeing it 'freighted with a cargo of materials for building up a British constitution'. That was in 1819, but Mackintosh was quickly proved right.[51]

Henry Grey Bennett, MP for Westminster, a well-connected parliamentary opportunist and a 'prodigious puppy' according to Bathurst, was joined by Joseph Hume, an Indian nabob, and together they proved tenacious and methodical critics of Tory administration. Assiduously collecting statistics, Bennett proved that in New South Wales one in some 500 persons was convicted of a capital crime in 1817, while in law-abiding Yorkshire a comparable figure was one in 4,100; 'in this school of reform vice and criminality had arrived at a much higher pitch than in the mother country'. When action became unavoidable, it was to an associate of such critics that Lord Liverpool's government turned.[52]

Bathurst, always loyal to his subordinates, appreciating the difficulties which they faced, attempted to defend them against attack by discontented colonists – Macquarie was a particular target for personal abuse – but had to pay attention to the Treasury, the source of all government power. He adopted the prudent task of appointing a commission of investigation, which would at any rate ensure delay, and, with luck, might produce some helpful recommendations.

3

Whigs and Tories

'A body of really respectable Settlers'

Macquarie can be given credit for much, including the use of the term 'Australia' rather than 'New South Wales' to describe his vast colony, and he deserves his own assessment that he had arrived to find New South Wales 'barely emerging from infantile imbecility' and left it 'enjoying a state of private comfort and public prosperity'. One indicator of the colony's prosperity was given by the catalogue of goods to be auctioned by William Baker in October 1821.[1]

English prints; writing paper; boots and shoes; a quantity of earthenware; tumblers and wine glasses; hats; turpentine in bottles; metal spoons knives and forks; hyson and hyson skin teas; irons of different sizes; cupboard, box and pad locks; umbrellas; silk handkerchiefs; red frocks; russell; pen and packet knives; dungaree; English soap; a handsome 8 day clock; gold and silver watches; rush bottomed common chairs and cedar tables. Prompt payment in pork or grain at storeable prices.

The last sentence indicates how scarce currency remained.

Such unauthorized initiatives as founding the Bank of New South Wales, or his socializing with emancipists might have been passed over in London, but the Colonial Office machine demanded a constant supply of paper and the Governor had certainly been extremely lax in forwarding returns and information to London. However popular with the colonists, Macquarie had exhausted the Colonial Office's patience by his refusal to forward copies of his New South Wales legislation, thus vitiating one of the few methods by which London could exercise some control over its charges. In fact, few colonial Bills were rejected as incompatible with British principles – colonists shared the same ideals and prejudices as their home-based relations – but the power to reject them was essential. When James Stephen finally received ten years' backlog of Macquarie's legislation he declared that, although strictly speaking all was illegal, as not having been considered by the British government, it 'could not be annulled because this would have thrown the government of New South Wales into utter confusion'.[2] Similarly, since the Colonial Office were ignorant of what the Governor was doing they were in no position to defend his actions. The parliamentary agitators, Grey Bennett in particular, turned their fire on the unfortunate Governor, stimulated by complaints pouring in on London from an indignant and influential Samuel Marsden, with whom Macquarie had quarrelled bitterly, describing the colonial chaplain as 'the head of a seditious low cabal, and consequently unworthy of mixing in private society or intercourse with me'.[3] With such conflicting evidence aired in the House of Commons debates, the British government decided on an official investigation, entrusted to the earnest and industrious John Bigge, whose reports, when debated and accepted in London, were to define the political future of Australia. One recommendation in particular, his insistence that secondary penal colonies should be established, marked the transition of the core settlement in New South Wales from a convict society to one where traditional colonial institutions were able to develop.

John Bigge was one of the early nineteenth-century colonial administration's most remarkable figures. A reserved and studious Northumbrian lawyer (but not, as the *Australian Dictionary of Biography* has it, an aristocrat) he had served as Chief Justice in Trinidad before starting a ten-year stint of colonial investigations, in New South Wales, the Cape and Mauritius. Arriving in September 1819, when Macquarie had been in office for nearly ten years, Bigge had no conception of the advances that had been made in the Governor's long administration, but he saw only too clearly the general muddle that had evolved.

Commissioner Bigge interviewed almost all of the free population, and hundreds of convicts, during his two-year stay. Transcripts of the evidence, taken by his brother-in-law, Thomas Scott (formerly a wine merchant at Bordeaux), ran to over 15,000 pages, nearly one-third of which are records of personal interviews. Short on tact (his later investigations in the Cape Colony were made much easier by his being accompanied by a diplomatic colleague, Colonel William Colebroke), Bigge irritated Governor Macquarie. To a great extent it was a clash of centuries. Macquarie, eighteen years the senior, had a lifelong ambition to set up as a Highland patriarch on the island of Mull; he remained a man with the habits of the eighteenth century (or even the seventeenth century, perhaps cast as one of Oliver Cromwell's more amiable major-generals), and the nineteenth century was taking over. Bigge was a creature of Bentham, Malthus and Ricardo, political arithmeticians and philosophers; he was attached to statistics, an Imperial civil servant, a compiler of those voluminous Blue Books on which policies were based. Between two such men little personal sympathy was possible, and its lack was reflected in their cold official correspondence, occasionally enlivened by flashes of Macquarie's annoyance; writing of a complaint made to Bigge: 'I consider Mr. Loane to be one of the most turbulent, troublesome and litigious characters that ever came to this colony and that his quitting of it would be a happy riddance.'[4]

Bigge's tone was not only unattractively condescending ('convinced of the rectitude of his own intentions . . . fortified with the approbation of the Parliamentary Committee of 1812, Governor Macquarie has not only continued his support to the emancipated convicts . . . but has manifested on public occasions towards them a larger share of attention than he has manifested towards those of the free class'), but it also accurately reflected the sentiments of the more influential settlers, the exclusives. New South Wales was still predominantly a penal colony; 'A Penitentiary or Asylum on a Grand Scale', according to Macquarie. In 1820, of 17,271 adult inhabitants, 9,451 were convicts and another 5,768 former convicts at varying degrees of liberty. Only 2,802 had arrived as free persons, or had been born in the colony. Of the 5,448 adult Van Demonians, 2,588 were convicts, 961 former convicts and 899 arrived born free. The colonies' future – Bigge recommended that each must be given its own administration – must lie in the exploitation of that still untapped natural resource, the almost unlimited land. John Macarthur advanced cogent arguments as to how this should be done in a letter to Bigge of 19 December 1821: 'If His Majesty's Government proposes to retain this Colony, as a dependency of Great Britain, there is no time to be lost, in establishing a body of really respectable Settlers – Men of real Capital – not needy adventurers. They should have Estates of at least 10,000 acres, with reserves contiguous of equal extent.'[5] Bigge had been powerfully impressed by the ordered efficiency of the Macarthur estate at Camden Park, where the sheep were processed through a production line of sixteen vigorous washers who ensured their fleeces were sparkling clean before being shorn. 'The perseverance and intelligence' of Macarthur were accordingly praised, and encouragement of the fine wool industry singled out as the key to Australia's future prosperity.

Lord Bathurst, in spite of his reservations, was willing to be convinced. Bigge's recommendations, once received in London, had been refined by discussion with James Stephen, with Francis Forbes, nominated as the first Chief Justice to New South Wales, and with Edward Eager, an Irish lawyer transported for forgery and subsequently a strenuous advocate for emancipists. Two Australians, William Wentworth and John Macarthur junior, both Cambridge alumni, contributed to the deliberations. Young Macarthur, who had spent his life in England since the age of 7, was more persuasive and less frenetically arrogant than his father, whilst Wentworth had already made an English reputation by the success of his book, snappily entitled *A Statistical Historical, and Political Description of the Colony of New South Wales and its dependent Settlements in Van Diemen's Land, With a Particular Enumeration of the Advantages which these Colonies offer for Emigration and their Superiority in many Respects over those possessed by the United States of America*, then already in its second edition. Macarthur's smooth public relations moved government views in the directions advocated by the squatters, while Wentworth chose the more difficult task of advocating the emancipists' interests, pressing for an elected Legislative Council with authority over colonial revenues and full civil rights for ex-convicts, rights which were also demanded in two petitions (1819 and 1821) from the 'Gentlemen, Clergy, Settlers, Merchants, Land-Holders and other Free Inhabitants' of New South Wales. Others insisted on the 'convict stain' that permanently marked out the wicked from the righteous; Dr Thomas Arnold, the great spokesman of the serious middle classes, wrote to Sir John Franklin on his appointment to the Van Diemen's Land government:

Feeling this, and holding our West Indian colonies to be one of the worst stains in the moral history of mankind, a convict colony seems to me to be even more shocking and more monstrous in its very conception. I do not know to what extent Van Diemen's Land is so; but I am sure that no such evil can be done to mankind as by thus sowing with rotten seed, and raising up a nation morally tainted in its very origin. Compared with this, the bloodiest exterminations ever effected by conquest were useful and good actions. If they will colonise with convicts, I am satisfied that the stain should last, not only for one whole life, but for more than one generation; that no convict or convict's child should ever be a free citizen; and that, even in the third generation, the offspring should be excluded, from all offices of honour or authority in the colony.

Arnold was admittedly a prig, but an influential one, and any Australian Governor was bound to take such views seriously.[6]

The New South Wales Act of 1823 (amended in the following year), the legislative fruit of the Bigge reports, went some way to meeting the different demands. It provided for the first stage in a classic Crown Colony constitution, in which the Governor was to be assisted by a Legislative Council composed first of nominated officials, to be joined in due course by similarly nominated civilians – 'unofficials' – who in due course might be elected, and increased in numbers. As had been recommended eleven years previously, government would be by an Executive Council, whose advice a Governor would be expected, but not obliged, to take: the same Executive Council continues in the present Australian government, with the Governor General in the chair, advised by the Cabinet ministers – advice which today is taken as commands, except under the most exceptional circumstances. Members of the Executive Council, who at that time included the Chief Justice and the General Officer Commanding, were nominated by London, frequently without consultation with the Governor, and since their posts were of indeterminate tenure, incoming governors often inherited them from earlier administrations. Clashes between members were therefore continual. The key figure in the Executive Council was that of the colonial secretary, the administrative head of government (to avoid confusion with the Secretary of State for the Colonies, the Whitehall minister in charge, usually also known as the Colonial Secretary, lower case is used when describing the Australian position). The first of these officials was Major Frederick Goulburn, brother of parliamentary under-secretary Henry, who arrived in 1821 to serve both as colonial secretary and private secretary to the Governor. Another of Bigge's recommendations was effected in 1823 when Colonel George Arthur was selected to become the first independent Lieutenant Governor of Van Diemen's Land, which was to be recognized as a separate colony.

Sir Thomas Brisbane, who replaced Macquarie in December 1821 at the Duke of Wellington's suggestion, was given the responsibility of implementing Bigge's recommendations and instructed to create the nominated Legislative Council, which would consider laws initiated by the Governor and certified by the Chief Justice as not contrary – 'repugnant' – to British law. This proviso was to be for long a subject of dispute. James Stephen for the Colonial Office recognized the difficulties. Admittedly, 'The law of England is the birthright of English subjects, which they carry with them when they quit their native land to make settlements on waste and unoccupied territories', but equally this could not be always applied: 'It certainly has never been required that the Law of England should be made the inflexible model for all Colonial Legislation.' How this dilemma was resolved occupied much subsequent argument, at each occasion moving nearer to the complete freedom of colonial legislatures.[7]

The same Act allowed for the creation of a Supreme Court, over which Chief Justice Forbes was to preside, and to allow for trial by jury in civil cases. An unconnected but highly significant development, and one which assumed that 'the birthright of English subjects' included the freedom of the press, was the establishment of a newspaper, the *Australian*. The founders were two self-confident young men in a hurry, William Wentworth and Richard Wardell, who had been contemporaries at Cambridge and the Middle Temple. Wentworth, who quite clearly had no gift for catchy phrases, declared his intention to 'pursue our labours without either a sycophantic approval of, or a systematic opposition to, acts of authority, merely because they emanate from government'. Newspaper censorship was at that time a controversial issue in Britain, where attempts to exercise official control led to hundreds of prosecutions. In Sydney, Governor Brisbane sensibly decided not to interfere; the paper cost a shilling, which would keep it out of the hands of the masses.

Like Macquarie, Brisbane was a Scot, but a Sassenach from Ayrshire rather than a 'Hielanman', and one of Wellington's personal friends, an officer who had fought in the Peninsular War and arrived in the colony a general, a Fellow of the Royal Society and a knight, altogether a much more dignified figure than the disappointed Macquarie, but an amiable and sensible man who found colonial quarrels irritatingly incomprehensible. Serious-minded and prayerful, Brisbane took his responsibilities weightily: reflecting on his authority to grant pardons, he wrote in his journal after reprieving twenty-six criminals condemned to death:

more particularly I pray on behalf of Duffey, sixty-two years of age, ordered for execution last Thursday, but whom I freely forgive O Lord, as I freely forgive, may I, through the merits of the son Jesus Christ, be as freely forgiven all the sins of my life . . . if I may have been the instrument of saving one soul from death, that I may have that soul for my reward!

Such actions help to explain the increasing change from New South Wales as a penal colony to its new status as a humane society. It was, however, far from becoming overburdened by 'respectable inhabitants'. The more obviously painful aspects of penal life had been ameliorated: floggings were replaced by that useful institution, the treadmill (vulgarly known as the cockchafer) and chain gangs were seen less often in the streets. Captain Count Francis de Rossi, the energetic Corsican appointed in 1825 the first Superintendent of Police, had begun to implement Bigge's regulations. Captain Hyacinthe de Bougainville, son of the great explorer, who had been on Baudin's expedition, revisited Sydney in the same year and was appalled by the treadmill as earlier visitors had been by the triangle and the lash: 'I could only look at this spectacle for an instant, and I didn't dare stare at these unfortunate men reduced to such a pitiable state.'[8]

While constitutional issues, being well understood, could be settled by consultations in London, the land question exposed British misunderstanding of the sheer vastness of New South Wales and the difficulties of farming there – indeed, these were only beginning to be painfully appreciated by the colonists themselves. Macquarie had been generous in handing out, or allowing his officials to distribute, land grants in an almost casual manner. Brisbane found that over 500 square miles of land had been granted without much indication of where these were located, and that 'many confused permissive occupancies and nebulous promises' of more donations had been made. It was not easy for an officer accustomed to the discipline of Wellington's army to act through the quarrelsome, insubordinate and poorly qualified officials at his disposal in New South Wales, or to control the voracious and aggressive settlers: 'Every person to whom a grant is made receives it as the payment of a debt; everyone to whom one is refused turns my implacable enemy.' In his relatively short period of office (December 1821–December 1825), Brisbane succeeded in tidying up the promiscuous disposal of lands by appointing a commission with powers to ensure that the conditions of grant were being properly complied with, and starting a system of selling land rather than giving it away. In the first six months after this was established (May–December 1825), more than half a million acres were sold at the price of 5s. per acre.[9]

This total, however impressive in British terms – about the same area as Northamptonshire – was but a tiny proportion of the region already claimed by the settlers, who had well outrun the surveyed area. British governments could hardly criticize successive New South Wales governors for expansionist generosity after November 1824, when Lord Bathurst, sedulously cultivated by young John Macarthur, agreed to grant a million acres, to be chosen by the newly chartered Australian Agricultural Company, very much a Macarthur enterprise: 'a pretty tolerable job', as Governor Gipps later ironically described the transaction. Since 1812, the young naval officer John Oxley, appointed as Surveyor General, had spent more time exploring and looking after his own business interests than in the hard work of preparing a general survey. Following the foundation of Bathurst, two apparently major rivers, the Lachlan and the Macquarie, had been identified. It seemed logical that these must either flow into the sea at some hitherto unnoticed point, or feed a great inland lake. Oxley was therefore instructed by Macquarie, prior to an 1817 expedition: 'First, to ascertain the real course or general direction of the Lachlan River, and its final termination, and whether it falls into the sea, or into some inland lake. Secondly, if the river falls into the sea, to ascertain the most exact place of its embouchure, and whether such place would answer as a safe and good port for shipping.'

Oxley's failure to find either lake or estuary was baffling and bafflement continued for many years thereafter. Oxley had nevertheless made two significant discoveries, the sites of the next New South Wales settlements outside the Sydney–Newcastle area, those of Port Macquarie and Moreton Bay, which in due course became Brisbane. Thomas Mitchell, who succeeded Oxley in 1828, was altogether more professional. Another Peninsular War veteran, Major Mitchell had made a name by his careful survey of the battlefields, continued after the war. Although he was as inclined to embark on extensive exploration as Oxley, Mitchell at least accompanied his Australian journeys with accurate surveys and some very competent illustrations. Only in 1834, after some harrying, did he produce the first general survey of the settled area, those nineteen counties defined five years previously, covering an area some 300 miles in length, from north of Newcastle (then little more than a village) to south of the present site of Canberra, and some 150 miles inland past the town of Mudgee. For the next generation until his death in 1855, Mitchell, able but insubordinate and aggressive (he fought one of the last duels in Australia in 1851), was an indispensable and aggravating figure in every administration.[10]

The second great breakthrough, after the crossing of the Blue Mountains, was effected when in 1824 a route to the coast near Port Phillip Bay was discovered. That was the work of the Australian-born Hamilton Hume, an explorer since the age of 17, and William Hovell, a sea captain turned settler, who together pioneered the overland route from Hume's Station, near Goulburn, to reach the coast at Port Phillip Bay in 1824. Hovell, who as a seaman ought to have done better, miscalculated his position and fixed their coastal point of arrival one degree further east than it actually was. When, therefore, a seaborne party set out they got no further than Westernport, which they reported as being unsuitable for agriculture, leaving Port Phillip for the moment undisturbed and the safe and good port for shipping which Macquarie had wanted still unconnected with the hinterland.

Another step towards civil society was the establishment of formal Anglican government, previously in the hands of the colonial chaplain, Samuel Marsden, often preoccupied with his evangelical missions in the Pacific and his own farming concerns.[11] Bigge's former secretary Thomas Scott, newly ordained, but well connected – another brother-in-law was the Earl of Oxford – was appointed archdeacon of New South Wales, in the diocese of Calcutta, with almost complete control of ecclesiastical affairs and ranking next after the Lieutenant Governor. Brisk, competent and a high Tory, Scott attracted angry opposition from the radical press – Wentworth's *Australian*, joined in 1826 by Edward Hall's *Monitor*, which specifically supported emancipists. 'The injured and oppressed,' Hall assured his readers, 'high or low, bond or free . . . [would] meet with firm, consistent, persevering and *prudent* friends.' Jealousy from clerics of other denominations was inevitable, sharpened by the privileges extended to Anglican education by the Clergy and Schools Lands Corporation. The permanently irascible Presbyterian cleric John Dunmore Lang was doctrinally and socially at the opposite end of the spectrum from Scott, and continued to be an irritant, sometimes a very productive irritant, to the authorities for the next half-century. Vituperative and entrenched in prejudice, Lang's irrepressible energies led him back in London only eighteen months after his arrival in 1823, returning with a Doctorate of Divinity (very speedily acquired) and Lord Bathurst's agreement to be appointed as a colonial Presbyterian minister, all at the age of 25. Lang could claim to be a representative of the Scottish established Church, but the claim cut little ice with the predominantly English colonial structure. The Roman Catholic chaplain, John Joseph Therry, a less abrasive character, enjoyed better relations with the administration, especially under the devout Brisbane; but Brisbane's successor, General Ralph Darling, distrusted Therry's influence with the convicts and abominated his support of the New South Wales radicals. However disputatious the behaviour of the clergymen, their labours did much to improve the general tone of the community and began the organization of education.[12]

Brisbane, intellectual and pious well beyond the usual standards of general officers, but totally inexperienced in civil government, was not an ideal choice: his relations with his colonial secretary Frederick Goulburn were strained, leading to numerous complaints being made to Lord Bathurst; and complaining to one Cabinet minister about the misdeeds of another minister's brother was dangerous. Goulburn had also quarrelled with the Macarthurs, also influential in Whitehall. The outcome was that both Brisbane and Goulburn were recalled.

'A perfect martinet'

Governor Ralph Darling (1825–31), 'bustling with optimistic activity and energetic plans for a reform of all departments', was not a fighting soldier, but a renowned administrator. He was not, however, recognized by his contemporaries as a gentleman – his custom of always appearing in uniform being one distinguishing mark of unacceptable behaviour – and was socially clumsy. The colonials attached considerable importance to having a Governor who behaved with viceregal affability; one of the complaints against the very gentlemanly Brisbane was that he had not been sufficiently sociable. The son of a sergeant-major, Darling had much of the senior warrant officer about him, a man, James Stephen conceded in 1825, 'with little reach of thought or variety of knowledge, unreasonably stiff in his manners and I suspect a great formalist in business and a perfect martinet in military matters'. (Stephen was writing to Lieutenant Governor Arthur of Van Diemen's Land: such frankness when writing to one technically Darling's junior illustrates Arthur's great influence in London.) 'I confess,' Lord Bathurst had admitted to Wilmot Horton, 'I think the new Governor will prove a troublesome gentleman', and Bathurst was right. Darling attempted to rectify his personal defects by lavish entertainment, but his unfortunate character negated their effects – 'a cold, stiff, sickly military person . . . of somewhat forbidding appearance . . . a great stickler for all forms of Etiquette' – but whose parties appeared 'a congregation of renegades from the worst society at home, of Godknowhereians and of Godknowhenerians whose right of admission consists in the possession of sheep, cattle, corn, merchandise, money, whale-oil, or daughters – a motley crew confusedly scrambled together'.[13]

Darling's patience – never his best quality – was severely tried by the 'incredible succession of incompetents' imposed on him as officials. He suffered from five Attorney Generals within four years, each more impossible than the last, culminating in the appalling Alexander Baxter, ignorant, violent, and a 'habitual sot'. Many detailed abuses were ferreted out by Darling, who complained that 'the common routine and forms of office were totally neglected', but, more importantly, the brisk Governor reorganized the whole government structure by expanding the functions of the colonial secretary.[14]

This official had previously been the chief administrative officer; Darling advanced the post to that of chief executive, with 'an immediate controlling power' and 'the special and indispensable duty to see that all orders and regulations are properly followed up and carried into effect'.[15] Alexander Macleay, an elderly entomologist sent out with Darling, made a start, but it was his successor, Edward Deas Thomson, who effected the transformation that enabled colonial secretaries to change their title to that of Premier when colonial self-government was established.

It was another misfortune that Darling was in office at a time when the British government was beginning a period of fundamental reform, and more than willing to concede further measures of self-government to New

South Wales. He had been instructed to impose discipline in place of Brisbane's leniency, and was initially supported in this by Whitehall; his efforts to restrain his critics in the press 'by no means should be neglected', wrote R. W. Hay in 1826, but the times were changing. The succession of post-war Tory governments ended in 1830 with the triumph of the Whig party, led by the 2nd Earl Grey and committed to parliamentary reform. Such Tory reformers as George Canning and William Huskisson had already been edging the party forwards; Huskisson, in his brief six-month career as Colonial Secretary was able to scrap the ancient 'mercantile' policy of monopolizing colonial trade in British interests, allowing the colonial territories thereafter to constitute something very like a Free Trade Area with the United Kingdom.

After the Whig government had forced through their great Reform Bill of 1832, which marked the move – hesitant as it was – towards a democratic franchise, Lord Grey's more liberal colleagues could be expected to sympathize with colonial demands for a greater say in their own affairs. Some recent Australian writers, seeking early indications of a national identity, have fretted over the absence of any real struggle for colonial freedom from imperial bonds. At least until the Second World War, little trace of what might be termed decolonization is manifest except at the fringes of political society. Nineteenth-century British governments proved embarrassingly ready to grant self-government; the critical figures in Canadian constitutional progress are not the rebels – Papineau, Riel or Mackenzie – but John Lambton ('Radical Jack'), the Earl of Durham, and his son-in-law, Lord Elgin; Natal was given a self-governing constitution so early that it had to be temporarily revoked; and the Australian colonies were presented with an open invitation to design their own constitutions. One consequence is the absence of an unequivocal national day of celebration, an equivalent to the Fourth or Fourteenth of July. Australia Day, 26 January, commemorating the arrival of the First Fleet, has less meaning for those states founded later, and is tarnished by the understanding that it also marks the beginning of Aboriginal dispossession; Anzac Day, 25 April, marks the anniversary of the landings in 1915 at Gallipoli of the Australia and New Zealand Army Corps, a solemn and emotional experience. Attempting to find some evidence of a hard-fought struggle for independence from the imperial yoke, historians have uncovered examples of indignant nineteenth-century petitions and lively public meetings, only to find these deflected by the condescending suavity of British politicians masking a mild irritation with those they perceived as uncouth colonials.

With improved communications, the day-to-day powers of a Governor were in practice reduced throughout the nineteenth century, but as late as 1992 the Governor of the Crown Colony of Hong Kong, Chris Patten, could, on his own authority and without much comment, remove elected members of the Legislative Council from their newly acquired seats on the Executive Council – effectively the government. Crown Colonies, the numbers of which had been greatly increased by the recent conquests, were administered by the Colonial Office alongside older colonies, those which had not declared their independence in 1777. Of these Jamaica was the senior, having been captured from the Spanish by a Cromwellian fleet, and having had an elected legislature since 1662. The bitter experience of the American war had been applied in 1791, when Pitt's administration established a representative Canadian government with an elected Legislative Council (which the Tories hoped might develop into a Canadian House of Lords) and an Executive Council. The Canadian constitution was the first example of how the lesson taught by the rebellious American colonies had been learnt – and by a Tory government. Its development was to serve as a pattern for Australian constitutional progress.[16]

The administration of Crown Colonies could be modified as British governments judged appropriate. When the Legislative Council had a majority of elected members the constitution was 'representative'. The next stage was usually the creation of a separate Legislative Assembly, thus, with two houses of the colonial Parliament, mirroring the British arrangement of Lords and Commons, with the Governor representing the Crown. It was, however, open to colonies to chose a single-chamber legislature; Queensland, always an odd man out in Australia, now has such an arrangement. Further progress towards a 'responsible' government could be gradual rather than formal. If a liberally minded governor, backed by a sympathetic Whitehall department, appointed his administration from a majority in an elected Assembly, the succeeding administration would then be 'responsible' to the electorate. How democratic this system might be depended on other factors, such as the franchise requirements, which might eliminate all but the well-to-do, the comparative size of constituencies, and the nature of those powers 'reserved' to the British imperial government. What the Crown granted the Crown could revoke. At least two colonies were made to revert to Crown Colony status when the conduct of their governments was felt to have departed too far from accepted standards – Jamaica in 1866 and Natal in 1876. In Australia, however, progress from representative to fully responsible government was to be unimpeded and, except in Western Australia, remarkably quick.[17]

For much of the nineteenth century British governments evinced only sporadic interest in the colonies. India, with the rapid expansion of imperial hegemony, dotted with exciting wars, followed by the recruitment of former enemies into the British Indian armies, attracted much more public interest, although even the great subcontinent remained for most of the time an object of secondary importance to successive governments. Among the colonies of settlement – those in Canada, Australasia and South Africa – neither Canada, with its increasingly powerful neighbour, nor the Cape of Good Hope could be for long ignored. The latter's persistent squabbles with Dutch and black neighbours and its importance on the route to India, obliged British administrators, although seething with indignation at the cost of the wars, to devote some attention to constructing, by painful fits and starts, what became the Union of South Africa (the pain was appreciably relieved by the discovery of gold and diamonds in prodigious quantities). Other than the excitements caused by local wars, the other colonies of settlement were the object of only intermittent attention by politicians who had developed a particular interest; notoriously, parliamentary debates on colonial matters were very poorly attended.

At a time when British constitutional theory and practice were evolving with bewildering rapidity (the unhappy Tory MP John Wilson Croker was horrified at the prospect of 'revolutionary Reform' which would be accompanied 'certainly by confiscations and persecutions'; the baffled Duke of Wellington, accustomed to the gentlemanly pre-Reform Act Parliaments, looked astounded at the collection of members elected under the new franchise of 1832: 'I have never seen so many shocking bad hats'), a neat and well-detailed model for colonial constitutions was not available. Wellington himself would certainly not have accepted without qualification the Earl of Durham's analysis: 'Since the Revolution of 1688, the stability of the English constitution has been secured by that wise principle of our Government which has vested the direction of national policy, and the distribution of patronage, in the hands of the Parliamentary majority.'[18]

Some Australians had been specifically calling for 'representative government', although without any clear definition of what this entailed, since at least 1822. Much more general was a feeling that being a British subject carried inalienable rights wherever such a subject happened to find himself, in Toronto, Cape Town, Sydney or even, just then beginning, in Hong Kong. A summary of these rights might be understood as a compound of Magna Carta, the 1689 Bill of Right, the rule of law generally, freedom of expression and the ability of the House of Commons to vote a government out of office, with the corollary that any government must have the support of a majority in an elected lower house – which amounted to 'responsible government'.

Most British politicians shared the same assumption. What was questioned was the fitness of any specific colonial society for such government, and the dangers that might be involved in delegating powers. Leading Whigs differed in their own assessments. The Earl of Durham was concerned specifically with Canada, where he advocated in 1837 the immediate grant of responsible government, the policy eventually carried out by Lord Elgin, but it could not be taken that Canadian precedents should be immediately followed in other colonies.

In the 1820s, the politically active among the Australian colonists would not have agreed with 'Radical Jack'. They aspired to fill the position occupied by the nobility and gentry of England, and complained that 'a race of Men, already arrived at an adult state, who, scattered in the distant and silent woods of their country, are yet destined to be the fathers of the succeeding generations . . .' required more legislative powers. The authors of this address to Governor Darling would have been horrified if a more democratic constitution were to be effected. They were the colonial establishment, the squatters, the occupiers of millions of acres of Crown land, in the process of making fortunes from the wool trade: the last thing they wanted was control passing to the emancipists and free workers.[19]

The Colonial Office refused to move. The vast extent of the colony – which from 1834 also included a new settlement at Port Phillip – and the nearly complete absence of suitable candidates with leisure and education enough to take an active part in a central council, militated against any precipitous advance towards representative government. On the other hand, British public opinion was moving in a generally liberal direction, and the permanent civil servants at the Colonial Office were themselves sympathetic to moderate colonial aspirations.

When, therefore, Darling attempted to muzzle the newspapers, as his contemporary Lord Charles Somerset had attempted to do in South Africa, the Governor found himself opposed both by his own Chief Justice, Francis Forbes, who was in constant private communication with London ministers, and by the Colonial Office. The Governor angrily told the 115 'members of the respectable classes' who had 'assured him that they deplored malign attacks on his administration'[20] that the criticism was all the fault of that triumvirate, Forbes, Wentworth and Hall, insultingly described as 'Americans at heart', who, fortunately, would therefore never be believed in London. His opponents were, however, presented with a wonderful opportunity when Darling had two soldiers, Joseph Sudds and Patrick Thompson, ritually punished in a public ceremony of his own devising and imprisoned in ghoulish fetters, also of his own design. When Sudds obligingly died a few days later the press was handed a story that ran and ran, in Britain as well as in New South Wales. 'Murder, or at least a high misdemeanour', cried Wentworth, somewhat bathetically, demanding Darling's recall. The Governor responded by accusing Wentworth, that 'vulgar, ill-bred demagogue', of seditious libel; in the subsequent trial Wentworth and his fellow editor Wardell came off clearly the better. An amendment to the Newspaper Act, which Darling proposed late in 1829, imposing a mandatory sentence of banishment on any editor convicted for libel a second time, was disallowed by the Colonial Office as 'repugnant'.

Governor Darling had committed the irrevocable error in public life, that of failing to have understood the shifts of political power. The Whigs' 1830 victory had been clearly foreshadowed in the previous year, when the Catholic Relief Act, to accommodate Roman Catholics, altered the oath required by Members of Parliament. This allowed Daniel O'Connell to take his seat, thus adding another powerful critic to the list of Darling's enemies. After the 'bad hats' had taken office in November 1830, young Lord Howick, the new Prime Minister's son, became parliamentary undersecretary at the Colonial Office. In theory run by old 'Goody' Goderich, who had painlessly moved from being a Tory Prime Minister to a Whig Secretary for War and the Colonies – equally ineffective in both offices – the Colonial Office was in fact a separate department, and, since Goderich sat in the Lords, Howick (the title being a courtesy one) controlled the Office, relying on the counsel of the experienced James Stephen. Howick, although suspicious of New South Wales, was an ardent supporter of civil liberties, and a dedicated opponent of slavery ('He had slaved out his life for the last two years on the question of the Niggers,' complained his father in March 1833). Howick therefore brusquely rebuked Darling for his attempted interference with the freedom of the press, a warning that liberal values were, at least for the time being, in the ascendant.[21]

Darling's Instructions, which had saddled him with a Legislative Council, were confirmed by the New South Wales Act of 1828, which took the colony a step nearer self-government as the number of Legislative Councillors was increased and their powers augmented, with the Governor obliged, subject to the usual caveats, including his power to reserve Bills, to abide by a majority decision. The unofficials, one of whom was the veteran John Macarthur, now declining into terminal insanity, were now in a majority of eight to seven. With that modest advance towards self-government – the Legislative Council members were still all nominated, and the Executive Council remained oligarchic – and with guaranteed freedom of the press, further progress was inevitable, but while New South Wales continued to serve as a convict colony this was likely to be slow. Towards the end of his first stint in office, in February 1834, Howick confided his views to Lord Melbourne, now the Prime Minister. In spite of his liberalism, he was appalled by 'the close correspondence between the state of society in the West Indies and in the penal colonies', in both of which the landowners had been corrupted by cheap labour – and by cheap land, too, in New South Wales – while the 'very depraved society' of emancipated convicts seemed not to have developed habits of industry and responsibility.[22]

When Darling left Sydney in October 1831 he was replaced by a Governor much more receptive to the Whig government's reforming principles and more likely to transmit a less damning account of colonial misdemeanours than his predecessor. An Irish gentleman and another Peninsular veteran, General Sir Richard Bourke had already proved himself a liberal and humane colonial Governor in the Cape Colony – characteristics that did not necessarily make for general popularity, either in Africa or Australia – and he contrived to smooth out colonial quarrels with great ease. The new Governor was in a strong position, arriving as he did with the full support of the incoming Whig government, and being a personal friend of Thomas Spring-Rice, an Irish neighbour and an influential member of Lord Grey's administration, who briefly became Colonial Secretary between June and December 1834. Bourke was thereby enabled, with London's approval, to pass two colonial acts strengthening control over existing grants and allowing annual licences to occupy grazing lands outside the limit of authorized settlement. 'Sheep', observed Bourke, 'must wander or they will not thrive, and the colonists must have sheep.' Charles Grant, later Lord Glenelg, who retained the Colonial Office portfolio for four years after April 1835, agreed that attempts to restrain settlers, 'especially in these days of general peace and increasing population', were 'wholly irrational'.[23] With expanding settlement legitimized by this new policy, Bourke was able to organize the little community at Port Phillip, on the south coast bay originally discovered by John Murray in the *Lady Nelson*, where the first hopeful settlers had landed with their flocks in November 1834. In September 1836 Captain William Lonsdale was appointed as police magistrate, Protector of Aborigines and head of whatever civil service might eventually be organized. Three surveyors, two customs officials and a commissary clerk thus formed the first administration of what, within twenty years, was to be the self-governing colony of Victoria. The following year Bourke visited Lonsdale's settlement and took great pleasure in naming it after the Whig Prime Minister, Lord Melbourne.

Bourke had been instructed to meet one of the most insistent colonial demands by introducing trial by jury in criminal as well as civil cases. It took him two years to push this through the Legislative Council, opposed by the exclusives, who were fearful of a system in which cattle-stealers would be tried by their comrades, and receivers of stolen good tried by each other. But before the Whig government could pay much more attention to colonial affairs, the remarkable Edward Gibbon Wakefield had transformed British public opinion.

Until the 1830s, colonies were considered either as valuable pieces of real estate on the grounds of their commercial desirability – the West Indies, for example, producing the essential sugar and rum – or strategic importance as naval bases, that scatter of red dots on the world's sea routes from the Falklands to Singapore. Colonies of settlement, along the pattern of the lost American colonies, were less appreciated. Those in Canada were viewed with general apprehension by most British governments as being both a permanent source of possible friction with the United States and of limited commercial and strategic value, furs and the naval base at Halifax being the two most significant items. One hope entertained by many British politicians was that an amicable arrangement could be reached with the United States – much more important as a trading partner – to take the various other bits of North America under its wing. A limited experiment had been made in 1820 to encourage settlement in the Cape of Good Hope, where it was judged desirable to reduce the Dutch majority by subsidizing emigrants to populate the Eastern Cape, and £50,000 had been granted by Parliament for this purpose. But New South Wales and its subordinate colony of Van Diemen's Land were still considered primarily as penal settlements; this, however, was about to change.

A Letter from Sydney

'Goody' Goderich, now Earl of Ripon, had given his new title to the Ripon Regulations which ended the system of land grants, substituting sale by auction at a minimum price of 5s. an acre, as Brisbane had done five years previously, but applying the proceeds to be used to subsidize emigration. It was an idea calculated to appeal to contemporary political economists; the industrious poor, left to fend for themselves at home in a harsh economic climate, might well turn to crime; this way, they could be sent to Australia under their own steam, as it were, and by hard work earn enough to buy themselves a small plot of land in one of the 'settled' districts where an eye could be kept upon them by a benevolent colonial authority.

Ripon's Regulations were inspired by the theories of Edward Gibbon Wakefield, and were Howick's work rather than that of the ineffectual Earl. At leisure in prison – for abducting a schoolgirl heiress, and that the second offence – with time to consider the issues of crime and punishment, the unstable but industrious Wakefield had composed 'A Letter from Sydney' (never having been nearer to Australia than Turin). His condemnations of the practice of uncontrolled land grants and the uninhibited spread of settlement in New South Wales convinced many readers of the *Spectator*, an influential journal which publicized his theories in December 1829, that the author was an expert on Australian affairs, and persuaded the new government of the merit of Wakefield's ideas.[24]

Wakefield had proved himself to be a man of 'of extraordinary powers of persuasion, of restless energy and ambition', and these were now demonstrated in more reputable activities. He gathered some notable supporters, the most influential of whom was Sir William Molesworth, the eccentric (he fought a duel with his Cambridge tutor), brilliant (his edition in sixteen volumes of Thomas Hobbes's works remains the standard work) young Member of Parliament (22 at the time of his election in 1832).[25] Wakefield argued that granting large tracts of land without any assurance that it would be usefully developed sterilized future growth. The wiser course would be to sell the land, at a modest but realistic price, the proceeds to form a development fund from which loans might be made available. Immigrants would therefore be encouraged to work for cash wages in order to save whatever was needed for the purchase price of their own freehold land.

Moreover, new settlements should be concentrated around urban centres, from which orderly expansion could be controlled, rather than the free-for-all that had affected New South Wales. Subsequent discussions, in which Wilmot Horton played an active part, led to initial confusion and delay, but progressed towards an agreement on ending the land grant system, which had previously proved generally popular. Governors, kept on the tightest of financial strings by the Treasury, found it convenient to pay officials and placate supporters with land rather than cash. They were supported in this by the War Office, anxious to persuade its retired officers to accept payment in Australian acres rather than gold sovereigns. Wakefield's adept public relations, and his vision of colonies populated by industrious settlers subsidized by the proceeds of land sales, cut across these arguments and reservations.

As not infrequently occurs, political enthusiasm was not sullied by practical experience. Neither Wakefield himself nor any of his prominent supporters had strayed far from Europe; until Charles Dilke made his round the world voyage in 1866–7, no British politician had a synoptic view of the colonial Empire; before Robert Lowe's return to England from his incursion into Australian politics and his election to Parliament in 1852 no parliamentarian had any experience of Australia – and Lowe as a Liberal minister showed little interest in Australia apart from opposing the 1855 Bills which were to establish the colonial constitutions. Robert Cecil, later Prime Minister as Lord Salisbury, had seen a good deal of Australia when straight down from Oxford, before his return to England and election to Parliament in 1854, but he only interested himself in colonial affairs when they were forced upon his attention in office. Wakefield and his supporters were therefore under the illusion that Australia was a country as apt for settlement by yeoman farmers as might be Yorkshire, where a few hundred well-managed acres would confer prosperity and justify the prices they expected – appealingly low by Yorkshire standards, acceptable in well-favoured Australian areas, but excessively high for most – and all, of course, without accounting for that permanent over-arching disadvantage, the Australian climate.

It was remarkable how quickly nineteenth-century British governments could act when occasion seemed to demand it. The National Colonization Society was founded within months of 'A Letter from Sydney'. By the end of the year the old system of free grants had been terminated. Land would in future be made available at a price of 5s. per acre, and some of the proceeds would be used to subsidize immigration. Not only New South Wales but all subsequent Australian colonies were to adopt the same principle, although the price might vary in different colonies. Those lands which were 'the rightful patrimony of the English people formed the ample appanage which God and Nature have set aside in the New World for those whose lot has assigned them but insufficient portions in the old' would be populated with the full encouragement of the British government. Lord Durham was here writing of Canada, and was somewhat dismissive of any rights Scots or Irish might have (to say nothing of the Welsh). In New South Wales there was another section of the population who might question the Earl's assignment of the 'rightful patrimony of the English people': the Australian Aborigines.

'People whose proprietary title to the soil we have not the slightest grounds for disputing'

When it was decided, in Whitehall offices, by people who had never seen any part of the land concerned, that Britain should claim half the Australian continent, the precedent set by Pope Alexander was being followed. British right was asserted against that of France, Spain, Holland, the United States or any other Western power. The Aborigines were not consulted, and could hardly have been consulted, since only the little communities around Port Jackson were aware of the British settlement. After the Battle of Trafalgar in 1805 had asserted the Royal Navy's global supremacy (later a little dented by the 1812 conflict with America), no other power was in a position to challenge British claims. What, then, of the Aborigines?

Britain claimed sovereignty over New South Wales: the power to govern all parts of the territory, to make and enforce laws and to defend the inhabitants, well defined by J. S. Mill as 'the supreme controlling power in the last resort'. It was a claim which in practice could hardly be contested. Even in South Africa, where black societies controlled lands with recognized boundaries and were organized in a structured fashion, acknowledging the supreme power of Britain 'in the last resort' was commonly accepted; King George III could be accepted as a paramount chief within traditional laws. What was not accepted, and indeed was vigorously contested, was the British right to expropriate black lands. Ten wars were fought in South Africa before an enforceable land settlement was pushed through. Australian Aborigines, however, were in no position to offer the sort of resistance made by the Xhosa or Basuto, who could defeat not only colonial levies but also British regulars; but their attachment to the land was quite as great, and, since almost the sole support of hunter-gatherers is access to natural food resources, Aborigines could be expected to defend these to the best of their ability. Their right to do so was acknowledged by Britain; writing of South Australia (but with current events in South Africa very much in his mind), the Colonial Secretary Lord Glenelg cautioned against intrusion into the lands of 'People whose proprietary title to the soil we have not the slightest grounds for disputing'. That was in 1835, when for nearly half a century Australian lands, amounting to some 4 million acres, had been granted, or more recently sold, to all of which the Aborigines had some title.[26]

The contrast with South Africa is instructive. Occupation of the Cape of Good Hope was an essential factor in the world war of 1793–1815, but brought with it the unwelcome responsibility for an inconveniently large colony, with no established boundaries. Powerful black tribes pressed on the frontiers, but the indigenous colonial population was a mixture of Khoikhoi – 'Hottentots' – and imported slaves, the present 'Coloureds'. Governor Bourke, while in charge previously at the Cape, had issued a famous ordinance, often called the 'Hottentots' Magna Carta'. This name is something of an exaggeration, but the ordinance did nevertheless declare uncompromisingly that 'Hottentots and other free persons of colour' enjoyed 'all the rights of law . . . to which other of His Majesty's subjects are entitled'. Legally, the position of Australian Aborigines must have been the same, but so robust a declaration was never forthcoming in colonial New South Wales.

Pastoralists and hunter-gatherers could coexist, and over long periods. Hottentot cattle ranged over the hunting-grounds of the Bushmen without more than occasional disagreements for a thousand years; even when Dutch colonists infringed on the Bushmen's territory such expressions of goodwill as the occasional gift of a sheep could keep local peace for over a century. In Australia, the rapid expansion and the scattered Aboriginal population should have made compromise easier, but two essential factors were missing.

In both New South Wales and Tasmania the first generation of occupation was essentially that of penal settlements, supposedly restricted to limited areas, where local agreements with the Aborigines were possible, and where widespread colonization was not envisaged. From 1793, for over twenty years, British governments were too occupied with the war to pay much attention to New South Wales. Governor Phillip's original draft instructions had been to make no grants of land, but the need to keep starvation at bay, to recompense officials and provide for emancipated convicts had led to widespread alienation of land. Organized settlement, which could have been accompanied by negotiations with Aborigines, never caught up with the uncontrolled expansion of the pioneer pastoralists.

Secondly, missionary activity, that essential moderating influence, was sparse in Australia. As soon as British forces had taken the Cape of Good Hope from the Dutch in 1795, the London Missionary Society despatched a team of four missionaries to instruct the natives and to act as intermediaries between them, the colonists (established for nearly 150 years) and the authorities. They were followed by colleagues and rivals, from the Anglican Church Missionary Society, the Methodist missions, the Glasgow Mission Society and the Basel Missions. Between them the missionaries learnt and analysed the languages of their flock, established a network of schools, and taught the gospel of redemption through hard work. From the mission schools a generation later came the first black and brown community leaders (and, eventually, President Nelson Mandela) who were able to play a part in political life (and, with the parliamentary vote in the Cape Colony, on the same basis as the whites). Above all, missionaries were the great facilitators of communication. To them, the great imperative was to save souls, and this could be done only by direct appeal in their flocks' own languages; it was missionary application that produced the earliest grammars of African languages. Settlers and administrators could supplement their commands with physical force, but missionaries had to persuade and convince.

In Australia, only a shadow of this creative force was able to operate. The first clergymen despatched with the prisoners were only peripherally concerned with the Aborigines, seeing their primary responsibility as the welfare of the settlers and – a good second – the convicts in the small urban centres. Except when they infringed on settled areas, Aborigines were neglected. Macquarie had recognized this deficiency, and appointed William Shelley, 'a man of very comprehensive mind' according to his friend Marsden, to establish a school for Aborigines at Parramatta in 1814. Under the initial direction of the London Missionary Society, the enterprising Shelley had nearly twenty years of Australasian experience as missionary to Tonga, ship's captain and trader. The school promised well, but folded on Shelley's death the following year; subsequent attempts at missionary activity were sporadic. Macquarie's expectations that Aborigines would become 'progressively useful to the country as labourers in Agricultural employ or among the lower class of mechanics' betrayed a complete ignorance of Aboriginal culture and proclivities.

The Church Missionary Society for Australia and Tasmania was founded in London in 1799, but did not begin any work in Australia until 1825. Its representative in Sydney, the Reverend Samuel Marsden, held out little hope for the Aborigines – 'they have no Reflection' – and preferred to concentrate on New Zealanders as 'a very superior people in point of mental capacity, requiring but the introduction of Commerce and the Arts, [which] having a natural tendency to inculcate industrious and moral habits, open a way for the introduction of the Gospel' – as good a guide to early nineteenth-century mission policy as can be found. The missionary societies agreed; all their Australasian efforts were concentrated on the Pacific islands and New Zealand.[27]

Marsden's lack of interest in Aboriginal ministry was sadly damaging, since he was by far the most percipient analyst of missionary work, deploring 'absurd' attempts to confine Aboriginal children since 'a roving life in the wilderness is not of necessity a barbarous one', and asserting that the 'true missionary must track the wandering savage in the desert' rather than prepare 'the savage mind for Christianity by the preliminary discipline of a civilising process'. Only in 1825, and almost accidentally, was a missionary enterprise begun which might have rivalled the African endeavours, by the Reverend Lancelot Threlkeld of the London Missionary Society, a Nonconformist body. Threlkeld was merely passing through Sydney on the way back from Moorea when he perceived the need for such an enterprise and convinced Brisbane to permit and endow his efforts. Threlkeld's station near the town of Newcastle became a showplace of mission endeavour. Working closely with the Aboriginal leader Biraban (John McGill), the two men published the first grammar of an Aboriginal language and began a translation of the New Testament. But 'conversions' were few. Biraban himself was 'punctilious in observing his ceremonial obligations' and preferred to live in traditional style, although he played a full part in the work of the mission, being bound to Threlkeld by 'mutual respect' and affection, and impressing judges by his ability as an interpreter. Threlkeld's pugnacious temperament led him into clashes with prominent Sydney churchmen, most especially with the unsympathetic Marsden, the London Missionary Society's agent in Australasia. Threlkeld was recalled and his stipend ended, but Governor Darling, though no unconditional admirer of missionary activity, agreed to finance his employment. During the next sixteen years as a missionary Threlkeld published four books on the Aboriginal languages represented in his district. Measured by the rate and permanence of conversions, Threlkeld's work was a failure, and his linguistic studies were not followed up, but for more than half a century his accounts of Aboriginal life remained the most serious attempt to explain their beliefs and customs. The eventual termination of official support may well have been a result of Threlkeld's presumption in chiding King Louis-Philippe of France for demanding compensation from his friend the Queen of Tahiti on behalf of 'emissaries of the Roman Pontiff' who had been expelled by the Queen.[28]

Threlkeld himself was not a missionary of the calibre of Robert Moffat or David Livingstone, who could affect the destinies of whole countries; he was opinionated and angry, a man of only limited education and restricted imagination. Worse, he did not possess the same sort of authority in London that South African missionaries often possessed, able to marshal parliamentary sympathy and extensive popular support. And Threlkeld was one of the very few missionaries working among the Aborigines of Australia, in contrast to the scores of settlements and schools established in South Africa. In December 1831 Lord Goderich's complaint that 'the attention of my predecessors having hardly been called to the lamentable state of ignorance and barbarism in which the Aborigines of New Holland continued to remain' ensured that a Church Missionary Society mission was established under the superintendence of Mr William and Mrs Watson, who were instructed to 'repair the wrongs inflicted by the settlers'. Their efforts, like almost all others, were misguided and short-lived.[29]

British attention, hitherto limited to the Oceanic islands, focused more closely on Australia after the reports of the Quaker missionaries James Backhouse and George Walker were published. Travelling among penal settlements first in Tasmania and then in New South Wales, Backhouse and Walker also visited some government-established Aboriginal settlements and Threlkeld's mission station. Their reports, through their friend Sir Thomas Fowell Buxton, were forwarded to Lord Glenelg. Not the most efficient of Colonial Secretaries, Glenelg was nevertheless sincerely dedicated to protecting native rights. The eventual success of the Anti-Slavery Society in obtaining the suppression of slavery throughout British territories in 1833 (the trade itself had been banned in 1807, and slavery had never been legal in England) had diverted the reformers' interest from abolition to the protection of native interests against colonial aggressions. Glenelg needed little convincing. As Charles Grant, he had been a reforming Tory before joining the Whigs. Politically a lightweight, something of a ditherer, known for his 'proverbial indecision and supineness', according to Molesworth, Glenelg had attended Magdalene College, Cambridge, a hotbed of evangelistic fervour, and he embodied all the liberal prejudices against exploiting settlers and anxiety to protect native peoples. His successors, however, although decently concerned with Aboriginal rights, did not share Glenelg's devotion to the subject, although with the spread of settlement pressure on the Aborigines increased exponentially. As British enthusiasm for protecting native peoples waned, their future looked precarious, and as power passed progressively to the colonists themselves, the very existence of Australian Aborigines became questionable as the tides of settlers, respectable and otherwise, swept into their ancient hunting-grounds.

4

Occupied Notices

Land of Lags and Kangaroo
Of Possums and the scarce Emu,
The Farmer's Pride, the Prisoner's Hell,
Land of Bums – Fare – thee – well!

Francis MacNamara,
convict (Frank the Poet)

'The moral Governor of the world will hold us accountable'

In May 1819 the Duchess of Kent gave birth to a daughter, Princess Alexandrina Victoria. In due course the princess would become Queen of Great Britain and Ireland and her dominions beyond the seas, which were to include a very fair proportion of the world's surface and about a quarter of the human race. Very nearly the whole history of Australian development, from the arbitrary pragmatism of penal administration, through the end of transportation, to the emergence of a new nation, the Commonwealth of Australia, took place within her long life. The convict colonies of New South Wales and Van Diemen's Land became self-governing states, joined by four more, two – Victoria and Queensland, named after the princess, and two others – South Australia and Western Australia, with unimaginative geographical titles. 'Occupied' notices had been served on all potentially acquisitive nations; but there was little to fear. Britain had taken possession of Australia simply because it was the only nation that could; nineteenth-century imperialism, like nature, abhorred a vacuum. Inside the protective shield of Victoria's Empire the Australasian colonies were able to develop their own characters and points of view. This chapter outlines the beginning of this process.

Even today the Australian states retain strongly individual characters.

Their great size – Western Australia is bigger than the whole of the Pacific United States, including Alaska, and even New South Wales is more extensive than Texas – make the comparison with American regions apter than that with American states. Tasmania, previously Van Diemen's Land, by contrast, is an exception; it is by some way the smallest, about the size of mainland Scotland, marked by a milder and more reliable climate, and has its own species of flora and fauna – although many of these, including the Tasmanians themselves as an unmixed race, have disappeared. The aspect of the state, with its elegant stone buildings and European trees, is strikingly like that of England, and the place names are resolutely British – Launceston, Devonport, Ulverston, Bridport, Lewisham and Richmond. The convict-built infrastructure remains visible – Tasmania is a conservative place – as schools, official buildings, roads and bridges, evidence (that of Richmond being a fine example), but an enterprising scheme to conduct water from the South West river to Launceston was abandoned in the 1820s over disputes about funding.[1]

In 1802 David Collins had been instructed to establish a straightforward penal colony, with 300 male convicts and only 14 free settlers. New South Wales was too pressing in its demands for labour and few prisoners were subsequently sent; by 1808 their number had shrunk to fewer than 200. The balance was drastically changed in that year by the arrival of more than 500 colonists removed from Norfolk Island, where the settlement had fallen victim to the constant confusion in British official minds regarding their New South Wales responsibility. At first, as early as 1785, Norfolk Island had seemed a promising outpost of Empire. Only a fortnight after the First Fleet landed, Philip Gidley King's party was sent to relieve pressure on the Port Jackson supplies; after King returned for the first time in 1790 to give London an accurate account of the colony's troubles, the incompetent and irascible Major Ross had created an atmosphere of discontent and simmering mutiny on the island. King's return in November 1791 as Lieutenant Governor restored a better frame of mind (he had found 'discord and strife on every person's countenance'). As free settlers emerged – mainly ex-marines and emancipists – who could make a success of farming, within two years the island was able to export grain to Sydney.

In spite of constant difficulties with the New South Wales Corps who replaced the Marines, and who were supported by Acting Governor Grose in Sydney, King kept the balance between disciplining convicts and encouraging settlers until he left once more for London in October 1796. Thereafter the island reverted to military rule; Captain Robert Townson, in charge for three years, continued King's humane and efficient policies, but Major

Joseph Foveaux, from July 1800, ensured that the island became an effective place of secondary punishment rather than a productive settlement. 'The nature of this place', he explained to his London masters in September 1801, excusing the harshness of his administration (he had hanged two Irish mutineers without trial), 'is so widely different from any other part of the World. The Prisoners sent here are of the worst Character, and in general only those who have committed some fresh crime since their arrival in Port Jackson, in short most of them are a disgrace to human Nature.'[2]

By 1804 the British government had decided to abandon the Norfolk Island experiment, but procrastinated in effecting their decision. It was not until 1808 that the plan began to be implemented, by which time the island's population was near-equally balanced between convicts and free settlers. This factor, together with the inconvenient distance from the mainland and the real dangers involved in sea communications, finally convinced the authorities that there was little point in maintaining the settlement. New South Wales was now self-supporting in foodstuffs and other well-isolated penal colonies could be found; Coal Harbour, shortly to be renamed Newcastle, but then best known as the 'Hell of New South Wales', began its career as a prison settlement in 1801. Accordingly King, in his new capacity as Governor of New South Wales, was ordered to close the Norfolk Island colony and transfer the inhabitants, bond and free, to Collins's struggling colony of Van Diemen's Land. The convicts were offered no choice, but the free settlers, now numbering about a thousand, were reluctant to move, in spite of generous relocation offers. Eventually the deed was done, and 554 of the islanders arrived 'to plague' Collins in the twelve months after November 1807, and to establish the district of New Norfolk to commemorate their coming.

It was the beginning of the end for the native inhabitants of Van Diemen's Land, who might have survived the introduction of one or even two guarded and restricted penal colonies, but to whom extensive European settlement proved fatal. Tasmanians differed ethnically and culturally from Australian Aborigines and by the time of the white incursions their numbers were perilously diminished, perhaps fewer than 5,000 scattered in small groups over 26,000 square miles. Some outside influences had affected the northernmost Australian Aborigines, but the Tasmanians' isolation had been absolute for 12,000 years. Cut off from continental Australia when the seas rose, Tasmanian culture stagnated; the dog never came to Tasmania, neither did the later technology developed by the mainland inhabitants. Over the following innumerable generations – perhaps six hundred – the population declined further. Those living on the Bass Strait islands died out over 2,000 years ago, and it is possible that even without European intervention the remnants would have perished; they were not, however, to be given the chance of surviving. They had few of even the limited range of implements common among Australian Aborigines – no boomerangs or woomeras, no stone axes or barbed spears and no bone implements of any sort. It appears that at the time of the Great Flood Tasmanians possessed some of the Aboriginal tools, including bone tools, but that these too had been gradually lost. Habits also changed: the richest food source, exploited by the first European arrivals, was fish, together with seabirds and seals; but Tasmanians had given up eating scaly fish some 3,000 years previously, although they continued to gather molluscs and crustaceans.[3]

The first intimate contact with the outside world was that of Captain Marion-Dufresne's crew in 1772, when, after an attempt by the French to land was repelled, the body of a Tasmanian was recovered. In the interests of science, the corpse was thoroughly examined. Its head was well shaped with a flattish nose, thick lips and magnificent teeth, but the eyes were 'reddish and ill-tempered', which was in the circumstances hardly surprising. Thereafter, apart from the contacts with the Bass Strait sealers and the visits of the later French expeditions, there was little sustained intercourse with the Europeans until Collins's arrival. From the first, the new Lieutenant Governor announced to the white population, convicts, settlers and troops, that 'the Aborigines of this Country are as much under the Protection of the Laws of Great Britain as themselves', and that they had been 'placed in the King's Peace' in order to afford 'their Persons and Property the Protection of the British Laws'. Gubernatorial decrees were one thing, but ensuring obedience to them was another. Collins's struggles to establish some sort of order in Van Diemen's Land were a repetition of those experienced seventeen years before at Port Jackson, with the added aggravation that he was permitted no direct contact with London, all instructions and requests being required to go through Sydney, where after the clash with Governor Bligh little attention could be spared for any of Collins's problems (although Collins, who never lacked initiative, did not hesitate to write direct to the Colonial Office). Until land could be cleared and crops grown, his provisions were grossly inadequate: 'the Governor himself, the officers, the entire settlement for eighteen months, were without bread, vegetables, tea, sugar, wine, spirits, or beer or any substitute except the precarious supply of the wild game of the country.' In such an emergency distinctions were, if not abandoned, then relaxed; convicts were given guns and sent to shoot kangaroo, extraordinarily plentiful in the hinterland, which inevitably led to clashes with the Tasmanians. It was easier, too, for convicts to abscond into the bush and since many of them would face the death sentence if recaptured, they were frequently desperate, living off the land and whatever they could steal from the stores or from the Aborigines.[4]

'Bushrangers' – 'the banditti of Van Diemen's Land' – outlaws who lived off the land by theft and violence, who later became an almost heroic icon of Australian myth – formed a real hazard to Van Diemen's Land settlers. The authorities could provide no effective defence, leaving it to the farmers themselves to fight off their attackers. As on the American frontier, free use of firearms led to many accidental deaths – William Abel shot his own son, and William Roadknight his neighbour's convict servant (he was sentenced to seven years for that, which would have been unlikely in the United States, then or now). When patrols were sent off, they sometimes managed to break up a small party, but absconding convicts and even discontented settlers made up the bushrangers' numbers.

Both settlers and bushrangers turned on the Aborigines, much to Collins's consternation, and the Governor followed Phillip's example in attempting to reverse the 'evil impressions' created. This was to some extent successful, since in spite of some attacks on settlers – often, it was admitted, justified – in 1818 the *Hobart Town Gazette* could ask:

Are not the Aborigines of this Colony the children of our Government? Are we not all happy but they? And are they not miserable? Can they raise themselves from this sad condition? Or do they not claim our assistance? And shall that assistance be denied? Those who fancy that 'God did not make of one blood all the natives upon the earth,' must be convinced that the Natives of whatever matter formed, *can* be civilised, any can be Christianized. The moral Governor of the world will hold us accountable. The Aborigines demand our protection.[5]

Inevitably, the Tasmanians responded with attacks on the settlers' huts, but for the first twenty years cohabitation seemed to be possible. Proof was given that thousands of years of isolation had not deprived Tasmanians of adaptability. With astonishing speed the Aborigines responded to the new challenges. Many, if not most, were soon able to communicate in English. In one Aborigine raid, that destroyed John Sherwin's house in 1830, the attackers demonstrated their command of the vernacular: 'Go away, you white buggers. What business have you here?' Some of the leaders were able to write tolerable English; dogs were trained to a degree that British observers found remarkable, considering that no dog had arrived on the island before 1800; the 'profound social and psychological adjustments necessary to setting up an affectionate relationship to a new animal' were made with 'extraordinary ability'. Guns were eagerly sought after, well maintained and expertly used (contemporary Africans were rarely able to acquire similar skills). New articles of diet were welcomed; a veritable passion for sugar, tea and tobacco developed.[6]

What caused relations to deteriorate, as they did markedly after 1824, puzzled the colonists. Between 1803 and 1824 only five Europeans had perished in Aboriginal attacks. Probably more Aboriginals were killed by bushrangers, and the only major clash between troops and an Aboriginal hunting party, which left some dead, was in the very early days, in May 1804. The change from comparative peace to near-continuous violence was probably the point when the European invasion – and the word is appropriate to Van Diemen's Land at least – reached a critical point. Richard Dry, a United Irishman transported in 1799, who became one of Tasmania's most prosperous farmers – his son, also Richard, became the first Tasmanian-born knight – writing in 1830, believed that the change was due to 'the rapid increase of Settlers who now occupy the best portions of the Land, extensive plains and fine tracts, where formerly Emu and Kangaroo fed in such numbers, that procuring subsistence was pastime to a Black Native . . . From this land they are excluded and daily witness our encroachment in the extensive Fences erected by the Settlers.' Certainly by that time all the best of the accessible land, stretching from Launceston to Hobart, had been allotted to the colonists.[7]

Subject to the authorities at Sydney, some two weeks' sailing away, and to London, another six months', Tasmanian Lieutenant Governors had a hard time of it. Collins had to cope with sharing responsibility with Colonel Paterson, Macarthur's old duelling opponent, as Commandant in the north, County Cornwall. In spite of easier access from Sydney, Cornwall was not successful, having attracted only sixteen settlers by 1810; two years later the division was abolished and Hobarton, now often also known as Hobart, became the seat of government. Collins's successor, after a three-year interval, was the Royal Marine Colonel Thomas 'Mad Tom' Davey (1813–16), so distrusted as 'so dissipated in his Manners and Morals, so very thoughtless and volatile, and so very easily imposed on by designing plausible Characters' and given in drink to 'an extraordinary degree of frivolity and low buffoonery' that Governor Macquarie insisted that he be 'tied down with rules'. William Sorrell (1816–24), an able and energetic officer, was able to sort out the confused administration and to deal with the problem of escaped convicts who had turned 'bushranger', the term first making its appearance in January 1817. It was Sorrell who terminated the career of Michael Howe, a Yorkshire highwayman, 'Lieutenant Governor of the Woods', who remained at large for five years, terrorizing settlements, and said to be in collusion with the colonial chaplain, the impecunious Cambridge graduate Robert Knopwood. The most interesting of bushrangers, Howe kept a journal in which he recorded his dreams and botanical observations. Eventually killed by the initiative of Private William Pugh of the 48th and a convict, Howe was described as

of athletic make; he wore at the time of his death a Dress made of Kangaroo Skins, had an extraordinary long beard, and presented altogether a terrific appearance. His face, perhaps in some degree from his associating with it the recollection of his crimes, exhibited strong marks of a Murderer. During his long career of guilt, he was never known to perform one humane act.[8]

As an attempt to confine recidivists Sorrell began the construction of a secondary prison at Macquarie Harbour on the bleak west coast, where the near-impassable forested hills made a successful escape unlikely. The 'disorderly and irreclaimable convicts' who were to be accommodated must 'dread the very idea of being sent there'. Accused men sent for trial to Hobart had 'declared that they would rather suffer death than be sent back to Macquarie Harbour'. If so, the Lieutenant Governor dryly commented, 'It is the feeling I am most anxious to be kept alive'. The first Commandant, the Ulsterman John Cuthbertson, set the style, being described by one convict as 'the most inhuman Tyrant the world ever produced I think, since the reign of Nero'. James Backhouse, the Quaker writer, analysed the causes of 85 convict deaths at Macquarie Harbour between 1822 and 1833: 35 from natural causes, 35 from drowning or accidents, 12 murdered by their comrades, and 3 shot by guards at Macquarie Harbour. Certainly, several convicts later committed capital crimes in order to be sent to Hobart for trial and execution as the only method of escape.[9]

Sorrell's brisk methods invigorated the Tasmanian economy, importing New South Wales merino sheep to begin the wool industry (in a demonstration of the difficulty of communications between Sydney and Hobart, 119 of the 300 valuable animals died on the voyage). By 1821 Van Diemen's Land, with a population of some 5,500, comprising 2,588 convicts, 2,168 emancipists and only 712 free settlers, was exporting wheat and salt meat to Sydney. In the following year the Leith-based 'Australian Company' began large-scale development in the north, and this led to the immigration of hundreds of ambitious Scots, among them a quite disproportionate number of newspaper men. The *Hobart Town Courier*, *Hobart Town Gazette*, the *Tasmanian*, *Colonial Times*, the *Trumpeter* and the grandly named *Tasmanian & Australian Asiatic Review* all had tiny circulations but provoked lively dissent and discussion.[10]

John Bigge had recommended that the Van Diemen's Land government should be separated from that of New South Wales, and this began to be done during Sorrell's term of office, to be completed by his successor after Sorrell was recalled, in spite of the colonists' earnest support. Like Collins, Sorrell had a somewhat unconventional home life, living with another officer's wife, having left his own in London with six children. In the tolerant Regency style this was not regarded as unforgivable – Sorrell was undeniably competent and popular – and it was only after eight years that the errant Lieutenant Governor's period of office was, regretfully, terminated. No such immorality could be expected from Sorrell's successor, for both Colonel George Arthur and his wife Eliza were earnest and devout evangelicals. Arthur's protracted and methodical administration (1824–36) saw the foundation of Van Diemen's Land as a self-contained Crown Colony, with its own Supreme Court and appointed Executive and Legislative Councils. Although formally titled Lieutenant Governor, Arthur and his successors were to all intents and purposes independent from Sydney, and indeed, Arthur's personal reputation and force of character gave him more influence in Whitehall than any of his contemporaries.

Unlike his predecessors, Arthur had moved from the army, in which he had seen only limited active service, to the new Colonial Civil Service, and served in the British Honduras, a challenging post. Arthur was a serious penologist – indeed, he was tediously serious on most subjects – and saw his prime responsibility as ensuring that Tasmania became, as the British government wished it to be, an efficient gaol. His colony was receiving the rejects of a prison system, and had to be strictly controlled and reformed. 'Evil-disposed' convicts must be separated from those who were well behaved, maintaining 'a continual circulation of convicts, a distribution of each in his proper place; in short a natural and unceasing process of classification'. Assignment and tickets of leave for the good, the chain gang and penitentiary for the troublesome, were always in prospect. Arthur's diagnosis of the causes of crime would hold good in the twenty-first century:

If we ask from what class do thieves chiefly spring? We are answered from among the poor and ignorant, from those who have been the victims of an unwilling and unavoidable ignorance of the force of moral obligations, from the circumstances in which they have been placed in infancy . . . If the rich and educated not so often expose themselves to penal inflictions, we are not to attribute the exemption to any inherent mental superiority. There is in truth no such natural inequality.

Measuring the effects of Arthur's strict attention to his reform-based activities is not easy. The influx of convicts after 1815 was inevitably accompanied by an increase in the number of secondary offences committed by convicts. Not that the increase was proportionate to the increased convicted population; the distinguished Australian historian A. G. L. Shaw calculated that some 36 per cent of the first post-war Van Diemen's Land convicts re-offended; between 1821 and 1824 the proportion fell to 31 per cent and thereafter regularly declined until 1832–3, when only 14 per cent were reconvicted, even though these were twice as likely to have been found guilty of other crimes before their sentence of transportation – figures which indicate the success of Arthur's reform policy. These figures relate to 'major' crimes, which would have carried a prison sentence in Britain; it was, however, a different story so far as minor crimes were concerned. Nearly three-quarters of the Van Diemen's Land convicts were arraigned every year, mainly for infraction of prison discipline. Emancipists, who might have been presumed to have learnt their lesson, were notably better behaved; between 1831 and 1837 about one-fifth of time-served convicts were convicted of serious crimes, a figure which approximates to 3 per cent annually, contrasted with the 14 per cent rate of those still under sentence.[11]

Control was effected by sentencing malefactors to work in chain gangs, and to work hard, even if their labour was useless. Macquarie Harbour would be replaced by a new high security penal settlement isolated on the Tasman peninsula, Port Arthur, while encouragement to the better-behaved convicts was given by careful awards of tickets of leave, conferring provisional liberty. In the first five years after Port Arthur was established in 1830, 1,711 Tasmanian convicts were sent there for secondary (in fact, often tertiary) punishment; only one in ten re-offended sufficiently seriously to justify a second spell, a low rate of recidivism by any standard. By the time Arthur left the colony he was able to reflect with some satisfaction that 5,000 of the convicts transported to Tasmania had settled into the community as model citizens.[12]

Governor Arthur enjoyed some substantial advantages over his colleagues in Sydney. Geographically restricted as they were, his subjects could not perpetually be extending their boundaries to bring fresh troubles on his head. In a modest farming community a Governor was not expected to keep up the style of the rising New South Wales metropolis. Nor was society divided between exclusives and emancipists to the same extent as in New South Wales, where Governor Bourke's liberalism, and his support of the Catholic barrister Roger Therry, was to bring down on him the wrath of the exclusives, precipitating his resignation in January 1837. Few Van Demonians possessed an ancestry that would bear too thorough an investigation; a semblance of respectability was enough to gain admittance to polite society. Arthur was, however, similarly saddled with officials who had been appointed from London, more due to the influence of their friends and relatives than their own talents. 'The Colonial Treasurer', Arthur ironized,

ought in my opinion to be as seldom as possible taken from his office: and the Police Magistrate never, if it can be avoided. Again, the two latter gentlemen never speak to each other, nor have they done so for the last three years. The Executive Council is consequently not the most comfortable assembly and as all feel it an intolerable burden to meet, I have convened them as seldom as a sense of duty would allow.

In the Legislative Council, established as was that of New South Wales in 1828, the Lieutenant Governor was obliged to assent to any measure supported by all the unofficial members, who were in a majority of eight to six, but he was able carefully to select decent and reliable citizens who would support his administration of what was still principally a penal settlement and who did not insist on regular or meaningful debate. When Mathew Forster, a blunt Berwick soldier, was appointed as police magistrate, and John Montagu, a Waterloo veteran who had married Arthur's niece, took over from the ill and incompetent John Burnett as colonial secretary, the administration was much improved.[13]

The radical feminist Mary Leman Grimstone, who spent three years in Van Diemen's Land between 1826 and 1829, left a dry portrait of Hobart Town, 'alias Humdrum Stadt':

In the first place you could hardly imagine that a country like England could produce such an illiterate cub as this Colony . . . mercantile classes are animated by an avaricious (or I should rather say *voracious*) spirit of money-getting, which engenders jealousy and ill-will when there is the least collision of interest or chance of rivalry . . . but if Settlers expect beyond that, unless to eat, drink, sleep, and mope, any thing requisite to render their lives endurable, let them not attempt it. I don't think a superannuated Dutchman, 'although furnished with *tobacco gratis*' would stay here if he could help it.[14]

Slowly, however, something not unlike an English provincial society was developing. A defining moment in the evolution of Van Diemen's Land into Tasmania was the June morning in 1826 when young Charles Arthur, the Governor's nephew and aide-de-camp, married Mary Allen Reibey, daughter, it is true, of the respectable Thomas Reibey, merchant of Launceston, but a daughter also of the remarkable Mary Haydock, transported for horse-stealing in 1790 while dressed as a boy, who, left a widow with seven children, became a prosperous farmer, hotel-keeper and ship-owner – and Charles went on to play in the first inter-colonial cricket match against Victoria in 1851.[15]

The Black War

Governor Arthur was least successful in dealing with Aboriginal resistance.[16] The new spurt of defiance which began in 1824 was to continue for seven years, in what might be called the only war ever to have been fought on Australian territory. His sympathies were with the Aborigines: 'all aggression originated with the white inhabitants; and . . . therefore much ought to be endured in return', and he began by reiterating Collins's declaration of the 'King's Peace' on 23 June 1824. Since 'several settlers and others are in the habit of maliciously and wantonly firing at, injuring and destroying the defenceless Natives', the Governor 'commanded . . . and strictly enjoined that the Natives of the Colony, shall be considered under British Government and protection.' Aggressions must cease, and Aborigines be treated 'on all occasions with the utmost kindness and compassion'. It may have been that the Governor's intentions were understood by some Aborigines, who later proved that they fully understood the concept of treaties, for in November a party of sixty-four arrived in Hobart, to be met by the Governor in person, accommodated in the Market House, and given food and clothing; but they departed without explanation.[17]

For some time bushrangers rather than Aborigines continued to constitute the most urgent problem – 103 men were hanged as bushrangers in the two years 1826–7. In the years before 1824–6 Aboriginal attacks averaged 18 a year; by 1828 they had reached 144, and by 1830, 222. Forced from their lands by the inexorable advance of settlement, robbed of their sustenance, the remaining Tasmanians were driven to raiding settlements as the only means of keeping alive. After 1826, captured Aborigines were treated as prisoners of war rather than criminal offenders. The contrast was underlined by the treatment on the one hand of Matthew Brady's bushranger gang in April 1826, marched to gaol in chains before their trial and execution, and, on the other, the surrender five years later of 26 Aboriginal survivors of the Big River tribe, who had killed far more Europeans than the bushrangers, but who walked free, carrying their spears, not to prison but to Government House, where 'kind looks and smiles fell gently on the war-tossed ones. Presents came before the Governor's feast; lollies or sweetmeats, toys, pictures, dresses were showered upon them.' The sixteen men, nine women and one child had fought on successfully for seven years.[18]

During these seven years of war, 170 settlers and troops were killed, with some 200 wounded; the Aboriginal casualties are undefined, but are estimated by Henry Reynolds as being not dissimilar to those of the Europeans. With the Tasmanians' ancient bushcraft allied to their mastery of more modern weapons, British army detachments were useless. In near-desperation Arthur adopted the principle of a big game drive, the 'Black Line'. For six weeks in 1830, nearly 3,000 men, including 550 soldiers, moved across the island in a south-easterly direction towards the Tasman Peninsula with the object of flushing out the hostile tribes and driving them into a corner. For six weeks the well-equipped cordon advanced, at a cost of £30,000, an enormous sum in the small colonial budget. It was totally unsuccessful, this attempt to carry water in a basket; the final 'bag' was one man and a small boy, and while the Black Line was moving ponderously across country the attacks continued; another four settlers were killed.[19]

It makes for easy indignation to denounce the Tasmanian 'genocide' as yet another example of the evils of British imperialism, but the fate of this free people is more an instance how the best-intentioned of interferences can have disastrous effects. Arthur, as a devout Christian, expressed his regret at 'being reduced to the necessity of driving *a simple but warlike* and AS IT NOW APPEARS noble-minded race, from their native hunting grounds'. It could, he believed, have been avoided, for

It was a fatal error in the first settlement of Van Diemen's Land that a treaty was not entered into with the Natives, of which Savages well comprehend the nature, – had they received some compensation for the territory they surrendered, no matter how trifling, and had adequate laws been from the very first introduced and enforced for their protection, His Majesty's Government would have acquired a valuable possession without the injurious consequences which have followed our occupation and which must ever remain a stain upon the Colonization of Van Diemen's Land.[20]

The Black Line had to be the last attempt to subdue the Tasmanians by physical force, for the British government had changed the policy as more liberal politicians came to power. The Colonial Secretary, Sir George Murray, wrote firmly instructing that 'any person who may have been instrumental to the death of a Native' must be brought to a trial, which might have 'serious consequences' for the accused. The war had to be settled by negotiation, and a potential arbitrator was at hand. This was the religious jobbing-builder George Augustus Robinson, who came to Van Diemen's Land in 1824, at the start of the Black War. When Arthur advertised, with the war at its height, for 'a steady person of good character . . . who will take an interest in affecting an intercourse with this unfortunate race', Robinson immediately applied and was just as quickly given charge of those Tasmanians living on Bruny Island, at the mouth of the Derwent River. Of these the best-known is Truganini (Trugernanna, or Trucanini). Robinson quickly gained the confidence, both of his charges and of Governor Arthur. With official backing, and accompanied by his Aboriginal wards, Robinson spent much of the five years between 1830 and 1835 quartering Van Diemen's Land, meeting, on a friendly basis, with all the black communities, convincing them to cease fighting and to accept the protection of the government.[21]

For this long period of hardship and often danger, Robinson and his Aboriginal friends have been sternly criticized by many recent writers. Robert Hughes stigmatizes Truganini as 'the arch-traitor to her race', who was 'busy becoming a sealers' moll, sterile from gonorrhoea, hanging around the camps and selling herself for a handful of tea and sugar'.[22] In truth, Truganini and the Big River Aborigines, brought in by Robinson and entertained to tea at Government House, were making a prudent choice. Further resistance, Robinson argued, was useless, and it was time to compromise. Truganini herself made the reasons for her decision clear: 'I knew it was no use my people trying to kill all the white people now, there were so many of them always coming in big boats . . . I hoped we would save all my people that were left.'[23] Robinson obtained permission, and the necessary substantial funds, to house his Aboriginal followers in the Bass Strait islands, where the climate was kinder and where they could be safe from interference. The settlement at Wybalenna (Black Men's Houses) on Flinders Island was begun in February 1833, and decently equipped, the cottages 'extremely well-built, with lime wash over brick and limestone, and carefully made and laid bricks', and boasting brass door handles, together with 'every article of domestic use far more numerous than usually fall to the lot of the English cottager'. The Tasmanians were not subject to rules, or confined to the settlement. Men could take up their weapons to go hunting in the bush, but in spite of liberty, adequate rations, abundant leisure – all the work was done by convicts – and medical care, Wybalenna became a death camp. The major cause was respiratory disease, especially pneumonia, but including tuberculosis and influenza; 132 died between 1834 and 1847, a period during which there were few births.[24]

The survivors continued to show the courage that had distinguished their previous life as warriors. Although they were sufficiently provided for, two articles of their agreement with the authorities had not been kept. Robinson, in whom an absolute trust was reposed, had promised to stay with them on Flinders Island; lured away by a higher salary and greater responsibility, he left to become Protector of Aborigines in Port Phillip. Another promise, that they would be allowed to return 'to visit their native districts', was also left unfulfilled. Robinson had a bad conscience about his failure to ensure that the promises 'made to them on which they surrendered their liberties' had been 'so faithlessly kept'.

The outcome is well known. By 1867 Truganini, thought to be the last of the Tasmanian Aborigines, was dead. (In fact she was outlived by Suke, who died in South Australia in 1888.) Not so well known is the petition addressed to the Colonial Secretary, Lord Grey in 1847, by the remaining Aborigines on Flinders Island, protesting against the failure of Tasmanian governments to keep the promises made to the Queen's 'free children' who

were not taken prisoners but freely gave up our country to Colonel Arthur then the governor after defending ourselves.

Your petitioners humbly state to your Majesty that Mr. Robinson made for us and with Colonel Arthur an agreement which we have not lost from our minds since and we have made our part of it good.

Your petitioners humbly tell Your Majesty that when we left our own place we were plenty of people, we are now but a little one.[25]

Although the petition was written by the teacher and catechist, Robert Clark, at the request of 'the free Aborigines inhabitants of Van Diemen's Land' the gravamen of the petition was a protest against the proposed return of an unpopular superintendent, Dr Jeanneret. Its first signatory was Walter George Arthur, chief of the Ben Lomond Tribe, then about 28 years old, who had less than three years' schooling but had learnt to read and write as well as the common run of colonists. He, and his wife Mary Anne, had both accompanied Robinson to Port Phillip, and on their return to Wybalenna four years later became activists pressing for what they understood as their agreed rights. Their petition was described by the superintendent, Dr Joseph Milligan, as 'almost the first evidence of their appreciation of the nature and value of civilized institutions and Government', and was successful. Lord Grey authorized the dismissal of Dr Jeanneret and agreed that the Tasmanians should be returned to their own lands.[26] Walter Arthur's spirited stand for his rights did not end with the dispersal of the settlement in 1847. As free farmer, in Oyster Cove, Arthur and his family lived in a house which had 'many tokens of civilization and gentility wanting in most of the country cottages of England . . . A few prints adorned the walls, and books lay on a side-table . . . the daily newspaper was there . . . the table was laid with quite a tempting appearance'; and like any English yeoman, Walter continued to defy the authorities when he believed that they were wrong.[27]

A similar account of an island family was given by Captain McTaggart, wrecked off King Island in 1843. 'Old Scott', a British sailor who had lived reasonably comfortably on the island with two Aboriginal women for fifteen years, was drowned helping the crew, leaving three children and their mother:

he had rather a comfortable house, with about 4 acres of land cleared away, where he grew vegetables and potatoes; but the land was not good, and the potatoes seldom grew larger than walnuts; their chief dependence was on ten splendid kangaroo dogs, which would always bring in – whenever wanted – an unlimited supply of kangaroo and wallaby . . . the old man must have taken great pains with his children, for the boy and eldest girl could read and write very well; they had the morning and evening service of the English pray book by heart; and invariably said grace with their meals. They are really fine children, and it was most pleasing to see them.

The mother, when I was coming off the island, begged me to try and do something for the children; knowing full well that, as the old man was dead, the children would forget all they had learned, and get as wild as the wallaby they hunted.[28]

Like other authoritarian governors, Arthur was distrustful of anything like a free press, invariably critical of authority (journals which do not promote indignation are, after all, rarely successful and an industrious attention to the truth has rarely been a journalistic habit). Andrew Bent, an unsuccessful burglar, transported in 1812, founded the *Hobart Town Gazette* and *Southern Reporter* in May 1816 – an enterprising convict could at the age of 26 succeed quickly enough. Within months of Arthur's arrival Bent found himself imprisoned for libelling the Governor; three years later the 'Tasmanian Franklin' was in prison again. Bent's mantle fell on Henry Melville, a free settler, dramatist, editor, occultist, pamphleteer and historian, whose book *History of the Island of Van Diemen's Land*, published in London in 1836, was a sustained attack on Governor Arthur. As had Darling in New South Wales, the Governor attempted to restrain the press by a Licensing Act, but he was out of touch with changing opinions in London as reformers, Whig and Tory, were coming to power. His Act was disallowed, and colonists were free to press for such British rights as trial by jury and responsible government, rights for which Arthur, quite rightly, considered that Tasmanian colonists were not yet ready.

The passions aroused among some colonists were illustrated by a flysheet published by the venomous William Goodwin's *Cornwall Chronicle* when Arthur's final recall was announced, demanding a 'General Thanksgiving':

For the deliverance from the iron-hand of Governor Arthur. We have now a prospect of breathing. The accursed gang of bloodsuckers will be destroyed. Boys will be seen no more upon Police Benches, to insult Respectable Men. Perjury will cease to be countenanced, and a gang of Felons will be no longer permitted to violate the LAWS OF CIVILISED SOCIETY.

By the time of Arthur's departure in October 1836, weeping bitterly and supported by the Chief Justice John Pedder ('a man of great talents and the purest integrity ... he is so tedious and so minute that life is much too short to wait for his opinions and decisions', according to the exasperated Governor), to receive acclaim and rewards from the Colonial Office, becoming a baronet, Privy Councillor and Lieutenant General, the administration of Tasmania had been greatly improved to an extent which ought to have meant a smooth ride for his successor. This was not how things turned out, as Sir John Franklin, the famous polar explorer, discovered when he became the next Governor. Europe being at peace, there was little advancement to be hoped for in the Royal Navy, although Sir John had taken part in the Greek War of Independence. In many ways, Franklin was both too senior and too inexperienced for the governorship of a colony moving towards self-government, reporting to a Colonial Office that demanded regular, frequent and comprehensive information, which Sir John did not give; 'inadequate ... unsatisfactory ... defective ... imperfectly reported' were among James Stephen's epithets. It might have been expected that a naval officer would be capable of keeping discipline, but the easy-going Franklin 'with the best disposition, does not appear to be possessed of sufficient firmness and self-reliance to control and govern the discordant elements by which he is surrounded'. On the other hand the new Governor had previous Australian experience, having sailed with Matthew Flinders in his great voyage of 1801–4.[29]

Thirty years later, the penal settlement of Van Diemen's Land was only slowly being transformed into the colony of Tasmania. A milestone was reached in July 1843, when Francis Nixon arrived as the first Bishop of Tasmania, making St David's church a cathedral and creating Hobart a city, but the island remained primarily a depository for British convicts. In 1836 when Governor Arthur left, nearly three-quarters of the population were convicts, ex-convicts, or had convict parents – and the 17,000 male convicts outnumbered the 14,000 male free settlers. When transportation to New South Wales ended in 1840 the stream of convicts, some 5,000 annually, was diverted to Van Diemen's Land, until by 1846 the island's convict population totalled 29,900, making it by far the biggest open prison in the world. Sir John Franklin, and his more remarkable wife Jane, were faced with the first results of this policy. They did their honourable best but Sir John was baffled by the furious internecine quarrels and conspiracies.

His staff, however, were unusually talented; Pedder remained as Chief Justice; John Montagu, the colonial secretary, was unequalled as an administrator, John Gregory, Colonial Treasurer, had been the commissioner John Bigge's assistant over a period of nine years, itself a powerful tribute; but both Gregory and Montagu were cold and difficult personalities, and had been closely attached to Arthur. Montagu, in particular, resented Franklin's inexperience, and contrived to spend many months in London, undermining the Governor's reputation with the Colonial Office. Personal animosity, fierce and protracted, characterized most nineteenth-century British colonies, and Tasmania was no exception. Northerners were jealous of southern hegemony – the first railway was constructed in the now more populous north, where the Leith Company was developing agriculture with Scottish efficiency, but the seat of government remained at Hobart; Methodists resented the superior attitude of Anglicans; free settlers looked down their noses at ex-convicts; and townspeople complained about the privileged landowners. Bishop Nixon quarrelled with his prison chaplains, with his archdeacon, Fitzherbert Marriott, with the Irish low churchman the Reverend Henry Fry as well as the Catholics and Methodists; the irascible Northumbrian, Thomas Gregson, later Premier, horsewhipped Governor Arthur's nephew and shot another political opponent, Henry Jellicoe. The beautiful Julia Sorrell, the previous governor's grand-daughter, had many admirers, but eventually married Thomas Arnold, son of Dr Arnold of Rugby, and became, in the fullness of time, Julian and Aldous Huxley's grandmother. In this small colonial society Jane Franklin effervesced. She wanted to see and understand everything. Her diaries read like those of her contemporary, Emily Eden; one account of a visit to Port Arthur gives a flavour of Jane's activities:

The Commandant, Charles O'Hara Booth, was 'not a little surprised to find ladies and all dive first thing into the Mines – descended and ascended the Shaft with her Ladyship – after minutely examining everything in the mines and afterwards the Jetty'. Lady Franklin was probably the only woman in the island, or in all Australia, who would minutely examine a jetty.

The next day they all examined Eagle Hawk Neck, then went to Port Arthur. Good Friday was kept holy: Saturday was very wet, but Lady Franklin went all through the workshops and dockyard. On Easter Sunday she missed church and visited the semaphore station. By Wednesday she had seen everything, met the ladies, tasted the prisoners' soup, tried on handcuffs, seen men at work, found out how to make 'steamer' out of pork and kangaroo, inspected a canoe made by convicts of hollowed gum tree, and a 'curious raft', and counterfeit dollars also produced by convicts. She visited the boys' establishment at Point Puer, and was impressed when one boy asked her for a Bible; but Captain Booth said the boy was a hypocrite.[30]

Lady Franklin interested herself particularly in the Female Factories, those curious products of nineteenth-century social practices. Newly landed convicts could be assigned to domestic service or boarded – not, as some indignant modern writers have it, 'incarcerated' – in what might today be called 'secure accommodation'. The Factories also served as maternity wards and nurseries, and also, as Lady Franklin explained to Elizabeth Fry, as places of detention.

You will ask what is the nature of this punishment with which she is now to be visited, and may perhaps suppose that on re-entering the prison where, in compassion to her situation she was before treated with tenderness, instead of severity some signal mark of the reprobation in which her offence is held, will be inflicted on her. You might conclude perhaps that she is subjected to that most harmless yet most efficacious of female punishment, the being deprived of the ornament of her hair, as practised I am told in the Milbank Penitentiary. Oh! No!
  At least then it will be concluded that these abandoned inmates of the Factory, go into solitary cells, or are put to hard labour. But this would be a mistaken supposition. They are put into that class or yard in the Factory which has the best ration, are in no way separated from the rest, have no harder labour than the picking of a little oakum and sleep in the same common room with the other women of their division. The only shadow of punishment they receive is the detention in the factory itself which is of 6 months duration.[31]

Compared with Holloway Prison in the twenty-first century, the Van Diemen's Land Female Factories sound positively humane.

'Persons of violent and uncontrollable passions'

Elizabeth Fry undertook to help Lady Franklin improve conditions in the Female Factories, but the greatest effect of Franklin's rule was procured unintentionally, by the Governor's secretary, Captain Alexander

Maconochie RN. Like Franklin, Maconochie was a distinguished geographer, although more of the armchair variety, the first Secretary of the Royal Geographical Society and the first professor of that subject in the new University of London. Coming as he did to Van Diemen's Land armed with commissions from the Society for the Diffusion of Useful Knowledge, the Religious Tract Society, the Religious Reform Society and the Society for the Improvement of Prison Discipline, Maconochie appeared an exemplar of the earnest reformer, the provider of detailed information to the Blue Books; and so it was to prove, as the Captain began to draft detailed reports on conditions in Van Diemen's Land.

The great clearing out of the English law and penology, to which Maconochie hoped to contribute, began with the appointment of Robert Peel as Home Secretary in 1822. Two hundred and fifty ancient statutes were repealed, and by 1830, when the reforming Whig government took over, only four crimes were punishable by execution; eleven years previously there had been some 180. Theoretically, high treason, piracy, murder and arson in a naval dockyard were capital offences, but after 1838 only murderers were executed (although in the twentieth century execution for treason was revived). In 1831, 1,601 death sentences were passed, but only 52 executions took place; by 1838, 116 death sentences were passed with only 6 executions, 5 of which were for murder. All executions were by hanging, and although the additional sentence of drawing and quartering was kept to delight conservative lawyers until 1870, it was never imposed, nor was it regarded as much more than an additional slap over the wrists. (Scotland was, as ever, different: until 1887 rape, robbery, arson and incest remained capital offences.)[32]

These decisive changes in the legal code were accompanied by a reorganization of the prison system, then gaining impetus under the leadership of Captain Joshua Jebb, a Royal Engineer, appointed in 1837 as Surveyor General of Prisons. American experience of solitary confinement in individual cells had impressed public opinion, and in 1839 an energetic building programme was authorized. Within a few years of the start, in 1840, of Pentonville, the first modern penitentiary, no fewer than fifty-four new prisons were constructed (of which a regrettable number still remain in service). Given that the initial sentences to be served in the new prisons were intended to be short – eighteen months was the original period, later shortened to nine months, to be followed by what might be called 'community service' on official building-sites – more than sufficient modern accommodation would be coming on stream.

It was also true that British parliamentarians and officials were becoming more closely informed of conditions in the Australian colonies, and began to appreciate that a convict colony was no longer a practicable proposition. Reflecting Whig opinions, Governor Bourke was personally sympathetic to the New South Wales liberals' claims for a greater say in their own affairs, and prepared a draft Bill which provided for a Legislative Assembly of 36 members, 12 nominated and the remainder elected, half by urban and half by country constituencies, with emancipists able to vote, but not to sit in the Assembly. Both Bourke's proposals, and those of the Australian Patriotic Association, established by Wentworth and his supporters in May 1835, were lost at sea, and copies reached London only in July 1836. In the meantime James Stephen had prepared his own not-dissimilar Bill, which was not well received by Howick, now in the Cabinet in his own right as Secretary at War from 1835. Whereas Stephen recommended a single 'blended' Legislative Council with an elected majority, Howick believed an elected assembly would fall into the hands of 'Adventurers or Attorneys and Lawyers of the Capital' (a not unreasonable fear, as things turned out), and proposed instead a system of local authorities which might later act as an electoral college to vote for Council members.

For the next few years constitution-making for New South Wales became a persistent political issue in Britain, as Howick, Glenelg and Sir George Grey (Howick's cousin, who had succeeded him as parliamentary under-secretary in 1835), assisted by James Macarthur for the exclusives, and Chief Justice Forbes and the radical MP Henry Lytton Bulwer for the Australian liberals, argued things out.[33] The most influential voice was that of Lord John Russell, a younger son of the Whig magnate the Duke of Bedford, who held astonishingly liberal views of colonists' rights and privileges. Howick, although with very little support, continued to argue for revising his local government scheme which would give the councils only the right to criticize legislation proposed by officials. The discussion continued without effect until overshadowed by another question, whether or not transportation should be continued.[34]

The common feeling that transportees 'have too easy a time' in Australia, expressed by Stephen in 1828, led to unwise interference with the ticket-of-leave system, and to an even more drastic policy of establishing different degrees of severity, with the widespread use of chain gangs in public works. Both Arthur, the most experienced of Australian administrators, and the newcomer, Bourke, protested. Arthur complained of attempts to dictate details of administration by persons 'who know nothing of the mental degradation or summary laws' to which the convicts were already subjected. 'The pernicious effect', he insisted, of 'long punishment without prospect of relief would render men even more desperate'; and he reassured critics that 'the great mass of the convicts in this colony is already as truly miserable as can be desired'. For New South Wales, Bourke, although not objecting to chaining as an extra punishment, warned against the dire effects of shutting out 'hope, and with hope excluding reform'.[35]

Fortunately the new policy was found to be not only ill-judged, but illegal. As the number of convicts grew inexorably, the practice of assignment grew. At the start of Bourke's term, in 1832, the total convict population in New South Wales was 21,635; by 1836 this had swelled to 31,486 of which 20,934 were assigned, compared with 13,486 in 1832; the proportion of those undergoing punishment had dropped slightly. The problem was passed to one of those useful committees, chaired this time by Sir William Molesworth, who had made a name for himself as Wakefield's most prominent supporter. The committee, appointed in 1837 was powerful, including as it did Lord John Russell, Home Secretary in Lord Melbourne's government, Lord Howick, Charles Buller and Sir Robert Peel, and its conclusions were unanimous. Into their deliberations were injected Captain Maconochie's reports, detailed and voluminous, forwarded by Sir John Franklin in February 1838, and published as official documents; these revelations influenced the committee profoundly. Once in Van Diemen's Land, Maconochie had been shocked – and as both a fighting sailor and a former prisoner of war he was presumably not easily shockable – by penal conditions. The secondary punishments were, he claimed

severe, even to excessive cruelty. Besides corporal punishment, to the extent of fifty to seventy-five lashes, and even, in some rare instances, a hundred lashes, solitary confinement, and months, or even years, of hard labour in chains (on the roads, or at a penal settlement), are lightly ordered, for crimes in themselves of no deep dye: petty thefts (chiefly in order to obtain liquor), drunkenness, indolence, disobedience, desertion, quarrelling among themselves, and so forth.

And the chain gang, Sir George Arthur had observed, was 'as severe as can be inflicted on man'.

Maconochie argued for a radical change in the system, convicts no longer being allocated to free settlers as servants but rather employed directly by government under proper supervision, as in the Pentonville scheme. He pertinently observed:

The fretfullness of temper which so peculiarly characterises the intercourse of society in our penal colonies, may be attributed I think, almost exclusively to their convict system. Degraded servants make suspicious masters; and the habit of suspicion being once given, masters soon begin to suspect their equals, and superiors, as well as their inferiors; whence, among other symptoms, impatience and irritability under Government regulations and judicial decisions, however, just or well founded.

However justified Maconochie's criticisms, both in their accuracy and as reports meant for the societies who had requested them, their publication in parliamentary papers was a grave breach of etiquette, and aroused indignation among Van Demonians, settlers and officials alike, who heaped complaints upon the innocent Franklin.[36]

Even without Maconochie's papers, the committee's conclusions were, given the well-known views of its members, inevitable. They were reinforced by the influential Richard Whately, Professor of Political Economy in Oxford and Archbishop of Dublin, who had been inveighing against the system since 1829, and whose evidence commanded great respect. The accounts the committee received of Sydney were as horrifying as those of Maconochie. Observing that, of a population of some 20,000, half were convicts or emancipists,

persons of violent and uncontrollable passions, which most of them possessed no lawful means of gratifying; incorrigibly bad characters, preferring a life of idleness and debauchery by means of plunder, to one of honest industry. Burglaries and robberies were frequently perpetrated by convict servants in the town and its vicinity, sometimes even in the middle of the day.

This account was based on the testimony of Judge William Burton, who later protested that the horrors of Sydney were not, usually, repeated in other regions of the colony; needless to say, none of the members of the committee had ever been to Australia. In some ways their views on sentencing were less severe than those of many politicians today.

With regard to the duration of punishment in penitentiaries, your Committee are of opinion that no offender of any description should be sent to penitentiaries for life, as such a punishment destroys all hope, and renders the culprit reckless; they recommend that the severest sentence should not exceed fifteen years; on the other hand, as a substitute for the lowest sentence of transportation, that for seven years, they would not venture to recommend a shorter period of punishment, in a penitentiary, than that of two years.

Transportation, the committee recommended, should be abolished as soon as practicable, replaced by prison sentences, and secondary punishments should be controlled following Maconochie's recommendations; a 'system of reward and punishment not founded merely upon the prospect of immediate pain or immediate gratification, but relying mainly on the effect to be produced by the hope of obtaining or the fear of losing future and distant advantages', should be investigated. Penal colonies were to be distanced from the free settlers, convicts who had served their sentences in the United Kingdom would be assisted to settle abroad, and finally, in what was from the beginning a quite unrealistic condition: 'That convicts who have been punished abroad should be compelled to leave the settlement in which they have been punished within a limited period after the expiration of their sentences, and that means should be afforded them by the Government for this purpose.'

Molesworth reported in 1838, and Parliament acted quickly. Assignment, which terminated the supply of cheap labour, ceased the following year and the end of transportation to New South Wales followed; in November 1840 what was intended to be the last shipload of convicts moored in Sydney Cove. Public opinion there was divided. General relief that theirs was no longer a convict colony was expressed, but employers, exclusives and emancipists alike, seeing themselves forced to pay their workers cash down for labour, were apprehensive; the free settlers, however, rapidly increasing in numbers, were equally keen to see the end of competition from unpaid convicts.

Batman's Colony

Interest in the south-east coast had subsided since George Bass in his open boat had landed at Westernport in 1798 and John Murray had named Port Phillip four years later. Thereafter only occasional parties of explorers, including the French expedition led by Nicolas Baudin, touched at Westernport, in addition to David Collins's short-lived attempt to begin a colony in 1802. Only in 1826 was any attention paid to the area, again as part of the general apprehension of French interference. The French Minister of the Navy and Colonies, Hyde de Neuville, had asked J. S. C. Dumont d'Urville to report of the suitability of New Zealand as a penal colony, as part of an extensive circumnavigation. Ignorant of this particular, but – with some reason – suspicious of d'Urville's motives during his visit to Sydney, Governor Darling prudently sent a small party – twenty convicts and a similar number of soldiers – who pottered about Westernport, attempting to establish some sort of settlement, before giving up. Darling had also been encouraged by reports of Hamilton Hume and William

Hovell's overland expedition to reach what they believed was Westernport but which proved to be the western shore of Port Phillip Bay, near Geelong. The subsequent uncertainty as to which was which contributed to a further period of neglect.[37]

What became the country's second most important state (a description with which many Victorians would not agree) was founded almost as a colony of Tasmania. The Sydney authorities, worried about the difficulties of administering the already extensive settled area of New South Wales, had prohibited expansion elsewhere, but were defied by the formidable Henty family. When they were denied an expected free grant of Tasmanian lands by the 1831 Act, the Hentys simply moved across the Bass Strait, bringing their sheep with them in November 1834 to Portland Bay. The following year John Batman took an even bolder initiative. Batman (his family name seems to have been spelt 'Bateman'), son of a convict, married to an absconding convict, 'sufficiently literate for any practical purpose' but keenly aware of the advantages of education, was a capable hunter of bushrangers and Tasmanian Aborigines. He was, however, also a leader in attempting to conciliate 'that much-injured and Most unfortunate race' and originator of the only formal treaty with Aborigines, thus embodying many of the complexities of the early settlers. As early as 1827 he had unsuccessfully applied, jointly with John Gellibrand, the Van Demonian Attorney General, for a land grant on the mainland. Seven years later, after Thomas Henty and his extensive family had begun to establish themselves at Portland Bay, Batman founded the Port Phillip Association with the intention of beginning an organized colony, and in May 1835 agreed a 'treaty' with the local Aborigines. This purported to entitle him to some 600,000 acres of land, lying more than 100 miles east of the Hentys' stations and including the Bellarine peninsula and the coastal strip up to the Yarra river – today's Geelong to Melbourne. Batman's agreement was immediately countermanded by the Governor, who insisted that all land belonged to the Crown and could only be disposed of by the government. But the Hentys and Batman were followed by a veritable Tasmanian invasion.[38]

The potential of the Port Phillip district was amplified after Surveyor General Thomas Mitchell's expedition in 1836. Charles Sturt's explorations of the river systems, made between 1828 and 1830, had failed to find the much discussed great inland lake but had penetrated down the main stream of Australia's great river, the Murray, to its mouth. Striking south from the Murray River, Mitchell found himself in a region that seemed so fertile and pleasant as to justify his name of 'Australia Felix' – the region of which Horsham is the centre, and where the spectacular Mount Arapiles commemorates Colonial Secretary Sir George Murray's service in the Peninsular War. Three years later the Scot, Angus McMillan, who had only arrived in the colony the preceding year, began his exploration of the extreme south-east of the continent, and by 1840 had established claims on the shores of Lake Wellington. This promising region was named 'Caledonia Australis' by the patriotic McMillan, but the equally patriotic Pole, Paul Edmund de Strzelecki, who followed some of McMillan's path, named the highest point in Australia after the Polish hero Tadeusz Kosciuszko: Mount Kosciusko. Between McMillan's property in the east and the western limit of settlement, some 400 miles of the coast, and inland for perhaps half that distance, were rapidly occupied. When the Tasmanian farmer John Robertson arrived with his flock of 1,000 ewes in 1840 he chose to settle on the Glenelg River, traced only four years previously by Thomas Mitchell, over 200 miles west of the new town of Melbourne. Letters for Melbourne were sent by sea from nearby Portland to Van Diemen's Land, thence again by sea to Melbourne, as the fastest route.

That settlement, which in 1836 had consisted of three weatherboard, two slab and eight turf huts, had developed into a small town of some 4,500 in which the Melbourne and Port Phillip Bank and the Melbourne Fire and Marine Insurance conducted business, where the Pastoral and Agricultural Society of Australia Felix encouraged farming, and where gentlemen relaxed in the Melbourne Club of 1838 and the Regatta Club founded two years later. Such social leaders as Mrs Patricius Walsh were able to give tea to the whole population – those acceptable members of society, naturally – in Northumberland Cottage. In 1840 hers was 'the ball of the season'.[39]

The New South Wales government was forced to accept a fait accompli. In 1839 the Port Phillip district was acknowledged as an official entity under the rule of Superintendent Charles Joseph La Trobe. His was a completely unexpected appointment; all previous governors had been naval or military officers, while La Trobe was a civilian, Swiss-educated, a writer of travel books and poetry, with no administrative experience, who had come to the attention of the Colonial Office through some reports he had been asked to prepare on West Indian slavery. But London had chosen well, for the Superintendent, later Lieutenant Governor, was patient, generous and firm, all qualities that helped to make him the unquestioned founding father of Victoria. Accompanied by an exiguous military force, La Trobe arrived in September 1839, with his wife and children and a prefabricated house (still standing in Kings Domain, Melbourne), to an enthusiastic welcome. His account of this to Governor Gipps gives a flavour of the man: 'the grave amongst them got up grave addresses and received grave answers – the gay made bonfires, put light in their casements and fired off fowling pieces: and the lower class got jovially drunk and were fined – all in my honor.'[40]

Such a considerable extension of colonial territory caused the home government concern – and justified concern – about the future of the native inhabitants, and La Trobe's attention was drawn by Lord Glenelg to 'the state of the aborigines and the relations between them and the settlers'. A Select Committee of the House of Commons had exhaustively enquired into the conditions of the Empire's native populations and had recommended the establishment of a Protectorate in Port Phillip, to be an independently funded body with its own staff. George Robinson, who had unparalleled experience of the problems, was the obvious choice to head the project, and was accordingly appointed by Gipps and La Trobe in January 1838. His remit was to provide reserves for Aborigines where support would be provided and encouragement given for them to become farmers on the European model. Robinson and his four assistant Protectors doubtless did their best, but there was no sign among the Aborigines of a willingness to settle, nor among the Protectors to follow the Aborigines on their wanderings. Once responsibility passed from London to the colonial governments the experiment petered out and by 1850 the system was reorganized. Henceforward, some of the Protector's functions would be transferred to Commissioners of Crown Lands, and the 15 per cent of land sales which had been earmarked for Aboriginal purposes was left to the judgement of colonial ministers, with predictable consequences.[41]

Given the chance, sheep are insistent wanderers, voraciously searching out new pastures (and after a few years, spoiling the land they have grazed). Anticipating a rapid increase in their flocks, new settlers laid claim to areas far in excess of their immediate needs. The farmer John Robertson described how 'Messrs Addison and Murray' who arrived on the same day 'ran about putting up frames of huts [to signify development of their claim] thinking to secure country by that means that would have kept 200,000 sheep (if they had got leave to keep it) with 700 sheep'. The local Aborigines were naturally alarmed and resentful of this invasion of their lands, which threatened their sources of food and the survival of their society. When settlers violently asserted what they saw as their rights (and almost invariably the first aggressions were those of the colonists), the Aborigines retaliated. Insults and injuries were answered by raids on homesteads and killings of shepherds. Such events, the common currency of frontier conflict, were exacerbated by the Aborigines' theft, not of the occasional sheep for food, but of whole flocks which were indiscriminately slaughtered.[42]

Such cruelty was guaranteed to infuriate any stockman, perhaps even more than personal violence, but was not seen as constituting grounds for an appeal to expensive and uncertain legal processes. The alternative of vengeful raids on the Aboriginal culprits – or those assumed to be so – was inevitable and sometimes devastating. The settlers took the law into their own hands; reasonable people, like the splendid Mrs Gibson, of Roseneath on the Glenelg River, could frighten off aggressors with a broken pistol, but when the neighbouring Whyte brothers had fifty sheep stolen in March 1840 they caught up with the raiders and killed at least twenty-six of them. Thirty-five more blacks were reported killed on the nearby Taylor Station. Both these massacres lacked any legal sanction. True, the Whytes reported the killings to the authorities, and were prepared to be sent to Sydney to answer an inquiry, but both they and the settler community were quite confident that no charges would ever be brought. They were of course, quite right.[43]

'Real black gentlemen'

It appears to have been Alexander Maconochie who in 1837 made the suggestion of recruiting an Aboriginal police force on the pattern of British experience in India, where Indian troops formed the permanent backbone of British forces.[44] Governor Bourke, to whom the suggestion was passed, had a different example in mind, based on his service in South Africa. This was the Cape Mounted Rifles, a corps of Khoikhoi (Hottentot) troopers with British officers who served in the bloody Frontier wars against the Xhosa. The 'Totties', given a horse, gun, uniform and rations, responded to a looser form of military discipline than that exercised on British troops, and constituted a formidable force, often allotted the most skilled and dangerous tasks.

Captain William Lonsdale, the police magistrate and administrative head, welcomed the idea, and was fortunate enough to have an experienced South African to hand. Christiaan de Villiers had served under the great African administrator, Sir Andries Stockenstrom, a personal friend of Governor Bourke, and had arrived in July 1836 looking for a post. Lonsdale appreciated that not only could an Aboriginal police force serve to supplement the existing fifty men of the border police, who were 'chiefly composed of nominally well-conducted convicts and others not of high character', but might offer Aborigines a place in the new settler society. The Port Phillip Native Police Corps was formed, under the command of de Villiers, with instructions that 'The men forming the Corps . . . should be led to believe that belonging to the police places them in a very superior situation . . . to consider themselves as a body distinct from all others.' In this respect the Corps was eventually to succeed, but after a turbulent beginning. De Villiers was a prickly character; he got on much better with the Aborigines than with Lonsdale, who expected more military obedience than was forthcoming from any Afrikaner, or with Lonsdale's nephew, the aggressive missionary George Langhome, with whom he was in constant conflict.

After two resignations, the last in 1839, the Aboriginal police faded away, but La Trobe was quick to see the potential benefits, and revived the Corps on a more formal basis. He had been encouraged in this by the success of seven Aborigines, some of whom had served under de Villiers, and all of whom were to join La Trobe's new corps, in tracking down the murderers of two whalers at Westernport. By a macabre coincidence the culprits were Tasmanian natives who had been brought to Port Phillip by the Chief Protector, George Robinson, who seems to have subsequently neglected them. Two men were hanged (the first executions to take place in Port Phillip), but three women were released; one of these was that great survivor, Truganini. Once again, there was a suitable candidate at hand to take command. Henry Dana, a well-connected young Englishman 'evidently a thorough gentleman', was appointed in January 1842, with the support of Robinson. To the Aborigines it was vital that they should be commanded by a 'thorough gentlemen' since they, like their contemporary South African blacks, had a very sensitive conception of social status (Sir Harry Smith, High Commissioner at the Cape, of middle-class background, was despised on that account by the Xhosa aristocrats).

Dana insisted that his men – never more than sixty – were well equipped with elegant uniforms, carbines, pistols and swords (very important, as a signifier of prestige) and mounted on fine big horses (17 hands was the standard). Allowance was made for Aboriginal social customs, ritual absences tolerated, and authority maintained with the assistance of clan chiefs (the senior, Billobolary, chose what duties he was prepared to perform, but kept the others up to the mark). While it lasted, the Port Phillip Native Police Corps was undeniably effective. The presence of the troopers, distributed in twos and threes around the district, discouraged attacks on settlers and the much more serious retaliations. 'Collisions' between troopers and 'wild blacks' were few. When the force was assembled for the annual parade, the policemen, splendidly uniformed on their magnificent horses, attracted widespread admiration, and gave onlooking Aborigines a warm new sense of their own worth. One such, the schoolboy Charles Never, saw them as 'real black gentlemen'. Their horsemanship was much admired, and, so was perhaps more remarkable, their horsemastership, since they kept their mounts in good condition on the longest of journeys.[45]

But such an enterprise was an Imperial creation, created, supported and administered by Imperial officers, and it could not survive under colonial governments. As early as 1847 the New South Wales Legislative Council rejected La Trobe's proposal to establish the Corps on a permanent basis: 'The Committee believes this Corps has hitherto been found very useful in checking the aggression of the blacks . . . but entertains great doubts about the propriety or necessity of constituting it on a permanent footing or as a Police to be employed against the white population.' That was the real objection: colonists could not stomach the idea of Aboriginals holding any sort of authority over the white population. When, after the discovery of gold, the responsibilities of patrolling the goldfields were shared by the Corps, and diggers were arrested, its future was abruptly curtailed.

La Trobe's limited powers – he was not, for example, allowed to make any appointments carrying a salary of more than £100 p.a. – were aggravated by the distance from Sydney, whence all decisions had to come. Bourke had been made conscious of this by his own visit to Port Phillip in 1837, and wrote to Lord Glenelg emphasizing this difficulty; the 550-mile journey would take at least ten days on horseback (the weekly postal riders actually reduced the time to seven days in 1839). The sea passage, in the teeth of the prevailing westerlies, was strenuous – La Trobe took thirteen days to make Port Phillip from Sydney in that year. Had a regular steam packet service existed (it came finally in 1843 and that via Launceston, a town that continued to be the most important economic link with the outside world), a direct voyage would need only four days. Sydney officials did not bother themselves overmuch about Port Phillip complaints; a four-oared gig was dispatched without oars; the essential flood-control system was underfunded, the main dam being a 'Barbarous Unsightly Discreditable Thing'; the new lighthouse was underpowered and soon had to be re-equipped. Matters improved somewhat after Bourke's successor as Governor, Sir George Gipps, visited the settlement in November 1841, but the pressure for economies unrelentingly applied from London was passed on from Sydney to Port Phillip.[46]

Progress towards securing some sort of self-government for the district was slow. From 1841 Port Phillip got its own resident judge; from 1844 this was the Irish Catholic Roger Therry, one of the two most able barristers in New South Wales, according to Gipps (the other was John Hubert Plunkett, also an Irish Catholic). This limited recognition of Port Phillip's independent existence was not much improved by the district's inclusion in the New

South Wales elected Legislative Council of 1843, when 6 of the 36 seats were allocated to Port Phillip and the town of Melbourne. The 'tyranny of distance' ensured that most, and often all, of these seats could only be held by Sydney residents. One of the first members to be elected was the energetic Dr John Dunmore Lang of Sydney, who took up the cause of the Port Phillipers, proposing in 1844 the separation of the district from New South Wales as an independent colony. It was perhaps not much of a potential colony; 26,000 Europeans, producing a revenue of some £60,000 p.a., but South Australia and Western Australia, separate entities from the first, were both even smaller.

Melbourne had become a real town, with a population of nearly 4,000. The theatre, performances in which had been suppressed 'owing to the disorders attending them', was revived, and under a new management 'engaged as respectable a company as could be secured in Australia'. Mr Murray, a Scottish visitor, also rather sniffily observed the attempts to create an exclusive society 'among a community of trade, where all are in fact buyers and sellers ... and therefore, to a great extent, on the same level'. Another Scot, William Westgarth, admired Mack's Hotel, 'completed on a scale of unwonted magnificence', and its clients: 'no spectacle of the kind is more exhilarating than that of the Australian traveller fully accoutered in his saddle with his black and well-used pipe, his spurs and massive whip, cantering leisurely over the grassy surface – a finished picture of ease, independence, and anxious enjoyment.'[47]

Colonial Secretary Lord Stanley was sympathetic to the idea of Port Phillip becoming a 'separate and independent colony' but required a comprehensive report from Governor Gipps before agreeing. Gipps had long advocated separation, recognizing 'a very general desire' for it, but pointed out the very real dangers of inter-colonial feuding. Lord Howick, now the 3rd Earl Grey, once more in office when Gipps's recommendations were received, believed that an inter-colonial conference would avoid the threatened peril of internecine dissension. Matters continued to move slowly. Gipps made his recommendations in April 1846; in July the following year Grey outlined his proposals for the new colony, to be named Victoria, and for amendments to the New South Wales constitution. These were not well received by the Legislative Council, who had no desire to relinquish control over so important a part of their territory and income, and little enthusiasm for the prospect of any inter-colonial body; when, half a century later, colonial federation was imminent, New South Wales held out until the last moment. No immediate action on separation was therefore taken. What was worse, the New South Wales majority on the Legislative Council continued to refuse to allocate Port Phillip a fair share of expenditure, and also made 'insulting attacks on the weaker', so that 'instead of spoliation alone, the district had to bear with spoliation and the most wanton abuse'. Surely, Port Phillip petitioners argued, 'the succession of injustices . . . heaped upon Port Phillip is quite unexampled in the history of British colonies'. Since no Port Phillip resident could reasonably function in Sydney, in the 1848 Legislative Council elections the exasperated settlers refused to return any local members, but elected Lord Grey himself as one of their representatives 'as one known to and held in respect by the people'.

'The whole of New Holland'

In what might be called the pre-Wakefield era, British governments needed to be galvanized, usually by the unwelcome expense of a war, into paying any attention to colonies, and Australia was usually at the bottom of any colonial priorities. It was the perpetually worrisome French who forced the birth of Western Australia. Louis-Claude de Saulses de Freycinet had already raised suspicions in the course of his expedition with Baudin, in which de Freycinet had decided to name the whole southern coastline 'Terre Napoléon'. This indiscretion had been glossed over, but when de Freycinet appeared again, between 1817 and 1820, his brother Louis-Henri was becoming a rising star in the French colonial services, and British apprehensions were aroused. These increased in 1826 when the explorer Dumont d'Urville sailed bound for Australasian waters, causing an agitated Lord Bathurst to write three letters to Governor Darling on the same day (1 March 1826), followed by another ten days later, instructing him to annex that third of Australia which had previously been overlooked. On 4 November 1826 Darling wrote to Major Edmund Lockyer: 'As the French Discovery ships may possibly have in view the establishment of a settlement on some part of the coast of this Territory', it should be made clear to any French the Major might encounter that 'the whole of New Holland is subject to His Britannic Majesty's Government'. Accordingly Lockyer, with twenty soldiers of the 39th Regiment and a similar number of convicts, sailed to King George's Sound in order to take over a million square miles of Australia, on 26 December 1826. He was thereby just a month too late to catch Dumont d'Urville's arrival in the *Astrolabe*; but d'Urville had in fact been despatched with primarily scientific instructions and harboured no predatory intentions.[48]

As part of the same preventative exercise Captain James Stirling had been sent to scout out the west coast of the new British possession. He reported that the Swan River, 400 miles north of King George's Sound, was an excellent base which would afford a good harbour on a navigable river. Moreover, he insisted, the land was as good as or even better than that of New South Wales. Governor Darling was convinced that it was 'of great importance that so advantaged a position should not be taken possession of by the French'. The Colonial Office, however, remained dubious, believing, with some reason, that such plans 'always ended in becoming sources of expense to the mother country' and therefore 'trembled at the thought of the expenditure involved'. But Stirling was well connected, having married into the rich and influential Mangles family, for long senior in the Honourable East India Company, and being a friend of both the then Colonial Secretary, Sir George Murray (a generous distributor of public funds, who came to office in 1828), and of his genial second-in-command, Horace Twiss. Whereas the eastern coast of Australia was out of the way for the East India Company's vessels, the Swan River was well placed as a way station to China (then beginning to be appreciated as a yet unexploited market for Indian goods – always excepting the thriving, but officially illegal, opium trade). Sir John Barrow, the influential Secretary of the Admiralty, had initially been opposed to the scheme, pointing out that the Swan River coast was, as the Dutch had so painfully discovered two centuries earlier, extremely dangerous. Barrow changed his view after he discovered from the Paris Embassy that the French were indeed considering the possibility of founding a penal settlement of their own in Australasia, eventually established in New Caledonia. That was enough. A solution was propounded by Thomas Peel, a kinsman of Sir Robert Peel, then Home Secretary, later Prime Minister, and the most influential Tory politician. A syndicate would guarantee to fund 100,000 settlers, with the requisite stock, Peel himself accompanying the first settlers, in return for a grant of 4 million acres. Negotiations resulted in this being limited to one million, and conditions were attached which, it was hoped, would minimize any risk to the government. The Treasury remained suspicious; Stirling, were he to be given charge, could expect no salary, and the pernicious practice of paying officials in land grants must be adopted.[49]

Stirling was therefore appointed Governor of the new, and to all intents and purposes still non-existent colony, the Swan River settlement, which was to become Western Australia and which comprised 'all that part of New Holland not included within the territory of New South Wales'. This generous grant amounted to about a third of the area of the United States minus Alaska; but the intention was not to attempt a great colonization, but to prevent any other power claiming possession. Once again, British dominion over a considerable slice of the world was proclaimed, this time by Captain Fremantle, in HMS *Challenger* at the mouth of the Swan River, near the site of the present port of Fremantle. The first settlers arrived in June 1829 and the capital was established at Perth.

From the beginning, the dice were loaded against the Swan River settlement. Lying some 3,000 sea miles from Sydney, far from any hope of relief – the nearest, or at least (given the wind patterns) the most accessible, British ports were Trincomalee or Cape Town, both acquired from the Dutch after 1815 – it was part of Australia only as a geographical expression. And Stirling had got his initial assessment badly wrong; far from being more fertile than New South Wales, the immediate hinterland was sandy and barren; Perth was a day's journey from the port of Fremantle, from which it was separated by what proved to be an unnavigable Swan River – and Fremantle itself was merely an unprotected anchorage; Albany, 300 miles south across country, was the only practicable sheltered harbour. Progress was painfully slow. Thomas Peel did his best, succeeding in settling himself and over 500 settlers in the district south of Fremantle. Working capital was provided by the Sydney merchant Solomon Levey, who had arrived as a convict in 1815 and who within ten years had become a prosperous merchant and a proprietor of the Bank of New South Wales. Peel failed to look after his partner's interests (Levey being both Jewish and an emancipist, the agreement had been initially kept secret) and it was only twenty years after Levey's death, in 1851, that his heirs obtained their rightful share of Western Australian acreage. Stirling found the post which he had struggled to win unremunerative and constantly difficult. London refused to provide any more public money – Stirling's Tory political friends had been ousted by Whigs – and the supporters of Wakefield were vociferously hostile to the Peel grant. By 1839, when Stirling left after a hard ten years, the colony's population was only 2,154, scattered over a coastal strip 400 miles long, administered with the help of a parsimonious British government to the tune of some £11,000 a year supplementing what could be extorted from the settlers, from which colonial salaries had to be paid, legislation funded and some sort of order maintained.

One major difficulty in the maintainance of order was the opposition of the local Aborigines. Many were seduced by the frugal benefits obtainable on the fringes of settlement, but others were prepared to fight. One such was Yagan of the Wajuk tribe, who is commemorated by a statue in Perth, partly for his killing of two transport drivers in 1833, but mainly perhaps because his head was subsequently sent as a trophy to Liverpool, its recovery in 1997 causing fresh dissension as its ownership was disputed. Another Aboriginal leader, Kal-yute of the Nyungar people, took part in the 'Battle' of Pinjarra. This encounter, one of the few frontier skirmishes that did not resemble a straightforward massacre, has been seized upon by writers exploiting Australian concern about the treatment of Aborigines. Far from 'a sleeping camp of eighty Aboriginal men, women and children' being 'butchered', there were deaths and injuries on both sides; probably fewer than twenty Aborigines were killed by an organized official expedition commanded by Stirling in person following the murder of a soldier. Stirling, who had made a treaty with another Aboriginal leader, instructed his troop that their duty was 'to protect the Aboriginals from injury, and to pursue by legal process, all those persons who may invade their Rights'. One of the combatants was Lieutenant John Rae RN, Flinders's successor in charting the Australian coastline, who was the first Western Australian Surveyor General, a post he held for the remarkable period of forty-two years, during which he personally explored and surveyed great tracts of the countryside.[50]

Another commercial effort to colonize the region was launched in 1839 by the Western Australia Company, which sought to develop nearly 200,000 acres on the coast some 90 miles south of Perth, where there was already a whaling station. Again, the Western Australia Company had influential support, numbering Wakefield and Sir William Hutt, Wilberforce's successor as MP for Hull, among its directors. As a Whig, Hutt was successful in gaining Colonial Office support. Grand plans were drawn for the new town of Australind, with churches, hospitals, parks and colleges, but they remained on paper. Ironically, it was William Hutt's brother, John, who irreparably damaged the project. Appointed as Governor to succeed Stirling in 1839, John Hutt had acted quickly to tidy the disorganized land tenure, taking land back from grantees who had not fulfilled the original conditions and raising, as required by the Colonial Office, the prices at which land was to be sold. Unfortunately, one of the areas reserved by John was 93,000 acres of the land just bought by his brother's company. An alternative site, 400 miles north, was proposed, but confidence had collapsed. Only 476 immigrants were attracted, and many of them subsequently decamped. By the end of Hutt's term of office, in February 1846, Western Australia's population had struggled to top 5,000, a figure which included a consignment of seventy-three juvenile delinquents fresh from the new penitentiary at Parkhurst on the Isle of Wight. Settlers blamed the Wakefield-inspired policy of land sales rather than free grants, but since the same practice obtained in the other colonies the fundamental reason was the comparative unattractiveness of the west. By mid-century a comfortable urban life could be had in Sydney (which had acquired a zoo, a circus and a fine art society) and in many small towns in New South Wales, while in Tasmania both Hobart and Launceston had good schools and theatres. In the neighbouring colony of South Australia the capital, Adelaide, founded eight years after Perth, already had a population more than twice the size of that of the whole of Western Australia, boasting a theatre, two grammar schools and a botanic garden. With such alternatives, few settlers were likely to be lured to Western Australia: Perth's first grammar school was established in 1876, and Western Australia did not get a theatre until after 1890.[51]

Like his contemporary George Gipps in New South Wales, Hutt endeavoured to 'civilize' the dispossessed Aborigines; a Department of Aboriginal Affairs was created, with two Protectors, appointed and paid from England; a subsidy was given to settlers who undertook to train Aborigines, schools were established by Methodists and Anglicans in Perth, Fremantle and Guildford, but their success was limited; Samuel Marsden had been right when he insisted that missionaries must follow the savages into the wilderness. Francis Lochee, the young editor of the *Inquirer: A Western Australian Journal of Politics and Literature*, accurately described the only alternative:

Unless constant employment be found for the adult natives, in the towns; unless they are properly wived, and they and their families considered to form part of the general society; in short, unless a full equivalent be given to them for the adoption of our forms in the relinquishment of their own, we much fear that all that is now being done will have little ultimate good.

Such a liberal policy was unlikely anywhere in Australia, and particularly in Western Australia.[52]

It was the Roman Catholics, rather than the Protestants, who made the most successful Western Australian missionaries. In 1845 Joseph Brady, newly appointed vicar-general of Western Australia, personally petitioned the Roman Curia to provide the means to evangelize the colony. His request was granted almost too generously. Created bishop of Western Australia, with a staff of French, Irish and Spanish missionaries, Brady, a charming and gentle Irishman, was soon in difficulties with his coadjutor, archbishop, creditors and Rome itself. He resigned, and most of his followers dispersed, but the Spanish Benedictine, Dom Rosendo Salvado and his first colleague, Dom Joseph Serra, established a mission at New Norcia (or Nursia), some 100 miles north of Perth. Overcoming the initial hardships – Dom Rosendo raised money by giving piano recitals in Perth, finding as many as seventy listeners – New Norcia became the most successful of mission stations, attracting praise from Florence Nightingale herself. The Benedictines had followed Marsden's counsel of pursuing the Aborigines into their own territory, but displayed a grace in attracting the local Murara-Murara to Christianity which Marsden could never have attained. Successful as New Norcia was, it came too late, and was too localized, to do more than temper Western Australia's subsequent history of Aboriginal marginalization.[53]

Only one alternative, it seemed, could jolt the colony into life, and that was the introduction of convict labour. The worried citizens of Perth complained to the Colonial Secretary in January 1846 that since 'there appears under existing circumstances no probability of the future arrival in this Colony . . . of the continued essential to prosperity – capital and labour', and in spite of the settlers' protracted aversion to the idea, their only hope was that 'Her Majesty's Government may be induced to convert the colony into a penal colony on an extensive scale'.[54]

At a time when transportation to New South Wales had ended, and when Tasmania was due to receive its last convicts in 1850, the fact that some colonists actually wanted to receive convicts came as welcome news to the British government. Opposed by the strictly religious Ulsterman, Colonel Frederick Irwin, Acting Governor after Hutt's departure, transportation was postponed. A variety of desperate expedients were attempted, including the despatch of the colony's schooner to Singapore to recruit labourers, a project overruled by Lord Grey, but the commissioners at Pentonville were not satisfied that the colony was indeed a suitable destination for its 'reformed' convicts. It was not until 1850 that the first convict ships moored at Fremantle.

Three years later a formal administration, with Legislative and Executive Councils was established, but little enthusiasm was manifested for the latest addition to the British Empire. By 1850, when South Australia was booming, its western neighbour had a population of fewer than 6,000, with only some 7,000 acres cultivated. Even at this early stage Western Australia had shown a distinctive character, something of the Wild West, and it was to remain relatively backward and defiantly independent for another generation. Its new neighbour on the eastern border, South Australia, developed in a very different manner.

A Nonconformist Eden

Considering that South Australia's persistent claim to distinction has been its freedom from 'the convict taint', it is pleasantly ironic that its first advocates were former prisoners – Wakefield himself, Robert Gouger, imprisoned for debt for a short time in 1829, and Anthony Bacon, a dashing but indebted cavalry officer. No important strategic interest dictated the establishment of a southern Australian colony, as it had done in Van Diemen's Land or in the west. The southern coastline of New South Wales, east from Port Phillip, had been used in a desultory fashion by sealers and whalers, but it was Charles Sturt's discovery of the Murray River mouth and the overland route to Sydney in 1830 that revived interest in the region.[55]

While in the King's Bench prison, Bacon and Gouger had heard a description of the southern coast by Captain Henry Dixon. On their release, they prepared a very sketchy plan, for which they claimed 'monied friends in the city' would provide all the necessary finance. The Colonial Office was not impressed, repeating that such plans 'always end in becoming in some way or another a source of expense to the Revenue of this country'.[56] Wakefield, who had been visited while *he* was in prison by Bacon and Gouger, had somewhat better success. The first attempt, an application for a company established by royal charter, with freedom to take over an area of New South Wales approximately equal in size to the Iberian peninsula, with complete control over its constitution and activities once a population of 50,000 was achieved, was to be entirely financed by the sale of the land. James Stephen killed that proposal stone dead, pointing out one or two obvious flaws that had somehow been missed – no paid-up capital nominated, English administrative expenses benefiting from a prior charge – and concluded 'this prospect is wild and impracticable. There is no reasonable prospect that it would be sanctioned.'[57]

The proposals were not helped by the fact that one of the backers, George Fife Angas, a Newcastle upon Tyne shipowner and founder of the London National Provincial Bank, was also a Dissenter, and something of a radical, who had made no secret of his desire to fashion any new colony according to such ideals, perhaps even 'to erect within the British monarchy a government purely republican'. No other Australian colony has a founder as distinct as South Australia. Almost as William Penn personally fabricated the constitution of Pennsylvania, so in a not dissimilar way did George Angas create South Australia as his ideal colony. He was by no means the sole initiator, nor particularly interested in constitutional details, but his single-mindedness combined with his financial resources prevailed over short-term scepticism. South Australia seemed to promise solutions to many diverse problems: philanthropists saw an opportunity to give honest labourers a better future, with the added incentive to taxpayers of removing paupers, extant or potential, from the parish rates; Dissenters welcomed a society where they would not have to pay tithes to an established Church that did not allow them to be educated at the universities or buried in its churchyards; immigrants could be carefully selected to ensure that the colony would not be afflicted with the criminal elements prevalent in Van Diemen's Land and New South Wales; the convict stain would never exist; and the opportunities for profit seemed enormous. For five years, committees, societies and associations produced memorials, proposals, pamphlets, suggestions and books. Jeremy Bentham was enthusiastic, having seen the first prospectus, that the colony should be called 'Felicia or Felicitania, or best of all Liberia'.[58]

A South Australian Association was formed, with the respectable MP Colonel Robert Torrens as chairman, and succeeded in negotiating the 1834 South Australia Act, which established the British Province of South Australia. An area of over 300,000 square miles, about the size of France and Germany combined, was arbitrarily carved from New South Wales (a pointless strip of desert some 400 miles long was left between the new colony and the western boundary of New South Wales). Once more, enthusiastic London investors prepared to risk their money in unknown Australian lands; but both investors and settlers in South Australia were more substantial than the unhappy Western Australians.

The Board of Commissioners of the new Association was empowered to dispose of the new lands, which included an extensive tract which Sturt had been able to assure the investors was particularly promising. Not, however, promising enough to justify the unreasonably high price of £1 an acre; the Commissioners were unable to raise the guarantee of £30,000 demanded by the Government, and George Angas had to intervene personally. This he did, in 1836, by purchasing the unsold land at 12s. an acre, floating the South Australian Company to do so. With his extensive contacts, Angas was able to fund the Company to the tune of £320,000, making it by far the largest investor in the new colony. The situation was now confusingly complex. Responsibility was to be divided, with little precision, between the underfunded Board of Commissioners and the Colonial Office, whose officials were becoming increasingly worried, and with the financial responsibility largely resting on George Angas personally.

Nothing was said in the 1834 South Australia Act regarding Aboriginal property rights. Previous extensive dispossession of the Aborigines had passed without more than occasional annoyed comments from the Colonial Office, but now, for the first time, the question was brought before the attention of the House of Commons and of the nation. The negotiations had taken place with a shaky and equivocal Colonial Office – the two years between Goderich leaving in April 1833 and Glenelg's appointment in April 1835 had seen altogether five Colonial Secretaries – and the Bill had been passed with great haste in an almost empty House of Commons. When the terms of the Act became known, critical comments began to flow. The immensely distinguished soldier, Colonel Charles James Napier, who had been invited to become the colony's first Governor, expostulated that the Act would 'seize by force' a populated region, declaring it to be uninhabited, and so rob 'an inoffensive race of people of their property without giving them the slightest remuneration'. He was not prepared to take responsibility for this, especially without a force large enough to control, not the Aborigines, but the settlers! The Colonial Office began to think again, and over a period of six months anxious negotiations took place. John Brown, the Company's emigration agent, agreed: 'That measures should be devised and enforced for their [the natives'] protection and civilization is not only just and humane but politic', but he complained that after 'people have embarked their money and spent their time' it was hardly reasonable that the Government 'suddenly finds out that there are natives and native rights which they ought to have first enquired about.'[59]

Sir Charles Grey, the parliamentary under-secretary, warned the South Australia Commissioners appointed under the Act that they must avoid 'petty encroachments on the aboriginal inhabitants', and Glenelg himself pontificated: 'before His Majesty can be advised to transfer to his subjects the Property in any part of the land in Australia, he must at least have some reasonable assurance that he is not about to sanction any act of injustice towards Aboriginal natives of that part of the Globe.' Assurances were duly forthcoming. Colonel Torrens, Chairman of the South Australian Commission established under the Act, saw the colony as a potential exemplar:

If the Colony of South Australia can be so conducted as not only to protect the natives in the enjoyment of existing rights but extend the guardianship of legal government, offer them subsistence and comforts of civilized men, win them to regular industry, and secure reserves of improving value for the endowment of schools and Christian teachers; may not colonization on these civilizing and Christianizing principles be extended without limit to other savage lands?

As for dispossession, although 'the case of native occupancy has never yet been provided for before hand . . . they are not only willing but desirous that South Australia should in this respect be made an exception to the general rule'. 'Positive orders' would therefore be given 'to protect the Natives in the unmolested exercise of their rights of property in Land', but Torrens qualified this guarantee with the clause 'should such a right be anywhere found to exist'. John Brown commented that there was 'nothing

... of any consequence' in the Colonial Office caveats: 'What is to be the interpretation of the word "occupy" is the question', and the land was 'not occupied according to any law regulating possession which is recognised by civilised people'.[60]

Immigrants trickled in during 1836, disembarking individually from the Company's whalers, or accompanying the preliminary surveying party. By December they had been joined by the official party in HMS *Buffalo*, and South Australia began its existence as a hermaphrodite entity, part Crown Colony and part commercial enterprise.

The dangers in having a colony owned by shareholders 10,000 miles away, dependent for capital on land sales made on the spot, should have been evident. Angas had to manage the Company's affairs as best he could from his home in Dawlish, Devon. In one querulous letter of 17 November 1836 he complained that his company had already sent out six ships with supplies, and that 'they do not intend to purchase any more until they hear of the arrival of the governor and the organisation of the Colony unless it be a small fast-sailing vessel of from 60–80 tons'.[61] With astute management Angas's Company quickly established a commanding position in the new colony, which Angas began to shape according to his own vision as a land of free settlers, in which the Church of England would have no special position, and where the Aborigines would be fairly treated.

This was not necessarily the position adopted by the harassed Board of Commissioners. Local officials were nominated by the Board and had their own ideas. The Treasurer, Osmond Gilles, was foul-tempered, an intractable republican, but he had the invaluable merit of being rich and willing to advance his own money as colonial funds. James Fisher, their representative Resident Commissioner, had prepared his own terms of reference, which had not been disclosed to the Colonial Office's Governor, Captain John Hindmarsh.[62] A heroic but choleric naval officer, Hindmarsh quarrelled with Fisher, which was perhaps inevitable, but also committed the irretrievable error of personally antagonizing both George Stevenson, the editor of the only newspaper, the *South Australian Gazette and Colonial Register*, and the British Treasury, by issuing unauthorized bills. In London, Colonel Torrens was spending the money that was accruing from land sales – which were going well – on sales promotion, rather than on assisting the colonists. The earliest arrivals had a hard time of it. One of the first was Captain Robert Hill, formerly of the East India Company, who arrived in August 1836, to be followed by his wife Fidelia in December. Living in a tent for some months before moving into a decrepit shack, Fidelia stuck it out for five years, during which time she wrote perhaps the best poetry to be published in Australia up to that time, and the first to be written by a woman. A devoted Wordsworthian, Fidelia aspires to his style, as when describing the disappointments of South Australia:

> Some who unceasingly, had lent their aid,
> And Time, and information, to promote
> The interests of the rising colony –
> Still flattering hope on the dark future smil'd,
> Gilding each object with fallacious dyes,
> And picturing pleasure, that was not to be.[63]

In due course pleasures came; by mid-1837 the new city of Adelaide, named after William IV's popular consort, was laid out by Colonel William Light, but conditions continued precarious. Within little more than eighteen months the London Commissioners were sufficiently alarmed to have both Fisher and Hindmarsh recalled. They were replaced by Colonel George Gawler, who had fought through the Peninsular War to take a prominent place in the Battle of Waterloo. Unusually, Gawler did not seek a post, and caused some surprise to the Board and the Colonial Office when he accepted an offer to act as Governor in the troubled colony, also taking responsibility as Resident Commissioner. A man of energy and initiative, Gawler found a muddle of incoherent land allocation and the shaky outline of an infrastructure. In the short term of his administration – less than three years – Gawler had transformed the situation; more than half a million acres had been properly surveyed, with a rural population of some 5,000 with 200,000 sheep and 15,000 cattle and a promising acreage under plough. The lifeline proved to be the overland route from eastern Australia, pioneered by the enterprising Durham man, Joseph Hawdon, who by the age of 25 had driven cattle from New South Wales to Port Phillip and established the first overland mail route. In 1838 Hawdon and Charles Bonney drove a mob of cattle 750 miles along the Murray River to Adelaide, ensuring a supply of stock to South Australia much more economically than by the risky sea voyage. Hawdon and his colleagues began the Australian droving trade, by which thousands of animals made the arduous journeys between the railheads, and formed an enduring national legend, comparable with that of the American West.

The contrast between the two cultures is, however, informative. Early drovers appeared very much like their cowboy counterparts taking their cattle along the trails to the yards of Chicago, but the Australian tradition has been more enduring. The outback remains open country to a much greater extent than the American West, and the great Australian cattle drives

continued until after the Second World War. It was only in 1924 that Cobb
& Co. ran their last stagecoach on routes that stretched over Australia
for 4,000 miles – and whereas the classic Western vehicle was merely a
four-in-hand, Cobb's coaches had eight, and often twelve horses to draw
them, a daunting task for any driver. Many cowboys were black or Hispanic,
but 'Native Americans' rarely figure in the myth except as scouts or enemies,
whereas some of the most skilled Australian drovers were Aborigines.[64]

From the first, South Australians were a different breed from those of the
other colonies, with none of the raffish habits that were prevalent elsewhere.
Not only were no convicts allowed, but the immigrants had been selected
with some care by the Board of Commissioners and the South Australian
Company. George Angas had been successful in attracting a substantial
German contingent from the Prussian province of Silesia after old King
Frederick William attempted to force all his Protestant subjects into a
state-approved orthodoxy. Those more rigid German Protestants who
objected to the imposition of a new Church order were subjected to quite
harsh treatment, and were personally funded by Angas to populate his new
colony. Just as in the late seventeenth century French Huguenots emigrated
to South Africa as refugees from religious persecution, and thereafter transformed the static Cape Dutch economy by beginning what became the
famous vineyards, South Australia benefited by the influx of skilled
Lutherans.[65] They adapted quickly to British rule and exhibited traditional
German initiative; a settlement was established at Hahndorf, still today a
placid Germanic community, where a market-gardening industry developed.
Under the leadership of their pastor, Augustus Kavel, more Lutherans
acquired land further north, in the Barossa valley, now famous for its many
fine wines. Kavel's immigrants were not the first to plant vineyards in South
Australia; that distinction could be claimed by the Devonian John Reynell,
who in 1841 began the Reynella vineyard, south of Adelaide and still
producing, a hundred and fifty years later, but the Germans were not far
behind. One of Australia's most famous labels, that of the Seppelt family,
had its origins in the Barossa valley, where the Silesian Jacob Seppelt and
his son Oscar built their first winery in 1867. Quantity rather than quality
marked Seppelt wines for many years until the gastronomic revolution
after the Second World War transformed all Australian wine-making. (In a
pleasant tribute to South Australia's benefactor, one wine-maker markets
'Angas Brut', a respectable méthode champenoise fizz.)[66]

Although Gawler had brought order out of chaos, and transformed a
temporary settlement into a functioning miniature colony, with public
buildings, roads and a thriving rural economy, in so doing he had spent

both the Company's money and the British government funds without always obtaining due authority. Angas had exhausted most of his available capital, and the Commissioners continued to be dilatory about providing their share of the funds. When they realized the full extent of the Governor's commitments – he was more than a quarter of a million pounds overspent – they panicked and appealed to the Colonial Office. Gawler was in turn recalled, bitterly criticized and told that his career was over, but it was now clear to all that the experiment of a self-financing commercial colony had failed and that South Australia must revert to the status of a Crown Colony. The two original culprits, Fisher and Hindmarsh, both fared better than the unlucky Gawler. Both were knighted, Hindmarsh as Governor of Heligoland, that sandy North Sea Island, the smallest British overseas possession, and Fisher as first Mayor of Adelaide, and President of the colony's Legislative Council. George Angas, who had done more than any other individual to assure the colony's success, prospered. As a founder of the National Provincial Bank in London, he was instrumental in creating the Bank of South Australia and the Union Bank of Australia, which became a constituent member of the present ANZ banking group. He decided to make his life in South Australia, became one of the first members to be elected to the Legislative Council in 1857, and died at the age of 90, protesting, in the best Nonconformist tradition, liberal principles and tolerance to all except members of the Church of Rome.

Western Australia saw the beginning of Sir George Grey's remarkable official career, as leader of a Colonial Office-sponsored expedition in 1837, but it was in South Australia that Grey first assumed real responsibility as Gawler's successor. Still only in his twenties when appointed in 1841, Grey (born in 1812) was the first Australian military Governor who had not seen service in the Napoleonic wars. South Australia was only the beginning; after decisively altering New Zealand history first as Governor and later Premier, and shaping that of South Africa as High Commissioner, Grey concluded his career by encouraging the new Australian Labor Party and stimulating – half a century after his first appointment – the movement towards Federation. The reputation of this explorer, naturalist, scholar, bibliophile, administrator and politician remains equivocal. He was arrogantly – though with some justification – convinced of his own superiority to anyone who crossed his path, and a shifty, if talented, self-promoter.[67]

As Governor, Grey vigorously and with much criticism of his predecessor Gawler pursued a policy of retrenchment, examining every detail (he refused a payment of 8*d.* to an office boy for sharpening pencils) and declaring that he would 'grant no single indulgence' to the indigent, but would not allow any to starve. Such rigour brought the colony through the economic crisis of the early 1840s in good shape. Grey's policies towards native races, Aborigines, Maoris or Xhosa, never deviated. His report to the Colonial Office on 'the best means of promoting the civilization of the Aboriginal Inhabitants of Australia', made in 1840 after a brief but intimate experience (he was nearly killed in one clash with Aborigines), achieved the status of a handbook. Natives were to be weaned from their unpleasant habits and encouraged to adopt such British fashions as wearing trousers and playing cricket, which would assist them in understanding the functions of democracy.

In South Africa, Grey's methods, assisted by the bloody suppression of armed objections, worked surprisingly well. His colleges at Zonnenbloem and Lovedale, open to girls as well as boys, black and white, were intended to produce leaders capable of holding their own in public life (even the girls were expected to learn Greek); from the middle of the nineteenth century black Africans began to participate in the political process. In Australia, Grey's approach to educating the autochthonous population was never tried. No Aboriginal leader such as John Tengo Jabavu, whose influence could swing parliamentary elections in the 1890s, has ever emerged in Australia; and Jabavu was born a century and a half ago.[68]

Moreton Bay and Places North

There had never been any question but that Van Diemen's Land, Western Australia and South Australia must stand on their own, and the separation of Port Phillip was clearly inevitable, but the suggestion that the northern regions of New South Wales might separate themselves from Sydney was by no means certain. Interest in the region was, for the first forty years of the British occupation, very limited. As part of the policy of establishing far-off outstations as secondary penal colonies, the surveyor John Oxley and his botanist colleague Allan Cunningham had been instructed to place a convict settlement on Moreton Bay. Port Macquarie, some 280 miles north of Sydney, Brisbane considered 'would suit very well a place of detention for the first grave offences; Moreton Bay for runaways from the former and Norfolk Island the *ne plus ultra* of convict degradation'.[69] A miserable Lieutenant Millar was therefore installed at Redcliffe with his wife and family, twenty convicts and a file of infantry; within weeks three had been killed by Aborigines. Governor Brisbane, seeing for himself in November, assented to a move 28 miles upstream, at a spot to be known by his own name. Millar's successor, Captain Patrick Logan, pushed through the initial development of Brisbane with great energy, enforcing discipline with savagery that became notorious, giving Moreton Bay the reputation of an unparalleled place of misery:

> I've been a prisoner at Port Macquarie, Norfolk Island and Emu Plains,
> At Castle Hill and cursed Toongabbie, at all those settlements I've worked in chains,
> But of all those places of condemnation, in each penal station of New South Wales,
> To Moreton Bay I've found no equal: excessive tyranny there each day prevails.[70]

During Logan's rule 126 prisoners, from a total population of under 800, escaped into the bush, to be killed by Aborigines or to starve; 69 of them were recaptured or made their own way back. Reports of the Moreton Bay region were eagerly seized on by Edward Hall of the *Monitor*, anxious to discredit Darling, who had consistently supported Logan; but before an inquiry could be mounted Logan, an adventurous explorer, was killed either by Aborigines or convicts, and the convict settlement abandoned. It was the French who now focused their attention on the region.

After a revolution in 1830 the 'Citizen King' Louis-Philippe came to power, determined, for public relations purposes rather than for strictly practical reasons, to restore something of the battered French prestige by creating a new empire to replace the country's lost dominions; the miserable state of Algeria is the most notable heritage of his ambitions. Covetous eyes were also turned on the Pacific, and an attempt was even made, in 1840, to create a French settlement there. Govenor Gipps of New South Wales, at that time responsible for New Zealand, managed, by the barest margin of four days, to get his blow in first, but the warning was heeded. Just as the southerly settlements had manifested the British claim in Western Australia and South Australia, so must some visible signs of Imperial possession be extended north.[71]

The first settlers arrived in 1840, well-equipped young Scots, like the Leslie brothers. They followed the lead of Captain Logan who, with one convict, explored the area discovered by Cunningham twelve years earlier, the Darling Downs. About the same size as Berkshire, the Downs' soil and water supply deserved better stock than the sheep brought by the Leslies, who were soon followed by other squatters, especially after the area north of the settled districts was declared open. Within a very short time a vast expanse of grazing land was claimed, although very sparsely settled. Only two factors restricted expansion: the stubborn opposition of the Aboriginal tribes and the shortage of convict labour. Transportation having ceased in 1840, frantic attempts were made by the indefatigable John Dunmore Lang to encourage emigration which would be reliably Protestant. Rushing about the British Isles in 1845, this unscrupulous cleric convinced a shipload of emigrants to sail to Moreton Bay on the promise of receiving land grants in proportion to their passage money. When these were not forthcoming Lang made a harsh attack on Lord Grey, and began a fervent campaign for a republican United States of Australia. But he was at least successful in attracting some thousand industrious Scots to Moreton Bay.[72]

By the closing years of the next decade, when the transformation of Moreton Bay into the new colony of Queensland was tabled, the population was still less than 24,000, a quarter of whom lived in Brisbane. Some devolution of government was nevertheless inevitable; Brisbane was 600 difficult miles north of Sydney, provoking resentful impatience at what was seen as incompetent interference (a century and a half later the sentiments have not much faded; Queenslanders are frequently at odds with whatever government is in power in Canberra). What the boundaries of the new colony were to be was a moot point. By 1853, with South Australia and Victoria separated, New South Wales was an impossible shape. No obvious natural frontier defined a border between New South Wales and Queensland, and, that chosen, the 29th parallel to within 300 miles of the coast, thence along the Dunmore River, gave no satisfaction to ambitious Queenslanders such as the Reverend John Dunmore Lang – apart from the satisfaction of his geographical immortality.

On the other side of the Tasman Sea a more complex situation concerning the New South Wales government was developing. British interests in New Zealand began with Samuel Marsden's evangelical efforts. Between 1814 and 1837 Marsden made seven voyages to New Zealand and won the friendship and trust of many Maori; Chief Ruatara translated (shortened) versions of Marsden's sermons and eagerly adopted Marsden's advice in agricultural improvements. There was much in common between Marsden and the Maori leaders; both were impatient of insubordination, authoritative and immensely practical, and it was an alliance between equals who understood each other, in stark contrast to the treatment accorded to Australian Aborigines. 'How', one Maori chief asked, 'do the Pakeha behave to the black fellows of Port Jackson? They treat them like dogs.' The same chief signified, along with all other Maori, his determination not to be relegated to the same position. By 1840, the year of the celebrated Treaty of Waitangi, which marked the beginning of British sovereignty, Sydney's initial responsibility for New Zealand had lapsed, but the experiences of the new colony constituted an informative parallel with those in Australia, as discussions for a possible unification continued for the rest of the century.

In this way, when the little Princess Victoria succeeded her uncle in May 1837, New South Wales, Western Australia, South Australia and Van Diemen's Land proclaimed British sovereignty over the whole of the continent, while markers had been clearly posted in New Zealand. Fifty years after the First Fleet had sailed the Great South Land had become what William Wentworth had prophesied in his 1813 prize poem: 'A new Britannia in another World.'

5

Representative Government

'Extravagant and absurd pretensions'

With the end of transportation to New South Wales the force of arguments against self-government was weakened. In a very few years a normal, free society would develop as conditional discharges and pardons sharply reduced the convict population, with only the dispersed penal settlements housing incorrigible re-offenders. The original demands of the colonists for the 'freedoms of Englishmen' had been met by acceptance of freedom of the press and by the extension of trial by jury, granted by Governor Bourke himself, against the objections of his nervous Legislative Council; and far more privileges than those available in the home country were to be found in New South Wales, by the liberty to take over at will huge areas of land. Government, however, remained in the hands of a nominated oligarchy.

The constitution-making debate had begun to alter its character after 1839. In London the cast had changed. Glenelg, whose reputation had been badly damaged by a narrowly rejected vote of censure moved by Molesworth, was replaced – loudly protesting – in February, at the Colonial Office, first by a pompous incompetent, the Marquess of Normanby, then in September by the much more influential Lord John Russell; Howick, unable to get his own way, resigned in August. James Macarthur, the forceful 'exclusive' spokesman in London, returned to New South Wales. For the next two years Russell was to be the unquestioned arbiter of colonial policy, and Russell at that time was much more liberal than most of his colleagues, and very much the coming man.

In New South Wales the situation had changed even more radically than in Britain. Free emigration had increased from only 407 in 1831 to 3,477 the next year, followed by a dramatic upturn to 10,549 and more than double that number in 1841. In that year the total population had shot up to 130,856 – a 70 per cent increase in five years. Nearly 27,000 of these were convicts still serving their sentences, plus another nearly 20,000 who had arrived as convicts. Whatever truth there had been in Judge Burton's description of Sydney before 1837, only two years later the city must have presented a much less unattractive image. The fiftieth anniversary of the First Fleet's arrival was celebrated in a seemly fashion; construction of Government House (still extant), designed by the immensely industrious Edward Blore (his most visible British work is the Pitt Press in Cambridge), was begun; the first Sydney regatta was held, and swimming from numerous secluded spots along the harbour shore had become a popular pastime – a hulk had been converted into a public bathing establishment at Woolloomooloo. Plans for the first installation of gas lighting were approved, completed in 1841. Samuel Terry, transported in 1800 for the theft of 400 pairs of stockings, died in 1838 a Director of the Bank of New South Wales and President of the Australian Society for the Promotion of the Growth & Cultivation of Colonial Produce and Manufactures, worth half a million pounds, his funeral attended by the regimental band of the 50th Foot.

Australia – the word was increasingly used to denote all the colonies – had ceased to be a joke in Britain, and been promoted to an object of sporadic interest; in 1850 *Punch* depicted Australia as a handsome youth who had outgrown his sibling colonies and required a new suit of clothes. But the colonists themselves enjoyed the reflected glory of belonging to an empire which was emerging as the undisputed world power. Men of unchallengeable distinction in Australia were few, and almost all of them immigrants, Wentworth being the great exception. As emancipists died off, petty distinctions between 'country born' or 'currency lads and lasses' and British newcomers, 'sterling', were substituted. British social rules were jealously observed, imported to the very different conditions of Australia. *Dods Peerage* devoted thirty-two pages to a minute gradation of Anglo-Saxon precedence, doubtless of inestimable value to London society hostesses, but of little use in New South Wales, where most of the inhabitants claiming respectability fell into group 173 (of 178) which included 'solicitors, attorneys, proctors, engineers, architects, medical practitioners, artists, literary men, merchants, master manufacturers, scientific professors, and others, not engaged in manual labour, farming of land, or retail trade, [who] are considered to possess some station in society'. Only clergymen (169) or barristers (171) among the civilian population could claim any superior station, which they accordingly did, with great vigour. Unofficially, possession of a certain minimum of freehold land was regarded as a qualification for acceptance in polite society, and indeed, was essential to qualify for the parliamentary franchise (until 1827 possession of property in England worth £10 a year and in Ireland £2 conferred the right to vote). In a colony, where land was allocated by government, it would be some years before anything resembling a native aristocracy could develop.

In so far as debate in England was concerned, Canada was the priority. The wars of 1812–14 had proved that Canadians wanted nothing to do with American republicanism, and that it was impracticable, if not impossible, for the United States to force integration on Canada as it did on Texas in 1849, although many British politicians would have been happy to have British North Americans joined with their southern neighbours. After an unsettling rebellion in 1837, which united English and French-speaking Canadians against the government and resulted in a number of Canadian 'politicals' being sent for short spells of exile in Australia, Lord Melbourne's government was goaded into action. In a typically Whig reaction they sent a representative of one of the great Whig families to sort things out. Lord Durham, rich, young and charismatic, was, however, also known as 'Radical Jack' for his advanced democratic ideas. Arriving early in 1838, he spent less than six months in Canada, but in that short time was able to collate his observations in the Durham Report, a document of decisive importance. Durham was also Lord Howick's brother-in-law, and was to become father-in-law of the useful Scottish peer, Lord Elgin, son of the famous purchaser of the Acropolis marbles, and himself responsible for establishing diplomatic relations with China by destroying the emperor's summer palace. Neither Howick nor Elgin was as radical as Durham – Elgin was generally to be found on the Tory benches and Howick was only very slowly converted to the idea of colonial self-government – but both were greatly influenced by his ideas. The north of England Whigs formed almost a separate party, living as they did in a society which had more in common with lowland Scotland than southern England; indeed, it might be said that the future of the Australian colonies was decided in the house parties at Lambton Castle and Howick Hall. Elgin's appointment was urged by Howick (who by that time had succeeded to the title of Lord Grey), and John Cell, the authority on British colonial policy, records that by 1846 Howick and Elgin had 'obviously settled the whole thing' (the implementation of responsible government in Canada) already; but whether Elgin had to be converted, or whether he helped Grey to arrive at a definite conclusion himself, cannot be determined.[1]

Durham's trenchant solutions to Canada's problems, embodied in a Bill presented to Parliament in 1839, formed a pattern for all succeeding colonial constitutional reforms. Durham was a follower of Wakefield, and his Report was strongly influenced, if not largely written, by the ubiquitous Charles Buller, who accompanied him to Canada as secretary. Not surprisingly, therefore, the Report advocated subsidized emigration, but also the establishment of 'responsible' government, in which the Governor was obliged to select his government from the elected majority in the Legislative Assembly, as in Britain, subject to the overriding authority of the Crown. It was, and remains, a system dependent on party organizations, which were only then cohering in Britain, and which had still to emerge in any colony.[2]

As Colonial Secretary from September 1839 to August 1841, Lord John Russell had great difficulty piloting the Durham recommendations through a suspicious Cabinet, highly conscious of their precarious position in the House of Commons – the government had actually resigned in May 1839, and only the Queen's reluctance to be saddled with the Tory leader Robert Peel, a man she described as 'cold, odd', a bleak contrast to her beloved Lord Melbourne, had enabled the Whigs to resume office. The concept of responsible government itself was ill-defined, easily confused with the idea of 'responsible' as indicating wise, prudent and dignified government (a confusion quickly dispelled by actual experience), but generally taken to mean the system which had evolved at Westminster whereby the Crown's prerogatives, with a few exceptions still remaining to the Sovereign, were to be exercised by the Prime Minister, the First Lord of the Treasury, who could rely on the support of a majority in the House of Commons. In this way the executive depended upon and was responsible to the elected representatives in the legislature; this contrasts with the American or French system, where the executive is not infrequently opposed by the legislature, a Republican President saddled with a Democratic Congress or vice versa. In the colonies, the monarch's representative, the Governor General or Governor, was expected to take the advice of his elected ministers, always excepting the provisions written into colonial constitutions. The British North America Act of 1840 therefore skated lightly over the whole question of responsible government, which was left to the Governors General to work out during their periods of office. After a rapid succession of three Governors General in as many years, the definitive formula was established under Lord Elgin, in post between 1846 and 1851, the Maritime province of Nova Scotia being the first to have the principle of 'government through the instrumentality of a parliamentary majority' accepted.

After the Canadian precedent had been established, no Australian colony was likely to be content with anything less than such 'responsible' government, but the first stage, of 'representative' government, which had been initiated in Canada itself a century previously, had first to be established in Australia, and the British government was likely to have reservations on such matters as the colonials' treatment of the natives and the prudence of allowing inexperienced politicians unfettered control of the purse strings. The fact that Charles Buller, held in high regard by Lord John Russell, was also the London agent of the Australian Patriotic Association might also have been expected to encourage rapid advance towards Australian self-government. Founded in 1835, inspired by William Wentworth and the emancipist Dr William Bland as a pressure group for representative government, with a strong pro-emancipist tinge, the Patriotic Association was matched by Macarthur's Petition Committee urging a more conservative form of representative constitution, with power retained by those already possessing it, and conceding nothing to the dangerous democrats. The struggle for colonial self-government was fought in the lobbies of the Palace of Westminster and the clubs of St James's, and in the correspondence flowing between Elgin in Toronto and Grey in London.

Sir George Gipps, the Governor who arrived in February 1838, was at first equally sympathetic, fresh from Canada and following subsequent developments there with great interest; his experience of working with New South Wales politicians speedily disillusioned him.[3] His appointment was itself an indication of the British government's changed attitudes. Although a long-serving soldier, who had been present at one of the bloodiest actions of the Peninsular War, Gipps's subsequent appointments had been civilian for twenty years before his arrival in New South Wales. Still only holding the rank of major, Gipps had nevertheless been knighted for his services, an indication of how clearly his civilian status predominated, in striking contrast to the senior military officers who had preceded him. Frank to the point of offensiveness, Gipps was a powerful and efficient administrator, able to get the best out of his staff. Unprecedently, all the senior departmental heads in post at his appointment remained in office under him, with the exception of those who were promoted. His relations with La Trobe, his junior at Port Phillip, were always cordial and constructive. Candour and effectiveness did not, however, necessarily command unanimous support from the colonists who were starting to flex their still limited legislative muscles.

Gipps rejected Lord Howick's cherished ideas of local councils in favour of the plan originally advanced by Bourke and Wentworth, of a single 'blended' legislature, with the proviso that after nine years the colony should be ready for a conventional two-chamber Parliament, with the progression to responsible government implicit therein. Such a plan would probably have passed without difficulty had not Russell, prompted by the Colonial Land and Emigration Commissioners, chosen to introduce the land issue. The first years of representative government in New South Wales were absorbed with three major questions, those of land policy, immigration and education. Squatters, those enterprising pioneers who had penetrated the unexplored land beyond the settled areas, had simply taken over large tracts as sheep runs. They now demanded regularization of their holdings and security of tenure, insisting that the Legislative Council should be allowed to control land disposal, a demand strenuously resisted by the Colonial Office. Since income from sales and leases of 'Waste Lands' was by far the major source of colonial revenue, ceding this to a local government would not only increase the likelihood of abuse, but constitute an irrevocable step towards colonial independence.[4]

Lord John Russell proposed that New South Wales should be divided into three separate districts, each of which would have a land sale price fixed, the proceeds to be applied to assisted emigration, and each eventually to form a separate colony. Coming on top of the Durham Report, that idea proved too complex and disputatious for a weak British government to press through the House of Commons, and it was allowed to drop in July 1840. It was then agreed that the existing arrangements were to remain in force for a year, and New Zealand, which had for a brief time been attached to New South Wales, was allowed to begin its own independent existence.[5]

New South Wales was bitterly disappointed; James Macarthur, recognized as head of the family since old John's collapse into madness and subsequent death in 1834, spent two years in London between 1836 and 1838 pressing the Petition Committee's case, had become friendly with Buller, and on his return to the colony formed a limited alliance with Wentworth, agreeing on the need for representative government, but differing on its form. When Lord Melbourne's government finally collapsed in June 1841 it was replaced by that of the Tory Sir Robert Peel, the new Colonial Secretary being Lord Stanley.

Nineteenth-century history is bedevilled by the proliferation of titles and the habit of politicians to change parties. That particular Lord Stanley had previously been Mr E. G. G. S. Stanley, Whig Colonial Secretary for fourteen months in 1833–4. In 1841, now with the courtesy title of Lord Stanley, and having joined the Tories but still a commoner, he was again appointed Colonial Secretary; in October 1844 he moved to the House of Lords, still as Lord Stanley, and in 1851 he succeeded to the family title as the Earl of Derby, eventually becoming Prime Minister. The Greys were almost as confusing, but at least remained loyal Whigs. Earl Grey was Prime Minister in 1832 with his son Lord Howick as colonial under-secretary in the House of Commons. In 1845 Howick succeeded his father as the 3rd Earl Grey, and sat in the House of Lords. General Sir Charles Grey, Queen Victoria's private secretary was his brother and Sir George Grey, colonial under-secretary 1834–8, his uncle, but Sir George Grey, of Western and South Australia, South Africa and New Zealand, whose career spanned sixty years of Australian history was no close relation. Such family connections were often significant, especially among the great Whig clans, and were to have a powerful influence on colonial developments.

Unsympathetic to demands for responsible government, and frustrated in his ambitions to make a name in the House of Commons, Stanley neverthe-less introduced the first elected representatives to the Australian colonies, and with considerable speed. After consultation with the Macarthur brothers, James and Edward, and Charles Buller, Stanley's Australian Con-stitutions Act of 1842 passed through Parliament without a dissenting voice. New South Wales was given a part-elected Legislative Council – twenty-four elected members, six of whom were to be chosen by the Port Phillip electors, and twelve nominated by the Governor. Former convicts, time-expired or pardoned, were allowed to vote and to sit on the Legislative Council. The franchise qualifications were set so high, however – twice as great as those in England – that a majority was captured by the old 'exclusives', with no heart for greater democracy. Gipps was caught between two fires, that of the Legislative Council members vigorously prosecuting their own interests, and that of the Colonial Office, still at least an eight months' round trip away (the first regular steam line, that pioneered by the revolutionary new *Great Britain* from 1852, was no faster than the better of the sailing clippers) and headed by a bewildering succession of masters – Glenelg, Normanby, Russell, Stanley and, for a short time, William Gladstone, all serving as Colonial Secretaries during Gipps's term of office.

After the first elections, the campaign for which lasted from December 1842 to June the following year, many long-prominent figures found their way into the new assembly, including Hannibal Macarthur, the Reverend Dr Lang and Roger Therry, but the leading spirit was William Wentworth. One of his first proposals, the right for livestock and the next season's wool clip to be registered as security for bank loans, was to be invaluable in financing Australia's staple industry. Altogether less impressive was Wentworth's demagogic attack on the Governor. 'There are', Gipps con-fided to La Trobe, 'about 5 or 6 men in the council who are personally my enemies . . . for no better reason that I am aware of than because they were not received . . . as dinner guests at Government House.' Wentworth became the squatters' spokesman, driven by a personal grudge against Gipps, who had blocked a ridiculous pet scheme of Wentworth's to 'purchase' a third of New Zealand from the Maoris (not 'jobbery', as any reasonable person would have described Wentworth's plan, but 'Elizabethan in spirit and characteristically splendid and defiant', according to the *Australian Dictionary of Biography*'s eccentric view). 'Eternal enmity' was therefore vowed by Wentworth against the upright and industrious Gipps, who feared the 'calamitous results' if such voracious Legislative Assembly members were allowed to parcel out Crown lands, 'each grasping at, or rather, I should say each higgling and bargaining for the greatest share.' With considerable acumen, the Governor used his powers to appoint a new member, the young barrister Robert Lowe; aggressive, albino, greatly talented and equally tactless, Lowe was to become a senior figure in British if not Australian governments. For nine months Lowe mounted astonishingly successful defences of Gipps's policies before demonstrating his capacity for quarrelling by resigning in a huff, only to return as an elected member.[6]

When Stanley incorporated Howick's old proposal for district councils in the 1842 Act he found that the idea still did not commend itself to the socially conservative Legislative Council, particularly worried about the probable effects on local rates; the Council waxed indignant:

Nothing can more clearly evince the evil tendencies of that entire separation of the Legislative and Executive powers which exists here at present, than the perfect indifference, if not contempt, with which the most important decisions and resolutions of your Honorable House have been treated by the head of the government during the course of this session. Notwithstanding the insignificant minorities – in which the confidential servants and advisers (if any such there be) of the government have been left on every important subject – which has engaged the attention of the House during the present session, the condemned policy and measures of the executive are still persevered in, as if they met the fullest concurrence and support of overwhelming majorities . . . decisions, in many of the most important of which some of the most experienced, and influential of the unofficial nominees of the Crown have concurred, have been utterly disregarded, and every possible expedient resorted to – in order to deprive the Council of that control over the public purse, which the Imperial Legislature on the one hand, and successive Secretaries of State, with the sanction of the Lords of the Treasury – on the other, have over and over again placed at its disposal.[7]

Since the Act was permissive rather than mandatory it was easy for the Legislative Council to do nothing at all to promote local self-government, which they accordingly did. The Legislative Council's principal grievance was financial. Paralleling the constitutional measure was the Australian

Land Sales Act which was to apply to all colonies, and which implemented Wakefieldian principles; free grants were everywhere to be abolished, replaced by sales at £1 an acre. Half the total proceeds were to be appropriated to assisted emigration, and the remainder to be spent on public services but in accordance with London's instructions. This drove Legislative Council members, anxious to control these substantial sums themselves, to rebellious fury. The 1842 New South Wales Act had imposed the burden of paying administrative expenses – a 'civil list' – on New South Wales. Both the amount – some £6,600 more than that of the much more-populous Canada – and the principle of 'no taxation without representation' were, somewhat ominously, invoked: 'no tax or aid can originate from . . . any other than the representatives of the people as recognised in 1778.'[8] The principle had been acknowledged in Canada, and 'It will be manifest, that the [Australian] Colonists have . . . an equal right to it'. This was not a cause likely to win much sympathy from a Tory government, and it was not until the Whigs were back in power, in July 1846, that the issue was positively addressed.

'If you wouldn't become a kangaroo'

The Legislative Council, dominated as it was by the squatters' interests, and kept in power by the skilful lobbying of the Macarthurs in London, consistently pressed for unrestricted expansion into the interior. Bourke had realized the impossibility of confining pastoralists and their animals to what the Colonial Office perceived as the administratively tidy 'settled area', the 'Nineteen Counties'. These had been surveyed by Thomas Mitchell in 1834 and extended more than 300 miles down the coast from Taree in the north to Moruya, and inland for some 150 miles, but even this extensive area – enormous, to English ideas – was not enough to satisfy the settlers. 'Not all the armies of England – not 100,000 soldiers scattered throughout the bush – could drive back our herds within the limits of our 19 counties.' By the time Bourke left (December 1837) sheep stations stretched from the southern boundaries of what is now Queensland to South Australia for well over 1,000 miles. Bourke had no difficulty therefore in supporting his Legislative Council in the 1836 Act which legitimized the squatting system by charging settlers outside the 'iron band of settlement' the flat rate of £1 per acre, for the homestead lot, in return for which the settler could have as much land as he could take possession of, subject to the ineffective supervision of newly appointed Commissioners of Crown Lands. Three years later the charge was augmented by a levy on the number of stock said to be run, and the Commissioners' supervision improved with the establishment of a Border Police Service. Well over a million sheep, on more than seven hundred extensive stations, were established as the foundation of what was to remain Australia's staple industry; the colony's prosperity subsequently rose or fell according to the success or failure of the wool clip.

This was clearly illustrated during the miserable years between 1841 and 1844. Following the uncontrolled expansion, it seemed – irrationally enough, but bearing in mind the very sketchy information available concerning the outlying districts – that all the best land had been sold. Certainly many of the squatters were over-extended financially and land sales plummeted from £324,072 in 1840 to a derisory £9,174 in 1844. Denied its main source of income, the New South Wales government was forced, for the first time, to raise capital in London; local credit dried up and three banks failed. The price of wool fell even as the sheep themselves multiplied. Thousands were simply allowed to die; many more were boiled down for tallow, until even that market was saturated. One bush ballad mourned the unsuccessful squatter's fate:

> Now all, intent to emigrate,
> Come listen to the doleful fate,
> Which did befall to me of late,
> When I went to the wilds of Australia.
> I sailed across the stormy main,
> And often wished myself back again,
> I really think I was quite insane
> When I went to the Bush of Australia.
> > Illawarra, Moneroo, Paramatta, Woolloomaloo,
> > If you wouldn't become a kangaroo,
> > Don't go to the bush of Australia.
>
> And when I came to look at the land,
> Which I got by his Excellency's command,
> I found it was nothing but burning sand,
> Like all the rest of Australia,
> But I bought flock of sheep at last,
> and thought that all my troubles were past,
> but you may believe I stood aghast,
> When they died of the rot in Australia.
> > Illawarra, Moneroo, etc.

My convicts were always drinking rum,
I often wished they were up a gum-
tree – or that I had never come,
To the horrible bush of Australia.
The bushrangers my hut attacked,
And they were by my convicts back'd,
And my log-hut was fairly sack'd
Of all I had got in Australia.
　　Illawarra, Moneroo, etc.[9]

Wheat prices collapsed after a disastrous two-year drought, imported goods could find no ready markets, and land values followed the downward trend. One run was sold for a pound of tobacco and two gallons of rum. As sales of Crown lands slowed to a trickle, assisted immigration was brought almost to a halt, and the New South Wales government was forced into its first public borrowing, a modest £50,000. The Bank of Australasia was driven to the expedient of a lottery, in which the prizes were foreclosed properties – early indication of an Australian fondness for gambling. Colonial prospects seemed bleak.

One of Gipps's first problems, therefore, was to convince the Colonial Office that the squatters must be tolerated. Echoing his predecessor's views, he assured Lord John Russell that Bourke had been right, and that

As well might it be attempted to confine the Arabs of the desert within a circle drawn on the sands, as to confine the graziers or wool-growers of New South Wales within any bounds that may possibly be assigned to them; and, as certainly as the Arabs would be starved, so also would the flocks and herds of New South Wales, if they were so confined, and the prosperity of the colony would be at an end.

Politely enough, he satirized the official view of theoretical crown supremacy which would claim that

it were as unauthorised an act of presumption for an Australian squatter to drive his flocks into the waste recesses of the untrodden wilderness, without Her Majesty's express sanction first obtained, as for a Berkshire farmer to feed his oxen, without rent or licence, in the Queen's demesne of Richmond or Hampton Court.[10]

At the same time the squatters' pretensions had to be faced down: they were being allowed to occupy vast areas at a merely nominal cost, and if they suffered in bad times they prospered exceedingly in good. Gipps was unrepentant in the face of vociferous opposition, and promulgated a set of regulations in April 1844. Squatters were allowed to stay put, but a separate licence was required for each run, which must not exceed 20 square miles or carry more than 4,000 sheep; after five years the squatter must purchase 320 acres as a homestead, and thereafter an equal area every eight years, at a price of £1 per acre. Arithmetically, this amounted to a payment of £40 a year for freehold possession of the land purchased, and permission to occupy 20 square miles of New South Wales. After a great deal of agitation – the regulations would drown the colony in 'one common vortex of ruin' – Gipps's regulations were incorporated in the 1846 Imperial Waste Lands Occupation Act and the Order in Council of 1847. The latter defined three types of land: 'settled' suburban areas, in which leases would be annual; 'intermediate', which included most of the existing stations, on eight-year leases, with the land to be offered annually for auction; and the unoccupied outback, where fourteen-year licences with an option to buy would be granted.[11]

A shift in New South Wales politics was thereby caused. From being agitators for change, the squatters became defenders of acquired rights and therefore in opposition to democratic advances. As the Order in Council was extended to other colonies with some local variants, a similar dichotomy emerged.

New South Wales was also agitated by the warning given both by Russell and Stanley that new colonies might be created north of 26 degrees, about the present position of Gympie, and that Port Phillip would, in due course, be given its independence. The Legislative Council's complaints to the Colonial Office, accusing Gipps of treating with 'perfect indifference if not contempt, the most important decisions and resolutions of your Honourable House', did nothing to convince the British government that New South Wales was ready for responsible government. Gipps, disgusted with what he saw as the 'extravagant and absurd pretensions' of the New South Wales Legislative Council, was more than willing to support the Port Phillipian separatists. James Stephen was unhappy with both of Lord Stanley's Acts, believing that it was high time the colonists were given control of the land revenue, and condemning the principle of a council composed of both elected and nominated members. Writing in 1848 he complained that 'Former administrations devised in Newfoundland and New South Wales the scheme of a single chamber. Having predicted with earnestness the failure of these schemes, I am probably under a bias when I conclude that they have failed . . . the longer they are tried the more complete the failure will be.'[12] The subject, however, was not allowed to drop, but dissension was replaced for the moment by the revival of that old issue, transportation.

A Convenient Change of Nomenclature

The greatest disturbance caused by the defeat of the Whigs in 1841 was that surrounding the future of transportation. Russell had come to the Colonial Office in September 1839 fresh from the Home Office, where he had successfully implemented the massive organization of the new Poor Laws. He had developed clear views on penology, but had no experience or understanding of Australian conditions. As Home Secretary he had succeeded, not without difficulty, in introducing a progressive domestic regime, greatly reducing the number of offences punishable by transportation, and in stopping transportation to New South Wales. But it remained too convenient a penalty to be abandoned entirely: some 4,000 prisoners were still annually sentenced to transportation for whom accommodation must be found.

'With some diffidence', Lord John proposed that, pending the completion of the experimental penitentiary at Pentonville, convicts should be continue to be transported to any part of the Empire that might be willing to accept them – the Cape, Corfu, St Helena and the Falkland Islands were among the suggestions reluctantly abandoned. A few hundred especially well-behaved, generally young, offenders, might be sent to Bermuda, and it was for some time hoped that others could be employed on the Halifax–Quebec railway construction. Some would be sent to Norfolk Island, whither Captain Maconochie, following the complaints of the Van Diemen's Land officials, had been sent to apply his modern methods as subjects for his experimental regime; but Van Diemen's Land remained by some way the most convenient – and much the cheapest – receptacle for what an Inspector General of British prisons was later to describe as 'the criminal sewage flowing from the Old World to the New'.[13] Once arrived, the convicts would be set to work in gangs, on probation and under strict supervision, after which they would, subject to good conduct, be free to work for wages.

Accustomed as he was to habits of obedience, Sir John Franklin did not question his instructions, although he protested when Russell instructed him to increase the time spent on gangs from one or two years to as long as four. Matthew Foster was appointed as director of the probation gangs and prepared for the reception of 2,000 convicts, searching both for suitable instructors and overseers and for projects on which they might be employed. Whitehall, however, enthused by the potential savings – an extra 2,000 sent would save £150,000 over four years, to say nothing of the improvements their work would surely effect in Van Diemen's Land – and totally ignorant of the difficulties facing the colonial government, decided to double the number. And Franklin's troubles were then increased by changes in London.

The new Tory Colonial Secretary, Lord Stanley, one of the richest men in England, heir to the Derby earldom and unquestioned potentate of Lancashire, was aggressively ruthless, 'haughty and domineering' and convinced of his own correctness. A firm believer in transportation, he proposed to continue sending the 4,000 or so convicts annually sentenced to transportation to Van Diemen's Land and to revive the penal settlement on Norfolk Island. Any system of convict administration that attempted more than mere control was expensive, and without adequate funding Maconochie was to find efficient implementation impossibly difficult. Stanley was no more generous than his predecessor, who considered that Maconochie had failed in making 'the penalty of the law a punishment for evil-doers', and was unsympathetic to such innovations, complaining that 'they made an efficient system almost impossible'. All such liberal follies, Stanley insisted, were to be stopped, and rigorous discipline imposed, but his own variation of the probation system would, he was confident, encourage virtuous conduct – and be even less expensive. An elaborate scheme was therefore prepared by which those sentenced to only seven years, who under the previous government would not be transported at all, would spend one to two years on public works in the Van Diemen's Land gangs, after which they might be given 'probation passes' enabling them to work for wages. When half their sentence was served they could be eligible for tickets of leave; or a pardon might be granted. Potentially dangerous prisoners accused of serious offences would be softened up by a two- to four-year sentence on Norfolk Island, where Maconochie's experimental system was to be replaced by a much tougher regime.[14]

In Whitehall offices, such a system sounded eminently sensible, but on the ground the practicalities of controlling what became tens of thousands of offenders, both those still under sentence and requiring supervision and support, and those released into the community, proved impossible. On Norfolk Island Major Joseph Childs, the commandant who replaced Maconochie in February 1844, initiated a system which did little to fulfil Lord Stanley's behest to maintain 'constant vigilance and inflexible vigour in enforcing the appropriate punishments'. There was plausible logic in Stanley's conception: a straightforward penal settlement, uncomplicated by problems of interacting with a free society that had developed in New South Wales and Van Diemen's Land or with any programme of reformation, was intended only to contain the men, to break their spirit and render them amenable to eventual transfer to a less stringent regime. The French prison settlements in Cayenne, graphically recorded in Henri Charrière's book *Papillon*, continued to fulfil for French governments most of Lord Stanley's requirements for well over a century; but the virtue of Norfolk Island – its remoteness – also nullified any proper monitoring of conditions there. When, at the same time as Childs' appointment, control of the island passed from Sydney to the even more inaccessible Hobart, effective supervision collapsed. Childs proved a disastrous choice, and Lord Stanley's good intentions were perverted. Punishments were frequent enough (26,000 lashes in sixteen months) and ingenious to the point of revolting tortures, but vigilance was noticeably lacking; homosexual rape and violence among prisoners was common; informers were punished by being beaten to death or having their nose and ears bitten off. The inevitable mutiny erupted, but not before the chaplain had written to London and Sydney exposing Childs' brutal incompetence.[15]

Another of Lord Stanley's proposals was the foundation of an entirely new mainland penal settlement, sufficiently far removed from existing populations to present no threat of pollution, and which would accept three categories of well-conducted convicts: 'exiles', those already selected as having been of good behaviour in a British prison, 'emancipees', holding conditional pardons, and time-expired convicts. A more radical suggestion of appropriating the distant Auckland Islands, 380 miles east of New Zealand, was unsuccessfully canvassed; the scheme outlined by Lord Stanley demanded that the settlement be part of a large new mainland colony. If New South Wales refused to accept convicts, and Western Australia was too underpopulated to allow more than a limited number to be absorbed into the community, a large part of New South Wales could be separated and re-established as a new convict colony. The *Sydney Morning Herald* was horrified, anticipating 'hordes of marauding and bloodthirsty reprobates' descending on peaceful Sydneysiders, but the plan went ahead. A site was found with an excellent harbour at Port Curtis in the tropical north, and named after the next Colonial Secretary, W. E. Gladstone (December 1845–June 1846). Lieutenant Colonel George Barney of the Royal Engineers was appointed as superintendent, arriving with some 150 potential settlers in the summer of 1847. They had a miserable time of it for six months, stiflingly hot, wet and plagued by mosquitoes, before the new settlement and colony was temporarily shelved, and with it all convict transportation to New South Wales. At that time Gladstone was a Tory, and lost his post with the fall of Peel's government, to be succeeded by that uncompromising Liberal, Lord Howick, now in the House of Lords as Earl Grey. Stanley's particular plan had therefore to be abandoned, and the settlement of Gladstone began its life as a useful small trading port, eventually forming part of the colony of Queensland.[16]

Stanley's policies were complete failures. The economic depression which had affected New South Wales did not spare Van Diemen's Land; given the requirement that a minimum period must be spent in strictly controlled work gangs, the difficulties of finding work for the men to do and honest supervisors proved insuperable. A flood of convicts swept into the colony, 5,500 in 1842 alone: as men served their time on the gangs and sought work things worsened; by 1844 the 4,603 new arrivals joined 3,179 unemployed pass-holders. The costs, both to the home country and the colony, grew unmercifully. Franklin, whose reputation had suffered grievously at the hands of John Montagu, who had gained Stanley's confidence and during his leave in London slandered the Governor unmercifully, was recalled in 1843 to be replaced by a staunchly conservative nominee, Sir John Eardley Eardley-Wilmot. Eardley-Wilmot was already 60, and, if not quite the muddle-brained blockhead that Stanley called him (but it was, after all, Stanley who had appointed him), he was certainly incapable of coping with the task of administering 30,000 convicts and a similar, but declining, number of free settlers.[17]

Unlike previous governors Eardley-Wilmot had no military experience, being an inoffensive country MP, with vaguely liberal views (although a proponent of the lash in regulating juvenile offenders), but he was due a reward after siding with Lord Stanley in his objection to the Whigs' intention to divert some of the revenues of the Church of Ireland, then a bitterly contested issue, to more useful purposes. With these qualifications, his attempt to lead a hard-bitten collection of convicts and settlers was an entirely predictable failure. Even a better man, however, would have been hard pressed to square the Colonial Office demands for economies with the colonists' insistence that they should not be required to pay so much of the expenses of running a penal colony for the benefit of the British taxpayers. Had it not been for his officials, the amiable James Bichen as Colonial Secretary and the excellent Peter Fraser, fourteen years as Treasurer, Eardley-Wilmot's life would have been impossible.

Unpopular with the settlers, Eardley-Wilmot was detested by the Colonial Office for his laxity in correspondence, and Gladstone, when he assumed office, moved swiftly to replace him. Stephen, who disliked Gladstone, admitted in his diary that at least he was nevertheless grateful to the Colonial Secretary for having got rid of 'his greatest incubus Governor Eardley-Wilmot'. Spicy stories of rampant buggery among the convicts, allied to (probably untrue) reports of the Governor's own libidinous behaviour (although if that were a genuine pretext for dismissal many more colonial officials would have suffered), raised shocked eyebrows in Whitehall. The crisis came in October 1845 when the unofficial members of the Legislative Council, smarting at the end of the assignment system, resigned en bloc: the 'Patriotic Six' refused to pass expenditure bills, declaring that 'not one shilling more' would be paid until the British government agreed to meet the cost of police and gaols. This unprecedented action by so innately conservative a body was denounced by the alarmed Governor as 'radical, in fact Jacobinical', and when the news of it reached London in April 1846 the letter of dismissal was speedily despatched. Eardley-Wilmot was replaced for a few months by the reliable La Trobe and then by William Denison; Eardley-Wilmot himself obligingly died in February 1847.[18]

Many of the most distinguished nineteenth-century Imperial officials and colonial governors were officers of the Royal Engineers. The great Lord Kitchener and the remarkable General Gordon, hero of Khartoum, were both Royal Engineers, as were, in Australia, George Grey, George Gipps, and William Denison. Sappers, reliably literate, professionally trained, were usually preferred to infantry officers (cavalrymen were rarely offered responsible civilian posts) but were also commonly regarded as being either 'mad, married or Methodists'. Denison had his share of oddities, the most obvious of which was the effort he expended in attempting to rebut Darwinism, and he was sometimes obstinately wilful, but he proved a competent and energetic administrator. Competent though he was, Denison was faced, on his arrival in January 1847, with the difficult task of reconciling his duties as Governor of what was still a penal colony with his responsibilities towards the discontented settlers, suffering as they then were from the effects of the recession. In these circumstances Stanley, reluctant to concede that transportation should be ended, was willing to consider some modifications to his policies. Van Diemen's Land pass-holders would be surely be welcomed in Port Phillip where labour was urgently needed; those convicts conditionally pardoned in one colony would therefore be allowed to move to any other spot in the Empire, except that from which they were originally banished, so enabling Van Diemen's Land convicts to cross to the mainland. Much consternation was aroused by this last measure, especially among South Australians fearing 'pollution' of their respectable and hitherto convict-free community by wild Van Demonians.

Sir Robert Peel's government had finally collapsed in June 1846 after the controversial repeal of the Corn Laws, in force for a generation to protect farmers' incomes at consumers' expense. The Tory party was left divided between such reformers as Gladstone, drifting towards the Whig-Liberals, and the new Conservatives inspired by the brilliant Benjamin Disraeli. Lord John Russell was able to form his first administration, with Lord Grey in his old post. Grey is the only nineteenth-century Colonial Secretary to have presented a studied justification of his career, which also marked a turning point in Imperial affairs. At the time of his first appointment, in 1830 at the age of 27, as second to the ineffectual 'Goody' Goderich, no coherent policies had been evolved, and opinions differed fundamentally on the utility of any colonization. In 1854, when he left office, after one of the longest periods of any individual in charge of colonial affairs (surpassed only later by Joseph Chamberlain), it was accepted that settlement colonies should have what was to most intents and purposes self-government, generally on a more democratic basis than that of the home country. Grey's personal views developed from that of the angry young radical who horrified Charles Greville by 'hold[ing] language the most revolutionary, and such as might more naturally be uttered at some low meeting in St Giles's or St Pancras' than in such a place' (the Palace of Westminster), to that of the elder statesman who lived to criticize both Gladstone and Salisbury. Grey's opinions were not coloured by any undue experience of colonial affairs; on his first appointment, confronted with a request concerning the Auckland Islands, he had to write to Stephen to discover whether they were British. His initial reluctance to allow responsible government to the Australian colonies was modified by the advice of Elgin from Canada, which led to Grey's eventual acquiescence in the 1850 Act that was to give carte blanche to the colonists to write their own constitutions. One of his first actions in office was to cancel the Port Gladstone scheme, arguing that a settlement there would only result in the freed convicts 'as it were to pass through a sieve into New South Wales'. Transportations to Tasmania, Grey announced in February 1847, would be suspended for two years after 1848 and the cessation would, he informed the Governor, thereafter become permanent. James Stephen also assured the Treasury that 'Her Majesty's Government had decided upon altogether abandoning transportation to Van Diemen's Land'.[19]

Before the ban was fully effective Grey was forced to change his mind, in spite of the fact that this would lay him open to 'a charge of breach of faith'. It appeared that his message had been garbled; his despatch to Denison had originally read: 'it is not the intention that transportation (under the present system) should be resumed at the expiration of the two years', but in transmission the words in brackets had been omitted; as received in Van Diemen's Land, however, the intention was unqualified.

Grey had feasible reasons for ending transportation. Unemployment

seemed to be no longer a problem in Van Diemen's Land, sinc
leave men had been allowed to move to other colonies; Britain, n
was gravely unsettled. British society had been changing, and
radically, well before the critical year of 1848. The Municipal Co
Act, which, after much agitated resistance, established elected loc
ments in 1835, stimulated widespread participation in the demo
cess, which led within a generation to the emergence of such ex
political families as the Chamberlains of Birmingham and the C
Newcastle. Trade unions, legalized in 1825, spread from their
combinations of skilled artisans to comprehend unskilled la
Workers' own initiative founded the co-operative movement in 18.
the 1847 Factory Act defined ten hours as the maximum industrial
day. Parliament, however, remained distant from most workin
concerns, but political skills honed in such extra-parliamentary a
were developing; and were, together with new expectations, taken
tralia by the hopeful new emigrants. Revolutions were breaking out
Europe; Chartists, those dangerous democrats, were menacing to th
that thousands of special constables (who included the future
Emperor Louis-Napoleon) were enrolled and the army readied; hu
of thousands of Irish were starving in the Great Hunger, driven to
and a few dozens under the ineffectual leadership of William Smith O
MP were actually taking up arms. Under these circumstances the
valve afforded by transportation could hardly be prudently abandon

Politicians have never found it easy to resist the lure of semantic
solution to their problems; it is easier to change the name from 'illiter
'educationally disadvantaged' or 'poor' to 'socially deprived' than to
expensive solutions to illiteracy or poverty. Grey was no exception.
months after taking office, on 2 September 1846, he wrote to James Ste
now retired but still very much the authority on colonial matters, s
out his new policy. Grey had accepted the criticisms of his predeces
policies; in future, 'that part of the punishment which consists in confine
and penal labour' should be inflicted in Britain. After this was satisfact
completed a pardon would be given, conditional on the convict remai
in the colony to which he would be transported until his sentence had b
completed; 'I would proclaim boldly that such men were considered a
their punishment as in all respects free, except as to remaining at home,
that they had a right to go where they pleased.' Families would have hou
prepared for them 'in the situations where their labour would be m
useful', while single men would be assigned 'just as convicts were . . . on
old system except in this very important particular that they would recei

wages'. Given that the preliminary imprisonment would have included 'not only moral, intellectual and religious instruction but also industrial instruction . . . every man should come out knowing how to read and write and also how to use his strength with advantage in at least two useful arts . . . [they would be] men who would turn their hands almost to anything – could dig – cobble – hew a stone, or use a saw or an axe, in short the sort of men who are invaluable in a young settlement'.[20]

Only slightly amended, Grey's letter formed the basis for his proposals. 'Transportation' would certainly be ended, and replaced by compulsory emigration. Pentonville prison had been opened four years previously, and under Joshua Jebb's supervision the first results were encouraging. After even eighteen months of near-solitary confinement, the only distractions being hard and tedious labour on the treadmill, the spiritual consolations of the chaplains and the earnest moral uplift of the warders, convicts were more than ready to face exile. Grey's plan was little more than a modification of Stanley's earlier scheme, with the nomenclature modified. After a limited period of imprisonment in the modern British prisons, convicts would labour in public works, either at home or on the fortifications of such places as Gibraltar or Bermuda. When that was done – and the two periods together would represent only a portion of the original sentence – the doubtless repentant sinners would be given a one-way ticket to the colonies. Even this limited step was, however, vigorously opposed by conservative opinion in Britain; the judiciary collectively but unsuccessfully lobbied for transportation, as a deterrent excelled only by capital punishment, to be retained.

The new arrivals were therefore no longer to be 'convicts', but 'exiles' who could be accompanied by their wives and families. They did not arrive in great numbers – some 500 a year in 1846-8. Given the much greater numbers of free settlers who were arriving, the 'Pentonvillains' were of little advantage to employers – they too, like free workers, had to be paid – and they were unwelcome competition to the new immigrants on the labour market.

Grey persisted, and found the New South Wales Legislative Council not unwilling to co-operate. In 1846 a Select Committee considered the 'Renewal of Transportation' and advanced some ingenious arguments as to the potential advantages (at least to the employers whose interests the Legislative Council jealously safeguarded). Groups employed on public works were anathematized: 'It seems to your committee that as, in the physical world it is an invariable law that all agglomerations of animal or vegetable matter heat and putrify and decay; so, in the moral world, there can be no aggregations of human beings, whether in Hulks or Gaols, or Penitentiaries or

Gangs, without calling this putrescent agency into existence . . .' Prisoners would be much safer put to work by benevolent employers than if allowed to mix with other depraved characters. Solitary confinement as practised at Pentonville might well be redemptive, but what could be more solitary and more conducive to future good than the life conditions of a convict working on a squatter's station?

Contemplate the life of a shepherd or hutkeeper, thus situated; placed two or three in number at most, in a small hut composed of bark and slabs, their nearest neighbours persons circumstanced like themselves, seldom within three miles, frequently not within ten; two out of the three of these men obliged in all weather to follow their flocks from sun-rise to sun-set; the third man, the hut-keeper – left all day alone to guard the hut, shift the folds, cook for his companions the out-going shepherds, and afterwards to watch their flocks by night, in order to protect them from the native dogs; there is evidently among persons thus circumstanced (and in our boundless wilds thousands are, and tens of thousands more, may be so placed), but brief time for converse after the labour of the day, and before retirement for the night to their pallets, and briefer time still between their rising in the morning, and departure with their flocks on their daily round. To the profligate, who has been accustomed to the bustle and dissipations of cities, what life can be more monotonous and irksome?[21]

The assignment system, the Legislative Council argued, should be revived for convicts of proven good character (no employer wanted to take on the old lags). If no fewer than 5,000 convicts annually were guaranteed, to be accompanied by an equal number of women (Van Diemen's Land was reported to be worse than 'the worst days of Sodom and Gomorrah', full proof of which allegations was available 'in the fearful records of the Jericho Station'), the Legislative Council would be willing to concur.

Reasonably enough, the free workers did not agree. Robert Lowe, conveniently forgetting that he had until recently been an advocate for continuing transportation, now energetically took the lead in opposition to it: 'The spirit of a better age is abroad,' Lowe predicted, speaking to an appreciative Sydney audience.

Unsupported by slave labour – unsustained by the profits of the lash – the landed aristocracy of the colony – the holders of princely domains – will sink overwhelmed by their own greatness.

I shall let it go forth through every British possession proclaiming that no faith is so hollow – no promise so rotten – no word so valueless, as that pledged by the head of the Colonial Office. There is no weapon in the artillery of subterfuge, –

no trick, no evasion – no falsehood or contrivance, that is not practised at the Colonial Office, that grave of colonial hope and colonial liberty. (Cheers)

Lord Grey was ironic:

I think the apprehensions of the colonists as to being demoralized by convicts are not a little visionary and that the danger would be rather that even the worst of our convicts would find that they had something to learn from the speakers at public meetings in . . . [respect to] truth and decency.[22]

But he was to be obliged to concede the point. The first shipload of 'exiles' under the new dispensation was greeted with defiance when it touched at Port Phillip in March 1849, the inhabitants were no longer willing to 'consent on any terms to the importation of British criminals', and the *Hashemy* was sent on to Sydney, to be met on 8 June with public indignation but some private gratitude. A rally was addressed by Lowe threatening armed resistance to 'the worst and most degrading slavery' and 'oppressive tyranny'. He concluded to 'immense cheering':

I can see from this meeting the time is not far distant when we shall assert our freedom not by words alone. As in America, oppression was the parent of independence, so shall it be in this colony . . . As sure as the seed shall grow into the plant, and that plant to the tree, in all times, and in all nations, so shall injustice and tyranny ripen into rebellion, and rebellion into independence.[23]

The Governor refused the demands of Lowe's supporters to return the convicts, more than half of whom had already been engaged by labour-hungry squatters, but in London Lord Grey accepted the inevitable; transportation would be ended, but the Order in Council would not be withdrawn. New South Wales had proved notoriously fickle in its communal views; indeed three more shiploads of exiles, one of which had also been rejected by La Trobe at Melbourne, unloaded their cargoes at Sydney and at Moreton Bay without further objection. But other colonies might be more accommodating. Surely the Cape of Good Hope, where John Montagu, previously of Van Diemen's Land, was now colonial secretary, would take some decent young Irish convicts? But the Africans would not, and the Governor, Sir Harry Smith, had to seek military protection against the enraged citizens. For a time it seemed that the southern ocean was to be populated by wandering convicts looking for a home as another shipload was turned away from Cape Town by vociferous protests and diverted to that inescapably convenient receptacle, Tasmania. Opinion there, as in the mainland colonies, was divided. Earnest moralists pointed to moral contamination – one convenient case of cannibalism was much publicized, although it had occurred thirteen years previously – and they were strongly supported by workmen, objecting to wage competition; by contrast, the large landowners enthusiastically advocated the importation of cheap labour. Some landowners were prospering mightily: Roderic O'Connor, who had admittedly arrived already rich, in his own ship, owned more than 70,000 acres (his half-brother, Fergus, was the leading English Chartist, but Roderic had few democratic leanings) and was for long able to influence his Legislative Council colleagues in resisting popular clamour. All Tasmanians, however, were united in protest against the British government's reluctance to pay for the expense of the convicts.

Only one colony seemed unequivocally willing to welcome convicts. Western Australia was bankrupt and could only be kept going by admitting 'exiles'. The colonists' plea for help was answered once a minor difficulty, that the commissioners of Pentonville prison did not consider Western Australia a suitable place for their reformed convicts, was overcome. The Western Australians wanted their convicts 'neither too wicked nor too good' – not 'lifers', in short, but men with nevertheless a substantial sentence to serve. They were unsure what to expect. Captain Edmund Henderson, another sapper, who brought over the first contingent, reported that the general view was to see 'men all chained together guarded with loaded firelocks, clothed in yellow and cursing horribly'. In fact, the well-conducted, carefully selected and industrious exiles, subsidized by Imperial funds, and supervised by the intelligent and liberal Henderson, proved the salvation of Western Australia. The convicts were so well behaved that the new gaol built for the confinement of second-offenders proved unnecessary, although some of Henderson's good work was undone when the humane Arthur Kennedy was replaced as Governor in 1862 by John Hampton, whose experience in Tasmania led him to use methods of considerable brutality. But during the eighteen years when transportation continued the influx of nearly 10,000 convicts revived the flagging economy.[24]

'Extreme inconvenience and loss'

In one sense, the New South Wales politicians had brought upon their own heads the separation of what was to become Victoria by dragging their feet on the district councils. 'The municipalities have only a nominal existence,' Lord Grey complained in July 1847. 'The Legislative Council has absorbed all the other powers of the Colonial State. The principle of self-government in the districts the most remote from Sydney is therefore acted upon almost as imperfectly as if no action had been taken . . . The Port Phillip representation has become an unreal and illusory, not a substantial, enjoyment of representative government . . .' – a conviction which his own election, by the Port Phillip voters, *in absentia*, to the New South Wales Legislative Council doubtless strengthened.[25]

Grey was also convinced, and with good reason, of the need to establish some form of co-ordinating central body. The inconveniences of having independent competitive states, whose differences could be settled only by extended and protracted judgements from London, were made clear in the 1840s, when New South Wales imposed a duty of 1s. a bushel on all imports of wheat. Van Diemen's Land retaliated in 1846 by abolishing all existing concessions made in favour of New South Wales products, thus provoking a serious debate in the Sydney Legislative Council. The prudent and experienced Edward Deas Thomson, clerk to the Council since 1829 and colonial secretary from 1837, politely pointed out that the problem was initially one of the Legislature's own making, and advised that some central control over all the Australian colonies should be established. After Gipps left office in July 1846, tired and ill – he died within a twelvemonth – Sir Charles Fitzroy, the amiable and newly arrived Governor, responded by suggesting to London the appointment of a Governor General. Suitable precedents existed; Sir Henry Pottinger had been sent out to South Africa earlier that year as High Commissioner to straighten out the tangled affairs of the Cape Colony, Griqualand, British Kaffraria and Natal. High Commissioners were needed only when contact with foreign powers or tribes was involved; in colonial Australia, where Aborigines could not, or would not, present such a united front as the Griqua or Afrikaners did in Africa, a Governor General would be the appropriate grade, and indeed in 1851 Fitzroy was himself created the first Australian Governor General.

In London, however, Lord Grey had more radical ideas. Whatever might happen to Port Phillip, Van Diemen's Land, South Australia and Western Australia were already separated, to different degrees, with Lieutenant Governors and administration appointed by the Colonial Office, and enjoying de facto independence of Sydney. It would reduce his officers' workload and make future developments easier if there were to be a federation, at least of the Australian colonies which had already achieved representative government – New South Wales and Van Diemen's Land, with Port Phillip awaiting formal separation. He pointed out that 'altogether independent legislatures, each exerting absolute authority' on tariffs would produce 'only extreme inconvenience and loss'. Some method must be devised to control such inter-state affairs as tariffs, post 'and the formation of roads, railways or other internal communications.'

Anticipating some move towards centralization, Grey had informed Fitzroy, on 31 July 1847, that

Some method will also be devised for enabling the various legislatures of the several Australian colonies to co-operate with each other in the enactment of such laws as may be necessary for regulating the interests common to those possessions collectively: such, for example, as the imposition of duties of import and export, the conveyance of letters, and the formation of roads, railways and other internal communications traversing any two or more of such colonies. I will not attempt at the present moment to do more than to indicate the general principles on which it is proposed to legislate. The details will be the subject of further and of very attentive consideration.[26]

'Very attentive consideration' was duly given by a parliamentary committee, which recommended, in April 1849 that

one of the Governors of the Australian Colonies should always hold from Your Majesty a commission constituting him Governor-General of Australia. We think that he should be authorized to convene a body to be called the General Assembly of Australia at any time and at any place within Your Majesty's Australian dominions which he might see fit to appoint for that purpose.

The General Assembly would be:

empowered to legislate on import and export duties, postal services, inter-colonial roads, canals, railways; beacons, lighthouses, shipping dues; weights and measures; the establishment and jurisdiction of a Supreme Court: all other common matters by consent of the colonial Legislatures: and the distribution of money in proportion to the receipts from a colony.

Once again, these were purely recommendations, to be implemented only when the colonists themselves wished.[27]

That they did not. That useful device for avoiding issues, the nomination of a select committee, was resorted to in both New South Wales and Victoria. Only old William Charles Wentworth persisted in attempting to persuade the Colonial Office to press ahead; but by that time – 1857 – Grey had moved on. It was an idea whose time had not yet come. Federation would only be possible when colonial administrations had matured and jealousies subsided, and when British governments were seen to be capable of more than intermittent attention to colonial affairs. As it turned out, the Australian colonies would have done well to heed the Colonial Office's advice. If there had been even a short experience of local governments, then the chaos of the early years of responsible administrations would have been, if not entirely avoided – government succeeded government with bewildering rapidity – at least improved. Had some inter-colonial body been established, much unproductive squabbling, and the lasting absurdity of multiple railway gauges, would have been avoided.

Little enthusiasm was shown. Wentworth, worried that the seat of a federal government might be moved to Melbourne, produced a draft Bill, but the New South Wales Legislative Council refused even to discuss it. The only constitutional sign of any Federation was the titular post of Governor General, but even this was quietly abolished in 1861.

One proposal that the Colonial Office succeeded in suppressing, and which would certainly later be regarded as a narrow escape, was the importation of Chinese or Indian labour to replace the now-ended supply of convicts, an issue pressed in 1843 by the New South Wales merchants. James Stephen had refused to agree, warning of the potential effects in words that a few years later would have won the warmest approbation in New South Wales. Paul Knaplund, Stephen's biographer, records that

employers in Sydney fearing a shortage of laborers, petitioned for the importation of coolies. To this Stephen offered the strongest objections. Calling to mind the results of the introduction of Negroes into the West Indies, he warned of the evil results flowing from the immigration of a new alien race so different from European in religion and in social habits.

James Stephen himself laid down the principle of

It being the most arduous if not the first duty of a Government to consult for the permanent interest of Society as opposed to the immediate interest of the most active and powerful of its members, and to watch over the welfare of the many rather than the present advantage of the few; and to protect those whose only property is in the power of labour against the rapacity of the rich.[28]

Another problem agitating New South Wales was that of education, which paralleled very closely that which had arisen in Britain and Ireland. Control of schools was fiercely contested between the denominations, each anxious to inculcate their particular brand of religion, and the reformers, dedicated to achieving national standards that could approach those obtaining on the Continent, especially in Germany. In his previous post as Chief Secretary for Ireland, Lord Stanley had introduced a system of 'National' non-denominational education, and hoped that its real, if limited, success, might be reproduced in New South Wales. The Church of England's position was equivocal: it was not, as in England and Ireland (although soon to lose its position there) the 'established' but the 'official' Church. In Scotland the established Church was Presbyterian, which gave the aggressive Presbyterian minister Lang a strong position among the many Australian Scots. Already by 1833 Governor Bourke had ensured the end of Lord Bathurst's attempt to appropriate Crown Lands exclusively to the Church of England through the Clergy and School Lands Corporation, and the restoration of this dominance was one of the guiding ambitions of Bishop William Broughton.[29]

Broughton was first appointed as archdeacon of New South Wales in 1829, and then as the first bishop of Australia in 1836. In an interesting link with the colony's past he was enthroned by old Samuel Marsden, who had first arrived as assistant chaplain to the penal settlement forty-two years previously. Broughton had vehemently opposed Governor Bourke's plans to bring in non-denominational education. A powerful common sentiment was that education should be, following the French example, 'free, compulsory and secular'; to this the Churches all objected, insisting that Christian education – that is, of course, their own particular brand – should be taught. Catholics were particularly vehement against national schools as 'seed-plots of future immorality, infidelity, and lawlessness, calculated to debase the standard of human excellence, and to corrupt the political, social and individual life of future citizens'. The eventual result was a draw, with both systems working side by side, but the sectarian animosity continued and flourished. Both Ireland and Australia remained ahead of Britain in primary education (Scotland, with a school in every parish since the Reformation, was always in the lead). Whereas, in spite of Lord John Russell's arguments, England only established a National Board of Education in 1870, the New South Wales Legislative Council created such a board twenty-three years earlier; public finance, which was given in England only in 1833, had been provided for educational purposes from Governor King's day onwards. Australia soon became a literate society, but not one where intellectual distinction was too highly regarded.

In all these issues the New South Wales Legislative Council found itself at odds with British government policies. In so far as Legislative Council members represented the majority opinion – and as they usually pressed graziers' interests, this was by no means invariable – the controversies encouraged demands for self-government. Yet more democracy was still hardly welcome to the well-entrenched landed classes.

The Systematic Violation of the Law

One issue proved intransigent, that of the fate of the Aborigines. Something of the initial concern so fervently expressed by Lord Glenelg had subsided. Russell had never shared the full enthusiasm of the 'Exeter Hall' men, and Grey, concerned with the affairs of forty-three colonies, refused to be worried overmuch about powerless and scattered communities of the original inhabitants. In his six years of office he had to cope with a full-scale war and the reluctant acquisition of a new colony in South Africa, Maori resistance and colonial land-grabbing in New Zealand, new constitutions in Canada, deadlock over old constitutions in Jamaica and an incipient war with the Chinese empire; colonial governments must be expected to keep order in their own backyards without the Colonial Office being involved. Previous British government initiatives had resulted in some action on the ground, the standing of Aboriginals as British subjects having been reinforced by an Act of 1843 admitting unsworn evidence to be heard in Court (unsworn because it was considered that uninstructed Aboriginals could not appreciate the significance of an oath). Following George Robinson's example in Tasmania a Protectorate system had been initiated and aboriginal reserves established in Victoria, but there was not much official enthusiasm for them. The Aborigines Committee of the House of Commons pointed out that until recently the Port Phillip district had been the undisputed property of the Aborigines: 'it is demanding very little indeed on their behalf that no expenditure should be withheld which can be incurred judiciously for the maintenance of missionaries, who should be employed to instruct the tribes, and of protectors whose duty it was to defend them.' Protectors should 'take seriously their duty to protect. They should inquire into all cases where any Aborigines were killed or injured or their property damaged, and they should defend in court any who might be accused of offences.' In the circumstances of the great spaces of pastoral Australia this was absurdly unrealistic; Protectors were men of only modest standing in colonial society, generally unwilling to do as both Marsden and Gipps insisted was essential, to 'itinerate, to traverse their districts attaching themselves to the different clans, identifying them, learning their languages and assessing their numbers and condition'. One, the Methodist William Thomas, Protector of the Port Phillip and Gippsland district from 1839 to 1848, a 'man of almost childlike simplicity of manners and . . . goodness of heart', faithfully did so, following the Aborigines in their wanderings, living in a tent and collecting what knowledge and understanding he could.

Thomas might be credited with 'striking success in settling intertribal disputes and preventing racial strife', but he was a rarity. The sheer speed of the settlers' advance and the Aboriginal dispossession prevented any extensive official protection.[30]

Even so, it could be argued that colonial authorities sometimes showed themselves capable of defending Aboriginal interests. Sordid small horrors perpetrated on remote stations were often unrecorded and some stories of atrocities were probably invented or exaggerated, but others have the ring of truth. The Reverend Lancelot Threlkeld, by no means an unprejudiced witness, recorded the account of a magistrate who saw forty-five Aboriginal skulls boiled down for export to Britain, the result of a mounted police massacre near Bathurst; the number may well be questioned, but many skeletal remains did end up in British collections. Only when a major incident was followed by a methodical investigation could action be taken. The best known of these took place at Myall Creek, near Inverell, in the New England Ranges, in July 1838. It was an area of new settlement – the botanist, Allan Cunningham, was the first European to penetrate the region in 1827 – where the influx of pastoralists had provoked indignant Aboriginal resistance. Attacks on isolated shepherds, five having been killed in the area, resulted in an expedition under Major James Nunn, instructed by Lieutenant Colonel Snodgrass (Dickens did not invent all of his improbable names) to 'use your utmost exertion to suppress these outrages'. An affray took place in January 1838 at Waterloo Creek, a long day's ride away from Myall Creek, in which a troop of mounted police charged an Aboriginal camp, killing at least nine and probably more, although nothing like the 300 that some commentators have advanced. A later inquiry produced evidence that some members of the Aboriginal party had indeed been implicated in the original murder of the white shepherds.[31]

Nunn's raid was nothing more than one of the inevitable brutalities of a colonial frontier, but Myall Creek was a very different affair, carried out by an unauthorized band – almost all serving or former convicts – who fell on a group of twenty-eight Aboriginal men, women and children, killing them all, and attempting to burn the bodies. When the station overseer found the bodies, he reported the killings to the authorities. Threlkeld described in some detail what was said to have occurred:

This year a party of Blacks consisting of almost 26 were at work at a station, the overseer told them to go away as the stockmen were out after the Blacks to punish them, they *did* not go, the stockmen came, ripped open the bellies of the blacks, killed the women, took the children by the legs and dashed their brains out against the trees. They then made a triangular log fire to burn the bodies, and reserved two little girls about 7 years old for Lascivious purposes and because they were too small for them they cut them with knives.

Threlkeld was able to provide witnesses to this particular outrage.

The two lads marked in the list, named *David* and *Billy*, are both witnesses to the Atrocities which have been committed in that Quarter, and both must be obtained to render affectual the Evidence, as the lad *Billy* was the Eye witness to the murders, but does not speak good English; whereas *David* speaks not only good English, but, understands the language beyond the Gwider, as well as that at Liverpool plains down to Patrick's Plains; he was also at the station at the time of the murders – Their wives are the two girls who were so inhumanly cut for lascivious purposes by the White men alleged to be the murderers, and who gave the two girls to those two lads to be their wives, they also should be obtained with the two lads to complete the chain of evidence. They were at the station alluded to, two or three months back and no doubt can be found near those parts.

The men involved – who seemed not to realize they had done anything particularly wrong – were identified and charged. A public subscription was raised to provide defence counsel, and the men were acquitted. 'It was with exertion that the Chief Justice could prevent the audience from *cheering*' the *Sydney Monitor* reported: 'What will the Colony come to if Gentlemen feel justified in soliciting subscriptions to pay Counsel to defend their pet murderers?'[32]

This was too much for Governor Gipps, newly arrived in February 1838 and supported by J. H. Plunkett, the Irish Catholic Attorney General, dedicated to impartial justice. Plunkett was himself an example of Irish Catholics not unduly hampered by the restrictive laws of his native land. Under eighteenth-century penal laws, Plunkett lands in Roscommon had been held in trust on their behalf by Protestant neighbours. Plunkett attended Trinity College Dublin, anathema to rigid Catholics. He benefited by the Catholic Relief Act of 1793 to become a barrister and at the early age of 29 was appointed Solicitor General of New South Wales. It helped, of course, that he was a valued supporter of Daniel O'Connell, and nephew of the Earl of Fingall.[33] A second trial was ordered by Plunkett, at which seven of the accused were found guilty and subsequently hanged. A storm of infuriated public opinion broke over the Governor's head. The executions were held privately, in the prison under military guard, to avoid anticipated violence. The *Sydney Gazette* for 12 December 1839 sagely commented:

Reason and experience alike conspire to impress us with the belief that the unhappy beings who have just suffered, if they did not actually act under the orders of some higher and concealed party, were at least persuaded that in doing as they did they were acting in accordance with the wishes of their superiors, whom it was both their interest and desire to please.

Eliza Dunlop, an Irishwoman married to a police magistrate and Protector of Aborigines, commemorated the massacre in one of the better known pieces of nineteenth-century Australian verse, 'The Aboriginal Mother':

> Now who will teach thee, dearest,
> To poise the shield, and spear,
> To wield the *koopin*, or to throw
> The *boomerring*, void of fear;
> To breast the river in its might:
> The mountain tracks to tread?
> The echoes of my homeless heart
> Reply – the dead, the dead![34]

One interesting result of the Myall Creek massacre was the start of a rumour, in the same issue of the *Sydney Gazette*, that mass killings of Aborigines were being effected by means of poisoned flour.

After the usual salutations, the countryman asked – 'Have they hanged the men?'

'Yes' replied the citizen. 'I understand they have.'

'It's a damned shame,' said the countryman. 'But we have fallen on a safer game in our part of the country.'

'Indeed, pray what is it?'

'Oh we poison them, and have done so to a good many already,' explained the countryman. 'Serves them right too.'

It is well-known that arsenic is used in great quantities by the shepherds of our interior in curing scab in sheep. It is kept in every hut at every sheep station in the country. The hut-keepers make 'wheaten cakes' and they have only to mingle a portion of arsenic in a particular cake and mark it, and give it to the Blacks as a present. It will despatch them rapidly or lingeringly, according to the quantity infused.

Ten years after Myall Creek, one Thomas Coutts was accused – by his fellow squatters – of giving poisoned dampers to his Aborigines, and taken in custody to Sydney. In his defence the *Sydney Morning Herald* claimed that two of his men and a boy had been murdered and half his flock killed. It does not seem that Coutts was ever tried for the allegations. Governor Fitzroy was very much on the settlers' side, but since Plunkett was still Attorney General, and would certainly have wanted to prosecute, it may be that the evidence against Coutts was shaky, but colonial governments would find it more difficult to ensure justice for the Aborigines, once deprived of Colonial Office support.[35]

Back in London, Lord John Russell concurred:

You cannot mistake the solicitude of Her Majesty's Government on the subject of the Aborigines of New Holland. It is impossible to contemplate the conditions and prospects of that unfortunate race without the deepest commiseration. Still it is impossible to forget that the original aggression was our own, – that we have never yet performed the sacred duty of making any systematic or considerable attempt to impart to the former occupiers of New South Wales the blessings of Christianity, or knowledge of the Arts and advantages of civilised life. To the Aboriginal Race of New Holland protection against injustice, and the enjoyment of every social advantage which our superior wealth and knowledge at once confer on us the power and impose on us the duty of imparting to them.[36]

The truth of the matter was that the effective power London could deploy in Australia was limited. In the not very long run, what a vocal majority of colonists wanted would be given to them; only in the Cape Colony, reluctant to bear the costs of defence, and Western Australia, still lagging behind, was responsible government delayed. The thinly populated, widely dispersed Australian colonies could only be governed by mutual consent, by the commonly accepted traditions of the rule of law, traditions which could only be asserted in some places and at some times. James Stephen accepted this frankly enough. Attempting to mollify the South Australian Commission indignant at the competition coming from Port Phillip, the under-secretary wrote;

In the remoter part of the vast regions comprised within the range of the Australian Colonies, the power of the law is unavoidably feeble when opposed by the predominant inclinations of any large body of the people. In such a country, unpopular regulations, unless supported by a force either of police or soldiery irresisting and overwhelming must become little more than a dead letter . . . Their proceedings instead of being condemned and opposed, are countenanced and supported by the society to which they belong. Consequently an extensive territory at a distance from the seat of Government has been occupied by unauthorised settlers of all classes, by the wealthy not less than by the poor, and, in this systematic violation of the law, each class find support and encouragement in the example and common interest of its various members. With the most earnest desire to repress this growing evil, local authorities have experienced the impossibility of making an effectual resistance to the general will.

The case of Port Phillip is but an example and illustration of this prevailing triumph of popular feelings over positive law. In the commencement of the year 1835, a large body of persons appeared in that vicinity, and have formed themselves into an organised association, took possession of considerable tracts of land under grants from neighbouring chiefs. With this semblance of title, they readily attracted new settlers, and established a correspondence and agency with a wealthy society in this country from whom they made arrangements for obtaining pecuniary and other aids. So strong had become the desire of joining the new settlement, that it is described by Colonel Arthur as a 'Mania' affecting all classes in that Colony. Within a very short space of time, Port Phillip assumed the appearance of an established settlement with extensive and valuable flocks and herds.

Such has been the progress of this adventure that it seems not unreasonable to infer that, before any instructions from this country could arrive at the place, the population would have become so numerous as to render hopeless any attempt to dislodge them either by authority or by force . . .

If it be answered that the Governor should have been directed to coerce this lawless invasion of the lands of the crown by force, it might be replied that there is not in the Australian Colonies any power, civil or military, available for such a service. The troops and the police in New South Wales and Van Diemen's Land are not more than adequate to the ordinary demands upon them. Further Lord Glenelg could not contemplate without insuperable repugnance the employment of hostile measures against the King's subjects for such a purpose.

That was in October 1836; it was another fourteen years before what amounted to colonial self-government was established, the delay being partly attributable to the interlude of Tory government between 1841 and 1847, but also, and in large measure, to the failure of the colonists to agree among themselves.

6

The Capacity to Govern Themselves

'The freedom and the institutions of the mother country'

If New South Wales had ever been a factor of strategic Imperial importance, as its first advocates had suggested, rather than a convenient penological experiment, by mid-century this seemed no longer to be so. Singapore had been acquired in 1818 by Stamford Raffles on behalf of the Honourable East India Company, followed a few years later by the percipient Captain Charles Elliot's selection of Hong Kong as a base for British merchants (his chief, Lord Palmerston, was indignant; complaining that such a useless island would never become 'a mart of trade'). Together with Trincomalee in Ceylon, ceded by the Dutch in 1815, a chain of naval stations thus safeguarded the route to China and the Pacific. Fremantle was later to be of some utility as a naval base, but the Australian colonies remained low among British priorities. They were less of a nuisance, however, than South Africa, where frontier wars ensured that military expenses continued high, or even New Zealand, where the Maori were formidable opponents; and the scattered Australian settlements at least denied the continent to foreign competitors.

It was not, however, the complaints of New South Wales legislators that eventually moved the British government towards action, but the revived outbreak of violence in Canada. Until 1847 the Canadian government had been precariously Tory, but in that year an election gave a majority to the Liberals – the Canadian parties being even then much more clearly defined than those in Australia, and remaining so until the turn of the century. Governor General Lord Elgin immediately appointed a Liberal Cabinet, headed by Robert Baldwin, who had previously played a considerable part in shaping Lord Durham's opinions. The disappointed Tories took to the streets, the excuse being a Bill to compensate those who had incurred losses in the 1837 rebellion. Elgin's carriage had to be galloped away under a hail of missiles from an aggressive crowd, who subsequently burned the

Parliament House; the violence was followed by a call for annexation by the United States. While this last was not a danger that had to be feared in Australia, the possibility of civil unrest seemed real enough, at least from the viewpoint of London. Even the Cape Colonists, solidly loyal after the recalcitrant Boers had moved themselves off to the interior on their Great Trek, but with their discontent fired by the threat of shiploads of convicts being forced upon them, had obliged High Commissioner Sir Harry Smith to protect his gubernatorial ball with the bayonets of British troops. The alternative to such measures, that of renouncing control over colonial affairs, became inevitable.

The parliamentary committee chaired by Lord Grey which had reported in April 1849 had been principally concerned with the separation of Port Phillip and the provision of a new constitution that would also apply to Van Diemen's Land and South Australia, although not, as yet, to Western Australia. As a starting point the committee recommended that each of those colonies, together with New South Wales, should have a Legislative Council, two-thirds of whose members would be elected, on an extended franchise, with control of local government and the judiciary. The committee were perhaps confused by the opposing arguments coming from New South Wales, and few specific recommendations were made for the future of that colony. It was better, they considered, not to depart 'from the general principle which leaves to the local legislature of every colony the creation of other local institutions, and the enactment of any laws which are to have their operation within the local limits of that colony'. (This left open the undecided question of what such limits might be.) Each colony had the right to 'A legislature in which the representatives of the people at large should enjoy and exercise their constitutional authority' – a very general prerogative indeed, one which might well give rise to apprehension among those nervous of 'the people at large', and which could easily be interpreted as signifying 'responsible' government, although this phrase appeared in no official document.

Grey's initial doubts as to the suitability of Australians for self-government, which he continued to discuss with Elgin in their personal correspondence, were not entirely countered by Elgin's reasoning: what was acceptable in Canada, with its by then eighty years of experience of local governments, might not be suitable in colonies which had been so recently penal settlements. Grey specifically denied that it was his intention to introduce any important constitutional changes in Australia, and rejected any claims from New South Wales for more extensive legislative powers. He was not prepared to vary the legislative procedure which was followed

throughout the Empire, of measured progress from Crown Colony to elected councils and representative government, merely in order to apply 'an untried scheme in New South Wales', but he was at least mollified by Elgin describing the evolution of responsible government in Canada, that 'community so full of lusty life'; Lord John Russell, however, always more liberal than most of his colleagues, needed little convincing that colonial self-government should be pushed forward.[1]

The Bill introduced in the House of Commons in June 1849 was based on the report of Lord Grey's committee and established the principle that 'representative' governments should be formed in the Australian colonies. The committee had not gone so far as to extend this to 'responsible' government, although clear indication that such a step would be almost inevitable was contained in the powers that would enable colonial governments to amend their own constitutions – subject always to Crown confirmation. Objections that were raised in parliamentary discussion concerned inter-colonial questions, mainly about protective tariffs and the projected inter-colonial council – this last being opposed by the smaller colonies, concerned that they would be swamped by the overwhelming predominance of New South Wales. June, however, was a little late in the year for serious parliamentary discussion, as London society began its annual transhumance, and the Bill ran out of time, which gave another opportunity for colonial views to be considered. It was reintroduced the following February by the Prime Minister, Lord John Russell, himself.[2]

The debate in the House of Commons on 8 February 1850 considered the committee's findings, now embodied in a second Bill, and in so doing settled the future of Australia. It was unusually well attended, with 345 members voting, a very great number for any colonial question. Molesworth, in the course of two long speeches in which he advanced his own model Australian constitution, specifically raised the spectre of violence, complaining of the ten years' delay since Russell had first introduced his abortive Bill on the New South Wales constitution: that 'it was by rebellion that Canada obtained responsible government, that it is by threats and menaces that the men of the Cape are successfully striving to save their colony from convict pollution.' He perceived the same threat of rebellion for New South Wales, due to the government's 'ignorance, negligence, vacillation, breach of faith and tyranny'.

Most of the speakers concerned themselves with the speculative question of whether a single-chamber parliament was to be preferred to the traditional pattern of two chambers – a Legislative Assembly corresponding to the House of Commons and a Legislative Council playing a similar part to that

of the House of Lords – but Russell cut right across such arguments, appealing to his ancestor's part in the Glorious Revolution of 1688: 'wherever Englishmen have been sent, or have chosen to settle, they have carried with them the freedom and the institutions of the mother country.' Once established, they should be left to govern themselves with the least possible interference. 'It is only in rare cases that the authority of the Crown ought to be interposed . . . with reference to local affairs, the executive and legal authorities of the colony are the best judges.'[3]

According to Australian colonists, the 'freedom and institutions' were nothing more nor less than the rights of contemporary Britons (the United Kingdom had included Scotland since 1707 and Ireland since 1801, but Englishmen often brushed aside the claims of the other countries) though these were, at the time, distinctly limited – a restricted suffrage, open voting at the hustings rather than a secret ballot, a hereditary upper house, and so forth. Australia very soon acquired institutions that were much more democratic, but such progress was not foreseen by the Bill. The Australian Colonies Government Act (13 & 14 Vict., c. 59) provided that Victoria, South Australia and Van Diemen's Land were all to have Legislative Councils, two-thirds to be elected on a restricted franchise, following the New South Wales model. This was a modest advance, and its chief merit, from the colonists' point of view, was that the Governors would be expected to follow the advice of the majority of their Councillors.

But however wary the Bill had been of constitutional innovations, the Act contained one decisive clause (number 32). While each colony was to be given a similar initial constitution, the Legislative Councils were allowed extensive powers to modify their own constitutions, to alter the electoral laws and 'to establish instead of the Legislative Council, a Council and a House of Representatives . . . to consist respectively of such Members to be appointed or elected respectively by such Persons and in such manner as . . . shall be determined' by the colonial legislatures. In plain language, this provision was equivalent to allowing the colonies to select whatever form of government they wished; in effect, to act as constitutional conventions in shaping their future forms of government. It was a remarkable concession, and one which carried with it some dangers – when this permission was repeated seventy-two years later in the Better Government of Ireland Act, and subsequently exercised by the Northern Ireland government to perpetuate Protestant Unionist hegemony, it spawned a multitude of troubles.

The House of Lords was naturally suspicious of such radical innovations. Grey had succeeded in squeezing through approval of Elgin's actions in the House of Lords by only three votes, and Clause 32 was, Grey admitted

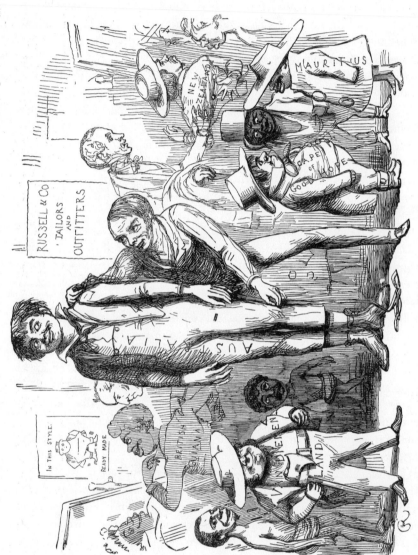

Even before gold was discovered Punch saw Australia as more than ready for new constitutions.

when he introduced the Bill, 'of a novel character', but without it 'he had no hesitation in saying that the Bill was most materially imperfect'. Once free institutions had been established in the colonies 'they ought not to be lightly altered by Parliament without the desire and sanction of the local legislatures'. There were to be some controls, in that Bills could not be immediately ratified by the Governors, but must be reserved for thirty days in the British Parliament before the Queen assented. Stanley, now in opposition, was suspicious and asked what 'power of interference either House would have under such circumstance'. Lord Grey was forced to acknowledge that this was very little: 'They would have the power of interposing a check by an address to the Crown', a statement which Stanley greeted with outspoken incredulity.[4]

Russell quite specifically saw the 1850 Act as the first step in colonial independence, telling the House of Commons:

I anticipate . . . that some of the colonies may so grow . . . that they may say 'Our strength is now sufficient for us to become independent of England. The link is now become onerous to us. The time has come when we think we can, in amity and alliance with England, maintain our independence'. I do not think the time is yet approaching. But let us give them, as far as we can, the capacity to govern themselves . . . and whatever may happen, we of this great Empire shall have the consolation of saying that we have contributed to the happiness of the world.

Writing privately, James Stephen was more specific: the policy was one of 'cheerfully relaxing, one after the other, the bonds of authority as soon as the colony itself clearly desired that relaxation . . . It remains for the Canadians to cut the last cable which anchors them to us. But it is for them to take that step and to assume the consequent responsibility. The same is in progress with the Australian colonies.' He went on to dismiss the rest of the Empire – always excluding India, not part of his own job description – as 'detached islands . . . wretched burdens . . . which in an evil hour we assumed but which we have no right to lay down again'.[5]

The decision to allow the Australian colonies to design their own constitutions was unprecedentedly bold. Vast in extent and potential wealth – South Australia and New South Wales before 1860 were each larger than Western Europe, yet the whole of Australia had a smaller population than that of many an English county (in 1857 Yorkshire had 300,000 more inhabitants) and only in New South Wales had there been a few years' experience of an elected council. At that time – the situation forty years later, when a new Federal constitution was being discussed, had greatly changed – the only constitutional model available was that of Britain. All other major countries had undergone drastic and rapid changes since the French Revolution; the only other democratic country whose institutions might serve as an example was the United States, and in the 1850s it was only too clear that America was heading for disaster. Even with this restriction the potential choices were extensive: a parliament could be composed of two chambers – Assembly and Council – or only one; qualifications for membership and the franchise could be whatever the colonists wished. Plural voting could be retained or abolished, electoral districts could be redesigned, the ballot could be public or secret – even women might be admitted to the vote. Apart from any powers retained by the British government, the new colonial governments would approach the status of sovereign states. The communities' views were canvassed, and a vigorous public debate ensued (although it was often only a minority that participated). Public opinion, as reported by the Governors, was weighed alongside the recommendations of the existing governments. It could have been disastrous; very few of the African governments hurried into independence after the Second World War did not degenerate into corrupt oligarchies or blatant dictatorships, but the Australian colonies (although corruption was not, and is not, unknown) shook down into self-governing states within a very short time. In some respects they became exemplars of democracy; adult male suffrage without property qualifications, equal electoral districts, votes for women, secret ballots, payment of MPs, were all achieved in some Australian colonies well before they were effected in the United Kingdom.

The task was initially harder because no powerful political parties had developed, or were indeed to develop for many years. Even in Britain the lines between Whig/Liberals and Tory/Conservative/Unionists were only beginning to solidify. In the Australian colonies some interests were prominent, those of the pastoralists being the most powerful, and some individuals attracted personal support almost irrespective of their policies, which often fluctuated unpredictably, but neither interests nor individuals coalesced into distinct and disciplined parties. Few Australians had experience of government except as officials; local government, which in Britain was becoming a school for national politics, had not developed extensively in the colonies.

Much depended on the abilities of those Governors who found themselves at the head of the first responsible Colonial administrations. New South Wales was fortunate in Gipps's successor. Sir Charles Fitzroy, who took post in August 1846, was affable, well connected (grandson of one duke and son-in-law of another), and experienced – briefly – in Parliament and more extensively in colonial administration. Tact and flexibility, both of which Fitzroy possessed in abundance, were very much needed in New South Wales, where politics were becoming acrimonious. The constitutionalists formed if not a party, at least a pressure group, akin to the British radicals, made up of individuals of diverse views; old William Wentworth, yearning for a colonial aristocracy paralleling the aristocratic Whigs, and Robert Lowe, able and acerbic, who went on to become (a very unpopular) Chancellor of the Exchequer at Westminster, were uneasy colleagues for the perennially active and quarrelsome Lang, who published a stream of books and letters warning Britain that only immediate and unconditional self-government would avert revolution in Australia, or for that matter in Ireland.[6]

The colonists, or at least their conservative leaders, were not much impressed with the 1850 Act, and the British concession on future emendation was brushed aside in an outburst of indignation from New South Wales. The old grievance, that of control of the public purse, remained; the most important objection of the New South Wales Legislative Council was that the 'Waste Lands', the vast unallocated areas of New South Wales, remained under control of the Colonial Office and of the Governor. Only when the colonists themselves were allowed to dispose of these and retain the income generated from them did they feel properly in control of their own destinies.

If what might be called the landed interests had been successful in securing their own position by the 1847 Order in Council, they had no desire to concede any of those privileges to others. Clause 32 of the 1850 Act had given the projected colonial legislatures power not only to alter their constitutions, but to change the qualifications of electors and of elected members. If, perish the thought, manhood suffrage were to be forced upon them, political power might in time pass to the populace! Manhood suffrage did in fact follow quite speedily, but political power has nevertheless shown a remarkable tendency to stay in the hands of comparatively few. Constitutional advance in Australia after 1850 was not delayed by reluctance of British governments to concede self-government but by colonial Legislative Councils fighting a protracted rearguard action against the threat of democracy.

There were many in New South Wales ready to agree with Grey that their colony was far from ready for democracy. 'We should very soon have anarchy and confusion' if responsible government were to be introduced, it was claimed. Constraints, it was argued, must be enforced on what Molesworth had called 'Communities the offspring of convict emigration, more hideously vicious than any recorded in sacred or profane history'. A single chamber was inadmissible; an upper house composed of Crown nominees was the least that should be provided to avoid irresponsible legislation. Most colonists, however, objected vigorously to the proposals; the old social division between emancipists and exclusives had been replaced by a new economic divide between landed and bourgeois interests and the 'operative tradesmen and mechanics', who intended to have their voice heard. James Macarthur, showing his quick appreciation of this changing society, had proclaimed (in the *Sydney Morning Herald* of 6 February 1841): 'We are all anxious for representative institutions'; he thought the time had arrived when 'the long agitated emancipist question might be dropped'.

The Legislative Council spoke for all in expressing 'deep disappointment and dissatisfaction', and this was reinforced by its successor elected in 1851 under the new legislation. As in England, the property qualification, and indeed the willingness of voters to elect such established leaders as William Wentworth even when their policies were quite contrary to majority opinion, resulted in the landed interests dominating the 1851 Legislative Council; only eleven of the fifty-four members (which still included eighteen nominees) came from urban constituencies. The Legislative Council's 'Declaration Protest and Remonstrance' was a very cross document: 'our reasonable expectations have been utterly frustrated . . . The exploded fallacies of the Wakefield theory are still clung to . . . thousands of our fellow subjects . . . are annually diverted from our shores, and thus forced, against their will, to seek a home for themselves and their children in the backwoods of America.' The Colonial Office was stigmatized as 'an inexperienced, remote, and irresponsible department'. The Council went on to claim:

the unrestricted right to legislate in all matters whatsoever. That with regard, however, to legislation affecting the prerogatives of the Crown or imperial interests, the Crown should continue to exercise its power of dissent or disallowance through its minister for the colonies, while, with regard to legislation of merely local or municipal concern, the assent or dissent of the Crown should at once be given or withheld by the Governor through his responsible advisers.[7]

That, however, was as near as the Council came to advocating responsible government, and in London this objection seemed unrealistically theoretical. Grey pointed out that since 1843 over two hundred colonial Acts had been submitted to London, and of these a mere seven had been disallowed; only one public office had been filled by Whitehall, that of Keeper of the Botanical Gardens. The colonists' demands therefore got a dusty answer from him. Grey believed that the 'Remonstrance' reflected the view of an oligarchic clique of landowners rather than general public opinion; and there was much truth in his charge. But dissatisfaction there certainly was: the young

Robert Gascoyne-Cecil, later Marquess of Salisbury and Conservative Prime Minister, one of the very few British politicians to have any direct experience of the colonies, remarked on 'the din of indignation . . . People are apt to be riled at having their minutest affairs settled for them . . . by a staff of clerks who cannot have the faintest ideas of the questions they are handling. From the Cape to New Zealand, from Bishop to potboy, the cry is the same.' Nor was the Colonial Secretary willing to accede to the colonists' demand that they be allowed to control the income from land sales, at any rate for the moment; it was 'a question of expediency and not of right – of expediency respectively both to the local community and to the Empire at large'. New South Wales could still, even after the separation of Victoria, claim huge areas of the continent, and the spectacle of these being filled with uncontrollable squatters was alarming. Stimulated by the foundation of the Aborigines Protection Society in 1839, the problem of colonial aggressions became the subject of parliamentary debates, and Ben Hawes, parliamentary undersecretary for the colonies, had confirmed 'with satisfaction' that under British rule Aborigines were entitled to 'every privilege of British-born subjects'. This was not a decision likely to fit comfortably into colonial prejudices, even if Hawes qualified his ruling by adding that the privileges could be claimed only when the Aborigines 'complied with provisions made and provided'. Again, if control of land sales was to be given to the colonists it should not be abandoned to the 'utterly unbalanced democracy' of Sydney, but more properly be vested – as it was in the United States – in a federal authority, an idea to which New South Welshmen were proving resistant.[8]

Australians might well have objected that Britain was not doing very well with its own institutions. Russell's administration never enjoyed a majority in Parliament, being sustained only by the failure of the opposition to achieve unanimity; even after the government's defeat in 1850 Stanley, then leading the Tories, had failed to provide an alternative administration. The Whigs' eventual collapse in February 1852 was brought about by one of their own defectors, Palmerston, in what he called his 'tit-for-tat with John Russell!' and when Stanley – now the Earl of Derby – did contrive to assemble a government it only lasted until December of that year.

In that short-lived Tory administration Sir John Pakington acted as Colonial Secretary. Pakington was an undistinguished and pedestrian politician, whose appointment was greeted with amused surprise. 'Sir Roger de Coverley' had been 'disinterred' in order to 'stick him on the Colonies'; but Sir John proved sympathetic to colonial demands.[9] While denying control of land allocation as an 'absolute right', Pakington confirmed that the British government, now 'after full consideration . . . under the new and rapidly changing circumstances of New South Wales', considered that 'the administration of these lands should be transferred to the Colonial Legislature'. This was a critical concession, for with the administration went the revenues. By handing over the potentially enormous income to be gained from the disposal of those 'Waste Lands' – a misleading term for all the rest of Australia that had not specifically been inalienably sold or granted – in addition to the other sources of government income, the Australian colonies were rendered financially independent of the British government, and at the same time retained a preferential access to the London capital market. Pakington also specifically agreed to the Council's request that the new New South Wales legislature should consist of an elected Assembly and a nominated Council, thus erecting a barrier against unrestrained democracy; but added the proviso, reflecting Clause 32, that 'It is scarcely necessary to add, that Her Majesty's Government do not consider that the power which the Legislature of New South Wales at present possesses of changing its Constitution is to be considered as exhausted by this exercise of it; that power must be retained in case further reform should at any time appear expedient.'[10] Such reform, however, would be restrained by the requirement that a two-thirds majority of both houses would be needed for any alteration to the constitution.

Although Pakington remained in office for only a matter of months, his successor in Lord Aberdeen's coalition government, the liberal-conservative Henry Clinton, Duke of Newcastle, confirmed and extended these concessions. Newcastle, although an ally of Molesworth and the colonial reformers, quickly made it clear that he harboured none of Grey's reservations about responsible government. Specifically referring to the Canadian precedent, Newcastle wrote to all the Australian Governors in August 1853 that 'All will agree as to the extreme difficulty of . . . keeping our fellow-subjects in Australia on a different political footing from those to whom these rights have been fully conceded in America', while his under-secretary assured some Newfoundland delegates that 'it was not the policy of the Imperial Government to refuse responsible government to any colony which was generally desirous of having it'. Whereas Pakington had agreed on an upper house composed of nominees, this condition was therefore removed by Newcastle; New South Wales was free to write its own constitution. Taken together with the allocation of the financial capital and income, the colonists were very nearly independent in all matters except foreign policy and defence. For the next half century, until the important political issue of colonial federation was raised, changing faces at the Colonial Office made little difference to Australian politics.[11]

The 1850 Australian Colonies Government Act struck at the pretensions of New South Wales to be in some respect superior to the more recent colonies. Its provisions were to be applied equally to Van Diemen's Land, South Australia and the Port Phillip district, which was to become the new colony of Victoria in 1851; in addition, New South Wales was warned that its territories to the north of 30 degrees might be detached to form a new colony, which became, in due course, Queensland. This provision, a revival of Stanley's idea of forming a new northern convict colony, owed much to a strange agreement between Grey, chafing at the end of transportation to New South Wales, and the remarkable Archibald Boyd, who made several journeys to London in the 1840s, advancing the colonists' cause and becoming an experienced interlocutor at the Colonial Office. Boyd had been successful in smoothing the passage of Gipps's land regulations, but in 1848 was ruined by his cousin Ben Boyd's spectacular business failure. Returning to London to begin an unremunerative career as a novelist, Boyd suggested to Grey that the communities around Moreton Bay would be sympathetic to the renewal of transportation. 'At Moreton Bay,' he declared,

it is the squatters who rule everything, and the inhabitants of the two villages of Ipswich and Brisbane could not, even if they desired it, offer any effective resistance to the wishes of the pastoral community. At Sydney, in short, the dominant interest is that of the labourer, at Moreton Bay that of the employer of labour. Each is despotic in its individual locality, and the same reorganisation of the penal system, which has been opposed with so much asperity in the one would, in the other, four hundred miles up the coast, be received with positive acclamation.

Boyd's suggestion was in essence a revival of Stanley's Gladstone project, shifted a few hundred miles further south into more moderate climes.[12]

In spite of some Colonial Office reservations concerning the location of the boundary between the new and old colonies, Grey jumped at the idea. New South Wales might well refuse to accept convicts, but a new northern colony would surely be more accommodating. At a meeting in July 1850 a petition was prepared, adopted in Brisbane in January 1851, asking for separation for the territory north of the 32nd parallel – a much greater slice of New South Wales, which would include the desirable lands of Australian New England, centred around Armidale – while the New South Wales Legislative Council were insisting on no cession of anything south of the originally projected 26th parallel, which would have retained even Brisbane in New South Wales. The northerners also demanded a constitution comparable with that of New South Wales, and the resumption of transportation. By December Grey had had second thoughts: the Moreton Bay project might be necessary 'by and by' but for the moment the northern population was still too sparse to make separation feasible.[13]

Pakington was already less enthusiastic about the scheme than his predecessor had initially been, since his government had announced their intention, in the Queen's Speech, 'to devise means by which . . . transportation to Van Diemen's Land may . . . be altogether discontinued'. It would have been difficult after that to send convicts to New South Wales, even if this was to a part of the colony now bearing another name. One of history's little ironies is that Australia, at least until the advent of Afrikaner-dominated governments in South Africa, usually lagged behind that country in its acknowledgement of human rights. The Cape Colony's Legislative Council, in spite of the mixed population of the country, had agreed on a responsible constitution soon after Russell's offer was received, and in March 1853, two years before New South Wales, the Cape had received an advanced – for that period – representative constitution; Newcastle insisted that both houses of the new Parliament were to be elected, and on a franchise low enough not to 'leave those of the Coloured Classes who in point of intelligence are qualified for the exercise of political power, practically unrepresented . . . we believe through the exercise of political rights enjoyed by all alike will prove one of the best methods [of ensuring unity]'. The Duke was a more convinced democrat than the once-radical Australian William Wentworth.[14]

In his letter to the Australian governors of August 1853 Newcastle underlined the interim nature of the existing constitutions, and warned that they should 'prepare themselves for "Responsible Government", as a change which cannot be long delayed, and which should be smoothed as far as possible'. Each colony was able to propose what form of government it thought suitable, without reference to any other, and the differing choices subsequently made reflected the varying circumstances of colonial societies. The colonists' freedom of choice was underlined; the upper houses could, if they so wished, be elected, on whatever franchise might be chosen. A hundred and fifty years later the British upper house has still to see the introduction of any electoral element.

This was well in advance of what New South Wales conservative opinion felt to be safe. 'Conscious of their own good intentions, superior education and great local knowledge', such conservatives as Sir Charles Nicholas, speaker of the Legislative Council, and James Macarthur considered 'the too evident disposition of the Colonial Office to hold the scales of justice between the competing factions was ill-informed, dangerously liberal, and subversive of every attempt to reproduce British society and politics in

Australia'.[15] The debate was now one between the 'squattocracy' and the democrats, who might respectively be compared with Tories and Whig/Liberals in Britain. Responding to the invitation (proffered by Russell, and extended by Pakington and Newcastle) to design their own constitution, the New South Wales Legislative Council appointed a select committee, chaired by William Wentworth, to prepare a draft. His arguments were those which would have been accepted by the British Parliament twenty years previously, if not by the people themselves, but which were now becoming dated. The 1832 Reform Act had been intended to allow commercial and industrial interests to share power with the landed aristocracy and gentry. There was no intention to permit the working classes, excluded by the property qualifications, any direct voice in the legislative process; of a population of more than 20 million, the Act increased the electorate only from 435,000 to 652,000; indeed, since the rural 'county' seats were increased from 188 to 253 the influence of territorial magnates was increased. Wentworth's 'firm conviction', that 'the representation of the country should be based on, or proportioned to, not the mere population, but the great interests, of the country', was also that of the second Lord Grey in preparing his reform Bill, but the world had moved on since 1832, and more rapidly in Sydney than at Westminster. It would have taken a British Tory of the old school to have advanced Wentworth's ideas of 1853:

The wealthy class of the city consists chiefly of these men of business – these lords of the Exchange as they call or think themselves. (Great Laughter.) There is my hon. friend from Darlinghurst (Mr. Baker) who is a manufacturer in a certain sense; he manufactures flour out of grain. My hon. friend the member for the Sydney Hamlets (Mr. Smart) is in the same position. Then there are some leather manufacturers, one or two brewers, an iron founder or two, and these I believe, with some trifling exceptions, are all. There is really nothing to represent here except a large mass of labour. (Great Laughter.)

And the 'large mass of labour', of course, did not enter the political equation. New South Wales was to have a 'lasting' constitution, 'a conservative one – a British, not a Yankee constitution'.

That being so, Wentworth's draft Bill proposed that membership of the new upper house should be not merely for life, but hereditary:

Is there not a class peculiarly fitted for hereditary distinctions? A class which has been great and powerful in all ages and in all countries where it has existed; which must continue to be great and powerful here as long as the great interior wilds of this country can be applied to no other purpose than the sustenation of sheep and cattle? Yes, sir, we have among us, and we shall have among us to the latest generations, our Shepherd Kings. And I believe that, as they are a body peculiar to this colony, so are they, as a general proposition, the body most fitted of all in the colonies – I mean the principal men among them – to receive these hereditary distinctions. I can afford to say this now.[16]

Wentworth's proposal was simply laughed out of court, principally due to the wit of the brilliant, boyish Daniel Deniehy, solicitor, journalist and later member of the New South Wales Legislative Assembly. His description of

these harlequin aristocrats (laughter) these Botany Bay magnificos (laughter), these Australian mandarins. (Roars of laughter) Let them walk across the stage in all the pomp and circumstances of hereditary titles. First then, in the procession stalks the hoary Wentworth. But he could not imagine that to such a head the strawberry leaves would add any honour, (cheers). Next came the native aristocrat Mr. James Macarthur, he would he supposed, aspire to the coronet of an earl, he would call him the Earl of Camden, and he suggests for his coat of arms a field vert, the heraldic term for green – (great cheers and laughter) – and emblazoned on this field should be a rum keg of New South Wales ... But their weakness was ridiculous, he could assure them that these pigmies might do a great deal of mischief? They would bring contempt on a country whose interest he was sure they all had at heart, until even the poor Irishman in the streets of Dublin would fling his jibe at Botany Bay aristocrats. In fact, he was puzzled how to classify them. They could not aspire to the miserable and effete dignity of the grandees of Spain. (Laughter) They had antiquity of birth, but these he would defy any naturalist properly to classify them. But perhaps it was only a specimen of the remarkable contrariety that existed at the antipodes. Here they all knew the common water mole was transformed into the duck-billed platypus, and in some distant emulation of this degeneration, he supposed they were to be favoured with a bunyip aristocracy.[17]

After this rhetorical triumph even the Legislative Council could hardly side with Wentworth, but the important points were won. The constitution drafted by the New South Wales Legislative Council and sent to London for approval, escorted by Wentworth and Edward Deas Thomson, was essentially conservative, with an entirely nominated upper house and a restrictive franchise for the Assembly calculated to exclude all but the most respectable of the working classes, but in one particular the British government decided on a more flexible approach. The safeguards that had been built in against constitutional change in a democratic direction, by insisting on a two-thirds majority in both houses, were dropped. At Russell's insistence a simple majority would be entitled to pass laws amending the constitution; which they promptly did. Herman Merivale, the perceptive parliamentary under-secretary, rightly pointed out that 'The able and wealthy leaders of the old Australian legislatures wanted to transfer power from Downing Street to themselves: they succeeded in transferring it to their inferiors'.

The colonial proposals were reviewed by the Colonial Office's legal advisers, reporting to Frederic Rogers, then a Commissioner for Lands and Emigration, later, when permanent under-secretary at the Colonial Office scornfully referred to as 'a person named Rogers' who in reality governed the colonies. There was some truth in that, since Rogers had been at Eton with Elgin and Gladstone, who remained a close friend. School and university friendships are often a valuable guide to the pecking order in Victorian society, and Rogers, later Lord Blachford, exercised unusual personal influence. Whatever the future might hold, the Colonial Office agreed that, for the time being, some control had to be kept over the colonies, but it was recognized that this must be flexible. 'The general principle', Newcastle wrote, was that 'in matters of purely local policy he [the Governor] is bound, excepting in extreme cases, to follow the advice of a ministry which appears to possess the confidence of the legislature'. But this was a counsel of perfection, based on the relatively stable tenure of British government; in South Australia, where forty-two ministries came and went in forty-five years, or New South Wales and Victoria, which saw twenty-nine and twenty-eight respectively in the same period, it was often all but impossible to determine which colonial ministry at any one time 'possesses the confidence of the legislature'. Moreover, the British government was 'fully aware that the power granted must occasionally be used amiss. But they have always trusted that the errors of a free government would cure themselves.' There remained, however, some matters touching 'the honour of the Crown or the faith of Parliament or the safety of the state' which must be finally settled in London, and it was impossible to define precisely what they might be.[18]

The New South Wales and Victoria Bills both attempted to define 'Imperial' subjects on which colonies might not legislate – allegiance, naturalization, treaties, foreign relations, defence, treason and, in Victoria only, divorce. Such a rigid division between imperial and colonial powers was recognized by the experienced Colonial Office administrators to be thoroughly impracticable. Rogers's view was therefore that a general right of referral by Governors to the Colonial Office in the first instance, followed by disallowance if this were judged necessary by the Judicial Committee of the Privy Council, must be retained. Herman Merivale pointed out that, once embodied in a written constitution, all future dissensions between colonies and mother country would have to be argued out as points of law before a tribunal. The existing system of potential disallowance by the Crown provided for compromise, under the 'arbitrary, but timid and manageable, control of the executive' (the British Government). Supported by Russell, Merivale's view prevailed. Eventually the instructions (8 October 1855) given to Sir William Denison on his promotion from Tasmania to New South Wales included an obligation to reserve specified matters. It was a power rarely to be used; in the succeeding forty years only four New South Wales Bills were reserved, together with eight from Tasmania, nine from South Australia, six from Victoria and five from Queensland; of all these only five were eventually disallowed. Australian democracy was to be constrained, not by imperial control, but by Australian conservatives.[19]

Victoria Victorious

When the news finally came on 11 November 1850 that the Port Phillip district was to become the independent colony of Victoria (brought by a coach galloped from Port Melbourne with a publican sounding a trumpet and waving a Union Flag, shouting 'Hooray! We've got separation at last'), rejoicing was widespread. Separation had long been promised, and did not take effect until the following June; some complained that the boundary, established on the Murray River, should have been extended north, but the news was properly celebrated. Beacons were lit, rockets fired, thanksgiving services attended, a 'Separation Anthem' composed, a fancy dress ball held, and hundreds of gallons of rum consumed. When the excitement died down, Port Phillipians, now Victorians, got down to the more serious business of preparing for the future and electing the first Legislative Council under the new dispensation.[20]

New South Wales, very naturally, did not approve. Compared with that thriving state, four times as populous, Victoria was small beer. Minute by Australian standards – about the same size as Great Britain – and occupying only 3 per cent of the continental land area, Victoria was a complacent pastoral state, with a population of some 70,000. Its success had certainly been astonishingly rapid. Within a dozen years of Mrs Walsh's being able to house the select society of Port Phillip in her little house, Melbourne was a thriving society of some 23,000; the port of Geelong, on the western side of the bay, had a population of 8,000, with streets 'somewhat spacious and laid out with great mathematical regularity'. Melbourne's unimaginative grid pattern was relieved by spacious surrounding parks, and the first of its fine municipal buildings were beginning to appear. Victoria was, however, almost entirely dependent on sheep. Almost the whole of the rural area was divided into nearly a thousand sheep runs, all unfenced and for the most part unsurveyed, on which 6 million sheep thrived. As early as 1851 Victoria was exporting more wool than New South Wales; at that time the cultivated area of Victoria was 52,000 acres, compared with New South Wales' 223,000, but within seven years Victoria had outstripped the older colony, with 299,000 acres under plough. From its inception as a near-colony of Tasmania, immigrants from other parts of Australia had been outnumbered by new arrivals from Britain. Strictly speaking, Victoria, like South Australia, could claim never to have been a convict colony. Although many of the original Van Diemen's Landers had been time-expired or pardoned convicts, and in the 1840s their numbers were reinforced by some 1,700 'exiles', the 'Pentonvillains', conditionally pardoned in England, they were far outnumbered by the free emigrants, more than 40,000 of whom arrived between 1838 and 1842. After that the stream began running temporarily dry. It was, however, soon to become a rushing river.

Given the relatively restricted area of land available and the consequent potential for profit arising on resale, application for allocations was brisk, and led to misunderstandings and opportunism. If the £1 an acre figure specified under the legislation were to be applied to suburban land an expenditure of some £60,000 could yield, on the first or subsequent resale, a profit of over a million. Even good agricultural land was fetching £4 rather than £1 an acre. The Wakefieldians assumed that no one would cultivate land for which a valid title could not be claimed, but squatters had limitless opportunities to move on. Real fortunes could be made almost instantly by speculation in suburban lots. Such people as Henry Deady could obtain an order in London for up to 5,120 acres (8 square miles) on payment of £1 an acre, with the ability to choose the land he wished. Deady's order permitted him to choose land near Melbourne and would, Gipps calculated, be worth £100,000; a very tidy profit. Some adept procrastination enabled Deady to be diverted to a beach region (the present suburbs of Brighton and Bentleigh) which nevertheless made him immediately a very rich man. Such examples persuaded Russell, 'writhing a little' Gipps thought, 'to revert to sales by auction'.[21]

Once the news of impending separation was received, the ground was prepared for the agreement of the new Victorian constitution. The Irish barrister, William Stawell, appointed Attorney General by La Trobe, was given responsibility for drafting the Bill, which not unnaturally, since the existing Legislative Council was also dominated by conservative pastoralists, followed similar lines to that proposed for New South Wales by William Wentworth.

Victoria was able to count on the services of some outstandingly able colonists, although the most brilliant of these, Hugh Childers, in charge of the colony's finances at the age of 26 and first Vice-Chancellor of the new University of Melbourne, returned to London in 1857 after participating in the first government. Two very different Irish lawyers pursued glittering careers in Victoria: the Catholic Charles Gavan Duffy, a Young Ireland rebel, who had narrowly escaped transportation to become an MP, introduced useful parliamentary experience into the Victorian Assembly and became Premier; Sir Redmond Barry, a Trinity College Dublin Anglican, first Solicitor General of Victoria became also the first Supreme Court judge. Two more influential lawyers were also at opposite ends of the political spectrum, the radical George Higinbotham – another Trinity College graduate – and 'arch-Tory' Thomas Fellowes.

The Victorian Legislative Council's drafting of their Constitution Bill provoked a pale shadow of the excitement that had been felt in Sydney when constitutional debate had been linked with the future of transportation. The permanently vexed question of state aid to religion alone aroused interest and only four public meetings – none in Melbourne – were convened on any other points. Although the question of hereditary Councillors was raised, it was speedily dropped. Guided by the skilful Childers as interim administrator, with William Stawell and J. L. F. V. Foster ('Alphabet Foster') the most influential members, the constitution intended 'to direct the overflowing stream of democracy into a proper channel: to develop that conservative element in it which is too often overlooked' – a colonial reflection of the new conservatism then being developed in England by Benjamin Disraeli.[22] The *polloi* were not to be irritated, as they were in New South Wales, by a Legislative Council nominated for life; a high property qualification would surely suffice to preserve the rights of the squatters, and a figure of £10,000 was canvassed. Thanks to the militancy of the ambitious John O'Shanassy and the diplomacy of Childers, the qualification for the Council was reduced to £5,000 with £1,000 qualifying for the vote – still high enough to ensure that the Council would be a substantial barrier against what Childers called 'the levelling flood of ignorance and prejudice to which every nation is subjected', especially when reinforced by allowing the vote to poorer but respectably educated persons such as lawyers and doctors. Without going to the lengths of establishing a hereditary aristocracy, the new Legislative

Council was intended to be as well entrenched a citadel of privilege as the House of Lords. As another protection against radical change, further constitutional amendments would need a two-thirds agreement in both houses of Parliament.

Stawell had some reason for nervousness in 1852, 'a time when the bonds of security were loosened, when most of our people had gone mad, and the rest were paralysed with fear, when the dregs of the colonies and those of Europe were daily poured upon us, and there was scarcely a policeman left to enforce order'.[23] These 'vagrants and wandering vagabonds' who were to upset the pastoral tranquillity of Victoria had come in search of gold.

Gold

In June 1848 gold had been discovered in the Sacramento river of California. Such 'alluvial' gold is obtained by separating gold from silt by the simple process of washing, requiring little capital but much persistence. Almost immediately, thousands of eager prospectors from all over the world swarmed in the first modern gold 'rush'. At the time California was without a formal government, being in the process of transfer from Mexico to the United States; no real control over the prospectors was possible, even with the help of United States forces. 'Nothing', reported Commodore Jones of the US Navy, who found himself representing the government, 'can exceed the deplorable state of things in California growing out of the maddening effects of the gold mania . . . no fear of punishment is sufficient.'[24]

The existence of gold in Australia had already been established; in 1844, when the Reverend William Clarke presented his first samples to Sir George Gipps, the Governor ordered the news to be suppressed. 'Put it away, Mr. Clarke, or we shall all have our throats cut.' When the California goldfield was proved, Gipps's successor, Sir Charles Fitzroy, very sensibly asked London for the services of a geologist to verify the potential of Australian ore. Thus, when Edward Hargrave, who had been tolerably successful in California, reported his discovery of gold near Bathurst in February 1851, the authorities were forewarned and the subsequent rush was controllable. 'All the horrors of California' with 'murders, riots, lynchings and general unrest' were not repeated in New South Wales, where the government was able to cope. Continuity had been established by the competent and level-headed Scot, Edward Deas Thomson, clerk to the Executive and Legislative Councils since 1829, colonial secretary from 1837 to 1856. Deas Thomson rejected demands from the reactionary squatters that, to discourage their workers from joining the rush, 'martial law be proclaimed, and all gold-digging peremptorily prohibited in order that the ordinary industrial pursuits . . . should not be interfered with'. A system of moderate licence fees to be paid by prospectors was established. This worked well enough in the more settled conditions of New South Wales, with adequate policing and competent administrators, but it was to cause uproar in the Victorian goldfields. Soldiers did not desert, nor servants leave their employers in such numbers as to endanger the New South Wales economy, which received a valuable boost from the increased demand for such items as 'Blue and red serge shirts, Californian hats, leather belts, "real gold-digging gloves" mining boots, picks pots and pans'. Charlotte Godley, an English visitor, was distressed: 'you hear endless stories of ladies who have been used to large establishments, and giving parties, now obliged to give up all thoughts of appearance, and open the door even, themselves.' Within weeks of the first rush, prices had resumed their normal level; wages, however, did not and the economy was thereby given a powerful boost.[25]

In Victoria, jealous alarm at New South Wales's luck was instantaneous, as the *Sydney Morning Herald* jeered at 'our dear sister Victoria, who went mad with joy at separation' and who would now see 'the old colony . . . take the shine out of her' (16 July 1851). For a short time this hubris seemed justified as labourers and shepherds streamed off for New South Wales; hundreds of workmen gathered to discuss co-operative ventures and the price of food soared, almost doubling the cost of bread as speculators cornered the wheat market. The spectre of 'impending ruin' led the Gold Discovery Committee of Victorian businessmen to offer a reward for the discovery of a profitable find within 200 miles of Melbourne; within five weeks the reward was successfully claimed. By August the immensely rich Ballarat field was discovered, and the Cavanagh brothers were able triumphantly to display 60 pounds weight of gold, which at £3 an ounce promised an impressive sum. Speculators poured in by the thousand. Their rewards could be astonishing; one man obtained 80 *pounds* of gold in a single hour; nuggets were dug out with no tool other than a penknife.

As Victoria suddenly became international news, shipping companies competed to charter vessels and to pioneer quicker routes – the overland voyage via Panama was touted, not very successfully; the Admiralty invited tenders for a steam service, to average eight and a half knots and to make only one stop, at the Cape – an impossible demand. Scores of helpful pamphlets were published, including *The Australian Colonies: Where They Are and How to Get to Them* – a title which indicated the prevailing ignorance of the subject. Not only the chance of instant wealth but the happy condition of the average colonial was instanced: 'It is in this colony [Victoria] that the English labourer is seen in his true character: he is no longer the abject cringing half-starved pauper; he is now bold, independent and fully conscious of the importance of his position.' While perhaps few English labourers would have accepted the description, it was true that wages at 10s. a day, and the astronomical sum of £20 a week paid for a two-man sawing team, were well in excess of anything to be earned in the home country. Dissenting voices were also heard: the anonymous author of *Australia a Mistake* warned of the plight of the disappointed emigrant who, if 'spared the pangs of absolute starvation', would find himself stranded in the wilds; but since it was the chilly Canadian state of New Brunswick that the author was recommending as an alternative some hyperbole was essential.[26]

Even more astonishing were the highly coloured accounts which reached Britain. One digger, George Reid, wrote home denying the 'strange things that you read of in the London papers. There are no Diggers ordering butts of Port and requesting passers-by to drink their health; no knocking men's eyes in or out with nuggets; no giving half crowns to have their teeth picked for them, etc, that I can hear.' Somewhat complacently, although acknowledging the 'state of feverish excitement alike perplexing to the moralist and statesman', Lieutenant Governor La Trobe congratulated himself on 'the love of order inherent in the Anglo-Saxon character, and to the prompt vigilance of both the home and local governments' which would soon result in quieter times. It was not the goldfields themselves that were disorderly. In Bendigo, Robert Cecil, even though wearing a white top hat, found 'more civility than I should be likely to find in the good town of Hatfield' and 'not half as much crime and insubordination as there would be in an English town of the same wealth and population' – but Bendigo was always more peaceable than the rival town of Ballarat.[27]

It was Melbourne that suffered. While gold fever was contagious the capital became like an abandoned city; by January 1852 only two policemen remained on duty; ships on the wharves were deserted by their crews. Transients and immigrants replaced the absconders; between 1852 and 1853 more than 100,000 people entered Victoria from foreign ports. The pressure on resources stretched housing, water and sewerage provisions past breaking point; such building controls as existed were abolished, a canvas town was erected in South Melbourne, and towards Richmond small wooden houses shot up; 'a balder and more unattractive scene cannot meet the eye of man'. It was to be very many years before Melbourne recovered from this inauspicious start, a 'deadly legacy of muddy streets, gimcrack housing and polluted streams. Visitors were nauseated by the stench of night soil and dead dogs decomposing in the streets.'

Five years later the population of Victoria alone was greater than that recorded in the 1851 census for the whole of Australia. At least 20,000 of these were Chinese, a figure which had doubled by 1859; racial antagonism was added to the dangerous mixture, although violence against the Chinese never reached the levels it did in California. Little could be criticized in the demeanour of the Chinese themselves, who arranged their own affairs in a usually peaceful fashion, and learnt to appreciate the quick and impartial justice that was available from the colonial courts, of a quality quite unknown in contemporary China. Ararat, a small town on the road from Ballarat to Horsham, was founded almost entirely by Chinese immigrants. Potentially more dangerous were the American diggers, accustomed to the lawless ways of the Californian fields, and the European refugees from the failed rebellions of 1848, imbued with frustrated political ambitions; but few of these apprehensions were fulfilled, for the goldfields in general were, as Cecil found, acceptably well ordered.[28]

Victoria was less well equipped to cope with the unprecedented situation than New South Wales had been. The 1850 Government of Australia Act, which had given its new status to the Port Phillip area, only came into force on 1 July 1851. The new Legislative Council was inexperienced, and La Trobe was promoted from his old office as Superintendent to the more elevated rank of Lieutenant Governor, responsible to London direct, in January 1851. Only from May 1852 did La Trobe receive the full salary to which as Lieutenant Governor he was entitled, £5,000: for ten years it had remained at the much more modest level of £1,500. His colonial secretary was William Lonsdale, a retired army officer, conscientious but hesitant, who had been police magistrate since the establishment of Port Phillip. The most formidable figure was that of William Stawell, supported by his fellow Irishman Redmond Barry (they had been together at Trinity College Dublin and Lincoln's Inn) as Solicitor General. Their administration was faced with the colossal task of regulating tens of thousands of eager prospectors who poured in through Melbourne. The system that had served well enough in New South Wales, that of charging prospectors for a licence, was adopted in Victoria, under the control of resident commissioners, commanded by the admirable William Wright, formerly a Commissioner for Crown Lands.

Wright was well aware that with the much greater numbers of diggers present on the Victorian goldfield, the collection of a monthly licence fee would be near-impossible. Recruiting the numbers of police needed to monitor licensing, as well as to settle disputes and convoy the gold to banks, was quite impossible. 'The very character of the service', Wright complained, 'exposes them to temptation of various kinds, which it is no wonder that men of ordinary character or principle would scarcely be proof against. I can only report that little or no dependence can be placed upon a purely civil police under existing circumstances.' Many of the police were ex-convicts and convict superintendents, 'long practiced in savagery and sadism'. Corruption in the early days was widespread, and the right of the police to retain half the fines they collected was a certain way to ensure persecution of the diggers.

The ability of the Commissioners and their assistants to control administration varied: some assistants were described by one discontented digger as 'the most extraordinary collection of incompetent empty-headed buggers, a set of young insolent and imperious men'. A more polite witness,

a very intelligent digger from Dorset . . . agreed that one of the greatest evils of the digging life was the constant and close contact into which they were brought with the police. At home, he truly observed, you know that such things as laws, magistrates, and police, exist, and you find the benefit of them, though they seem to pass at a distance from you; but here the man-hunters are out every day, and you are constantly favoured with their visits. He said, as many had said to me before, 'Three and four times a day I have been summoned to show my licence, and threatened with handcuffs if I murmured.'[29]

As numbers rose, production became more difficult. In the first full year, 1852, more than £16 million worth of gold was extracted by some 35,000 diggers. Two years later 100,000 men produced little more than half that sum. Although the income produced by licence fees was substantial, it was less than the extra administrative expense, and its collection was therefore all the more essential. Unsuccessful miners who could not, or would not, afford the licence fee were then liable to be carted off to gaol. La Trobe, denying reports of the 'universal unchecked prevalence of crime and disorder at the workings', was able to assure Lord Grey that 'the orderly bearing and conduct of the great proportion of the people on the ground is undeniable' and instanced the fact that Sunday was universally observed as a day of rest and quiet, at least until nightfall.

Commissioner Wright, aided by his assistant John Bull, whose huge size must have helped his 'tact and sense of justice', were able to restrain discontented diggers for the better part of three years, but the situation was aggravated when La Trobe was replaced in June 1854 by Sir Charles Hotham, a naval captain who only reluctantly accepted the governorship. He had pleaded with his former chief Lord Malmesbury to intervene with the Duke of Newcastle to find him a sea-going command instead, but had been told brusquely that 'if he did not take what had been given him he should have nothing'. Lord Malmesbury sympathized, writing that 'they have packed him off to Australia to get him out of the way'. Hotham was indeed to have a miserable time of it during his truncated stay. Even a more conciliatory character or experienced negotiator would, however, have been given a hard time, for the diggers were increasingly angry.[30]

The nature of the goldfields had changed since the first arrival of the eager prospectors, individualists each with their own basic equipment, or at most small groups of friends, working individual claims. Once the original alluvial deposits – the wet diggings – had been scoured down to bedrock, and the original diggers departed, rich or more usually disappointed, claims were bought up by larger syndicates, able to provide capital for the construction of dams and watercourses which could be more than 20 miles long. Excavations were still shallow as the 'wash dirt' was pursued under the creek-bed, 10–20 feet at most, but continued to require co-operative effort. By December 1853 the Ballarat field had become a 'rich man's diggings' where steam pumps were used to pump out the deep shafts. The sense of community thus engendered was consolidated by the existence of a common enemy, the Goldfields Police.

While the quality of these police had improved since the earliest days, and their services in conveying the gold safely to the Melbourne banks were appreciated, the diggers resented having to interrupt their work to find their licences on demand, and even to endure the long wait needed to obtain them from one of the two issuing points. And many diggers were by no means so law-abiding; those who had run out of the ready cash needed for the licences, or who lacked that 'love of order inherent in the Anglo-Saxon character', or who saw the risk of being caught as merely a part of the stakes involved in seeking a fortune on the goldfields, developed their own strategies for avoiding payment of the licence fee.

Nevertheless, compared with the Californian gold rush, the Australian diggers were decidedly tame. 'For all their raffish appearance and reputation, the early Victorian goldfields seem hardly to have loosened conventional codes of feminine (and even masculine) respectability.' Great political effects were initially expected from the gold strikes, especially in New South Wales. Wentworth predicted that the discovery of gold 'must, in a very few years, precipitate us from a colony into a nation'. The old agitator Dr Lang saw the opportunity of establishing a republic; a certain result confirmed by a 'Divine Providence' of this 'wonderful discovery', he wrote, 'is that Australia will, in spite of every effort to the contrary, very soon be free and independent'. Young Henry Parkes, editor-proprietor of the *Empire*, who won a seat on the Legislative Council in 1854, had young Australia telling Mother Britain: 'I can take care of myself. Let us make a bargain Mother. Let us part as friends.' But a century and a half later Australia is still a constitutional monarchy. The 'New Britannia' that Wentworth had long expected to arise remained, in his mind, New South Wales, with the other colonies being dragged along in the train of the Mother Colony. The Victorian discoveries brought such confident predictions to an abrupt end as New South Wales was supplanted by the smaller southern colony; and the reasons why Lang's predictions of an Australian republic have still not been realized run as a constant strand though all subsequent Australian history.[31]

Eureka

The fight at the Eureka stockade in December 1854 is perhaps the most dramatic event in Australian domestic history, the country's only battle – if one omits the periodic clashes with Aborigines as too one-sided to be so dignified – and has been well over-dramatized. It has been variously identified as an outburst of Irish 'hatred against "Saxon" oppression' and (by Karl Marx) as 'a concrete manifestation [of] the general revolutionary movement in Victoria'. The flag flown at the fight, 'exceedingly chaste and natural in design', seemed to be 'a thing of beauty under which free people could stand upright and proud' and subsequently took a leading position in nationalist iconography. A more reasonable view was advanced by the historian Neville Meaney, who described the fight as an 'incident, dressed up in borrowed robes, often ... given a ludicrously inflated importance, even as a Declaration of Independence'.[32]

Some sort of dispute was inevitable, given that the designers of the constitution of Victoria had been thinking in terms of a dispersed pastoral population with a couple of urban centres and had not envisaged the presence of tens of thousands of miners. The very high property qualifications demanded, which had to be confirmed by a period of residence in the colony, meant that very few of the diggers would have been entitled to a vote. Men's expectations of their political rights were also constantly being raised. Britain's great Reform Act of 1832 had been followed by agitation, mainly among skilled urban workers, for a much wider participation in political life. Under the guidance of Francis Place, a London tailor experienced in radical politics since the beginning of the century, the London

Working Men's Association drew up a programme of political reform. Expressed in the 'People's Charter' of May 1838 this was summarized as:

1. Adult male suffrage.
2. A secret ballot in place of the public hustings.
3. Electoral districts equal in numbers – the aim being to ensure fair urban representation.
4. Annual elections to Parliament (an impossible demand, the absurdity of which did much to damage the reputation of the 'Chartists').
5. Payment of MPs, in order to enable wage-workers to stand.
6. No property qualifications for MPs.

Although these demands, with the exception of annual parliaments, were all eventually to form part of normal political discourse and were achieved in Australia very speedily, the movement soon escaped from the founders' control into the hands of a verbally violent but ineffective leadership, the chief representative being the erratic Fergus O'Connor. The threat of an armed rebellion fizzled out in 1839, in large part due to the sympathetic General Charles Napier, who explained exactly how his forces could deal with any violent uprising, but the democratic demands had gained wide currency. Some prominent Chartists, accused of seditious libel (a conveniently loose charge) were arraigned – Lord Melbourne's Whig government was no friend to democracy – and a few transported to Australia, including John Williams, the Mayor of Monmouth. Many more of the free immigrants were imbued with Chartist ideas and, once arrived in Australia, founded Chartist organizations. The energies of many British Chartists were diverted into other channels. Some were, perhaps, unfruitful; the remains of the Chartist National Land Company may still be seen at Heronsgate, near Rickmansworth; such organizations as 'The Institution of the Intelligent and Well-disposed of the Working Classes for the Removal of Ignorance and Poverty by Means of Education and Employment' funded libraries and encouraged debate; but it was rather the Anti-Corn Law League, the Ten Hours Committee and the trade union movement that demonstrated real efficacy. Protective tariffs that had sheltered farm incomes while raising staple food prices were abolished in 1847, breaking the old Tory party in the process; in the same year, ten hours was established as the maximum working day. When in February 1848 the deposition of King Louis-Philippe of France and his replacement by a republic, together with the accession of a reforming Pope, Pius IX, sparked off revolutions throughout Europe, it seemed that Britain was in danger. But the reviving Chartists, like so many later left-wing organizations, could not agree between themselves.

O'Connor's proposal for a British republic with himself as President was abandoned in favour of armed revolt. Some skirmishes actually took place, at Bradford and Bingley in Yorkshire, where a policeman was killed, but the London insurrection, scheduled for Whit Monday 1848, was rained off.

If Chartism was overwhelmed by English inertia, in Australia it was reinforced by another phenomenon of the 1840s, the Irish diaspora. In what was perhaps the greatest human disaster of the nineteenth century, and certainly a defining moment of Irish history, the 'Great Hunger' – the famine of 1845–7 – resulted in nearly a million Irish deaths, and forced more into emigration. British governments coped with only limited success in combating the worst effects of the famine, and Irish resentment at British influence (unwarranted, since nineteenth-century British governments after 1830 went out of their way to remedy Irish grievances, but the memory of a million dead requires much effacing) was fuelled by very real suffering. This mixture of British political radicalism and Irish discontent, with the stress of alternate hope and disappointment, the separation from families and the solace offered by the grog shop, inseparable from a digger's life, combined to generate a touchy and unstable society.

The Victorian government had compromised – dithered might be a more appropriate word – over the diggers' complaints. An attempt to double the 30s. monthly fee was aborted; in September 1853 the fee was reduced to £2 for three months or £8 for a year; and on 1 February 1854 a Bill was introduced into the Victorian Parliament which would give the franchise to yearly licence holders, although these were also required to have a residence qualification. No change, however, altered the basic facts, that huge numbers of workers, often transient, were crowded together in the goldfields with no political institutions to represent them, and that the police were inadequate, untrained and recruited without enquiry from almost any applicants capable of locomotion. Able and tactful commissioners such as Wright and Bull could smooth things over, but once a weak link developed the whole system was placed at risk.

The weak link came in the shape of Deputy Commissioner Robert Rede, appointed in Ballarat in May 1854. Rede had no service experience, had spent nine years in Paris – surely no preparation for Ballarat – but he had good family connections, and was given ample freedom by Governor Hotham. Hotham had been in post less than four months before the events which led up to Eureka began. In that short time he had learnt little, disregarding the advice of his officials and Executive Councillors, and behaving more as a military governor than as an official preparing an emergent colony for responsible government. In La Trobe's time the Executive Council had met more than once a week but under Hotham it met only six times in five months, and not at all for two months after his arrival. In an attempt to avoid having his autocratic conduct limited by the Executive Council, Hotham consulted its members individually, although warned by Stawell that this device was 'legally so objectionable' that he was bound to object. Hotham also disregarded the advice of the Tory colonial secretary, Foster, demanding that even junior officials reported directly to the Governor.

Prior to taking up his post, Hotham had been warned by the Duke of Newcastle that 'There is an enormously extravagant expenditure going on in that colony which if not arrested will cause its ruin'. Faced with a budget deficiency of £1 million, Hotham cracked down on unpaid licences, which were now to be inspected twice weekly – an impossible frequency, exacerbating the discontent. Although the worst of the police had been removed, their replacements were open to criticism. In September the *Ballarat Times* reported:

The habits of officers also tended to augment the evil. They lived in a style totally unsuited to the duties they had to perform. Dressed in a smart uniform, and messing together according to military custom, they moved with a dignity more suited to a capital than a Gold field, and having an unpopular duty to perform, they invited hostile criticism and enmity, by the apparent pains which were taken to separate them from the diggers, and maintain the class to which they belonged.

If such law-abiding citizens as the respectable Dorset digger found the police distasteful, more independent spirits were less patient.[33]

In October a banal scuffle outside the Eureka Hotel in Ballarat led to the death of a digger. Evidence pointed to the landlord as a principal culprit, but the local magistrate quickly dismissed the case against him. The ensuing riot led to the destruction of the hotel; very properly, Hotham ordered a new trial which found that the magistrate concerned, who owed money to many Ballarat residents, had been open to improper influence and that the policeman, Sergeant Major Dawes, had taken outright bribes. Both were dismissed, the landlord and his accomplices found guilty and some of the rioters sentenced to short terms of imprisonment.

The incarceration of their comrades undid any benefits that the retrial might have produced, and an indignant deputation visited the Governor; the language of their demands was threatening, harking back to the Cromwellian Levellers and the American rebellion:

That it is the inalienable right of every citizen to have a voice in making the laws he is called upon to obey. *That* taxation without representation is tyranny. *That* being as the people have hitherto been unrepresented in the Legislative Council of the Colony of Victoria they have been tyrannized over and it becomes their duty as well as interest to resist and if necessary to remove their responsible power which so tyrannizes over them.[34]

When the deputation 'demanded' the release of the Eureka rioters on 27 November, the naval officer in Hotham perceived this as nothing less than mutiny; he had gone, he believed, as far as he reasonably could, and would not interfere again in the processes of the law. One of their major grievances, he assured the deputation, was already addressed since he had sent to England legislation which would confer the franchise on any miner who purchased an annual licence, the cost of which was to be reduced to £1; moreover, if the diggers themselves would elect one of their number as a representative the Governor would immediately appoint him to the Legislative Council. Otherwise Hotham was ready to support Rede in sterner measures. Troop reinforcements sent to Ballarat were received with hostility; a mass meeting of miners resulted in thousands of licences being defiantly burned; Rede ordered the police to weed out unlicensed miners, who began to make the mutiny a reality.

Those prepared for violent action were a minority, but they could rely on much sympathy from the rest of the mining community and had thrown up at least one effective leader. Peter Lalor was an unlikely rebel, the son of an Irish MP who had experience enough of the mode of conducting politics in Ireland 'not to want to be involved with them'. One brother, Richard, who had accompanied Peter to Australia, also became a Westminster MP, but although another, Fintan, had been involved in the abortive revolt of 1848, Peter's own subsequent political career was entirely constitutional. When Speaker of the Victorian Parliament from 1880 to 1887, Lalor adopted a pragmatic conservative stance; if democracy meant 'Chartism, Communism or Republicanism' he repudiated it, but if by democracy was understood 'opposition to a tyrannical press, a tyrannical people or a tyrannical government' then he would 'ever remain a democrat'.[35]

But Peter Lalor was Irish, with a powerful sense of solidarity in resistance to unfairness and, when elected leader by a miners' meeting on 30 November, accepted with some diffidence: 'I expected someone who is really well known to come forward and direct our movement.' A barricade, 'nothing more than an enclosure to keep our own people together', was thrown up, followed by much discussion and some warlike preparation. In the early morning of 3 December the army moved in. The fighting was done by the regular soldiers, but the Melbourne *Argus* correspondent protested against the 'barbarities practised by the mounted troopers. Those who had taken the law into their own hands were punished by the soldiers; those who were warned and perfectly innocent of rebellious notions, were murdered, fired at, and horribly mangled by the troopers.' Four soldiers and some thirty rebels were left dead; the police troopers appeared to have suffered few casualties. Lalor was among the wounded, losing an arm, but establishing his popularity. Hotham redeemed himself to some extent by not insisting on any punishment for the rebels, and within a few months Lalor was elected a member of the Victorian Legislative Assembly.[36]

Although the Legislative Council was solidly behind the Governor, popular opinion in Melbourne was indignant at the violent suppression of the rising. A public meeting called to support the Governor had to be abandoned, as dissidents prophesied a general rebellion if those responsible for the 'illegal and murderous' action were not 'brought to justice'. A worried Hotham found convenient scapegoats, and appealed on 3 January 1855 to the Colonial Secretary for Secret Service funds in order to combat 'the French Red Republican, the German political metaphysician, the American Lone Star Member and the British Chartist [who] here meet not to dig gold but to agitate, overturn the Government and seize the Land'. This was pure hysteria. The investigators Hotham had sent to the goldfields in mid-December were confident enough to recommend a general amnesty, petitions for which poured in. 'Politically more than two-thirds of us are . . . downright rebels', one gentleman wrote home; but rebels only in the strictest constitutional sense, more like liberals agitating for no taxation without representation. The trials of those diggers who were arraigned became farcical as the accused were acquitted to loud cheers, until their defence counsel no longer bothered to present a case. When a commission of inquiry presented its conclusions these condemned both the rebels and the government:

they most unequivocally condemn the resort to arms on the part of any section of the people. This is to betray the popular cause by placing it at the mercy of authority rendered despotic by the necessity of the case. It is a procedure which levels at once the boasted superiority of British character and civilisation; a movement alike illegal and unworthy.

The subsequent Mining Act of June 1855, which established a system of elected miners' courts, gave the miners almost complete control over regulations; combined with the grant of the franchise their triumph was complete.[37]

With some diffidence, and against many objections, Victoria also decided to adopt the secret ballot for the new parliamentary elections. British conservative opinion was alarmed; voting was a public duty, and should involve public responsibility; secrecy was suspiciously un-British and it was only in 1872 that British elections ceased to be fought on the hustings, often noisily enough. Together with the miners' franchise, the secret ballot went a long way to ensure that the Victorian Assembly would be much more representative of public opinion than the Council – but also that clashes between the two houses were thereby guaranteed.

7

The Transition to Responsible Government

New South Wales

The colony's new constitution, inaugurated in November 1855, made few concessions to democracy. The Legislative Council was to be entirely nominated and to sit for life. If the colonists believed this to be a reflection of the British system, the British politicians who had drafted the permissive legislation did not. Both Gladstone and Newcastle attacked the idea that Britain had some anti-colonial interests that needed nominees to defend them. 'The House of Lords', Grey insisted, 'was an institution altogether peculiar to this country [and] Parliament could no more create it than it could a full-grown oak.' Property qualifications were retained for both the franchise and the right to sit in the Legislative Assembly; and although the Act included the power of the legislature to amend the constitution this was subject to a two-thirds majority in both the Legislative Assembly and the Legislative Council. In particular, there was no mention of responsible government, but every precedent indicated that all concerned assumed that, as in Canada and New Zealand, ministries must be able to command support in the elected Legislative Assembly. The parallel with New Zealand was especially convincing. With a white population of only some 30,000 (Maoris were enfranchised on the same basis, but insistence on English literacy drastically reduced any Maori influence), the New Zealand colonists had been assured by the Colonial Office in December 1854 that 'Her Majesty's Government have no objection whatever to offer to the establishment of the system known as responsible government in New Zealand. They have no reason to doubt that it will prove the best method for developing the interests as well as satisfying the wishes of the community.' The only condition imposed was provision for retiring officials, 'of which the necessity appears to be fully recognized by the General Assembly'. No legislative enactment was required to bring the change into operation since 'In this country the recognized plan of Parliamentary government . . . rests on no written law, but on usage only.' No Australian expected anything less, and Clause 32 gave them the opportunity to bring it about.[1]

The 1855 election in New South Wales was indecisive, returning about thirty members who could be classified as 'conservatives' with twenty liberals, but these definitions were fluid in the extreme; Denison, who had taken over from Fitzroy in January 1855, complained to his friend Sir Roderick Murchison, the famous geographer, 'I have as many parties as there are individuals members of the legislature'. The *Sydney Morning Herald* of 22 May mused on the future: the youth of New South Wales would surely live to see 'the colony expanded into a nation, the government raised into a federal state. Perhaps still united to England by some silken thread.' Would the expanded New South Wales 'improve on the pattern of the USA' or degenerate into one of those 'wretched republics, ever torn by anarchy, ever defiled by blood, with whom liberty is but the shrieks and capers of an unhanded madman', which characterized the rest of the American continent? It was not until June 1856, after the first general election of March, that a ministry was actually formed. Denison's first responsible minister was Stuart Donaldson. He was not the Governor's first choice; Denison would have preferred that Deas Thomson should continue in office, and the latter continued to advise him informally. Donaldson was impeccably conservative, rich, well travelled, founder of that bastion of the establishment, the Australian Club (although he had fought a duel with old Sir Thomas Mitchell – knight and Oxford DCL since 1839, but still not quite respectable; both men missed).[2]

Donaldson was asked to form a ministry in January. By April he was losing patience, writing agitatedly to his friend James Macarthur:

I do not see how the Governor can go on many days longer in his present state of uncertainty. He has *no ministry – no Executive Council even*, which can prepare – or mature – the necessary plans for 23rd May by which time the Assembly must be called together. *A responsible ministry must be found immediately* (it appears to me) and a great deal of most important discussion must take place, as well as the *nomination of the upper House by that responsible ministry*. The elections are now *most in favour of the liberal-conservative party to which both you and I, I think, belong* – and if they conclude as they promise to do, the majority will be both *large and powerful*.

Macarthur himself might not have accepted Donaldson's description of his own politics, unhappy as he was at what seemed to be the triumph of democracy, but he gave his temporary support to the first responsible administration as Minister without Portfolio. Only one member of the new Cabinet, William Manning, Solicitor General since 1844, had any administrative experience. The new ministers found parliamentary life 'so intractable and we could not go on from night to night with majorities of only two or three'. They lasted out for less than three months, after which Denison turned to what, broadly speaking, was the liberal opposition.[3]

Sir Charles Cowper, 'Slippery Charlie', brought out to Australia at the age of 2, had become a zealous opponent of transportation, and was considered 'too radical' to become the first Premier – the term generally used in the Australian states – but within months was recognized as an inevitable choice. Although his first ministry lasted only four weeks, in the next fourteen years Cowper headed four more administrations. Together with the even more radical John Robertson, a ruggedly independent squatter, who had arrived as a 6-year-old but identified himself with the native-born, the New South Wales liberals were the dominant force in ten of the eleven ministries, and were successful in carrying two radical amendments to the colony's constitution. Cowper's failure to assemble a stable majority faced Denison with the decisions expected of a constitutional monarch; if it were clear that neither party – or combination of persons, as was more likely in New South Wales – could secure a majority in the Assembly, the Governor had a choice. Either Parliament could be dissolved and a new election called, or the politicians told to go and try again. Denison rightly concluded that an election would be unlikely to produce any clear result, and refused the dissolution that Cowper requested. There followed a year of reconstituted Donaldson government under the 'precise and methodical' Henry Parker, a period long enough for the opposition to cohere rather better, and for the Governor to lose patience. 'For Heaven's sake,' he wrote exasperatedly (to Donaldson on 25 February 1857), 'get your loan bill and all other bills as fast as you can.' Parker could not contrive to manage business expeditiously, in particular to secure the passage of a new electoral law, too liberal for such former supporters as James Macarthur but vociferously demanded by the townsfolk. Cowper, back in September, could only hold on until December of that year; this time Denison agreed to a fresh election, which led to Cowper's return and nearly two years of stability.[4]

For many years the nominated members of Legislative Councils continued to represent the propertied interests, solidly conservative and frequently clashing with the elected Assembly members, foreshadowing what became in the twentieth century a division between Labor majorities (always so spelt) in the lower house, heavily influenced if not dominated by trade unions, and a shifting coalition of urban and rural conservatives which usually held power in the Senate. For the first years of responsible government this distinction was often overlaid by divisions on domestic matters.

British parliamentary life is still governed by conventions, often solidified into rules. In the nineteenth century these were still being established, and the House of Commons was very much a gentlemen's club, whose members whatever their politics were bound by a common code of conduct and similar views of society. When John Bright, well read, much travelled, immensely influential and popular, but a Lancashire factory owner, who had not experienced the purifying effects of education at a great public school and ancient university, and was a Quaker to boot, became a Cabinet minister in 1868 his colleagues were baffled. They realized he was unused to the round of country house gatherings at which so much business was done, and which would now have to accommodate him; would Bright require special nourishment? What topics of conversation might not be ventured upon?

Australian politicians were more robust. It was to be many years in England before such a man as Sir Henry Parkes could become prominent in British politics. Parkes, who was to become the nearest approach to a national Australian leader before the end of the nineteenth century, was a near contemporary (four years younger than Bright).[5] Five times Premier of New South Wales between 1872 and 1891, and one of the founding fathers of the Australian Commonwealth, Parkes was accepted abroad as 'the most commanding figure in Australian politics'. Son of a gardener and odd job man, an ivory turner whose business had failed, Parkes had come to Australia in 1839 'compelled', as he put it, 'to seek the means of existence in a foreign wilderness'. Like Bright, Parkes was self-educated, liberal-minded but lacking the insulation of wealth that protected the English politician, and having to operate in a society where agreement on codes of conduct was less common than in British politics; his first ministry fell partly because it was felt that in one inter-Cabinet dispute Parkes had not displayed 'the frankness of a gentleman or the sensitivity of a friend or colleague'.

A more radical bloc was forming within the liberals, but one without an acknowledged leadership. Henry Parkes had emerged as proprietor and editor of the *Empire*; 'The politics of the *Empire*', Parkes declared, 'will best be indicated by the word Radical; and it will be a bold and uncompromising champion of its creed.' But Parkes made heavy weather of his entrance into politics, hampered by financial problems which led in 1858 to his bankruptcy and the sale of the *Empire*. Together with Daniel Deniehy and John Robertson, Parkes supported Cowper in a programme of electoral reform. In November 1858, taking advantage of Clause 32, the New South

Wales Assembly passed (with the full support of the Colonial Office, were it needed) a constitution more radical than that secured in Britain for some years to come. Voting was to be by secret ballot with manhood suffrage; property qualifications for members were abolished, and membership of the Assembly increased to seventy-two; electoral districts were reorganized to give a more equitable representation in place of the original system which had favoured the dispersed rural districts. Some mollification was offered to the conservatives by the introduction of plural voting – extra business and other votes, a system which continued in the United Kingdom until after the Second World War – but Donaldson was scandalized by the thought that 'every beggar in the street with his bludgeon at his back' would be admitted to the vote on equal terms.

All Cowper's reforms were resisted, unavailingly, by the nominated Legislative Council, clearly out of touch with public opinion. He was brought down, in October 1859, by a quarrel over religious versus undenominational education, a troublesome subject for all nineteenth-century governments, but the liberals came back in March 1860 under the leadership of John Robertson (there had been a short and ineffective interim conservative ministry led by the rich and eccentric William Forster, playwright and satirist).[6]

By October 1859, after Cowper's defeat, Denison wrote wearily to a friend:

I have now been working responsible government for three years and a half, and have to report that the anticipations of those who hailed its advent as the introduction of a political millennium have been grievously disappointed. During this period I have had five sets of ministers, besides numerous individual changes; not one single measure for social improvement has passed, and the only acts of importance which have stood the ordeal are those of very questionable advantage . . . since the commencement of the present session in a House elected by universal suffrage, Mr. Cowper, the head of the government has been obliged to resign twice. The first time the House ate its own words, and he was able to come back; on the second occasion, the decision was so unmistakeably against him, that he and his colleague were obliged to resign altogether. I have now got a set of untried men, the outsiders in the political race, but I hardly expect to have them in for the remainder of the session. Indeed I do not feel sure that I shall not have to turn them out this very day, for they appear inclined to override the law, instead of considering themselves bound to carry it out honestly.[7]

Cocky Farmers

James Macarthur and his fellow squatters had been apprehensive that a democratic responsible government would upset their existing comfortable status, and it was not long before their fears were realized. The Order in Council of March 1847 had transformed the squatters from struggling pioneers to privileged occupiers of land – often very large areas; in central New South Wales just over a thousand properties held some 44 million acres, only a fraction of which, thanks to the generous land policies, had actually been paid for. On these holdings cultivation was strictly limited to the immediate needs of the ranchers themselves, thus sterilizing much potentially rich arable land. In the better areas, such as the Riverina, eighty estates of over 40,000 acres had been amassed 'from which human habitation had been all but obliterated'. It was not an auspicious beginning for responsible government.

Resisting popular pressure is a skill highly developed by sensible democratic governments – consider how for half a century British governments have avoided the reintroduction of capital punishment, during a time when there was every indication that this would command an enthusiastic majority in a referendum – but it was quickly put to the test in both New South Wales and Victoria. The democratic effects of manhood suffrage could be diluted by altering the size of constituencies so that reliable conservative voters were grouped in relatively small numbers, while dangerous urban democrats had to produce large numbers of voters in order to elect a candidate. Electoral districts had therefore been skewed to give excessive political power to the pastoral districts at the expense of the towns and settled areas. Urban workers and idealists found this imposition of a rural aristocracy intolerable, and insisted that the 'land must be unlocked', demanding a homesteading policy similar to that of the United States which would make the equality of representation – one vote, one value – more easily attainable:

The ingenious mechanic, the stalwart yeoman, and the industrious labourer – those classes of society which form the bulk and basis, the bone and sinew of every Anglo-Saxon nation, – have failed in every fair effort to find a home of their own, and, in despair, have at last, in too many instances, been obliged to submit to the remorseless exactions of that class of men whose special and peculiar business it is to reap where they have not sown, to gather where they have not strawed, and to grind the faces of the poor.[8]

John Robertson, energetic, popular, uncouth and vehement in debate, made himself their champion. His success was embodied in the Land Acts of 1861 which allowed anyone who could muster the sum of £80 to choose a plot of 320 acres, which would become his freehold property within three years, on a further payment, and on condition he was living on and developing his farm. The land could be selected anywhere except in towns, suburbs and on goldfields, but often on land already occupied by squatters on short leases. 'Selectors' were also allowed to stake claims to land which was still unsurveyed. It was an extraordinary measure, negating previous arrangements and, in theory at least, allowing anyone to choose their share of the colony's land. Chaos was inevitable, and a wild scramble for land ensued. Well-established squatters with access to credit and with a cavalier disregard for the law could employ a series of man-of-straw 'dummies' to act as intending purchasers; the condition that a house must be erected could be evaded by renting a de-mountable 'flying hut'. Astute selectors could 'pick the eyes' out of a run by choosing strategic sites, for example around a waterhole, and demand ransom money from the squatter. A painstaking investigation made in 1883 was scathing: the 1861 Act which 'professed to open the country to settlement' had instead 'Barred the advance of honest enterprise in all directions, and has at the same time opened a door for the entrance of every phase of abuse and fraud, to be shared in by persons of all classes and conditions'.[9]

It was generally accepted that 320 acres was the minimum necessary for profitable agriculture, and that plots should be made available to all comers, with very little attention paid to their experience, ability to clear, equip and stock their holding, or to the suitability of the land. A low price would be fixed, and easy payment offered. The cry to 'unlock the land' which could be answered without expense to government was irresistible, but the dangers considerable. The prudent Victorian lawyer George Higinbotham pointed out that however ingeniously legislation was framed, its purpose could be easily defeated by the superior economic power of the defensive squatters:

It is idle to say that land legislation can meet and defeat the various contrivances of fraud. Those contrivances are so numerous, and the means of resisting them, if absolute power be not given, so weak, that – I care not how carefully your Acts are framed – if men are tempted by strong inducements of avarice, and are provided with legal means to effect their object, the State will be defrauded, and the poor man for whom you wish to legislate will be utterly defeated.

Higinbotham was proved right.[10]

Those selectors who succeeded in obtaining their acreages often had a hard time of it. If they were industrious, lucky, had family help and enough capital to get them fairly started, a modest prosperity was attainable. Three hundred and twenty acres was in fact usually insufficient, but a successful man could acquire more, and when other colonies followed the New South Wales initiative 640 acres was established as a permissible maximum. Caroline Chisholm, who did much to help new settlers, had told the House of Lords Select Committee on colonization from Ireland (1847) that she had 'known families who to secure a Homestead have gone for years without tea or sugar'. Such small farmers – 'cockatoo, or cocky farmers' became figures of Australian legend, the 'battlers' wresting a living from the land. Many gave up, the temptations of drink, idleness, or sheer blank discouragement driving them to sell their selection for what it would fetch and hire themselves out as labourers. Others flourished; one Highland family was able to select between them 1,920 acres, and within twenty years was able to boast seven good horses, ten cows 'of aristocratic lineage', pigs, turkeys and chickens, a small plain house, surrounded with vines, almonds, apples, pears, peaches, apricots and mulberries; the visitor was given a supper of 'a sirloin of beef, a sucking-pig, a boiled and stuffed turkey, four boiled fowls, a ham, early potatoes, peas, radishes, cucumbers, bread, scones, oatcake, fritters, a plum-pudding, curds and cream, pitchers of cream'. It was a feast that it would have been impossible for a farmer in contemporary Scotland to have furnished and an extraordinary contrast to the Highlands they had left, devastated by famine and clearances. 'It's a good country for a steady man', was their unanimous verdict.[11]

'Constitution-tinkering is here continual'

In the aftermath of Eureka, Hotham was obliged to fight a rearguard action against the newly enfranchised radicals, who would be able to exercise their vote in the election due in October 1855. John O'Shanassy, a friend of Gavan Duffy, who had been elected to the first Legislative Council in 1851, had announced his intention to move a resolution denouncing the 'system of irresponsible government' in Victoria which had 'provided itself most injurious to the highest interests of her people, confessedly unsuited to their wants, opposed most flagrantly to their deliberate wishes, destructive alike of their unalienable rights, and most cherished constitutional liberties', and which must be replaced by a government responsible to the majority in the House of Assembly. Lord John Russell brushed the Governor's concerns aside: 'I am not aware that any special directions are required from myself.'

Grappling with the problem as he saw it, Hotham prepared a minute on 23 November 1855, the day the new constitution was proclaimed, putting the point of view that

the Colonial Governor is the Queen's agent, and he is responsible to his Sovereign, the Parliament and the British people.

The Governor of this Colony will always require, that previously to the introduction of any measure into Parliament, his sanction be obtained. Should he refuse his sanction, and this measure be of sufficient importance to warrant such a consequence, he may, should he think proper change his administration, or they may, should they feel aggrieved, tender their resignations, but in no case can they be justified in submitting a measure to Parliament without the cognizance of the Governor.[12]

Although eminently conservative, the incoming administration could not accept this view, and demanded its withdrawal; on 3 December Hotham replied that his minute was not a 'dictation' and that he recognized that 'the forebearance of all Parties Concerned' would be necessary. On the thirtieth of that month Hotham died.[13]

A year's interregnum followed, in which old General Edward Macarthur took over, the last of Wellington's officers to administer an Australian colony. He was succeeded, after a quiet year, by Sir Henry Barkly (1856–63).[14] Barkly had the invaluable qualification of having been a Westminster MP, as well as governor of two other colonies, and was able to guide the first responsible governments. He inherited a caretaker administration, headed by a Cambridge doctor, the reliable William Haines, which had been appointed by Hotham entirely from members of the Council, and which did not have majority support in the Assembly. Sir Henry came with the firm intention of making self-government work, and a 'total lack of fear of the participation of the masses in politics'. Although a Tory, he believed in the Disraelian concept of conservative democracy, and conscientiously accepted that 'the action of the ministry is entirely independent of the Governor, except in the extreme resort of a dismissal, and the business of the executive is consequently confined to the registration of the recommendations brought forward by the responsible head of each department'. He appreciated that a Governor was appointed by and responsible to the Colonial Office in London, but was obliged to act, except in very unusual circumstances, on the advice – for which read direction – of the elected colonial ministers. A good example of the difficulties facing Barkly, and of his skill in handling them, was the ministerial crisis of February 1858, when the Haines administration was defeated on an electoral reform Bill. The opposition leader, John O'Shanassy, would accept only the post of colonial secretary, as it was still commonly known; only one of his colleagues had actually opposed Haines's reform Bill, although they were now pledged to bring forward a new Bill. When that was introduced it was rejected by the Legislative Council, to great popular agitation by 'the scum of our back streets'. Rather than appeal to the voters, O'Shanassy chose to try again – if he could continue in office for two years both he and his colleagues would qualify for a substantial pension. In October a much less radical Bill was quickly accepted by the Council and the O'Shanassy government continued clock-watching, counting the days towards the happy date when they would qualify for pensions, confident that however many times they suffered defeat in Parliament, no alternative was readily available. Higinbotham fulminated: 'the present Assembly is in a state of utter demoralisation. It is a mere rabble of political desperadoes ... to gratify a coarse personal malignancy is the common and primary object of almost all.'[15]

As in New South Wales the first years of responsible government in Victoria were characterized 'by political instability, faction and intrigue'; between November 1855 and June 1861 seven governments struggled for existence. 'Constitution-tinkering is here continual', observed the shrewd young politician Charles Dilke in the course of his world tour in 1867: 'the new society is ever reshaping its political institutions to keep pace with the latest development of the national mind.' Tinkering was effective: – manhood suffrage, the secret ballot, and triennial assemblies were all quickly accepted – before some continuity was given by Sir James McCulloch, a decisive Scot, in power with two short intermissions, from 1861 to June 1871. The real political struggle, however, was not within the Assembly, whose individuals could often agree to differ in the general interest, but between an increasingly democratic Assembly and a solidly reactionary Council, still composed of prosperous conservatives.[16]

It was hardly surprising that the new Australian governments would take some years to shake down; what is much more remarkable is the controlled and law-abiding evolution of colonial administrations. That of Victoria is particularly striking. Before 1851 no local institutions had existed; the only experience of government had been the opportunity, often ineffective, to send members to the New South Wales Legislative Council. The election of September 1851 was the first opportunity to elect a part-representative body; five years later the first responsible government was formed – twenty-four years after the first settlers had arrived – and by 1861 stable administrations were formed on the basis of a democratic system that only a few years earlier was viewed with nervous distrust. The Australian colonies moved towards democracy much more rapidly than did Britain. By 1861 New South Wales, Victoria, South Australia and Queensland all had secret ballots and manhood suffrage – one man one vote – the last not attained in Britain for many years to come. Even after the 1867 Reform Act (bitterly opposed by Robert Lowe, whose Australian experiences had led him to distrust democracy), only 2 million of the 8 million adult men in England and Wales could claim the franchise; the succeeding 1884 Act brought the proportion only up to about 60 per cent; it was not until June 1918 that Britain finally caught up with the example set seventy years earlier by its Australian colonies in adopting the principle of one man one vote (votes for women followed in two stages, in 1918 and ten years later, a generation after South Australia had begun the process in 1894).

The growth of Melbourne was as remarkable as the development of self-government. By 1861 – sixteen years after the town's foundation – the population had risen to 140,000, bigger than that of Bristol, soon to become larger than Edinburgh and, to the disgust of New South Welshmen, considerably larger than Sydney. Melbourne had also become the undisputed financial centre; in 1861 the first officially constituted stock exchange was established, ten years before that of Sydney. In the same years deposits held by Melbourne banks totalled £2,259,000; ten years later this had risen to £6,228,000, while the comparative figures for Sydney were £1,012,000 and £1,484,000 respectively.[17]

South Australia

The other established colonies, Van Diemen's Land and South Australia, were given the same carte blanche to design their own constitutions as had New South Wales and Victoria. After its shaky start, South Australia bounced back into prosperity with the discovery of extensive silver, lead and copper deposits, and with the adoption of a variant Wakefield system in 1842 which brought a steady stream of subsidized emigrants, 56,000 of them before the gold rush arrivals of 1852. The responsibility for selecting emigrants was vested in the London Emigration Commissioners, who took their responsibilities seriously. Attempting to correct the imbalance of the sexes, and to provide for the victims of the Irish Famine, the Commissioners began to send out numbers of orphaned Irish girls. It was a doubtful success, as colonists complained that many of the girls were flighty, dirty or immoral, and the experiment ceased after a few months during which 621 girls were sent out. Only after some debate, and on condition that proportionate numbers of English and Scottish girls should be sent, and those with 'domestic experience and high moral character' be selected, were more women accepted. The standards were not met, Poor Law governors being only too anxious to reduce their expenses by deporting their most expensive responsibilities, and 4,000 Irish girls were duly shipped. By June 1855 the South Australian *Register* reported that 700 Irish women were lodged in disgraceful conditions in the immigrants' depot: 'The result is that the moral tone of the colony is being fearfully undermined, while the institutions of British pauperism, in their worst form, threaten to establish themselves permanently amongst us.' The Colonial Office protested that 'As we were aware that the original founders of the colony of South Australia were English and Scotch . . . we endeavoured to keep the immigration of the Irish as low as we could', and promised to do better. By 1862, 62 per cent of the assisted emigrants to Southern Australia were English and Welsh, and 24 per cent Irish; in neighbouring Victoria the proportions were 44 per cent and 30 per cent and in Western Australia 47 per cent and 40 per cent; these differences were to have a lasting effect on the character of the colonies.[18] Charles Dilke noted the contrast between the nations:

The Scotch are not more successful in Adelaide than everywhere in the known world. Half the most prominent among the statesmen of the Canadian Confederation, of Victoria, and of Queensland, are born Scots, and all the great merchants of India are of the same nation. Whether it be that the Scotch emigrants are for the most part men of better education than those of other nations, of whose citizens only the poorest and most ignorant are known to emigrate, or whether the Scotchman owes his uniform success in every climate to his perseverance or his shrewdness, the fact remains, that wherever abroad you come across a Scotchman, you invariably find him prosperous and respected.

The Scotch emigrant is a man who leaves Scotland because he wishes to rise faster and higher than he can at home, whereas the emigrant Irishman quits Galway or County Cork only because there is no longer food or shelter for him there. The Scotchman crosses the seas in calculating contentment; the Irishman in sorrow and despair.[19]

The noisy democracy of Sydney and of the Victorian goldfields had no reflection in sedate Adelaide or in the prosperous farms and vineyards. Growth in South Australian farming had been even more successful than in Victoria, and as early as 1865 it had become the largest farming state. The issue that both agitated and united the colonists was that of education; a cardinal principle of the founders and immigrants had been that all religious denominations should have equal treatment, and Lieutenant Governor

Frederick Robe, who succeeded the remarkable Charles Grey in 1845, was a High Church Tory and a supporter of Anglican primacy. The early dreams of religious equality and laicity had been dimmed with the failure of the Commissioners and the reversion to Crown Colony status, under which South Australia's Legislative Council could make its own arrangements. The 1846 census proved that Dissenters were in a minority, and Robe's proposal, supported by the equally conservative Sir John Morphett, to give state aid to all Churches aroused general indignation. The arrival of a bishop in December 1847, although a bishop with limited privileges, on a par with clergymen of other denominations, caused further irritation. Many Nonconformist Churches refused their state grants and a disconsolate Robe applied for a transfer after only six months in the colony. Reforming zeal characterized both voters and candidates in the first election of a representative Assembly in 1851. From the 5,912 registered in the contested seats (7,279 in all, from an adult male population of some 20,000), 4,918 voters turned out, returning members who 'almost to a man had committed themselves to some form of change'. Their very first action was to reject a Bill continuing the system of state-paid priests, thereby re-establishing South Australia as an unequivocally secular state.[20]

Boyle Finnis, one of the earliest immigrants, a member of both Legislative and Executive Councils, had been colonial secretary under the accommodating Governor Sir Henry Young since 1851, and continued as Premier under the much brisker Sir Richard Graves MacDonnell. Young, in post between 1848 and 1854, was one of that new breed, a professional colonial civil servant, one of the first Australian governors without military or naval experience, who had eighteen years colonial service before being posted to Australia. His initiative was demonstrated when the colony was faced with the same sort of currency shortage that had plagued Macquarie in New South Wales. With Finnis's support Sir Henry agreed to the issue of a Bullion Act in 1852 making gold legal tender, and to the circulation of stamped gold tokens. This was equivalent to coining colonial money, very much frowned upon by any British Treasury, but the Colonial Secretary, Sir John Pakington, defended his Governor, and ensured that sufficient sovereigns were exported. Rather unfairly, it was Sydney that was allowed to establish the Australian mint, which it did in 1855, much to the mortification of the Victorians, who refused to accept New South Wales gold as legal tender, an attitude in which Melbourne persisted for two years.[21]

Young was altogether less successful in constitutional matters. As might have been expected, the South Australian Legislative Council was even more conservative than most, and reluctant to let slip any part of its control.

Much discussion ensued, when after 1851 the Legislative Council was given a majority (16:18) of elected members, leading Young to the somewhat desperate measure of drafting a constitution himself. His proposal, which hedged the question of responsible government and provided for a nominated upper house, as in New South Wales, was rejected by the existing Legislative Council, who considered that they had been 'misled' and that the colonial administration had acted 'unfairly'. When Young nevertheless sent his draft to London, it was followed by an indignant petition and in turn rejected by the British government. Arriving in June 1855 the energetic and opinionated Governor MacDonnell threw himself into the debate. Very justly pointing out that because of the 'intelligence and orderly' character of the South Australians and the nature of the colony,

where the subdivision of landed property prevails to great extent, giving to an unusual number a fixed interest in the soil, and where the general population is settled, and regards the country as the home of their adoption, in whose good government and general progress they must therefore feel a deep and lasting concern, a very democratic form of constitution might be adopted with greater safety than in almost any other of the British colonies.[22]

MacDonnell suggested an odd single-chamber Assembly, usually regarded as dangerously democratic, but with some modification by ensuring a minority core elected on a restricted franchise. Abandoned as quite unworkable, 'a Governor's fancy', South Australia opted instead for a conventional House of Assembly and Legislative Council, both entirely elected, with a moderate property qualification imposed for the Council, but with the Assembly elected by all resident adult men. Old George Angas, who had been a member of the Legislative Council, had every reason to be pleased with his colony's rapid progress to self-government.

South Australia was also the first colony to institute triennial Parliaments, in 1856. Chartists had demanded that fresh elections should be held every year, and three years was a compromise between that practically impossible demand and the five years established in Britain and specified in the original colonies' constitutions. The precedent was followed by the other colonies, and carried on to the Federal constitution of 1900. Combined with the later decision to make voting compulsory, this was to lock voters into political life, and to make governments spend a great proportion of their time planning to win the next election – a practice which brought some decidedly negative consequences. In addition, since those colonies with elected Councils retained their previous tenures – in South Australia for example, six members of the eighteen-member Council retired every four years – elections for Assembly and Council were pushed permanently out of phase.

Tasmania

The Van Demonians, or since the bishopric of Tasmania had been established under that name in 1842, the Tasmanians, were less enthusiastic about the prospect of responsible government than the other colonies. Two factors combined to influence their attitudes: their colony was so much smaller than the others that little remained unallocated of the 'Waste Lands' which elsewhere represented potential income; and the government costs involved in supporting the high proportion of convicts made a financial agreement with the home government a matter of pressing urgency. As a penal colony, Van Diemen's Land had not benefited by the 1842 Act that introduced an elected element into the Legislative Council, but when the 1850 Act providing for the addition of elected members to the Council was passed the news was received with only modified excitement. Ending transportation was the central subject occupying public attention and dividing the Governor and his Councillors. Only when convicts ceased to arrive could Tasmania claim equality with the eastern mainland states and be allowed the same freedom to draft its own constitution. Lord Grey, however, clung to the hope that the eastern Australian colonies might still admit some convicts, especially if agreement could be reached with the northern settlers, and the 1848 order authorizing transportation had not been revoked. But Van Diemen's Land remained the only practicable possibility for the time being; and both the Governor and many influential colonists wanted more exiles.

After the rush to the goldfields, labour was unprecedently scarce, and the restricted number of prisoners who arrived were eagerly recruited. When 292 convicts arrived in 1852, 1,259 applications for their services were received. Sir William Denison, who did not have a high opinion of the fitness of his charges to assume the responsibilities of self-government, was anxious to have, as in New South Wales, a nominated upper house to act as some restraint on that 'egalitarian, envious and democratic society'. Free workmen were moving to the mainland, lured by the higher wages paid in those areas where there was no competition from convict labour. Denison vigorously defended Van Demonian employers. He abjured the 'intense appetite for work operating upon a coarse and grovelling mind that prevailed in South Australia. Higher wages led only to drink and debauchery; lower wages, although providing 'a fair share of the necessaries, the comforts, and even the luxuries of life', prevented servants from dictating to their masters. And did not informed visitors, including Fitzroy and Deas Thomson, agree that Tasmanian landowners kept up their property better than those in New South Wales? Lord Grey concurred; Australia contained

not less than 68,000 persons upon whom the sentence of transportation has been passed and who are now living in a state of perfect or qualified freedom and in general earning their bread by honest industry, but who would have had no resource but to fall back into the commission of crime, if removal had not been made a portion of the punishment of transportation.

His plan was working well. In March 1851 Grey was able to claim that

Out of 1,618 convicts sent out to New South Wales between June 1849 and April 1850, with tickets of leave under the existing plan, there were only forty from whom it had been necessary for misconduct to withdraw the tickets of leave, and of those only ten were cases of a serious description.[23]

To be sure, some influential colonists agitated for the end of transportation, but they were unlikely to be as violent as the Cape population had proved. Lady Denison poked fun at Lord Grey for dispatching a man-of-war to Hobart to overawe any rebellious Van Demonians: 'Could he only take a peep at us, he would find everything going peaceably; a noisy party indeed *talking*, and *eating* public dinners, but *doing* nothing in the way of opposition.'[24]

Opposition in Britain was not, however, to be lightly dismissed. The following February the Russell government fell, and Grey was out of office. But it was the discovery of gold that finally ended transportation to Van Diemen's Land, as ticket-of-leave men streamed across the Bass Strait to join the rush. In the circumstances, 'there are few English criminals who would not regard a free passage to the gold fields of New South Wales, via Hobart town, as a great boon'. When Colonel Joshua Jebb, the eminent Surveyor General of the new prison service, added his view that transportation had ceased to be an effective deterrent, and that the new prisons were taking so much greater a share of convicts, and reforming them with some success, the decision was taken. On 31 December 1852 the last convict ship sailed for Van Diemen's Land and only Western Australia remained open as a destination for transported criminals.

Tasmania was now free to claim the same status as the other colonies and was given a similar constitution in October 1856, at the same time as South Australia and less than a year after New South Wales and Victoria. The

Here there are no paid idlers or sinecurists; every man, from the Governor downwards, is emphatically a working man. Nor have we a Church establishment, a House of Lords, or hereditary privileges of any kind to which democratic sentiments and prejudices are hostile . . .[27]

but it was not until 1872 that the franchise was restored. Governing so tiny a population did not demand great personal qualities, which was just as well since Bowen possessed few, other than superb self-confidence and a superficial charm; he was a consummate bore, idle, inordinately pleased with his lofty acquaintances and immensely conceited. His superiors viewed him with scorn. Lord Granville described him as a 'pompous donkey'; Kimberley noted his 'ridiculous egoism'.[28]

Responsible government came to Queensland in an oddly reversed fashion. Bowen had been sent out to govern in an orthodox Crown Colony manner, and accordingly appointed his secretary, Robert Herbert, as colonial secretary. Herbert was a peculiar figure to initiate a new Australian government; aristocratic (a cousin of the later Colonial Secretary Lord Carnarvon), completely inexperienced (a few weeks' service as Gladstone's private secretary) and at 28, unusually young. Herbert never married, and he tolerated colleagues with pronounced hauteur, befitting a Fellow of All Souls College. In spite of these disadvantages he enjoyed a notable success. Unlike the other colonies, where no government lasted for more than a few months, Herbert continued serenely in charge, enjoying a substantial majority in the Legislative Assembly. This was continued at the second general election, in 1863, but by February 1866 he found himself 'weary and sick and disgusted with colonial politics', and resigned. During more than six years of leadership, an unequalled continuity in any Australian colony, Herbert had set Queensland off to a remarkably good start. With the full support of Governor and Assembly, Herbert had forged ahead with development of colonial infrastructure, and with the English aristocrat's disdain for mundane financial details. His programme was necessarily an expensive exercise – railways, roads, bridges, harbour facilities and public buildings were all needed, and these were financed through the Union Bank which placed loans in London. Persistent bank warnings that investors' patience was wearing thin, and counsels advocating restraint were ignored. By early 1866 the Queensland government was in desperate straits. One £1 million loan had failed, leaving the bank perilously exposed, refusing to advance new money; the government then tried the dangerous expedient of trying another bank, Agra and Masterman's Bank, anxious to break into Australian business. Within weeks a London banking crisis brought down both Agra and Masterman's and the most important of the government building contractors, Peto, Brassey and Betts. The Union Bank immediately cancelled an advance of £100,000, driving the government to such desperate measures as issuing unconvertible notes. It was hardly surprising that John McMullen, the Union Bank's inspector, wrote: 'I hate government accounts, and do not believe they are ever in the long run any real benefit to banks.' With the help of the London financial market the colony's finances were restored, but only after a march by the thousands of men thrown out of work had spread panic in Brisbane.[29]

Since Herbert had resigned in February 1866, four months before the crisis broke, his successor Arthur Macalister, was left holding a very unattractive baby. Macalister, an undistinguished solicitor, a failed shop-keeper and dismissed as a local postmaster, could not cope, and resigned when Bowen vetoed the proposal for the controversial note issue. Herbert was recalled, and in a couple of weeks had piloted stop-gap agreements through with the local banks, before leaving for London to negotiate the resumption of colonial finance, and to begin a creditable career in the civil service.

With his departure, Queensland resumed the pattern of quickly changing ministries, although at a less rapid pace than that of most of the other colonies. Only Western Australia lagged far behind, excluded from the privileges of self-government. In striking contrast to his admiration of South Australia, Charles Dilke found Western Australia detestable:

The contrast between the scenery and the people of West Australia is great indeed. The aboriginal inhabitants of Albany were represented by a tribe of filthy natives – tall, half-starved, their heads bedaubed with red ochre, and their faces smeared with yellow clay; the 'colonists' by a gang of fiend-faced convicts working in chains upon the esplanade, and a group of scowling expirees hunting a monkey with bull-dogs on the pier; while the native women, half clothed in tattered kangaroo-skins, came slouching past with an aspect of defiant wretchedness. Work is never done in West Australia unless under the compulsion of the lash, for a similar degradation of labour is produced by the use of convicts as by that of slaves.[30]

In the rest of the continent, or at any rate in the great semicircle that spread from Port Augusta to Brisbane and beyond, more than a million people had settled into a system of self-government – ten years after Lord John Russell had made his first proposal that the colonists themselves should decide on their own future.

8

Exploration and Expansion

Waiting 'for something to turn up'

It was little more than forty years between the time when the Australian colonies began to settle into their new self-governing status, with constitutions agreed by their own voters, and the day in January 1901 when the Commonwealth of Australia emerged as a nation, independent to most intents and purposes; a very short period in a country's life, comparable with that in the United States between the presidencies of John F. Kennedy and George W. Bush, but one which saw tremendous changes. From being a largely pastoral country, with agriculture concentrated in Tasmania and favoured parts of the eastern colonies, Australia by the turn of the century was a mixed economy with flourishing industries, its population concentrated in the capital cities, and one beginning to realize that it might have a place in the world other than that of a British colony, that there was indeed a genuine, distinct and inimitable Australian-ness.

Towards the end of the nineteenth century, when young Australians were seeking for evidence of a specifically Australian identity, it was sometimes asked why Australian history and geography were not taught in the schools; 'why were Leichhardt, Sturt and Burke and Wills not eulogised as Mungo Park and Livingstone were?'[1] As far as the latter part of the question went the answer is not far to seek. Australian explorers were simply not as exciting as Richard Burton, exploring the male brothels of Karachi and fighting off Arab attackers with his sabre; or as influential as Livingstone, whose missionary activities accompanied his exploring ventures, and who was responsible for transforming an entire African region. Australian explorers did not have to fight their way through 'hostile tribes and kingdoms' accompanied by dozens of armed escorts and porters – indeed, they usually relied on Aborigines as guides, and often depended on their help for survival. Apart from Burke and Wills, of whom more later, Australian explorers were decent, well organized, subfusc and sober (at least while travelling).

Self-discovery first got under way in the 1860s with the expansion of exploration. For a century after Cook's first voyage the interior of Australia beyond the expanding pastoral frontiers remained almost entirely uninvestigated. The northern littoral itself had been tolerably well explored, some strategic points temporarily garrisoned, and farms established. These had succeeded well enough to encourage the New South Wales government to consider the possibility of discovering a suitable transcontinental route to the north coast. Until 1860 the whole of the original area first claimed by Britain as New South Wales was, except for the colonies of South Australia and Victoria, still part of the 'mother colony' governed from Sydney. The first important journey to this unexplored interior was made by the German-born, Berlin-and-Göttingen-educated Ludwig Leichhardt, who flashed briefly across the Australian scene between 1842, when he arrived in Sydney aged 28 hoping for some official scientific post (for which he was well equipped), and 1848, when he disappeared. Quite inexperienced in the hazards of bush-travelling, Leichhardt raised enough money to lead an expedition from the border of settlement in the Darling Downs to Port Essington on the Coburg peninsula, a journey of some 3,000 miles. Of the original ten expedition members, only one, John Gilbert, was lost, the least incompetent of a very scratch party, killed by Aborigines. Leichhardt's methodical industry, his collection of specimens and his meticulous journals, excited the scientific community, won the young explorer international esteem, and encouraged him to try again. However brilliant as a scholar, Leichhardt was no leader of men; the second expedition was a failure, and a third, intended to cross the whole country and arrive at Perth, disappeared completely some time after April 1848. Attempts to discover traces of Leichhardt and his men, however, led to some profitable journeys.[2]

Almost wiped out, too, was Edmund Kennedy's expedition from Rockingham Bay on the Queensland coast to the tip of Cape York. A trained surveyor, Kennedy was second in command to Sir Thomas Mitchell in an 1846–7 expedition to Queensland, and was both an experienced bushman and a lively and popular leader. Theirs was a terrible route, though thick forest and mangrove swamps, beset by fierce Aborigines. Just short of his objective Kennedy, accompanied only by his young Aboriginal colleague, Jacky Jacky, was fatally speared and Jacky Jacky struggled through alone to reach Cape York and the waiting ship. Adventurous young Aborigines penetrated unknown territories with much the same motivation as the young Europeans; but the comradeship and excitement could not last once the adventure was done – as it proved for Jacky Jacky, whose subsequent history forms a sad commentary on the difficulty of being even a successful Aborigine. Widely honoured and given a cash reward, within five years he was burnt to death, having fallen drunkenly into a campfire.[3]

Explorations in southern Australia began with the work of Edward Eyre, who learnt his trade in droving, beginning at the age of 19 as a new chum fresh from Sedbergh School in England, taking sheep and cattle across country from Sydney to Port Phillip and Adelaide. By 1840, still only 25, Eyre had reached the dismal lakes Torrens and Eyre, great dreary salt wastes, on rare occasions filled with a few inches of water; the great Australian lakes, which Macquarie had hoped to find, exist only after extraordinary rains. The discouraged Eyre, determined to 'waste no more time or energy on so desolate and forbidding a region', named his farthest point Mount Hopeless.

With a much better equipped expedition than Eyre had been able to mount, but in what turned out to be a devastating drought, Charles Sturt set out in August 1844 to find a way around Eyre's salt lakes to the inland sea he was convinced must exist. Nearly 50, his health seriously impaired as a result of his earlier explorations, Sturt's expedition dragged on for nearly eighteen months, and penetrated beyond 25 degrees south in terrible conditions, with the thermometer bursting at 127 degrees Fahrenheit. Reluctantly abandoning hope of finding a great lake, together with the boat they had dragged for over 1,000 miles, the explorers returned, with only one helpful discovery, that of a fragile system of watercourses – Cooper's Creek – in the middle of the 'Great Stony Desert'.

Soon after his return to Adelaide, Eyre chose to strike off in another direction, and in February 1841 attempted an east–west crossing, with one assistant and three Aborigines, along the coast and across the horrible Nullarbor Plain from Adelaide to Albany (the name, which might sound Aboriginal, is in fact dog Latin). Aborigines were unpredictable companions, sometimes saving whole expeditions from disaster, but in this instance proving treacherous, killing Eyre's assistant, leaving the leader to struggle on, relieved by a chance meeting with a French whaling crew and accompanied by the remaining loyal Aborigine, the dependable Wylie.[4]

Augustus Gregory's explorations were more successful. Gregory's parents had come with the first Swan River settlers in 1829, and he had practised in Western Australia as an enterprising surveyor. His 1855–6 expedition, sponsored by New South Wales and the British government, included a scientific team headed by the distinguished German-born botanist Baron Ferdinand von Mueller. It was a model expedition, well equipped, prudently led – there was no trouble with Aborigines, always treated with respect – which earned Gregory the Royal Geographical Society's gold medal. Starting in September 1855 from Point Curtis on the eastern coast, Gregory traversed much of Leichhardt's route, but also carried out a thorough exploration. Cool, even cold, in his personal relationships, Gregory was the ideal Australian explorer, but his very success militated against popular fame, which is generally ensured by a spectacular and material failure. The greater part of the journey was done by Gregory and six others, all of whom returned safely, which did not make for exciting stories. In 1858 Gregory set off again to try to link up with Sturt's discoveries, approaching from the north, which he did successfully, following the course of the Barrow River to Adelaide through 'some miserable territory . . . sandy desert or worthless scrub without any sign of change in advancing into the interior beyond that of increasing sterility'.

In 1858, also, one of Sturt's party, John Macdouall Stuart, financed by the enterprising stockdealer, speculator and pastoralist, James Chambers, began commercial explorations in the south. Gregory and Stuart were both experienced explorers, although of very different characters. A professional surveyor – he later became Sir Augustus, Surveyor General of the new state of Queensland – Gregory was well organized and competent, one of three exploring brothers. Stuart, by contrast, was a loner, a heavy drinker, who sought out challenges. He had spent a year and a half with Charles Sturt in his exploration of the South Australian desert, and travelled light on his 1858 expedition (in recognition of which he was awarded a lease over 100 square miles of the new country) accompanied only by an assistant and an Aboriginal tracker, who gave up before the end. Well rewarded for his discoveries, which were advanced further in 1859, Stuart set off north in 1860, and reached Attack Creek, within 300 miles of the northern settlements. By that time Gregory, striking south from the Timor Sea coast, and skirting what is now the Gregory National Park, and Stuart, moving north from Adelaide, had overlapped, but had not succeeded in joining each other's tracks.[5]

With success so near, the race to cross the continent began in earnest, and the potential rewards for a successful transcontinental expedition increased. The muddled colonial boundaries that followed the separation of Queensland had left an enormous territory cut off from New South Wales, 710,000 square miles stretching in a dog-leg from north to south, and from the tropical marshes on the Timor Sea to the dreary shores of the Nullarbor Plain. This cartographical anomaly was rationalized, largely at Gregory's instigation, by South Australia taking over the immensely unattractive dog's-paw, bringing its boundary up to Western Australia, while Queensland pushed its frontiers west to include the much better lands of the Barkly Tableland and the Mount Isa mineral deposits. The future of the rest, the region north of 26 degrees south, that now constitutes the Northern Territory, remained to be settled.

One of the few attractions of this new piece of real estate was the possibility of establishing direct connection between the north and south coasts, eventually perhaps by rail, but in the meantime by the rapidly extending electric telegraph which could connect to the international telegraph terminal in eastern Java. Sir Richard McDonnell, South Australia's governor from 1855 to 1862, was himself an enthusiastic bushman, and persuaded his government to finance Stuart for a final attempt to cross the continent. Such potential competition annoyed the other colonies, who would have very much liked to have the telegraph terminal on their own territory, but an overland route to the north coast, which would reduce the more expensive underwater cable to a minimum, would be preferable. Given Stuart's experience, South Australia had a sporting change of pioneering a suitable route, and in August 1859 offered a prize of £2,000 for the first successful south–north crossing to be made west of 143 degrees east – about the position of Ballarat – and which would follow Stuart's tracks. The Victorians would have none of that, and determined to launch their own expedition which would be, as befitted the richer colony, an altogether more splendid affair than anything South Australia could manage. So indeed it proved to be, funded on a much grander scale by £12,000, in contrast with Stuart's £2,500 in all from South Australia.[6]

Commanded by Superintendent Robert O'Hara Burke of the Victoria police, the Victorian party was unprecedentedly well equipped, having twenty camels, with their drivers, numerous horses and wagons, six tons of firewood and 45 yards of green veiling against the sun, setting out in August 1860. Burke was a strange choice, a temperamental Ascendancy Irishman, brave to the point of rashness, opinionated, a poor leader and a worse judge of men, with little experience of work in the bush. The second in command, William Wills, could serve as an English stereotype as well as Burke did for an Irish. Self-contained, reserved and methodical, he had all the qualities that Burke lacked, but little capacity for decision-making. Along the painful route, the expedition's expensive equipment was jettisoned, and most of its personnel dispensed with. Only Burke and Wills with two others made the final dash for the north coast, and only one, John King, survived. Wills's last letter is a splendid example of the literature of exploration, as almost without emotion Wills described his impending death:

My dear Father,

These are probably the last lines you will ever get from me. We are on the point of starvation, not so much from absolute want of food, but from the want of nutriment we can get.

Our position, although more provoking, is probably not near so disagreeable as that of poor Harty and his companions. We have had very good luck, and made a most successful trip to Carpentaria and back, to where we had every right to consider ourselves safe, having left a depot here consisting of four men, twelve horses, and six camels. They had provisions enough to have lasted them twelve months with proper economy. We had every right to expect that we should have been immediately followed up from Menindie, by another party with additional provisions and every necessary for forming a permanent depot at Cooper's Creek. The party we left here had special instructions not to leave until our return, unless from absolute necessity. We left the creek nominally with three months' supply, but they were reckoned at little over the rate of half rations. We calculated on having to eat some of the camels. By the greatest good luck at every turn, we crossed to the gulf through a good deal of fine country, almost in a straight line from here. On the other side the camels suffered considerably from the wet; we had to kill and jerk one soon after starting back. We had not been out a little more than two months, and found it necessary to reduce the rations considerably; and this began to tell on all hands, but I felt it far less than any of the others. The great scarcity and shyness of game, and our forced marches, prevented our supplying the deficiency from external sources to any great extent; but we never could have held out but for the crows and hawks, and the portulac. The latter is an excellent vegetable, and I believe secured our return to this place. We got back here in four months and four days, and found the party had left the creek the same day, and we were not in a fit state to follow them.

I find I must close this that it may be planted, but I will write some more, although it has not so good a chance of reaching you as this. You have great claim on the committee for their neglect. I leave you in sole charge of what is coming to me. The whole of my money I desire to leave to my sisters; other matters I will leave for the present. Adieu, my dear father. Love to Tom.

WJ Wills

I think to live about four or five days. My spirits are excellent. My religious beliefs are not in the least bit changed and I have not the least fear of their being so. My spirits are excellent . . .

and in his last diary entry Wills commented dryly: 'my pulse is at 48 and very weak, and my legs and arms are nearly skin and bone. I can only look out, like Mr Micawber "for something to turn up".'[7]

Suffering, success, and courageous death were all the ingredients needed for a successful legend to be born, and the most incompetently conducted of Australian explorations remains the best known. The only member of the transcontinental group to survive was the Irish soldier John King, the first man known to have made the return journey across the continent, rescued 'half-demented by starvation and loneliness' by some Aboriginals, and retrieved by a relief expedition on 15 September 1861. Meanwhile, Stuart's official party had succeeded in advancing only a short distance beyond the point previously reached, and returned to Adelaide on 23 September. Hearing of the tragic success of Burke and Wills, Stuart immediately mounted another South Australian expedition. The government's generosity had been nearly exhausted, and the venture was funded largely by Chambers and local tradespeople. After terrible privations, Stuart's party succeeded in reaching the north coast in July 1862. The race had been won by Victoria, but the miserably funded South Australians all returned, although Stuart himself was in a terrible condition, carried on a stretcher.

Eyre's explorations in the west were succeeded by those of Ernest Giles, who made two crossings in different directions in 1875 and 1876, and by the great John Forrest, in 1870 and 1874. Giles was supported by von Mueller, now Sir Ferdinand, who had been one of Gregory's companions on his epic journey of 1855-6. A determined but prudent leader, Giles nevertheless lost one of his companions, Alfred Gibson, commemorated in the name of the desert which they traversed. John Forrest, who commanded his first expedition at the age of 21, later became the first Premier of Western Australia, and the first native Australian to receive a peerage. His two west–east crossings in 1870 and 1874 from Perth and Geraldton respectively to Adelaide, were satisfactorily crammed with peril and adventure, and won Forrest acclaim in London and Australia as the 'Young Explorer'. To the majority of Australians, who by 1880 lived in towns, the almost immeasurably great and terrifyingly hostile outback was quite unknown, but the knowledge that it existed, with so much still waiting to be discovered, permeated Australian consciousness; nothing could be further removed from the safe restrictions of the British Isles.[8]

Adventurers in the twenty-first century can follow, more or less, in their predecessors' tracks, but the east–west road crossings can hardly be recommended. Stuart's route is easier to trace, since it is represented, in a general way, by the Stuart Highway, some 2,000 miles of (usually) all-weather road from Port Augusta in South Australia to Darwin in the Northern Territory. The highway follows the route of the Overland Telegraph Line, the building of which was one of the most significant events in Australian history, and which caused the massive temporary expansion of South Australia. Stuart's journeys had proved that the construction of a telegraph was possible, and it seemed that, if the project were to be properly handled, it must be South Australia's responsibility. Inaccessibility from the rest of Australia had resulted in any northern settlement being useful only as a warning to other powers to keep off, hardly necessary any longer, and as a way station for any traffic proceeding through the Torres Strait, which, after the opening of China to trade, had virtually disappeared. However, with the demonstration that good pastoral lands might be found north of the existing settlement, interest quickened. New South Wales, to whom the territory had ostensibly belonged ever since Cook's original proclamation, was in no position to object, since the creation of Queensland had cut off the mother colony from the northern regions. Queensland's ambitions were satisfied by the extension of its western boundaries, and although offered all the territory north of the Tropic of Capricorn, she sensibly declined to accept the responsibility for vast tracts of difficult land up to 2,000 miles distant from Brisbane. South Australia, on the other hand, was eager to add to its territory, and the Duke of Newcastle, looking at the map, saw no reason not to oblige.

From 6 July 1863 more than half a million square miles, hitherto very nominally administered from either Perth or Brisbane, were handed over to South Australia by the New South Wales government to constitute the Northern Territory. For South Australia it was a classic case of colonial hubris, of biting off more than could conveniently be chewed; some South Australians saw the dangers, but many clamoured for even more land, to include the adjacent Burketown region of Queensland. South Australia now appeared to have the advantage of a potential telegraph terminus at what was intended to be the capital of their new acquisition at Palmerston, prudently named after the then Prime Minister, on Adelaide Bay, and conveniently near to the international connection in East Java. The construction of some 1,800 miles of landline and 1,000 miles of submarine cable would connect Australia with the rest of the world; but the contract entered into demanded that the landline should be completed in the frighteningly short term of 18 months. With enormous efforts, which included the temporary installation of more than 200 miles of 'pony express' despatch riders, the task was completed under the enthusiastic direction of Charles Todd, Postmaster General of South Australia, although the northern terminus had been changed to the new port at Darwin. Todd had already persuaded South Australia and Victoria to co-operate on adopting a standard telegraphic system, a considerable achievement given the acerbic inter-colonial jealousy, and had negotiated the link between Adelaide, Melbourne and Sydney by 1866. In October 1872 the transcontinental work was done, and one of the first messages was from Queen Victoria, notifying Todd that he was now a Commander of the Order of St Michael and St George. London remained a little confused about Australian geography, as appeared from Foreign Secretary Lord Carnarvon's request to the Governor of Victoria to allow American telegrams to pass over the Adelaide–Darwin line; 'Apply to the South Australian Government' was the aggrieved reply. The *South Australian Advertiser* was furious: 'People have an idea that Australia is one colony, containing a few thousands of inhabitants, whose manners are rude and almost lawless . . . and that Melbourne is the capital city and seat of government of this wild and uncultivated country.'[9]

The telegraph was not allowed to function uninterrupted. The line had sliced through Aboriginal communities; though widely dispersed, they were resentful of this intrusion into their previously undisturbed and ancient lands. Two years after the first transmissions, an incident occurred which eerily foreshadowed the last telephone messages sent by the victims of the atrocities in New York on 11 September 2001. The Barrow Creek telegraph station had been attacked by Aborigines, killing two of the operators; as John Stapleton lay dying he was able to send a farewell message to his wife in Adelaide, 1,200 miles away, over the telegraph wires. In the latter days of the nineteenth century such a violent reaction by Aborigines was rare in the southern populated regions. There the days of poisoned flour and organized battues were passing, largely because the remaining Aborigines presented less of a threat – and in Tasmania, of course, no threat at all – but in vast northern regions, still largely unexplored, Aborigines were able to resist unwelcome intruders. With colonial independence, the Aborigines lost the protection, sometimes unreliable, but always present, of the British government. The colonists themselves were often resentful of what they saw as the dangerous interference of misguided idealists, ignorant of the problems faced every day by the men on the spot. James Stephen was certainly an idealist, but he was entirely accurate in his description of colonial attitudes, writing of the

hatred with which the white man regards the black. That feeling results from fear – from the strong physical contrasts which intercept the sympathy which subsists between men of the same race – from the proud sense of superiority – from the consciousness of having done them great wrongs and from the desire to escape this pain of self reproach by laying the blame on the injured party.[10]

Persecution was replaced by open neglect; Victoria spent about 1 per cent of its land revenues – derived from the sale of lands to which the Aborigines had at least some claim and on which they depended for their existence – on Aboriginal welfare; South Australia, with its strong streak of conscience, intended to do better by committing 10 per cent of land revenue to Aboriginal purposes, which was the figure required by the Colonial Office, but in 1860 decided that this was grossly excessive and that 'natives were to have what was absolutely necessary' – which was not very much. One of the first acts of the Queensland self-governing administration was to restrict Aboriginal rights to the issue of one blanket a year.

Some limited imperial protection remained by the continuance in force of the 1846 Waste Lands Occupation Act, which recognized Aboriginal rights to use the land for their own purposes. Queensland leases included a clause reserving to the Aborigines 'free access to the said parcel of land' or to any portion of it including the trees and water which would 'enable them to procure the animals, birds, fish and other foods of which they subsist'. In Western Australia the blacks had 'the full right' at all times to enter upon any but enclosed and cultivated land 'for the purpose of seeking their subsistence therefrom in their accustomed manner'. The South Australian/ Northern Territory leases went into most detail, allowing the Aborigines

Full and free right of ingress, egress and regress into upon and over the said Waste Land of the Crown . . . and in and to the Springs and surface water thereon and to make and erect such wurlies and other dwellings as the said Aboriginals have been heretofore accustomed to make and to take and use for food birds and animals . . . in such manner as they would have been entitled to if this demise had not been made.

It was not effective, being 'recognised in a poetic rather than a practical sense'; some tolerant and humane pastoralists did contrive to co-exist with what remained of the Aboriginal communities but Aboriginal welfare was low on the list of colonial priorities.[11]

Even had the colonial governments been properly concerned with their Aboriginal citizens, other less obvious inroads were being made into Aboriginal life. On 26 December 1859 the clipper *Lightning* began to land its cargo, which contained a consignment of animals for Thomas Austin of Barwon Park, near Geelong, who was anxious to establish some decent shooting (the Austins were a sporting Somerset family), and 72 partridges, 5 hares and 24 wild rabbits joined the Australian fauna. They were not the first rabbits to come to Australia, for Phillip had brought five with the First Fleet, the Reverend Samuel Marsden jealously guarded his own warren, and rabbits were welcomed in Tasmania, but Mr Austin's were disastrously successful. Within a few years a grey tide of rabbits threatened to engulf Western Victoria. Fifteenth-century English labourers, their lands turned into sheep runs, had complained of the sheep that ate up men: in nineteenth-century Australia it was the rabbits who ate up the sheep. Previously prosperous runs were abandoned as thousands of rabbits devoured the grass and barked the trees. One South Australian farmer described how he met

a swarm coming from the hills, I never saw such a thing before. The ground was scarcely to be seen for about a mile in length. Five weeks since I could not find a rabbit on my land, but since then we have killed thousands. When the sun is hot you can go along the fences or any place where it is shady and kill hundreds with a stick. Today has been cool but still I several times killed two or three at a blow. The paddocks stink with the dead ones.

The value of land was halved, and many of the newly established settlers were ruined, but what was financial hardship to the whites was death to the Aborigines, whose resources were destroyed by the invasion.[12]

Not that many Aborigines survived in the south, where by 1860 the Aboriginal population had drastically shrunk – fewer than one thousand full-bloods were believed to remain in Western Victoria. The 'hatred' that Stephen had detected was replaced by a complacent reflection that this unfortunate race was doomed to extinction and that therefore further persecution was unnecessary; self-interest and decency both indicated that the remaining Aborigines should be, if not integrated into, at least accepted by white society. At best, they were at least as unequivocally and distinctively Australian as the kangaroo, and could be trained to make themselves useful. From the earliest days Aborigines had guided explorers; they were often able to follow well-used trails, from which stones had been cleared. Watkin Tench described two expeditions, intended to be punitive (Phillip's patience, which had survived a previous serious wound, was finally exhausted). They had a terrible time of it, nearly drowning in a bog after having insisted that they press on 'without heeding difficulty or impediment of road', and their predicament afforded the Aboriginal guides 'an inexhaustible fund of merriment and derision'. Aboriginal help was essential in the literally vital discovery of waterholes. Eyre acknowledged their assistance, in that chance-met Aborigines would walk with him for miles to indicate the nearest water. The extent of their knowledge amazed some travellers; Sturt recorded that while preparing for his 1844–5 expedition, Toonda, a local man, drew in the sand 'a plan of the Darling for 300 miles, also of the Murray a good distance both above and below its junctions. He drew all the lagoons and gave the names of each; by comparing afterwards the bends he drew with major Mitchell's chart, they both agreed.'[13]

Assistance was often demanded rather than freely given, by the simple expedience of temporarily capturing a likely guide, and chaining him to ensure that the promised water was actually discovered. Most Aborigines were, however, willingly incorporated into expeditions, where they could act both as guides and as diplomats, negotiating with other Aboriginal bands. Sir Thomas Mitchell himself insisted that his guide, John Piper, whom Mitchell had previously styled 'conqueror of the interior' was 'most essentially required' on his 1845–6 expedition, and he acknowledged that 'in most of our difficulties by flood and field, the intelligence and skill of our sable friends made the "white fellows" appear rather stupid. They could read traces on the earth, climb trees, or dive into the water, better than the ablest of us. In tracing lost cattle, speaking to the "wild natives," hunting, or diving, Piper was the most accomplished man in camp.'[14]

Acceptance in European society was easier in the outback, where Aboriginal stockmen proved their adaptability by combining the new skills of horseman- and marksmanship with the ancient familiarity with the country, which enabled them to outlast their white co-workers. In 1852 the commissioner for Crown Lands reported that Aboriginal shepherds looked after their animals better than Europeans, and clipped 'much more closely and cleanly than it is possible to induce hired Europeans to do'. That was, however, the judgement of an official, who was not asked to depend upon Aborigines or to live in close proximity with them, and who could afford to be just and liberal. To the small farmer or white labourer, the Aboriginal hand represented either the only labour available or a potentially dangerous competitor to those who 'don't want to see the bread taken out of a white man's mouth by a nigger'. At this level, the black man was either a social inferior to be kept in his place or a threat to be pushed aside and denigrated.[15]

It was true that as a hired worker the Aborigine left much to be desired. For a period, perhaps of months, he would work willingly enough, but he would invariably feel the need for change – to go 'walkabout'. The Port Phillip Native Police Corps had recognized this, and provided for the absence of their men, but an anxious farmer was in no position to be so tolerant. Domestic service was often attempted, with some success, but this sometimes verged on straightforward slavery. John Batman, sometimes lauded for his attempt at treaty-making, took two Tasmanian boys and refused, in spite of George Robinson's demands, to restore them to their parents. They were, Batman insisted, 'too useful'; one looked after the pigs while the other milked the cows, and they were not allowed to go home until after Batman's death. Blatant exploitation took the form of employment at 'nothing a year, paid monthly' but with food and clothing provided. One Queensland pioneer was able to snatch a 14-year-old from his tribe, and reported: 'Kindness, plenty of good food and clothes soon made him a happy little nigger and he remained with me for years.'

The fact that such abductions were recorded without any attempt at dissimulation, or even any indication that the actions were regarded as wrong, indicated their commonplace nature. Lucy Gray recorded that her husband bought a little boy from 'an old gin for a couple of handkerchiefs', although when the child was chained at night, 'to prevent him on a sudden fit of homesickness, going back to his Mammy in the night', she admitted that 'it looked like making a slave of him'. Some more commercial transactions were officially frowned upon; one squatter informed the magistrate when two men stole a couple of Aboriginal boys to sell in the goldfields, but such actions were rarely, if ever, prosecuted.[16]

Instances of young Aboriginals of full or mixed blood – and these last were becoming increasingly common – making their way in white society were unusual. The surveyor John Wedge, a Tasmanian Legislative Councillor, acquired a full-blood Aboriginal boy, Mayday, who was 'always correct and well-behaved, and would compare favourably with most European boys of the same age', but who died of pneumonia. Death from respiratory ailments or relapse in drunkenness and prostitution was a common outcome from such attempts, however well-meaning, at integrating Aboriginals into white society. Once again, the contrast with South Africa is noteworthy. By 1880, in Cape Colony, Africans were taking their place in white society as teachers, newspaper editors and clergymen; voters were registered and jurors sworn in, while in Australia, most Aborigines were not even counted in the census; officially, they had ceased to exist.[17]

South Australia's Delusions of Grandeur

White Australia, on the other hand, was prospering mightily. In 1866 the total population – only the whites being counted – was something over 1,100,000 of whom 538,000 lived in Victoria, now comfortably the largest colony. Melbourne had 130,000 inhabitants, about the same number as Bristol, Sydney with 96,000 being comparable with Newcastle upon Tyne; both were therefore already cities of note in the British Empire and internationally (Chicago was just passing the 30,000 mark). Victoria had taken the lead in more than mere head-counting: while at this date New South

Wales bank deposits struggled to exceed £4,800,000, those in Victorian banks were well over £7 million. Once all colonial governments were placed on an equal constitutional basis (Western Australia always excepted) the prestige of seniority previously enjoyed by New South Wales was also lost.

For nearly thirty years after 1860 Australia really earned the title of 'Lucky Country', with its economy expanding at an average of 5 per cent per annum; between 1861 and 1890 the GNP in real terms nearly quadrupled. Gold had provided the most powerful impetus, but continued prosperity was based on sheep. Inventions and improvements transformed the pastoral system of the 1840s with its wandering flocks of underbred animals, dependent on bullock carts for transport. The total sheep population had quintupled to over a hundred million by 1891, but scientific breeding had also produced new types of merino, introducing French, German and American lines (the Americans, strange animals with crinkly fleeces, later proved lacking in stamina and were bred out). As a result the average weight of fleeces more than doubled during the period, so that by 1891, 634 million pound weight of wool was clipped. The Devonian Peppin family, who had begun raising sheep in England with some of King George III's own flock, were the leaders, and their Wanganella strain is now dominant in Australia, and much further afield. Ten thousand miles of railtrack enabled the wool clip even from the furthest stations to be brought economically to the ports, whence the sailing clippers, for many years until the eve of the Second World War, proved able to compete against the more expensive steamers.

The export of sheep meat was pioneered by the partnership between the French investor, Eugène Nicolle, and the entrepreneur Thomas Mort, who invested over £100,000 in the effort to develop a practical sea-going refrigerated vessel (Mort, who contrived to be both an idealist and rich – he died worth over £600,000 – handed over half of his considerable business to the workers at Mort's Dock and Engineering Company in Balmain, where the first Australian locomotive was constructed). The first shipment of frozen meat reached London in February 1880 and attracted great interest. Although an anonymous correspondent in the *Field*, after experimenting himself, was sceptical, the Australian meat was generally reported to be in a satisfactory condition. Not only meat, but butter could be exported after the introduction of the cream separator and refrigeration in the 1880s. From a negligible share of the British market in 1890, by the end of the century Australia and New Zealand had shot ahead to become the second largest supplier, although still a good distance behind the market leader, Denmark.[18]

Such rates of expansion necessitated bringing millions of acres into agricultural production, especially for dairy farming, which tended to require expansion into well-wooded areas. New techniques were developed; scrub clearance by mallee rolling – simply dragging an old boiler or large trunk across the ground and burning off the residue – and the 'stump jumping' plough (basically one with independently suspended multiple shares) developed in South Australia. The enterprise of the Victorian pastoralist Edward Lascelles in rabbit-control converted huge areas that had been dismissed as unproductive into profitable cereal-growing land. In 1860 the five Australian colonies, excluding Western Australia where there was little agricultural development during the period, had just over 1,100,000 acres under crop; by the end of the century this had increased nearly sevenfold, to 7,500,000. The biggest increase had been in Queensland, from 3,300 acres to nearly half a million, but the two great agricultural colonies were South Australia and Victoria, together having 5,500,000 million acres.

William Farrer, a Westmorland farmer's son, Cambridge-educated, who had settled near Lake George in the 1880s, worked for twenty years on developing new disease-resistant strains of wheat; Baron von Liebeg's work in Germany from the 1850s had made economic chemical fertilizers available, although Australian farmers were slow to use them until encouraged by the new agricultural colleges, the first of which was founded in 1883, at Roseworthy, South Australia. Large-scale irrigation began in 1886 with the Irrigation Act which asserted Crown Control over all water rights in Victoria. Alfred Deakin, barrister and journalist, the Victorian Commissioner for Public Works, had made a special study of irrigation in the United States, and brought back two Canadian brothers, George and William Chaffey. Using powers under the Irrigation Act, Deakin pushed through an agreement with the Chaffeys to initiate an extensive scheme on the Murray River, in the unpromising district of Mildura. Problems were encountered, but Mildura developed into a thriving fruit- and wine-producing area, providing an example quickly followed in the other colonies.

The map of Australia, as drawn in 1863, after the by-now misnamed South Australia had extended its boundaries to the far north of the continent, was not definitive, as the inescapable facts of distance asserted themselves. Hobart was nearer to the great ice shelf of Antarctica than to the new settlements of northern South Australia, and these were 2,000 miles by sea, the only possible means of communication, from Sydney. Perth, by the same measure, was as far from Sydney as Paris is from Moscow; indeed, Batavia, the capital of the Dutch East Indies, was closer to Perth than was the capital of New South Wales. Railways, when they were built, assisted only to a limited degree. No railway connected the south with the north until, after many procrastinations, the line from Alice Springs to Darwin was finally completed in 2003. Western Australia had shared the other colonies' prosperity to only a very limited extent and felt its isolation, indeed eventually developing its own separatist movement. When the Union Bank of Australia first considered opening a Perth branch in 1860 it found the prospects poor, and abandoned the project. In 1858, when South Australia was able to boast a population of 118,215, that of Western Australia had risen only to 14,837. Pleas were sent to London for more convicts. Governor Arthur Kennedy protested that the objections from some colonists constituted a 'groundless panic', stimulated by 'willful and malicious representations', and that the West Australia Pentonvillains formed 'a class of men . . . whose general conduct will bear a fair comparison with the "free emigrants" to any Colony'.

Transportation, which had helped to rescue the colony's faltering economy, was finally ended in 1868; those convicts already in the colony were obliged to serve out the remainder of their sentences, although these were now under conditions which could approximate to 'community service' rather than a form of confinement. Even so, Western Australia retained the stigmata of a convict colony until nearly the end of the century. In all towns, strangers were looked at with grave suspicion. The curfew bell rang at 10 p.m. 'Bond or Free? the policeman asked all those whom he met after that hour in the streets.' The other colonies felt obliged to protect themselves against ticket-of-leave men infiltrating; Anthony Trollope was indignant at having to accept, before leaving for Adelaide, a magistrate's certificate to prove that he 'is not and never has been a prisoner of the Crown in Western Australia'.[19] Sir Frederick Weld, who supervised the first representative Council of 1870, with elected members, was a Governor with exceptional qualities. A pious Roman Catholic, he had previously settled in New Zealand, where he had headed a government in 1864–5. Distrustful, with some reason, of his Western Australian colonists, Weld nevertheless piloted the colony through the early stages of self-government. Any further steps were fraught with problems. Emancipists had been kept firmly in their place by a series of local laws between 1873 and 1879 which excluded them from sitting on the Legislative Council or on juries and from membership of the Western Australian Bar. All these restrictions would have to be lifted if Western Australia was to be given responsible government. Only in 1887 did the Legislative Council begin the preliminary negotiations to achieve this, concluded in 1890 when Western Australia finally assumed its place among the self-governing Australian colonies.

Enthusiasm for self-government in Western Australia, and willingness to bear the extra costs involved, had been increased by the discovery of rich mineral deposits. Another gold rush began in 1887, which gave the colony access to the London capital market – during the great bank collapses of 1896–7 Western Australia was the only Australian colony able to raise funds in London. Coolgardie, 350 miles inland from Perth, and nearby Kalgoorlie, became the new gold centres, with the Golden Mile rivalling the contemporary riches of Johannesburg and the Rand, although everything in Western Australia was more difficult than in the South African fields. Railways had reached the Rand within four years of the first finds, but the Western Australian goldfields were isolated in the semi-desert. Supplies came from the coast via camel train, and water had to be brought by bullock cart until a single-line railway was built in 1894, reducing the price from half-a-crown to 4d. a gallon; several prospecting parties died from thirst before this was completed. The delivery of water necessitated a major civil engineering project, a pipeline pumping water over 300 miles from the Darling Range at a cost of nearly £3 million. Within a few years of the gold strike the population of Western Australia had risen to 138,000 and, just as the immigrant 'Uitlanders' in the South African Boer republics had caused a revolution and eventually precipitated a war, so the newcomers to Western Australia stimulated constitutional change. Regarding the existing colonists as a mixture of smug urbanites – Perth's population increased to 44,000 in the decade – and unreliable ex-convicts, the Australian uitlanders, who came mainly from the eastern colonies, insisted on being granted the franchise on equal terms and began their own agitation for a separate goldfields colony. 'The government of Western Australia', a contemporary noted 'has hitherto been that of a huge land development company: constitutional questions have been kept in the background; but "items of democratic legislation to which they have been accustomed" were being demanded by the new-comers.' If these were not forthcoming, the miners would continue their pressure.[20]

The miners' complaints were deftly fielded by John Forrest – from 1890 Sir John – the first Premier of the new responsible government, a position that determined reactionary was to retain for over a decade. Forrest's administration is an unequalled example of how quickly a self-governing state could develop. Other colonies had got off to a hesitant start, with rapid changes of government; Western Australia, perhaps because responsible government had been so long delayed, experienced no such problems. Although very much a second-division Governor of a minuscule colony (the Colonial Office had its stars and its also-rans), Sir Frederick Napier Broome, in charge from 1883, had prepared the ground well, and Forrest had little domestic opposition. Some of the miners' demands were met, but only in stages – the abolition of a property qualification for Legislative Council membership in 1893 and adult suffrage (women having been given the vote on the same restricted terms as men since 1899) not until 1907, nearly fifty years after most of the other colonies.

The goldfields extended the settled districts of Western Australia a long way to the east, giving the colony for the first time a hinterland backing the coastal strip of settlement, but a thousand miles of desert still separated Western Australia from the eastern colonies.

South Australia was attempting to expand in a different direction by developing its newly acquired northern coast. Efforts, made as early as 1823 to establish a trading station which could cut into the profitable Dutch Torres Strait trepang trade, had misfired: Raffles Bay commemorates this connection with the originator of Singapore. Melville Island was chosen for the first attempt, but the handful of settlers and convicts left there in 1824 by Captain Gordon Bremer RN suffered from the weather, which was very hot, alternately very wet or very dry, and exacerbated by fevers, termites and resistance from Aborigines resentful at the disturbance. Raffles Bay, whither the Melville Island settlement was transferred in 1827, fared no better, and Fort Wellington was in turn abandoned two years later, in spite of the industrious Commandant, Collet Barker, the later explorer of South Australia. The year 1837 saw another attempt at Port Essington on the Coburg peninsula, again made by the optimistic Captain Bremer. Captain John Macarthur of the Royal Marines was appointed Commandant of what it was hoped would become the new town of Victoria. Once more, hopes were disappointed. T. H. Huxley, who visited Victoria in 1848, described it as 'about the most useless, miserable, ill-managed hole in Her Majesty's dominions'. Reluctantly, in the following year the Colonial Secretary Lord Grey decided to abandon the unhappy settlement, after Lord John Russell had refused to sanction colonization.[21]

Following the success of the transcontinental expeditions, interest was renewed. Owing largely to the initiative of the extensive Elder family, a close and talented Scottish network, a new colony was planned. The Elders left their mark in South Australia; Sir Thomas advocated the use of transport camels and bred them on some of his 7,000 square miles of runs, importing their Afghan drivers with the original beasts – these pioneers left their name on the railway that runs north from Adelaide to Australia's centre at Alice Springs, and now on to Darwin: the Ghan. Brother Alexander, who had pioneered Elder interests in 1839 and become an elected member of the Legislative Council, had returned to London, where he was instrumental in floating a North Australian company to finance colonization. At a time of political flux – there were nine changes of administration between 1862 and 1868 – successive Adelaide governments dithered. Two years were spent mapping out a theoretical colony and selling the rights to take up land, which had to be settled within five years, all without any examination of the ground. Only in March 1864 was a Resident appointed, the widely regarded Boyle Travers Finnis, who had been the colony's first Premier under responsible government, and instructed to find a suitable place to reside. His survey was troubled with the usual northern problems – disease, climate, disloyalty and Aborigines; and the Resident, who never resided, was dismissed, condemned for wasting £40,000 of public money. John McKinlay, who had led the South Australian Burke and Wills relief expedition, and Francis Cadell, the pioneer of Australian inland steam navigation, were subsequently commissioned to find a better location, but it was Finnis's assistant, J. T. Manton, who finally convinced the colonial government to adopt the excellent harbour of Port Darwin for the still-theoretical settlement's site.[22]

In Adelaide the government continued to debate, prey to the shifting policies of evanescent administrations; Sir Henry Ayers, who gave his name to the famous rock, now known by its Aboriginal name as Uluru, was Premier no fewer than seven times between 1863 and 1873. Only after five years had elapsed since the original decision to allow settlement was Port Darwin finally selected as its site, and by that time £100,000 had been wasted, Elder's shareholders had lost their capital – although £73,000 was subsequently awarded for breach of contract – and South Australia's reputation for competence had been badly dented.

The credit for forcing a decision must go to the indefatigable Surveyor General, George Goyder, famous for plotting the hydroiset which divided potentially agricultural land from pastoral land and desert. Persisting through the bewildering changes of government – he served under twenty-four different Commissioners of Crown Lands and through thirty-four changes of administration – Goyder, together with Forrest of Western Australia, did more to develop Australian resources than any Governor or Premier. The new settlement at Port Darwin, which retained the name of the previous site at Palmerston until 1911, continued to be a drain on Southern Australian resources, owing its survival to the artificial stimulus afforded by the overland telegraph line's operation (the terminal station is still visible, the oldest of Darwin's historic sites) and the discovery of gold in 1872 at Pine Creek, some 150 miles away. Never as dramatically successful as the other fields, Pine Creek's gold rush nevertheless kept the community from total collapse. But after fifty years of expense, some

£4 million, South Australia's Northern Territory had a population of only 3,000.

Queensland was able to view South Australia's misfortunes with quiet satisfaction, but was experiencing for itself the tyranny of distance. Two factors had contributed to the progress of Queensland's north – gold and sugar. An abortive rush in 1858 left stranded thousands of miners who had to be rescued by ships chartered by voluntary subscriptions. Others decided to stay, and began a settlement on the coast at Rockhampton. A much more successful field was opened fourteen years later, at Charters Towers, inland from Townsville: once again this led to the foundation of a new port, named after Captain Robert Towns. For a short time Charters Towers, surrounded by mines, with its own stock exchange, was a centre of feverish activity and speculation – and much of its elegant architecture still remains.

Australian sugar had been pioneered by an Irish-Caribbean co-operation. Captain Francis Allman, of the 48th Foot, a Clare native, had been appointed Commandant of the new penal settlement of Port Macquarie in 1821; a good practical farmer, judging the climate suitable for sugar cane, Allman used the services of a West Indian convict, James Williams, to begin cultivation. Port Macquarie proved too far south for reliable growth, and the first commercially successful enterprise was that of the Scots aristocrat Captain Louis Hope, son of the Earl of Hopetoun, in collaboration with a Barbadian, John Buhot. In 1863 Hope was able successfully to produce 3 tons of sugar from his plantation on Moreton Bay, using labourers recruited from Polynesian islands.

It was assumed at the time that Europeans could not engage in manual labour in the tropics, and that recruitment from outside would be essential. Indian labourers had been successfully employed in the Natal canefields, but the Government of India was insistent that Indians should enjoy the protection to which they had a right as British subjects, and privileges that in Natal included the right to remain in the colony and to bring their families to join them. The thought of having to put up with non-whites as fellow citizens was abhorrent to Australian feeling and the matter was not pursued. Polynesians, who could be recruited on fixed-term contracts and expelled at their termination, seemed a suitable alternative.

Captain Robert Towns, an old sea captain who had learnt his trade in the same fashion as Cook – with North Sea Collier brigs – was the first to import the islanders. His fast schooner *Don Juan* sailed from Brisbane River in May 1863 with detailed instructions for Captain Grueber. Towns was particularly anxious to assure the island missionaries of his good intentions; Grueber was to tell them that his object was to engage men 'for a short season to serve me in cultivating cotton; the labour will be light in weeding and cleaning and picking cotton, and I engage to provide them comfortable huts and regular rations of rice, meat, pumpkins, potatoes, and yams, if they will grow'.

Subsequent ventures were not as highly principled. When Ross Lewin, a deserter from the Royal Navy who had acted for Towns in the early voyages, set up a business on his own, what had been a decently conducted commercial venture – Towns' labourers were indeed returned home on time, bearing large chests with their new acquisitions – looked very much like a revived slave trade as Lewin advertised his willingness to provide labourers at £7 a head. Fraud and violence replaced persuasion, and efforts by the Queensland authorities to regulate the trade were widely ignored. For seventy years, since the slave trade had been banned in British possessions, it had been the Royal Navy's duty, and particular pleasure, to arrest the perpetrators. When, in 1872, Captain George Palmer of the sloop HMS *Rosario* discovered Lewin's schooner *Daphne* in Fiji with 108 islanders crammed into the tiny hold and the ship's papers clearly fraudulent, Palmer arrested the ship and crew, and sailed to Sydney for their trial. Charged with 'knowingly, wilfully, feloniously and piratically ... receiving and conveying the islanders ... with a view to their being dealt with as slaves', *Daphne*'s captain and supercargo were instantly acquitted by the Sydney magistrate. Even although another Australian 'blackbirder', Albert Hovell of *Young Australian*, had been sentenced to death for murder only a few days previously (the sentence was commuted and Hovell released some years later), the acquittal of the *Daphne*'s crew served as a green light for the Pacific raiders. The Royal Navy's guns had been spiked by a colonial court, and the islanders were left unprotected.[23]

Countless murders must have subsequently occurred, those which were identified being discovered only accidentally, the worst being the exploits of the Victorian brig *Carl*. Its owner, the Irish doctor James Patrick Murray, turned Queen's Evidence, confessing to at least seventy murders; two of the crew were sentenced to death, but the disgraceful Murray escaped all punishment.[24]

As the islanders retaliated, the blackbirding trade became notorious. Only when the Welsh-born lawyer, the incorruptible Sir Samuel Griffith, became Queensland's Premier in 1884 was decisive action taken. The 'respectable' Queensland firm of Burns, Philp (Sir James Burns and Sir Robert Philp being the founding partners) had imported labourers from New Guinea; the crew of their ship *Hopeful* was proved to have kidnapped hundreds and murdered at least thirty-eight. A Brisbane court sentenced two of the seamen to death and many others to imprisonment; Sir James and Sir Robert continued their successful careers. As usual, none of the death sentences was carried out, and within a few years all the culprits had been released by a government headed by Boyd Morehead, an unscrupulous grazier. When Sidney and Beatrice Webb visited Brisbane in 1898 they left a vivid account of the unsavoury atmosphere:

The Legislative Council was made up of elderly gentlemen with financial 'pasts' who were quarrelling over the management of the refreshment room ... the Capitalist government has an evil odour of past financial frauds ... as well as plentiful petty pilfering, whilst the Labour members, although a respectable and well-conducted set of men ... would make a blatant fiasco of their attempt to take over the reins of government.[25]

It might be added that the morality of Burns, Philp did not improve. During the First World War their New Guinea trade rose from £225,416 in 1915 to £1.2 million in 1919, 'on the backs of the Melanesian population, forcibly recruited and then kept in check with corporal punishment. British observers were appalled as Australian entrepreneurs and German planters drove forward a policy determined principally by racism and profit-making.'

'They must act in the matter as they please'

In both New South Wales and Victoria two other issues consumed the first responsible governments, as they continued to bedevil Australian politics for another century. The Treaty of Nanking, which in 1842 had ceded Hong Kong to Britain, had also opened five Chinese ports to international trade, allowing Chinese the opportunity, for the first time in the Middle Kingdom's history, to emigrate. Many thousands took advantage of this to join, first the Californian gold rush, then that of the Australian diggings. Canton, and the new colony of Hong Kong, were the centres of the 'pig trade' organized by Chinese entrepreneurs who sold tickets on usurious credit terms to desperate local men, often completely unprepared for their new conditions – 128 of 332 passengers on a single voyage to California committed suicide during the passage. Standards were improved after 1855 when the Hong Kong Governor Sir John Bowring passed a Chinese Passengers Act, and with the improvement came increased numbers. Between January and June of that year fewer than a thousand Chinese were landed in Australia; in the same period of 1857, 14,000 arrived, by which time Victoria harboured 35,000 Chinese. Disputes were inevitable, but thanks to Hotham's introduction of the Protectorate system, and the generally law-abiding character of the diggers, together with the care taken by the Chinese themselves to avoid irritating their hosts, were rarely accompanied by serious violence. An attempt was made by the Victorian government to restrict immigration, but this only had the effect of encouraging immigrant ships to dock elsewhere. One observer described six or seven hundred Chinese plodding their way to the Victorian border from Guichen Bay in South Australia 'winding across the plain like a long black mark'. It was just such a party that discovered the famous Ararat seam, where the first serious clash took place – with American diggers – in July 1857.[26]

Compared with California, it was all fairly mild. In 1854 the California Supreme Court ruled Chinese evidence to be inadmissible, a decision which 'invited the murder and robbery of the Chinese'. The invitation was accepted. Two years later the Shasta *Republican* reported that 'Hundreds of Chinamen have been slaughtered in cold blood during the last five years by desperados . . . The murder of Chinamen was of almost daily occurence. Yet in all this time we have heard of but two or three instances, where the guilty parties have been brought to justice and punished according to law.' Eighty-two Chinese murders were recorded; in only two of the cases were the murderers tried and punished. In Victoria, white Americans were as likely to be the objects of indignation as the Chinese. 'In the towns . . . they have given much trouble . . . One was lately fined [$100] . . . and the Court regretted it could not make the penalty heavier, for committing an assault upon a man of colour, whom this barbarian ejected from a place of public amusement for no other reason than that he was black!'[27] Although newspaper reports deplored the 'ruffianly behaviour, unmanly violence and unbounded rapacity', they were able to add that 'Had it not been for the interference of several white diggers loss of life must have ensued' but was prevented 'by the force of arms and example'.

Far from a general resort to force against the unwelcome Chinese, the diggers seemed 'disposed to rest satisfied with any measures that may be adopted by the Legislature'; and the government duly obliged. A Victorian Legislative Council report was unambiguously racist: 'In this country there is no Asiatic or other race with whom it is desirable they should intermarry.' These 'pagans' were 'addicted to vices of greatly immoral character'. The pagans were to be discouraged by an entry tax of £10 a head, and a limitation of the numbers that could obtain passage on a ship; they were restricted to one per 10 tons measurement. An annual tax of £1 was added, later increased to £6 and paid by perhaps half the Chinese.[28] These measures succeeded only in transferring hopeful Chinese to New South Wales, where no such restrictions yet existed, and in 1860 ten thousand Chinese moved over the Murray River to the diggings in the Young area. By that time anti-Chinese attitudes had been hardened by international events. A convenient little war with China had been fomented by the British which resulted, in 1860, in an expedition to Peking. This being accompanied by some satisfactorily bloody Chinese atrocities (the young Henry Loch, later a Victorian Governor, was nearly one of the victims), an excuse was thus presented to destroy the magnificent Imperial Summer Palace and to remind China of her power-lessness.

Compared with the violence in the United States, such as the 1885 massacre of fifty-one Chinese by miners at Rock Springs, Wyoming, and that two years later in the Log Cabin Bar, Chinese miners in Australia did not have too much to complain about. The Chinese had done well enough in Victoria to provoke vicious verbal attacks, 'a festering mass of animal existence', according to a *Bathurst Free Press* correspondent in 1857, and some riots in the same year, but the most serious disturbances were in New South Wales near to the town of Young. The riots at Lambing Flats in July 1861 were the last occasion on which the British army was used in Australia, and foreshadowed the establishment of the 'White Australia' policy. The *Sydney Morning Herald* reported that a crowd of 3,000 savaged the Chinese: 'Men, or rather monsters, on horseback armed with bludgeons and whips, with a fiend-like fury' beat, robbed and even scalped the helpless Chinese:

unarmed, defenceless, and unresisting Chinese were struck down in the most brutal manner by bludgeons provided for the occasion, and by pick handles. The previous excitement had done its work, and now the wretched Mongols were openly and unblushingly searched for valuables, and robbery was committed without the slightest attempt at concealment. Very few of the poor creatures here attacked escaped with their pigtails, none of them without injury of some kind, whilst every article of the property they had endeavoured to take with them was plundered of all that was valuable, and then burnt. Some of the acts of barbarism said to have been committed here were such, that Englishmen can scarce be brought to credit that their country men could be guilty of them – for who amongst the British people could ever believe that men of their own country – Britons, would take the Chinese pigtails with the scalp attached. That this was done in more than one instance there can be no doubt, since the possessors of these trophies made no concealment of them, but rather prided themselves on their possessions.

Perhaps more remarkable than the diggers' attack on the Chinese was the colonial authority's sustained effort to keep the peace, and to act against the rioters – actions quite unparalleled in the United States. After the first demonstration by the miners, led by a brass band, the message came from Sydney: 'the law must be upheld – the Chinese must have the same justice and protection attended to them as other people', backed up by the arrival of two hundred soldiers and the Premier, Charles Cowper himself. Before the violence was finally suppressed a detachment of infantry and sailors from HMS *Fawn* had to be called in, and a number of rioters were shot. Once the immediate danger was over, Cowper was successful in soothing the white diggers, suggesting that the law would be changed to restrain Chinese immigration. A bill to this effect was indeed passed in the Assembly, but rejected in the Council, where one member pointed out that the Chinese were, after all 'no lower than French or Germans'. Such liberal sentiments were probably, however, less important than Legislative Councillors' anxiety to secure a continued supply of cheap and industrious labour.[29]

Racist Australian legislation proved a great embarrassment to the British government, both on humanitarian grounds (although these were slowly weakening) and as threatening imperial stability and trade (both growing in importance). The 1860 Convention of Peking provided for a British minister at the Chinese capital, and began the modernization of the Chinese empire under the leadership of Chinese reformers and their largely British officials. The commercial opportunities this offered, although these later proved to have been overestimated, aroused great interest in London, where the spectacle of Australian colonists irritating the Chinese government was greeted with alarm. Furthermore, a consistent concern of British governments was the insistence that all British subjects, of whatever race, must be accorded the same legal protection – and this included all the races of British India. Racist colonial legislation therefore presented a dilemma; if responsible governments were empowered to legislate on all internal matters, when could London intervene? A New South Wales Act of 1861, refusing Chinese the opportunity to naturalize, was accepted there under protest; the principle was 'repugnant to British traditions', but British governments, Colonial Secretary Lord Derby regretted, 'were in the hands of the colonists, and they must act in the matter as they pleased'.[30]

More reluctance on the part of British governments to authorize repressive colonial legislation was exhibited in 1876 when a Queensland Bill attempting to impose higher licence fees for 'Asiatic and African aliens' residing on the goldfields was rejected by the Colonial Office. These goldfields were the new finds in north Queensland and especially the remote Palmer field in Cape York. Unlike the New South Wales and Victoria diggings, with good communications and near centres of population, the north Queensland fields were impossible to police with any degree of thoroughness. 'A dead Chinese in the bush was unlikely to provoke questions, and Aborigines could always be blamed.' Reports of any major violence would, however, have been impossible to suppress, and serious trouble was unlikely enough, especially since the Chinese were considerably in the majority on the Palmer goldfield. Violent racism in Australia was never institutionalized as it was in America, where such despicable demagogues as Denis Kearney and Dr O'Donnell were able to organize political parties, one of which, the Workingmen's Party of California, was able to elect the chief justice of that state, five of his six associates, eleven Senators and two Assembly men. As in New South Wales, however, a British government had to depend on persuasion, and an amended Queensland Bill, which received Royal assent in 1877, re-imposed the restrictions which had previously been in force in Victoria, but which had been removed by 1867.[31]

'A happy application of good sense'

The second continuing cause of dissension was constitutional. One man was pre-eminent in defining the relative powers of Colonial Secretary in London and those of the colonial governments, together with the often uncomfortable position of the colonial Governor as intermediary. George Higinbotham was an Irish barrister who, like Trollope's Phineas Finn, made another career as a journalist in London which he continued after his arrival in Melbourne in 1853.

Higinbotham's liberal sympathies and remorseless logic, exercised first in the Victorian Legislative Assembly as Attorney General 1863–8 and after 1880 as a member of the Supreme Court – Chief Justice from 1886 – led him to insist on a colonial government's sole responsibility for its domestic affairs. 'The million and a half of Englishmen who inhabit these colonies' were not to be governed in London by 'a person named Rogers' (the irreproachable Sir Frederic Rogers, permanent under-secretary at the Colonial Office). This principle led Higinbotham to insist that a colonial Governor was the representative of the Sovereign, and not of the British government of the day. As such, Governors should refuse even to communicate with the Colonial Office on items of domestic policy. Only on matters of foreign affairs, specifically reserved in the Australian constitutions, was the Governor to act on London's instructions. In all other respects he was 'a local Sovereign', who must possess 'every power necessary to carry on the government of a colony and to maintain its peace and welfare' – and of course, as the central principle of responsible government, bound to follow the advice of his ministers.[32] Given the evanescent nature of colonial governments, which had an average life of only eighteen months throughout the nineteenth century, and where a permanent party system only began to emerge towards the end of the period, Governors were frequently called upon to exercise their discretion and to act, when they could, as instructors in parliamentary procedures. Should they, for example, attempt to find another grouping which might command a majority after the current administration had suffered a parliamentary defeat, or allow a dissolution which would result in a general election?

At bottom lay the difficulties of translating an unwritten British constitution, which depended on acceptance of many conventions and traditions, into written colonial constitutions. Interpretations had to be decided through a series of legal confrontations, which continued throughout the nineteenth century, and even in the twentieth, as exemplified in the case of Governor General Sir John Kerr's dismissal of a Labor government in 1975 or Sir Philip Game's removal of New South Wales Premier Lang in 1932.

One area of continuing uncertainty was the exact nature of the relationship between the Governor of a colony and its Executive Council – the ministers enjoying the support of a majority in the Legislative Assembly. Although theoretically equivalent to that between a British Prime Minister and the Sovereign, both the distance and the powers of delay, and even rejection, possessed by a Governor, meant that practice was very different. A Prime Minister was expected to visit the Queen every week when she was in London and Windsor, and wait on her during her holidays at Balmoral. Any objections she might express could be accommodated, usually fairly quickly. In addition, Queen Victoria was able to form close relationships with her Prime Ministers: even Gladstone, whom she disliked, had regular conversations with her over many years. For the last thirty-three years of her reign, Victoria had to deal only with three Prime Ministers – Disraeli, Gladstone and Lord Salisbury, with the exception of a few months when Lord Rosebery filled a gap. A governor, on the other hand was in post only for six years, during which he might have to cope with four or five different colonial Premiers.

Definitions had therefore to depend on precedents developing from specific cases, the most important one that of Sir Charles Darling in 1866. Darling, as nephew of Sir Ralph, had begun his colonial career early as secretary to the New South Wales Governor. Arriving in Victoria in September 1863 as one of the most experienced colonial servants, having served in the West Indies, the Cape and Newfoundland over a period of twenty years, he inherited a political situation which, while clear, was fraught with possibilities of conflict. Unlike the other colonies at the time, Victorian governments were stable, with only two administrations between 1861 and 1868 (John O'Shanassy 1861–3, Sir James McCulloch, 1863–8). McCulloch owed his continued success to the coalition between a liberal middle class and radicals concerned with land legislation. Conservative opposition in the Assembly was only feeble, and was concentrated, as the framers of the Victorian constitution intended, in the Legislative Council. Between 1856 and 1863, in the first seven years of responsible government, the Council rejected forty-four Bills passed by the Assembly, making constructive legislation almost impossible.[33]

Armed with a convincing popular mandate in the November 1864 general election, McCulloch presented a series of Bills, which were, as usual, rejected by the Council. The device was then adopted of tacking one of these to a supply Bill – the provision of funds to carry on government – which the Council could constitutionally only reject, but not amend. At the time the dispute between 'free-traders' and 'protectionists' had assumed an almost religious intensity, and continued to be a vital element in Australian politics – indeed, it has still not disappeared from the political agenda. McCulloch's Bill to introduce a protective tariff would, it was quite clear, suffer the fate of its predecessors and was therefore sent to the Council together with the supply Bill; as expected, both were rejected, leaving the administration without funds. The government thereupon decided to seek bank finance to bridge the gap, but only the London Chartered Bank, of which McCulloch was the sole local director, agreed to make advances on the basis of hypothecated future revenue.

This venture was probably illegal or at least constitutionally questionable, but had the undoubted merit of enabling government to be continued and its obligations honoured. At every stage Darling, although doubtful, was guided by the influential Attorney General – George Higinbotham. McCulloch's opponents counter-attacked by preparing a petition, given to Darling for transmission to the Queen, accusing the Governor of participating in these possibly unlawful acts. In his despatch to the Colonial Office accompanying the petition, which largely concerned itself with criticisms of the signatories, Darling expressed his opinion of them by hoping that 'the future course of political events may never designate any of them for the position of a constitutional adviser of the Crown, since it is impossible their advice could be received with any other feelings than those of doubt and distrust'.

With those words Darling sealed both his own fate and a vital constitutional principle. Just as Queen Victoria could not avoid accepting William

Gladstone, so no colonial Governor could refuse to accept the advice of responsible ministers for any reasons of personal distaste. This was made clear to the unhappy Governor by Newcastle's successor at the Colonial Office, Edward Cardwell:

It is one of the first duties of the Queen's Representative to keep himself as far as possible aloof from and above all personal conflicts. He should always so conduct himself as not to be precluded from acting freely with those whom the course of Parliamentary proceedings might present him to his confidential advisers. While on the one hand, it is his duty to afford to his actual advisers all fair and just support, consistently with the observance of the law, he ought, on the other hand, to be perfectly free to give the same support to any other Ministers whom it may be necessary for him at any future time to call to his counsels.

The colony is entitled to know that the Governor gives this support to his Ministers for the time being, and that he is able and willing, if the occasion shall arise, to give the same support to others.

I regret to say that in the present instance you have rendered this impossible. It must be evident to yourself that you occupy a position of personal antagonism towards almost all those whose antecedents point them out as mostly likely to be available to you in the event of any change of ministry.

Cardwell was famous for his intolerant toughness, and, in a rare example of Colonial Office sanctions, Darling was promptly recalled in November 1865. In Victoria this was generally seen as an unacceptable interference in colonial affairs, and Darling departed 'amidst extraordinary scenes of public mourning'.[34]

Darling's period of office also contributed towards the case studies of gubernatorial powers, when the Confederate commerce raider *Shenandoah*, calling at Melbourne in 1865, was allowed to take on supplies and recruit crew. After the end of the American Civil War, claims, primarily for the activities of the British built *Alabama* but also including the depredations of the *Shenandoah*, totalling $15 million, were adjudicated against Britain, but, perhaps fortunately for him, Darling was by that time dead. Charged with allowing the ship to dock, Higinbotham wriggled. Yes, Darling had acted following consultations with some people who also happened to be ministers but 'We did not offer a single piece of advice in the character of responsible ministers ... Sir Charles Darling thought proper to ask the opinion, counsel, assistance of those Executive Councillors who happened then to be nearest to him ... But whatever advice was given ... was given not as ministers of the Crown.'[35]

The year 1864 was not the last trial of strength between the Victorian

Council and Assembly, as Darling's successor, Sir John Manners-Sutton (later Lord Canterbury) was caught in just such a crossfire, over a grant to be made to Lady Darling as some compensation for what many thought to have been the harsh treatment accorded to her husband. Then Sir George Bowen, promoted in 1873 from the governorship of Queensland to that of Victoria, was asked to decide between the radical Premier Graham Berry and the consistently conservative Council over the question of payments to members. Berry, the protectionist equivalent of free-trade Henry Parkes in New South Wales, working class and populist (although more vociferously democratic than the subtler Parkes), proposed a different solution to a deadlock, which was not to seek a bank loan, but to dismiss civil servants. Black Wednesday, 8 January 1878, saw County Court judges, coroners, police magistrates and some fifty other civil servants dismissed, ostensibly as a financial expedient, but also, since many might be expected to be conservative sympathizers, as a warning to the Council.

These crises were all referred to London in search of clarification, but the Colonial Office could offer little help. The Victorians had chosen to saddle themselves with a constitution which was unworkable unless Council and Assembly conducted their relationships more reasonably. Westminster would not amend the constitution; the Victorian Parliament alone had powers to do that, but could not muster a sufficient majority of both houses for the necessary action. Higinbotham expostulated that any 'representative not of the Crown but of the foreign nobleman who is at the head of the Colonial Office' who 'without any authority or law whatsoever, constantly interferes in our local affairs' must be firmly told: 'This must not be.' Walter Bagehot was, however, surely in the right when he blamed the excessive powers of the Council:

The evil of two-coequal Houses of distinct natures is obvious. Each House can stop all legislation, and yet some legislation may be necessary. At this moment we have the best instance of this which could be conceived. The Upper House of our Victorian Constitution, representing the rich wool-growers, had disagreed with the Lower Assembly, and most business is suspended. But for a most curious stratagem, the machine of government would stand still.

No Governor, however deaf to Colonial Office advice or commands, could be expected to adjudicate this self-inflicted conflict.[36]

Sir John Young, who succeeded Denison in New South Wales, had an easier time. Unlike Darling, Young was an experienced parliamentarian, having represented County Cavan for twenty-four years, and was adept at adjudicating between the parliamentary factions, also taking great pains to advise ministers totally inexperienced in parliamentary procedures and conventions. Although between 1857 and 1872 New South Wales had experienced eight administrations, these had been led by the same three people, Robertson, Martin and Cowper, which presented many problems to a conscientious governor in deciding who should be commissioned, but did produce some individuals experienced in parliamentary practice. Young was immediately faced with a constitutional crisis when Premier Charles Cowper made an attempt at reform by replacing the system of nominating Legislative Councillors by election. Inevitably rejected by the Council, Young was ready to cut that Gordian knot by swamping the Council with Cowper supporters. This was unduly democratic, the Duke of Newcastle believed, but Young had made the point that responsible government required that the Assembly's will predominate.[37]

Like Young, his successor the Irish peer Lord Belmore had parliamentary experience, although in the Westminster House of Lords. He had been warned shortly after his arrival in January 1868 that the Colonial Secretary hoped 'you will keep Sydney out of any [constitutional] mess similar to that now existing in Victoria', and this Belmore did skilfully. New South Wales politicians were slow to develop ministerial discipline, being 'apt to act independently of their colleagues', to 'keep the Governor in the dark' as to what they intended doing and to act 'too often in departmental matters independently of the Governor and each other'. The arrival of Sir Hercules Robinson in June 1872 (like Young and Belmore, an Irishman, as were so many of the best colonial Governors) brought a less suave style to government. After a few years' service with the Royal Irish Fusiliers, and a period superintending famine relief works, Robinson had become a colonial civil servant, very much the coming man in the Colonial Office with three previous successful governorships, while still only in his forties. Popular in Australia for his sporting proclivities, especially after his horse Kingsborough won the Australian Derby, Robinson was called upon to cope with a major row, ostensibly about the prerogative of pardon, but in reality as part of a parliamentary opposition to Henry Parkes. The question eventually found its way to the House of Lords, where it was claimed that 'The fact is, in these matters, we cannot be too logical'. The Earl of Kimberley, an experienced Colonial Secretary, confirmed that opinion: 'Constitutional Government in this country had not grown up by a rigorous application of . . . logic, but rather by a happy application of good sense.'[38]

9

Federation

Colonial Quarrels

The clear potential advantages of some sort of inter-colonial agreement had been obvious since Lord Grey's abortive legislation of 1848, but the first generation of responsible governments were too involved in experimenting with constitutions and with defining their own priorities to consider the subject further. One of the first contributions to a renewed debate came in 1853, and from an unexpected source, when William Smith O'Brien, shortly before his return to a comfortable retirement in Ireland, published his suggestions, anonymously, in the Launceston *Examiner* (30 August 1853). O'Brien thoughtfully listed the matters that should be handled centrally: 'Among the subjects which may become matters for discussion and agreement . . . the following may be specially enumerated: – Inter-colonial tariffs, postage, electric telegraphs, light-houses and beacons, a penal settlement, extradition of criminals, copyright and patent for inventions, professional qualifications, a mint, bankruptcy . . . naturalisation, minimum price of public land, defence against a common foe', and he pointed out the necessity for a Federal Court of Appeal. Charles Gavan Duffy, O'Brien's former colleague in Young Ireland, becoming a leading figure in the Victorian Parliament, took up the issue in a Select Committee called four years later to consider a Federation of New South Wales, Victoria, Tasmania and South Australia. Meeting from late 1857 to 1859, Duffy's committee foundered on the persistent rivalry between Victoria and New South Wales.[1]

Social rivalry between Sydney and Melbourne was sometimes bitter. Sydneysiders viewed Melbourne as a New Yorker might have regarded Chicago; a Russian observer in 1863 quoted Melbourne residents' opinions of the rival city: 'You are going there, you can judge for yourself the difference between that town and our Melbourne . . . you won't see such beautiful buildings . . . and the streets are narrow; no life there such as we have here. Of course, there are frightfully rich people there – but mostly descended from convicts – and as for their behaviour!' The Austrian ethnologist Karl Scherzer, aboard the K&K frigate *Novara* in 1858, agreed. Visiting the richest man in Australia, Sir Daniel Cooper, a liberal supporter of Henry Parkes, at his 'almost princely' mansion in Rose Bay, Scherzer observed: 'you can sense straight away that you're in the house of a parvenu, where they're trying to ape certain manners, yet keep slipping up. You notice everywhere evidence of their lowly origin.'[2]

One striking, and literally concrete, demonstration of the Sydney–Melbourne rivalry was the erection of two great exhibition buildings for the Sydney Garden Palace International Exhibition in 1879 and for the Colonial Exhibition in Melbourne the following year. The Garden Palace Exhibition complex was an amazing example of what Victorian engineers and contractors could do, and contrasts interestingly with the muddled delay a century later suffered in the building of the Sydney Opera House. The decision to hold an exhibition was taken on 17 December 1878; within a few days the Colonial Architect James Barnet, trained in London, prepared plans and a first estimate of £50,000. These were approved on New Year's Eve and by 7 January John Young had been appointed as chief contractor on a cost-plus basis – which would today be looked upon as a licence to print money. The project was enormous – 333,750 square feet, built on a modular basis – a fruit of Young's experience in the Crystal Palace project, with a dome on the main crossing which would be, at a diameter of 100 feet, the sixth largest in the world, and only five feet lower than St Paul's. As well as using prefabricated iron and timber panels, reinforced concrete was employed in the foundations, cantilevers and vaulting, one of the earliest uses of this material. Within nine months the whole enormous structure was finished, within the agreed costs, by working twenty-four hours a day, using the new electric arc lights, and on 17 September 1879 the International Exhibition was opened. The whole enterprise demonstrated a courage, efficiency and speed not matched until Sydney carried off the millennial Olympics with such style.[3]

Young and Barnet's triumphant structure did not last long, being destroyed by fire in 1882; Melbourne's has lasted better. The main hall of David Mitchell's 1880 colonial exhibition still stands grandly in Carlton Gardens adjacent to the new Melbourne museum. (Mitchell, a practical builder rather than an architect, was responsible for one other internationally famous product: his daughter Helen, better known as the diva Dame Nellie Melba, and the dessert named after her.) Melbourne naturally set out to trump Sydney; the exhibition attracted more visitors – 1,485,896 – cost more – £250,000 in all – and was larger – 30 acres of buildings.

Again, it was designed and built in an amazingly short period.[4] The other four colonies, at liberty to fashion their constitutions and frame their laws as they wished, had developed their individual characteristics. Richard Twopenny, author of *Town Life in Australia*, published in 1883, judged:

Of the three societies, that of Sydney is on the whole, I think, the best. At Melbourne there are probably a larger number of cultivated persons, but the distance between the suburbs and the more extravagant mode of living limits their sphere. The Adelaidians are perhaps the most English of all in their way of thinking, but they are also by far the most narrow-minded. For pure Philistinism I don't think I know any town that equals it ... And yet for kind-heartedness these gossip-loving Philistines are not easily to be surpassed. As long as things go well with you they will talk against you; but no set of people are less open to the charge of neglecting friends in misfortune.

The evolution of Tasmanian society was marked by the progress of the Reibey family. Thomas Reibey the younger, born in 1821, grandson of the convict Mary Haydock Reibey, was sent to Trinity College, one of Oxford's smartest, came down without a degree, was ordained and was promoted to archdeacon, a post from which he had to resign in 1870 over a sexual scandal. Trying again, the irrepressible Thomas entered politics; the 'ecclesiastical debauchee' became Premier for a year after July 1876, but his greatest success was in horse racing (very much in the Trinity tradition). Reibey was the first native-born Tasmanian Premier, his predecessors having been largely Scottish. None had much success in dealing with the economic problems of Tasmania.[5]

Tasmania's experience of the 1840s depression, was prolonged by continuous emigration, principally to Victoria, which reduced governments to desperate straits in scraping together income, to the extent that a movement advocating annexation by Victoria prospered. Lack of public funds caused obvious damage to the infrastructure. Smallpox, typhoid and diphtheria were endemic, and the sailors of HMS *Wolverene* were laid low by a particularly virulent strain of syphilis in 1877. Sewerage and water supplies were deplorably defective, and education lagged behind that in the other colonies. Only in 1869 were teachers subjected to examinations, and a relatively modest Public Works appropriation was passed only in 1880.

Conditions improved after 1872 when James 'Philosopher' Smith discovered extensive tin oxide deposits on Mount Bischoff, which became the world's richest tin mine. Within the next ten years silver lead had been found near Mount Zeehan and at Mount Bischoff, copper at Mount Lyell, and gold at Beaconsfield. With the orchards developing along the north coast, Tasmanian governments could be assured of a modestly reliable source of income, which in turn led to more stable administrations. The first of these was that of William Giblin, a talented young Tasmanian-born lawyer, Attorney General at the age of 30, and Premier at 38. During his five-year administration Giblin was able to put Tasmanian finances on a sound base, establishing income and land taxes; between 1870 and 1891 the Tasmanian population increased from 99,000 to 146,000.

Not counted in those figures, but very much alive and insistent on continuing their own preferred way of life, were the descendants of the Tasmanian Aborigines, now gathered on Cape Barren Island. Much to his credit, Archdeacon Reibey found time, among his other pursuits, to visit the islanders in 1862. His invitation came from the schoolteacher Lucy Beedon, the teacher on Gun-Carriage island, herself half-Aboriginal. Between them, Lucy and the Archdeacon arranged for two more teachers and also for the Reverend George Fereday to act as the islanders' agent. Bishop Sir Henry Montgomery, in Tasmania between 1889 and 1901, bustled about in an attempt to improve the islanders' conditions, happily convinced that if the people could be 'kept from drink, encouraged to become farmers by judicious grants; prevented from inter-marrying too much, the islands would be a very happy region, famed for its salubrity and out of reach of the greater temptations.' The bishop was in Tasmania long enough to realize his errors, admitting that the islanders had developed a 'settled hatred' for himself, the schoolmaster and the constable, and had expressed a wish not to become 'like white people'. He perhaps shared his lack of psychological subtlety with his more famous son, Bernard, Viscount Montgomery of Alamein.[6]

Tasmania remained the most conservative of colonies. Manhood suffrage was introduced only in 1901, when Federation obliged this step to be taken, at the same time as the abolition of plural voting and the ending of property qualifications for members of the lower house; triennial parliaments were delayed until 1935. Disputes between Council and Assembly were rarer than in the other colonies, partly due to the absence of radicalism, but also because the Council claimed an absolute equality of power with the Assembly and was constitutionally permitted to amend Supply and Taxation Bills. The crises (inevitable when Council and Assembly locked horns) which arose in 1879 resulted in Giblin's election, and although the Council continued to be obstructive, Giblin was able to rally enough public support to extend the franchise for both houses, so restricting the Council's more obstreperous members.

Although telegraphic communication with the rest of Australia was established in the 1870s Western Australia remained isolated from the other colonies, sharing the same continent, but with little in common except the common bond with Britain. There was little in common, either, between Perth and the north, the border with the Northern Territory being 2,000 miles distant, with most of the population concentrated in the south-western corner of the colony. British control of the Aborigines continued much longer in Western Australia than in the other colonies, only being delegated in 1897. As a result, some Aborigines enjoyed better conditions than those elsewhere; in the pearling trade off the north-west coast employees had to be given a written contract of employment, which provided, *inter alia*, for return home at the end of the period. After 1897, and in the pastoral industry after 1886, the Western Australia government was free to enforce a much less equitable contract, with no provision for payment of wages in cash, but allowing flour, tea, a blanket and one pair of trousers. When a Royal Commission investigated in 1905 it was found that less than 10 per cent of those employed enjoyed even this dubious contractual protection; in the remoter districts, 'cruelties and abuses existed which cannot be longer hidden or tolerated.'[7]

Nearly as isolated, almost as large and considerably more populous, Queensland was also distanced from the Sydney–Melbourne axis. Western Australia and northern Queensland, together with the Northern Territory of South Australia, remained largely frontier regions, where clashes with the Aboriginal population continued long after the troubles in the southern colonies had subsided. Whereas the north-west of Australia is arid, incapable of affording more than occasional sparse pasture, the north-east is, thanks to the sometimes over-abundant rains, fertile. Settler expansion was rapid, one example being the development of the 2,500 square mile Thurulgoona estate by Melbourne wool-broker Richard Goldsborough in 1883 at a cost of more than half a million pounds. Such large-scale expansion displaced dozens of Aboriginal communities, a displacement often accompanied by violence. Henry Reynolds estimates that, while perhaps five thousand whites from northern Australia have died in all Australia's wars, more than twice that number of northern Aborigines have been killed in the same period; the statistics may be unproven, but the fact remains that mass killings continued into the 1920s. Further north, the growing sugar industry claimed to be a special case. The right to employ 'Kanakas' – Melanesians working in the tropical areas – was jealously guarded at a time when all other 'coloured' workers were strongly objected to in the southern colonies. Since no white workers wanted employment in tropical plantations, settlers and labourers were at one on the topic. And Queensland, with a consciousness of being part of the Pacific world, was developing its own imperial aspirations.

One serious consequence of these intercolonial disputes was a failure to agree on that most basic item of infrastructure, a railway system. Thanks to George Stephenson, most of the world's railways run on track with a gauge of 4 foot 8½ inches. This inconvenient module is that of a typical horse-drawn two-wheeled cart; the original railways used for transporting coal accommodated first the horse-drawn tubs, superseded by the same tub dragged up by a stationary steam engine at the top of an incline. Stephenson simply used the same rails for his first locomotive engines, and the world followed; or at least most of the world. In 1846 the British government adopted Stephenson's gauge as the standard for Britain, although permitting Ireland to retain a wider, 5 foot 3 inch gauge; and the Great Western Railway, for much longer, stuck to Isambard Kingdom Brunel's original 7 foot standard. The New South Wales government – at that time New South Wales still included Port Phillip – agreed in 1848 to accept the Stephenson gauge, but two years later the Sydney Railway Company asked the Colonial Office if the Irish standard might be adopted instead. The Colonial Office offered no objection, and the Australian plan – this time with the approval of Victoria and South Australia, by then separated – was approved. But Sydney then unilaterally decided to revert to the 4 foot 8½ inch gauge, and began construction of its system. Since the other two colonies had already ordered engines and rolling stock on the previous basis, furious dissension was expressed. London did its best to persuade New South Wales to stick to its agreement, but could hardly interfere in the domestic concerns of independent colonies; New South Wales therefore went one way, South Australia and Victoria another.

The issue became more complex when in 1870 South Australia decided to construct feeder lines, some of considerable length, connecting the 5 foot 3 inch main line to a narrower gauge, of 3 foot 6 inches. Goods or people moving between Sydney and the South Australian back country would therefore have to transfer twice, adding considerably to the costs and time taken for the journey. When Queensland, prompted by Robert Herbert, pressed ahead in 1864 with their own rail system on a 3 foot 6 inch gauge, followed in 1879 by Western Australia, the complex jigsaw was completed.

Although the most obvious result of inter-colonial rivalry was the proliferation of railway gauges that harassed train travel for more than a century, the most persistent was the argument over inter-colonial trade. A great stir had been fomented in 1846 between Van Diemen's Land and New South Wales, each attempting to establish protective tariffs against the other, which had formed one of the reasons for Grey's federal initiative, but the more serious problems manifested themselves in the 1850s, beginning with the Murray River trade. Forming the frontier between New South Wales and Victoria for most of its length, before flowing through South Australia to enter the sea near Adelaide, and passing as it does through extensive farming districts, the Murray should have been a great artery of trade, but the three colonies could not agree on its management. The first inter-colonial conference called in 1863 to discuss the matter collapsed; neither Queensland nor Western Australia saw any point in attending. The free-trade Melbourne *Argus* congratulated Victoria on its escape since 'The half-developed, unconsolidated communities of a continent are wholly unfit for anything like a systematic consolidated policy, such as that proposed'. After the conference's failure the New South Wales government threatened to establish customs stations to levy tolls unless Victoria made over part of the import duties imposed at Melbourne on goods which then crossed the river into New South Wales. That colony had some reason for annoyance since its most important agricultural centre, the Riverina, north of the Murray, was a good deal nearer Melbourne or Adelaide than Sydney, and its farmers preferred to ship their goods through Victoria or South Australia, to the detriment of Sydney. An alarming example of this competition manifested itself in 1864 when an armed confrontation seemed likely as the Victorian government sent policemen to protect Murray River shipping from 'seizure, search or illegal interference' by New South Wales officials. When Inspector Hare, of the Victorian police, confronted Mr Gordon, of the New South Wales customs, he was threatened with being shot; he countered by promising to throw Gordon overboard if the customs officer put a foot on his boat.[8]

An uneasy agreement between the two colonial governments followed, which should have been helped by the extension of the rail systems. The Melbourne line reached the south side of the Murray River at Wodonga in November 1873, and the Sydney line the north bank at Albury in February 1881. For two years the two termini then remained confronting each other, with passengers and freight having to change into carts and carriages to make the transition, while the colonial governments argued about the cost of building a bridge. Only in August 1883 was the junction completed – and even then the different gauges necessitated trans-shipment. Five years later the line was extended both to Adelaide and to Brisbane, leaving only Western Australia isolated by the interminable Nullarbor Plain until the connection was finally established in 1917.

The improved postal services made possible by the rail links were augmented by the new telegraph lines, which connected even Western Australia by 1877, but any general agreement proved illusory. New South Wales and

Victoria reached an agreement on the Murray trade, on condition that goods coming upriver from South Australia could be taxed on entry to Victoria. This neat stitch-up, in 1867, naturally aroused indignation in both South Australia and Tasmania. Another inter-colonial conference was held in 1870 to discuss the foundation of a customs union which would share revenue among the colonies: this was scuppered both by Victoria's insistence that the others all adopted the Victorian tariffs and by Queensland's continued absence. Victoria's policy was 'pernicious', the *Sydney Morning Herald* expostulated: 'It is of course useless to discuss the question so long as this temper shall prevail.' London was worried; the troubles that Earl Grey had foreseen were burgeoning, and since the British government was then religiously pursuing free-trade policies, the whole idea of tariffs was anathema. More conferences resulted only in the Colonial Office washing its hands of the whole business (Australian Colonies Duties Act, 1873) and leaving the colonies to agree or disagree. They chose the latter course.

The most serious effect of this was the adoption of contradictory policies by the two largest colonies. Victorian liberals, abandoning the free-trade policies of British Liberals, plumped for protecting the colony's industries by tariff barriers. Against the protests of the Legislative Council, protection was formally adopted as the base of Victorian commercial policy, with its most prominent politician, Alfred Deakin, its standard-bearer. Inevitably, New South Wales adopted the opposite position, for which sound reasons existed. With a considerably larger land area, and a smaller (at the time) population, New South Wales could rely on an income from land sales and did not need to insist on customs dues. Victoria accordingly abrogated the 'treaty' with New South Wales, and erected their own customs houses beside the Murray; South Australia and Tasmania introduced their own protective tariffs, and internecine strife continued. The influential, rich and opinionated David Syme, who controlled the Melbourne *Age*, was able to persuade Victoria's public opinion, and to influence parliaments towards protectionism, but a protectionism allied to radical policies. Even conservative free-traders such as Sir James McCulloch had to adjust their policies to those supported by Syme, characterized as 'the apostle of protection, preaching it in and out of season'.[9]

'The magnitude of their ideas is appalling'

Individual colonies had previously displayed nervousness about the ambitions of European powers. It was the Crimean War that prompted the old salt Hotham to purchase the colonial steam sloop HMS *Victoria* for colonial defence, and the passing of a Volunteer Act (1854) to authorize recruitment from the 'highly respectable classes of all persons' in rifle and cavalry units. Such enthusiasm suited the British government very well, since it was felt that colonies should be responsible for meeting their own defence costs, beyond that of the all-powerful Royal Navy which remained, for the time being, a purely Imperial instrument. Little objection was therefore raised when British troops, who had been much appreciated for their band concerts, cricketing ability and construction projects – Captain George Barney RE, later Surveyor General of New South Wales, was merely the most prominent of an industrious group – were finally withdrawn in 1870, the last to go being the 18th Foot, now the Royal Irish Regiment. The *Sydney Morning Herald* saw the move as 'the first step towards nationality, not the result of direful conflicts and years of suffering, but the well-considered decision of men who rule the destiny of a great nation' – and who, it could be added, were anxious to spare unnecessary expense.

Would this troop retirement encourage the ambitions of other European countries? The half century after the first Australian responsible governments were established saw widespread changes in the Asian-Pacific region. Some alarm had already been manifested in 1839 when two American warships, with intentions entirely innocent, were able to anchor undetected in Sydney Harbour, and in the 1840s United States' interests had been advocating the annexation of Tahiti. After the Mexican War of 1847 America, with its newly acquired west coast, began developing a Pacific policy, and from 1869 transcontinental railways linked the eastern and western coasts of the United States, which was then beginning its post-Civil War reconstruction, built on the forced expansion of the war effort. Stimulated also by the gold rushes, first to California, then to the Klondike and the Yukon, the west coast ports developed rapidly, asserting the United States' position as a Pacific power. In the 1890s a series of plots, culminating in the first use of the US Marine Corps in unprincipled empire-building, led to the annexation of Hawaii and the construction of the great naval base at Pearl Harbor, which brought American sea-power into the Pacific centre. Although Anglo-American relations were, on at least three occasions during the nineteenth century, very cross indeed, the US and Royal Navies remained good friends, and frequently acted together. But if the United States was never seen in Australia as a threat, European nations certainly were.

With a much weaker strategic rationale than that of the United States, France was disturbing the other side of the Pacific in south-east Asia. Beginning in 1839 with the dispatch of a secret agent to Canton by King Louis-Philippe, France had been searching for a foothold in the region, which might then be expanded to counter the Dutch in the East Indies, the Spanish Philippines, and even, God willing, the diabolical British in India. Initial success was achieved only in 1862, when the port of Saigon was taken. The Emperor Louis-Napoleon, disappointed by his failure to install a puppet government in Mexico, consolidated further French conquests into the new province of Cochin China. His republican successors proved even more aggressive. By 1886 French rule had been imposed on Annam and Tonkin, while French hegemony was recognized in those parts of the Siamese empire now called Laos and Cambodia. A slice of the world bigger than France itself passed under French control, to be a source of much later trouble.

During the great days of Ming China such territories would have been claimed as part of the Chinese empire, and even an enfeebled Ch'ing dynasty had been able to bring France to the brink of defeat, but China itself was falling victim to foreign aggression; Russia as well as France nibbled at the coast to claim areas of influence, but the most perilous of all threats to China came from its ancient feudatory, the Meiji empire of Japan. It took only a decade after the first treaty with America was signed in 1854 for definite agreements to be reached between Japan and the West, now, after the collapse of the Tokugawa shogunate, ruled by the young emperor Mutsuhito. Within a single generation the 'enlightened government' had transformed Japan from a feudal to a modern state, and one as bent on expansion as any European power.

Somewhat apprehensively, the governments of Spain and Holland looked to the security of their own empires in the face of these new threats. The Dutch East Indies, even after the loss of Ceylon to Britain and the establishment of British authority in the Straits Settlements, still stretched in a great arc through 50 degrees of longitude from Sumatra to New Guinea, and the Philippines remained a Spanish possession, commemorating the old Treaty of Tordesillas; even Portugal retained the tiny territory of East Timor and, by courtesy of the Chinese government, their trading station at Macao, but Portugal could not be perceived by any other country as a threat.

The Pacific islands had become a confused and scandalous region as the European powers scrambled to gain footholds in this hitherto unappropriated region. Maps convey different meanings to observers depending on where they find themselves. To British governments, the scatter of islands across the South Pacific represented little more than navigational hazards. If some other power wanted to assume responsibility for any, Britain, knowing well how unprofitable and thankless the task would be, was content to let them; but to Australians, perils lurked in such inaction. France had already, in 1844, declared a protectorate over Tahiti, and in 1853 annexed the island of New Caledonia. Tahiti was far distant, but New Caledonia lies opposite the Queensland port of Mackay, about the same distance from the mainland as Norfolk Island, and from New Caledonia north a chain of islands, from the New Hebrides through the Solomons to the Bismarck Archipelago, parallels the Australian and New Guinea coasts. Britain had acquiesced in the earlier annexation of New Caledonia by Louis-Napoleon – a 'cowardly policy' according to the *Sydney Morning Herald* (3 November 1853). At the time, Australian public opinion was not too greatly exercised; Britain and France were, for once, close allies, preparing to go to war with Russia, but Anglo-French relations were volatile. Following the British example, France established a penal colony in New Caledonia, and it was rumoured that the Second Empire had designs on the New Hebrides for the same purpose. Australian apprehensions quickened. Presbyterian and Methodist ministers in the New Hebrides were threatened by a Catholic takeover, and New South Wales dreaded an invasion of absconding convicts. As early as 1860, Gavan Duffy wrote to John Lang, still a furious radical at the age of 62, blaming Louis-Napoleon, together with the other European powers for letting the French emperor have his own way in meddling with the Pacific regions. 'In the present condition of Europe it is surely our duty to be in a condition to invite our resources for defence, or at least to take council together.' The Victorian navy, represented by HMS *Victoria*, was readied for action, but that particular threat evaporated as Louis-Napoleon turned his attention instead to Mexico, with disastrous results.[10]

Victorian sentiment was more expansionist than that of New South Wales. The suggestion that, as some sort of compensation, Britain should annex Fiji, conveniently situated east of the New Hebrides, was enthusiastically canvassed. When, however, in 1871 Gladstone's Colonial Secretary, Lord Kimberley, suggested that New South Wales, rather than Britain, should take over the island (and the attendant expense) the Premier, Sir James Martin, politely declined. The Governor, Lord Belmore, explained that although 'It might have suited a few Sydney Merchants . . . a much more legitimate way of spending money' would be to improve internal communication, although 'Victoria which is richer and more ambitious than New

South Wales might perhaps have entertained the idea'. Benjamin Disraeli, now leading what had become the Conservative Party, coming to power in 1874, proved more sympathetic. Encouraged by his cousin, Sir Robert Herbert, previously Queensland's first Premier, now in London as permanent under-secretary at the Colonial Office, the new Foreign Secretary Lord Carnarvon agreed to make Fiji a British colony.

It was, however, neither Victoria nor New South Wales, but Queensland that proved acquisitive, and German rather than French ambitions which provoked a reaction. The various attempts made to arrive at some sort of common Australian trade policy had the model in view of the German Zollverein, first established in the 1820s, which had become, under the guidance of Prince Otto von Bismarck, the foundation of the immensely successful German empire. Impetus towards agreement between the Australian colonies, which had so signally failed to establish their own customs union, was given a powerful reinforcement by Bismarck's own expansionist policies in the 1880s. Once German hegemony in continental Europe had been assured by the defeat of France in 1871, nationalist pressure for colonial markets, which might rival England's, developed. Bismarck, previously indifferent – 'colonies for Germany would be like the silks and sables of the Polish nobles who had no shirts to wear under them' – changed tack in response to pressure from such bodies as the Kolonialverein, founded in 1882 to agitate for colonization 'as a matter of life and death', and the disreputable Gesellschaft für Deutsche Kolonisation.[11] Two areas signalled as targets for German ambitions were the south-west coast of Africa, and New Guinea, together with the offshore islands of New Britain and New Ireland, which with the Solomon Islands stretched through 15 degrees of longitude to form a substantial barrier to any Australian expansion into the Pacific.

Plentiful excuses for intervention in the region were offered by the helpful murder of missionaries, by the horrors of the quasi-slave traders, the 'blackbirders', and by the enterprising pirates, as Germany, France and the United States put down their various markers. Only Britain, confident in her possession of so considerable a quantity of the earth's surface, remained aloof; but such disinterest did not extend to her colonies, and Queensland was not exempt from territorial ambitions. That colony's jurisdiction extended, after May 1872, to all islands within 60 miles of her coast, which included those in the Torres Strait. Extended by the acquisition of the offshore islands of Tauan and Sabai in 1879, Queensland was brought to within a few miles of New Guinea, and Australian pressures to annex 'the magnificent island', as well as a great deal more Pacific real estate, mounted.

It was Graham Berry of Victoria who had first suggested, in September

1877, that 'a kind of Monroe doctrine should be established that all the islands in this part of the world should be held by the Anglo-Saxon race'. Victoria remained ambitiously acquisitive, but Queensland was more intimately concerned and continued to press for some sort of gesture extending imperial authority over New Guinea. Alerted to German intentions, in February 1883, by the colony's Agent General in London, the Queensland Premier Sir Thomas McIlwraith moved swiftly. Acting on his own initiative, the Premier on 3 April 1883 authorized the annexation by Henry Chester, a police magistrate, on behalf of Queen Victoria, of the eastern half of New Guinea. It was a bad time to have chosen for such an initiative. The Liberal Prime Minister Gladstone, unlike the Conservative opposition, was adamantly opposed to any further colonial expansion, and was being currently harassed by two much more pressing problems – the recalcitrant Boers in South Africa and the threatening situation in Egypt. Moreover, there was a strong and probably justified suspicion that McIlwraith's move was, as William Redmond, the Irish Nationalist MP and an acute observer then visiting Australia, put it: 'simply a design to obtain better facilities for procuring black labour for the sugar plantations [but] . . . of course you don't hear this declared from the housetops.' The Colonial Secretary Lord Derby, although mollified by McIlwraith's offer that Queensland would meet all expenses, and initially sympathetic to the idea, was obliged to disown the annexation, explaining that 'Our responsibilities are already heavy enough' and 'our possessions, scattered as they are over every part of the world, are sufficient to require the utmost care and vigilance.' The Victorian government had complicated matters on 12 June, by requesting that Britain should please annex all the rest of unclaimed Melanesia. By now thoroughly nervous, Lord Derby wrote to Henry Ponsonby, the Queen's private secretary, on 29 June:

[The Australians want to] annex, or at least undertake a protectorate, of 1. New Guinea 2. New Hebrides 3. Samoa. 4. all islands north and northeast of New Guinea. I asked them whether they did not want another planet all to themselves? And they seemed to think it would be a desirable arrangement, if only feasible. The magnitude of their ideas is appalling to the English mind . . . It is hardly too much to say that they consider the whole of the South Pacific theirs *de jure*, and the French possession of New Caledonia they regard as an act of robbery . . . it is certainly hard for four millions of English settlers to have only a country as big as Europe to fill up.[12]

Some compensation was offered to the colonists, who were 'proving very wild on the question of annexations', by Derby's decision of 2 July, disallowing the annexation but offering to reconsider, should the Australasian colonies be prepared to foot the bill. At any rate, the Colonial Secretary announced that the eastern part of New Guinea was to be regarded as within the British sphere of influence and that any foreign occupation would be seen as an unfriendly act. This was not enough to satisfy the colonies, where widespread indignation was aroused by what seemed to be a cowardly reluctance by the British government to assert Australian interests. A public meeting on 16 July 1883 in Sydney, saw the other colonies united behind Queensland. Higinbotham of Victoria insisted that: 'the interest of all these colonies requires that long string of numerous islands extending along the north east spurs of Australia from New Guinea to New Hebrides and thence to Fiji ought not to become the property of any nation in the world other than Great Britain' and therefore Great Britain 'should exercise a right which is assumed to belong to all civilized countries' to 'take possession of islands not occupied by peoples who are recognized to be within the ranks of civilized nations'. Continued indignation resulted in another inter-colonial conference in December 1883, at which, for the first time, all, including New Zealand, with Fiji indicating informal concurrence, were represented. The resolutions passed were politely phrased; the first stated:

1. That further acquisition of dominion in the Pacific, south of the equator, by any foreign Power, would be highly detrimental to the safety and well-being of the British possessions in Australasia, and injurious to the interests of the Empire.

But the second conceded:

2. That this convention refrains from suggesting the action by which effect can best be given to the foregoing resolution, in the confident belief that the Imperial Government will promptly adopt the wisest and most effectual measures for securing the safety and contentment of this portion of her Majesty's dominions.[13]

In May 1884 Derby reminded the Australasian governors of his previous year's offer, and indicated that he would additionally be prepared to appoint a Deputy High Commissioner for the Western High Pacific, to be quartered in New Guinea, and to contribute towards the costs involved. The Colonial Office was, however, becoming mildly concerned about German ambitions after Bismarck had, in June of that year, publicly rejected the idea of an Australasian Monroe Doctrine. Apologizing for his insistence, Lord Derby pressed Gladstone for a Cabinet meeting: 'New Guinea is very urgent indeed', and on 6th August the Cabinet did decide to declare a protectorate over the whole of East New Guinea, that part not occupied by the Dutch.

Since all government and society adjourned for the grouse-shooting on 12 August, nothing was said or done until 30 September when a worried Lord ('Pussy') Granville, Gladstone's Foreign Secretary, told the Prime Minister that 'a very awkward question has arisen'. The German ambassador had informed him that the Germans intended to press ahead with their annexation of northern New Guinea, and that the cruisers were on their way. The wisest course, Granville considered, was to say nothing publicly and to attempt to convince the Germans in private of the error of their ways. The news broke in Australia only on 9 October; the British protectorate would be limited to the south coast, and this was followed on 19 December by newspaper reports that the Germans had indeed annexed the north together with the Bismarck Archipelago. 'The German government has behaved very shabbily', Robert Meade, who was even then negotiating with them, crossly wrote to the dejected Pussy. Papua, the southern region, would become the protectorate of British New Guinea, with its capital at Port Moresby, while the Germans would erect a base at Rabaul.[14]

Australian opinion was even more inflamed, at least in Queensland and Victoria. The *Anglo-New Zealander and Australian Times* (3 July 1885) may have decided to bite the bullet, since 'Everyone must agree that the Germans are far and away the most acceptable rivals', but many were furious. 'The exasperation here is boundless,' wrote James Service, the brisk radical Premier of Victoria. 'If England does not save us from the danger and disgrace . . . the bitterness of feeling towards her will not die out in this generation.' That was going too far, and four years later the protectorate over British New Guinea was formally changed to annexation, with the administration confided to Queensland: Australia might claim to have her first colony, but the seeds of distrust of Britain's willingness to defend Australian interests were sown. Another valid point was made by Lord Derby: if the Australians wanted to expand 'the most practical step that they could take . . . would be the confederation of those colonies in one united whole'. For the first time the colonies now appeared prepared to consider the matter and Federation became a serious issue.

The Federal Council

The Victorian Premier, James Service, had taken the initiative in calling the Inter-colonial Convention in 1883 to consider movement towards a federation of all the colonies – indeed, the choice of the word 'Convention' implied the intention to design a constitution. Although the Convention's first meeting was held in Sydney, New South Wales was a reluctant participant. It became, Deakin recorded, 'a point of patriotism with many New South Welshmen to belittle and oppose' what they saw as 'a Victorian invention'. Many felt, with old John Robertson, that Victoria was nothing but a 'cabbage garden' and that the only acceptable federation would be one in which the other colonies crept back into the bosom of the mother colony. Though never as brash, the New South Wales Attorney General, native-born of convict parents, William Bede Dalley, agreed with Robertson sufficiently to have any proposed federal responsibilities well restricted, and was finally instrumental in New South Wales' refusal to participate in the Federal Council of Australasia, which held its first session in Hobart, in January and February 1886.

Only Victoria, Queensland, Tasmania, Western Australia and – giving the Australasian touch – New Zealand and Fiji were represented. The absence of South Australia and New South Wales was itself enough to doom the Council, never uncommonly active – the records of its deliberations over the years fill only five slim volumes – to impotence. The Council's limited legislative powers included many of those legal matters indicated previously by Smith O'Brien, but the chief concern was with the Pacific islands. Suspicions of Britain's reluctance to support annexations were expressed. The Council would 'have to jealously watch over the interests of the Australasians in that direction', there being 'an uneasy feeling, a feeling of apprehension ... that English statesmen, in their endeavours to meet present exigencies, are but too apt to remove those exigencies by the cession of territory in the Pacific of which they have a very imperfect and inadequate knowledge.' It might well have been remarked that most Australian politicians had a 'very imperfect and inadequate knowledge' of the great issues that even then were occupying the minds of the British government, but British politicians were indeed dismissive, on the rare occasions when colonial concerns were forced upon their attention. A central object of British policy was the security of imperial communications through the 'All Red Route' of submarine cables, essential both for trade and to control naval operations; but technically excellent communications were hampered by traditional bureaucracy. The only mode of communication between the Federal Council and Whitehall was through the Governor of Tasmania, where the infrequent meetings of the colonial Premiers continued to be held. Enthusiasm for inter-colonial action was limited; the two largest colonies remained jealously opposed to each other; the smaller colonies were fearful of being squashed into impotence; organized labour and the radical democrats saw both advantages, in that a strong nation would be better able to keep out coloureds of all sorts, and dangers that a constitution could reflect the most illiberal of the existing colonial constitutions – to say nothing of the likely provisions for an upper house and the continuation of the Governor Generalship, both regarded by ardent socialists as decaying monuments of a colonial past.[15]

Colonial Federation was not the only show on the road, but faced competition from an Imperial Federation League formed in England in November 1884, with the Liberal peer Lord Rosebery presiding, but with a strong Conservative following, advocating in place of the Empire a federal union of Great Britain with the colonies of settlement, Canada, Australia, New Zealand and South Africa (India posed a problem, but timid steps towards eventual self-government there were already beginning). The League itself did not last long, but the sentiment, later expressed by Alfred Deakin, that the Empire's position was 'unstable, untrustworthy, impermanent and required to be replaced gradually, but surely, by a fuller and more complete organisation', flourished; and it would be much easier for a united Australia to participate in a Federal empire than it would be for the constituent colonies.[16]

William Dalley of New South Wales, in spite of his reluctance to associate with the Council, being temporarily Prime Minister pulled off a spectacular coup in March 1885, upstaging the Council's formation by volunteering a contingent of 500 infantry and two batteries of artillery to join the expedition against the Sudanese, in rebellion against Egyptian rule and who had besieged General Gordon in Khartoum. Gladstone's government, with little appetite for action, accepted the offer only reluctantly (similar offers from Victoria, South Australia and Queensland were politely refused) and took the first opportunity to withdraw (but it took ten years and two expensive campaigns before the Sudanese were subdued). Stimulated by the news of Gordon's death, the expedition's despatch was greeted with unbridled enthusiasm as an unprecedented crowd of some 200,000 gathered to see the soldiers off. The famous historian J. A. Froude, who was in Australia at the time, shrewdly commented: 'The New South Wales colonists cared nothing about the Soudan. They were making a demonstration in favour of national identity.'[17]

Taking part only in one minor action, with three wounded, the Australian troops had little opportunity to distinguish themselves. The bathetic withdrawal, and the return of the contingent only three months later, caused a speedy deflation of belligerent enthusiasm, but the Australian representatives to the first Colonial Conference, held in London in 1887 to coincide with the Queen's Golden Jubilee, arrived trailing clouds, if not of military glory, then at least of good intentions demonstrated. Called at the suggestion of the Imperial Federation League, this Conference was the first of a succession of such meetings, still continuing, at which leaders of the colonies deliberated together with the British government. It was this 1887 conference that saw Alfred Deakin appear on the international stage, still in his twenties, the only Australian politician (other than Henry Parkes) to have more than a local celebrity until the advent, more than thirty years later, of Billy Hughes.[18] Undeterred by the presence of the Prime Minister, the Marquess of Salisbury, and other notables, Deakin attacked what he termed 'the natural *vis inertiae*' of the Colonial Office and insisted that colonies, in Australia at least, would demand their rights. Following the Duke of Cambridge at a banquet on 20 April, Deakin commented on 'the innocence without spot or blemish' that characterized British knowledge of the colonies. Such remarks met with a cool reception by the Conservative Lord Salisbury, who had a poor opinion of Australians:

the most unreasonable people I have ever heard or dreamt of. They want us to incur all the bloodshed and the danger, and the stupendous cost of a war with France, of which almost the exclusive burden will fall on us, for a group of islands which are to us as valueless as the South Pole – and to which they are only attached by a debating-club sentiment.

Salisbury's reference was to what he saw, not without reason, as Australian agitation about the French occupation of the New Hebrides as part of their existing colony of New Caledonia and its possible use as a penal settlement. Victoria was the leader in this, somewhat surprisingly considering its geographic position, while Sydney, so much nearer, took little interest. Service was particularly virulent on the subject: a historian of Federation, John Hirst, comments: 'In Sydney's governing circles, they thought he was mad, which is how nationalists appear to those who are not.' Deakin later revealed a bold Victorian plan in 1888/9 to invade the New Hebrides, which had hitherto remained unsuspected:

There were more rumours of French preparations for the seizure of the New Hebrides which on enquiry seemed to be well founded. It was therefore decided to forestall them by despatching a detachment of the Victorian permanent military forces in a swift steamer with orders to hoist the British flag and keep it flying. The boat was to be chartered privately and the men taken off when supposed to be away at Westernport in practice. This time it was not intended to allow the flag to be hauled down except upon express instructions from the Home Government.

Fortunately the project was abandoned – its consequences, Deakin admitted, might have been the gravest. It was left to normal diplomatic channels to solve the question by agreeing, in October 1907, an Anglo-French condominium of the islands, and the end of transportation by France to the Pacific.[19]

Australian defence against aggression or contamination by escaped or released convicts (a sensitive subject, this) depended upon Britain's command of the seas. While this endured, as it did until 1941 (and then ended largely through bad diplomacy), Australian safety was assured; when it failed Australia would be in danger. The most productive result of the 1887 Conference was therefore the colonial agreement to contributing towards the cost of the Royal Navy. Since 1821 the navy had maintained a presence in Australian waters, as part of the East Indies station, based on Sydney. A modest enough squadron – the biggest ship being the fifth rate 26-gun frigate *Calliope* – the Crimean War agitation led to some improvement. In 1865 a grant was made to the Victorian government to provide a new ironclad, the *Cerberus* – still only a coastal defence ship of 3,480 tons – supplemented by an antiquated converted three-decker, the *Nelson*. New South Wales boasted its own small navy, the old steamer *Wolverene*, and South Australia bought a well-designed and powerful small cruiser *Protector*, but Victoria's was by some way the most significant Australasian force. Given French ambitions, and with France at that time striving to construct a navy that might challenge Britain's, some greater deterrent was arguably needed. As part of a major reorganization of imperial defence, Admiral Sir John Colomb's publications had alerted British governments to the imperative necessity for a chain of well-defended naval stations in the Pacific and Indian oceans, and Major General Bevan Edwards was sent to report on Australia's potential role in Imperial defence. The naval recommendations provided for five fast cruisers and two torpedo boats, paid for by the colonies, to be stationed in Australasian waters, under Royal Naval command but not to be removed from their station without the agreement of the colonial governments. On 5 September 1891 therefore the *Sydney Morning Herald* was able to greet the arrival of the first Australasian squadron, as 'marking a distinct epoch in the onward march of Australian nationality . . . All going well, the berths that the British warships have occupied so long in Farm Cove will this afternoon be taken up by a far superior class of ships.'

On his return from the celebrations in 1887 Deakin had reported that the people of Great Britain had been educated on colonial matters. He believed 'the people of the mother country will come to recognise that the people of the colonies are of common blood, common kin, and common aspirations, and, I believe, the interests of the colonies will yet be regarded as their interests, and be guarded by politicians in Great Britain as zealously as those in any part of the kingdom. (Applause).' While the first part of Deakin's sentence was true even at that time, and quite especially true towards Australia and New Zealand, where family relationships were and remain more common than with Canada or South Africa, the second remained an aspiration. Democratic politicians, at best, will take the interests of their voters reasonably seriously (more usually, special interests with personal benefits attached command their attention) but will very rarely concern themselves with anyone not capable of influencing their next election. It would take the threat of war to make British politicians take colonial concerns seriously.[20]

After the New South Wales Prime Minister Alexander Stuart resigned in October 1885, and Dalley refused the offer of succession, three uncomfortable free-trade administrations led by George Dibbs, the septuagenarian John Robertson, and Patrick Jennings, were followed in 1887 by another headed by the indestructable Henry Parkes, Prime Minister for the fourth time. Apart from claiming that his predecessors were soft on free trade, Parkes had few other distinctive policies, but represented both continuity and New South Wales assertiveness. Moving towards the end of a long political life – he could recall arguments with Gipps and Wentworth – Parkes was fortunate to be in power during the New South Wales centenary in 1888. Never short of ideas, the Prime Minister suggested that New South Wales should celebrate by taking to itself the name of 'Australia'. The other states were indignant and horrified, and much enjoyment was had by those suggesting alternatives – Albertia, Guelphland, Neo Cambria, Lagsland or Convictoria were advanced with greater or lesser degrees of seriousness. Parkes was, however, talked out of his scheme by the new Governor, the tactful and experienced Lord Carrington.[21]

Once the excitement of Jubilee year was over, and the usual problems of New South Wales politics – which at one stage saw the Prime Minister besieged in his office by a White Australia mob – reasserted themselves, Parkes had to find a new issue, and that of Federation fell conveniently to hand. Now 74, with thirty years of parliamentary experience, white-haired and -bearded, Parkes was genially known as the Grand Old Man. The sobriquet was borrowed from William Gladstone, although apart from political longevity and free-trade principles there was little in common between the High Church Oxonian and Homeric scholar, and the financially embarrassed and socially equivocal Parkes, who had just married his faithful mistress. The impetus towards Federation had come mainly from Victoria, and Parkes chose a Victorian occasion in February 1887, at a dinner given in his honour by the Victorian Prime Minister and the Mayor of Melbourne, to announce his own conversion:

However interesting, therefore, it may be to guide the destinies of an old and renowned state, it is still more interesting, still more meritorious, still more glorious, to awaken all the latent ambitions and to lay deep and broad the safe foundations of a young nationality in a land like ours . . . if we are only united we may found an empire – whether affiliated to the mother country or not remains to the wise dispensation of God alone to determine – that in all which has distinguished our parent land shall be equally grand, and without any of the stains which rest upon the mother country's history through the ravages of civil war and misgovernment in past ages. (Cheers) I would for the moment forget all the local matters, and would meet your representative men here, and would extend to them not only the right hand of fellowship, but try to act with them as true patriots seeking to promote the great Australasian nation.[22]

The occasion taken by Sir Henry in September 1889 to announce his subsequent campaign for a united Australia was well chosen, at a banquet in Tenterfield, just inside the colonial border, on his return from a conference with Queensland ministers on the subject of a possible federation. After doubtless raising a laugh at the expense of the Federal Council – 'They must have heard something of the Federal Council, on which New South Wales had not yet taken a place, and which sat in Tasmania, and which held sessions which never appeared to interest any one' – the Prime Minister came to the main point, referring to General Edwards' recommendations on defence, which had just been laid before the colonial parliaments. If these were to be implemented, a united Australian command was essential:

The great question they had to consider was whether the time had not now arisen for the creation on this Australian continent of an Australian government, as distinct from the local Governments and an Australian Parliament (Applause). In other words, to make himself as plain as possible, Australia had now a population of three and a half millions, and the American people numbered only between three and four millions when they formed the great commonwealth of the United States. The numbers were about the same, and surely what the Americans had done by war, the Australians could bring about in peace. (Cheers) Believing as he did that it was essential to preserve the security and integrity of these colonies that the whole of their forces should be amalgamated into one great federal army, feeling this, and seeing no other means of attaining the end, it seemed to him that the time was close at hand when they ought to set about creating this great national government for all Australia.

At the time Parkes's *ballon d'essai* was greeted with only modest interest. Given the defence point, which was concerned only with possible future dangers, more pressing issues had to be addressed. New South Wales continued strongly in favour of free trade, while all the other colonies were protectionist and New South Wales' dismissal of the Federal Council was resented by its members. Their Prime Ministers, when approached by Parkes, insisted therefore that the process should begin by New South Wales joining the Council; and Parkes's own supporters were lukewarm: 'I am sorry to see how lost the Legislative Council is on the Federation Question', he complained.[23]

It was Parkes's great moment. With his party and his colony fervently supporting free trade – and having won two successive elections on this issue – any agreement with the other, protectionist, colonies could only be achieved by sacrificing the principle. This he did in a speech in the Sydney suburb of St Leonards in November 1889: 'The question of free-trade and protection', the Premier declared, 'was trifling compared with the necessity, the grandeur and the duty of giving to Australia an Australian government'. It should be the responsibility of such a government, free from inter-colonial rivalries, to decide on the issue. Such realism was too much for the electors of New South Wales who at the next election two years later dropped the old pilot in favour of the ardently protectionist George Dibbs, with George Reid succeeding to the leadership of the free-traders. That single word, 'trifling', thus robbed Parkes of any hope of remaining in office and becoming the first Prime Minister of the new federal state, but at the same time conferred the necessary credibility in the other colonies to enable him to be accepted as the apostle of federation – and he had gained a valuable partner in the person of the rising politician Edmund 'Toby' Barton, a handsome and convival lawyer, previously a minister in the Dibbs government, who had been the youngest speaker of the New South Wales Assembly.[24]

Although Parkes steadfastly refused to join in the Federal Council, a compromise was arranged whereby an informal Council meeting was arranged, in Melbourne, which the New South Wales Premier would attend. At the meeting held in February 1890, although the Victorian Premier, the undistinguished Duncan Gillies, was in the chair, Parkes took the lead; as Alfred Deakin wrote:

First and foremost of course in every eye was the commanding figure of Sir Henry Parkes, than whom no actor ever more carefully posed for effect. His huge figure, slow step, deliberate glance and carefully brushed-out aureole of white hair combined to present the spectator with a picturesque whole which was not detracted from on closer acquaintance.

The meetings, which were open to the press and widely reported, attracted much greater public interest than had ever the humdrum gatherings of the Federal Council. To the principle of a Federation there was little objection, although fears were expressed as to the difficulties which might lie in wait. Nor was there any suggestion that the new Australia would not remain a loyal member of the Empire; Parkes's famous reference at Tenterfield to the 'crimson thread of kinship' aptly summarized the Melbourne meeting's commitment to Britain and the British system. What minor disagreements emerged were glossed over, and the informal meeting transformed itself into a Federation Convention, agreeing to assemble a twelvemonth later, to prepare a draft constitution.

Accordingly, in March 1891 delegates appointed by the colonial parliaments, seven from each together with three from New Zealand, met in Sydney. The two historic names in the First National Australasian Convention were those of Sir Henry Parkes and Sir George Grey, whose remarkable career after his pioneering efforts in South Australia had included governorships of the Cape Colony and of New Zealand, where he had been also, and uniquely, Prime Minister. Neither veteran was able to contribute much, Parkes incapacitated by an accident and Grey now well past his best. It was the Queensland Premier, Sir Samuel Griffith, who chaired most of the committees and who was entrusted with preparing the final draft of the proposed constitution. Griffith's austere persona, incisive legal brilliance and administrative energy, hid a romantic Welsh nature; in his 'gap year' – an early example of this phenomenon – Griffith had toured Britain and Europe, fallen in love and learnt Italian, later devoting himself to translations of Dante.

Even though Parkes's success in deferring the tariff problem had removed the most controversial subject, formidable difficulties confronted the Convention. Its members were all experienced in the working of the Westminster system, dependent as that was on accepted conventions, and to which the whole idea of a written constitution was alien. A federal constitution, in which states' rights must be balanced against an effective central government, had to be approached by studying foreign examples. Of the various models of a federal structure then available, that of Canada seemed the most relevant, and there were attractions in following an Imperial precedent which had stood the test of a generation's experience. As the Australian colonies had been encouraged towards Federation by apprehension of German or Japanese intrusion, so the Canadian federation of 1867 had been pressured by American aggressiveness, led by the sabre-rattling of William H. Seward, Lincoln's Secretary of State. With Britain's undertaking to defend

Canada east of the Manitoba frontier, the apprehensions of the smaller colonies had been assuaged, and Canada was able to safeguard her advance towards the Pacific and to enjoy thirty years of undisturbed political development, providing an encouraging example to the Australians.

The British North America Act of 1867, drafted by Sir John MacDonald, the Conservative Prime Minister of Canada (the former provinces of Upper and Lower Canada brought together after the Durham Report and now renamed Ontario and Quebec) had united Canada with the Maritime provinces of New Brunswick and Nova Scotia (Prince Edward Island and Newfoundland held out for independence until 1873 and 1949 respectively). MacDonald envisaged a strikingly conservative constitution, with an entirely nominated upper house holding life tenure, frankly stating that the Senate was designed to protect minorities and that 'the rich are always fewer in number than the poor'. Australians were not going to fall for that piece of special pleading and preferred the then current American pattern, whereby Senators were to be elected by the state parliaments.

Much admiration was expressed for the American model, at least as first drafted by the founding fathers, but the horrible shadow of the Civil War, which had ended only twenty-five years previously, and a perception of American society as 'brash and materialistic', afflicted by economic inequalities and by racial problems mercifully (it was thought) absent in Australia, 'militated against uncritical acceptance of the American system'. Andrew Inglis Clark, the young and talented Tasmanian Attorney General, and an ardent republican, put the contrary case, 'describing the great variety of American life, and wealth and industry and variation in climate, population and social life, the strength of community and local public life' (he had never been to the United States, but a subsequent visit did not modify his views). Many of Clark's ideas did find their way into the eventual Australian constitution, but other important innovations came from Switzerland – the use of the referendum – and from the German empire – the role of the central state in industrial matters and the provision of old-age pensions.[25]

Opinions were, however, divided on the responsibilities that should be given the Senate. Conservatives and the representatives of small colonies, both alike suspicious of democratic pressures, pushed for a powerful Senate, whereas liberals clung to the idea of responsible government in which the lower house was the repository of power. Sir John Winthrop Hackett, a conservative Western Australian representative, forecast that 'either responsible government will kill federation, or federation in the form in which we shall, I hope, be prepared to accept it, will kill responsible government'. In the event, the Convention avoided so drastic a solution, compromising on leaving the essential power of passing money bills with the lower house, but allowing the Senate to 'request' amendments to them.[26]

It was an uncomfortable solution, that carried with it many risks. Under the Canadian constitution, the Senate lacked democratic authority and became a refuge for distinguished or embarrassing party personages, not unlike the British House of Lords. In Australia, however, Senators were to possess real, if limited, power. Whenever there was dissension, or even simple failure of communication, between the Australian Senate and the House of Representatives, the authority of the Governor General had to be invoked, as had frequently happened in Victoria and New South Wales between the Council and Assembly, and was to occur again, spectacularly, in 1975 when Sir John Kerr dismissed the Labor government of Gough Whitlam over just such an issue.

Surprisingly, given the nature of committees, within three weeks a draft had been prepared and passed to Griffith to perfect. This he did with masterly concision, and although the next ten years were to see many additions and amendments, the armature of Griffith's work still shapes the present Australian constitution – union under the Crown, a House of Representatives representing the people, a Senate in which all states had an equal number of members, and a High Court to adjudicate on constitutional cases. Following the American rather than the Canadian precedent, only specified powers would accrue to the central government, all others remaining with the states. It was intended that the agreed draft should be sent to the colonial parliaments, not for further discussion – that would surely have been fatal to any decisions – but for popular approval; but before this was done Australia was in crisis.

The Great Depression

There seemed to be no limits to the potential wealth of Australia in the early 1880s. Mount Morgan, near Rockhampton, the 'Mountain of Gold' was discovered by the Morgan brothers in 1882, revealing an exceptionally rich auriferous vein that produced a ton of gold every month; the adjoining copper ore supplemented the miners' receipts when the gold became worked out. Even more important was the development at Broken Hill, in the far west of New South Wales, near the border with South Australia. A German prospector and station hand, Charles Rasp, with some colleagues, pegged out a claim of what they thought to be tin and zinc; in fact it turned out to be high quality lead silver ore. A public offering of shares in the Broken Hill Proprietary Company at £2 saw the value rise to over £400. Broken Hill developed into a flourishing community, and although the initial boom did not last, BHP continues as a major international company, BHP Billiton.

Such seemingly inexhaustible mineral riches, backed by the reliable staple, wool, had led to a surge in Australian investment; between 1881 and 1885 over £37 million was borrowed in the London market by the colonial governments, and not much less by private borrowers; the next five years saw the total top £100 million, of which more than a half was absorbed by the still comparatively small Victorian community. Melbourne was the unquestioned financial capital of Australia, and property development there mushroomed: 'There was no limit to the prices buyers would contract to pay, for nobody intended to pay until he had re-sold at higher price.'

Australian developers and their banks eagerly sought more British money. The London *Bankers' Magazine*, 'torn between awe and alarm', noted that Australasian colonial debts were the highest per capita in the world, at over £50, compared with £12 in Canada (Queenslanders were the most extravagant, borrowing nearly £70 each). Competing between themselves, twelve new banks opened their doors between 1877 and 1885, as did many more institutions calling themselves banks, but without proper management, policies or controls – there were no fewer than forty-nine building societies in Melbourne alone, six mortgage banks and fourteen real estate financiers. Most were grossly underfunded; the Metropolitan Bank had an authorized capital of a million, but only £175,000 was paid up.[27]

Foreign borrowings, used to finance urban expansion, were not covered by earnings; the gap should have been filled by exports, but the strain was too great. South Australia and Queensland had already expanded their pastoral industries beyond economic geographical limits, and the collapse was inevitable. Between 1884 and 1891 wool prices declined from 12¼d. (5.1p) to 8d. (3.3p) per pound, allied to the increasing burden of debt assumed by the pastoralists in fencing and the constant pressure of borrowing repayments. Investment slumped, collapsing from over £22 million in 1888 to £9 million three years later, and to only one and a half million pounds in 1897. Mining suffered equally; within a few months after September 1888 copper fell from £99 a ton to £35. With the Australian economy in so parlous a state British investors became wary, their nervousness increased by a banking crisis in November 1890, which forced the ancient and highly respectable Barings Bank to near collapse. Colonial depositors looked nervously at their own banks, whose money supply was being swiftly depleted, and beginning in July 1891 the 'land banks' began to topple, the first being the British Bank of Australia and the Anglo-Australian Bank. Although later investigations proved that mismanagement and fraud had been rife, the crisis, and the loss of small savings, prompted in some radical quarters an outbreak of anti-plutocracy, especially of the London variety. More sensibly, the Melbourne journal *Table Talk* pointed out, in October 1891:

Our credit was excellent, and for a very good reason. The country is rich in natural products, which only required developing. The money thus borrowed in England was understood by the lenders, to be required for developing our resources. Have the Building Societies which are now stopping payment developed the natural resources of Victoria? Let their books be examined, and what will be found? Loans on land, loans on houses erected by speculative builders: in fact loans to everybody except the persons who really could and would like to develop the country if they had an opportunity. The cry is always . . . 'The assets are good'. Are they good? Then try and convert them into ready money.

Other parts of the Empire were in no doubt where the blame lay. John X. Merriman, the austere Premier of the Cape Colony, grumbled that without proper financial controls Australian ministers had been 'plunging wildly into the unknown, which seems to me to be at the bottom of half the messes these Australians get themselves into'.[28]

Such an enfeebled economy could not withstand the two extraordinary blows of drought and strikes. Two key sectors of Australian labour were seamen and shearers. With so much of the economy dependent on sea transport a stoppage on the wharves could bring the country to a standstill, while shearers were, in effect, the production line of pastoralism, converting millions of sheep, eating their heads off behind expensive wire fences, into cash income. Labour had become organized during the good years and had agreed a code of working practices with the pastoralists. Trade unions protected by legislation were established in all colonies, with the usual exception of Western Australia. Much of this had been due to the organizational talent of William Spence. A typical example of early trade union organizers – evangelical, teetotal, serious minded and socialist only in a woolly emotional fashion – the Orkney-born Spence had extended his success in running the Victorian Amalgamated Miners Association to the shearers, where by 1890 he had achieved closed-shop status for his members in New South Wales, Victoria and South Australia.

The strike weapon had been used in Britain since 1871 when the third annual meeting of the Trades Union Congress established its 'Parliamentary Committee' and the stoppage by Tyneside engineers won a new nationally accepted nine-hour day, but the most dramatic strike was that by the London dockers in 1889. Claiming a standard wage of 6d. an hour – which indicates the appalling conditions of dock labour – the strikers were generously funded, to the extent of more than £30,000 by the Australian workers, and their success, competently organized by Bill Tillett and Tom Mann, served as an example to Australian unions. Australian seamen had been out between November 1878 and January 1879, protesting against the employment of Chinese in the coastal trade. That action ended in a compromise, but was followed in 1890 by the first major Australian strike, again on the waterfront, but this time as a grievance of the ships' officers, which spread to the dockers and eventually to Spence's shearers. After three months, which saw much hardship among the strikers (the grateful London dockers contributed to the strike fund) and some unofficial and official violence – although never as bad as that which took place in the Yorkshire and Welsh coalfields in 1893 – the men had to return to work on worse terms than they had previously enjoyed. A strike at Broken Hill in 1892, after the miners' refusal to accept imposed variations on a previous agreement and a consequent lockout, was equally unsuccessful, but entered Australian labour history by stimulating the embryonic Labor Party to parliamentary action.

Queensland was the scene of the most dramatic incidents. Blacklegs employed to break the strike provoked violent reactions from the Queensland shearers, directed by the journalist William Lane, an intellectual and internationalist who had organized the collection in support of the London dock strike. As the stoppage dragged on for many months, attitudes hardened. Pastoralists had been hard hit by the prolonged and excessively severe drought which began in 1888, and were in no mood to surrender. A strong government, the coalition between McIlwraith and Griffith, popularly known as the 'Griffilwraith', formed in 1890, was prepared to exert its authority. When workers in the isolated district of Barcaldine, characterized by Chief Justice Darley as 'a closely knit band of criminals . . . devastating sparsely inhabited country, holding the few inhabitants in terror', resorted to force in excluding blacklegs, mounted police and artillery were used to suppress the 'insurrection'. The strike ended only in May 1891, with several of the leaders imprisoned; the intemperate reactions of the authorities shocked all Australian labour into a recognition of their lack of political power, and established Queensland's reputation for edging towards the extremes of politics, of left and right. 'Politics in Queensland', the Labor Party historian Ross McMullin has written, 'have been conducted with a coarseness more pronounced than elsewhere in Australia', which, considering that Australian politics rarely scale heights of refinement, is something of a meiosis.[29]

The lesson driven home to labour organizers was that in order to be effective strike action needed to be accompanied by the exercise of political power, and that an immediate aim must be the imposition of industrial agreements; labour parliamentary representation was therefore essential. The New South Wales Trades & Labour Council, first formed in 1871, accordingly prepared, in April 1891, an election programme for the Labor Electoral League. There was little specifically socialist in the manifesto, and indeed the Australian Labor Party has rarely been more than tinged with Marxism: electoral reform, improved education, a gesture towards the then fashionable land-tax theories of the American publicist Henry George, and the inevitable diatribe against the unfortunate Chinese, formed the basis of Labor's initial programme. One of the most unlikely founding fathers of the Australian Labor Party was the veteran Sir George Grey, who turned up to represent New Zealand at the 1891 Federal Convention. The historian John Fitzgerald describes his effect:

I shall never forget the scene in the Town Hall, Sydney, early in 1891, when Grey addressed an immense audience, which filled the hall and galleries and spread away into the remotest corridors and out into the adjacent streets. He was over eighty years of age then, and very feeble, so that his voice could not be heard further than a few yards from the platform, but not a soul of that great audience stirred, not a man left; they stood watching with rapt attention the frail figure and white bearded face . . . During the election which followed soon after, the name of Grey was constantly invoked, and received always with enthusiastic cheers; while at that meeting this phrase – 'They say we are leaderless, but we shall never want a leader while Grey lives' – evoked a storm of applause.[30]

Investors' confidence crumbled further after the strikes, and demands for cash withdrawals continued. The collapse of the quasi-banks was followed by that of solider institutions; the Federal Bank of Australia was the first to go in January 1893, followed by others, in New South Wales, Queensland and South Australia as well as in Victoria. In Melbourne the Australian Club, a haven of middle-class comfort, was driven to the desperate expedients of relaxing membership standards and reducing fees. Arthur Eager, son of the influential convict lawyer, resigned in protest against the 'Ten-pounders' who had not 'improved the tone of the club'.[31] Public funds dried up as colonial governments found that they could no longer raise loans on the London market. An unlikely offer of help – politely declined – came from Cecil Rhodes, then Prime Minister of the Cape Colony, who offered to buy the bonds of Victoria and New South Wales and to offer a cash loan. The Victorian Premier, James Munro, assented to a Voluntary Liquidation Act, which should have saved some of his immense fortune, but he, like many other politicians, including Alfred Deakin, was bankrupted, victims of a colonial hubris particularly affecting Melbourne. New South Wales managed better, and emerged from the depression sooner. By draconian action the colonial governments saved the situation; the original banks were liquidated and new banks, with the same names, took on the assets and liabilities; liquidity was assured by the single device of converting, willy-nilly, 50 per cent of depositors' funds into equity. It was drastic, but it worked. The colony of Victoria declared a week-long moratorium, giving a valuable breathing space, but it was Sir George Dibbs, New South Wales Premier, who emerged as the hero. Not much regarded by his contemporaries – the waspish Deakin remarked that 'his many charms of manner and some powers of mind were ill-conjoined' and he was written off by Parkes as 'a man of a weedy nature and a sprawling mind' – Dibbs (knighted in 1892) nevertheless 'saved New South Wales the extremity of disaster by his courageous action' – the government advance to depositors of 50 per cent of their assets in the form of government guaranteed treasury notes. These were original and pragmatic solutions – one is tempted to say typically Australian. Payments of loan interest were maintained, and colonial credit survived unscathed. By January 1894 Dibbs could say: 'the monetary cyclone which recently developed so rapidly in our midst . . . has now passed away, leaving, happily, in banking circles, more damage than actual destruction behind it.'[32]

The real lesson, however, was not appreciated; one senior British Treasury official commented: 'Would that Australia during 1893 possessed some one institution of established credit, similar to the Bank of England!' It was to be many years before such a central bank evolved, but Australian financiers were inventive, and the country's credit was good. In the following year Australian government loans were once more successfully placed on the London market, and spirits rose with the news of yet another mineral bonanza, this time in the Western Australian goldfields.

A Second Commonwealth

Throughout the first century of modern Australian history the pace of development had been staggering, even by comparison with such countries as the United States of America and Japan. Perhaps the rise of Melbourne to a world city within a generation might be paralleled by that of Chicago or Tokyo, but both nineteenth-century America and Japan inherited established political and legal institutions and an economic infrastructure, whereas Australians, to a very considerable extent, developed their own solutions.

That speed of change had not slowed was exemplified by the rise to power of the Labor Party. Only seven years separated the foundation of the Labor Electoral League from the formation of the first Labor colonial government: admittedly one of mayfly duration, as the Dawson ministry in Queensland lasted only six days in 1898; but the next decade saw a national Labor government firmly installed with a majority in both houses of Parliament, the first in the world of its kind. George Dibbs and Henry Parkes had been playing musical chairs in the Premier's office since 1887, but in October 1891 a new force emerged when Labor claimed an immediate success in New South Wales parliamentary elections, winning 35 seats (of 141) in the Assembly, thereby giving it the balance of power. It was an astonishing achievement, and the current discussions of Federation could not neglect this new point of view; Alfred Deakin believed that 'the rise of the Labor party in politics is more significant and more cosmic than the crusades'. At the first sitting of the Assembly the Labor leader, George Black, declared a policy of 'support in return for concessions', that 'reformism' so despised by true socialists, yet so remarkably more effective in improving workers' lives than the application of Marxist formulas. Less promisingly, New South Wales Labor adopted the principle of delegated members of parliament; all candidates were obliged to sign a pledge to – as W. S. Gilbert had it – 'vote just as their party told them to'. Some discipline was certainly essential, since ideas on policy were so diverse and diffuse, but this sacrifice of individual and collegiate rights to an extra-parliamentary body was to prove a poor principle for a party in government, albeit an excellent method of maximizing influence in opposition.[33]

Concessions did not appear immediately: Dibbs did enough to command support from some Labor members, including a substantial reform package in 1893, to enable him to continue in office through the financial crisis. With emotions heightened by the strike at Broken Hill and its questionably brutal suppression, Labor solidarity wavered; four of the most outstanding, including John Fitzgerald, the most intellectual of Labor Party men, were expelled. At the 1894 election Labor had to pay for its errors; 15 official representatives were returned, 20 fewer than previously, plus 13 more who objected to the party's dictation – but all could be relied upon by the new Prime Minister, the reforming George Reid. Fitzgerald was defeated by the rising young Welsh shopkeeper and jack of all trades, Billy Hughes, the first entrance of that remarkable man into Australian parliamentary life. With Labor's continuing support, New South Wales could enter the renewed federal debate with an unprecedently strong government.

In the other colonies, Labor's success was less dramatic. All three Labor candidates were elected in South Australia's 1891 poll; Victoria, with its strong liberal tradition, had two members backed by the Melbourne Trades Hall Council in the Assembly in 1889, but in Queensland, where two Labor men had gained seats by 1889, the 1891 election was disastrous. Nevertheless, the Queensland members of the Intercolonial Trades Union Congress had initiated an Australian Labor Federation, which presaged what was to become the Australian Labor Party (ALP). The Labor Federation was largely the creation of William Lane, who later turned his attention from journalism and politics to the establishment of a Utopian community in Paraguay. 'New Australia' was a predictable failure, and converted Lane into a conservative imperialist, but his place in labour history was secure.

During the banking disasters, progress on Federation ground to a halt. Deakin had been forced into bankruptcy, and in New South Wales Parkes lost his seat in 1895, while Barton was struggling against the popular Reid, who although a federalist in principle was primarily concerned with ensuring his own colony's interests. It was not until 1895 that the process was revived, with potent support coming from the Australian Natives Association (ANA). Founded in 1884 as a mutual friendly society, along the lines so popular in nineteenth-century England, such as the Oddfellows, Foresters or Templars, which collected weekly payments to fund medical and other benefits, the Australian Natives Association restricted its membership to those (white, of course) born in Australia. Together with the trade unions, self-administered friendly societies gave working men valuable experience in administration, but the ANA also developed, from its origins on the Victorian goldfields, a specifically Australian nationalism, which brought with it a demand for Federation. Nationalism, however, did not imply any desire for independence; the ANA wanted an Australia securely within the British Empire. Nor was New South Wales anxious to identify with Victoria; it was not until 1888 that a branch was established in that colony, with membership also allowed to immigrants resident for at least ten years.[34]

With the support of the ANA, Barton and Deakin founded Federation Leagues in Melbourne, Sydney and Adelaide, and Parkes, licking his wounds after his supersession, created a Federal Party, intended to unite both free-traders and protectionists. Popular enthusiasm for union grew, and in 1893 the Victorian and New South Wales Federation Leagues combined to call a conference at the border town of Corowa. For the first time it was the people rather than the politicians who were taking the initiative, and it was a Bendigo lawyer, Dr John Quick (subsequently knighted for his efforts in forwarding the cause of Federation), who proposed a resolution:

That in the opinion of this Conference the Legislature of each Australasian colony should pass an Act providing for the election of representatives to attend a statutory convention or congress to consider and adopt a bill to establish a Federal Constitution for Australia and upon the adoption of such a bill or measure it be submitted by some process of referendum to the verdict of each colony.[35]

Quick's resolution was subsequently adopted by the Federation Leagues, and George Reid scented a promising issue; Federation was again popular, and its adoption would also afford an opportunity finally to dish Henry Parkes. New South Wales had always been the most reluctant and the most important of the colonies and Reid, who continued in office until 1899, had the power to permit or to block any moves towards Federation. Grossly fat, a gift to caricaturists and a master of broad repartee, Reid was also a skilled and astute politician, whose prime objectives at the time were to secure both his own position in New South Wales and the passage of some long-delayed reforms, especially those essential to give the colony a healthy tax base and to clean up the abuses of the Selection laws. Like many Australian politicians, Reid was well aware that a safe position of power in the home state had many advantages over the perilously insecure prospect of office in a federal government – and Reid, in fact, was to experience only disappointment on the national stage. His first action promised progress, a suggestion to convene a Premiers' meeting in Hobart for January 1895 to coincide with a meeting of the Federal Council, so ensuring that all the colonial heads of government, whether members of the Council or not, would be present. Many Federal Councillors were cross, considering that their constitutional authority was being ignored, 'thwarted or overshadowed by a meeting of individuals elsewhere', but Reid's stratagem worked, and a 'Premiers' Plan' was adopted. This was essentially Quick's Corowa proposal, somewhat modified to allow a review by the colonial parliaments of any draft a convention might agree. Parkes was furious, his thunder having been stolen and his chance of figuring as the father of a new Australia dissolved. He died a disappointed man in April 1896, but to subsequent generations he remains the greatest figure – indeed probably the only recognizable figure, apart perhaps from William Wentworth and Alfred Deakin – among nineteenth-century Australian politicians.

Reid followed his proposal by introducing a measure in the New South Wales parliament providing for the election of Convention delegates and the eventual submission of a constitution to a popular vote; Victoria, Tasmania, South Australia promptly followed the mother colony's example. Conservatives scented danger in the idea that delegates should be chosen by the entire electorate; parliaments themselves were surely better fitted to select sober and experienced men, and allowing a referendum introduced direct democracy, a perilous concept. Queensland's conservative administration, preoccupied with its own problems, wriggled and prevaricated. Western Australia, still lagging a generation behind other colonies in constitutional affairs, also delayed. Sir John Forrest was insistent that his voters' interests should not be submerged in any federal arrangements and his position was complicated by the eastern goldfields' demands for secession, where the journalist John Waters Kirwan had assumed the lead in a campaign insisting that, should Western Australia decide not to join in a Federation, the goldfields would do so as an independent state. Although Kirwan's campaign was essentially a device to force Forrest's hand rather than a realistic attempt at secession, it was powerful enough eventually to succeed, after a great deal of agitated dissension.[36]

Some impetus was provided by yet another gathering, the Federal People's Convention held at Bathurst in 1896. Very much a New South Wales affair, support was nonetheless widespread, and as a popular rather than a parliamentary initiative the Bathurst meeting proved the strength of general pro-Federation sentiment. More encouragement for unity was given by the appearance in the region of a new and dangerous potential enemy. In an incident anticipating Pearl Harbor (by sinking a British registered ship carrying Chinese troops), Japan attacked the Chinese empire. The subsequent 1894–5 war was short and decisive, the corrupt and ineffective Chinese forces disintegrating under the modernized army of Japan, and the resultant treaty was a degrading humiliation for the Chinese. At the war's end Japan controlled Korea, Taiwan and Weihaiwei, a strategic port, and was admitted to all the privileges enjoyed by Western nations in China; it was unlikely, however, that this would permanently satisfy Japanese ambitions. Any effective defence of Australia against such an experience could only be assured by a united command acting within the British Imperial structure.

It was a measure of the 'deadweight of apathy' deplored by Deakin, that two years elapsed before the elections envisaged under the Hobart Premiers' Plan were held. Only in March 1897 were forty delegates, ten from each of the four participating colonies, elected to the first of the second round of

Conventions. The turnout was low, and most of the successful candidates were serving parliamentarians, Quick being one of the exceptions. There might have been another in the imposing shape of the Catholic Archbishop of Sydney, Cardinal Moran, who had attended the Bathurst convention, but Protestant opposition combined with a general feeling that religion was best left out of the equation resulted in his defeat. No ministers of religion were elected, more than half the delegates to the conventions being lawyers or pastoralists; surprisingly, considering the success of the Labor Party only one trade union official was present.[37]

Taken very much as a matter of course at the time, it was nevertheless an impressive demonstration of a mature democracy in a new society. Fifty years previously Lord John Russell had given the oligarchic colonial governments the authority to design their own constitutions, which they promptly fashioned in a more democratic way. In 1891 it had been representatives of the colonial parliaments rather than the people who had drafted a constitution, but now the voters themselves chose delegates to design a Federal constitution which would then be submitted for their approval in a referendum – all to be done openly, with contributions invited from all sources. Anywhere but in Australia it would have been a perilous experiment, watched with bated breath by those responsible, and perhaps only in Australia could so successful an outcome have been confidently expected. The 1880 Education Act, which provided for free, compulsory and secular education, had ensured a high degree of literacy, and widely circulated newspapers provided extensive coverage of political discussions. The existence of colonial governments brought political questions nearer to home than in the highly centralized British society; decisions made in colonial legislatures could have immediate impact on the voters, and while this carried with it the risks of 'pork-barrelling' and corruption, political discussion reached into every household and saloon. Altering constitutions had also, since the start of responsible government, been a regular topic of discourse, as each colony exercised the freedom to amend its own institutions.

Colonial susceptibilities demanded that meetings were shared between them; Tasmania had been given its turn in the Federal Council, and the Federal Convention held their sittings in Adelaide, Sydney and Melbourne (Queensland still being absent, and Western Australia too distant). The National Australasian Convention met in Adelaide in 1897 and demonstrated that peculiar mix of liberal and racist attitudes that still characterizes Australia. One colony, South Australia, presented a delegation chosen by all qualified adults, including women, twenty years before Britian took that bold step towards recognizing the equality of the sexes, but there was no agreement at the Convention about who would be held to qualify as an Australian citizen. Aborigines, it seemed, might have to be included, but that minor problem could be left for the future parliament to solve; it was essential, however, to exclude any other non-Europeans. Although the discussions centred around the original Griffith draft, it was Barton who acted as chairman, conciliating opponents and sifting irrelevant objections from constructive suggestions. After an interval to receive comments from the colonial Parliaments – 286 were submitted – the Convention reconvened, first in Sydney and then in Melbourne, to approve a final constitution, in which the chief cause of dissension would be the division of power between the states, as the colonies would become, and the new Federal nation, the Commonwealth of Australia.

The choice of name provoked some stirrings and many alternatives were proposed. Sir John Macdonald had wanted to call the Canadian Federation 'The Kingdom of Canada', but Lord Derby had insisted on the 'Dominion of Canada' in order to avoid injuring American republican susceptibilities. But did not 'Commonwealth' revive memories of the interregnum and King Charles's head? (A few years later King George V was to overrule Winston Churchill's suggestion that a new battleship should be named *Cromwell*.) And was it not a direct translation of 'Republic' – *Res Publica*? Queen Victoria's worries on the subject were calmed, and the name accepted.[38]

If the British model were to be adopted as the basis for the Australian parliamentary system, it offered little guidance on the federal aspect of the new constitution. Although an element of federalism persisted in the United Kingdom, and indeed was to develop as Ireland moved towards Home Rule, and while Scotland had always retained its own laws and religion, the doctrine of responsible government remained opposed to any dilution of parliamentary power. In the United States the executive, under a directly elected President, and the legislature, sometimes in opposition to the chief executive, remained clearly separated; any British government, on the other hand, was absolutely dependent on being able to sustain a majority in the House of Commons. Carrying the British example to its logical conclusion, the proposal of a centralized and unified Australian government which would abolish the colonial legislatures, or reduce them to quasi-municipal status, had its partisans. Its most influential proponent was Sir George Dibbs, with his bitter experience of the banking crisis: 'How far more beneficial in every way; how far more likely to extend our revenues and minimise our expenditure; how far more impressive to the outside world and to our creditors in England, would be the complete pooling of our debts, our railways, our national establishments generally.'[39] This would have been to follow the Canadian example, and the rest of Australia would have none of it. Five conditions were attached to the 1897 resolution to safeguard existing colonial powers – the principle of 'supreme states with limited federal powers' – prescribing 'absolutely free' intercolonial trade, thus leaping one major hurdle, but handing over control of customs and excise to the new Commonwealth. Subject to these provisos the new constitution would establish:

(a) A Parliament, to consist of two Houses, Namely, a States Assembly or Senate, and a National Assembly or House of Representatives: the States Assembly to consist of representatives of each Colony, to hold office for such periods and be chosen in such manner as will best secure to that Chamber a perpetual existence, combined with definite responsibility to the people of the State which shall have chosen them; the National Assembly to be elected by districts formed on a population basis, and to possess the sole power of originating all Bills appropriating revenue or imposing taxation.

(b) An Executive, consisting of a Governor General, to be appointed by the Queen, and of such persons as from time to time may be appointed as his advisers.

(c) A supreme Federal Court, which shall also be the High Court of Appeal for each Colony in the Federation.[40]

The names adopted underlined the American precedent – the House of Representatives and the Senate mirroring the United States Congress – but the question was left open as to whether or not the Senate should be elected by all states on an equal basis, regardless of population, as in the United States, where each state, from California and Texas to Rhode Island, is entitled only to two Senators. Having settled these preliminaries, the Convention adjourned to allow the Premiers to attend the Queen's Diamond Jubilee celebrations and to receive their share of those imperial honours distributed to mark the occasion. It was significant of changing attitudes that neither Deakin nor Barton chose to accept what might have been their due, but this did not signify any falling off of loyalty. Even such stalwart opponents as old Paul Kruger could admire the old lady who had for sixty years both symbolized, and had a very fair share in controlling, the destiny of the most powerful country in the world, and the display in London was stunningly impressive. Twenty-two regiments of Indian cavalry provided officers for the Queen's close escort; the colonial escort, commanded by Colonel Lasseter of New South Wales, contained troops from Canada, the Cape, Natal, Ceylon, Trinidad, Cyprus, Rhodesia, Malta, Jamaica, Bermuda, St Lucia, Hong Kong, Singapore, the Malay States, Mauritius, British Guiana, North Borneo, the Gold Coast and Sierra Leone, as well as detachments from all the Australasian colonies: an incarnation of the empire upon which the sun never set.

More practical meetings were held in the course of the rejoicing, during a conference of colonial governments under the chairmanship of Joseph Chamberlain, the Colonial Secretary. Chamberlain, perhaps the most talented and original politician of his day, was something of an oddity. His career solidly grounded on an industrial fortune and an impressive record in local government, Chamberlain had disagreed with Gladstone on the Irish Home Rule question and left the Liberals to found the new Unionist Party. Although able to demand whatever post he might have chosen in Lord Salisbury's Conservative–Unionist coalition, Chamberlain had chosen the comparatively humble Colonial portfolio, traditionally held by good second-raters or bright men on the way up. A convinced Imperialist, and later primarily responsible for bringing about the Anglo-Boer War, Chamberlain was a persistent advocate of Imperial federation as a method of combining Britain and the self-governing colonies into what could become a worldwide united power. Few colonial governments, and not many of Chamberlain's colleagues, were much interested, and Chamberlain had to accept the conference's decision that 'the present political relations between the United Kingdom and the self-governing colonies are generally satisfactory under the existing condition of things'.

Back in Australia, the prevailing sentiment was characterized by the acting Premier of Queensland, H. Tozer, who quoted a local poet:

> Behold how strong that throne may be
> Whose firm foundations stand,
> Not on a despot's tyranny,
> Nor strength of armed band,
> But on a people's love and trust.

Such sentiments were, however, not quite universal.

Republicans and Nationalists

It was not only federalism that made the 1890s a time of excited debate on the future of Australia. As in England, republicanism was a lively, although very much a minority issue. Charles Bradlaugh, who, backed by the insistent electors of Northampton, in 1886 finally won the right of atheists to take their seat in the House of Commons, was the hero of Australian republicans. His portrait adorned the first issue of the *Republican*; and his friend, Joseph

Symes, published the Victorian journal the *Liberator*. Like Symes, most of the prominent Australian republicans – George Black, who became a Labor member of Parliament, David Buchanan, who had opposed the Sudan contingent in the New South Wales Parliament, and the Queensland idealist, William Lane – were British born.

But as the English republicans declined into respectability after the boost given to the monarchy by the 1887 Jubilee celebrations – the House of Commons honoured Bradlaugh in 1891 by expunging all references to his previous rejections – Australian republicans were stimulated both by the festivities of the 1887 Jubilee and of the centenary of the First Fleet's arrival the following year. Young Henry Lawson, whose mother Louisa may be said to have founded the republican movement, described how he 'wore the green in fancy, gathered at the rising of the moon, charged for the fair land of Poland, and dreamed of dying on the barricades to the roar of the Marseillaise – for the Young Australian Republic.'[41]

Not that there were many injustices for young Australians to rebel against. To all intents and purposes, the Australian colonies were in charge of their own destinies; in the forty-eight years between the establishment of responsible governments and federation only five colonial Acts had been rejected by British governments. The only live issues were those of British unwillingness to support Australian imperial adventures and to admit the persistent racialism of Australian exclusion policies, neither nourishing food for young idealists. The Sydney *Bulletin*'s uncompromising statement that 'Australian and Republican are synonymous. No nigger, no Chinaman, no lascar, no kanaka . . . is an Australian' sat uncomfortably with support for the Rights of Man.[42]

Most Australians regarded their rights as those guaranteed by the British constitution, to which appeal was constantly made by such earlier agitators for colonial rights as Wentworth. John D. Lang, almost alone of politicians, took republicanism seriously, going so far as to delineate a future country of seven provinces (the reference being to Holland) – Flindersland, Leich-hardtsland, Cooksland, Van Diemen's Land, New South Wales, Victoria and South Australia. Daniel Deniehy added his voice to that of Lang, but his visionary eloquence was 'a cry in the wilderness' of mid-nineteenth-century Australia. Nor was more than the occasional spark of republicanism visible in the dramatic episode at the Eureka stockade, where most diggers wished to be seen (and probably saw themselves) as British constitutionalists rather than Australian nationalists. Certainly the monarchy did not always attract fervent loyalty (nor did it in England, where criticism of 'the widow of Windsor' mounted in the 1870s and 1880s) but it did command widespread support. When in 1867 the Duke of Edinburgh, 'Affie', the Queen's favourite son, was shot in Sydney by a deranged Irishman (the Duke was saved from death by his solid braces, but the assailant was hanged, in spite of the Duke's objections), Australian indignation was universal. Lord Belmore had to work hard, and in the end unsuccessfully, to prevent a savage Treason Felony Act being passed, in a single day, by James Martin's government. The visits of the young Princes Albert Edward and George (later King George V) in 1881 provoked demonstrations of intense loyalty; the fact that the two young men were serving as midshipmen, under naval discipline in a warship, did much to dispel any ideas of a pampered and effete monarchy. The 1887 Jubilee celebrations, designed by Disraeli to boost monarchical sentiment, proved popular in Australia. Thomas Walker, a 'protectionist democratic republican' New South Wales Legislative Assembly member, proposed giving the sums to be spent on the festivities to the needy; but Walker, poet, playwright, medium, who shot at a clergyman while drunk, was hardly representative of colonial opinion. Parkes immediately called a huge meeting to denounce the 'disgrace' of Walker's proposals, and promised to 'tread disloyalty into the dust'. Another poet, Bernard 'Barney' O'Dowd had included republicanism among his early enthusiasms, but was changing his views. Writing to his poetic mentor Walt Whitman on 9 June 1890, O'Dowd admitted that he had been 'foolish enough to start a movement for the separation of Australia from England'. Whitman approved of these changed views; Britain had been on the whole, 'a loving parent, indulgent and liberal'.[43]

More serious debate on republicanism was generated by Louisa Lawson, founder and editor both of the *Republican* and the feminist journal *Dawn*, and by the *Australian Nationalist*. George Black, who helped establish the Australian Labor Party, pressed for 'The abolition of the office of Governor, of the Upper House, and of British titles; payment of members of parliament; penal code reforms; nationalisation of the land; "championship of liberty"; and "Federation of the Australian Colonies under Republican rule"'.[44] Few of these aims were carried through in the century which followed.

Republican enthusiasm was short-lived. At the time of the 1887 Jubilee a glorious row had broken out in Sydney Town Hall as republicans denounced a plan for a celebratory school picnic as 'a threat to democratic values'. Ten years later, when the Diamond Jubilee celebrations were being organized, the lively nationalist journal the *Bulletin* was resigned:

one section of Australian republicanism dropped out of sight to a great extent when the frantic loyalism of ten years ago became ingloriously defunct for want of sufficient interest in itself to keep itself alive. The Throne and Person are not objected to in Australia with quite the old vigor of language, because there is an increasing tendency to forget that such things exist. A continued study of the British papers seems even to suggest that JOHN BULL doesn't grovel with quite his old abundant worminess, and in this theory, doubtful as it is, there seems to be some slight hope for better things in the future. If a constitutional monarchy like that of Britain could exist absolutely without the element of grovel, then THE BULLETIN might possibly give up preaching republicanism.[45]

The True *History of the Kelly Gang*

Federation formally created Australia as a nation-state, but a common sense of national identity was still evolving. Participation in three major wars was to exercise a powerful influence, and indeed it might be said that with the influx of non-British citizens after the Second World War, together with the current near-obsession with Aboriginal matters, Australian nationality continues its evolution. Support for Federation both nourished and fed upon a feeling of a shared culture, expressed by the young poet William Gay in 1895: 'A Man from Ballarat does not in Hobart, in Cooktown, or in Coolgardie, feel among foreigners. There is less diversity of local prejudice, of dialect and custom between north and south and east and west of the whole of this Continent than there is ... in England' – and even more obviously, Gay might have written, in Britain. At that time, however, and until the emergence of Billy Hughes on the international stage during the First World War no politician appeared to represent an integrated nation; Henry Parkes and Alfred Deakin were prominent figures, but they were perceived primarily as representing New South Wales and Victoria respectively. Popularity, even eminence, in one colony did not guarantee recognition in any other – indeed, probably militated against it.

In spite of the flurry of republicanism which accompanied the negotiations on Federation, and which was very much concentrated on New South Wales, the new Commonwealth saw itself as an extension of Britain on the other side of the world, part of an Empire which was indisputably the world power (and which under Lord Salisbury's Conservative government lost no opportunity of inflating its own greatness). The most striking fact about the Australian population in 1891 was the solidly British – if the term is taken to include Irish – character of the population. Of a population (full-blood Aboriginals not then, or for long after, included) of 3,174,392, just over two-thirds were Australian-born. The ethnicity of these two groups has been calculated in percentages as:

English	48.8
Irish	25.7
Scottish	14.5
Welsh	1.5
Channel Islanders etc.	0.3
total	90.8

At that time the population of the British Isles was

England	27,483,490	Approximate %	71
Ireland	4,450,546		13
Scotland	4,025,647		12
Wales	1,720,609		4
	37,680,292		

The Irish therefore comprised a considerably higher proportion of the Australian population than that which held in Britain, but there was another significant variation. Irish Catholics formed almost all the Irish in Britain, since there was at that time little reason for Irish Protestants to move to Britain, whereas in Australia Irish Protestants formed a very noticeable minority of all Irish: about a quarter, as was then the figure in Ireland.[46]

Some interesting comparisons emerge. Although the proportion of Scots was not dissimilar in the United Kingdom and Australia, there were fewer Welshmen in Australia, and the proportion of those of English birth or ancestry was smaller, though still much the largest, than in Britain. On the other hand many of those listed in the English census were Irish immigrants themselves, who formed a steady stream throughout the nineteenth and twentieth centuries. In 1891, first-generation Irish formed some 2 per cent of the English population; given the much higher earlier rate of emigration, British residents with Irish ancestry must have formed a considerably greater proportion of the whole. Between 1876 and 1880, for example, a third (32.6 per cent) of all Irish emigrants, to all parts of the world, went to Britain rather than further afield. Even when allowance is made for that, however, Australia was still more Irish than was England. So, too, was the proportion of Roman Catholics; but it is quite wrong to assume that at the time of Federation Irish = Catholic and Catholic = Labor. It was only in the 1920s that the Labor Party became powerfully identified with Irish Catholicism.

Although Australia was low on the list of countries to which Irish people wished to emigrate – apart from the proximity of mainland Britain, the United States and Canada were their preferred destinations – Irish immigrants did well in Australia. The Ulster Scottish were always a formidable group, and flourished in all climates, but Catholic Irish often had a hard time of it in America. Despised by American workers as lowering wages, the Irish Catholic population of the cities, where hostility to abolitionists and hatred of the free blacks was proverbial, met the reform movements of the age with determined opposition. Riots were frequent: a series of Protestant–Catholic disturbances in 1844 in Philadelphia left thirty dead. Irish racists, hearing of Lincoln's Emancipation Proclamation, began riots in New York in July 1863 which lasted for four days with many hundreds killed and wounded, and dozens of blacks lynched and tortured.

Colonial Australia was more welcoming than was the Land of the Free, and from early days the Irish played a much more active part in Australian national life than they had been able to do in America. From Bourke onwards, many Governors were Irish, and Duffy and O'Shanassy were only two of the more prominent Irish colonial Premiers, a century before the first Irish Catholic was elected to the American presidency – and although Britain has had three Irish Prime Ministers, none have been Catholic. The most absurdly restrictive 'Penal Laws', which denied Catholics the right to vote or enter the professions, among other shocking restraints on freedom, had been removed in Britain and Ireland in the 1780s, but it was many years before Catholics were able to find senior posts in the United Kingdom; Daniel O'Connell, 'The Liberator', was one of the first to be allowed to practise as a barrister in 1798. Opportunities were better in the colonies. Colonel Christopher Bird, an English Catholic, after having been assistant military secretary to the Commander in Chief became colonial secretary at the Cape in 1818. Roger Therry and John Plunkett were the first Irish Catholics to gain senior office in New South Wales, Therry as a court commissioner and Plunkett as Solicitor General. Both men had been educated at Trinity College Dublin, illustrating the fact that social standing was at least as important as religion in achieving success.

Patrick O'Farrell, in his authoritative work *The Irish in Australia*, explains how the Irish immigrant had to adjust his own culture and ideas to the shock of Australia. 'The Irish, one might say, were compulsorily anglicized by the materials of physical environment in Australia . . . Those who now expect much culture transfer with Irish Immigrants are romantics, and the implication of their interest a fixation on the Australian failures.' Why then were not the Irish in America similarly 'anglicized'? Few elements of Gaelic folkways survived in the new world, but anglophobia flourished among some. O'Farrell points out that the exiled leaders of the 1798 rebellion (who deplored the excesses of their followers; 'a band of ruffians . . . desperate and bloody-minded', wrote Joseph Holt) readily accepted the version of British rule applied in the colonies, especially under the generally benevolent rule of Macquarie. 'Thus', concludes O'Farrell,

was established a duality vital to the practicalities of Irish behaviour in the colony. Rebels conformed in peace, setting up a marvellous tension between myth and reality which gave the Australian Irish the best of both worlds – the proud and fearsome reputation for rebellion, heroism, and devotion to principles of freedom; and a quiet profitable stake in the new country. The rebel 'chiefs' had done sufficient in Irish rebel history to assure them of automatic dominance of the Australian Irish scene and to ensure that whatever they did locally would be consecrated as a proper and acceptable course. They opted into the Australian colonial enterprise, and their previous revolutionary eminence not only made this conformism the Irish norm, but a posture unchallengeable by the extremism of wild nonentities: the heroes had taken the quiet path.[47]

Later in the century some attitudes hardened, as the twin Protestant and Catholic religious revivals of the 1840s and 1850s excited sectarian antipathy. The Catholic revival, stimulated by the need to combat the new doctrines of liberal and lay democracy, was the most active as new cults and fresh saints were discovered to stimulate popular fervour. What sympathy existed for the violent pursuit of Irish independence was dwarfed by the support for the Irish parliamentary party created by Charles Stuart Parnell, and whose chiefs, John and William Redmond and John Dillon, all made successful Australian tours. Another Irish nationalist MP, Michael Davitt, reported that his countrymen in Australia 'were as a rule, sharers in the sentiment of Australian attachment to the Empire' and that their cabins often had a picture of the Queen, 'almost always flanked by that of Mr. Gladstone, and not infrequently, by either Mr. Parnell, Mr. Dillon, or Mr. William O'Brien' (the last being the contemporary Nationalist MP, and not the unhappy Young Irishman William Smith O'Brien).[48]

Underlying this tolerably satisfied society there remained – and remains, to some extent – a violent undercurrent. Crime statistics are notoriously unreliable, and may reflect the effectiveness of policing, but at the end of the twentieth century Australia was reported to lead the world in serious assault and came second (to Denmark, which sounds unlikely) in theft. It is probable that these otherwise incredible statistics are a result of the disturbed condition of Aboriginal society, but in the later nineteenth century distrust of the law, and a willingness to resist its execution was more widespread.

To some extent this was due to defects in the system. At a time when labour was a scarce resource police recruitment was impossibly difficult:

the constables, a motley collection of cripples, ex-convicts, drunkards and old soldiers, divided their time between the public house and dancing attendance on the Justices. But even without these human frailties, a system that fragmented the guardians of law and order into a piecemeal jumble of Metropolitan, Water, Horse Patrol and Gold, Native, and Rural Police, was bound to be found wanting.

Even after the Cowper ministry in New South Wales established a centrally controlled force, complaints continued, the police accused of being 'sluggish, incompetent, drunken and cowardly'.

Rather than being modelled on the London or Dublin Metropolitan Police, who patrolled unarmed, the Australian country force was, following the example of the Royal Irish Constabulary, mounted and armed; by the end of the century even the urban forces in Victoria were issued with revolvers. An armed police is rarely popular, and the Australian police have been no exception. Both the enforcers of law and its breakers were disproportionately Irish – 479 of the 803 New South Wales troopers in 1872 and 21 from 27 of those convicted of armed robbery and born outside the colony were Irish (and 42 of 59 native-born offenders were Catholics, and therefore for the most part almost certainly Irish).[49]

One enduring, even flourishing, Australian myth has been the elevation of rural criminals into national heroes. 'Bushrangers' – rural robbers, usually operating in gangs – had been a particular menace to Governor Arthur in Van Diemen's Land and had to be repressed with military force. Their successors in New South Wales were perhaps less brutal – they did not actually eat their companions, and killed only when frightened or trapped – but can hardly be accounted admirable. Frank Gardiner came closest to the popular ideal of a gentleman highwayman, robbing only the rich (there is after all little profit to be had from robbing the poor), employing threats rather than actual violence, and ending his life as a respectable saloon keeper (in so far as the phrase is not oxymoronic) in San Francisco, thanks to the intervention of Governor Sir Hercules Robinson, who insisted on pardoning Gardiner in spite of popular clamour and parliamentary opposition. The most successful was Ben Hall, who also avoided personal violence when possible, and whose gang escaped capture for three years, only being finally disposed of after having killed two policemen. Some took to violence as a last resort, like the ex-soldier and Anglican lay-reader Andrew Scott, a lecturer on prison reform. Scott was approaching 40 when hanged, but one of his associates was only 15. Others were uncomplicated brutal killers, like Daniel 'Mad' Morgan, who shot down anyone who got in his way.[50]

It was the last of the bushrangers, the Ned Kelly gang, who have become heroes of Australian legend. The Kelly boys, Ned, Dan and Jim, sons of an unsuccessful selector, drifted in and out of petty crime, well acquainted with the law. Their uncle, Jack Lloyd, was a successful police informer, but the boys seem to have been treated as convenient 'usual suspects' by the sometimes corrupt and usually ineffective Victorian police. Jim survived to live to a respected old age, but Ned and Dan, joined by two other young men, were cornered by the police after a scuffle. Ned personally killed three troopers, after which the group's fate was sealed; but it took two years and some dramatic events before the Kelly gang was brought to account. The final scene took place in the little Victorian town of Glenrowan, where the gang took some thirty of the community hostage while they tore up the railway tracks, intending to derail and ambush a special train which they assumed would be coming after the news of their latest murder reached Melbourne. To a decent set of human values, the true hero would be the local schoolmaster, Tom Curnow, who evaded his drunken captors and managed to stop the train, or the Queensland Aboriginal policemen who eventually tracked down the gang; but Curnow is forgotten and the trackers' descendants are left still attempting to claim the originally promised reward, while Ned Kelly is commemorated by a huge effigy, a memorial cottage and dozens of badly informed justifications, the latest of which is Peter Carey's *The True History of the Kelly Gang* which won the Booker Prize for Fiction in 2001.

Much of Kelly's fame is due to his having left his own spirited justification, the 'Jerilderie letter', and having the idea – ineffective but highly dramatic – of forging a suit of armour from plough mould boards. Sidney Nolan's dramatic paintings have provided powerful icons for those Australians who are so inclined to adopt the Kellys as a paradigm of Australian culture. Outsiders remain puzzled; Bill Bryson, a perceptive traveller, comments:

The story of Kelly is easily told. He was a murderous thug who deserved to be hanged and was. He came from a family of rough Irish settlers, who made their living by stealing livestock and waylaying innocent passers-by. Like most bushrangers he was at pains to present himself as a champion of the oppressed, though in fact there wasn't a shred of nobility in his character or his deeds. He killed several people, often in cold blood, sometimes for no very good reason.[51]

Perhaps influenced by the convict ethos of abominating the informer, white rural Australia's culture of communal self-reliance was transmitted to urban society as the labour movement developed. 'Larrikins' became the urban version of the romanticized bushranger. Nuisances, more than serious threats, given to brawling between rival 'Pushes' and rape, larrikins were primarily a Sydney phenomenon. At the time, and even today, Sydney was a more violent and disturbed city than Melbourne, with more than twice the Victorian level of crime. A not-unsympathetic novelist, Louis Stone, describes a typical gang:

They were still young – from eighteen to twenty-five – for the larrikin never grows old. The Cardigan Street Push, composed of twenty or thirty young men of the neighbourhood, was a social wart of a kind familiar to the streets of Sydney. Originally banded together to amuse themselves at other people's expense, the Push found new cares and duties thrust upon them, the chief of which was chastising anyone who intruded on their pleasures. Their feats ranged from kicking an enemy senseless, and leaving him for dead, to wrecking hotel windows if the landlord had contrived to offend them. Another of their duties was to check ungodly pride in the rival Pushes by battering them out of shape with fists and blue metal at regular intervals.[52]

When the worst larrikin crimes, such as the gang rapes in Waterloo and Woolloomooloo in 1883 in which both of the victims died, were brought to trial the public support for the offenders paralleled that often offered to the bushrangers (offered, of course, by those who had not been victims of either). The four Mount Rennie rapists (who, it must be said, did not actually kill their victim) were hanged in 1886 to cries of 'Shame'. On the other hand, the rape of an elderly Aboriginal woman in Victoria two years later was punished by the two guilty men being sentenced to long prison terms and to be flogged, without overt public dissent. Support for criminals, however unpleasant their crimes, was not confined to New South Wales, being not untypical of earlier British society, when public hangings were often accompanied by loud expressions of sympathy; but by the end of the century the performance and reputation of the British police had gained general support.[53]

Given that transportation to New South Wales only ended forty years previously, it was natural that a certain sympathy for lawbreakers lingered. It was perhaps more remarkable that within a single generation great cities had emerged with orderly law-abiding and industrious populations. One French visitor, Albert Métin, writing at the turn of the century, believed that the Australian working man had 'placed himself in the category of the "respectable people"', who changed after work; he 'is housed . . . and behaves like a person of good society', observing the proprieties and showing deep respect for religion. 'More and more one can observe the external difference between the worker and the bourgeois diminishing except during working hours.' One manifestation of sober propriety was the spread of 'temperance' hotels, which did not serve alcohol; many were commodious, the Melbourne Federal Hotel built for the 1888 exhibition was the largest in Australia, accommodating 400 guests on seven floors, with six lifts, gas lighting and an ice-plant. At the extreme of respectability were the 'wowsers', condemning all deviations from the strictest standards, who secured the closure of the Victorian Public Library and National Gallery after a female nude had been exhibited; *Chloe*, the guilty lady, is still on show, more appropriately, at Chloe's Bar off Swanston Street.

Nineteenth-century visitors were struck by the physical development of young Australians. The novelist Anthony Trollope saw that the 'born colonist is superior to the emigrant colonist' – but he was referring to the workers, and not to the middle classes. Michael Davitt went 'so far as to say that the Australian born of British or Irish parents is the best physically developed man of either of these races'. Contemporary statistics confirmed these views, which horrified the War Office when they began statistical comparisons of recruits' physique; the malnourishment which dragged behind the Industrial Revolution had taken a heavy toll of English workers, although this was not uniform throughout the country. Later research identified young London convicts as being considerably shorter than their contemporaries from the rest of England, especially those from Northumberland, or from Scotland or Ireland.[54]

Australian girls were much appreciated for their 'freshness, beauty, good sense and lack of affectation. The colonial miss was the salvation of English visitors trapped into endless colonial balls and tea parties.' Dr Constance Stone, the doyenne of Australian medicine, assured Beatrice Webb in 1898 that Australian girls had 'stronger passions than English or American' (corroboratory evidence is unfortunately lacking). Beatrice, however, pointed out that contemporary English, the 'new women' – Girton girls, bicyclists, tennis players, – were noted for much the same qualities: 'the difference was that whereas in Britain these qualities were attributed to youth, in Australia they were more likely to be attributed to being Australian.'[55]

Well before Federation, with the goldfields exploited no longer by the romantically individualist 'diggers' but only large corporations using modern equipment, Australia had become primarily an urban nation, with 35 per cent of the population living in the capital cities, and a quarter of the nation concentrated in metropolitan Sydney and Melbourne. Australians, crammed into a suburban sprawl in often poor conditions – the outbreak of bubonic plagues that swept Sydney in 1900 evidencing the primitive urban sanitation – sought solace in claiming kin with the hardy men of the outback, the shearers, drovers and range-riders. The young poet Henry Lawson became the bard of the untamed wilderness, but, embodying the contradictions of bush myth and urban reality, Lawson spent his adult life in Sydney, with interludes in Brisbane, Albany, Wellington and London. As Lawson expressed in his verse, the idea of 'mateship' was beginning to be regarded in some way as particularly Australian, embodying the virtues of the hardy bushman. Apart from its implied relegation of women to a somehow lower standard of consideration, it is at least questionable whether these characteristics are peculiar to Australia. Any dangerous activity, from soldiering to scuba-diving, imposes reliance on one's fellows. Squaddies have their 'oppos' or 'muckers', miners their 'marras', southerners their 'mates', Americans their 'buddies', each watching the others' backs, guarding their blind sides, checking their gear. In this sense, 'mateship' is by no means a peculiarly Australian concept. Nor is the exclusion of women from masculine society the preserve of Australians; in Durham or Memphis, just as much as in Rockhampton or Hay, women were expected to know their place, which was emphatically not in bars. Not, to most observers, a very attractive concept and one declining rapidly in Australian society as wine bars and family clubs replace bars and pubs, 'mateship' has nevertheless been elevated, with almost religious intensity, into a potential pillar of the constitution. Casting around for something to shore up his waning popularity (eventually reinforced by a stern anti-immigrant policy), Prime Minister John Howard seriously proposed, in 1999, to include 'mateship' as one of the Australian defining values, along with the respect for human rights, to be formally embodied in the Australian constitution.

Republicanism may have been very much a minority concern, but radicalism, especially in Sydney, flourished, expressed chiefly in the vigorous columns of the *Bulletin*. Founded and edited by the dedicated John Feltham Archibald, who reinvented himself as the French Jules François, the paper was given bottom by the Scots immigrant William Traill, whose experience on a Queensland cattle-station gave him an authority (rare among urban Sydney intellectuals) to write on back-country affairs. The *Bulletin* became not only the 'Bushman's Bible' but, with Archibald's cosmopolitan outlook, a home for all varieties of young Australian talent. Phil May's cartoons and Archibald's 'polished nib' pierced hypocrisy and self-satisfaction, while A. G. Stephens as literary editor encouraged the efflorescence of a native Australian literature. Later writers, searching for evidence of a specifically Australian culture, have made much of the *Bulletin*'s writers, but, as with republicanism, many of the literary trends identifiable through it were common to contemporary Britain. Later-nineteenth-century English novelists had begun to draw their material from the working classes: quite specifically, and with a defined social purpose, in novels by Charles Kingsley (whose brother Henry wrote a famous Australian novel, *Geoffrey Hamlyn*, as early as 1859); Thomas Hardy published *Tess of the D'Urbervilles* in 1891 and *Jude the Obscure* in 1896. Vernacular verse in both Britain and America became popular at all levels of society when Kipling published *Barrack-Room Ballads* in 1893, and W. W. Jacobs' stories of the London river appeared in the *Strand Magazine* in the 1890s. It was therefore entirely natural that parallel developments occurred in Australia, and took their place in both national cultures: George Ridley's 'Blaydon Races' became the quick march of the Coldstream Guards, and A. B. (Banjo) Paterson's 'Waltzing Matilda' the unofficial Australian national anthem; and his ballad hero, 'The Man from Snowy River', an exemplar. Paterson was a real bushman, but most of the other *Bulletin* writers were urban Sydneysiders: Henry Lawson wrote verses praising the manly virtures of the outback on the basis of six months' experience. Professor Manning Clark selected one (surely not very impressive) sample:

> No church-bell rings them from the track,
>   No pulpit lights their blindness –
> 'Tis hardship, drought, and homelessness
>   That teach those Bushmen kindness:
> The mateship born, in barren lands,
>   Of toil and thirst and danger,
> The camp-fare for the wanderer set,
>   The first place to the stranger.

On the other hand, Lawson's short stories can be very good indeed, but the work of another iconic notable outback writer, Joseph Furphy's novel *Such is Life*, is now barely readable.[56]

By some way the most popular Australian writer and the only one with a contemporary reputation abroad was T. A. Browne ('Rolf Boldrewood'). With an unequalled experience of backcountry life – half a century as squatter and stipendiary magistrate – Browne's *Robbery Under Arms*, published in 1888, remains *the* nineteenth-century Australian novel. One colonial curiosity of *Robbery Under Arms* is that the police inspector is based on the actual Sir Frederick Pottinger, son of the Hong Kong and South Africa Governor, Sir Henry Pottinger. Browne's literary rival was the English-born Melbourne novelist Marcus Clarke, whose *For the Term of his Natural Life* (1874), became a popular classic of convict society – and as misleading as popular classics usually are. Perhaps the most interesting of the Australian writers were both women, Ethel ('Henry Handel') Richardson (1870–1946) and Miles Franklin (1879–1954). Although both spent long periods abroad – most of Richardson's life was spent outside Australia – their two best-known works, respectively, the trilogy *The Fortunes of Richard Mahony* (1917, 1925, 1929) and *My Brilliant Career* (1901) – are informed by their Australian upbringing in much the same way as their contemporary Katherine Mansfield's New Zealand childhood informed hers.[57]

Sport

All observers agree that Australians are keen sportsmen, enjoying the advantages of a climate which makes outdoor activities pleasantly accessible. (Given that national performance at that weather-sensitive game, cricket, must vary according to the weather it is a wonder that England ever manages to win a test match.) As early as 1804, the Sydney *Gazette* drawing attention to the weather, wrote:

The late intense weather has been very favourable to the amateurs of cricket, who have scarcely lost a day for the last month. The frequent immoderate heats might have been considered inimical to the amusement, but were productive of very opposite consequences, as the state of the atmosphere might always regulate the portions of exercise necessary to the ends this laborious diversion was originally intended to answer.

Twenty-six years later the *Gazette* recorded a match, the forerunner of many Australian victories, played between 'military experts at the game and . . . native-born youths', in which the experts were beaten (210 to 188 runs) by the young colonials. It was the beginning of a rivalry which has continued, and which cements the relationship between many of the countries of the present Commonwealth of Nations.

The first Australian cricket team to tour England had a strange genesis. Horatio Wills, born in 1811, the son of a transported highwayman, succeeded his stepbrother Robert Howe as editor of the *Gazette* in 1832, and launched his own journal, *Currency Lad*, which became an advocate of 'native-born' rights.

> prate not to me of foreign land
> of beauty o'er the sea
> This is my own – my native land
> the only land for me![58]

Very sensibly deciding that small newspaper proprietorship was rarely profitable, Horatio chose marriage as an alternative, acquiring a young wife and a large property in the Grampians, winning a seat in the new Victorian Legislative Council and eventually taking over a huge station in Queensland. Within a few days of taking up residence in October 1851 nearly all the Wills party were massacred by local Aborigines; of the family only one son, Tom Wills, survived.

Tom had been educated at Thomas Arnold's Rugby, where he had demonstrated a precocious proficiency at cricket, captain of the first XI, appearing with extraordinary impartiality for Oxford, the Gentlemen of Kent, the All Ireland XI and the MCC. After the massacre Tom returned to his native state of Victoria. One initiative, surprising after his experience, was to accept an invitation to coach an Aboriginal cricket team, and to captain them against the Melbourne Cricket Club in December 1866. It was not a successful debut, Melbourne winning by 9 wickets, but shortly afterwards two of the Aboriginal players, Bullocky and Cozens, represented Victoria against Tasmania. After serious practice the following year, under the tuition of Charles Lawrence, a Sydney publican, the Aboriginals' performance improved to the extent that they were able to draw with an Australian Army and Navy XI, and to convince Lawrence that an English tour was feasible and potentially profitable.[59]

It was true that Lawrence's men, taking the field in a picturesque kit of red Garibaldi shirts and white flannels, each with his own individually coloured cap, were regarded more as curiosities than as serious opponents, and that their display of skills with the boomerang and woomera after each match was perhaps more appreciated than their cricket. Once in England, however, and after evading an attempt to stop the tour by the Aborigines Protection Board, who feared that they might be exploited, insulted and depraved by social contact with white society, the visitors performed well enough. In their first innings against the MCC the Aborigines made 185 against Marylebone's 117, all the wickets being taken by the all-rounder Cozens, who was also the second-highest scorer. The English newspapers were on the whole welcoming, describing the tour as 'the event of the Century', and the cricketers as 'stalwart men' of 'manly, dignified and pleasantly confident gait and carriage' who 'showed conspicuous skill at the game' (the last was W. G. Grace's assessment, which must be taken as authoritative). Perhaps the *Daily Telegraph* was condescending in judging that 'nothing of interest comes from Australia except gold nuggets and black cricketers', but the tour had to be judged a conspicuous success.

The sequel was less happy. In 1871 the Aborigines Protection Board won the right to prohibit further Aboriginal tours. Most of the team died prematurely and obscurely, often of drink. Only Mullagh, the opening batsman and star bowler (831 maidens in 1,877 overs with 2,489 runs scored against him) remained in the game, with the Melbourne Club, to play against Lord Harris's English XI in 1879, when he was the team's highest scorer in the second innings. Whereas in England the visiting Aborigines had been received without discrimination (there was one racial incident, naturally enough in Yorkshire), back at home Mullagh was subjected to racist abuse, called a 'nigger' and sent to sleep in a stable rather than in the hotel which accommodated the white team, treatment which he much resented. Such discrimination was to remain commonplace for many years; the great fast bowler Eddie Gilbert, who once dismissed Don Bradman for a duck, was made to sleep in a tent in the Queensland Cricket Association's Secretary's backyard.[60]

A little brisk violence contributed to the development of winter games. Soccer has never been as popular in Australia as either rugby or its variant, Australian Rules, described by the *New York Times* as being 'by no means so dangerous to the participants or so exciting to the spectator'. Safety was indeed the intention of its inventor, the same Tom Wills. Having played rugby at school in the 1850s Wills believed that the game was not suitable 'for grown men engaged in making a living' and together with his brother-in-law H. C. A. Harrison developed an alternative code, Australian Rules, an elegant and speedy variation. New South Wales and Queensland have remained loyal to the older game, but Australian Rules has become the leading winter sport in the other states. (Quite why William Webb Ellis's initiative in changing the rules of soccer has developed so many local and national variants could be a fruitful field of research: American football, Australian Rules, Rugby Union and Rugby League all have their devotees, and have been joined by 'Gaelic Football'; but it is a subject which will not be pursued further here.)[61]

Football's variations are many, but there is only a single canon of the finest of games and it is cricket where Australian prowess has been most striking. Not without its own dangers (Frederick, Prince of Wales was killed by a cricket ball in 1751), cricket remains suitable for grown men engaged in making a living, the most gentlemanly of team games and still a central feature of Australian life, perhaps the most significant relic of Englishness (cricket has never taken root in Scotland and such things as the rule of law and parliamentary government are more properly British) in Australia.

'What will it cost us to join?'

After the conclusion of the Diamond Jubilee festivities the debates in Australia were resumed, at first in Sydney in September 1897, followed by the final session in Melbourne between January and March the following year. It was up to the colonial liberals to modify the initially conservative document drafted under Sir Samuel Griffith's watchful eye. All colonial Legislative Councils, elected on a restricted franchise, had been reliably protective of the propertied interests; it was naturally hoped by the pastoralists and merchants that a Federal Senate could be elected, not directly, but by the colonial Legislative Councils. This sentiment was reinforced by the small states who wanted a strong upper house to protect their interests against the overwhelming majorities which the Big Two could deploy in the new Assembly. The eventual compromise was to have the Senate indeed elected by universal adult suffrage (women were included after 1903) but to guarantee, as in the United States, an equal number of Senate seats to all states. Representation in the lower house would be proportionate to population, except that the smaller states would be entitled to a minimum of seats, five each for Tasmania and Western Australia.

The question was not so much about the form a Federal constitution would take, which changed not greatly from that first advanced in 1891, but on how many individual colonial powers must be ceded to a central government, and how such sacrifices might be made more equal. 'What will it cost us to join? What will we lose? What will we gain?' were the central questions. And, as the answers emerged, 'How can we explain this to the voters?' Much depended on the economic situation of individual colonies. Victoria had suffered most in the depression and had been slow to recover, while New South Wales had weathered the storm more comfortably; Queensland and Western Australia were enjoying the benefits of the recently developed goldfields, but Tasmania and South Australia experienced difficulties in expanding their agriculture. The weaker states were therefore more anxious to seek the shelter of a Federation, whilst prosperous New Zealand, seeing no point in being yoked to the poor relations across the Tasman Sea, did little more than keep a watching brief on negotiations.[62]

Labor opinion, generally unenthusiastic about Federation which 'would do nothing to meet the social and industrial problems so urgently pressing for solutions', and with the experience of the Barcaldine strike in mind, feared that a federal force would have no such compunction in suppressing strikes as that colonial troops might be thought to display:

If New South Wales soldiers, actuated by patriotic motives, refused to fire upon their own countrymen it should be competent to march in Victorians or Western Australians, to offset the purpose. Thus can Queensland squatters get their sheep shorn with Victorian bayonets; South Australian bullets arbitrate with Victorian dock-labourers; while New Zealand gatlings and Tasmanian Nordenfeldts would be a strong argument to return to work in a coal miners' strike in New South Wales.[63]

Such arguments were unlikely to carry much force with the general public, and only one Labor delegate, the right-wing William Trenwith of Victoria, was selected for the definitive Convention.

On one matter there was very little debate. The 1896 convention had resolved unanimously that the restrictions imposed on Chinese should be extended to all 'coloured races'. Reflecting a very general sentiment, the Melbourne *Age* declared that 'we wish to see Australia the home of a great homogenous Caucasian race, entirely free from the problems which have plunged the United States into civil war . . . There is no use in protecting our workers from the pauper labour of the Far East if we admit the paupers themselves.' Article xxvii of the Constitution's section 51 accordingly provided that the Commonwealth parliament would be empowered to make laws controlling immigration, while article xxvi enabled 'special laws' to be devised to control people of any race – except the Aborigines. It was of course unfortunate that certain members of the coloured races could hardly be so satisfactorily excluded, and constitution makers did not concern themselves with the Aboriginal population except in so far as to decide that their numbers were not to be included in any census; their future status was confided to a Commonwealth government. It was left to the New Zealand delegate, Captain William Russell, to protest. In contrast with his colony, in which politics had 'for years hinged almost entirely upon the native question', a Federal Parliament – in which New Zealand might be included – 'would be a body that cares nothing and knows nothing about Native administration and the members of which would have dealt with native races in a much more summary manner than they would have been in New Zealand'.[64] Russell had good grounds for his apprehensions. While New Zealand's treatment of her natives was not above reproach, the Maori had been given a sort of honorary-white status. Maoris had been allowed full adult male suffrage, and Maori residents in Australia were similarly enfranchised, as were those Australian Aborigines who had adapted to the customs of white society. When two Maori shearers were refused admission in 1905 a major row resulted in a climb-down by the then Australian Prime Minister.

Perhaps the most radical item of the new constitution was hidden in the long section 51 which specified the powers of the new Parliament. Paragraph xxxv gave the legislature responsibility for conciliation and arbitration 'for the prevention and settlement of industrial disputes extending beyond the limits of any state'. At the time – and for many years thereafter – this insertion of the state, albeit permissive rather than mandatory, into private industrial concerns, was almost revolutionary. Combined with paragraphs xxiii and xxiii(A) which anticipated that government would wish to provide 'invalid and old age pensions, maternity allowances, widows' pensions, child-endowment, unemployment, pharmaceutical services, sickness and hospital benefits, medical and dental services ... benefits to students and family endowment', this assumed the existence of a welfare state far in advance of any such provisions in the United Kingdom, or anywhere else in essentially capitalist societies. Given the fact that organized labour had played little part in drafting the constitution, these provisions were surely remarkable, as reflecting the general opinion of politically involved Australians. The Commonwealth was to begin with a programme of social legislation supported by a great majority, and which did not have to be wrangled over by opposed factions, as it was to be for many years in Britain.

Financial arrangements were the most sensitive subjects for discussion, since the states' representatives were extremely anxious to keep control of those appetizing 'pork barrel' items to which they owed, in large degree, their continued political survival. It was agreed that the main source of Federal government revenue would be from customs duties, but it was by no means agreed how this should then be distributed. Very much as the least of potential evils, the proposal of Sir Edward Braddon, Premier of Tasmania, who had learned the ways of negotiation in the Indian Civil Service, was grudgingly accepted, although the settlement offended the basic principle of Federalism, that each government, both the separate states and the Commonwealth, should be financially independent. The Commonwealth was to return three-quarters of the customs and excise revenue to the individual states; and an initial period of ten years was required before what discontented New South Welshmen dismissed as the 'Braddon Blot' could be obliterated; haggling over funding between states and Commonwealth was, however, to continue throughout the twentieth century. The delegation of authority to the Commonwealth Parliament, although extensive, left the states as independent sovereign powers, with their own Governors, and having direct access to the Secretary of State in London. Nor could state laws be vetoed by the Commonwealth, a matter which long continued to prove an embarrassment. Parkes was proved right in that internal tariffs, once so hotly disputed, had indeed become a 'trifling' question. Braddon's proposal had ensured that external tariffs would underpin the nation's finances, while the inter-colonial tariffs simply faded away.

Agreement on all issues was finalized by the delegates on 16 March 1898, and was well described by the Melbourne *Argus* as 'a compromise, or rather a series of compromises', but which concluded that it was now or never: 'It is, as far as this generation is concerned, the choice between federation or no federation; between Australia with a common policy, a common flag, and common interests, and Australia as it is today – a cluster of divided colonies, parted from each other by hostile tariffs, and made helpless against a common enemy by their very divisions.'

Although the draft constitution was agreed by the delegates *nemine contradicente* it could not be taken as a definitive expression of the political will: Queensland and Western Australia were not represented, and two of the New South Wales delegates refused to recommend the resultant Bill to their voters – and those two were particularly influential personages, Premier George Reid and W. J. Lyne, soon to be Reid's successor. It was not necessary to the success of Federation that all colonies should be included; Canada had federated without two of the Maritime Provinces, and an Australian union would not be be materially damaged by the absence of Western Australia, but without New South Wales nothing could be done. Two points in particular offended New South Wales susceptibilities: now once more the most populous colony, she would have only the same number of senators as Tasmania, with less than one-tenth of the population; nor was her dignity as the mother colony to be acknowledged by having Sydney chosen as the Commonwealth capital. That issue had been the subject of some amused discussion. Braddon advocated Hobart on the grounds of its equable climate, while Josiah Symon defended South Australia's Mount Gambier, a pleasant coastal town near the Victorian border. Reid prevaricated, saying that although he disagreed with the proposals, he intended to vote for them, thus earning himself the sobriquet 'Yes/No Reid'.[65]

A more serious point was that of the Senate membership; it appeared grossly undemocratic if it were to take eleven New South Wales votes to elect a Senator, but only one Tasmanian. This might not be too objectionable if the Senate was to be, like the British House of Lords, limited in its powers, but this was not the intention of the founding fathers. Constitutional technicalities are not the most exciting of historical topics, but Australian history in the twentieth century has been so bedevilled by the relations between Senate and House of Representatives that some description is essential. Bluntly, the founding fathers misjudged matters: the Senate was intended to represent the states, to be a body in which grave and reverend signors, not obedient to any party loyalties, would argue out any inter-state as well as state and federal questions. They had in mind something like the United States Senate, which at that time was elected collegiately rather than by popular vote (that came about in 1913); but at the same time the example of the British House of Lords was before them. The Lords was very much a party house; invariably dominated by Conservatives, it could be regarded as a safeguard against demagogues, and the Australian fathers were a conservative bunch. But the House of Lords' powers were comparatively restricted, and after the 1911 Parliament Act were to be more limited still.

The inherent dangers in combining the two systems were clearly seen at the time, especially by Deakin, the most percipient of Australian politicians:

If we are to create a House, with all the traditions, so far as responsible government and its authority are concerned, of the representative chambers which exist in these colonies and the mother country, and are then to introduce on the other side, clothed with equal power, a body entirely foreign to the British Constitution, and to which there is no sufficient parallel in the Australian colonies, we shall be creating at the outset certain conflict and inevitable deadlock . . . To introduce the American Senate into the British Constitution is to destroy both.

Deakin believed that it would, however, be possible to have an upper house

so intimately in relation with public opinion and composed of men so highly qualified that it should exercise a very large and salutary power indeed in controlling legislation.[66]

It was an unrealistically pious hope. In broad contrast to the limited post-1911 powers of the House of Lords, the Australian Senate had a firm grasp of one of the purse strings. Although Senators might not either initiate or amend money Bills put to them, they were able to send the proposal back to the Assembly for reconsideration, with their own suggestions for alterations. A government then had the difficult choice of either accepting the 'suggestions' of the upper house, perhaps after some discussions during which some senators might change their minds, or, should the possibility of a joint sitting of both houses be unfeasible, asking the Governor General in his vice-regal capacity to dissolve both houses, a 'double dissolution', and hold a general election. When Senate and Assembly were controlled by different parties, Senators could use their powers to harass the government and make the conduct of business extremely difficult; if the Senate felt strongly, as it did in the famous case of 1975, they could increase the pressure; if the result seemed doubtful, Senators would not force the issue.

If a crisis demanded a 'double dissolution' the Governor General would be most unlikely to refuse.

To governments, the Senate's powers were more annoying in that, unlike the House of Lords, the Australian Senate could claim a degree of democratic authority, being elected by direct popular vote; but the degree was affected by the calendar. Assemblies had a life of only three years, but Senators were appointed for six, with half returning every three years. It was therefore quite likely that Senators elected four or five years ago would be less representative of popular opinion at any given time than the government of the day.

Deakin, while appreciating the unusual nature of the Commonwealth constitution, believed it would, somehow, work. Admitting that the Australian Senate was to exercise a strong constitutional role, Deakin (in an article for the American press) commented that

Englishmen would probably marvel at the power entrusted to the Upper Chamber, but the fact that it is a Federal House distinguishes it entirely from an hereditary chamber like the House of Lords . . . the distinctive characteristic of the commonwealth will be that it associates a responsible government dependent on one chamber alone, with a second chamber strengthened by its federal origin and a kind of inviolable independence in its constituencies which will remain in some aspects, as they are now in all aspects, sovereign states. This combination is original, constitutes a type, and may properly be styled Australian.[67]

Original the proposal certainly was, but the powers of the Australian Senate were to cause many future problems, and subsequent alterations only aggravated the difficulties.

The constitution had been drafted by lawyers and politicians, but over the years the public's views had been thoroughly aired. How far the final validation, that of approval in a nationwide referendum, was going to be an expression of informed opinion was doubtful. Certainly the 4 to 1 victory over England in the 1898 cricket Test Series aroused far more popular enthusiasm than any constitutional issue. No colony had a turnout of voters higher than 50 per cent, although the majorities in Victoria, Tasmania and South Australia were substantial among those who had bothered to vote. In New South Wales the majority (71,412 to 65,954) was not high enough to meet the requirement of a minimum of 80,000 votes in favour. (Reid had negotiated a minimum figure as a device to ensure delay, which proved successful.) It was therefore back to the negotiating table for the colonial Premiers. New South Wales had to be satisfied, and both Queensland and Western Australia were still holding fire. It was another year before more

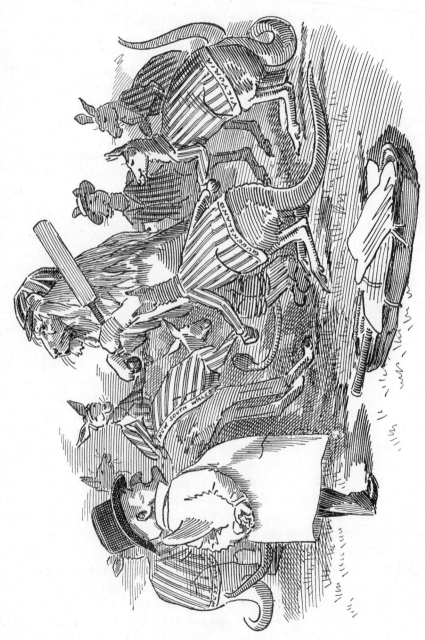

In 1899 Punch had already defined relations between the mother country and its colonies in sporting terms – Britain had lost the latest Test Series.

compromises were agreed, of which the two most important were the site of the new Federal capital and the provision for future constitutional alterations. Very logically, the new Commonwealth Parliament was itself to decide where it should have its being, which must be somewhere in New South Wales, but not in or near Sydney. Until a site was selected, Melbourne would act as a temporary capital. Amendments to the constitution would be acceptable, thus removing the Senate's power to block them, but subject to strict conditions (a majority of electors in a majority of states plus an overall national majority); but the equal number of Senate seats for each state was to be preserved.

Neither Queensland nor Western Australia had participated in the referendum, for their own particular reasons. Queensland's Premier, Hugh Nelson, a prominent squatter, and his deputy Horace Tozer were deeply implicated in financial scandals, and striving to ensure that the employment of Melanesians should be permitted in the north, which was vehemently opposed by the southern majority. Only after October 1898, when the respectable James Dickson became Premier was Queensland ready for participation in a second referendum.[68] In Western Australia John Forrest was having trouble with his Legislative Council, a querulous press and many of his own supporters. The Western Australian Legislative Council insisted on amendments which Forrest attempted to negotiate with the other Premiers, but it took the unlikely assistance of Joseph Chamberlain to bring Forrest under starter's orders. If Forrest put the unamended, original Bill to a referendum, Chamberlain would ensure that Western Australia would be treated, in spite of its tardiness, as an original founding state.[69]

Between May and September 1899 a second referendum was held, with Queensland participating. The result there was narrow, with 55 per cent voting affirmatively, the northerners having been won over to an acceptance of pure-white Australia by the threat of potential exclusion from the national market. Turnout generally was much higher than in the previous year, some 60 per cent voting rather than only 45 per cent in 1898, and New South Wales voted in sufficient numbers to confirm the previous vote; but it remained true that a considerable majority was either against Federation, or not concerned enough to come to the polls.

'To assist and explain'

It was in very few minds that the new Australia would not continue to be closely tied to Great Britain, although the idea of an Imperial Federation, which could unite Great Britain and the settlement colonies into a single political entity, had few Australian supporters. The Preamble to the Constitution Act stated that 'the people of New South Wales, Victoria, South Australia, Queensland and Tasmania, humbly relying on the blessing of Almighty God, have agreed to unite in one indissoluble Federal Commonwealth of Australia under the Crown of the United Kingdom of Great Britain and Ireland'.

Legally, any proposed Australian constitution had to be validated by the Westminster Parliament and a delegation was therefore invited to London in order 'to assist and explain' to the Colonial Office and to Parliament during the passage of the Bill. Edmund Barton, Charles Kingston, James Dickson, Alfred Deakin and Philip Fysh, representing the five federating colonies, were accordingly despatched charged with the duty of 'Unitedly urging the passage of the Bill through the Imperial Parliament without amendment'. S. H. Parker for Western Australia and William Reeves, the New Zealand London representative, were on hand to put their colonies' point of view; although there was very little chance of New Zealand joining it was accepted that Western Australia would join the Federation as soon as possible. It was a complex situation; rather than going, cap in hand, to obtain the permission of the mother country, the Australians freely admitted that some questions involved relations with not only Britain, but with all the other countries of the Empire, some of which might have different views. For his part, Chamberlain recognized 'fully the unwisdom – I had almost said impossibility – of pressing views on great self-governing communities to which they were absolutely opposed'. Going through Westminster was also, it might be added, much simpler and quicker than having all the colonial Parliaments pass their own Constitution Acts to restructure their own powers in accordance with the new Federal constitution.

Alfred Deakin left a highly readable and lively account of the discussions, in which he appeared in the best of all possible lights, while his fellow delegates were condescendingly dismissed. Dickson 'went boldly over to the enemy', while back in Australia William Lyne, the New South Wales Premier, was 'anxious to stab Barton in the back', Sir Samuel Griffith was 'obstinately declining to be bound by the Referendum' and the Australian press 'shrieked censure upon the daring delegates'. It was in fact probably a good deal less exciting. The sticking point was clause 74 which ended the right of appeal to the Privy Council in London. This was very much a lawyers' case, the Australian legal profession defending its own interests by insisting that the new Commonwealth High Court should be the final court of appeal, and one which had some popular attractions, as removing what could be said to be the last legal restriction on Australian sovereignty. In objection, it was urged that central control by appeal to the Privy Council provided a judicial link between all the countries of the empire, many of which had quite different legal systems – Dutch law in South Africa and French law in Canada still maintaining a reduced position within the common law systems.[70]

Nor were the Australians united on the point. Even the former republican Bernard O'Dowd expostulated that the House of Lords was 'the finest, fairest and soundest court in the world' while Australia only had 'lousy Lawyers'.[71] New South Wales, Queensland, Tasmania and Victoria delegates insisted that they had no authority to accept amendments to a document agreed in referendums; but Queensland, which had not participated in the final drafting of the Bill, was entirely opposed to the proposal. With some satisfaction, Chamberlain was able to point out that 'the delegate of Queensland, the Government of Queensland, the ministers of Queensland, and the people of Queensland are at the present time urging, with all the strength in their power, that her Majesty's Government shall restore the right of appeal'. So too was the Western Australian government, insisting that this 'bond between all British peoples be maintained inviolate' and New Zealand, still in the running – it had asked that the right to join the Federation be maintained for a seven-year period – both colonies supporting an amendment to the Bill. Supported by this dissent, by the fact that all the colonial Chief Justices backed the maintenance of the right to appeal, and that Australian public opinion, as evinced in newspapers, chambers of commerce and other public bodies, concurred (the Governor of Victoria reported that amendment would be enthusiastically approved throughout the colony), Chamberlain was able to persuade the delegations to agree that the right of the Privy Council to hear appeals from the Australian High Court should be preserved 'except in cases in which the constitutional rights of the Commonwealth and the States or the States inter se are concerned, in which case the decision of the High Court is final, unless it grants leave to appeal to the Judicial Committee of the Privy Council'. It was something of a fudge, unpopular with the new High Court judges – Mr Justice Richard O'Connor had 'no hesitation in saying, if we found that by a current of authority in England' it seemed likely that the Privy Council would decide a case 'in a manner contrary to the true intent of the Constitution as we believed it to be', then the High Court should disregard the provision. But the arrangement continued to work moderately well until terminated in 1982.

War

The Australian delegates' task in London had been facilitated by the reputation which Australian soldiers were even then winning in South Africa. Although Henry Parkes had hung his 1889 Tenterfield speech on the peg of defence, nineteenth-century Australian governments were slow to expand their own fighting services. In 1884, when the colonial militia was first organized, there were fewer than 500 regular soldiers, supporting some 9,000 volunteers, of whom only 145 were mounted. After General Edwards' reports were accepted progress speeded somewhat. More permanent staff were recruited, Irish and Scottish volunteer units were formed, and a light horse regiment raised. Much more was to be heard of them, and of one unlikely recruit to the garrison artillery, a prickly, seemingly unstable engineer-lawyer of Prussian-Jewish parentage, Lieutenant John Monash, who was commissioned in April 1887. Defence, however, remained a low priority. British army officers acting as commandants of the colonial militia often clashed with their political quasi-masters (having a dual responsibility to the British War Office and to the colonial government made for such difficulties). In particular, the energetic Colonel Edward Hutton, previously the Queen's aide-de-camp, quarrelled publicly with Premier George Dibbs, who insisted on reducing defence expenditure at a time when Hutton was extensively reforming the New South Wales militia.

With only 1,500 regular soldiers, Australian forces were poorly prepared for their first major military involvement. When the Transvaal and Orange Free State Afrikaner republics invaded the British colonies of Natal and the Cape in October 1899, Chamberlain, preparing for war (in fact largely instigating it), had already instructed the Governors of New South Wales and Victoria, together with Canada, to ask for 'spontaneous' offers of troops when fighting should begin. None agreed, sensibly refusing to sign what might well be an open cheque, but Queensland and South Australia both volunteered their own contingents. Once the first battles of the war resulted in shocking British defeats more volunteers poured in.

In years to come the patriarch nursing his grandchild on his knee will recount the history-making event of October 31, 1899. Even if the contingent never fired a shot no one will discount the fact that their departure for the Transvaal proclaims to the world the priceless truth that the silken cords still tightly bind the Australian daughter to her mother England, and that she is ready to do and die for the just and kindly parent who is peopling the earth.

The first to go went as colonial contingents, from New South Wales and Victoria, but were soon joined by others from all the colonies. Since the war continued for more than a year after Federation the Australians fighting in Africa became the first Commonwealth troops to see action.[72]

In all, perhaps fifteen thousand Australians served, for the most part as mounted infantry. The Queenslanders were the first in action, in a successful raid over Christmas 1899 on a Boer commando at Sunnyside in the eastern Cape. 'Banjo' Paterson was there as a war correspondent, and Colonel Hutton was able to see the fighting value of his colonial troops in action when he was given charge of the mounted infantry division, a third of which were Australians. South Africa, with its vast expanses of bare countryside, was an ideal site for horse soldiers, and the contingents from Australia, New Zealand and Canada, all cavalry or mounted infantry, were perfectly suited to small-scale mobile warfare. Organized conventional fighting was over within the year with the capture of the Boer capitals, but a harsh guerrilla campaign followed, which lasted for another two years. During this phase of the war conventional military standards collapsed; the Boers flogged and shot two members of a deputation who proposed peace terms, fired on ambulances (no morals, those Boers, one Tommy commented; 'they'll shoot at the helpless – why, they even attack the cavalry') and slaughtered hundreds of black fighters. Lord Kitchener's 'scorched earth' tactics, which included the burning of Boer farms and the wholesale deportation of families into the 'concentration camps' (not, as some writers hasten to claim, a British invention, but begun by the Spanish authorities during the Cuban War of 1898), were a desperate expedient to end hostilities which left a bitter legacy.

At that stage public opinion in Britain, and somewhat less in Australia, turned against the war:

some of us are willing – willfully, blindly eager mad! – To cross the sea and shoot men whom we never saw and whose quarrel we do not and cannot understand. Our cry is 'For England' or 'Blood is thicker than water!' and so we seek to blind and deceive ourselves as fools who are unanimous in their eagerness to sacrifice right, justice, truth – everything, to satisfy their selfish craving for what they consider a picnic – to have 'some fun' – to have a spree.[73]

Lord Salisbury's Conservative government had won the 'Khaki' election in 1900 on an appeal to patriotic sentiment, but the opposition leader Sir Henry Campbell-Bannerman reflected an influential section of informed opinion when he attacked Kitchener's methods. 'When is war not war?' he asked, and answered himself: 'when it is carried out by methods of barbarism.' One contributor to 'barbarism' was the Bushveld Carbineer, Australian Lieutenant Harry 'Breaker' Morant, executed for shooting Boer prisoners and a German missionary. At the time there was little sympathy in Australia for what was, quite correctly, appreciated as a just punishment, but later Morant was glorified as a victim of British rigidity and class prejudice. 'A myth', commented the Australian military historian Craig Wilcox, 'that had turned a murderer into a martyr.' What the Morant case really demonstrated was the difficulty of having inexperienced and often poorly disciplined colonial militia under the command of professional imperial officers, some of whom were slow to adapt their techniques of leadership – and whereas the early contingents had received training, the irregular units, such as Morant's Carbineers, were sent into action with little more than a passing acquaintance with discipline.[74]

From an Australian point of view, it was not an unduly hard war; about 600 dead, killed in action and died of disease in similar proportions, by comparison with 22,000 British dead, but for the first time Australians had formed a national force, which had performed well – the fighting qualities of the Australians were recognized by the award of five Victoria Crosses. Organization of an effective defence force became a priority of the new Commonwealth, a task entrusted to the abrasive former New South Wales Commandant, now Major General Sir Edward Hutton.[75] The Imperial bard Rudyard Kipling began his verses 'The Young Queen', which became widely adopted as a celebratory ode by recognizing the Commonwealth soldiers of the Young Queen:

Her hand was still on her sword-hilt, the spur was still on her heel,
She had not cast her harness of grey war-dinted steel;
High on her red-splashed charger, beautiful, bold, and browned,
Bright-eyed out of the battle, the Young Queen rode to be crowned.

She came to the Old Queen's presence, in the Hall of Our Thousand Years –
In the hall of the Five Free Nations that are peers among their peers:
Royal she gave the greeting, loyal she bowed the head,
Crying – 'Crown me, my Mother!' And the Old Queen stood and said: –

'How can I crown thee further? I know whose standard flies
Where the clean surge takes the Leeuwin or the coral barriers rise.

Blood of our foes on thy bridle, and speech of our friends in thy mouth –
How can I crown thee further, O Queen of the Sovereign South?'

Kipling provided his own answer: the Queen of the Sovereign South should
not seek for conquest or glory, but for the love of her people; which in good
measure she has indeed attained.

10

The Commonwealth Feels its Way

'That's the Empire . . . And that's what I'm painting'

The Commonwealth was inaugurated on 1 January 1901, with the blessing of old Queen Victoria, born when Lachlan Macquarie governed New South Wales, and crowned in the year Governor Bourke visited Port Phillip and changed the settlement's name from Beargrass to Melbourne.

All Australian colonies were henceforward to be states, albeit each retaining its own administration and with the Governor in Government House continuing as before. All the new states celebrated the occasion in their own fashion. As the mother colony, and the home of the Governor General, pro tem, Sydney began with a spectacular parade, organized by Premier Lyne, who, in spite of his opposition to Federation, flung himself into the task with great zest. Much impressed by the performance of colonial troops in Africa, the Queen took a personal interest in the celebrations, insisting that the Guard of Honour should represent the Empire as a whole, and that the Guards and Household Cavalry should take part; the War Office muttered at the expense, but the Australian public applauded. Some Labor members, mistaking costume drama for militarism, objected to the Household Cavalry, and Billy Hughes, then making his mark as a trade union organizer, was allowed to include a detachment of mounted shearers: they were not a success, for people wanted to see the troops. Subsequent events were anti-climatic; the swearing-in of the Governor General was held in Centennial Park, a huge open space where even 200,000 spectators seemed sparse, and the banquet was marred by rather too great conviviality.

Although the Commonwealth of Australia began its existence on the first day of the new century, for the first months, until an election could be held, the country was administered by a caretaker government. Seven ministerial posts were provided by the constitution – Attorney General, Defence, External Affairs, Home Affairs, Postmaster General, Trade and Customs, and Treasury, plus that of Prime Minister (so-called to distinguish the Commonwealth leader from the heads of states government, now to be known as Premiers). With one exception, all the states were represented in the first Cabinet, Victoria by Alfred Deakin and Sir George Turner, New South Wales by Edmund Barton, appointed as Prime Minister, and William Lyne, Queensland by James Dickson, South Australia by Charles Kingston and Western Australia by John Forrest – all former Premiers. Tasmania grudgingly accepted the appointment of Neil Lewis as an unpaid, supernumerary Minister without Portfolio. The new Governor General, Lord Hopetoun, had stumbled by first offering the prime ministership to Lyne, as head of the senior colony's administration, rather than to Barton, who was known to command more support, but the error was quickly rectified. The one serious incident that marred the celebrations was not attributable to the Governor General but to the Premier of New South Wales, who, in defiance of the official code of precedence, which placed a Roman Catholic cardinal higher than even an Anglican archbishop, demoted Cardinal Moran, representing a fifth of Australia's population, in the order of the inauguration ceremony. In a justifiable huff, the prelate boycotted the official celebrations.[1]

Aborigines, organized by Archibald Meston, the pioneer of Queensland's Aboriginal protection system, were accorded their part in the festivities, although more as anthropological curiosities than as members of the Australian community. Believing that the Aborigines were doomed to extinction, Meston considered that society should 'make all possible atonements for the past by brightening their declining years and guiding them gently and kindly over that bridge spanning the abyss between the present and the rapidly nearing final departure'. Meston's contribution to brightening the declining years of the First People in Sydney was to restage the landing of Captain Cook at Kurnell on 28 April 1770 with twenty-five Queensland Aborigines. Meston's men were more convincing than those representing Cook's crew, who appeared clad in 'astonishing' vestments that 'might have belonged to a comic opera or a pantomime', or than Miss Lilian Bethell, as ' "Australia, a nymph" ', sporting a helmet resembling those worn by the Metropolitan Fire Brigade'. Altogether more impressive were Meston's arrangements in Brisbane for the Duke of York's visit in May, when a triumphal arch was constructed, decorated with greenery and Aboriginal warriors, 'the best built and intelligent-looking coloured men' the Duke had seen, the tallest of whom was 6 foot 4 inches. With some reason – three of the men caught fatal chills as a result of their participation in the festivities – the Duke expressed concern for Aboriginal welfare, and on their future prospects, a subject still pursued by his granddaughter, Queen Elizabeth, during her visit a century later.[2]

Then it was Melbourne's turn when, as the home of the first Commonwealth Parliaments until a new capital was identified, the Duke and Duchess of York inaugurated its first session on 9 May. The Duke had a fair idea of what to expect, having visited Australia before, in company with his brother Prince Albert Edward, when both were midshipmen in HMS *Bacchante* and both princes had dutifully memorialized their impressions in their diaries. The ceremony faithfully followed the pattern of that held at the openings of each Westminster Parliament. With the Senators assembled under the dome of Mitchell's exhibition hall, the Duke directed the Usher of the Black Rod to tell the House of Representatives that His Royal Highness desired their immediate attendance, after which three verses of the 'Old Hundredth' were sung. Dignity was very soon broken as 'Fighting Charlie' McDonald, a republican Queensland Labor MP, questioned the standing orders, only to be squashed by Barton: 'It may be so in Queensland, but it is not so in most parliaments.'

Queensland had, however, signified its continuing determination to be different. Tom Roberts, probably the foremost painter of his day, recorded the opening ceremony. Best known as a landscape painter, a member of the Heidelberg School, the Australian equivalent of the contemporary 'Glasgow Boys', Roberts was an unusual choice. He worked for two years on the huge painting, *The Opening of the First Commonwealth Parliament*, explaining that when royalty, the Governors, Members of Parliament representing democracy and the people themselves met together, 'That's the Empire . . . And that's what I'm painting.'[3]

The first Federal elections held in March established the emergent Labor Party in a powerful position, with 16 of the 75 seats, to 32 for Deakin's protectionists and 27 for the free-traders led by George Reid. The new Commonwealth Parliament advanced only slowly, its problems paralleling those experienced fifty years previously in the first responsible colonial governments. Administrations succeeded each other at short intervals (eight in the first decade), although Cabinets often included many of the same figures. Most politicians had achieved eminence only in their own states; after Parkes's death in 1896, Alfred Deakin of Victoria, Edward Barton of New South Wales and Samuel Griffith of Queensland, almost alone, were recognizable as national figures, although John Forrest made himself notorious for his reactionary and particularist views and Reid was an accomplished self-publicist. Political parties were equally emergent, clustering around three positions – protection versus free-trade, with the new Labor Party representing trade union interests. But most of the new MPs (or MHRs, as they later became known) advocated social policies very similar to those which developed after 1906 in the British Liberal governments of Campbell-Bannerman and Henry Asquith – unemployment insurance, old-age pensions, plus some control of abusive employment practices.

In many respects the Commonwealth went further, to establish policies which made Australia the most politically and socially advanced state in the world. Among its first acts were the formation of an electoral commission to adjudicate on constituency boundaries, an example not followed in Britain until 1918; the nomination of a single polling day to allow postal voting, which in Britain was delayed until 1950; an agreement to pay salaries to MPs, which Britain allowed only ten years later, and, much the most important, to give women the vote, fully achieved in the mother country, only after much agitation, in 1928. To be sure, there were flaws in some of these advances: it is particularly disappointing that the representation of women in parliament and government has grown only slowly. But all were achieved almost effortlessly in the first elected Commonwealth administration, that of Edmund Barton (January 1901–September 1903).

In other ways, however, as befitted one of the very last creations of the Victorian age (the old Queen died on 22 January), the constitution seemed to hark back almost to the Middle Ages. The executive power was specifically vested in the monarch, as in the days of Queen Elizabeth I, to be represented in Australia by a Governor General, who was to exercise this in the Federal Executive Council: the same formula 'the Governor General in Council' being used as had been in the earliest seventeenth-century Crown Colonies. It was of course clearly understood that the Governor General acted on the advice of his ministers – his 'powers and functions' were to be used 'subject to this constitution' – but nowhere in that constitution did the words 'Cabinet' or 'Prime Minister' appear. Nor was it clear what reserve powers, still retained by the sovereign, were to be transferred to the Governor General personally as distinct from the Governor General in Council.

Few Australians can have been much troubled by these ambiguities. The practice of responsible government had been well understood for half a century, and the emotional ties to Britain and the Empire were strong enough to blunt the inherent absurdity of a head of state who lived 12,000 miles away. By no means a simple relationship, continued 'allegiance to the Crown' involved an acceptance of shared values – the rule of law, a free press, the protection of individual liberties, a claim on the protection offered by the then superpower and represented by the Royal Navy, a shared pride in being part of the Empire upon which the sun never set, and even an affection for the person of Queen Victoria (an affection paralleled by that demonstrated a century later on the death of the Queen Mother, when flags flew at half mast, and much of the population were glued to their television sets, following the state funeral). While it might be said that Australia was not truly a sovereign nation, since the rights (even if rarely used) to reserve questionable legislation were retained, together with the agreement that foreign relations remain an Imperial prerogative, and the deferential forms of communication continued (but this last was a widespread and meaningless convention: until well after the Second World War brusque letters from Inland Revenue officials in the United Kingdom were still signed by 'Your obedient servant'), it was clear the United Kingdom would do nothing to interfere with Australian governments' control of their own affairs. The relationship was more that of membership of a club, where common rules were accepted. But a period of radical change for the club then known as the British Empire was just beginning.

Only a modest contribution to the Commonwealth's early success was made by Lord Hopetoun, who had been released for this service by Queen Victoria with the greatest regret, so invaluable had his service been as Lord Chamberlain, but his qualifications were undeniable. His court connections made life easier for the Duke and Duchess of York when they came to inaugurate the new Parliament, and his previous experience as Governor of Victoria (1889–95) had given him some exposure to Australian habits and valuable experience on handling colonial politicians; moreover, his youthful likeability promised well for smooth relations. Deakin, reporting Hopetoun's arrival in Victoria, said: 'he promises to be popular among all classes, for he is young, active, with bright cheery ways and a nice style in public speaking.' These qualities were demonstrated in the inaugural procession, when a man in the crowd called out for three cheers for the Governor General; 'Not for me, old chap,' Hopetoun answered, 'for Australia.' Apart from his mistake in offering the caretaker administration to Lyne, Hopetoun moved elegantly through the required manoeuvres demanded of a viceroy whose functions were so largely decorative. Both he and the Countess were quite seriously ill during their time in Australia – Hopetoun died in 1908 – and it was perhaps fortunate that his friendly relations with the affable Barton were never troubled by constitutional issues.[4]

If the first Governors General were not much help to the new ministries, they at least did no damage. Lord Hopetoun resigned in May 1902, complaining, with some justification, that his salary was not enough to cope with the demands made on it by official duties; he managed to recoup the family funds by selling land at Rosyth for a naval base at a price commonly regarded as excessive. Lord Tennyson – Hallam Tennyson, the poet's son, an undistinguished personage – was briefly promoted from South Australia to fill the unexpected gap. His successor, Lord Northcote (1903–8), had worked his way though the ranks of the Conservative Party in the House of Commons and was therefore well schooled politically; when called upon to exercise his powers to dissolve parliament – or to allow a new government to be formed – his judgement proved apt and was never questioned. After a blameless period of office Northcote was replaced by the playboy Tory peer Earl Dudley, whose appointment and family title were due to his mother's friendship with the concupiscent Prince of Wales and to a distant relative who had left him an immense fortune. Deakin described Lord Dudley as having done 'nothing really important, nothing thoroughly, nothing consistently ... which is after all, very much what might have been expected'. For very different reasons Lord Denman, the youthful Liberal Chief Whip in the House of Lords, appointed in March 1911 at the age of 36, did little better. The Denmans – the wife considerably the stronger personality and later the founder of that most formidable of British institutions, the Women's Institute – got on well with the Labor government; rather too well, in fact, to suit the Colonial Office, who objected to the Governor General's support of Australia's claims to control her own fleet, and who were happy to accept his resignation. Afflicted by Australia's national plant, the wattle, which aggravated his asthma and bronchitis, the Governor General left in May 1914: five Governors General in twelve years was not a good beginning.

A constitution, like a new pair of boots, requires wearing in, and the process took some time; indeed, it has continued ever since. Barton, while not shining at party politics, was the right man to smooth out the wrinkles, and after a difficult start had an untroubled period of office, relying as he could on the support of the fourteen Labor members. His ministers were experienced, and included John Forrest, ideally suited for defence in a period which included the last stages of the Boer War and the formation of Federal forces; the irascible Charles Kingston of South Australia was an effective head of the Trade department; George Taylor proved an outstandingly able Treasurer, while Deakin as Attorney General held the fort during Barton's absences and piloted through the arrangements for the new High Court. But former Premiers, as all these ministers were, often do not take kindly to subordination and disputes were frequent. Reid was the notable absentee, heading a querulous opposition. The amount of business transacted by the first generation was impressive, including the extension of the franchise to all adults, the foundation of the 'White Australia' policy, the maintenance of external tariff barriers and the establishment of an internal free market, the extension of conciliation and arbitration beyond state boundaries, the establishment of the Commonwealth Bank, the construction of a railway link to Western Australia, and the introduction of a Federal old age pension, all measures dear to Labor voters. John (Chris) Watson, the leader of the Federal Parliamentary Labor Party (FPLP), had proved himself a capable manager of the disputatious New South Wales Labor Party and adapted quickly to Federal politics.[5]

'A working man's paradise'

One contentious issue overshadowed all others in the first years of Federation and has continued to plague Australia ever since – protection versus free trade. On the one hand, new Australian industries needed shelter from cheaper imports, but Australian primary producers wanted unimpeded access to foreign markets. Two parties formed in the Commonwealth parliament adopting opposite fiscal policies. Free-traders, led by George Reid, were generally conservative and Deakin's protectionists liberal, the opposite of the British situation when free trade was a venerable Liberal policy, and where protectionism had been made a central policy of Joseph Chamberlain's Liberal Unionists in coalition with the Tories. Imperial policy had been to create an Imperial free-trade area, and an obligation was laid on the Australian colonies not to impose tariffs. When Gladstone's Liberal government conceded to the colonies in 1873 the power to regulate their own custom duties, a controversy began which increased in pitch as Australian industry developed, demanding that its products be sheltered by tariff barriers. Federation changed the problem. No longer concerned about inter-state trade, it was Australia's relations with the rest of the world that demanded clarification. Article xx of the constitution, allocating customs revenues to the federal government, implied a substantial element of protection, which might imperil Australia's relations with her customers. Barton and Deakin, protectionists both, saw an answer in Imperial preference; that goods coming from Britain and the other dominions, which represented nearly three-quarters of Australian imports, should be admitted at lower rates than those from other countries, thus creating the world's most extensive single market. The tariff question was settled only with difficulty. Labor members were divided on the issue, and the Senate, where there was a majority of free-traders, exercised their delaying powers. Opportunities for filibustering on tedious matters of detail were legion. A 'frittering struggle over details and a shameless repetition of stock fiscal arguments', wrote the wearied Deakin, acting for Barton in the Prime Minister's absence, 'has proceeded until to the public the whole debate has become a nightmare.' Agreement was eventually reached in September 1902, only days before the ending of the first Parliament's first session and the initial compromise proved too low to finance the costs of government; but the same day that the new tariff was introduced in parliament, 8 October 1901, inter-state free trade was established.

Other legislation in Barton's original manifesto commanded near-unanimous support. The Immigration Restriction Act of December 1901, the first to be passed by the new Parliament, was the definitive expression of the White Australia policy. The Brisbane *Worker* had put Queensland's question:

> What about the coloured alien
>> And the Chow and the Hindoo,
> Men of Queensland ask Australia
>> What do you intend to do?

> Out from mill and shop and garden,
>> Hawkers, fossickers, and cooks;
> Wipe them once for all and ever,
>> From the Federal nation's books.

The sentiment was shared by almost all other Australians.[6] Complete exclusion of non-whites had begun with the anti-Chinese legislation of the 1880s, and was perfected in the following decade by Queensland's reluctant agreement to allow the coming Commonwealth parliament to decide whether or not black labour, then regarded as essential to the survival of the colony's tropical agriculture, should be admitted – which it certainly would not. All parties were in accord: Australia was to remain white. No blacks or Asians were to be allowed in to undercut Australian workers, and those who had already penetrated the citadel were to be repatriated. Australians, even Deakin, the least racist of contemporary politicians, said, were to be 'one people, and remain one people, without the admixture of other races'. From the Labor benches, W. G. Spence, a decent trade unionist, argued:

The influx of these aliens would so lower the aggregate standard of the community that in a very short time social legislation would be ineffective. But if we keep the race pure, and build up a national character, we shall become a highly progressive people of whom the British Government will be prouder the longer we live and the stronger we grow.

Less sophisticated politicians were more direct; 'Coloured aliens', one member complained, were 'not nice people to be seen in the lonely bush of Australia'. The heirs of more than 2,000 years of Confucian culture were put in their place; no Chinese could be expected to 'attain that level of civilisation which Australia had inherited from the centuries'. But it was the Queensland Labor supporters who were most explicit: 'The *Patriot* is sure the beautifully-dressed ladies who attend . . . Church must be pleased to think that perhaps a big fat buck nigger, reeking with the germs of all sorts of diseases carried from the necessary Yokohama, has warmed the seat on which she sits.'

Joseph Chamberlain, when Colonial Secretary, had pleaded with the Australian ministers to adopt some hypocritical cloak to 'avoid hurting the feelings of any of Her Majesty's subjects' – most of whom happened not to be white. This the Commonwealth contrived to do by insisting that intending immigrants take a dictation test in English, a device that had proved useful in excluding Indian workers from the South African colony of Natal while allowing entry to such educated Indians as the young lawyer Mohandas K. Gandhi, who, while not exactly welcome, were tolerated. Less liberal even than Natal, where blacks had been skilfully excluded from their legal political rights, the Commonwealth of Australia wanted to ensure that no person of the wrong pigmentation, however fluent in English (as were many Indians and Africans), should be admitted. It was therefore decided that the test could be imposed in any European language that happened to be known to the immigration officials: Scots Gaelic, for example, was sure to be a sound litmus test for the suitability of hopeful entrants.[7]

The elegance of this method of control appealed to Labor members, who felt that it could be extended; could it not be applied to Italians, for instance (an Italian was 'not civilised in the ordinary Australian sense' and in the habit of perambulating the cities 'with a knife in his hand and a razor in his pocket')? Unfortunately not, the government decided, since some 10 per cent of white Australians were not British – Germans, Italians and Greeks among them in substantial numbers – but another loophole might be closed by banning anyone who had no contract of employment. The arrival of six English hatters to work for Mr Charles Anderson of Sydney caused a political storm before healthy Australian irreverence and fondness for teasing authority allowed the 'mad hatters' to be admitted.[8]

Abominable though the White Australia policy sounds to modern ears, it seemed eminently reasonable at the time, buttressed as it was by very generally accepted racial theories which placed whites at the top of a developmental tree (a delusion not shared by Chinese or Japanese, equally convinced of their own superiority). The Labor Party was essentially a proletarian movement, which had already succeeded in establishing a high-wage economy in which workers' interests were protected, and which would in the course of the next few years secure what was rightly described as a 'working man's paradise'. Such gains would dissolve if cheap labour were to be admitted, and racialist rhetoric, rendered more acceptable by the social Darwinism of the period, merely added strength to the economic rationale. Even mail steamers operating on government service were required to employ all-white crews; the new Australia was to be boiler-plated, triple-hulled pure-white and overwhelmingly British, an ideal which remained far too popular to allow modification by more liberal politicians. E. L. Batchelor, Minister for External Affairs 1908–9 and 1910–11 in Andrew Fisher's Labor governments, could regret 'the extreme undesirability from every point of view of those occasional and discourteous comments that appear in our Australian journals', but insist that he firmly believed 'the immigration exclusion policy . . . to be of advantage to all concerned'.[9]

If a Labor government would not relax their racialist policies, no concessions could be expected from the opposition. Even the affable Barton adopted racist language:

There is no racial equality. These races are, in comparison with white races . . . unequal and inferior. The doctrine of the equality of man was never intended to apply to the equality of the Englishman and the Chinaman . . . Nothing we can do by cultivation, by refinement, or by anything else will make some races equal to others.

Pondering the fact that over 70 per cent of the competitive places in Sydney's best schools at the beginning of the twenty-first century are taken by Asiatic students, one might conclude that there was something in Barton's theory, if not quite in the way he intended.[10]

Barton's national government collapsed in September 1903. He had not been a continuing success as Prime Minister: convivial to the point of frequent alcoholic befuddlement, his geniality could carry him only so far. Thomas Bavin, Deakin's private secretary, judged Barton to have 'little or no interest in the game of politics for its own sake', but his acceptance of the chairmanship of the new High Court took him to a sphere where his admittedly keen legal mind served him well, and where sobriety was not strictly required. At the subsequent general election the parties produced an awkward result – 26 for protectionism, 25 for free-traders with Labor holding a decisive balance of 23 seats. Deakin took over, but found that he 'could not play cricket with three elevens in the field' and surrendered power to Chris Watson, who on 27 April 1904 became Australia's first Labor Prime Minister, and the first anywhere in the Empire, relying on the support of Deakin's protectionists. John Forrest could not believe his eyes when he saw Labor ministers on the Treasury benches. 'Mr Speaker,' he expostulated, 'what are those men doing in our places? Those are our seats!'

More than any other factor, modern Australian political life has been defined and characterized by the existence of the Labor Party. In spite of numerous splits, and long absences from office, the Labor Party, often with a fresh complexion, has emerged to face a shifting coalition of parties whose most distinctive feature is that they are *not* Labor. Including its first short period in office, there have been nine Labor prime ministers, the last being Paul Keating, 1991–6. In foreign policy their record has been chequered, but at home Labor governments have generally pursued progressive social policies and have been led, at least until after the Second World War, by honourable men; but too many Labor leaders have been lost after clashes with unreasonably jealous colleagues – three Prime Ministers, Chris Watson, Billy Hughes and Joseph Lyons, quitting, largely due to the control exerted by the party machine.

Like its British counterpart, the Australian Labor Party began as a creature of the trade union movement, but whereas the British Labour Party adopted the conventions of Cabinet responsibility, the Australian Labor Party was, for the first half of the twentieth century, subject to the overwhelming, often near-dictatorial, and still powerful influence of the party Caucus. The word itself, with its un-English, derogatory connotations (Disraeli used it to describe Chamberlain's Birmingham municipal machine, and, more famously Lewis Carroll described a 'Caucus-race' in *Alice's Adventures in Wonderland*) distances Australian from British Labour politics. The Australian Labor Caucus began in New South Wales when the Political Labor League attempted to insist that Labor parliamentarians pledge themselves to obedience. With some reluctance the principle was adopted by the other state Labor parties – with Queensland especially dragging its heels. From its inception, therefore, the Federal Labor Party began its existence committed to the acceptance of parliamentary decisions being determined outside Parliament, and with ministers selected, not by the parliamentary leader, but by Caucus, although the Prime Minister retained the freedom to allocate portfolios; but Watson, an adept conciliator, persuaded Caucus to allow him to arrange his own ministry, which included one Liberal, Henry Higgins, a distinguished Ulster-born lawyer.[11]

Watson's government lasted for only a little over three months, defeated by a temporary combination of free-traders and the anti-Labor protectionists under George Reid. It was to be Reid's only taste of power, shared with the Deakinite Alan McLean, and with a majority of only one in the lower house the government held on with difficulty until July 1905 when, once again in alliance with Watson, Deakin was able to form a protectionist government. Given that Labor voters were committed to protection, such a combination made sense, and this was duly implemented in Deakin's second ministry, which, with Labor support, continued for three and a half years. As with the British Labour movement, advancing much more slowly than that in Australia, socialism was debated rather than implemented; what mattered was to improve workers' conditions rather than to pursue Marxist theories. Throughout the rapidly changing succession of governments this improvement was steadily implemented; and, by that startling provision in the constitution which envisaged, indeed almost mandated, social reforms, no right-wing parties could justifiably object.

Watson was, however, immediately in trouble with the Labor Caucus, which censured him for agreeing to cooperate with Deakin. In his letter of resignation Watson put the constitutional dilemma precisely:

I may say primarily that the view I have held since the inception of Labor in politics is that the organisations should decide in conference what the policy of the movement should be, and lay down such conditions as may be necessary to ensure the solidarity of the Party. Once the Party enters Parliament it alone should, by its corporate voice, decide the course to be taken in any particular emergency. Having chosen its captains the party outside should be prepared to trust to their guidance while the battle continues. If they do wrong, that is reason for selecting fresh men when an election comes round; but I contend that the men in parliament are, or should be, the best equipped to deal with parliamentary emergencies.[12]

Watson was persuaded to withdraw his resignation, and reforms required by Labor continued, although Deakin refused to countenance the more socialist aspects of Labor's programme. No Labor members were included in the Cabinet, but the radical young Queenslander Littleton Groom represented Labor interests as Attorney General. Alfred Deakin was then at the height of his considerable powers, probably the most intellectually brilliant of all Commonwealth Prime Ministers, responsible more than any other for forming the pattern of Australian political life and establishing what could well be called the Deakin constitutional settlement. He took the additional portfolio of External Affairs – which at that time was almost exclusively concerned with Imperial relations – and also continued to act as the Australian correspondent for the respectable London newspaper, the *Morning Post*. His anonymous weekly articles, begun in 1901 and which continued to run for the rest of the decade (for much of which he was Prime Minister), provide an unequalled perspective on Australian politics.[13]

Of the many achievements of the 1905 Deakin government, which included the preliminary work on transcontinental rail routes, the beginning of Antarctic exploration, the introduction of old-age pensions and the establishment of a national defence system, the most innovative was surely what was known as the 'New Protection', which used tariffs as a social mechanism. Both New South Wales and Victoria had already enacted compulsory arbitration in industrial disputes, a major Labor policy, and the Federal constitution provided for a Federal conciliation and arbitration service, but it was not until 1905, during Reid's brief administration and after much acrimonious debate that a Commonwealth Court of Conciliation and Arbitration was established. It was an unprecedently radical move, this creation of a 'new province' of the legal system, and one reinforced the following year by the Excise Tariff Acts, which imposed a tax on local products, paralleling the tariff on imported goods, a tax which could be remitted if 'fair and reasonable' wages were paid. In 1907 Hugh MacKay, owner of the Harvester Company, which controlled the largest factory in the country, manufacturing agricultural machinery, applied for a tax rebate. As a test case, Henry Higgins, as president of the Conciliation and Arbitration Court, decided that a minimum wage of 42s. a week was needed in order to maintain an unskilled labourer, married and with three children, in frugal comfort, allowing for a certain amount of leisure and 'provision for evil days'. MacKay successfully challenged the ruling in the High Court, but the principle was commonly accepted that Australian men had the right to a fair wage at above subsistence level – a principle that suited employers too, as removing one element of competition in an emergent market. It was nearly a century later that a minimum wage was fixed for British workers, making the Higgins 'Harvester' decision a bold step. Inevitably in the context of the time, no minimum wage was fixed for women, who continued to be employed sometimes at near-starvation wages. Outsiders predicted economic collapse if workers, already protected by an eight-hour day, were to be cosseted still further, but this did not occur, for better and for worse, Australia was to be a high wage economy, and one insulated from external competition.[14]

Votes for Women

Support for White Australia was near-unanimous, but two other issues caused some heart-searching. Votes for women came about, like so many other Australian constitutional developments, remarkably quickly and painlessly. The first women's suffrage society was founded in 1884 by the Victorians Henrietta Dugdale, Annie Lowe, and Vida Goldstein. Mrs Dugdale, twice widowed, was the author of an indignant futuristic satire *A Few Hours in a Far Off Age* dedicated to Higinbotham, acknowledging his 'brave attacks' on 'the greatest obstacle to human achievement, the most irrational, fiercest and powerful of our world's monsters – the only devil – MALE IGNORANCE'. Her time traveller describes an earlier period – the nineteenth century, when

the males of these primitive people held their own sex so in veneration that quite young ones – puny in intellect, and without education – were, by act of senate, qualified to elect senators, enter upon the government of the world, and occupy the highest officials to the exclusion of the Infinite Intelligence, where possessed by women. So those poor vain creatures, with much assumption of wisdom, though still very apelike in various ways, made laws affecting woman's liberty, property, and even her children . . . the women up to the last years of the nineteenth century were really slaves in all but the name . . . However, woman's position greatly changed in the twentieth century.[15]

Seven years later New South Wales took up the cause with the establishment of the Womanhood Suffrage League, inaugurated in the offices of the radical Louisa Lawson's journal the *Dawn*. In its first issue (15 May 1886), the *Dawn* proclaimed that

Every eccentricity of belief, and every variety of bias in mankind allies itself to a printing-machine, and gets its singularities bruited abroad in type, but where is the printing-ink champion of mankind's better half . . . Men legislate on divorce, on hours of labor, and many another question intimately affecting women, but neither ask, nor know the wishes of those whose lives and happiness are most concerned.

Women were, however, far from unanimous. At one of the very first meetings of the Women's Literary Society, in the inoffensive setting of Quong Tart's tearoom in King Street, Sydney, one 'energetic and much-esteemed member rose and said, with white heat, that she hoped we should never discuss such a disgraceful matter' (as that of women's right to vote). Horror, too, attended the interesting suggestion of the journalist Eliza Ashton, who recommended that, since 'marriage was a failure, a lamentable one', it should be replaced by an amicably renewable contract.[16]

Louisa Lawson's strong republican sentiments introduced another element of discord. The ladies in Quong Tart's tearoom would have been equally shocked by her condemnation of 'abject grovelling to royal ermine and jewelled heads' and her suggestion that 'If our loyalty means neither more nor less than sacrifice of all our interests, hopes, and manhood to English avarice, cupidity and pride, undeniably the time has come when we should cut the painter'. Support, however, also came from a more conservative quarter, the Women's Christian Temperance Union, a well-organized and widespread movement which established its own franchise and suffrage departments.

By the time the matter came up before the first Commonwealth Parliament in April 1902, women had already been accorded the vote in South Australia from 1894 and in Western Australia from 1898 – that surprising concession being due to the Forrest government's hope that urban women's votes would counteract those of the goldfield radicals. Since it was agreed that no person having the right to vote in a state election could be denied that vote in the Federal Parliament, the principle of extending the franchise was already conceded (but this principle was weakened more than a little when it came to considering the Aboriginal vote). Nevertheless, hidebound members put up a fight. William Knox, a director of BHP, whose major contribution to Australian traditions was to ensure that, as in Britain, the parliamentary day began with prayers, insisted that 'It is a man's duty to be here, and it is a woman's duty to look after her family'. Senator Edward Pulsford, although liberal on other matters (he was one of the very few in either house to vote against the previous year's racist immigration Bill), believed it 'not desirable in the interests of the sex themselves, nor do I think that they themselves desire, that they should be immersed in political life'. Amid the plethora of quotations from Plato, Gladstone, Lincoln, Florence Nightingale, Huxley and many other authorities, the Bill for women's suffrage passed both houses without real trouble.[17]

In spite of the early grant of women's suffrage their progress in politics was tardy. Edith Cowan became the first woman elected to a state assembly, that of Western Australia, in 1921, and it was Western Australia that first saw, eighty-eight years after women had been given the vote, a female state Premier (Carmen Lawrence in 1990, pipped at the post a year earlier by Rosemary Follett of the ACT to be the first woman ever to head an Australian government). Advance at the Federal level was even slower. It was over forty years before the first woman was elected to the House of Representatives, where Enid Lyons (late Dame Enid) won a Tasmanian seat for the United Australia Party in 1943. By that time the United Kingdom, which had only reluctantly conceded the vote to women in the same terms as men in 1928 with the introduction of the 'Flapper Franchise' (older women, presumed to be as reliably responsible as their younger male contemporaries, had been admitted to the franchise in 1918), had produced such formidable female MPs as Lady Astor, elected to the House of Commons in 1919, and 'Red Ellen' Wilkinson, later a Cabinet minister, elected in 1924, to say nothing of the Irish republican Constance Gore-Booth, Countess Markiewicz, elected in 1918 but who refused to take her seat.

But two Australian swallows did not combine to make an Australian feminist summer. The year 1943 also saw the first woman senator, Dame Dorothy Tangney; thirty years later, in 1973, there were still only two women in the Senate, Dames Nancy Buttfield and Margaret Guilfoyle, both Liberals. In 1979, when Margaret Thatcher became Britain's first woman Prime Minister, no Australian women were sitting in the House of Representatives. In a world which had seen Golda Meir, Mrs Bandaranaike, and Indira Gandhi established as world figures this was a poor record. Only at the turn of the millennium, after an example had been set by the Australian Democratic Party, did the major parties demonstrate a real effort by committing themselves to a target proportion of women representatives. Women Cabinet ministers nevertheless continued to be rare birds. The most prominent feminine politician at that time was the egregiously eccentric Pauline Hanson, who attracted considerable support among redneck Queenslanders for her right-wing policies. With some effort, the 1998 election brought the total of women MPs to 22 per cent of the total, but Australian politics remain a predominantly masculine preserve.

Complacent masculinity, later joined by distastefully coarse language and crude manners, long remained a defining feature of Australian political life, in which women were rarely taken seriously. In Britain not only were the great society hostesses, usually Whig-Liberals, accepted as confidantes and advisers, but ladies on the fringes of good society and questionable social position were treated as having a judgement to be respected; even so staid a politician as Gladstone accepted Parnell's mistress, Mrs Katherine O'Shea, as a negotiating partner in the vexed question of Irish Home Rule. The admirable Caroline Chisholm, whose portrait appears on Australian twenty-dollar banknotes, a seeming exception, proves the point. Together with her husband Captain Arthur Chisholm of the East India Company's army, Mrs

Chisholm took charge of the reception of the flood of immigrants they encountered when on leave in Sydney in 1838–40. Meeting every immigrant ship, with the support of Governor Gipps, Mrs Chisholm found positions for newly arrived girls, established employment agencies and helped immigrants to settle. When the New South Wales government refused further assistance, Mrs Chisholm returned to England to persuade Britain of the need to assist emigrants, not only with passage money, but with hard information and help with settling in to the new country. It was due to her influence on such personalities as Angela Burdett-Coutts, Charles Dickens and Lord Ashley that Mrs Chisholm was able to transform the emigrants' conditions, an achievement well recognized in both Britain and Australia – but it was the openness of British society to this unknown middle-class woman (a Catholic to boot, which caused a stir in New South Wales) that enabled her to succeed.

It may be that one pathway for women's entry into politics was unduly restricted. The role of local government in Australia remained comparatively minor, the consequence of the resistance to Gipps's and Grey's desire to establish district councils and the subsequent removal to government boards of many of their responsibilities; the residual powers of shire and borough authorities were much less than those possessed by an English county council and their membership limited. Opportunities for women, either as officials – and as early as 1874 Mrs Nassau Senior was appointed as a Poor Law inspector in England, or as members – in 1870 Emily Davies was elected to the London Education Board, were not paralleled in Australia. Women did better, too, in New Zealand, where both Pakeha and Maori women were enfranchised in 1893, and in local elections all had the vote from 1874; Dame Catherine Tizard was appointed Governor General in 1990, and Jennifer Shipley became Prime Minister in 1997, succeeded by Helen Clark – a situation still difficult to envisage in Australia, although Queensland, New South Wales and South Australia have all had women governors.

Not much attention was lavished on another political community. Allied to the effects of the White Australia policy was the refusal to accept full-blood Aborigines as part of the community, which amounted almost to a denial of their existence. A peculiarly Australian perversity this, without parallel in other countries subjected to European colonization. New Zealand Maori had been given their place as – admittedly second-grade – citizens, and duly sanitized aspects of Maori culture were accepted. Given the extent of intermarriage, however informal, Afrikaners could hardly avoid accepting their 'coloured cousins', whilst the English Africans were pushed into moulding blacks along British patterns, a process culminating in that splendid nineteenth-century Gladstonian liberal, Nelson Mandela.

Not so in Australia. King O'Malley, the wildly eccentric American Labor MP, sometime bishop of the Water-lily Rockbound Church, Redskin Temple of the Cayuse Nation, who numbered the provision of lavatories on trains and the abolition of barmaids among his other enthusiasms, refused to accept the comparison with Maori, pontificating that 'an Aborigine is not as intelligent as a Maori. There is no scientific evidence that he is a human being at all.' Somewhat pointedly, Senator R. C. O'Connor, a political opponent, regretted that 'Unfortunately, they are a failing race. In most parts of Australia they are becoming very largely civilized ... and are certainly quite as well qualified to vote as are an equal number of persons who already possess the franchise.'[18] In North America, prolonged indigenous resistance, although ineffective in preventing widespread destruction, elevated 'Indian' chiefs into folk heroes; Tecumseh, Cochise, Sitting Bull and Geronimo are famous in United States history, but few Australians indeed could come up with the names of Aboriginal resisters; the chosen Australian hero remains the unsuccessful horse-thief, Ned Kelly. Until comparatively recently this distressing subject was tacitly avoided; it had not, after all, led to the disasters caused by the White Australia policy, but an increasing consciousness of past injustices, exacerbated by well-meaning attempts at reparation, is now a constant worry to Australian politicians, caught between the indifferent majority, more concerned with economic difficulties, and Aboriginal activists backed by liberal opinion.

Much later distress could have been avoided if the first Commonwealth Parliament had carried the logical extension of women's suffrage through to that of the Aborigines. Prior to 1902, Aboriginal men could vote in all states except – inevitably – Queensland and Western Australia, and in liberal South Australia Aboriginal women were also enfranchised; only in South Australia and Tasmania was the franchise given to all men without qualification. The horrid prospect of blacks, and especially of black women, being allowed to vote, and even to sit in the House, unnerved the House of Representatives:

If anything could make the concession of female suffrage worse than it is in the minds of some people, it would be giving it to any of the numerous gins of the blackfellow. It cannot be claimed ... that the aboriginal native is a person of very high intelligence who would cast his vote with a proper sense of the responsibility that rests upon him. And it can even less be claimed that his gin would give a vote which would be intelligible.[19]

Although the Senate was willing enough to admit Aboriginal men and women to the common electoral roll, objectors in the House of Representatives succeeded in tacking on a special disqualification on the Commonwealth Franchise Bill (1902): 'No Aboriginal native of Australia, Africa or the islands of the Pacific except New Zealand shall be entitled to have his name placed upon an Electoral Roll unless so entitled under section forty-one of the Constitution' – the section stipulating that any adult having a state vote must be entitled to the Commonwealth franchise. Accordingly black men and women were in principle admitted to political life in New South Wales, Victoria, South Australia and Tasmania (where comparatively few were left), but barred in Western Australia and Queensland, where many Aboriginal communities survived, and where they remained barred for another sixty years. When South Australia surrendered her northern region to become the Northern Territory, her Aboriginal inhabitants lost whatever shadow of rights they might have retained. Even when unpopular minorities had the right to vote, as in the American southern states, they could be discouraged; in 1896 Louisiana had 130,334 blacks on the electoral roll; eight years later 1,342 remained. The small number of Australian Aborigines who did qualify for the Federal vote – mostly of mixed race – were never fully integrated into political society.[20]

Some minor matters remained to be settled, among them what was to be the flag of the new Commonwealth and where the new capital. The first was made the subject of a competition, the unspoken assumption being that it would incorporate the Union flag, which it duly did, being a blue ensign bearing the five stars of the Southern Cross and a single larger star signifying the Commonwealth. This remains, in the face of attempts to replace it, the Australian flag. The winning design, submitted by five separate competitors, was flown from the Melbourne exhibition building for the first time on 3 September 1901.

Finding a site for the new capital was less easy. The stipulation that it should be in New South Wales, but not within 100 miles of Sydney offered a fair degree of choice, which took no less than nine years to finalize. The suggestion of Armidale, 350 miles off in New England was hardly serious, for New South Wales insisted that any distance much greater than the minimum would not be agreed – and since the state would be required to provide the necessary 100 square miles for the new Federal capital its agreement was essential. If Victorians were eventually to lose the Melbourne

Parliament they insisted that the new capital must at least be reasonably accessible. The first formal choices were Bombala or Dalgety, both isolated in the Monaro hills, near the Victorian border; but the key factor was the main railway line running from Sydney to Melbourne through Albury, a connection to which would be difficult and expensive. Only in October 1909, after eight years of argument, was the pleasant county south of Lake George settled on, which would enable a branch line to join with the mainline at Yass – 150 miles or so from Sydney. New South Wales agreed to provide nearly 1,000 square miles for what was to be known as the Australian Capital Territory and the city of Canberra, where building began in 1912.[21] The new capital's name was an approximation to an Aboriginal original, insisted on by Prime Minister Fisher when his own name was suggested, and very considerably better than the other suggestions received, one of which was Sydmeladperbrisho.

A Two-Party System

The main characteristics of Australian policies had been established by the Deakin–Watson collaboration. These were threefold, and remained central to national policy which no Australian government, of whatever political hue, could disturb except at its peril:

1. Centralized control of industrial relations, which protected workers and employers alike, at the cost of rigidity and reduced initiative.
2. Such industrial constraints, which relegated market influence to a secondary importance, necessitated the second essential, that of all-round tariff protection to shelter Australian industry.
3. The White Australian policy, which provided another barrier to competition.

If Australian development was to succeed so insulated from the rest of the world the Imperial link became even more essential. For better and for worse, these policies were continued for many years. Only in 1966 was the White Australian policy effectively abolished by Harold Holt's Liberal government; protection was officially renounced by Bob Hawke's Labor administration in March 1991, whilst the centralized industrial relations machine continues, although reduced in scale. In trade matters the Imperial link was eventually dissolved in 1973 when Britain joined the European Economic Community, thus ending the special relationship with the former colonies.

The progress of social legislation carried through by the Deakin government alarmed the conservatives, an alarm heightened by some Labor rhetoric which seemed to promise wholesale nationalization. The 1906 general election again returned the three teams in very similar numbers – Deakin's protectionists with 26 seats, George Reid's followers, now marketed as 'Anti-Socialists', with 23, and Labor with 25. John Forrest resigned in 1907 and began negotiations to unite the conservatives and free-traders into a formal anti-Labor front. Despairing of ever succeeding with free trade, Reid resigned as leader of the opposition in November 1908, which enabled his successor, Joseph Cook, to form an anti-Labor alliance with Deakin's followers. Since Reid could never have served with Deakin, this enabled the two right-wing parties to unite, at first as a 'Fusion' party. Reid's departure to become the first Australian High Commissioner in London marked the end of an era, as of the old colonial political figures only Deakin remained, already showing signs of the mental disturbances which were to force him out of political life. By that time the Labor Party had reason to believe that the Deakin alliance had served its purpose; old-age pensions were established that year, extending into their retirement the protection given to workers by the Harvester judgments; the white Australian policy insulated jobs against the immigrant population; tariffs, extended and increased, with rates nearly doubled, sheltered manufacturing jobs, and the salaries of MPs had been increased to a comfortable £600 a year. When Andrew Fisher, a Scots-born Queenslander who took over the leadership of the parliamentary Labor Party from Watson in 1907, was able to defeat the government in November the following year, and to become Prime Minister, the Labor Party had its second taste of office. It was not long-lived, replaced within months by Alfred Deakin at the head of the new 'Fusion Liberal' party, which now included Sir John Forrest's followers.[22]

By 1910 Fisher was back, reinforced by a general election victory, in which Labor won an absolute majority in both houses of Parliament – 47 of the 75 House of Representatives seats and 23 of the 36 in the Senate. The Cabinet contained many of the ablest Australian politicians: Fisher himself, tolerant and dignified, also ran the finance portfolio – Treasury – effectively; the cool and industrious Western Australian senator George Pearce, at Defence; and the phenomenal Billy Hughes as Attorney General. From such a position of power Labor was able to reinforce the Deakin legislation, to strengthen protectionism, increase old-age pensions, provide cash maternity benefits, and to establish a national bank, the Commonwealth Bank. The new bank, launched almost in spite of the advocacy of King O'Malley, had very little about it of socialist ideals, becoming a staidly orthodox and efficient government bank, but without the powers of a central bank in controlling the financial system.[23] Apart from the new bank, and the imposition of a land tax, Fisher's legislation was more a continuation of the Deakin settlement than a radical departure from it, although Labor sought to do more, especially by extending the powers of the Federal Arbitration Court, for which the constitution required a referendum. Theoretically an extension of democracy, this practice of placing specific issues before the electorate could be a weapon of conservatism, and had been used successfully by such authoritarian countries as Napoleon III's France, and it has continued to enable Switzerland to delay until recently such democratic rights as female suffrage. Australians were to prove resistant to referendums, agreeing very few government proposals thus submitted (the first two referendums, in 1906 and 1910, on relatively minor points, were approved, but the next thirteen were rejected; it was not until 1928 that the electorate again approved a referendum proposal), and this was duly rejected. It seemed that a broad consensus had been realized which narrowed differences between moderate right and moderate left to the question of competent administration. Only when specific issues thrust themselves forward, or when an extremist became prominent, were Australian politics concerned with great principles; and the unwelcome corollary was that pettiness and corruption became too commonly accepted.[24]

Fisher's proposals were far reaching, even, in an Australian context, revolutionary – the first referendum on 26 April 1911 asked for authority to extend Federal government control over trade and commerce, employment and financial corporations, and monopolies; the normal apparatus of central government control, but anathema to 'States Righters'. The second, in May 1913, was even more extensive and failed narrowly. Both were energetically supported by the Attorney General, Billy Hughes, who well understood the powers that efficient government needed but was, once again, frustrated.

One obligation incurred at Federation had to be fulfilled. South Australia, realizing the painful economic consequences of its grand ideas in taking over the Northern Territory, had insisted on the Commonwealth assuming responsibility, which was duly done, after much discussion, only in January 1911. At the inauguration in Darwin, Mr Justice Mitchell, the Recorder, complained that 'one of the saddest things to me about this particular town is the number of people ... who are always decrying the land'. Nearly a century later the sentiment has perhaps transmuted into a sense of wry pleasure in surviving the discomforts.[25]

Defence

In January 1901 the ultimate issue of the South African War had already been decided, although the terms of the Boer capitulation were not agreed until May 1902. Few then could have forecast the rapid transformation of the defeated Afrikaner republics into provinces of the Union of South Africa, governed by the great guerrilla leaders Botha, Herzog and Smuts, with Smuts becoming a British Field Marshal and a member of the Imperial War Cabinet. The struggle to force Irish Home Rule through a recalcitrant House of Lords had been abandoned after the defeat of Gladstone's second Bill in 1893, but Ireland was quiescent. The Campbell-Bannerman Liberal government of 1906 had undertaken to implement Gladstone's proposals, although it was another eight years before the Home Rule Act was placed on the statute book. Driven by South Africa and Ireland, and by developing Indian institutions and nationalist sentiment, the post-war Imperial club was to undergo decisive alterations. To these, Australia and New Zealand, uncomfortably isolated in the South Pacific, acceded sometimes reluctantly.

The new nation of Australia was born into a world of rapid and often threatening change. Both China and Japan had suffered cracks in their defensive carapaces at about the same time, by the 1859–60 Anglo-Chinese War, which reinforced the preceding Treaty of Nanking by establishing the right of diplomatic representation in Peking, and by the arrival of the American fleet off Yokohama in 1858, but Japan's reaction to Western customs was generally more rapid and effective than that of China, due largely to the centralization of power in the hands of the Meiji emperors. China's crushing defeat by Japan in 1895 cemented Japanese convictions of their own superiority, which made Australian attitudes more resented. The Japanese Minister in London complained to Prime Minister Lord Salisbury that it was not so much the prohibition which might exclude some Japanese visitors, but the fact that 'Japan should be spoken of in formal documents, such as Colonial Acts, as if the Japanese were on the same level of morality and civilisation as Chinese and other less advanced populations of Asia'.[26] That was in 1898; within two years the Boxer Rebellion, which was accompanied by the murder of missionaries, the famous siege of the British embassy, and the relief by British, Indian, American, Italian, Japanese and Australian forces had done nothing to enhance China's reputation. Two ancient nations, Russia and Japan, both modernizing and re-equipping at a rapid pace, came to blows in 1905. At the decisive sea battle of Tsushima the Japanese emerged decisively victorious, having driven home the point that Japan was a modern military power and an extremely effective one at that.[27]

By that time Lord Salisbury had been succeeded by Arthur Balfour, another master of foreign policy, first as Foreign Secretary and then, in July 1902, as Prime Minister. With the support of King Edward VII, Balfour had begun the process of putting together an alliance that was to result in the Empire, Italy, Russia, Japan and, eventually, the United States, joining together in the First World War. The Anglo-Japanese Treaty of January 1902, which was to continue in existence for nearly twenty years, provided that if either country were attacked by more than one other country the other party would provide assistance. If only one aggressor was involved, only neutrality was demanded. Although not informed of the arrangement until the public announcement was made, Australian public opinion, embodied in Barton's official endorsement, welcomed the alliance and gave an 'effusive' reception to a Japanese squadron visiting Australian ports the following year. But although the officers of HIJMS *Hiyei* and *Kongo* were doubly welcome as having defeated the dreaded Chinese, and the technical ability, discipline and personal civility of the Japanese were lauded, the barriers against Japanese immigration remained intact.[28]

As far as Australia was concerned, the bargain implicit in membership of the Imperial club was that the defence guaranteed by the Royal Navy would be reciprocated by Australian participation in Imperial quarrels. But as with all such understandings, misunderstandings were inevitable. Barton, that astute lawyer, made his government's attitude clear to Joseph Chamberlain. They were 'precluded from the discussion with external authorities representing Foreign Nations, of matters involving the relations between the Empire and these Nations, excepting with the express authority of His Majesty's Imperial Government'.[29] This neat pushing of Australian problems on to the British plate was reinforced by the Commonwealth government's initial reluctance to use the obvious channel left open to them, that of communication with foreign governments through their consular officials in Australia. When used by Alfred Deakin in 1905 this device ensured an American naval visit, which met with conspicuous success. The arrival of the 'Great White Fleet' – the American Pacific Squadron's men-of-war were painted in tropical white with tasteful yellow funnels – had been engineered by Deakin, who approached the United States government directly rather than going through the correct diplomatic channels via the British government.[30] A resentful Colonial Office could do nothing about it, and the fleet arrived to a tumultuous welcome in both Sydney and Melbourne. Deakin went further in the next year by reviving the proposal that a 'Monroe

Doctrine' of the Pacific should be established to exclude external interference, guaranteed by Britain and the United States plus Holland, France
and China – quite specifically excluding Japan. Since this would have caused
havoc in the Foreign Office, clinging to the Japanese Alliance and anxious
not to provoke Germany, the idea was not progressed and when the Anglo-
Japanese Treaty was renewed in 1911 the news was well received by Australia. 'External Relations', to Australian politicians, continued to mean
negotiations with the Colonial Office, and those through the Governor
General. In the fourteen years before the outbreak of the First World War
the direction of the Department of External Affairs changed hands ten times
– and for eight years the portfolio was held by the current Prime Minister.

After the Russian defeat Japan was now unquestionably the leading South
Asian power and a potential threat to Australia. The visit of the American
'Great White Fleet' therefore came as a welcome reminder that there was
another power, not so strong at sea as the Royal Navy, but with far fewer
responsibilities, which might join with the Australians in facing the 'Yellow
Peril'. The colonial navies inherited by the Commonwealth in 1901 were a
motley collection of gunboats, torpedo-boats and a couple of armoured
cruisers, responsibility for Australia's defence being confided almost exclusively to the British navy. Defence was therefore a vital subject for the
colonial conferences held at five-yearly intervals since 1897. That of 1907,
the first to be renamed 'Imperial', attended both by the Commonwealth of
Australia and the Premiers of the new South African states, was particularly
noteworthy. Barton had attended the 1902 conference, but the confused
state of Australian post-Federation policies deprived him of much authority.
Nor was Barton as experienced in international affairs as Deakin, his only
previous experience being the negotiations with Chamberlain three years
previously. He was therefore less effective in pressing for the creation of a
specifically Australian navy, accepting instead the payment of a contribution
towards imperial expenses. For this Barton was much criticized by Australian nationalists, who perhaps failed to appreciate the heavy expenditure
that would be involved in such a policy.

Deakin attended the 1907 conference as Australia's Prime Minister,
alongside such powerful characters as Louis Botha, who had been in arms
against the Empire only five years previously, the Québecois Wilfrid Laurier
of Canada, and Winston Churchill, enjoying his first taste of power as a
Liberal parliamentary under-secretary. Deakin was an old hand at such
negotiations, beginning with his attendance as a Victorian delegate at the
first Colonial Conference twenty years before, when he had met the venerable reformer John Bright, who earnestly recommended that the Australian

colonies should 'cut the painter'. Such action would have been the negation of all Deakin stood for, as he proved a passionate advocate of the pressing need for a common defence policy. It was a personal disappointment to him, after his earlier efforts in the Victorian government to prevent the French annexing the New Hebrides, that prior to the 1907 conference Salisbury's policies had been watered down by Campbell-Bannerman's Liberals, in pursuit of an entente with France, to establishing a condominium in that disputed territory. The New Hebrides subsequently became a French Overseas Territory (but Australian influence in the islands is however commemorated by that useful ejaculation 'bagarite').

Churchill wanted to invite the state Premiers as well, thinking that they might prove an antidote to Deakin who he believed to be 'the most hostile to our government of all the Australians' – at least on the question of Imperial preference – but his chief, Lord Elgin, demurred. The Premiers were 'in some cases by no means high class', and results were best obtained if the colonial delegations spoke with a 'single voice' of unquestioned authority. This centralizing reinforcement did much to secure both Australian Commonwealth control over the states, and the future British Commonwealth's influence over its member countries. Questions of Imperial preference did indeed occupy much of the 1907 conference's time, and Deakin, although unsuccessful in many of his proposals (both Laurier and the British government being against him), succeeded in establishing a favourable image of Australia in British public opinion.[31]

On defence, Deakin pressed for the creation of an Australian navy, a continuation of the forward policies he had advocated in Victoria. Accepted in principle, as part of the general reconsideration of Imperial defence, which continued to be developed with great energy by the 'hawks' (including Churchill, Kitchener and Haldane), it was, however, left to Andrew Fisher to implement the proposal by authorizing the formation of a flotilla of nineteen destroyers. A speedy rethink proved necessary when the consequences of HMS *Dreadnought*'s construction were appreciated. Built at great expense, and in record time, *Dreadnought* was the first of the fast, heavily armoured all-big-gun battleships, a type which survives today in the US Navy, and which immediately rendered all other capital ships obsolete. Joined by battlecruisers – ships of similar size and armament, but with better speeds made possible by reduced protection – Britain was committed to out-building all her potential enemies, and badly needed colonial support.

The revised strategy was to construct an entirely new Pacific fleet, composed of three squadrons, each with one battlecruiser, three light cruisers, six destroyers and three submarines. One of these squadrons would be paid for and controlled by Australia, and eventually manned entirely by Australian crews. With the arrival of the destroyers, *Parramatta*, *Yarra* and *Warrego*, the Royal Australian Navy was finally established in October 1911, the result of bipartisan Labor and Liberal policies. Fisher took great pleasure in reflecting that 'our ships will fly at the stern the white ensign as the symbol of the authority of the Crown and at the jack staff the Commonwealth flag'. Within a very short time, however, the Admiralty concentrated its capital ships in European waters, seriously depleting the Pacific fleet; the battlecruiser *Australia* was the only capital ship retained, at the insistence of the Australian government.[32]

At the Imperial Conference held at the time of King George V's coronation, in the summer of 1911, it was Andrew Fisher who led the Australian delegation. Fisher was an object of generally sympathetic curiosity as a Labor Prime Minister with a strong majority, in a country which had produced such advanced social legislation, a subject of great interest to Herbert Asquith's reforming Liberal government. Asquith's own reforms had been taken further by David Lloyd George at the Exchequer, and would have been advanced still more by Winston Churchill in his short tenure at the Home Office, to equal in some respects and even to improve on Australian standards (although on such great issues as that of women's suffrage even British Liberal governments lagged). Old-age pensions were established, trade union funds had been protected by the Taff Vale decision of 1902, and MPs were to be paid from 1911. In Parliament, the Labour Party, under the leadership of Ramsay MacDonald, was firmly established with a solid bloc of some 50 seats, but still very much a third party. Fisher was therefore seen as something of a portent, foreshadowing what might be expected if British Labour should ever succeed in forming a government, a prospect which, in view of the Liberal government's then unprecedented success in winning elections, seemed at the time to be far distant.

Fisher was something of a disappointment, a poor subject for lionization, refusing all honours, although reluctantly agreeing to being admitted to the Privy Council and therefore acquiring the title of Right Honourable, but displaying no overt signs of revolutionary socialism other than that of removing the lace from the court dress he was obliged to wear on his admission to the Privy Council.[33] On defence, however, Labor proved unexpectedly militaristic for a party which had hitherto been suspicious of defence expenditure. It was Billy Hughes who had most clearly seen the potential dangers, against vociferous Labor opposition – King O'Malley thought the party had gone 'mad on militarism' by adopting 'the most diabolical methods of Europe' and giving power to 'the gilt-spurred roosters'. Lord Kitchener was invited to assess the situation and reported that a national defence force was needed to protect Australia against invasion, which should number about 80,000 men of all arms, and that compulsory training should be extended to age 25. His suggestions were immediately implemented by the Fisher government, whose January 1911 Act providing for a militia force was actually a tougher version of one earlier prepared by Deakin. With certain exceptions, all 12-year-old boys were required to register and begin part-time military training, which was to continue until the age of 25. It was, by British standards, a remarkably severe programme, but was generally accepted by Australians as a necessary precaution. About 155,000 young men were registered in 1911, with 92,000 in training, and some 20,000 being added to their numbers in each subsequent year. A military college was established and armament factories built; much effort and money was expended, but very few officers and men had actual combat experience. By introducing conscription, Australia had gone much further than the mother country, where compulsion was only resorted to after the horrifying losses of the first two years of the First World War, but where the creation of an efficient voluntary militia had been implemented in 1907 with the foundation of the Territorial Army. At the Coronation Conference Australia's defence policy, and its integration within the Imperial structure, was left undefined, to be settled later; but before that could be done the world erupted into war.[34]

On the brink of the First World War, the war to end war as it was optimistically called, Australia was a very different country from that collection of colonies which had come together fourteen years previously. The population had grown by more than a third, from some 3,700,00 to 4,900,000, half a million of whom were immigrants, almost all from Britain, many attracted by government assistance. Such an influx inevitably brought problems as so many labourers, often unskilled, had to be absorbed into an economy in which industrialization was growing only slowly, in spite of tariff protection; but all benefited from a social security system unmatched anywhere, from free education, from – if they could find work – a basic living wage and the right to travel freely and settle in any part of the country, again with government support. The Commonwealth had absorbed the Northern Territory, taken over the administration of New Guinea, and placed its markers in the wastes of Antarctica. A national bank, a national defence force and a Commonwealth High Court, had all been established. Government had succeeded government, observing all the democratic and parliamentary proprieties and perfecting the constitutional settlement. All in all, it was an astonishing achievement, this quiet unification of a congeries of colonies into a modern state. But not yet, perhaps, in spite of the flag and the new capital under construction, a continental nation. The states retained solid power, combined with 'something like parochialism'; the historian Frank Crowley noted 'a breezy, buoyant imperial spirit. But a national spirit was practically non-existent.'[35]

And a great segment of the continent, a jagged semicircle from Townsville in the east, south to Broken Hill and west to Kalgoorlie, comprising more than half the total land mass, was inhabited mainly by Aborigines, some disinherited and dejected, others clinging to their ancestral traditions, but all banned from participation in the new country of Australia.

A Botany Bay savage: J. Ihle, 1795, from a sketch made in Port Phillip, dramatized for London buyers.

Aboriginal fishing methods: making those large and intricate nets demanded great skill and patience. Natives at Second Valley, Album of Sketches, E. W. Belcher, watercolour c.1843–75.

Sydney Cove in 1842, viewed from the Rocks to Bennelong Point, where the Opera House now stands. By Jacob Janssen.

Captain James Cook by
Bernard Hailstone.

Captain Matthew Flinders:
although both Cook and
Flinders were commissioned
by George III, Cook was
essentially a man of the
eighteenth century, Flinders
a romantic intellectual. By
Helena G. de Courcy Jones.

Governor Thomas Davey of Van Diemen's Land attempted this graphic depiction to explain the rule of law to his Aboriginal subjects.

Abandon hope: a Portsmouth hulk. The hulls of the old men-of-war formed convenient receptacles for convicts, but provided no opportunities of reformation such as were offered by transportation. By Samuel Prout.

The Gordon Riots, 1780, 'The Social Order as a Beleaguered City'.

The Conciliator: George Augustus Robinson persuaded some Tasmanian Aborigines to settle on Flinders Island, but did not see the project through.

Mathinna, a Flinders Island girl, painted by a convict artist, Thomas Bock, in 1842, aged 8. She died in 1856.

Boy with sulphur-crested cockatoo, c.1815. Attributed to John Lewin, Australia, 1770–1819.

Felling huge eucalyptus was a skilled and risky trade.

The first Cobb & Co. coach imported from America, delivering mail to the
Coranaderrk Aborigines. The last coach service ended in 1924.

Port Arthur: scientific, and not ineffective, penology. The hospital, and Smith O'Brien's cottage, are on the hill behind the barracks block.

Jane Franklin – 'sensible, agreeable & not unpretty' – who later organized the eight-year search for Sir John's lost Arctic expedition, recorded in the Cambridge Scott Polar Research Institute.

William Charles Wentworth, brilliant and unpredictable, the first great Australian of the nineteenth century.

The first Australian cricket team to tour England in 1868 was Aboriginal – from the Madimadi and Wutjubaluk people in Victoria. The organizer, Tom Wills, is at the back (*centre*) with Johnny Mullagh on his left.

Opposite page: The First Responsible Government of New South Wales: June 1856.
Left to right: Thomas Holt, Colonial Treasurer; William Manning, Attorney General; Stuart Donaldson, Colonial Secretary (Premier); John Darval, Solicitor General; George Nichols, Auditor General and Secretary for Land and Works

Above: The First Federation Conference, Melbourne, 1890. The impressively maned Henry Parkes is the unmistakable central figure. *Standing, from left:* Andrew Inglis Clark (Tasmania), Captain William Russell (New Zealand), Sir Samuel Griffith (Queensland), Sir Henry Parkes (New South Wales), Thomas Playford (South Australia), Alfred Deakin (Victoria), Bolton Bird (Tasmania), G. H. Jenkins (clerk). *Seated, from left:* W. MacMillan (New South Wales), Sir John Hall (New Zealand), John Macrossan (Queensland), Duncan Gillies (Victoria), Dr John Cockburn (South Australia), Sir James Lee Steere (South Australia).

Midshipmen Prince Albert and Prince George visiting Brisbane in August 1881.
Prince George (*right*), later Duke of York and King George V, opened the first
Commonwealth Parliament in 1901.

The Women's Christian Temperance Union was a formidable champion of women's
rights: the Brisbane Committee 1901.

This is the Empire: Tom Robert's sketch for his painting of the first Federal Parliament, opened in May 1901 by the Duke of York.

After the charge at Beersheba: a soldier of the Light Horse leading a large group of Turkish prisoners.

Men of the 24th battalion A I F waiting to go into action at Mont Saint-Quentin on 1 September 1918. Both the corps and division commanders, Generals Monash and Rosenthal, were civilian soldiers. The attack succeeded, at heavy cost.

Billy Hughes, 'The Little Digger', addressing the Anzacs in France: their achievements enabled Australia to take an independent line in post-war settlements.

The Kelly gang was finally cornered by Queensland Native Police Trackers. Their leader, Inspector Standish O'Connor, refused to accept his share of the reward in protest at his men's mean treatment.

Queen Elizabeth II with Prime Minister John Howard opening the Australian War memorial in Hyde Park, November 2003.

Don Bradman at the Adelaide Oval: that extraordinary institution, the Commonwealth, is held together as much by cricket as by constitutional affinities.

11

War and Peace

'The liberties of the smaller nations'

Twentieth-century Australian politicians have not, as a rule, made much impact on the international stage. Two names stand out from the ruck in the first half century – William Morris Hughes and Herbert Vere Evatt; both Labor lawyers with long careers, both highly individualistic and pugnacious. London-born, Welsh-educated (at Llandudno Grammar School, where he almost certainly learnt to speak Welsh, a subject of considerable later discussion), Billy Hughes emigrated to Queensland in 1884, at the age of 20. By turns seaman, boundary rider, locksmith, and bookseller, Hughes eventually made a name for himself as a trade union organizer and was elected to the New South Wales Legislative Assembly as a Labor member in 1894. It was the beginning of a political career that lasted until 1952 when he died at the age of 88, four times Prime Minister and still a member of the Commonwealth Parliament, although he had crossed the floor to become a Liberal.[1]

Hughes can have owed little of his success to his physical attributes; a small wizened figure, with a hoarse rasping voice, chronically dyspeptic for most of his career, he suffered from near-complete deafness; but the Governor General, Sir Ronald Crauford Munro Ferguson, in office between May 1914 and October 1920, not a man easily impressed, himself a former Liberal MP, described him to Prime Minister Asquith as 'a remarkable personality . . . a natural leader of men; a delightful companion; bold in adversity; clear in his views, and what is rare in Australia sound on the question of economy . . . probably considers himself a Socialist . . . He is a sincere Imperialist and to him more than any other is due the progress made in Australia in Naval and Military preparation.'[2] The seeming contradiction in terms is more apparent than real: neither the British Labour nor the Australian Labor Party were ever more than superficially socialist in a Marxist sense, and Ferguson's description of Hughes might equally well have later been applied to that English trade unionist and Foreign Secretary, Ernest Bevin.

In spite of his limited previous education (he had been a pupil-teacher for a short time), Hughes was admitted to the Sydney Bar in 1904, taking silk in 1909. When the first Commonwealth Labor government was formed he became Minister for External Affairs; after that short-lived administration he found himself once more in office under Andrew Fisher as Attorney General, a position which he again held in 1910. Australia's policy of allowing governments only three-year terms necessitated another Federal election in May 1913, which Labor narrowly lost. Ungrateful for the social benefits Fisher's government had produced, many voters objected to defence expenditure and the introduction of compulsory military training. Anti-Labor press comments were fuelled by new regulations restraining political advocacy, and by a dramatic strike of tramway drivers in Brisbane, which the Commonwealth government had supported. Labor was, however, able to hold on to its Senate majority, where the system allowed for only half of the seats to be resigned at triennial intervals. Joseph Cook came to power as Liberal Prime Minister, twenty-two years after his first election to the New South Wales Assembly as a Labor member, since which time he had drifted to the right. Dependent on a majority of only one in the House of Representatives, the pedestrian and uninspiring Cook found government difficult, but the task would have baffled a better man. Within three months he was obliged to ask for a new election for both houses – a double dissolution – which was for the Governor General to allow or deny; in such circumstances, where reasonable government had become all but impossible, there was no question but that a fresh election was essential and the dissolution was authorized. The September 1914 election returned Fisher once more at the head of a Labor government, for the third time, pledged to help in the Empire's war, to the 'last man and the last shilling'.

The Prime Minister's pledge was not welcomed by an influential section of his party, permeated by socialist objections to an imperialist conflict. Many others saw the war as an opportunity to increase government control over the economy, and some trade unionists objected to employment preference being given to returned soldiers. If Fisher's guarantee of the 'last man' had extended to a support of general conscription he would have been in even further trouble with the party Caucus, but it did not, for the Prime Minister resisted demands to conscript men for action abroad. The new militia would be available only for home service. In failing health, and faced with rebellious members of his own party, the strain of heading a wartime government proved too much, and in October 1915 Fisher reluctantly – he disliked and distrusted Hughes – handed the reins of government to his Attorney General, accepting the post of High Commissioner in London; for the next seven years Billy Hughes devoted himself to winning both the war and the peace.

The causes of the First World War – the Great War, as it was known at the time and long after – have been the subject of countless books, essays, theses and enquiries, and surely are to be found many years before that fateful August of 1914. Some sort of outbreak had been widely expected and was probably, at least since the beginnings of the Balkans conflict in 1912, inevitable; the Dominions had been specifically alerted on 29 July, following which they all signified their willingness to contribute troops. Fisher confirmed Cook's earlier offer to despatch 20,000 men for service anywhere that they might be needed. The formal British decision to declare war seemed almost casual, the result an almost foregone conclusion. Not only Parliament, but even the Cabinet itself was not consulted before the Foreign Secretary Sir Edward Grey sent the fateful ultimatum to Germany demanding the withdrawal of her forces from Belgium. The actual declaration of war was made by the King himself at a Privy Council meeting attended by only one minister, the very junior commissioner of works, Lord Beauchamp, who had been, fifteen years previously, Governor of New South Wales. That was Australia's only participation in the declaration of war. If the British Parliament was not consulted, it would have been odd indeed if colonial governments were; only one, that of Canada, subsequently formally expressed its approval.

Public opinion had moved since the 1890s, when the *Bulletin* very pertinently queried why Australia should become involved in any British war wherever it might be. The South African War had ended without too many Australian casualties, and the new Union of South Africa testified to its ultimately beneficial effects. Very few Australians had doubts about the inevitability, or the justice, of Australia's participation in a European war. Imperial solidarity had been reinforced in the first years since Federation by a wave of British immigrants who had helped to increase the population to nearly 5 million at the outbreak of war. Few Labor MPs actively opposed the war, the most prominent exceptions being the stridently anti-capitalist Frank Anstey, and Frank Brennan, strongly critical of British policies in Ireland. Henry Boote, the Liverpool-born journalist, editor of the *Australian Worker*, probably encapsulated the majority Labor view: 'We must protect our country. We must keep sacred from the mailed fist this splendid heritage. For that our Army of Defence was formed, and our Navy built. But we hope no wave of jingo madness will sweep over the land, unbalancing the judgment of its leaders, and inciting its population to wild measures, spurred on by the vile press.'[3] There could be no doubts about Hughes's own attitudes: the war was Armageddon, the supreme crisis of civilization, and must be won at all costs.

Labor had reinforced Deakin's initiative which resulted in Australia being prepared for war – but what sort of war was far from clear. Few of the protagonists had any experience of war, the last major European conflict having been the Franco Prussian War of 1870–71. Grey, for example, was 8 years old in 1870, the King 5; the German emperor was 12. None of those likely to be involved in the actual fighting had been engaged in a European war; the British armies were the most advanced in doctrine and equipment, well trained to fight the Boer War over again, as indeed all armies, at the best, are usually prepared only to re-enact the most recent campaign. The French were still relying on 'élan' and 'audace', while the German strategy was dependent on a quick successful dash for Paris. The Australian contingents were officered by men who had seen service in South Africa or in India, and who appreciated the effectiveness of fast-moving horsemen in the open spaces of the veld. Australia was well suited to provide mounted infantry, who needed less training than conventional cavalry but had to be physically tough and enterprising, skilled in horsemastership (although, as it turned out, the Australian horses were not as well treated as they might have been) rather than horsemanship, able to operate in relatively small numbers, at company or battalion level. Much less urban in 1914 than in 1939, with some half of the population living outside the great cities, Australia was able to provide impressive numbers of remounts in the shape of the indefatigable and obstreperous 'Walers'. Where Australian troops could be deployed in this way, as in Palestine and Syria, they were outstandingly successful, but the First World War was essentially, as far as the Imperial forces were concerned, fought out on the Western Front, and there conditions were very different.

The first Australian and New Zealand expeditionary force, the Australian Imperial Force (AIF), 20,000 strong, was recruited astonishingly quickly and sailed within six weeks, 'eloquent testimony to the near-unanimity of viewpoint within the Australian community which regarded the war as just and service in it as both obligation and privilege'.[4] It embarked in October 1914 for Suez, escorted by a squadron which included the Japanese battlecruiser *Ibuki*, one of the first benefits of the 1902 Anglo-Japanese Treaty. Their journey was enlivened by an encounter between HMAS *Sydney* and the German commerce raider *Emden* off the Cocos Islands in November which provided the first victory for the new Australian navy. Joined in the Egyptian desert by more shiploads of men and horses, the Australian and

New Zealand Army Corps, the famous ANZAC, was formed. Short on artillery and engineers, the Anzacs had a high proportion of mounted infantry, and unfortunately found themselves conveniently placed to participate in one of the war's great defeats.

It seemed unlikely that any European war would spread to the Pacific, where the existing alliances defined who would be Britain's enemies and who their friends. Treaties with France, Russia and Japan and friendly relations with the United States would ensure these countries' cooperation; China's internal struggle between the new republic of Sun Yat Sen and the failing Ch'ing empire kept her out of any equation, leaving Germany as the only likely local power to threaten Australia. Since the German navy would be very fully occupied in European and Atlantic waters there was little peril to be apprehended by Australia, and indeed the only action anywhere near Australian waters during the war was the battle between *Sydney* and *Emden*.

Those German ships in the East were ordered home, steaming to annihilation by Admiral Sturdee's squadron at the battle of the Falkland Islands in December 1914. The task of invading the nearest German colonies was entrusted to Australia, responsible for occupying German New Guinea and Rabaul, while New Zealand took over German Samoa. The first Australian shots of the war were fired on 12 September in a brisk little campaign which was to gain Australia a colony at the cost of six dead. German islands north of the Equator, including the Caroline, Mariana and Marshall groups, were occupied by the Japanese; although their formal surrender had been made to the Australians at Rabaul, the British government promised that Japan should permanently retain these conquests, while attempting to hide this unpalatable concession from the Australian government.

Turkey, which had drawn upon German assistance in the modernization begun by Kemal Ataturk, had joined in the war alongside Germany and Austria. An initial Turkish attack on the Suez Canal having been repulsed, the British War Cabinet had decided to cut Turkey off by severing internal communications, which necessitated forcing a passage through the Dardanelles. Although that should have been primarily a naval operation, conventional wisdom decided that after the fleet failed the commanding heights had first to be seized. The assault, which began on 25 April 1915, was led by the 3rd Australian Brigade. The strategic rationale was not unconvincing – a successful landing followed by a rapid breakthrough would transform the situation in the Middle East, protect the route to India and the vital Suez Canal link and take out both Turkey, one of Germany's most powerful allies, and Bulgaria, thereby relieving the pressure on the Russian front (Britain had already agreed that Istanbul would be handed over to Russia at the end of the war) – but the tactics were horribly inept. A landing in the face of strong Turkish forces, renowned for centuries as the toughest of fighting men, backed by the easily available resources of the Turkish capital, was doomed to failure. Sending in the inexperienced Anzacs, dismissed by the Commander in Chief Lord Kitchener as 'quite good enough if a cruise in the Sea of Marmora was all that was contemplated', was, at best, irresponsible. What followed was no cruise but a prolonged slaughter. For the next five months the Anzacs, British, French, Newfoundland and Indian troops fought bitterly against a determined Turkish resistance in a highly restricted battlefield. Australians and New Zealanders suffered shockingly heavy casualties, as many as 50 per cent in some actions, and proved themselves equal to the finest fighting men of any land.[5]

The most that can be said for the Gallipoli campaign in military terms is that it was good preparation for the horrors of trench warfare on the Western Front, and that the final evacuation was brilliantly executed; but the first large-scale action in which Australians participated shocked the country into a new consciousness of nationality, one which was unique, precious and distinct from a sense of being a distant Dominion of the British Empire. It also later gave rise to a myth which denigrated the British share of the fighting, and which has resisted many attempts to present the facts. On the seventy-fifth anniversary of the landings, in 1990, 'politicians, wishing to bask in the reflected glory of their veterans' were reinforced by a 'parochial' literature, 'preoccupied with heaping praise on Australian soldiers, and failing to compare them with those of the other nations present – apart from the usual disparaging comments about the British high command and the reputed poor physique of the British troops'. It also virtually disregarded the New Zealand element in the Anzac story, and it might be said, that of the French, who lost 9,798 dead at Gallipoli, rather more than the Australians of whom 8,141 died; the New Zealanders lost 2,431 dead and the British over 30,000. But Britain and France were miserably accustomed to their sons' deaths, while for innocent Australians and New Zealanders this was their first, bitter experience of modern war.

It was the initiative of a young Australian journalist that defined the shape of the Gallipoli story. Keith Murdoch was given his first important job in 1915 – four years earlier he had been struggling on £4 a week – as London managing editor of the cable service for Sir Hugh Denison's Australian newspapers. Helped by family connections, his father being a friend of both Fisher and Hughes, Murdoch obtained permission to visit Gallipoli, where he spent four days in September. In so short a time, and with no previous experience of battle, Murdoch relied on the views of an experienced war correspondent, Ellis Ashmead Bartlett, who had been on the scene from the beginning. On this frail basis Murdoch prepared a long and impassioned letter, ostensibly for Prime Minister Fisher, which contained bitter complaints – often justified – about the conduct of the campaign, but which also extravagantly praised the physique and fighting qualities of the Anzacs while denigrating the British soldiers as 'feeble, child-like youths'. The theme was taken up by the official Australian war correspondent C. E. W. Bean in a very successful publication *The Anzac Book*. Although Bean did not echo Murdoch's slander, he believed that the Australian soldier was 'a bushman in disguise' and that 'the wild pastoral life of Australia, if it makes wild men, makes superb soldiers' – which, considering that half the Australian population lived in cities and that many of the Anzacs were British-born, was the stuff of which myth is made. But the Anzac myth took time to develop; a more immediate effect was that Murdoch's letter was widely distributed and, published as a Cabinet paper, employed to great effect by the opposition to Prime Minister Asquith. Lord Northcliffe, who controlled the most authoritative newspaper, *The Times*, and the most popular, the *Daily Mail*, took up both the story and Keith Murdoch to reinforce his campaign to replace Asquith by Lloyd George.[6]

As the wounded survivors of Gallipoli trickled back to Australia, and as the bloody facts of the campaign became known, a feeling of national pride welled up. The men who had fought had done so, not as Victorians or Queenslanders, but as Australians. From the first anniversary of 25 April, the day was to be commemorated as a solemn occasion of national remembrance, together with a celebration of the heroism of the Australian fighters. By a nice irony the oldest Australian Catholic newspaper reflected on the first anniversary:

the price of nationhood must be paid in blood and tears; there is no country that truly loves its flag which has not made the supreme sacrifice – which has not freely offered up the lives of its best and bravest for a dream, for an ideal, for a solemn purpose. It is the fortune of Australia to find her true soul in that great and glorious struggle to preserve the liberties of the smaller nations, to crush a despotic militarism which would awe and subjugate the rest of the world . . .

There were patriots who protested against the slavish and sycophantic doctrine. But, generally speaking, it was assumed that Australia only lived by the grace of England, and the Empire Day orators had a better hearing than the faithful souls who clung to Australia Day and gave special honour to their own starry banner.[7]

The reference to 'the liberties of the smaller nations' was surely meant to refer to Ireland, where the Home Rule Act had been suspended for the duration of the war, but on the very day the newspaper appeared the Dublin Easter Rising began, in which the rebels welcomed the support of their 'gallant allies' – the very 'despotic militarists' against whom Australia was fighting in the 'great and glorious struggle'.

Gallipoli veterans were also horrified by the behaviour of some of the more recent recruits, who in February 1916 mutinied and rioted in Sydney:

Half intoxicated soldiers, drinking out of bottles in the middle of the streets and on the sidewalks, crowding into trams and hustling the passengers, jeering at those who reproached them, robbing shops and overturning barrows, and desecrating the flag, under which their brethren in Europe are fighting, by raising it aloft over a staggering crowd who had forgotten the obligations of their manhood – these men have dishonoured themselves and their country.

The Returned Soldiers' Association scathingly condemned the rioters, and offered to clear the streets of them: it was the first demonstration of the great influence that this organization has had on Australian society.[8]

Back in Egypt, the AIF was reorganized, the infantry formed into two Army Corps, destined for France; the mounted men, Australian Light Horse and New Zealand Mounted Rifles, with the Imperial Camel Corps, deployed in the Middle East. Under the command of General H. G. Chauvel the heavily outnumbered Light Horse repelled another Turkish attack on the Canal and pursued the Turks across the desert to Sinai, the same ground fought over sixty years later by Egyptian and Israeli tanks. A stubborn Turkish resistance along a line from Gaza to Beersheba was crushed in October 1917 by a reinforced Imperial army, commanded by General Edmund Allenby, probably the best fighting general in the British army, with Chauvel's Desert Mounted Corps forming the largest concentration of horse-soldiers in the armies of the Allies. Beersheba fell within an hour after a spirited, but unprecedented, charge by the Light Horse: mounted infantrymen were not intended to act as cavalry but the Light Horse rode straight at the Turkish guns.[9]

The AIF on the Western Front had much the worst of it. The Australians transferred from Egypt arrived in France in April 1916, to be introduced to a new and peculiarly horrible type of warfare. The assault on Gallipoli relied on Boer War tactics, with repeated efforts to storm Boer (Turkish) koppies (hills) at bayonet-point with depressingly similar results. In France, chemical, aerial and mechanized warfare were being introduced: all armies employed enormous artillery resources, with profligate expenditure of ammunition, unheard-of numbers of machine guns were sited on fixed lines behind extensive barbed wire, and cavalry was useless; but the trenches still had to be taken man-to-man. The Australians had not been trained for this sort of fighting, and their experience of the first offensive on the Somme in July was terrifying. 'Expecting death every second', one NCO wrote home. 'Men smothered in one trench, dead and dying everywhere. Some simply blown to pieces.' Confined to a few miles between Beaumont Hamel and Péronne, the army's every foot of advance was gained only at the expense of countless lives. Attempting to take the fortified German position at Pozières, in forty-five days the AIF lost 23,000 men in an area 'more densely sown with Australian sacrifice than any other place on earth'. Five Victoria Crosses were won at Pozières, aptly enough by an Irishman, an Englishman, a New Zealander and two Australians. It was hardly surprising that at home volunteers were falling off. Such casualties, bearing in mind their proportion to the population, incurred at a distance so far from home, would be enough to shatter the morale of any army; but the AIF was astonishingly resistant.[10]

What, it might be asked, was it all for?

Australian war aims were never clearly defined, but it was well understood that they must include taking possession of the German Pacific colonies. When, therefore, Japanese forces took over the German colonies north of the Equator, Australian opinion became agitated. After the German capitulation, German New Guinea was defined as 'the whole of the German Possessions in the Pacific lately administered from Rabaul' – which included the islands now taken by the Japanese. It was well understood in Britain that this situation contained 'the material for a tragic row' and that the Australians 'must hold their hand somehow until we come to an understanding with the Japanese'. This was going to be difficult, since the Japanese had made it clear that they intended to hang on to their acquisitions, and Japan was an important contributor to the war effort; had not Japanese warships escorted the Anzac soldiers to Europe? Edwin Montagu, then acting as a sort of Cabinet odd-job man, took angry exception to the Colonial Secretary Lewis ('Lulu') Harcourt's April 1915 explanation of Australian concern: 'He . . . fears that the Australians may be angry if the Japanese get some of the Islands . . . and yet I think the Japanese have been far more useful to us in this war than the Australians and would have been still more useful but for Mr. Harcourt himself.'[11] Such concern was one motive for Hughes's acceptance of a British invitation to confer, which resulted in his arrival in Britain in March 1916. It was a critical time of the war: conscription, introduced in January 1916, was beginning to bite, the House of Commons had held its first secret session, General Townshend was forced to surrender 10,000 British troops to the Turks at Kut-al-Amara, opening a strategic gap to be plugged at great cost, the revived submarine attacks in the Atlantic were bringing alarming casualties, and the Dublin Easter Rising was brewing. Lloyd George was the coming man, later that year to succeed to the prime ministership. Lloyd George and Billy Hughes were an uncomfortably similar pair. Born within a few months of each other, schooled in Welsh Wales although neither was born in the Principality, both lawyers, radical politicians, successful wartime leaders, although both splintered their parties; both survived through the Second World War. Although both were tricky, unscrupulous politicians, provoking bitter enmity as well as fervent admiration, Hughes was never accused of the extent of corruption which characterized many of Lloyd George's actions, and he ended his life as plain William Morris Hughes.

Hughes's visit to London was indeed a personal triumph; with the enthusiastic backing of the Northcliffe press, Keith Murdoch acting as a go-between and unofficial adviser, the 'Little Digger' became something of a popular hero both in Britain and in France. The Melbourne *Age* perceptively, if polysyllabically, recorded:

If we search for the reason for these evanescent idolatries we shall find none stronger than the supreme need of the good natured British to find a lion ... Winston Churchill was under eclipse and Lloyd George's more turgid oratory was at a temporary discount. Lord Kitchener's star had paled and Mr. Asquith had refused to coruscate. The advent of the Australian Prime Minister was a god-send.[12]

Invited, as Sir Robert Borden of Canada had previously been, and as, more significantly, Jan Smuts was in the following year, to attend meetings of the War Cabinet, Hughes pushed the Australian point of view on the Pacific islands, but did not succeed in reaching a firm agreement. In truth, with the casualties on the Western Front reaching horrifying proportions, it was a little early to reach clear divisions of potential future spoils. Moreover, German diplomats had proposed a separate peace with Japan and Russia. Although Japan had dutifully informed her allies of her rejection of these approaches, the danger had been made clear. Hughes's visit to Britain gave him his first opportunity of playing a part on the international stage. A conference, to be held in Paris, had already been arranged in order to consider post-war economic policy in relation to a defeated Germany. Quite without precedent, and unexpectedly, Lloyd George announced in the House of Commons on 23 March that Hughes was to attend: 'I have never met an astuter man of business,' was Lloyd George's tribute to Hughes; and Hughes was to go as a representative, not of Australia, but of the British government itself, which his status as a Privy Counsellor made constitutionally possible. The other two members were Bonar Law, the future Tory Prime Minister, now Colonial Secretary, and Lord Crewe, former Viceroy of Ireland and Secretary of State for India, which gives an idea of the importance of the affair. Nervous of Hughes's opinion – well known to be adamant that 'any German influence must be extirpated from British trade' – Bonar Law attempted to ban Hughes from speaking when the conference began in June 1916. That was to demand the impossible, and so it proved. Hughes was instrumental in securing a final resolution which declared the Allied intention to prohibit trade with Germany completely 'for some years after the war'. It was a decision of doubtful wisdom, but Hughes's part was applauded vigorously in France and bitterly criticized in Germany. Australia was no longer just a name in the international arena, but a country with its own interests, and determined to pursue them.[13]

Back in Australia at the end of July, stimulated by his reception in Britain, where Lloyd George had been particularly supportive, Hughes was faced with the news that recruitment was falling off. Considering the massive effort that Australia had made by contributing some 400,000 volunteers at a time when the total population did not exceed 5 million, and that casualties both in Gallipoli and on the Western Front had been shockingly high – 5,000–6,000 in a single day (19 July) during the Somme offensive of summer 1916 – this was a hard proposal to sell. A 'hot time', Hughes predicted, writing to Keith Murdoch, by then firmly entrenched in the Northcliffe camp, subserviently smoothing 'my dear Chief', and acting as Hughes's personal liaison in London. The joint efforts of Prime Minister and journalist produced appeals to the Australian public, from such diverse individuals as the labour leader Arthur Henderson, Lloyd George, Aristide Briand, the French Prime Minister and from all the former Australian Prime Ministers, to permit conscription, as New Zealand had already done and as Canada was to do the following year; but the question was quite peculiarly contentious in Australia. Although it was a Labor government that had begun conscription into the militia in 1911, wartime conscription for overseas service remained a bitterly contested issue. Some emotion had been generated by the aftermath of the Dublin Rising, in which thirteen of the leaders had been executed (some 500, civilians and military, perished in the Rising itself), but perhaps as powerful were the arguments based on race. If white men were sent to the front, surely their place would be taken by the dreaded coloured immigrants? Hughes fought this by guaranteeing that 'no coloured or cheap labour would be allowed to enter Australia' during the war. A boatload of Maltese workers was received, given a dictation test in Dutch, and promptly expelled. Public opinion, and not only that of the radicals and socialists, was outraged, and the Maltese were allowed in.[14]

Realizing that a Bill was unlikely to pass though Parliament, Hughes appealed to the country in a national referendum, an extraordinary step, taken by no other country. All the efforts of the government, reinforced by wartime powers, were exerted, but the referendum was narrowly defeated in October 1916. Governor General Ferguson's analysis of the reasons for defeat included employers' fears that they would lose essential workers, the women's vote and the soldiers' dislike of their elite force becoming a conscript army. 'I told him so', replied Bonar Law, saying that Hughes had sown the seeds of suspicion when in London by associating himself with 'a certain section of the press' – meaning the Northcliffe newspapers.[15]

Ferguson could have added another factor to his list. The Catholic Archbishop of Melbourne, Dr Daniel Mannix, was opposed to the whole war which he condemned as 'a trade war', and although he was reproved almost unanimously by other Australian Catholics his influence was very considerable. Realizing the importance of the Irish vote, Hughes had pressed Lloyd George (Prime Minister from December 1916) to take some action such as implementing the Home Rule Act, which was already on the statute book, but whose enforcement had been postponed until the end of the war. Lloyd George confessed to the Ulster lawyer Edward Carson, a member of the close War Cabinet, that he was 'a coward then not to insist on a settlement at the time. It has done much harm in Australia.' During the conscription campaign Hughes had pulled no punches, and some of the blows he landed were well below any permissible belt; with the remorseless extension of call-up for home service military training already permitted, many Labor supporters were alienated. The bitterness had extended to the Labor Caucus, when a motion was moved that the Prime Minister 'no longer possesses the confidence of the party as leader'. At a stormy meeting on 14 November Hughes, finding 'the prospect of a modus vivendi . . . hopeless', and that 'owing to the fact that members were acting under instructions from outside organisations, and were impervious to all argument', was forced to resign from the party, accompanied by twenty-six other Labor MPs, thus mirroring the division that was even then taking place within the British Liberal Party, which left Lloyd George as coalition Prime Minister and Asquith leading a rump of Liberal purists. It was the first of three major Labor splits, and a significant one. Hughes's 'National Labor' Party governed with Liberal support until February 1917, when it merged with the Liberal Party to form the National Party with Hughes at its head. In the coalition he was far more than *primus inter pares*; only George Pearce, as Defence Minister, was more than tolerably competent.[16]

Four former Labor ministers resigned over the affair, but two, E. J. Russell and William Higgs, later followed Hughes into the National Party. The division in the rank and file ran deeper. A high proportion of those who abjured Hughes's leadership were Irish Catholics, whose influence was therefore considerably increased within the party. One error made in the campaign was the failure to exclude seminarians and teaching brothers from the draft, arousing deep concern in the hierarchy that the structure of Catholic education would be gravely damaged. Sectarianism had hitherto not played a conspicuous part in Australian politics but henceforward it was to become a significant party issue: Labor politicians tended to be Catholics, and their opponents Protestant; the next three Labor Prime Ministers were Catholic (John Curtin later rejected the Church) and Liberal leaders have been, more or less enthusiastically, Protestant although Joseph Lyons, of the United Australia Party, and Archie Cameron, leader of the Country Party, were both Catholic.[17]

It was not only conscription that presented a challenge to the coalition government, for, just as in Britain, the Australian war effort was hampered by strikes, starting in November 1916 with a miners' strike. Hughes would very much have wished to attend the Imperial War Conference planned for March 1917, which was to discuss strategy, possible terms of peace, Ireland, and the future of the German colonies, but, given the situation at home where an election was mandatory some time that year, he could not be spared. His absence was perhaps desirable, since the issue of the German Pacific colonies had already been decided in Japan's favour. Anxious both to ensure that Japan increased her naval contribution to the war effort, and that a deal be struck before America's entry into the war (which was judged imminent: in fact declared on 7 April, and certain to bring with it President Wilson's well-known resistance to Imperial territorial expansion), an agreement was reached on 14 February. Reluctantly preoccupied with electoral problems, Hughes had grudgingly assented to this 'secret Treaty', an assent that was later to embarrass him, in so far as Billy Hughes could ever be embarrassed.[18]

It did not, however, need Hughes's presence at the conference to gain one of the points he had long been insisting on, the desirability of having all Australian forces acting together, preferably under Australian command. The Canadians had already succeeded in this from the start of the war, and had gained both in efficiency and in reputation by it. Once again, in 1917,

consulting with each other about their common affairs',[22] and was to be achieved by terminating the old arrangement whereby Dominion Prime Ministers communicated with the British government only through their Governors General. Hughes required instead that direct communication be established with the British Prime Minister; the Governor General should cease to be responsible to the Colonial Office and become instead the 'King's Representative in the Commonwealth'.

Much could be said in favour of the existing system. Governors General were familiar faces in London, their strengths and weaknesses well understood. They could be, and almost always were, in near-daily touch with their Prime Ministers in the Executive Council, and could be relied upon to provide an unprejudiced view. Moreover, they could expect a reasonably long period in office (Ferguson, in the exceptional circumstances of wartime, held post for nearly seven years), while Australian governments had proved evanescent – Hughes's first government in 1915 was the eleventh since Federation, fifteen years previously. But Hughes intended to stay in office, and in fact did so, to 1922, and he insisted on this new status being recognized. It was duly accorded, subject to the qualification that such communications be limited to important matters, day-to-day business continuing to flow through the Governor General and Colonial Office. George Higinbotham's stand on constitutional principles in the 1860s had eventually been justified.

Hughes did not seek agreement for his next major initiative, which was to despatch Sir Henry Braddon as Trade Commissioner to the United States, although he was able to see that Braddon was properly furnished by the British government with letters of introduction. Ferguson was injured by an act he saw as undermining his own authority, and considered resigning, but was pressed to stay, both by the Colonial Office and by Hughes himself, who was conscious of Ferguson's value as an ally.[23]

Hughes's authority at the Imperial Conference was bolstered by the continued magnificent success of the Australian and New Zealand troops. In the Middle East the symbolic success of Jerusalem's capture had been followed by the complete destruction of the Turkish armies. On the Western Front, in August 1918 the British, Australians and Canadians broke the German lines, and enabled the cavalry, now accompanied by armoured cars, to sweep through. Almost Australia's last feat of arms was to rescue the newly arrived American divisions, bogged down near Saint-Quentin; in two months the Australians suffered more than 20,000 casualties but took 29,000 prisoners.

'That's about the size of it, Mr President'

Anticipating final defeat, and judging the American President to be a softer touch than the Europeans, the Germans appealed to Wilson for an armistice on 4 October. Without telling his allies, the President sent his own terms, the famous 14 points, on 8 October. Lloyd George and Marshal Foch the Supreme Commander of the Allied forces, were naturally annoyed, and Hughes was furious, launching a personal invitation to the French Prime Minister, Georges Clemenceau, to insist on a more rigorous settlement, and pressing for Australia's representation in any negotiations. In this he was supported by the Colonial Secretary, Walter Long, who felt that since Australian sacrifices during the war had been 'a good deal more than the Americans', Hughes had as much a right to participate as had President Wilson. (The comparison rather depends on who was counting; American deaths in action were 49,000, those of Australians 60,000, but Americans also had 57,000 dead from disease, mostly in the influenza epidemic of 1918–19.) Seeing this as just another complication in a difficult process – for if Australia was to be included in the peace negotiations then all the other Dominions would claim the same right – Lloyd George was reluctant; but Hughes was implacable. In letters to the press, and in speeches to sympathetic audiences, the 'Little Digger' hammered home his points:

we, who are conquerors, we, who have suffered so much, who have given up those rights for which we went to war, to have not set out in the bond [armistice] that the islands shall be ours, that our rights to make economic treaties should remain, that indemnities should be exacted, is to me inexplicable. I can only regret from the bottom of my heart that this thing should be been done. Australia stands after four years of dreadful war, her interests grievously imperilled, her rights of self government menaced, and with no provision made for indemnities.[24]

At home, Hughes's Cabinet colleagues were horrified; the Acting Prime Minister W. A. Watt, cabled to Hughes that his claim 'was unreasonable and cannot be supported by cabinet'. Ferguson considered that 'Hughes had done the most mischievous thing possible and exposed his flank to all his enemies in a deliberate endeavour to stir up bad blood between England and Australia . . . One can never forgive him for this despite his personal charm and friendliness', but concluded: 'But my heart warms to him now in his attacks on the "high falutin" of Wilson.'[25] The fight was, however, being won by Hughes. In November he was appointed Chairman, no less, of the British Committee appointed to consider the potential German liability for war indemnities, and he was acquiring powerful allies. Sir Robert Borden, the Canadian Prime Minister, infuriated by the decision to place Kaiser Wilhelm on trial without consultation with the Dominions in Cabinet, threatened to 'pack his trunk' and return to Canada. Smuts started his own hare by insisting on South Africa's right to absorb German South West Africa, with the result that in all discussions the future of South West Africa and the Pacific colonies were linked as a special case.

When the question of representation at the Peace Conference came to be considered, after President Wilson's arrival in Europe on December 1918, Hughes let rip. Sir Maurice Hankey, the Imperial Defence Committee Secretary, recorded:

The Cabinet were much impressed with the critical power of the Hughes speech . . . it was their first explanation of the reason why this man of frail physique, defective hearing and eccentric gesticulations had attained such a position of dominant influence in the Australian government. It was a fine specimen of ruthless and pungent analysis of President Wilson's claim to dictate to the countries who had borne the brunt of the fighting.

Hughes thought it intolerable that Wilson should attempt to dictate terms when the United States had participated for so short a time, but it was probably Borden's supportive intervention the following day (31 December) that was critical; Canada must have its own seat at the negotiating table, and if Canada, then also the other Dominions. Among other matters, the Cabinet resolved that:

(b) The British Dominions and India should in all respects have the same powers as, and be on equal footing at the Conference with Belgium and other Allied States . . .
(d) the Prime Ministers of the Dominions and the representatives of India should be placed on a panel from which part of the personnel of the British delegation could be filled according to the subject for discussion.[26]

Lloyd George, whose authority had been reinforced by a sweeping victory in the November general election (and Wilson's reduced by his contemporaneous loss of control in the United States House of Representatives) pressed the Dominion case on the Allies, who agreed that Canada, Australia and South Africa should each have two seats, and New Zealand and India one each; if these were combined with the British delegation, the Imperial bloc would have ten seats. When, in September 1919, the Prime Minister finally reported on the peace settlement to the Australian Parliament he claimed that 'Australia became a nation, and entered into a family of nations on a footing of equality. We had earned that, or rather our soldiers had earned it for us ... Australia had to press her views, and to endeavour to insist upon their acceptance by other nations. Without such representation that would have been impossible.' Billy Hughes was entitled to take some credit for that achievement, but it rested principally on the sacrifice of the Australian people.[27]

Hughes had, however, some unsettled business. Accepting only with reluctance the formula agreed between Britain and Japan in the 'Secret Treaty' of 1917, in which he had in fact previously acquiesced, he pressed for New Guinea and the Southern Pacific Islands to be annexed by Australia rather than transferred under some limited League of Nations mandate. Smuts, even more anxious for undisputed control of German South West Africa, proposed the introduction of a 'class C' mandate under which the mandatory would exercise full control and administer the territories under Australian and South African law respectively – which of course would give Australia the essential control over immigration. The point was only won after an acerbic exchange between Hughes and President Wilson in which the President taxed Hughes with presenting an 'ultimatum' to the conference; in response, Hughes curtly replied: 'That's about the size of it, Mr President.' Australia was now able to add the former German mandated territories to its existing colony of Papua, thus controlling all eastern New Guinea and the adjacent islands.[28]

On two other issues Hughes did not show up well. As chairman of the British delegation to the Reparations Committee Hughes insisted on presenting an enormous and crushing bill for indemnities to be paid by Germany. This was completely unrealistic and in stark contrast to the appeal of the South Africans to treat a vanquished Germany with as much humanity as Britain had extended to the defeated Boers only twelve years previously. His attempt was, however, understandable enough; both Britain and Australia suffered grave financial losses as a result of the war and of their sustained efforts to pay off the borrowings that had been entailed; Australia, which could submit justified claims for over £100 million, eventually received something just over £5 million.

Equally understandable, but bearing lethal consequences, was Hughes's persistence in upholding the White Australia policy. This plank of the Deakin settlement had the overwhelming support of Australian voters, and any relaxation would have seemed suicidal to Hughes's Cabinet colleagues. Not that Hughes himself needed convincing; the old trade unionist was as insistent on excluding labour competition as any Australian worker. The electorate, it seemed, had appreciated Hughes's record as a war leader. In the December 1919 election, the first at which the new system of preferential voting was used (see below), the Nationalists retained their overall majority over both the four small 'Country' parties, and Labor – the last still bitterly divided by the conscription controversy, and by continuing bickering between state parties.

The immediate problem lay with that valuable wartime ally, Japan, where public opinion was equally unanimous in demanding the League of Nations' Charter should include some acceptance of equal treatment for all, 'without making any distinction on account of their race or nationality', a provision which could bring the whole weight of the League to bear on Australian immigration policies. It might well have been that the Japanese government had no intention of interfering with other governments' immigration policies, since Japanese racialism and resistance to foreign influence was notorious; but, as the experienced director of military intelligence, Edmund Piesse pointed out, the Japanese negotiators at the League of Nations 'knew that the racial equality movement was supported by a society of patriots which had committed more than one political murder, and it seems probable that their refusal to exclude immigration from this amendment was due in part to fears for their own safety.'[29] Hughes was adamant, resisting pressure not only from Lloyd George, President Wilson, Sir Robert Borden and Smuts, but from the faithful Keith Murdoch. Botha himself confided in the Japanese representative Baron Makino: 'Strictly between ourslves I think he [Hughes] is mad.' Besides his own obstinacy, aided by selective deafness, Hughes had another weapon. Quite as opposed to Asiatic emigration, and readier to express their objections violently, were the West Coast Americans – and Hughes was very capable of selective leaks to the Californian press. Wilson was therefore compelled to back down, his emissary Colonel House urging Makino to drop his insistence on racial equality: 'He knew that no clause, no matter how mild and inoffensive, could satisfy Hughes, who had made it clear that he would raise a storm of protest in the Dominions and in the "western part of the United States", something neither House nor Wilson would relish.'[30]

In the end Hughes was successful, but at a cost. The Japanese obtained significant benefits from allowing their opposition – which had led them to the brink of refusing to join the League – to subside. Their claims to the Chinese provinces of Kiachow and Shantung were explicitly acknowledged and there was an understanding that they would be allowed 'much the same guardianship over East Asia as the Americans asserted over Latin America', an implicit recognition of which later Japanese governments were to take unscrupulous advantage. Yet both Hughes and Pearce were conscious of the benefits that had been gained by the Japanese alliance; anxious not to lose these, they attempted damage limitation. At the Imperial Conference in June 1921, when the renewal of the alliance was discussed, Hughes asked 'What is the substantial alternative to the renewal of the Treaty? The answer is that if Australia was asked whether she would prefer America or Japan as an ally her choice would be America. But that choice is not offered her.' The Canadian Prime Minister Arthur Meighen was determined to follow the United States line, which ruled out any binding treaty with Japan. Hughes responded: 'Now let me speak plainly to Mr Meighen on behalf of Australia. I for one will vote against any renewal of the Anglo-Japanese Alliance upon one condition and one only, and that is that America gives us that assurance of safety which our circumstances absolutely demand.' This Australians were not then, nor for many years later, to receive.

The two Dominions were divided by geographical imperatives. Self-interest obliged Canada to follow the lead of her great southern neighbour, while Australia looked apprehensively to the north. When Meighen violently attacked the Japanese 'activities in Korea, Formosa and Manchuria', Hughes countered by saying that Canada counted on the Americans, but 'America speaks with two voices'. Dealing with Britain and Canada, Hughes did not avail himself of the more histrionic techniques employed when Australian security was at stake. Japan had been a reliable ally for twenty years. It could not be wise to 'alienate by a rude and abrupt refusal to renew this Treaty, our nearest neighbours, a great and powerful nation, whose circumstances compel her to seek new territory for her overcrowded population, and who has behind her effective means of making us feel the full force of her resentment'.[31]

Hughes had a powerful case. The war had been fought mainly in the Levant and in Europe and it had taken the massed resources of the Western Allies, plus the Dominions and a contribution from such other countries as Brazil and Portugal, to overcome Germany and Austria. There had been virtually no action in the Pacific region, where security had been guaranteed by the Japanese. Were there to be another European war with a similar balance of forces, the Japanese position could be vital. Britain simply could not deploy enough resources to counter hostile navies in the Pacific as well as in the Atlantic and the Indian oceans, especially in view of the now proven effectiveness of submarine warfare (and even more with the still unappreciated threat of carrier-borne aircraft) while the British army would never match the potential strength of the major European land powers. Australia's security had been greatly improved by the 'C' mandates in New Guinea and the Islands, but ultimate reliance still had to be placed on the

Royal Navy, and Admiral Beatty himself admitted that 'If Japan seized the opportunity of aggressive action in the Pacific at a time when the situation at Home was threatened from another quarter, reinforcements capable of dealing with the whole of Japan's main forces could not immediately be spared'. It would be up to the forces based on the impregnable new station of Singapore, together with whatever could be provided from Hong Kong, to hold off an attack. The only likely aggressor was Japan, and if Japan could not be secured as an ally, then America would be the only hope; and America was a much less willing supporter of Australia than Britain.

Under the Republican administration of the raffish and corrupt Warren Gamaliel Harding, the United States reversed Wilson's previous decision to build a fleet of equivalent size to Britain's, which would have ensured that, together, control of the Pacific could remain in Anglo-American hands. Britain was equally ready to reduce post-war expenditure, and welcomed an invitation to an international conference in Washington between November 1921 and February 1922. At Washington, Australia had no separate voice, with Pearce heading the Australian section of an imperial delegation led by Lord Curzon. British policy was to replace the Anglo-Japanese alliance with a tripartite pact which would include the United States, but this was rejected by both the Americans and the Japanese. In its place, no fewer than seven separate agreements were reached by the participants, who also included France and Italy. A Quadruple Pacific Treaty included France, and a Quintuple Treaty brought in Italy as well – neither of them more than agreements to agree. The central provision was a limitation of the building of capital ships – battleships and battlecruisers over 10,000 tons – in the proportions Britain 5, United States 5, Japan 3, the other naval powers having less. Japanese opinion was somewhat miffed at this implied inferiority, but when taken with the fact that the United States was concerned with two oceans and Britain with three, while Japan had only the Pacific in its sphere of influence, the proposal was in fact favourable to Japan – especially when combined with the Anglo-American agreement on restricting the expansion of their naval bases, although with Singapore and Port Moresby specifically excluded. Finally, a comprehensive Nine-Power Treaty bound the signatories, including Japan, to respect the independence and integrity of China. Taken with the other agreement to ban gas warfare and submarine attacks on merchant shipping, the Washington treaties were welcomed with international enthusiasm; Japan promptly returned the port of Tsingtao, acquired under the Versailles Treaty, and renounced the concessions previously agreed. From an Australian point of view there were grounds for only cautious optimism. It is perhaps possible that had Hughes, in his best hectoring form, been present at Washington the result might have been different, but as it was the effectiveness of British protection that could be afforded to Australia had been dangerously diminished; and the vague provisions of the multiple treaties were totally ineffective, as was subsequently proved.[32]

Before losing power, as he was to do in the 1922 election, Hughes was able to score one triumph against Lloyd George and again to demonstrate Australian independence. Lloyd George, beset by scandal over the sale of honours, by gloomy economics and an Irish civil conflict, hoped to retrieve the situation by demonstrating his old powers as a leader in war. A Turkish revolution had brought Mustapha Kemal Pasha – Ataturk, the founder of modern Turkey – to power, with the tacit support of Russia, France and Italy, and the violent resistance of the Greeks in Asia Minor. Lloyd George alone backed the Greeks, now desperate in the face of Kemal's successful armies, which had swept their forces from Asia and massacred thousands of Armenians and Greeks in Smyrna (although the Greeks had perpetrated previously a number of rather less spectacular massacres of their own). By the post-war settlement the region around Istanbul and the Straits had been declared neutral territory, garrisoned by the Allies of whom only Britain – and there practically only Lloyd George and Churchill – wanted to take their responsibility to the brink of resisting the Turks. Their only potential source of support seemed to be the Dominions, to whom appeals were accordingly sent, but apart from New Zealand and Newfoundland the response was reluctant. Hughes was particularly indignant. In spite of his hard-won concession that the Dominions must be consulted before such decisions were taken there had been no such consultation; worse, the appeal had been leaked to the newspapers; and, a particularly sensitive point, the storm centre was Chanak, the southern shore of the Dardanelles, just over the water from Gallipoli, that sacred ground.

In spite of his real anger, Hughes immediately announced publicly that, if needed, Australian troops would indeed be sent to help Britain defend 'the freedom of the straits and the sanctity of the Gallipoli Peninsula'. His wrath was reserved for his secret official communication:

This in a matter of such grave importance is most unfortunate as it precludes that full and judicial consideration of the position by Commonwealth which is its clear right as a national Government. It is not right that a Dominion should be stampeded into action by premature statements in the Press disclosing a position which, even admitting its gravity, is not set out in detail, and upon which no information had been previously received by the Commonwealth Government suggesting the probability of the Empire being involved in hostilities . . . The point the Commonwealth Government desires to emphasize most strongly is this, that consultation with the Dominions ought to take place before any action is taken or irrevocable decision is made by Britain, as then and then only can our voices be heard and our counsels heeded. Either the Empire is one and indivisible or it is nothing. If it is only another name for Britain, and the Dominions are to be told that things are done after they have been done, and that Britain had decided upon war, and are often asked whether they wish to be associated with her and to stand by her side, when they have in fact no other alternative, then it is perfectly clear, the relations between the Dominions and Britain being what they are, that all talk about the Dominions have a real share in deciding foreign and Imperial policy is empty air.

Fortunately, the crisis was defused by the sensible British Commander in Chanak, General Sir Charles Harington, who turned a Nelsonian eye to a Cabinet instruction to present Kemal with an ultimatum, thereby allowing yet another international conference to succeed in effecting a solution which gave the Turks all they wanted.[33]

Setting the Mould

Australia, Britain and the United States all suffered from undistinguished governments in the immediate post-war years. Bonar Law, Baldwin and Ramsay MacDonald, Warren Harding and Calvin Coolidge, all failed to rescue their countries from economic crises, but while in America the near-revolutionary figure of Franklin Roosevelt generated a national revival, both Britain and Australia continued under leaders at best mediocre right through the 1930s.

The war shattered all previous ideas of international relations: perhaps 20 million lives had been lost in a seismological catastrophe which might have been avoided if the mechanics of diplomacy and the entrenched concepts which lay beyond them had been less clumsy and the passions to which they gave rise more measured. A new society seemed to be forming, slowly and messily, in the old imperial Russia, and new nations were emerging. All the participants had been rudely shaken into a fresh awareness, and faced daunting problems of reconstruction, social and material. America and Australia had been spared material damage, but Australia had incurred tragic human losses. One hundred and fifty years of peaceful development (few at that time considered the Aboriginal point of view) had been brutally brought to an end, and Australia faced its own peculiar problems. The population was far too small to provide a tax base strong enough to finance the demands on the infrastructure imposed by a population concentrated in the coastal cities and so widely scattered over the immense distances of the interior. Wildly inflated estimates of the population increasing to 100 million by the end of the century inflated public expenditure schemes beyond any reasonable expectation of funding, and since development was a state, rather than a Commonwealth, responsibility, they stretched state finances dangerously. Nor had the old colonial rivalries subsided as states contested with each other for bigger and better schemes. Indeed, these became more strident with demands for new states to be formed in northern New South Wales, northern Queensland, Western Australia, and even the Riverina; they culminated in a royal commission presided over by Judge Cohen, designed to administer euthanasia to such schemes. It was not the last of such inquiries, for the issue refused to simmer down. Western Australia indeed went to the length of holding a referendum in 1933 in which a large majority voted for secession from the Commonwealth and the state's re-establishment as a self-governing colony.

Perhaps the most damaging, and longest, continuing restriction of economic improvement was the built-in effect of constantly increasing wages and associated costs authorized by arbitration boards, which in turn led to employers' demands for increased tariff protection. When economic recession obliged the boards actually to reduce wages, industrial conflict was inevitable. Australia might well lead the world in the support given by the state to its citizens, but there was a price to pay.

Post-war pressures were demonstrated on Armistice Day 1918 itself, when even placid Adelaide was torn by strikes and riots. The diagnosis was ominous, the strike being blamed on 'Bolshevism' – 'anti-war radicals and revolutionaries, anti-conscriptionists and Irish nationalists, pacifists, shirkers and strikers … all somehow related in a conspiratorial network'. Hughes was successful in ensuring that Australian servicemen were quickly sent home and demobilized, and went out of his way to work with Gilbert Dyett, the chairman of the Returned Services League (the Returned Soldiers' and Sailors' Imperial League of Australia). A Royal Commission was appointed to report on the relationship between wages and the cost of living, finding a wide gap. The cost of living, for example, had risen in Melbourne from £3. 7s. 9d. per week in 1914 for a family of five, to £5. 16s. 6d., and wages – the base wage stood at £4.2s. – had not nearly kept pace. The Arbitration Council then agreed that wages should be automatically adjusted to reflect the cost of living; it was another protection for workers, but also another rigidity built into Australian competitiveness.[34]

The Labor Party wanted to go much further. Its October 1921 conference carried the threatening, if vague, resolution to pursue 'The socialisation of industry, production, distribution and exchange', modified by explanations that this was not to be taken too seriously. A very similar experience was afflicting the British Labour Party at the same time, which resulted in the inclusion of the famous clause 4 of its 1918 constitution, in very similar terms, an undertaking which was to remain until 1995. A useful weapon to opponents in both Australia and Britain, the commitment was defended vigorously by only a small, if active minority, and its implementation carefully limited by Labour administrations.

Australia had indeed suffered terrible manpower losses during the war. Over half the eligible male population enlisted, and 80 per cent of these served overseas, mainly in France. Nearly 60,000 never returned; another 145,000 were wounded or gassed. Proportionate to the population Australia lost 1.2 per cent – only Britain, at 1.6 per cent and New Zealand at 1.5 per cent were higher – and Australian casualties in action were a higher proportion than any other of the Empire countries – 64.98 per cent of those embarked. The costs of the war were similarly great; the total public debt, which stood at £337 million at the outbreak of war, had risen to some £700 million at its end.[35]

However, unlike the European Allies, France and Britain in particular, Australia had many sources of post-war resilience. Industry had expanded somewhat during the war, both by military expenditure and the need to provide domestic substitutes for imported items – Australian manufacture of pianos, hitherto a German import, being one clear example – but large-scale production failed to develop, and the economy remained dependent on abundant mineral resources and a flourishing agriculture. Jobs needed to be found for the returning servicemen – 166,000 arrivals in 1919, including some ten thousand immigrants – and these could not be provided by displacing wartime women workers, for very few women had been employed in the defence industries. Optimistically, and following the principle that the white population must be expanded, the Hughes government encouraged immigration by devolving responsibility to the states, who were given substantial financial inducements to settle newcomers on the land. The response was lacklustre; only New South Wales, Victoria and Western Australia took advantage of the scheme, and New South Wales used only £100,000 of an allocated £6 million. Other states were suspicious, preferring to settle their own citizens rather than encouraging immigrants, even when they came bearing Federal gifts.

Queensland, faithful to its role as odd man out, proved distinctly difficult. On 23 March 1919 shots fired from the headquarters of the Russian
Workers Association began a week of riots between returned servicemen
and assorted left-wingers. The left-wingers, however, held the reins of
government with the brutally realistic Edward ('Red Ted') Theodore in
charge. The Labor-dominated Assembly persuaded the Lieutenant Governor, William Lennon, a former Labor minister quickly appointed during
a gubernatorial interregnum, to flood the Legislative Council with reliable
nominees (who included a Queen Street pieman). This 'suicide squad'
promptly abolished themselves, making Queensland the only Australian
state which still has a single-chamber legislature; supposedly more democratic, such an arrangement could easily become demagogic, which it
duly did.

The December general election of 1922 modelled future Australian politics for years. Apathy was widespread, with so low a turnout as to provoke
the institution of compulsory voting before the next election. Labor
remained unelectable: one member, the former minister Hugh Mahon, was
expelled for attacking the British government as 'a gang of false-hearted
hypocrites' while another one, Michael Considine, had been gaoled for
saying 'bugger the King, he is a bloody German bastard', sentiments which
did not go down well with many returned servicemen. Electoral fraud had
long been common in New South Wales, but Labor's introduction in trade
union elections of ballot boxes with sliding panels was thought to be going
too far; in Queensland the Labor government had practically to abdicate in
the face of Caucus dictates; Theodore resigned in disgust to take up Federal
politics from a New South Wales base. Victorian Labor was beginning to
take the palm for distinguished corruption under the leadership of John
Wren, the nearest Australian equivalent to a Tammany Hall boss.[36]

The election lost the Nationalist Party its previous overall majority,
leaving the Country Party with the balance of power. Originating as the
Farmers' & Settlers' Association and gathering to itself state-based parties,
the Country Party had the defects of any special interest group. Never
entirely an employers' association, for many of its demands for better
rural services in communications, health and education were very generally
supported, the party was always instinctively on the political right. Its
policies varied with agricultural economics; when times were good, any
government interference was abominated; if markets failed, then help was
demanded – and, in the shape of export subsidies and the foundation of
cooperative marketing organizations, such help was frequently constructive.
Without any distinctive philosophical or intellectual structure, although

perhaps not quite as described, 'a mob of disgruntled, wire-whiskered bushies', the Country Party was inevitably pragmatist, an ideal coalition partner, but with no potential for forming a national government.[37]

This pragmatism inspired Dr Earle Page, the party's leader from April 1921, to define their aims as being those who would 'switch on the lights when the burglar is about, to make him drop the loot'. Page, whose family were established in the little town of Grafton, 450 miles north of Sydney, had personal experience of rural disadvantages and his energy, reinforced by a reckless – even vicious – audacity, made him a formidable party politician; but he remained essentially, for better and worse, a country doctor and enterprising businessman. Page refused to serve in any government headed by Hughes – the two were too alike for comfort – and he drove a hard bargain with Hughes's successor as leader of the National Party, the ex-serviceman, Cambridge blue, Stanley Melbourne Bruce, later Lord Bruce of Melbourne. With only twelve members – the Nationalists had 31 – the Country Party was nevertheless allocated five of the eleven portfolios, and Page himself was appointed Deputy Prime Minister. Hughes, nursing the bitterest of grudges, was consigned to the back benches. Always anti-Labor, the Country Party was nevertheless by no means invariably in accord with their fellow-conservatives in the National Party.

The coalition administration in power between February 1923 and October 1929 is usually known as the Bruce–Page ministry, with good reason. Bruce had all the personal dignity and air of authority that the frenetic little surgeon lacked, a prudent appreciation of the possible, and a flair for international relations, but depended on Page's energetic command of detail. For sixteen of the next nineteen years Labor was kept out of office by similar right-wing coalitions, combinations between a classic moderate conservative party, under the names of 'Nationalist', 'United Australia Party', and, eventually, 'Liberal' supported by a special-interest group representing non-metropolitan electors, generally somewhat to the right of the Liberals.

The electoral advantage given to non-Labor parties was reinforced by the unyielding monolithic nature of the Australian Labor Party itself. Clinging to its tradition of insisting that the party Caucus elect not only the leader, but the Cabinet and shadow Cabinet members, hampered those Labor governments that did succeed in being elected, and pushed dissidents into opposing camps. Three of the non-Labor Prime Ministers during the first forty years of the Commonwealth – Hughes, Lyons and Cook – began their political careers in the Labor Party.[38]

Another constant factor was the essentially bipartisan nature of many domestic policies. No right-wing government queried the essential conditions of the Deakin settlement – conditions which amounted, at that time, to a decidedly liberal social programme. Opposition ingenuity was taxed to find a platform which might offer more to their proletarian supporters and which could be presented as financially viable. To gain power, Labor had to rely mainly on discontent with the government convincing the electorate that it was time for 'Buggins' turn'. It was not until after the long twilight of the Liberal Party, which culminated in the Gough Whitlam Labor victory of December 1972, that the conservative coalition ceased to regard itself as the natural party of government; the half century after 1922 saw only just over ten years of Labor government under three Prime Ministers.

Labor had its work cut out to recover from the split over conscription, which had divided the party on sectarian lines, many of the insistent anticonscriptionists having been Catholic, with influential hierarchical support. Hughes's supporters followed him into the National Party, leaving Labor disproportionately Catholic. A revival of Labor's fortunes may have been helped by the introduction of compulsory voting, initiated by Queensland in 1915, and which was followed nine years later by a similar measure, rushed through the Commonwealth Parliament, without much discussion or a division, by the useful workhorse Senator Herbert Payne of Tasmania, who believed that his measure would ensure that 'in a short time there will be a wonderful improvement in the political knowledge of the people'. Since the percentage of those who voted in the previous Tasmanian Senate election of 1922 was only 45.63 per cent, the lowest of any state, Senator Payne may have been unduly sensitive, and his expectations were to be sadly disappointed. Electoral apathy should act as a warning sign to politicians that they are seen by the electorate as irrelevant, and artificial stimulation of interest can be dangerous. On the other hand, compulsory voting ensured that women, previously often unenthusiastic voters, were called upon to cast their votes, although this did not seem to make much difference. Women tended to be more conservative and generally voted for the same party as their husbands, parties were reluctant to adopt female candidates and independent women candidates were very rare indeed.[39]

Any advantage compulsory voting may have given to Labor was eroded by another innovation. The survival of coalitions was much assisted by the replacement of the traditional first-past-the-post system of voting by one of 'preferential voting' in 1918 for both houses. By this, voters place a number opposite each candidate in order of their preference. Only if a candidate obtains an absolute majority of first preferences is he elected; if not, the candidate with fewest first votes is eliminated and the second preferences distributed. Carried far enough it is quite possible for a candidate with most first preferences *not* to win. Electors, if they could work their way through the complex voting papers, could therefore vote for both coalition candidates in the knowledge that their votes would not be wasted. Labor voters were much less likely to want to give second preferences to a non-Labor candidate. When this was combined with compulsory voting a powerful advantage was handed to right-wing parties.

Labor was also afflicted by another split, one over communism, encouraged by the emergence of Soviet Russia on the international scene, anathema to most of the stolid trade unionists who dominated the party, and truly anathema to those Catholics who heeded the Church's condemnation of communism as an atheistical materialistic creed. The outcome of the fight against communism was never in doubt. The Communist Party of Australia's first manifesto, suffused with the customary jargon of 'toiling masses', 'the overthrow of all the political machinery of the system' and the 'Dictatorship of the Proletariat' was never going to appeal to a society in which the worker was, by the standards of the day, remarkably well protected – child allowances and pensions all going up, house-ownership was becoming the norm, and unions were able to deliver a powerful industrial punch. Theodore had no difficulty in having a motion carried by the 1924 Federal Labor conference that 'No member of the Communist party be admitted to the Labor Party'. Australian unions could, however, be quite militant enough without communist reinforcements: indeed, union power seemed to be so dangerous (although in fact, compared with Britain or the United States, strikes in Australia were considerably less worrisome) that the Bruce–Page government resorted to that last desperate strait, a referendum. Influenced by the cold and authoritarian Attorney General, John Latham, Page lashed out against unions, attempting to deport two 'agitators' by means of an amended Immigration Act, altering the Crimes Act to suppress communist activities, which included making even advocating a strike under certain circumstances illegal, the Navigation Act to quell marine union activities, and the Arbitration Act to allow enforcement of court orders. Like its predecessor of 1919, the September 1926 referendum culminated in failure. Whatever the merits of the government's case, it is likely that many disgruntled electors, forced to the poll under financial penalties, would simply vote 'agin the government'.[40]

Extending the powers of central government was certainly desirable. Since states were responsible for development projects some vied with their neighbours to construct the biggest and the best. Victoria and New South Wales both built ambitious water-control projects, which contributed to the eventual exhaustion of the Murray River, today in danger – like the Orange River in South Africa – of never quite reaching the sea and with its waters reaching dangerous levels of salinity. Electricity generation was expanded for the electrification of the extensive suburban railways, to replace steam power in factories, and to provide domestic power and light. All states extended their railway system, thus meeting another Country Party demand, although South Australia, relying on an American consultant, ordered loco-motives from the United States that were too heavy to run on much of the existing track. Reliance on imported machinery remained very high; in so far as Australian industry developed, it was in the assembly of imported parts. Both Ford and General Motors established Australian factories, but even the sheet steel for car bodies had to be imported. Confiding in the protection offered to industry by the tariff, the states concentrated on settling returned servicemen and immigrants on the land, it being believed at the time that human felicity was best attained by tilling the soil (or in England by breeding chickens). Such settlement would bring the extra advantage of concentrating the rural population instead of its remaining dispersed in the pastoral areas. Queensland attempted to provide land by inflicting punitive charges on the pastoralists, a move stopped by the courts, and nowhere were the plans a general success. Western Australia tried establishing communal labour camps to clear land for dairy farming, while Victoria developed its brown coal mines; brown coal being a difficult fuel, little in demand, the project proved uneconomic. The great success in agriculture was in the capital- rather than labour-intensive wheatfields, where the total cultivated area rose from 9 million acres in 1920 to 18 million at the end of the decade.

'Men, money and markets' was Bruce's slogan, for the success of which the three constituents had to be balanced, and this was not achieved. Over 260,000 British immigrants arrived in the decade after 1921, the great majority of whom were absorbed into the general labour force, which, considering the expense of the land settlements, was just as well. State officials claimed that they had spent £278 million on soldier settlement, and although the Federal commissioner's calculation was somewhat less, either sum amounted to nearly half the total cost of the war debts. Money flowed, mainly from London, to finance the cost of the improving infrastructure and to provide consumer credits; by 1928 the public debt had risen to over £1,200 million, and this was in now overvalued pounds sterling. It was in the provision of markets, that essential third factor, that the Federal government failed. World commodity prices fell throughout the 1920s, more steeply towards the end of the period, and Australia could offer little in the way of exports other than her traditional farm and mineral deposits

– these last now much less in demand. Any solution to economic problems, it was generally accepted, had to be found within the Empire, and in 1925 this led to a decision with serious consequences. Britain had abandoned the 'gold standard' – essentially a method of fixing sterling against the dollar – in 1919, and in 1925 decided to return to this system, which had the great advantage of providing stable international exchange rates. Winston Churchill, the Chancellor of the Exchequer, had his doubts, but was persuaded by conventional wisdom. Whatever the merits, the entry rate fixed for sterling was too high, by some 10 per cent, a fact pointed out at the time by John Maynard Keynes. Since Canada and the major European trading nations had already reverted to the gold standard, Australia had little choice but to follow, and similarly overvalued its pound. Imports from all countries other than Britain therefore became cheaper by that amount, and Australian exports comparatively dearer, beginning the trend, as Keynes had warned, towards 'unemployment and downward adjustments of wages and prolonged strikes'.[41]

As the day of reckoning loomed near it was Earle Page, as Treasurer, who had to cope. By threatening to stop payments to the states – New South Wales was particularly recalcitrant – Page forced an agreement in December 1927 whereby all loans were to be negotiated through a Loans Council. In this way £972 million of state debts were consolidated into Federal borrowings, which ought to have greatly improved Australian borrowing powers. This time the necessary referendum received a convincing majority, but the anticipated benefits did not appear, largely since the national finances were not placed under the control of a true central bank, which indeed did not exist. Some progress had been made by reconstituting the Commonwealth Bank with 'some vague and ineffectual central banking functions', including note-issuing and discounting power, but it was not given the necessary authority over the banking system.[42]

What eventually proved fatal to the Bruce–Page ministry was its one attempt to roll back the Deakin settlement. In September 1929, after two more general election victories (in 1925 and 1928), the government struck out. Keynes's dire forecast was being neatly exemplified. Unemployment at over 200,000, or 8 per cent of the workforce, was followed by strikes of dockers and timber-workers, and a lockout of coalminers, all caused by workers' failure to accept reductions in Federal wage awards, during which readily available blackleg labour was harassed and assaulted and had their homes bombed. Seeking greater control, Bruce introduced a Bill to transfer the Commonwealth Conciliation and Arbitration Powers to the states. Scenting an opportunity for revenge, Billy Hughes held secret talks with

Theodore to prepare a Keynesian economic plan with which to tempt Nationalist waverers. In a tense vote over an unrelated issue – the Maritime Industries Bill – during which it is said that Hughes stood guard over one uncertain member in the billiard room to prevent him being 'got at' during the dinner break, the government was defeated.[43] Bruce was granted a dissolution by the obedient Governor General, the unremarkable Lord Stonehaven, but only of the House of Representatives: the subsequent election on 12 October 1929 returned a Labor government under James Scullin, with an impressive majority, 47 of the 75 seats – but with only 7 of the 36 Senators Labor's situation resembled that of the Colonial governments in the previous century when radical Assemblies faced conservative Councils.

Labor's Death Wish

Bruce, rejected even in his own constituency, was given unequivocal notice to quit. Hughes, expelled from the Nationalists, was prepared to support Scullin, but since portfolios were allocated by the still-resentful Caucus, had no hope of a Cabinet post – and Caucus had given Scullin some very difficult colleagues. The beginning of the Great Depression was the worst possible time for an untried and inexperienced administration to gain office, and Scullin was faced with a more than common set of problems. What Australian Labor desperately needed was an honest, decent and reliable leader, not implicated in the scandals and dissensions that had harassed the party in opposition. These qualities Scullin provided in abundance; a devout Catholic, with an irreproachable family life, he was radical enough to satisfy most left-wingers, at least until the harsh reality of power began to make itself felt.

The Melbourne *Argus* was right when its leader of 15 October 1929 stated baldly:

There is nothing more certain than that the Labor party cannot confer any advantages upon its supporters at the present time. There is no money for the purpose, and if it endeavoured to squeeze further resources from the taxpayers it would quickly find itself deprived of many of the forces that helped to place it in power. A policy of retrenchment is equally impossible for the same reason.

Almost immediately the effects of the Great Depression's onset began to be felt. Wool and wheat prices fell, and the industries encouraged by tariffs during the 1920s faced growing competition. The miners' strike continued, and the Labor government, unable to redeem a rash election promise to pay the full wage-rates demanded, was forced to watch the miners go back to work on the owners' conditions. Another proof of government power-lessness was provided by the forced removal of homeless unemployed men from their camps on Sydney's Domain, which infuriated the *Labor Daily*: 'EVICTED AND HARRIED LIKE DOGS IN CITY ... GOVERNMENT MAKES WAR ON STARVING. Mighty Ukase goes forth to "CLEAR OFF" OUTCASTS IN LAST STAGES OF DISTRESS.'

Australia's problems might well have baffled a more experienced adminis-tration. Unemployment was shooting up, to reach nearly half a million in 1931, although the true total was probably a good deal higher as workers made do with part-time jobs. Conditions experienced in England, mainly in the traditional mining and engineering industries of South Wales and Tyneside, were repeated all over Australia. The historian Manning Clark, who was there at the time, gave an impassioned account of conditions in Sydney:

Men and women, mad with hunger, were ferreting about in gutters and garbage bins in Sydney for scraps of food. To collect the dole, men and women stood for hours in chilly, draughty places herded like wild beasts. Government officers mocked them. The unkind branded them as the 'sussos'. The coal miners and their families on the northern coalfields were close to starvation. One unemployed ex-digger handed back the medal he had received from a 'grateful country' for his service in the war. Albert Jacka, a winner of the Victoria Cross, was knocking on suburban doors, and pleading with housewives to buy his soap.[44]

Remedying such horrors was negated by the government's inability to borrow; as the cost of servicing existing debt neared the frightening equivalent of half all Australia's export earnings, access to capital markets dried up. What reductions in expenditure could be envisaged were brutally effected; defence expenditure, which included the construction of the majes-tic Canberra War Memorial, was slashed from £6.54 million to £3.86 million. Some solutions were rejected by the Senate, whose conservative members proved much more anxious to destroy the government than to assist its efforts. A wheat marketing Bill, which might have dramatically increased wheat exports, and a measure to modernize the Commonwealth Bank, were both blocked, but it was Scullin's own colleagues who caused most damage.

The brunt of the government's difficulties naturally fell upon the Treasurer Ted Theodore, designated as his deputy by Scullin. 'Carefully attired, aloof, grave and measured in manner', with an 'air of brooding strength and confident grasp of the world at large', Theodore was an imaginative and constructive political economist, by some way the most competent available; but he was shunted off into a siding during a Royal Commission inquiry investigating his complicity in a mining fraud. During the Treasurer's absence, after 9 July 1930, his place was taken by the amiable Tasmanian Joseph Lyons, who came to occupy a place in Australian history not unlike that of Ramsay MacDonald in Britain. The administration was further weakened by Scullin's decision to go to England for the 1930 Imperial Conference, where he hoped, among other objectives, to play a part in restoring the confidence of the London bankers. (James Fenton, the Minister for Trade, acted as Prime Minister during Scullin's visit to London.)

A preliminary step in this direction had been made by the despatch of a British adviser, Sir Otto Niemeyer, a senior Treasury official and member of the League of Nations Financial Committee (and not, as some Australian writers have it, a banker, except in so far as he had been a few months previously appointed to the board of a French bank). Reporting in August 1930, Niemeyer presented the recommendations prompted by current orthodoxy, and even then being advocated by the British Labour government; financial stability was to be restored by strict controls and balanced budgets. It is doubtful whether the ministers understood much of the situation; in an unkind mixed metaphor Niemeyer described Scullin and Lyons as being 'entirely at sea . . . like a couple of rabbits popping their heads out of the hole'. Obediently accepted by both the Commonwealth government and the only two state Labor Premiers then in power, those of South Australia and Victoria, the Niemeyer scheme was violently attacked by Labor's left wing.[45]

Such resentment assisted the forceful Jack Lang, Labor Premier in New South Wales 1925–7, to regain power with a convincing majority, and his victory brought a new stimulus to the objectors. Quite unable to stem the flood, Lyons and Fenton had to stand helplessly aside as power drained from the government to the party Caucus, which in a tumultuous four-day meeting rejected the Niemeyer plans.

Lyons was furious at this seizure of executive power, and refused to obey Caucus's orders. 'Trembling with anger', he declared: 'I will not do it . . . I will go out of public life first.' The absent Scullin concurred, cabling that he would not accept a course he saw as 'dishonest and disastrous' and rebuked his colleagues: 'Our government floated a loan and guaranteed the public a safe investment. Thousands of people withdrew their savings from the Savings Bank to assist the Labor Government. To default on this loan would weaken the value of their investment: would destroy public

confidence, and would delay for years the restoration of economic prosperity.'[46] Leaving his self-imposed exile, before he was found not guilty on
the fraud charge, Theodore was able to persuade Caucus to accept an
alternative plan, which required the Commonwealth Bank to provide credit
for services and public works. In the meantime the repayment of government
debt due in December should simply be postponed for a year. A few years
later, when the works of John Maynard Keynes had been absorbed, such
proposals would have seemed eminently sensible, but in 1930 were taken
as near-revolutionary.

On his return in January 1931 Scullin was able to secure a semblance
of order, restoring Theodore to his post as Treasurer, an action which,
interpreted by Lyons and Fenton as gross ingratitude and an unacceptable
U-turn, led both men to resign. Compared with the ructions about to be
caused by Jack Lang this was a minor upset. A difficult man to classify,
personally formidable, dour and aggressive, on the right wing of his party
but a radical reformer, with a ferocious personal ambition that could lead
him to the brink of violence, Lang had some things in common with his
contemporary Benito Mussolini. On 9 February 1931 he 'stunned' the Labor
Premiers' conference by a proposal that Australia should refuse to pay
interest on British bonds, and restrict interest on domestic government
borrowing to 3 per cent. Furthermore, Lang would secure the safe seat of
East Sydney for one of his own nominees, Eddie Ward, pledged to implement
the 'Lang plan'. Both the plan and Ward were decisively rejected by the
parliamentary Labor Party, whereupon Lang's supporters in Parliament,
five in the House of Representatives and two in the Senate, left Labor to
form their own faction.

At the other end of the party spectrum, Lyons, Fenton and their supporters, convinced that economic salvation depended on accepting the
Niemeyer plan, moved to unite with the Nationalists in forming another
new party, to become, on 3 May, the United Australia Party (UAP). Too
late to prevent the split, Scullin belatedly decided to return to the orthodox
deflationary policies, agreed at a protracted conference with the three Labor
state Premiers, and now including Lang. The Premiers bound themselves to
implement promptly a programme of higher taxes, reduced interest rates
and a 20 per cent reduction in all government expenditure, including wages
and pensions. It was essentially the same programme that was to bring down
the British Labour government in August of that year.

Once endorsed, the 'Premiers' plan' was approved in Parliament in spite
of opposition by a minority of the Labor members. The most furious of
these was Frank Anstey, who declared the Premiers' plan to be

the annihilation of everything that the Labor party has produced during two long generations. This government has, since it took office, pursued a policy of drift. It has suffered ignominy upon ignominy . . . But are we justified in spitting upon the altar of Labor simply because others may desecrate it worse than we may? That is not the path of salvation . . . this Government is crucifying the very people who raised its members from obscurity and placed them in power.

Even those who had supported the plan did so without conviction, appearing 'beaten and broken . . . they drank their tea or their whisky amid gloomy and despondent self-criticism. Regretting the lost chances of the past, they clicked the balls around in the billiard room, or paced the long, lighted lobbies with saddening eyes.'[47]

Lang perceived an opportunity to advance himself in the general malaise. In spite of the fact that he himself had signed the Premiers' Plan, and that New South Wales was rapidly heading towards bankruptcy, Lang encouraged his supporters, headed by 'Stabber Jack' Beasley, to move a vote on a matter of confidence against their own colleagues in the parliamentary party. In this they were successful, and on 25 November 1931 the government was defeated by the vote of its own rebellious MPs, and Scullin obliged to ask for a dissolution.

The subsequent election was a staggering blow; the official Labor Party gained only 14 seats out of 75 in the House of Representatives. Vindicated by the electorate, if not by his former colleagues, Lyons and the new United Australia Party took over, with an absolute majority and no need to rely on Country Party support; it was to be ten years before another Labor government was returned to office. With Labor right-wingers following Lyons, and the Langites having either left the party or withdrawn their support, the parliamentary Labor Party was once more a demoralized rump. Isolated in New South Wales, and having had his own party ejected from Federal office, Lang continued his campaign of defiance. Previous New South Wales defaults on loan payments had been met by the Commonwealth government, but a price was demanded. An Enforcement Act demanded that banks holding any New South Wales state funds should remit them to the Federal Treasury. In answer, the Premier of New South Wales sent civil servants and police physically to remove the funds from the banks. Unemployed timber workers were engaged to guard the New South Wales Treasury against any attempt to enforce the law, and 25,000 special constables were recruited from the state public service. The Commonwealth government was warned that 'civil war' was the logical outcome of its main purpose – although the warning might more suitably have been addressed to Lang's supporters. Agitated right-wingers began to talk of physical force and quasi-fascist institutions along the lines of the Irish Blue Shirts started to mobilize. The Commonwealth government prepared for force, but the situation was saved by the New South Wales Governor, Sir Philip Game, who had earlier supported Lang in the fight against the Council.

A calm and sensible man, whose judgement was quickly proved right, Game used the powers invested in him by the New South Wales constitution, which had not been affected by Federation, to dismiss Lang and call a new election, in which Labor was annihilated. Lang supporters won only 24 of the 90 seats, and Labor loyalists none at all. 'A tremendous surge of relief, extending well beyond New South Wales', greeted the demise of the Langites; but Jack Lang himself survived for many years to trouble and inspire Australian politics.[48]

Bridges and Bowlers

Only a handful of world cities are instantly recognizable by an icon, a symbol that identifies them beyond a doubt: New York has the Statue of Liberty, Paris the Eiffel Tower, London Big Ben. Others, such as Tokyo or Los Angeles, cannot claim the same distinction. Sydney stands perhaps alone in boasting two such icons – the Harbour Bridge and the Opera House – unique to it (and Melbourne, alas, has none).

By the end of the nineteenth century settlement around Sydney Harbour had developed along the north shore to such an extent that 5 million people and some 400,000 vehicles crossed annually on the overcrowded ferries. A bridge, it was concluded in 1900, was clearly needed, and competitive tenders were invited. What with one thing and another, including the war, it was not until 1922 that the project finally began, to a design by the London engineer Sir Ralph Freeman. Given the wide span – 1,650 feet – and the high clearance – 172 feet – together with the necessity to provide for heavy road and rail traffic, the technical problems were considerable and the bold elegance of the engineering solution quite remarkable. The huge single arch, nearly 40,000 tons of steel, rests upon steel pins 14 inches in diameter and the visual effect of the whole is unforgettably stunning. Seen as it is from so many different angles, from the streets above and below, and from the ferries, still essential for passenger traffic, the Sydney Harbour Bridge must have the greatest public presence of any bridge in the world.

It was also a demonstration of the extent to which Australia was still an economic dependency of Britain, and a failure of protective tariffs to develop

Australian industry, that not only the design came from England, but Scottish masons were imported to cut the granite facings for the abutment towers and almost all the steel had to be shipped out from Middlesbrough by the bridge's builders, Dorman Long, who had also built a bridge to a similar design in Newcastle upon Tyne. Novocastrians, though claiming priority, have to admit that their bridge, with a sharper arc, is less elegant than the Sydney imitation – and a good deal smaller. Saturday, 19 March 1932, when the bridge was opened, should have been an affirmation of the future possibilities symbolized by the event. It was given a different twist by an unexpected interruption, when an opinionated warrior, Captain Francis de Groot, who had turned up mounted and in uniform, spurred forward to slash the ribbon before Premier Lang had a chance to perform the operation himself.

De Groot was a member of one of the many right-wing groupuscules that flourished in the 1930s. The Old and New Guards, the Sane Democracy League, the Soldiers and Citizens Party, the Empire Party, the All-for-Australia League and the Emergency Committee were united only by a general feeling that the ordered society in which they had been brought up, and for which many returned servicemen believed they had fought, was disintegrating.[49] Portents of doom abounded: unemployment and the current account deficit both continued to rise; the nation's favourite, the racehorse Phar Lap (who was actually born in New Zealand but is lovingly preserved in Melbourne by artful taxidermy), winner of 37 of the 41 races which he ran in his career, died, allegedly poisoned, in California.

One subject, however, gripped Australia in 1932, the bodyline bowling controversy.

To the uninitiated a brief explanation of the game of cricket and some of its myriad rules may be in order. In Britain, cricket has always been an English game (if Wales be included) never having caught on in Scotland or Ireland; its origins are ancient, but in 1882 an Australian victory over the English team was commemorated by an 'In Memoriam' notice in the *Sporting Times*, mourning the death of English cricket, and announcing that 'the body will be cremated and the ashes taken to Australia'. Since then the fight for 'the Ashes' has formed the highlight of the summer sporting season. Each test series comprises five matches, each lasting up to five days so that the dedicated follower may spend up to twenty-five days (matches can be curtailed by weather or by an indisputable win) out of doors watching cricket; any game that can command that sort of attention possesses extraordinary powers. From being primarily an England *v.* Australia affair, test matches have spread to all Commonwealth countries, with the exception of

Canada, where the existence of any summer game is perilous. New Zealand, South Africa, Zimbabwe, India, Pakistan, Sri Lanka, Bangladesh and the West Indies combine to meet in the cricket field even when political differences are acute. Conferences are often enlivened by statesmen taking the field themselves, as when the British Prime Minister John Major partnered the Australian Premier Bob Hawke in Harare in 1992.

The position of the batsman in cricket is lonely and perilous, faced as he is by eleven opponents thirsting to dismiss him (there is another batsman standing idly by on the pitch waiting his turn, and another nine lurking in the pavilion, but at any one moment all attention is centred on the lone man at the wicket). He may be dismissed either by the bowler striking the stumps, or by a fielder catching the ball he has hit (for the moment we disregard the l.b.w. rule and other complexities) The bowler bowls – not throws – the ball so that it will bounce once before rising, either to hit the wicket or to tempt the batsman to make a catchable shot. If the bowler chooses to make a fast delivery strike the ground near the batsman, it will rise steeply, making it both difficult to hit and imperilling the batsman's body.

Faced with the finest batsman of his day, possibly the most effective of all time, Donald George Bradman of New South Wales, the English captain of the 1932 test team, Douglas Jardine, decided to employ this technique. Using his impressively fast bowlers, Harold Larwood and Bill Voce, and grouping the fielders close around the wicket, Jardine was able to present an altogether intimidating prospect for the best of batsmen. When a fast bowler also directed his balls towards the leg stump – the right-handed batsman's left – the batsman was often forced to use the bat defensively. The method was by no means new, although it had not been much used, as being thought to produce a cramped and tedious game; but with Larwood's delivery it was fearsomely effective.

So effective, indeed, as to excite violent controversy. Christened 'bodyline' bowling by an Australian writer, it infuriated spectators and press, as injuries to the batsmen mounted. 'Of two teams out there, one is playing cricket, and the other is making no effort to play a game of cricket,' the injured Australian captain, Bill Woodfull, reproved the English manager. English newspapers sneered at the 'undignified snivelling' of the Australians; Australian Labor papers detected the fell hand of 'British Imperialism'. Nor were the English team uncritical; one fast bowler, Australian-born 'Gubby' Allen, refused to bowl as Jardine instructed.

The controversy was exacerbated by class distinctions. At the time English cricketers were either amateurs – 'gentlemen', or paid professionals – 'players', the distinction made apparent in the score cards where gentlemen were accorded the privilege of initials, while players were generally allotted only their surname. And D. R. Jardine, Winchester and Oxford, was very much a 'gentleman', cool and reserved, lacking the common touch; the fierce jeers of the Australian crowds were dismissed with cold contempt. Larwood on the other hand, a Nottinghamshire miner, was a quintessential 'player', and retained some crowd approval. The dispute's effects were lasting, and not without importance; the writer Philip Knightley comments that 'The bodyline tour's significance lies not so much in its sporting aspects but in its social and political ones. It defined a difference in Australian and British attitudes to life and the relationship between the two countries.' It was not that Australia was, or is, a classless society; the members of, say, the Australian Club are recognizably distinct from the railwaymen, but that English society at the time presented complex strata of social distinctions, exemplified in the cartoons of *Punch*. Nor was cricket acclaimed in Britain as a national sport in the same way that the game attracted Australian loyalties. Soccer was the passion of most British working men, while cricket supporters (Yorkshire and Lancashire always excepted) are concentrated in southern England. In the last seventy years both societies, and the game of cricket, have been much altered, but when a television drama series, *Body-line*, appeared in 1983, older Australians were moved to recall their feelings; Sir Anthony Mason, a former Chief Justice, disclosed that the tour and England's attitude had turned him into an ardent and lifelong republican.[50]

Recovery

Historians often, and politicians invariably, overestimate the importance of politics in a nation's life. It is, however, true that Australia is endowed with an unusual level of politicization. Its voters are obliged to elect state and Commonwealth representatives, state and Commonwealth Senators, and to vote in referendums as often as called upon; they may also vote in local and municipal elections. Many thus elected, perhaps not an unusual proportion but often a substantial one, turn out to be at best incompetent, and not infrequently corrupt. It was not therefore unexpected that, when later faced with yet another level of politics in the possible change from monarchy to republic, voters recoiled; politicians do not enjoy the highest of reputations.

Standing considerably higher in the public estimation are sportsmen, and the 1920s introduced licensed wireless broadcasting, which brought a new immediacy to sporting events by live commentaries, transforming sport from being essentially a series of local events into a national passion. It took some time for piecemeal regional development to emerge as a national network, but by 1929, 300,000 licences had been issued (and doubtless a good number of unlicensed radios were in use). Listeners could follow, ball-by-ball, that new art form, the commentary on a test match, especially such a series as that of 1926 in which Australia won all five matches. By 1928, when Donald Bradman, the man whom most Australians would still regard as *the* Australian hero, played in his first test, wireless had brought cricket into every home, bar, club and, very often, workplace. Other sportsmen were losing their traditional pastimes, 1927 was the last year of the koala-shooting season, in which over half a million of the little beasts were shot, but other marsupials remained fair game.

It took some time to surmount the peculiar difficulties of Australian broadcasting services – the communities scattered over great distances, the wide range of climatic conditions, the lack of rural electricity – but these were eventually overcome. The Reverend John Flynn of the Presbyterian Inland Mission, who pioneered that outstanding Australian initiative, the Flying Doctor Service, worked with a young engineer, Alfred Traeger, to develop a pedal-powered transceiver, easy to operate, which first brought medical services to the remotest outback station. Since the first flights, made by Dr K. St Vincent Welch in 1928, the service has developed into a national emergency network which also provides advice and educational services. The multi-talented George Taylor, cartoonist, inventor, soldier, publisher and advocate of town planning, urged national control of broadcasting (his equally remarkable architect wife Florence, who carried on her husband's publishing work for thirty years after his death, was the first Australian woman to attempt a flight, in one of George's gliders). Largely as a result of Taylor's advocacy, the Australian Broadcasting Commission (ABC) was established in 1932, following the example of the British Broadcasting Corporation. The Commission was fortunate to have William Cleary as its second chairman, from 1934 to 1945. With the help of his vice-chairman, Herbert Brookes, Cleary was able to turn the Commission into an enlightened music patron, establishing orchestras in all the states, subsidizing visiting artists, encouraging Australian composers and bringing a new dimension into cultural life. Taylor's personal toughness, forged in earlier conflicts with Jack Lang, was called upon during the Second World War, when he had to defend the Commission's independence from both Labor and UAP Prime Ministers, ultimately resigning in protest against political interference.

If the ABC encouraged Australian arts, the cinema, following the introduction of talkies in 1931, began that transformation which has affected the whole world – the introduction of American styles and habits. In the 1930s Hollywood was already *the* film industry, and its early products were enormous fun, moving at a pace that swept criticism aside and suspended disbelief. The three-hour session in the dark womb of a cinema, with two films, a cartoon and Movietone news, and, quite possibly a mighty Wurlitzer rising from the depths of the orchestra pit, was an escape into another world – and the fashions and values of that other world (which was not that of the actual contemporary America, wrecked by the after-effects of the slump and the Depression, but the ideal fantasies of the worried masses) became instantly desirable. It was, too, an art form in which Australians could excel. Ken Hall opened the first sound stage in 1931 with his production of *On our Selection*. Three years later Errol Flynn, the prince of swashbucklers, made his first appearance in Charles Chauvel's *In the Wake of the Bounty* – and in the same year another Australian star made his first international appearance in a different medium, when Robert Helpmann joined the Sadler's Wells Ballet.[51]

Increasingly, Australians were able to enjoy their leisure as the economy revived. Unemployment fell after 1936 to between 8 and 10 per cent, although the workforce had increased. In so far as interest rates were brought down, and stayed lower, and inefficient firms were forced into bankruptcy to make way for more profitable groups, the Premiers' Plan worked. For the first time, Australia gained a modern steel industry, as BHP took over the Port Kembla plant of Australian Iron and Steel. BHP paid abysmal wages and conditions were dire, but the company prospered. By 1934 the basic wage, which had been cut in the economy drive, had been restored. Three years later the Federal Arbitration Court added a 6s. 'prosperity allowance' to the basic wage. In 1939 a standard 44-hour week was introduced. As post-war electric generation came on stream the demand for consumer goods shot up; a cold beer was established as an Australian working man's natural right.

One great date in Australian history is 10 December 1919, when the two brothers, Ross and Keith Macpherson Smith, landed their Vickers Vimy bomber at Darwin, having flown from England in twenty-eight days. Both were immediately knighted, and the Commonwealth prize of £10,000 shared with their aircrew. The following year two other young airmen, Hudson Fysh (grand-nephew of the Tasmanian Prime Minister) and P. J. McGinnis, founded a company with its headquarters in the remote Queensland town of Longreach, to be known as Queensland and Northern Territory Aerial Services (Empire Airways) Pty Ltd., sensibly better known as Qantas.

International aerial communications, however, remained slow and expensive, even after July 1938 when the first flying-boat service was established. Three flights a week between Australia and Britain, in spacious machines, with overnight stops and meticulous service, constituted the most civilized form of air travel, but were not for the masses. Internal communications expanded more quickly, moved by the Holyman brothers, founders of Australian National Airways, and by 1936 all the capital cities were connected by regular passenger services, using reliable DC2 and DC3 aircraft.

Australia demonstrated its wonderful ability (surely very British) to be both conservative and innovatory in the early 1920s. The first air routes were established in 1922 on short hauls in both eastern Australia and Queensland, just as Melbourne was pensioning off its tramway horses (1923) and Cobb and Co. were regretfully closing down their last magnificent coach services (1924). With the introduction of reliable cars and diesel lorries, motor transport flourished. In mid decade both General Motors and Ford established Australian assembly plants which within a short time were producing over 70,000 vehicles a year. In 1931 General Motors bought control of Holdens, previously their body shop, and increased the local share of components; but it was not until 1949 that the first wholly Australian-built car, a Holden, was marketed. Road-building remained a state responsibility, but a Federal Roadbuilding Fund was established in 1926 to enable a motorable road network to be constructed. Given the great distances to be covered this was a massive undertaking, and one subject to the fluctuations of capital availability, but few improvements add more to the prosperity of country regions than the provision of good transport links. Only a small proportion of the total road system was bitumen surfaced – as late as the 1950s Sydney and Melbourne were the only two state capitals to be completely linked by hard-top highways – with the result that only the sturdiest of vehicles could cope with country roads. Since at that time British roads were being constructed to a more consistent standard, British car manufacturers found their products largely unacceptable in Australia, apart from the more luxurious models for urban use. American vehicles, cheaper, simpler and tougher, were better suited to Australian conditions.

State authorities, with vested interest in their own railway system, looked warily at road transport, but freight remained a near-monopoly of rail until the Second World War. For passengers, the proliferation of gauges and the slowness of even main-line trains, made motor transport attractive. (With wonderful hindsight a 1921 Royal Commission finally recommended a uniform gauge of 4 foot 8½ inches.) Even today, the line between Sydney and northern New South Wales, a distance of less than 500 miles, entails a full day's travel along a route for the most part single track: in France, a comparable journey takes three hours. When an air-conditioned rail service between Melbourne and Albury was inaugurated in 1936 the speed attained of 79 m.p.h. was hailed as a conspicuous success – but one which even British railways had been managing since the end of the nineteenth century.[52]

For Western Australia, the completion of the Commonwealth rail link to Kalgoorlie in 1917 brought the state rather closer to the rest of Australia, replacing the ocean voyage which had previously been the only link between Perth and the other capitals; but it remained a four-day journey from the east coast, with several changes needed.

The Far East is our Near North

Diplomats and Dominion Prime Ministers must have felt a gust of relief when Billy Hughes no longer represented Australia, and the Little Digger's harangues were replaced by the smooth silences of Stanley Bruce. With a more extensive international experience than any other contemporary Australian politician, including many years' residence in London and visits to central America, Bruce had been the Australian delegate to the League of Nations in 1921. In office he did not choose to consolidate Hughes's achievement in securing recognition of Australia's independent sphere of action, even when this clashed with British interests; the Bruce–Page government preferred to hold close to the Imperial apron strings. Excellent economic reasons existed for such a course. Between 1922 and 1926, 42 per cent of Australian exports went to Britain, not much less than the pre-war figure (45 per cent), and British capital continued to form by far the most important resource for Australian enterprise. Relations with Britain were nourished by the appointment of R. G. Casey as a liaison officer in London, working in the British Cabinet Office, independently of the High Commission. Casey, a man very much in the Bruce mould, with a Cambridge degree followed by a distinguished army record, remained in direct contact with Bruce's office in Melbourne (the move to Canberra was implemented only in May 1927). Foreign affairs should have been left to the prudent Senator George Pearce, who had represented continuity and commonsense in Australian foreign affairs from his first appointment in 1908 as Defence Minister in the Fisher Labor government, but Bruce took the portfolio for himself.

Alarmed by the potential consequences of Japan's victory in the 1905–6 war with Russia, Pearce had been convinced of the urgent necessity to improve – initiate might have been a better word – Australia's own military capacity. Remaining in charge of Defence throughout the war, when from 1915 until 1921 he acted virtually as Hughes's second in command, Pearce could claim credit both for acting as a restraint on Hughes's excesses and for creating, almost from scratch, a superb fighting machine. In doing so and in supporting conscription he had not endeared himself to that section of the Labor Party suspicious of 'militarism' and 'British imperialism', who were mainly to be found in the eastern states; coming from Western Australia, where his views were shared by the great majority, Pearce remained a favourite son.[53]

As Minister of Defence, Pearce had represented Australia at the Washington conference, where Arthur Balfour, the British Prime Minister, a reliable judge in such matters, found the Senator 'the greatest national statesman he had ever met'. Certainly Pearce's assessment, made in July 1922 was perceptive:

We are of European race. Our fathers came from Europe: we have grown up to think as Europeans, and our interests have been centred in that group of nations from which our stock has come. Whilst racially we are European, geographically we are Asiatic. Our own special immediate Australian interests are more nearly concerned with what is happening in China and Japan than with what is happening . . . in Belgium, Holland, Poland, or other countries farther removed.

The Japanese acceptance of the conference decisions mollified Pearce, previously suspicious of their intentions. He accepted that his fears of 1906 were no longer justified, and was gratified by what he saw as 'a friendly understanding, full and complete between the two great English-speaking Empires of the world'.[54]

Bruce, however, was not interested in consolidating good relations with Australia's northern neighbours, dismissing the representatives in China appointed by Hughes and abolishing the Pacific Branch of the Prime Minister's Department, which had been led by the persistent advocate of engagement with Asia, Edmund Piesse. Pearce, who alone among Labor Senators had thrown in his lot with the National Party, was demoted to the Ministry of Home Affairs. Bruce's election slogan in 1925 – 'Men, Money, Markets' – encapsulated government policy, and Britain was expected to be the prime source of the three. Given this 'little Australia' policy, the country played a minor role in the development of the new concept of a British Commonwealth which evolved during the decade, and in which the major participants followed their individual agendas. Both the Irish Free State and the Union of South Africa were led by individuals who only a few years earlier had been in arms against Britain; indeed, Ireland's representative at the 1923

Imperial Conference was Foreign Minister Kevin O'Higgins, who only two years previously had been a prominent member of the Sinn Fein forces (and who was in turn to be murdered by the IRA in 1927). Both South Africa and Ireland, with Canada in support, pressed for a more formal definition of the already largely de facto independence of the Dominions, but Australia remained reluctant to take advantage of any such opportunities. When the 1923 conference agreed that the Dominions should appoint their own diplomatic representatives to foreign countries, as a logical consequence of their representation in the post-war settlement and the League of Nations, Canada, South Africa and even Ireland promptly did so; but not Australia. The cost, it was believed, would be too heavy, and Australia 'was judged not to have a domestic constituency seeking public signs of national independence from Britain'. Similarly, the definitive Statute of Westminster of December 1931, which formalized Balfour's formula that Great Britain and the Dominions were 'autonomous communities within the British Empire, equal in status, in no way subordinate one to another in any aspect of their domestic or internal affairs, though united by a common allegiance to the Crown, and freely associated as members of the British Commonwealth of Nations', was unenthusiastically received in Australia. With the government divided, the opposition was able to secure a motion of amendment insisting that the statute would not apply to Australia until formally adopted by the Commonwealth Parliament; and, significantly, this was not done for another eleven years.

One potentially important step was, however, welcomed, which was the recognition that the Governor General should function as a representative of the King in Australia, and not of the British government. Scullin had insisted on this point at the conference when he put forward the name of Sir Isaac Isaacs, Henry Higgins's old colleague of the first High Court, as Governor General. King George V, who attached great importance to personal relations with his representatives (although not talented himself in personal affairs), objected that he had never met Isaacs. It was not perhaps so much the King, as his secretary Lord Stamfordham (a collateral descendant of the Australian Commissioner John Bigge) who was most agitated, claiming that 'a pistol had been put at the King's head', since only one name had been put forward rather than the usual selection of at least two, therefore giving the King no choice. Scullin pointed out that there were precedents for this, both in the Union of South Africa and in the Irish Free State, and described Stamfordham's reaction: 'Lord Stamfordham threw up his hands and excitedly exclaimed: "Do not talk to me about Ireland. That is a country of rebels and the man nominated for the position of Governor-General was himself a rebel." ' The later interview with the King himself was a much more sedate affair, in which Scullin's proposal was accepted. While non-Australians continued to be appointed, after the Second World War it was accepted by both parties that the Governor Generalship was best held by an Australian.[55]

With Lyons holding an unassailable majority and a divided Labor muttering in the background, the incoming Prime Minister's task was easy. This was just as well, as Lyons had only two years' experience of Commonwealth politics, and his previous career in Tasmania was no preparation for the task of leading the nation. Australian domestic policy continued without major dissension, recovering from the worst effects of the Depression. Abroad, prudent inertia continued, with External Affairs still being run as a branch of the Prime Minister's Office. Disarmament agreements were faithfully adhered to: HMAS *Australia*, welcomed into the fleet with such pride eleven years earlier, was accordingly scuttled; Australian representatives argued in the League of Nations in favour of banning chemical and bacteriological warfare; the arguments continue.

From its start, after the refusal of the United States to join, the League of Nations was doomed to impotence, and its essential weakness was exposed in September 1931 by Japan's invasion of Manchuria. Internal cohesion in Japan had been crumbling ever since the Washington conference limited, as the Japanese navy saw it, her ability to defend herself against American aggression, economic as well as military. With the armed services reporting directly to the timid and ineffective though well-meaning Emperor Hirohito, rather than to the elected government, it was easy for military plots and coups to be arranged (the most outrageous of these being the murder of the whole Cabinet by an air attack). What was by comparison a small bomb explosion on the Manchurian railway provided an excuse to occupy Manchuria – all without government agreement or that of the Army High Command.

It could be argued that the Ch'ing themselves were foreign invaders, who had brutally crushed the Ming empire and established themselves as a ruling caste; but that was three hundred years ago, and with the establishment of the Chinese Republic by Dr Sun Yat Sen in 1912 the last of the Ch'ing emperors could claim only a very restricted rule. Japan took advantage of this by disguising their rule as the re-establishment of Manchurian independence, with the last Emperor, Pu Yi, as their puppet ruler of Manchukuo. When China appealed to the League of Nations, the Tokyo government denied any territorial ambitions and promised to withdraw their troops, a promise neither the government nor the weak Emperor could enforce. A

League commission of inquiry was obliged by the evidence to rule against Japan, whereupon Japan withdrew from the League; like the fox blaming the rabbits for trouble-making, the Foreign Minister, Uchida Yasaya, blamed the turbulent state of China, which necessitated 'the general principles and usages of international law' being 'considerably modified in their operation so far as China is concerned'.[56] In accepting this flimsy pretence, Australia behaved no worse than the other Dominions; Canada and Britain were even prepared to defend Japan, and there was a general sense of relief that Japan's demands for *Lebensraum* were easily satisfied in a region conveniently distant from Australia. Japan was, after all, an increasingly important customer, taking, between 1932 and 1936, 12 per cent of all Australian exports, second only to Britain and well ahead of America (3 per cent).[57]

Paradoxically, as Australian public opinion was not greatly concerned with events in Europe or the remoter parts of Asia, and as Australian governments were only reluctantly drawn into foreign policy, former Prime Minister Bruce was taking a prominent part in international events. High Commissioner in London from 1933 to 1946, Bruce was also elected President of the League Council for 1935–6 and chairman of a commission to review League policy on non-aggression and armaments. He was an effective performer, but matters had passed beyond the possibility of reform, and Bruce's most important work, now largely forgotten, was his collaboration with Lord Boyd Orr, which eventually led to the establishment of the United Nations Food and Agriculture Organization, probably the most effective section of the United Nations.

Protectionism was sanctified as a policy at the Ottawa Imperial Economic Conference in 1932, when Britain and the Dominions agreed reciprocal preferences. Since 63 per cent of Australian exports were to the Imperial market, Australian primary producers were therefore well secured, but at the same time preliminary efforts were also made to expand trade with Australia's neighbours. It was, Lyons announced, 'a strange thing that no official visit has ever been paid by Australia to the countries of her near neighbours'. As a start, J. G. Latham, the External Affairs minister, was despatched in 1934 on an extensive visit which included the Dutch East Indies, the Straits Settlements, China, the Philippines, Hong Kong and, most significantly, Japan. Latham was able to assure his Japanese hosts that the Australians had never 'even considered' supporting any sanctions against Japan and reported to Parliament that closer relations with this area were essential 'not only in economic matters, but also in relation to the vital issues of peace and war'.[58]

Closer links with Japan were naturally economically hampered by continuing agreements on Imperial preference. Negotiations were entrusted to Sir Henry Gullett, who had served in the First World War and indeed written one volume of the official war history. The balance of trade, since 1930 at least, had been heavily in Australia's favour, and when British textile manufacturers complained about the threatening increase in Japanese sales to Australia, Gullett had to pay attention to their case. This he did with such vigour that it appeared to a contemporary observers 'that Australia was spoiling for a fight and the Japanese did not refuse the challenge'. Rather than an agreement, a brisk trade war ensued, settled to nobody's satisfaction in December 1936. By this time much of the goodwill generated by Latham's visit had been sacrificed. Australia and Japan were beginning to get the measure of each other. The dispute, wrote the Japanese Consul General, had given 'us a splendid opportunity to realise exactly how important each of our countries is to each other', or, included in the ambiguity, how unimportant. But at least the Australian government realized that the days of amateurism in foreign policies were ended, and the independence of the Department of External Affairs was rescued from its undignified subordinate position within the Prime Minister's Office and returned to Pearce's capable hands (October 1934–November 1937).[59]

When in his previous incarnation Senator Pearce took over the Home Affairs department in December 1921, his new responsibilities included the mandated territory of New Guinea, together with the previous Australian protectorate of Papua, and the two home territories. These were the Federal district of Canberra, site of the Commonwealth Parliament, and the Northern Territory, surrendered to the Commonwealth by South Australia in 1907, although the transfer was not effected – there was a matter of £6 million to be paid – until January 1911. Devising policies for these very different constituents proved a continuing embarrassment to Australian governments.

Events in New Guinea after 1888 provide an interesting study in colonialism. The island was divided between the western province of the Dutch East Indies and the eastern, split between the German colony of Kaiser-Wilhelms-Land with its capital at Rabaul, and the British Protectorate of Papua. German techniques were the simple and effective ones of shooting and flogging those natives who could not be simply ignored into submission, and the efficient construction of communications and harbours. Almost equally typical, the Protectorate, with responsibility shared between Queensland and Britain, was a well-intentioned and poverty-stricken muddle, governed as best he might by the professional colonial civil servant and doctor William MacGregor, sheltering the population from the worst abuses and attempting to introduce some logic into the confused system of control. In 1906, in a charged atmosphere of scandal and recrimination over the conduct of a punitive expedition led by the acting Administrator, responsibility for Papua was accepted by the Commonwealth. Australia's first colony was thus created and placed under the direction of the Department of External Affairs, with Hubert Murray appointed as Lieutenant Governor.

One of the extraordinary Murray brothers – Gilbert, the younger, became Regius Professor of Greek at Oxford and published translations which introduced a generation of English-speakers to the Greek theatre – Hubert was the ideal colonial administrator. Personally large (6 feet 3 inches) and powerful, English heavyweight amateur boxing champion with a first in Greats, a commander of mounted infantry in the Boer War, Hubert was a liberal Catholic 'keen on the protection of animals, children, foreigners, heretics, unpopular minorities and the like'. Until his death, still in charge, in February 1940, Murray was allowed to run Papua as he wished, always putting the interests of the native Papuans first, and doing very little to inflict the benefits of civilization on them.[60]

In September 1914 the situation changed radically when Kaiser-Wilhelms-Land surrendered to Australian troops and was placed under military government, the German settlers being allowed to continue running their plantations and the German brutality perpetuated by the Australian government. With peace in 1919, and at Billy Hughes's insistence, Australia was given a 'class C' mandate, which allowed a very full measure of control over what was once again known as New Guinea. Murray, distrusting with good reason the capacity of Australian administrators to control the planters' exploitation of the natives, tried to have the two territories, Mandate and Protectorate, jointly administered, but was over-ruled by his fellow commissioners. Papua continued under Murray's benevolent paternalism, while New Guinea was entrusted to Australian generals, who proved, as expected by Murray, so ineffective as to provoke the continuous wrath of the League of Nations: as an example, in the twenty years after 1920 Murray found it necessary to sentence only two Papuans, reputed untameable savages, to death; in the same period the New Guinea government hanged sixty-five.

Nevertheless, Rabaul, built by the Germans, was a more advanced society than that of Port Moresby and one which had a much larger European population and more amenities. A great general strike that took place in Rabaul in January 1929 exemplified both New Guinea's relative sophistication and the readiness of its rulers to use violence. The organizers, one Suysuma, a ship's captain, and several senior policemen, simply withdrew workers to the mission stations; in spite of their peaceful return to work many were sentenced to prison terms, and 'most were beaten by outraged, and anxious officials, while awaiting trial or during their sentences'. Murray would have kept his officials under better control.

Nearer home, Senator Pearce was rather more successful in the Northern Territory. Its population was overwhelmingly Aboriginal, although there were no accurate records of these; the white population consisted only of 739 men and 166 women (the disproportion indicating the frontier nature of the society) plus 132 Asians, mainly Japanese. Trouble had been brewing from the beginning, when John Gilruth, an abrasive Scottish veterinary surgeon, was appointed as administrator. Gilruth was a good vet, but a miserably poor administrator, who alienated the population to the point of an actual rebellion, forcing him to leave in 1919 under the protection of the Royal Australian Navy, to be followed by his senior colleagues. Reluctantly, and only after another revolt over 'no taxation without representation', the Northern Territory was granted a seat in the House of Representatives, although without a vote. The first member to be elected was Gilruth's chief opponent, the union organizer Harold Nelson, whose militant activities had brought about the closure of the Territory's only industry, the Vestey meat-processing plant. The British-based Vesteys, however, remained the largest landholders in the Territory, with some 27,000 square miles, including the 5,800 square mile Wave Hill station, later to become a focus of Aboriginal land claims.

The Northern Territory was, and remains, an anomaly, with a land area of 540,000 square miles and a population of some 165,000, half of whom live in the capital, Darwin, and another 30,000 in Alice Springs, 1,400 miles to the south, connected by an adventurous road and, since 2003, by a railway. It is one of the most sparsely inhabited areas on earth. In 1911 it was very much a frontier region, with many, perhaps most, Aborigines living out of contact with the authorities. The best legacy of South Australian rule was the Hermannsburg Lutheran Mission, founded in 1888 to serve the Aranda people, the only Protestant mission that can be compared with the Western Australian New Norcia. At Hermannsburg the admirable Pastor Carl Strehlow took up the work, in a more methodical and scholarly fashion, that Threlkeld had left unfinished fifty years previously, and among his pupils was Albert Namatjira, the first Aboriginal artist to be recognized internationally. Hermannsburg was well ahead of its times, since most missions still concentrated on converting the Aborigines to their own brand of Christianity, a process to which the black Australians proved frustratingly resistant. Perhaps misled by their success in Southern Africa, where black Christians were numerous, and became increasingly influential – Nelson Mandela was a member of the Methodist Church – Australian missionaries hoped for the same results. Only in the 1920s, with the work of the Presbyterian Robert Love, was it acknowledged that Aboriginal traditions and beliefs had an enduring worth, and that the missionaries' function was to offer other perspectives rather than insist on imposing their own values. Even then, such fundamentalists as the Apostolic Church missionaries at Jigalong, who believed Aborigines to be children of the Devil, steeped in sin to be redeemed by beatings and bullying, were able to continue until 1969. The Territory authorities were more concerned with imposing order than with Aboriginal advancement. In 1928 thirty-two Aboriginals were shot in retaliation for the murder of a dingo-shooter: ten years later Police Constable Murray was said to have accounted for some thirty on his own account. The Papuans had by far the best of Australian rule.[61]

Very different conditions obtained in the site of the nation's capital, the Australian Capital Territory (ACT) where on 9 May 1927 the Duke of York, later King George VI, opened the new Parliament House, with a verse of the national anthem sung by Dame Nellie Melba. After the decision taken in 1909 to site the new capital at Canberra an international competition resulted in an American, Walter Burley Griffin, being appointed as controlling architect. Griffin was a fine architect, a former associate of Frank Lloyd Wright, but little remains in Canberra to indicate this. All the earlier buildings, and all those outside the government centre are, at best, commonplace, but as a landscape designer Griffin was outstanding. Canberra, with its necklace of lakes and surrounding hills is stunning, if not inspected too closely, but to see Griffin at his best, Newman College in the University of Melbourne should be visited.

It was political incompetence and infighting that robbed Griffin of the credit and prevented his designs from being completed. The initial reviewing board, appointed by the Fisher government, with the grotesque King O'Malley in the chair, produced their own scheme; the next government, prompted by the imaginative Etonian William Kelly, scrapped O'Malley's scheme and appointed Griffin as director of design and construction, thus infuriating the original critics. With Labor back in power, the assault on Griffin, described by the philistine minister William Archibald, as a 'Yankee bounder', continued. A royal commission was appointed which accused Archibald and the civil servants of having acted as 'a combination . . . hostile to Mr. Griffin and to his designs for the city'. That conclusion, reached in

1917, and subsequently queried, was ignored under wartime pressure. By 1920 Griffin had had enough, and resigned, very publicly and indignantly, from all connection with the project. The whole episode was to be replayed, under very similar circumstances, a generation later in the construction of the Sydney Opera House. As thousands of other examples prove, democracies do not make good patrons of architecture.[62]

In 1936 Australia became responsible for nearly half the land area of another continent, Antarctica, which today places under Australian control a larger part of the world's surface than any other except that of the Russian Federation. This acquisition, of enormous potential importance given the mineral resources of Antarctica, was primarily due to one man, Sir Douglas Mawson. Yorkshire-born in 1882, Mawson was brought to Australia at the age of 2, and graduated with a degree in mining engineering from Sydney University. A brief encounter with Ernest Shackleton in 1907 led to Mawson's first visit to Antarctica as physicist aboard the Nimrod for Shackleton's first voyage south, together with his tutor and sponsor, the 50-year-old Professor Edgeworth David. Remarkably, David, Mawson and surgeon Alistair Mackay managed to complete both the first ascent of the 9,000-foot Mount Erebus, and to reach the neighbourhood of the magnetic south pole, hauling their supplies for 1,260 miles. Mawson's career bridges the gap between the bold pioneering reconnaissances of such explorers as Scott, Shackleton, Nansen and Amundsen and the later more specifically scientific expeditions. Shackleton's nomination of Mawson to command the search, should his own exploration party fail to return, places the Australian in the apostolic succession of adventurers, but Mawson was primarily a scientist and organizer whose work happened to take him into cold and dangerous places. The first Australian Antarctic expedition, between 1911 and 1913, produced an unprecedented quantity of geological, meterological and marine information, as well as providing yet another epic journey in which both of Mawson's companions perished, one through the toxic effects of eating their sledge dogs' livers; Mawson himself survived to earn a knighthood in 1914.

When the 1926 Imperial Conference asserted British rights over more than two-thirds of Antarctica no other European nation felt inclined to dispute the claim, and the United States Secretary of State, Charles Hughes, specifically renounced any American ambitions. Admiral Richard Byrd's first expedition in 1929 began to revive American interest but by then it was too late since Mawson's work had already established the Empire in possession. The British government, in the last large-scale exercise of Imperial powers, divided up its share of the continent between New Zealand,

Australia and Great Britain, with Australia taking the largest part. Mawson was back in the Antarctic leading the British Australian and New Zealand Antarctic Research Expedition (BANZARE) in 1929–31, which made use of Scott's old ship, the *Discovery*, and also one light aircraft. The other distinguished Australian to accompany both Shackleton and Mawson was the photographer Frank Hurley, whose pictures of the *Endurance* surrendering to the Antarctic ice rank among the finest of the twentieth century.[63]

Ambling Along

The Lyons government which took office in January 1932 was fortunate in that by that date the worst effects of the Great Depression were beginning to subside. Unemployment, which reached 30 per cent of the workforce during the year, moved to below 25 per cent the following year, as the stream of assisted immigrants was cut off. As might have been expected from a politician emerging from the parochial politics of little Tasmania and catapulted into the new world of Canberra, Lyons was not an effective leader. According to his predecessor, Bruce, the new Prime Minister was 'a wonderful winner of elections, and a helluva nice bloke, and that sums him up exactly'. Richard Casey, Honorary Minister from 1933, described the Cabinet's performance: 'We amble along as a collection of individuals doing the obvious things that come to our hand.'

Ambling along, however, for eight years, with so difficult a colleague as Billy Hughes was no mean achievement, but was positively dangerous as international prospects clouded. As he had done before the First World War, Hughes warned of the perils ahead. 'When Britain was mistress of the seas our security was assured', but 'despite all the good will in the world, the British Navy is no longer in a position to come immediately to our aid'.[64] That was in September 1933. The following year Hughes's book *The Price of Peace* warned that it was 'a matter for speculation whether the [still unfinished] Singapore base could be held against a determined attack'; and all that Australia could muster to help were two light cruisers, three destroyers and a survey ship.

In October 1934 an election saw the UAP lose its absolute majority, being once again obliged to accept a coalition with the Country Party under Page. The new government included the Victorian lawyer and politician, Robert Menzies, immediately appointed Attorney General, although a newcomer to the Federal Parliament; one of his colleagues was Billy Hughes as Minister for Health and Repatriation, a new and unaccustomed responsibility for the rogue elephant. If Hughes had not fallen out with the Labor Party earlier over conscription, he would have done so over the imposition of economic sanctions on Italy after the invasion of Abyssinia. The Labor Party, worried about the Catholic reaction to any opposition to Mussolini, described by Archbishop Mannix as 'the greatest living man', was not prepared to support economic sanctions. Frank Forde, temporary leader of the parliamentary Labor Party, declared that 'the control of Abyssinia by any country is not worth the loss of a single Australian life'. This supine attitude, which amounted at times to positive support for the dictators, was extended by refusing to support the Spanish republican government following Franco's revolt.[65]

British reaction to the Spanish Civil War was little more creditable, but at least Britain showed itself ready to take action against the Italian invasion of Ethiopia, setting the pace in imposing economic sanctions. Australia followed only reluctantly, with many Catholics supporting Italy. As a gesture, HMAS *Sydney* was sent to join the international force at Gibraltar. Hughes made it perhaps his finest hour. No one in Australian politics knew international relations better than he, and he made it, almost single-handed, his mission to prepare Australia for war. 'The League is powerless – that is the great outstanding fact. It talks; it appeals; it supplicates; it negotiates, but it cannot act.' All this was too much for his Cabinet colleagues, who forced his resignation; in March 1936 Hitler's forces occupied the Rhineland, in breach of the Versailles Treaty.

The next election, in October 1937, was a tougher test for Lyons. The coalition's majority was reduced, and – perhaps acknowledging that he had been right – Hughes was admitted back into the fold, as vice-chairman of the Executive Council. The Labor Party was recovering its unity and nerve; in failing health, Scullin was replaced in September 1935 by John Curtin, to general surprise, Forde having been expected to win, for Curtin was an unlikely successor to Scullin as leader of the Labor Party. A parliamentarian since 1928, he held no office under Scullin, probably owing to his history of alcoholism. An honourable and modest man – critics might say he had much to be modest about – Curtin had moved a long way from the red-flag-waving socialist editor of the *West Australian Worker*. He took over a shabby and disreputable party, shadowed by 'flagrant graft and chicanery' and 'intellectual bankruptcy'.[66] Compared with the left wing in Britain, Australian socialists made a poor showing. At a time when Victor Gollancz's Left Book Club publications were required reading for anyone with intellectual pretensions, when Harold Laski, R. H. Tawney and George Orwell were beginning to exercise their enormous influence, Australian

Labor produced little or nothing to nourish the creative imagination, but continued to tear itself apart. Curtin set about restoring some credibility. He could not be expected to revive creative debate in a party where his single intellectual sympathizer and potential rival was Herbert Vere Evatt, brilliant but enthusiastic to the point of instability, then making his name in the High Court. Among Curtin's other colleagues, however, were some men of real capacity. Disgusted by what he saw as Langite treachery, Theodore had renounced politics, but Queensland was held together by the cool apparatchik Forgan Smith, and a more stable character than Evatt was making his name fighting the Langites in New South Wales. This was the generous and reliable Ben Chifley, a former engine driver whose decency shone like a beacon in the middle of the squalor of Australian Labor. In his transparent honesty Chifley resembled such British Labour leaders as Ben Tillett and George Lansbury, but represented a peculiarly Australian tradition of the Catholic Irish working class, from which Lyons, Curtin and Scullin had also sprung. One would have to look hard before finding an English Labour leader from a similar background.

When Lyons died, still in office, in April 1939, sustained by his indomitable wife Enid, his political heir had already been named. Three years previously he had written to Robert Menzies: 'for some time I have felt that the time had come for you to step into my shoes both because you should be given the opportunity to use your talents for Australia's benefit and because I feel that I have done a pretty good job ... and I am entitled to a rest.'[67]

The Second World War and its Aftermath

A Public Lynching

In May 1935 that old warhorse Billy Hughes had sounded the clearest warnings of future conflict. In a new edition of his book, *Australia and War Today*, he foresaw that Germany

intends to recover all her former territories in Europe; to Germanize Austria; to incorporate in the new and Greater Germany most, if not all, the countries in the old Austrian Empire . . . Nor will even the realization of these immense ambitions satisfy her. After securing the hegemony of Europe, she will seek that of the whole world, certainly she will insist on the return of her former colonies and possessions.

Back in office as Foreign Minister in October 1937, after having been dismissed by Lyons for his outspokenness, Hughes relentlessly exposed the defence shortfall: Australia had a total tank force of 13, all obsolete; ammunition was not coming from government factories kept on short time; naval forces continued inadequate. When the Italian and German consulates protested against Hughes's denunciation of their countries' aggressiveness, Lyons refused to support his Foreign Minister and the Labor opposition continued weakly isolationist. Hughes scornfully replied to an intervention by John Curtin:

What are we to do when weak nations of the world are oppressed? The honorable gentleman says that we must close our ears to the piteous cries of the oppressed, because otherwise we may be endangered . . . The day may come when this small nation will cry aloud to the world for help, but what will the world say if we adopt and pursue the policy of selfish isolation outlined by the Leader of the Opposition?[1]

The wartime leaders of Australia were hardly worthy of their people. Robert Menzies, in power at the outbreak of the Second World War, clever, charming and socially adroit, was utterly inexperienced in warfare or international affairs: his lack of participation in the First World War was the subject of a bitter and unjustified tirade from his colleague Earle Page (whose own participation had been less than heroic); he had been educated entirely in Victoria and had only entered national politics in 1934. John Curtin, his Labor successor after a forty-day interlude under Arthur Fadden in September 1941, was even more inexperienced, but had been a somewhat discriminating pacifist; his newspaper described the First World War as 'a fight between German and British thrones, nobles, banks, shareholders and merchants', but had been prepared to support violence in the 'class struggle'.[2] Newly elected to the House of Representatives, Curtin had confidently expected to be given office in Scullin's government, as a member of the Federal Labor Party's executive committee, but Scullin, a teetotaller, found Curtin's drinking abhorrent; when appointed Prime Minister in October 1941 Curtin had therefore no ministerial experience. He displayed solid character, however, breaking his addiction and adjusting his prejudices to the inexorable logic of events. Menzies, vain and self-confident, wanted to make his mark on the central direction of the war, while Curtin took the more sensible attitude of attending to the home front. Two of Australia's most experienced politicians were well placed abroad. Stanley Bruce acted as High Commissioner in London for thirteen years after 1933, exercising considerable influence, which he rapidly lost after Churchill came to power in May 1940 by arguing for a negotiated peace with Germany: 'Rot,' exclaimed Churchill.[3] In Washington, Australia's first foreign diplomatic post, that of Minister to the United States, was held by Richard Casey, Federal Minister in the Lyons government, who continued a distinguished diplomatic career after the war. Independently rich, highly visible and personable, Casey worked the Washington circuit to great effect, raising Australia's public reputation as an independent Pacific power and acting as a valued intermediary between Britain and the United States. Less effectively, Earle Page was despatched to London for a few months in 1941–2 as a special envoy to the Imperial War Cabinet.

Lyons died in April 1939 leaving the UAP divided and in confusion and bitterness. Hughes very nearly succeeded in returning to power, being narrowly beaten by Robert Menzies, whose periods in office between April 1939 and August 1941, and then from 1949 to 1966 are a record for either Australia or Britain. For nineteen days in April 1939, while the UAP selected another leader, Earle Page became Prime Minister. When Menzies was chosen Page tore into his colleague in a vicious attack, claiming that Menzies was not 'fit to lead his country'. It was Page himself who was discredited by his intemperance, allowing Menzies the supreme revenge of forgiving Earle.

Menzies lost no time in making his own position clear; on 27 April, days after taking office, he wrote:

Britain's peace is precious to us because her peace is ours. If she is at war we are at war – defending our own shores. I cannot have a defence of Australia which depends upon British sea power as its first element. I cannot envisage a vital foreign trade on sea routes kept free by British sea power, and at the same time refuse to Britain Australia's co-operation at a time of any danger.[4]

Unlike Billy Hughes, Menzies had been an appeaser, a strong defender of the Munich agreement, willing to go far – probably too far – in avoiding war. He recognized that 'problems of the Pacific are difficult' but went on to claim that the 'primary risk in the Pacific is borne by New Zealand and ourselves' and suggested this might be avoided by increased diplomatic contact with other countries including China and Japan. While it was not entirely unrealistic to continue cosying up to Japan, by 1939 Menzies' optimism was looking threadbare.[5]

As with Neville Chamberlain in Britain, Robert Menzies could not rely on support from a united party. The embittered Page refused to serve under Menzies (he later changed his mind), which caused a division within the Country Party, only to be resolved in March 1940 when Page's successor, Archie Cameron, brought the party back into the coalition. A general election in September brought little comfort, with Coalition and Labor seats evenly divided, the balance of power being held by two independents, A. W. Coles and Alex Wilson, who supported the coalition. As in 1914, there was no hesitation in joining in Britain's fight: 'Great Britain has declared war', Menzies announced on the evening of 3 September, and 'as a result Australia is also at war'.[6]

Although Australia and New Zealand followed Britain in declaring war on the same day (Canada and South Africa debated the subject for a week and three days respectively, while Eire opted for neutrality), it was some months before the volunteers, as enthusiastic as they had been in 1914 although fewer in number, could be deployed on active service. The verdict of military historian Jeffrey Grey was that 'Ponderous mobilization, cabinet indecision, fluctuating perceptions of Japanese intentions, the unreadiness of the armed forces and a shortage of shipping delayed their departure until early 1940'. Unready the armed forces certainly were. As a sop to the Labor radicals, and following a 1919 commitment, Scullin had cancelled compulsory military training in 1930, replacing it with a volunteer militia force; in a single year army numbers fell from 47,931 to 27,454. Compulsory training was only reintroduced in January 1940 and Australia entered the war with a poorly equipped and sketchily trained militia and a pitifully small regular force. Militia could volunteer for the overseas service with the AIF – at lower pay – and many did, but the maintenance of two armies, one limited to home service, with two separate and often bickering chains of command, made direction of the war even more difficult. Jeffrey Grey comments: 'At times, it might be wondered whether some of Australia's most senior officers ever put as much energy into fighting the Germans and Japanese as they did into quarrelling with one another.'[7]

Unlike the British Labour Party, Australian Labor steadily refused to participate in a coalition government. The best that could be done was to form an all-party Advisory War Cabinet. Although Curtin always expressed himself ready to cooperate, the existence of an opposition which had only one fewer seat in the House of Representatives than the government, and which contained such dissidents as the unrepentant Langite Eddie Ward, who had opposed increased defence spending and had attacked his leader in 'virulent clashes', and the intensely ambitious Herbert Evatt, who left the High Court for Parliament in the 1940 election, made consistent bi-partisan action difficult. Curtin's task in papering over the cracks was to be made easier by the German abrogation of the Soviet pact and invasion of Russia in June 1941, which brought Australian communists back into the fold together with the re-admission of the Non-Communist Labor Party, but an important minority remained less than loyal to Curtin's cooperation with the Australian government.

The opposition objected to the AIF leaving and, while reluctantly accepting Australia's belligerent status, insisted that Australian forces should be retained to protect the homeland. It was an unrealistic and even dishonourable position, but one that has subsequently received some support.[8] In the first place the immediate threat, indeed the only threat to have taken tangible form, was in Europe, and, as was soon to be made clear in that dramatic summer of 1940, Britain and her Empire were to stand alone, with most of Western Europe under Germany's power. Australia could best be defended by keeping open communications with her allies, but with a navy which, although modernized in the 1930s, consisted only of six light cruisers, this could not be done without support from Britain, and from the modern ships of the French and Dutch navies.

Such support was to prove alarmingly ineffective. The Royal Navy could be relied upon for a substantial presence in the Atlantic and the Indian oceans, but was likely to be heavily strained in keeping open the sea routes in the face of German and Italian submarines and surface raiders. A decision had been taken in the spring of 1939 to strengthen the eastern squadrons, but in the great expanse of the Pacific this would take time, and time was not to be granted; and whereas in the First World War the Japanese alliance had blocked this gap, that country was now moving towards an alliance with Germany.

Much more potentially dangerous to Australian security than the despatch of land forces overseas was the relative neglect of the Royal Australian Air Force (RAAF). Although volunteers had rushed to join the air force – 68,000 of them by March 1940, in contrast to the 20,000 or so army volunteers – most were eventually sent to join RAF squadrons in Britain after passing through the Empire Air Training Service (EATS). Inspired by Bruce and his Canadian counterpart in London, Vincent Massey, EATS trained Dominion and British aircrews in Canada and Australia, under much more suitable conditions than those obtaining in beleaguered Britain. For the first two and a half years of the war, Europe and the Mediterranean remained the only theatre of action, and eighteen Australian RAF squadrons fought in Europe throughout the war, incurring heavy casualties and participating in some of the most hazardous sorties. After Japan entered the conflict many Australian pilots were posted to the Pacific, but the RAAF squadrons that should have constituted Australia's defence were at first dangerously few.

As Neville Chamberlain was doing in England, Menzies assumed emergency powers. 'All in' was his motto as he swept into action to initiate the 'New Despotism' by taking powers to control all aspects of civilian life by the National Security Regulations, effecting control over labour prices and restricting media freedom. Compulsory military training for home defence was introduced, and the Communist Party (and also, eccentrically, the Jehovah's Witnesses) banned; even in wartime Britain it was not found necessary to silence either of these dangerous sects. But, also like Chamberlain's preparations, those of Menzies were to a great extent paper creations, doing little to equip the country for war; and there was no Australian Churchill waiting in the wings to take charge of the nation's destiny, as the old warrior did for Britain on 10 May 1940.

Australia's volunteers were indeed a generous contribution to the hard pressed Imperial forces and one which might have left the homeland dangerously imperilled – if there was indeed a threat of Japanese invasion. The understanding with the British government was that Australian protection would be assured from the modern naval base of Singapore, a promise reinforced by Churchill on 10 August 1940 when he undertook that, if Japan invaded Australia or New Zealand 'on a large scale', he could give an assurance that we should then cut our losses in the Mediterranean and sacrifice every interest, except only the defence and feeding of this Island, on which all depends, and would proceed in good time to your aid with a fleet able to give battle to any Japanese force which could be placed in Australian waters, and able to parry any invading force, or certainly cut its communications with Japan.

It was an impossible promise and one which Anthony Eden rightly queried, although it might be said that the premise of a Japanese invasion on a large scale was a highly significant qualification. At that time, Britain's plight was desperate; the last army had been extracted from the Dunkirk beaches, badly mauled, with its equipment lost, an invasion imminent, and the skies of southern England witnessing the most decisive air battle in history.[9]

A naval base was useless without a navy, and that of Britain, weakened by the Washington accords, had been further damaged by official complacency. Previous planning had disintegrated as Nazi armies crushed Holland and France. Some Dutch warships escaped, but the powerful French fleet, which included the fast battleship *Richelieu*, seemed lost to Britain when the country surrendered on 22 June. When in the same month Italy joined with Germany the Royal Navy was alone (the Dominions offering what help they could), responsible for conducting a war in the Atlantic and Mediterranean, with little to spare for regions which remained peaceful, or at least, since the war between China and Japan continued, which were not involved in European hostilities.

Menzies, like Hughes before him, itched to be at the centre of power and as soon as possible took himself off, via the Middle East, to Britain, where he was a not entirely welcome guest. Even before his arrival in February 1941 Menzies had irritated Churchill by sending a telegram critical of the failed Anglo-Free French invasion of Dakar. The totally inexperienced Menzies lectured Churchill, with nearly half-a-century of active service, on the unwisdom of a half-hearted attack which did not have 'overwhelming chances of success'. Churchill ended his long reply:

Still, my dear Prime Minister and friend, as you have allowed me to deem you, I cannot guarantee 'clear-cut victory' in the Middle East, or that Cairo, Khartoum, the Suez Canal and Palestine may not fall into Italian or German hands. We do not think they will, and we are trying our utmost to resist the attacks which are massing against us. But I can make no promises at all of victory, nor can I make any promises that regrettable and lamentable incidents will not occur, or that there will not be disappointments and blunders. On the contrary, I think the only certainty is that we have very bad times indeed to go through before we emerge from the mortal perils by which we are surrounded.[10]

When, however, Churchill received Menzies at his official country house, Chequers, on 1 March, the Australian Prime Minister came trailing clouds of reflected glory, for Commonwealth forces had taken the leading part in sweeping the Italian army out of Egypt and for hundreds of miles across the Western Desert and were now urgently needed elsewhere. After the 1940 blitzkreig and the evacuation of Dunkirk no Imperial forces had been fighting in mainland Europe, but on the same day as the Chequers meeting the German army entered Bulgaria on their way to an invasion of Greece. Mussolini had attempted an invasion the previous November, and had been humiliatingly repulsed by the Greek army, but there was little prospect of that small and poorly equipped force for long resisting the *Wehrmacht*. If help was to be sent to Greece the only forces available were a British armoured brigade, one New Zealand and two Australian divisions. Strategically, the opening of a new front might have been expected to be the occasion of a serious debate, but there was little discussion in Canberra. Indeed, the probability of such action had been recognized in November 1940, when the Governor General's speech acknowledged that

Germany's intentions in relation to Greece, Bulgaria and Turkey, however, remain undefined, and consequently the problem of the defence of the Middle East is one which must continue to engage the attention, not only of His Majesty's Government in the United Kingdom, but also of Australia, which has large forces in Egypt and Palestine.

Australian participation was agreed by both Menzies in London and the Australian Cabinet. How far Menzies was properly consulted when the decision to send troops to Greece was actually taken is uncertain; there had been discussions with General Wavell, the Commander in Chief Middle East, and the Australian commander, General Blamey, but the head of the British Foreign Office, Sir Alexander Cadogan, thought Menzies had been poorly treated. Twenty-five years later, however, Menzies remained convinced that the decision was right, based on 'the overwhelming moral and political repercussions of abandoning Greece'. Assistance to Greece was perhaps inevitable, but the subsequent decision to continue the fight in Crete was disastrous. Not only had the German army cut through the Greek defences within days, but at the same time German reinforcements had rolled back the British in North Africa; Benghazi, captured from the Italians, fell to their German allies; Crete succumbed to a daring German assault by paratroops; of the 58,000 British, Australian, New Zealand and Polish troops engaged, 28,000 were killed or captured; Australian losses, including wounded, totalled 6,727. Menzies, concerned about the defence of Australia, attempted to insist that one or more of the three Australian divisions then in the region should be sent back, but all, after the mauling received in Greece, were absolutely essential in the Middle East.[11]

When Menzies returned to Australia in May 1941 he had been away for four months. So protracted an absence, with so slender a majority, was a major political error. It was not the Labor opposition that brought Menzies down on 29 August, but internal party squabbling. The feuds within the UAP had not subsided; Acting Prime Minister Arthur Fadden had sent encouraging messages to Menzies in London, but some of the UAP members were openly contemptuous of their leader, and many more stood in need of constant soothing and encouragement. Three of the most competent and reliable ministers, Geoffrey Street, James Fairbairn and Sir Henry Gullett were killed in an August 1940 air crash. Paul Hasluck, one of the official war historians, stigmatizes the UAP plotters: 'It would reveal a much less repulsive condition of Australian politics if one could believe that the members of the UAP who opposed Menzies and worked for his deposition in July and August 1941 were doing so simply because of their illusion that political stability and a united war effort might thereby be gained.' Helping the war effort was, however, far from the minds of the UAP rebels who 'set a low value on their conception of party responsibility'. A. W. Coles, the independent MP, bitterly described the dispositions: 'Mr Menzies has been offered as Australia's scapegoat on the altar of political ambition, under the coercion of constantly applied pressure. I witnessed a lynching organised by mass hysteria. It was something so unclean that it will never be erased from my memory – it was nothing but a public lynching.'[12]

It was true that Australia was less than convinced of the need for increased effort; before the Greek debacle there had been few Australian casualties, and the imminence of the Japanese threat had been proved exaggerated. Professor Elkin, the highly regarded anthropologist, conducted an opinion survey which concluded that

In the first place, very great numbers of our people have to be won over to a sense of urgency and of self-sacrifice. Secondly, the condition from which they have to be converted is only in a small minority of cases apathy. It is much more varied and complex. Thirdly, each one of us must make up his mind what are the moral and political objectives of the war. And, lastly, confidence in our political leaders must be regained.[13]

There might be a parallel between Menzies' resignation and the replacement of the shuffling Prime Minister Neville Chamberlain by the outstanding war leader Churchill, were it not that Menzies had run a reasonably competent wartime administration and that his eventual replacement, John Curtin, was anything but a natural leader in war. When Gerald Wilkinson, a British intelligence agent, described Curtin as 'a small and parochial man and obviously not equipped by experience and environment to take naturally to a global view of strategy', he was being accurate, if unkind.[14] Nor was there any immediate unanimity in the Coalition as to who should succeed Menzies. In some desperation, Arthur Fadden of the Country Party was elected, only to suffer a parliamentary defeat six weeks later as the two independent members chose to switch their allegiance to Labor, bringing John Curtin to the Prime Minister's office.

After the parliamentary defeat of the stopgap Fadden administration Curtin took over the government on 3 October 1941. It was an unpromising situation for a country at war. The new Prime Minister's team was inexperienced – only four of the nineteen Cabinet ministers had previously held office – but proved unexpectedly efficacious. Personal jealousies and feuds dissolved under the responsibilities of office, although Eddie Ward – 'that bloody ratbag', according to Curtin – remained bristlingly disloyal to such an extent that in any government not dominated by the extra-parliamentary Labor group he would have been instantly dismissed. Curtin himself was frail, ill and physically timorous – but he was to hold on to power for the next three years.

He was given very little time before the realities of war exploded in Australia's face. The restrictions on naval armaments imposed by the Washington treaties of 1922 had been abandoned in 1936, and both Japan and Germany had been quick to take advantage of this. Although Germany's splendid new battleships and heavy cruisers were potentially deadly as commerce raiders, they were never able to combine, deprived as the *Kriegsmarine* was of aircraft carriers and support ships, into a force capable of a fleet action. Japan's surface forces were much stronger, comprising as they did such huge vessels as the *Yamato*, at 64,000 tons the biggest warship afloat, and, given access to the raw materials of Manchukuo and northern China, the Japanese army and air force were able to equip themselves to a standard high enough, when combined with thorough training and a patriotism which bordered sometimes on the fanatic, to match any European or American troops.

Japan's democracy was a delicate plant – the first parliamentary institutions were more recent than those of the Australian colonies – and the martial traditions of the feudal shogunate still flourished, nourished by half a century of recent victories. During the 1930s military revolts had succeeded in assassinating a number of Cabinet ministers – including one admiral –

thereby fatally undermining the democratic process.[15] Saionji Kinmochi, who had succeeded Ito Hirobumi, the founding father of modern Japan, died in 1940. Like Prince Ito, Saionji was an experienced internationalist, who had headed the Japanese delegation to Versailles; while he lived he did his best to keep Japan a constitutional monarchy within the Anglo-American international order, but without Saionji no other politician could withstand the aggressive ambitions of the military. Konoe Fumimaro, Prime Minister in 1940–1, attempted to follow Saionji's diplomacy, but was unwilling to impose his will (and incapable of doing so) on the army. When General Tojo Hideki assumed control in 1941 prospects of peace evaporated.

Britain's isolation seemed almost to guarantee Germany success, and the prospects that might accrue to Japan as a partner, in picking up major parts of the British, Dutch and French Asian colonies, to be integrated in the 'Greater East Asia Co-prosperity Sphere', tempted the Japanese government to agree a Tripartite Pact with Germany and Italy in September 1940, followed by a neutrality agreement with Russia in April 1941. A foretaste of these benefits was given in May 1941, when the Vichy government allowed Japan access to French Indo-China, followed by the despatch of troops in August. By that time Japanese rule extended through 40 degrees of latitude, from Harbin to the Gulf of Siam.

What part a Japanese-dominated Australia might be expected to play in the Greater East Asia Co-prosperity Sphere is unclear. Occupied Indo-China was recognized by Japan as remaining French, and Thailand's political regime continued uninterrupted. The possibility of invading Australia was discussed in Tokyo, but plans were never developed. The imperial Japanese army was already stretched very thin, continuing the draining war with China as well as providing manpower for the new adventures. Had the Japanese occupation of New Guinea been successful, it might have seemed that air raids in the north, plus some bombardment of coastal cities by the 18-inch guns of the Japanese battleships, might persuade Australia to accept Japanese rather than its former British sovereignty. Without the transport needed for a large force, only the most opportunistic of Japanese commanders could have hoped for a successful invasion of the continent by land forces, which was surely never anything but a very remote prospect.

Within weeks Curtin was faced with the consequences of the Japanese attack on Pearl Harbor, on 7 December 1941, which transformed the war for Australians, bringing as it did hostilities into the Pacific and the promise of American help. All eyes switched to Singapore, designated as the strong point of Imperial defence in the Pacific region. Surrounded as it was by a bloc of allied French and Dutch territories, with all modern facilities for repair and supply, servicing the Royal and allied navies, Singapore seemed an excellent choice; but the navies it was meant to shelter were now scattered. In 1919 Admiral Jellicoe had reported that the fleet based on Singapore should consist of sixteen battleships and battlecruisers, four aircraft carriers and ten cruisers, together with four destroyer flotillas. The cost of this, estimated at £20 million, of which Australia and New Zealand were to be asked to contribute 29 per cent, left the Dominions 'aghast' – but the scheme was 'totally emasculated' by the Washington treaties. On the outbreak of war the *total* strength of the Royal Navy comprised only twelve battleships and battlecruisers and six aircraft carriers; the Italian navy alone had nearly as many battleships and destroyers, and three times as many submarines, to say nothing of the rapidly growing *Kriegsmarine*, or the potential Japanese threat. In these circumstances Churchill's undertaking to cut losses in the Mediterranean to reinforce Singapore was meaningless – and should have been known to be meaningless.

From June 1940 the conduct of the war had been a purely British Imperial affair, run from London by a government desperately trying to deal with its European enemies while subject to scrutiny in the House of Commons. With greater or lesser success, each Dominion with access to the War Cabinet pressed its own views and requirements, Canada, for example, banning the use of any of its troops from the Middle Eastern conflict, and Australia doing its best to make provision for its own defence. After December 1941 the war was primarily an Anglo-American affair, with Russia fighting a parallel war on its own front. Australian access to the Anglo-American High Command was limited, especially as policies were increasingly settled personally between Churchill and Roosevelt. In the First World War, Australia had been a vital ally, and continued to be so from 1940 to 1941 in the Middle East, while Australian pilots were prominent in both the RAF and RAAF. In the Second World War, Australia's role after the Japanese aggression was more limited, in strategic terms little more than a very useful local facility in the South Pacific, an invaluable supplier of strategic materials, but with its soldiers confined to a subordinate and limited role under American command. In such circumstances Curtin, even had he possessed similar personal qualities, was never able to make the same waves in the High Command that Billy Hughes had been able to create thirty years before; nor was Australia able to exert the influence on the United States that the long-established Imperial ties had facilitated.

Future strategy was settled in the vital 'Arcadia' conference in Washington, to which Churchill had hurried almost immediately after Pearl Harbor. Russia, which had the only army capable of facing the *Wehrmacht*, had to be kept supplied as a matter of priority until American and British forces could move into Europe. The Japanese, it was feared, would 'establish themselves fairly easily in British and American possessions', but Singapore was assumed to be the key, and frequent cables were sent from Washington to Curtin assuring him of Anglo-American intentions to reinforce the island. Australia's secondary role, and that of the other smaller allies, was underlined at the first meeting with Roosevelt, who agreed that no 'permanent body' could be established that would 'limit the action or capacity to take prompt decisions of United States, Great Britain and Russia'.

Pearl Harbor showed the effectiveness of a surprise attack by the Japanese air force, but very soon the ability of the imperial Japanese army was demonstrated in a very uncomfortable fashion. The Japanese advance which overwhelmed south-east Asia within months was one of the most brilliant feats of arms in the history of modern warfare. Operating many hundreds of miles from their bases, the troops, showing their superb fighting qualities, were supported by excellent logistics, all contributing to the complete surprise of the Allies when the Japanese landed on the Malay Peninsula on 8 December. Two days later Admiral Tom Phillips's squadron (augmented at Menzies' request with a modern battleship, but lacking the vital aircraft carrier that was intended to be included), steaming to the rescue of the British and Dominion troops, was attacked by Saigon-based Japanese planes. Within two hours the battle cruiser *Repulse* and the new battleship *Prince of Wales* were sunk; what had been intended as a bold Nelsonian enterprise, which might have changed the whole course of the war, had disintegrated, and with it all reason for holding on in Singapore.[16] Reinforcements were nevertheless rushed there: on Christmas Day Churchill was able to tell Curtin that Roosevelt would agree to support Singapore; on 14 January he informed him that a vital convoy had reached the island with 9,000 men including an anti-tank regiment and fifty Hurricane fighter aircraft. Five days later the Supreme Allied Commander, General Wavell, reported that Singapore was not defensible against a land attack. If the Japanese advance had been astonishing, British unreadiness seemed to prove that the phrase 'military intelligence' is indeed an oxymoron. The possible withdrawal from Singapore was therefore urgently discussed, and a copy of the memorandum proposing this was sent to Curtin via Earle Page, whereupon Curtin telegraphed that the evacuation of Malaya and Singapore 'would be regarded here as an inexcusable betrayal'. In reality, far from being a betrayal an immediate evacuation would have been by far the wisest possible course, and the 2,000 Australian soldiers who landed on the 24th were needless sacrifices. With just a dash of his usual cynicism, the historian

A. J. P. Taylor judged that the men had been sent 'into certain captivity in order to appease the Australians'.[17] On 15 February the British general commanding surrendered unconditionally, and some 100,000 Imperial troops were taken prisoner, marched off to a vicious captivity, constituting the worst defeat ever inflicted on a British force.

Four days later Australian civilians had their first direct experience of war, when Japanese aircraft attacked Darwin on 19 February, sinking nine ships in the harbour, destroying more than twenty planes and killing 233; it was Australia's Pearl Harbor, if on a smaller scale. Profoundly shocking as it was, Australia's first direct experience of war being brought to her own shore, the Darwin raid was not intended to herald an invasion of Australia, just as the attack on Pearl Harbor did not presage an invasion of Hawaii. The raid was the first of more than sixty in the next two years, and reinforcing Darwin, in the absence of a railway link, over the indifferent roads, was very difficult. Civilian morale was sadly damaged; the American Minister, N. T. Johnson, reported to Roosevelt describing 'near panic . . . a feeling of utter helplessness . . . presented to the onlooker a tragic picture'. Showing another side of his abilities Ted Theodore was appointed to head an Allied Works Council, where he proved briskly unsympathetic to union objections as civilian Australia was placed on a war basis.[18]

The new government's almost complete ignorance of foreign affairs had been demonstrated by a panic suggestion, made on 22 December 1941 in a cable to the British government, that Russia should be given nearly a free hand in Europe in return for waging war on Japan:

The attitude we are inclined to recommend is to accede to Stalin's wishes as far as possible, providing he undertakes to commence war against Japan in the near future . . . We think there is very urgent need for specific understandings with Russia regarding military, naval and air cooperation. We are not concerned to block Stalin's wish ultimately to gain territory at the expense of Germany and Japan so long as we can overthrow those powers.

But the concessions were to go further, implicating Finland, Poland, Czechoslovakia, Korea and Iran. (By 1944 Mr Curtin's education had been advanced: on 4 May, at a meeting of Dominion Prime Ministers, he raised the question of 'the risk that after the defeat of the Nazis, Communist or Leftist organizations might move into control in Germany, and indeed all occupied countries'.)[19]

To some extent this innocence was helpful in clarifying war aims. All other interests should be subordinated to the defence of Australia. It was not an attitude calculated to win friends. An article under Curtin's signature appeared in the Melbourne *Herald* on 27 December 1941 (it was drafted by the Prime Minister's press secretary), claiming:

We look for a solid and impregnable barrier of the democracies against the three Axis Powers and we refuse to accept the dictum that the Pacific struggle must be treated as a subordinate segment of the general conflict . . . The Australian Government therefore regards the Pacific struggle as primarily one in which the United States and Australia must have the fullest say in the direction of the democracies' fighting plan. Without any inhibitions of any kind, I make it quite clear that Australia looks to America, free of any pangs as to our traditional links or kinship with the United Kingdom.

Both Roosevelt and Churchill were angered. The American President declared that it did not 'ingratiate Australia with the United States. Quite the reverse: it smacked of panic and disloyalty.' It was not, however, Curtin who began the pressure to withdraw Australian troops from the Middle East, which was started by Menzies and reinforced by Fadden on 16 September 1941, the day after Stalin had – quite impossibly – asked for twenty-five British divisions to strike north through Persia. General Auchinleck attempted to resign his command, and Churchill, 'astounded' by the Australian government's decision, was 'sure it would be repudiated by Australia if the facts were known', but went on to add that 'personal feelings' must be 'subordinated to appearance of unity'. With forty years of parliamentary experience, Churchill was prepared to be sympathetic to any government with a majority of one.[20]

Curtin did not pursue Fadden's order, which would have at that time been militarily absurd, but after the Japanese attack, early in January the British government suggested that two of the three Australian divisions fighting in the Western Desert could be transferred to meet the Japanese advances, their destination at first to be the Dutch East Indies. Curtin, however, demanded that they should be returned to Australia. Grudgingly, and after much prevarication and some dissimulation this was agreed to, and the 6th and 7th, both experienced divisions, were returned to their homeland. While the troops were actually on their way Churchill, without informing the Australian government or even his War Cabinet, ordered their diversion to Rangoon in an attempt to shore up the defence of Burma. Curtin, supported by his Chiefs of Staff, expostulated angrily, and the troops were allowed to continue to Australia.

The Anglo-American strategy, evolved during the December 1941 meetings between Roosevelt and Churchill was reinforced in talks held in

April 1942 between Churchill, Roosevelt's personal representative Harry Hopkins, and the American Chief of Staff, General George Marshall. When Marshall expressed American reluctance to direct further forces to Australia and the south-west Pacific and agreed on the priority of the European war, Churchill noted that the plans could be 'fatally compromised by Japanese action in the Indian Ocean', where the allied navies, under the command of British Admiral James Somerville had suffered severe losses on 28 February. Five cruisers, including HMAS *Perth*, and five destroyers were sunk off Java and 13,000 British and Australians were taken prisoner after the Dutch surrender of the island. By contrast, the defence of Ceylon against Japanese attack in April was successful: six more Royal Navy ships, including the aircraft carrier *Hermes*, were sunk, but the Japanese lost many experienced pilots, and both fleets retired, Somerville seeking a base in West Africa, the Japanese to meet the American threat in the East. With five battleships intact, Admiral Somerville had to protect the Indian Ocean, but the threat was enough to deter the Japanese navy thereafter from attempting a fleet action there. Somerville's battle on 4 and 5 April marked the limit of Japanese intrusion westwards. A month later another fleet action between the Japanese and American fleets (though Royal Australian Navy ships also took part) in the Coral Sea prevented a planned Japanese invasion of south New Guinea. A month later on 4 June a Japanese attempt on Midway was foiled, with four Japanese aircraft carriers sunk by an American Pacific fleet recovered from the Pearl Harbor disaster. After Midway, Japan lost the command of the seas and the threat of a Japanese invasion of Australia receded to the verge of impossibility. The decisive contribution to victory by the Australian army was made on the Western Desert, when the 9th division helped to roll back Rommel's Afrika Corps at El Alamein in October 1942 and permit the invasion of Italy. After the Alamein battle the Australian soldiers were returned to the homeland to be employed under American command, in what were essentially sideshows – painful, unpleasant and dangerous, but peripheral to the strategic struggle.[21]

Ironically, the first actions fought by Australian soldiers in the Pacific theatre were victories, not for the experienced AIF troops but the much-criticized militia. Only volunteers could be employed abroad, the conscripted militia being for home service only, but 'abroad' did not include Papua, an Australian possession. When, therefore, the Japanese landed on the north coast of New Guinea in 1942, they were confronted by two Australian militia brigades. Advancing across the Owen Stanley Range over what became the infamous Kokoda track, the hitherto invincible Japanese were checked by the 'pathetically young warriors' of the 39th militia battalion in August and September 1942. Thereafter, until January 1943, the Australian soldiers, reinforced by units of the newly arrived AIF, forced the Japanese back over the Kokoda track and up the north coast to their landing beaches. From November they were joined by American troops, but these, inexperienced and poorly trained, were less helpful than the American sea and air support. It would also have been entirely reasonable to blame the Australian High Command for much. Two of the senior generals in Malaya, Tom Blamey and Gordon Bennett, were widely unpopular, Blamey for his dubious inter-war record and rowdy drinking, and Bennett for his inglorious and unauthorized flight from Singapore. Dissensions among both the army and air force High Command were public and did considerable damage to the fighting efficiency of the services; Lieutenant General Sir Sydney Rowell 'made no great secret of his contempt' for Sir Thomas Blamey, while the protracted feud between Air Vice-Marshals Jones and Bostock is described by Jeffrey Grey as 'disgraceful'. Fortunately, the fighting in which the 9th division found themselves involved as they pressed north into the Mandated Territory of New Guinea was carried out in small units, down to platoon level, at which the junior officers and men excelled; generals could do little to help or hinder, as long as the supply routes were kept open. It took eight months of bitter fighting before the mountainous Huon peninsula fell and the survivors of the Japanese XVIIIth army, reduced from 35,000 to 13,500, were penned up on the north coast. The Australian army lost 2,165 dead and 3,350 wounded, the Americans about half of that number, Papua was a genuine Australian victory, the first gained by Australians not fighting alongside British troops.[22]

A measure of Curtin's authority was his ability to persuade the Labor Party to accept conscription for service overseas, a complete reversal of previous policy, which had led to the disastrous split in 1916. It was done by the ingenious device of extending the region in which militia could be called upon to serve, to include the whole of the south-west Pacific area, apart from the Philippines and some areas of Java and Borneo. More symbolic than useful, since 200,000 militia conscripts volunteered to join the AIF, the move placated American critics, who unfairly characterized the restrictions as indicating Australian reluctance to fight. Labor opposition was bitter, and astonishing to those who believed in collective Cabinet responsibility. It was one thing for Arthur Calwell, as a backbencher, to attack the Prime Minister, but when members of his own Cabinet, such as Eddie Ward and Don Cameron, joined in 'vitriolic' and 'poisonous' tirades the magnitude of Curtin's task was apparent.[23]

It was perhaps as well that Curtin, inexperienced as he was, virtually abdicated responsibility for controlling Australian forces, handing over command to the egocentric American General Douglas MacArthur, who showed no interest in any Australian problems. In March 1942, after a dogged resistance (in stark contrast to that offered by the British in Singapore) the American and Filipino troops still holding out in Bataan and Corregidor surrendered to the Japanese. Their commander, MacArthur, was ordered to transfer his headquarters to Australia, which was henceforward to serve as the main American base for the re-conquest of the Japanese-occupied territories. If Australian politicians and soldiers had found some of their British counterparts dismissive, MacArthur gave a demonstration of what arrogance could really be like, leaving poor Curtin having little to do but agree. But with great numbers of American troops in Australia, all fear of a Japanese attack was over.

The Australian government had asked that Papua and New Guinea should be liberated by Australian troops, with a view to re-asserting Australian authority at the end of the war (not that the native inhabitants had shown much enthusiasm for membership of the Greater East Asia Co-prosperity Sphere) and many Papuans had won golden opinions for their brave support of the Australian forces. As well as continuing the advance up the north coast of New Guinea it was also politically sound that the Australian forces should eject the Japanese from the neighbouring islands of New Britain, which as part of the Bismarck archipelago had been included in the Mandate. Tactically, the wisdom of sending 35,000 fine Australian troops to New Britain to do little more than sit and look at a very much larger Japanese force until the end of the war was at least questionable. A full division and two independent brigades were sent to liberate the Solomon Islands, another part of the mandated territories. Unlike the calm that prevailed in New Britain, there was prolonged and tough fighting in Bougainville and therefore quite heavy Australian casualties – none of which contributed much to advancing the end of the war.

Strategic logic took second place to MacArthur's determination to keep the liberation of the Philippines in purely American hands (and to revenge his own personal humiliation). Casting about for some employment for the remaining Australian forces, he dispatched the last two divisions in May 1945 to assault Borneo, which would liberate the British and Dutch oil wells and possibly enable Australia to claim a post-war mandate; but the veteran Australian troops were not allowed to take part in the great battles then deciding the issue of the war in Europe. Once again some hundreds of Australians were killed for no strategic imperative.[24] From June 1944, as British, American and Canadian troops were landing on the Normandy beaches, the Australian government began demobilizing its soldiers.

The Home Front

Domestically Australians, like Americans, were insulated by geography from the worst effects of the war, but nevertheless felt its force. Drastic powers were taken to draft the civilian workforce into the war effort; all 'unoccupied' women – defined as those single or divorced or childless between the ages of 18 and 45 – were liable to be conscripted into industry. Enthusiastic female volunteers staffed a striking range of voluntary organizations – the Red Cross, the Air League, the Australian Women's Legion, which included a cavalry corps, the National Emergency Services, the Country Women's Association, the Melbourne Militors, the War Workers' Social Aid, Comforts Funds, and the Women's Auxiliary Service Patriots, all under the aegis of the Women's Auxiliary National Service and the Women's Voluntary National Register. More formally, women were recruited into the new armed services, the Women's Auxiliary Air Force, the Women's Army Service and the Women's Royal Australian Naval Service. Under the direction of the blunt Scot, Jack Dedman, a former British soldier, Australian society was forced to appreciate the virtues of austerity, but socially the influx of a million well-dressed, well-paid and generally agreeable American servicemen lightened the prevailing gloom. The Labor government, however, showed its usual disregard of the brotherhood of man by first resisting the arrival of any black servicemen, and then banishing most of them to remote sites in Queensland.[25]

All wartime governments attempted to gain wider powers and to hang on to them – the British Defence of the Realm Act, the unpopular Dora, passed in August 1914, continued for more than sixty years. Dora's fiat set limited hours for public houses, but was outclassed by the Australian legislation, which closed bars at 6 p.m., leading to the notorious six o'clock swill, with thirsty drinkers clamouring to get their shout in before the dreaded hour approached; like Dora, the six o'clock closing had a long life, only ending in the 1960s. By that time the intrusion of women into what had been an exclusively male preserve was beginning to be accepted, at least in the larger towns. Some of these powers were doubtless necessary, but in such a lively democracy as that of Australia more was achieved by spontaneous self-discipline and by the flexibility that open government can give to emergency management. One cheering development was the hoax perpetrated in

1944 by two soldier-poets, Harold Stewart and James McAuley, on the innocent editor of the avant-garde journal *Angry Penguins*, by submitting under the name of 'Ern Malley' verses concocted from a pamphlet on pest control, Shakespeare, and other disparate materials. All were accepted and given the highest critical praise.

In spite of the best efforts of Eddie Ward, who ran a scare about the 'Brisbane Line', or Menzies' alleged plan to abandon all of northern Australia in the event of a Japanese invasion, and whose 'loud-mouthed larrikinism' brought discredit on the government of which he remained a minister, Curtin gained a triumphant victory in the 1943 elections, winning 49 of 74 seats in the House of Representatives. Together with a respectable Senate majority this gave him an unassailable – and very rare – authority. During the campaign, Curtin began to qualify his famous comment about looking to America for leadership 'free of any pangs as to our traditional links or kinship with the United Kingdom'. 'Australia', he said, 'could not expect to hold indefinitely a large continent with a small population and a declining birth rate.' The only likely source of immigration (too many of those American servicemen who might have wished to stay were inconveniently black) was Britain; there must therefore arise 'a second Britannia in the Antipodes' in which the obligation would be 'to be a good Australian, a good British subject, and a good world citizen'; and this was to become a central policy of post-war governments. It was a sign of John Curtin's new enthusiasm for the British link that when the time came to replace Lord Gowrie, who as Governor General had been a close friend of the Labor leader, he chose, not an Australian, but another Briton – and not only a Briton but the King's brother, the worthy Duke of Gloucester.

For the time being, kicking against the pricks of devolved state powers, since five of the six states had conservative majorities, Curtin attempted once again, in August 1944, to go down the road of obtaining increased Federal authority by means of a referendum. Australian voters were to be obliged to decide whether or not to allow the Commonwealth government extensive new powers, fourteen in all, bundled into one take-it-or-leave-it proposal. Sensibly, the voters decided, with the end of the war in Europe at least in sight, to leave it, by a majority of two and a half to one million. One achievement that was, however, made possible by wartime conditions was Treasurer Chifley's legislation for a Federal income tax to replace the different taxes levied by the states, a valuable extension of central power.[26]

Reasonably enough, Labor governments attempted to fulfil their traditional mandates by advancing social legislation, aided by the pressures of war which concentrated power in the national government. In so doing the centralization of income tax provided a vital resource; in the budgets of 1937–8, £11.5 million was provided for defence; by 1943–4 this had risen to £545 million – and once these costs began to fall, the income could be, relatively painlessly, transferred to sponsor Labor projects. And fall the costs of combat rapidly did. Army expenditure, which in 1942–3 had reached nearly £300 million, fell to £216 million the following year. To some extent social priorities were bipartisan; Menzies had begun the child benefit scheme in 1941, followed by Chifley in 1944 with a comprehensive programme of unemployment insurance, sickness and maternity benefits and contributions towards prescription costs. The government wanted to go further and provide complete medical cover, through a National Health Service, such as was introduced in Britain in 1946. But Australia had no Aneurin Bevan capable of facing down the vested interests of the medical profession (and to an extent the British scheme had bipartisan support in that it was prepared by the Conservative Minister for Health in the Churchill government, Sir Henry Willink). A Universities Commission was established in 1943, followed by the foundation of the Australian National University as a graduate college in 1946. In a scene hitherto dominated by the Universities of Sydney and Melbourne, with the Universities of Adelaide, Western Australia, Tasmania and Queensland forming a second division, new institutions appeared – the University of New England in Armidale, Newcastle University and a second Sydney institution, the University of New South Wales, together with a host of state colleges and teacher training colleges.

For the last few months of Curtin's life before his death in July 1945 he was in and out of hospital, desperately ill, but clinging on in the knowledge that he was still capable of holding together a querulous and fragmenting Labor Party. He need not have worried overmuch since his successor, Ben Chifley, was more than able to keep both party and the country united. Tougher and a more talented administrator than Curtin, inheriting a sound majority – although with the headstrong Lang back in Parliament as a one-man party intent on harassing his old colleagues – Chifley also inherited the party's old albatross, the White Australia policy.[27]

Since Chifley had already been appointed Minister for Post-War Reconstruction the change, in domestic affairs, was seamless. At the first post-war election in 1946 Labor won its second successive general election victory, and although losing 7 seats in the lower house increased its senate majority; and, *mirabile dictu*, a referendum increasing the Commonwealth authority over social security was actually won (although two others were, as usual rejected). Labor's programme was reformist, and on the whole gradualist, unlike the more radical approach of the contemporary British Labour Party.

The extravagant incompetence of the post-1919 settlement policies was avoided. A Commonwealth Employment Service, preferential employment, gratuities and vocational training helped to slot returning servicemen into post-war life. Economic recovery was very much more rapid than after the First World War; indeed, in some respects Australia emerged from the conflict much more prosperous than it had been before, with the community's purchasing power 'vastly enhanced'. The devastation in Europe and in Asia had caused food prices to shoot up: by 1944–5 the index of Australian export prices (1936–9 = 100) had risen to 130, and by 1948–9 to 348; wheat sales had increased eightfold over the previous ten years. American servicemen brought an influx of welcome dollars, at a time when rationing reduced the choices available. The more limited role of Australian ground forces after 1943 enabled demobilization to be started the following year, thus staggering the flow of returning soldiers entering the job market. Women had played a much greater role in wartime industry, and had earned the right to be paid wages at 90 per cent of the men's rate in war-related jobs; not equal pay, but much fairer than the 54 per cent that had been traditional.

The administration of Chifley's Department of Post-War Reconstruction was confided to H. C. 'Nugget' Coombs as Director General, who later observed that 'While the war has left us . . . problems, it has also increased our capacity to solve them. We have built over the years of war a technique for handling our economic affairs which we need not throw aside . . . It did not take us long to discover that the working of the economic system was something within our capacity to control.' Coombs went on to demonstrate, as head of the Commonwealth Bank, how the Australian economy could be, if not controlled, at least guided, but not the least interesting aspect of his speech was that it was given in January 1944, at the time of the Anzio landings in Italy, six months before the Allied armies disembarked on the Normandy beaches – and Dr Coombs was speaking of the war, as far as Australia was concerned, already being over.[28]

In its policies towards the Communist Party, Labor reflected the extent to which Australian attitudes resembled those of America rather than Britain. The mass of the British parliamentary Labour Party was solidly centrist, with a numerically small, although often influential left wing given to occasional fragmentation, whose ideas nevertheless stimulated the rest of the party. Even the generous enthusiasm for the Russian peoples' determined resistance to Hitler did not translate into much sympathy with communism; and the introverted and fractious Communist Party of Great Britain rarely aroused emotions other than mild amusement. Australian

Labor, on the other hand, was fervently, although not unanimously, anti-communist.

In December 1942 the Curtin government had raised the ban imposed on the Communist Party by Menzies in 1940 and the revised ACP began to make headway in organizing industrial workers. Once wartime pressures were relaxed, communist-inspired strikes became frequent, and were met by Labor governments with repression as stern as anything that could have been expected from their political opponents. In Queensland, Premier Ned Hanlon passed draconian emergency legislation, backed by brutal police action, to suppress a 1948 strike; in the following year a coal strike resulted in 'hundreds of thousands of workers losing their jobs and the national economy being suddenly thrown into chaos'. Within a fortnight 'industry was brought almost to a standstill, unemployment reached half a million and soup kitchens dotted Sydney's industrial suburbs'. Chifley was forced to rush through Federal emergency laws which permitted stiff prison sentences to be imposed on miners' leaders.[29]

There were many, especially among Catholic voters, who believed, in spite of such evidence to the contrary, that Labor was not severe enough in its persecution of communists. Organized in Victoria, at first secretly, by Bartholomew Santamaria, the Catholic Social Studies Movement, commonly known as the Movement (or 'the Groupers'), developed into an effective anti-communist force. Santamaria had been a supporter of Franco, and a member of the shadowy but influential Catholic Action. Supported at all levels, from parish priests to Archbishop Mannix, who had fervently supported Franco and hailed Mussolini as 'the greatest man living', the Movement supplanted many communist activists in the trade unions. Once the confusion of sympathies caused by courageous Russian resistance and the Red Army's victories over the German armies had been dispelled, and as the oppressive character of the Soviet regime became apparent, Australian resistance to internal communism became more fervent, and demands for the renewed suppression of the Australian Communist Party grew.[30]

Theoretically, the Labor Party still clung to its socialist ideals of public ownership of the means of production, distribution and finance, and from time to time activists succeeded in pushing some aspects of these on to the party's attention. Wartime exigencies had already led to the establishment of some fifty government-owned factories, and it was hoped that the principle could be extended, as it was in Britain, to the most important sectors of industry. That these were generally unsuccessful was due not so much to the fact that nationalized enterprises were government controlled, but that they were not open to the scrutiny of shareholders, nor subject to market disciplines, nor capable of attracting competent managers. What would have been a disaster for Australia was avoided when the project to nationalize the entire banking system, a particular interest of the Prime Minister, was declared unconstitutional by the High Court. When the government decided, under the constitutional clause agreed with Joseph Chamberlain half a century earlier, to take the case to the Privy Council, the Australian court's decision was confirmed. The electorate recognized the project as dangerously rash – it was followed by the opposition gaining power in Victoria – and dimmed the lustre that Chifley and his colleagues had won.[31]

At the end of the war the Australian population was some 7.5 million, demonstrably far too low a figure to cope with the needs of industry and the demands of an improving infrastructure. One project alone, the Snowy Mountains Hydro-electric Scheme, which aimed to divert the east-flowing Snowy River waters over and through the mountains to generate power and to reinforce the Murray basin, was to require 100,000 workers. Immigration was essential, but was to be strictly controlled. The original reason for the White Australia policy, that of protecting Australian jobs, was no longer valid, but racism was entrenched in Australian society. Arthur Calwell, the Labor deputy leader, Minister for Immigration in the Chifley governments between 1945 and 1949, was an unabashed racist. Not only would no non-whites be admitted, but those Australians who had been so unpatriotic as to marry Chinese, Japanese or Indonesians were not allowed to bring home their spouses and children. 'No Japanese women, or any half-castes either, will be admitted to Australia', ran Calwell's instruction to his department; 'they are simply not wanted and are permanently undesirable', since 'a mongrel Australia is impossible'.[32]

Immigrants had to conform to the best Aryan traditions; and a ready source lay to hand. The Russian invasion and annexation of the Baltic Republics, Lithuania, Latvia and Estonia, provided thousands of prospective immigrants, not only well educated, but, more importantly, notably white. 'Many of their people were red-headed and blue-eyed. There were also a number of natural platinum blondes of both sexes,' Calwell observed with satisfaction. Great Britain, however, remained the principal recruiting ground. By an agreement in 1947 the British and Australian governments subsidized immigrants' fares, bringing the cost of passage down to £10 – less than a month's average wage. Another agreement with the International Refugee Organization allowed Australia to nominate immigrants with special skills who could receive free passage. The newcomers would be obliged to work for two years at the government's direction, a system uncomfortably reminiscent of nineteenth-century indentured labour.

It was not altogether successful. Certainly, nearly three quarters of a million 'New Australians' arrived in the first five years, half of whom were British, the remainder coming from other European countries, preferably from the north to conform with Calwell's prejudices but also, to some unease, including a fair number of Italians. Communists were of course banned, but no questions were asked of a number of former Nazis. After the horrors of war and occupation, Australia seemed a haven of peace and opportunity to the 'displaced persons' who accepted the harsh conditions of the initial labour camps with little demur, and later settled into the community with little difficulty, beginning the welcome diversification of what had been a stagnating monoculture. The rules could have been more generous, for a quota was applied to Jewish refugees which deprived Australia of much of the cultural nourishment and commercial ingenuity afforded to England (less so to Scotland, and hardly at all to Ireland, where the government imposed a near-absolute ban) by Jewish immigrants. Between 1938 and 1945 only 6,475 European refugees were admitted to Australia.

Philip Knightley brilliantly captured the experience awaiting the New Australians:

Who were these strange people? they looked like Europeans and they spoke a European language, but they were very different. They had peculiar eating habits. They ate spaghetti out of a tin. They loved cold spaghetti sandwiches. They had their main meal of the day not at 1pm or at 8pm but at 6pm and they called it 'tea'. But tea was also what they drank, not coffee. They knew what coffee was but had no idea how to make it. They had no knowledge of croissants or pastries and certainly would not consider eating them for breakfast. For breakfast they like chops or whatever was left over from the previous night's tea, all mixed together and then fried in dripping and called – for reasons no one could explain – 'bubble and squeak.' . . . They had restaurants but the food was bad, the service was appalling and many of them closed at the very time people wanted to use them – at weekends. In some parts of the country you could eat in a restaurant or drink alcohol in a pub, but you could not do both on the same premises without breaking the law.

The men drank large quantities of beer during the day but stopped promptly at 6pm. Many were then sick in the gutter . . . At parties and dances, the men stood at one end of the room and drank beer out of a barrel – the only time they were allowed to do it after 6pm – and talked about sport. The women stood or sat at the other end of the room, talked about babies and only spoke to the men to tell them it was time to go home. A woman who joined the men's group was considered to have loose morals. A man who joined the women's group was considered to be effeminate, probably a homosexual, or a 'poofter', whatever that was.[33]

Adaptation should have been easier for the British immigrants, escaping from the cold and the austerity of post-war Britain where rationing continued until 1954, and with few language difficulties, but to many newcomers the shock was considerable. Most came from close-knit working-class communities and retained family links, and in spite of the warmth of their reception were sometimes vociferous in their complaints; the 'whingeing Pom' became a figure of contempt. Over the years a fifth of the immigrants left, but the rest settled, and their children were absorbed into the comfortable mass of the Australian people.*

Foreign Affairs

The star of the Labor governments from October 1941 to December 1949 was undoubtedly the brilliant, wilful and eccentric Herbert Vere Evatt, Attorney General and Minister for External Affairs for the whole of that period. From September 1948 he was also elected President of the General Assembly of the United Nations, which could be taken to mark Australia's acceptance by the international community as an independent state. Although Evatt never achieved the prominence of Billy Hughes after the First World War, the effects of his work, good and bad, have perhaps been longer lasting.[34]

With the help of Casey, whose polished affability smoothed the disturbed waters left in the wake of the arrogant minister, Australia was reluctantly admitted to at least the fringes of American counsels. President Roosevelt, although not impressed by the arguments, conceded that a Pacific War Council 'with a fancy name' could be formed 'if it would make anybody happy'.[35] Curtin welcomed the news, declaring that 'Australia would now have a direct voice in the higher direction of the Pacific war', but this was hardly so; the Council was 'consultative' and 'advisory' only. Indeed, Evatt's agitation might have had an opposite effect. Australia was recognized in Washington as having a voice in Pacific affairs, but on the same level as the Philippines or New Zealand, while the real decisions continued to be taken between the United States and Britain, and later with Russia. Australia was

* My own first experience of Australia comes from the next decade, when there had been a notable improvement, but Knightley's description was still recognizable; some cynics might say that traces still remain.

not represented at any of the Great Power conferences in Casablanca in January 1943, Washington in May 1943, Quebec in August 1943, Moscow in October 1943, or Cairo in November 1943. In particular, the Cairo conference's decision that all territories seized by Japan since 1918 should be permanently removed from her control, an action which directly affected Australia, was first communicated to Canberra by the press.

This brusque intimation of Australia's secondary importance led directly to the Australia–New Zealand treaty (the Anzac pact), which protested against exclusion and insisted on representation in post-war settlements. The core of the agreement, which the New Zealand government made more acceptable to the United States and Britain by modifying Evatt's wilder notions, was the establishment of a regional zone of defence, directed primarily against American assumptions of regional hegemony. A line was drawn in the sea, asserting the Dominions' insistence on representation in any Pacific agreement. Evatt's insistence that Australian sovereignty should be extended in the Pacific islands was assessed by the American Minister in Canberra as 'a very clear statement of what might be called the First Imperialistic peace terms yet made by any leader among the Allied Nations'. Australia had painful justification for this self-assertion. Thousands of volunteer Australian, Canadian and South African pilots had flown for the RAF, and Australia's contribution to the war effort had been decisive in the Middle East. Although battle casualties – 34,000 deaths – were lower than in the First World War (300,000 British servicemen died in the Second World War, with 60,000 civilians and 35,000 merchant sailors: total American deaths were 300,000) the horrors endured by the prisoners of war taken by the Japanese made a deep impression. Moreover, Australia had proved an essential base for any Pacific operations, a vital source of raw materials, and emerged acknowledged as the foremost regional power.[36]

The formation of the United Nations, first adumbrated between Roosevelt and Churchill in their historic meeting of December 1941, was finalized in the San Francisco conference held in April, May and June 1945, at which Evatt led a strong Australian delegation. Preliminary negotiations had resulted in the British Dominions being recognized as independent states, which they undoubtedly were, but at the price of conceding the same status to the Ukraine and Belorussia, a complete fiction. Taking a lead among the smaller countries, Australia was elected to the Executive Committee and to the Co-ordination Committee responsible for preparing the final draft of the United Nations Charter. Australian influence was successful in strengthening the powers of the General Assembly against those of the Security Council, to the extent of allowing the Assembly to make recommendations on any matter deemed to fall within the scope of the Charter, and in having the importance of UNESCO (the United Nations Economic and Social Council) duly acknowledged. The Big Five (the United States, the Soviet Union, China, France and Britain) insisted, however, on retaining their power of veto, although conceding the right to have any item brought forward for discussion by the Security Council. Although essential at the time, and useful for many years afterwards, the composition of the Security Council as the executive body of the United Nations on which the five permanent members had a guaranteed seat and veto-powers, began to look increasingly artificial as the balance of world power changed at the end of the century.

Obedient to the exigencies of his country's White Australia policy, Evatt was instrumental in securing an amendment to Article 2(7), which ensured that the United Nations was banned from forcibly intervening in any matter considered to be essentially within the jurisdiction of a sovereign state. This was a repeat of Billy Hughes's performance at Versailles where – with the earnest support of South Africa – he had been successful in resisting League of Nations interference; both Hughes and Evatt had the same end in view, the preservation of White Australia. Very many unsavoury governments have since been happy to shelter behind this provision.[37]

One most important item of post-war international policies, the Bretton Woods arrangements of 1945, which established the International Bank for Reconstruction and Development and the International Monetary Fund, was greeted with many reservations. Since Federation, Australian governments had been accustomed to quite strict control over their own financial affairs, and to the exercise of substantial power over tariffs and domestic industry. Doubts, then expressed, sound almost prescient fifty years later. Would the agreements not 'sacrifice the sovereign rights of independent nations on the altar of another imperialism'? And Eddie Ward's rotomontade sounds perhaps a little less ridiculous today:

the Agreement will enthrone a World Dictatorship of private finance, more complete and terrible than any Hitlerite dream. It . . . quite blatantly sets up controls which will reduce the smaller nations to vassal States and make every government the mouthpiece and tool of International Finance. World collaboration of private financial interests can only mean mass unemployment, slavery, misery, degradation and final destruction.

Australia's signature to the General Agreement on Tariffs and Trade (GATT) in 1947 was pushed though by Chifley – Australia was one of the eight founding members, the only one outside Europe or North America – in the face of critical opposition from Menzies, who could not understand 'the complete passion ... for multilateral trade agreements'; he was supported by Thomas White, a former Trade minister, who believed that GATT represented 'the economic disarmament of Australia'. The conservatives had much to learn about post-war realities.[38]

If objecting to American imperialism, the Labor government was not averse to the home-grown variety, and the most pressing of Australia foreign policy concerns were those concerning their Asian neighbours. Those long-standing fears of Japan had proved only too well founded, and resentment against the Japanese was exacerbated with the return of the prisoners of war, and their truly shocking accounts of their inhumane treatment – although the vile conduct of Emperor Hirohito's army had been obvious ever since the atrocities perpetrated at Nanking in 1937 had been recorded on news film. The two hammer blows of the atomic bombs dropped on Hiroshima and Nagasaki in 1945 and their horrifying effects had done something to counter calls for vengeance, but it was also made clear by the United States that Japan was to be an American responsibility, and that no interference, however friendly, was to be permitted.

Elsewhere in South Asia the old colonial powers resumed their pre-war responsibilities, the French in Indo-China, the Dutch in their East Indian empire, and the British in the Straits Settlements and in Hong Kong, but the European imperial will was ebbing. Evatt's view, and that of many Australian diplomatic professionals, was that old-style colonial government should be replaced, not by independent self-governing states, since few if any Asian countries seemed ready for this (India was the great exception), but by enlightened trusteeship; and Australia was surely an ideal trustee, and in a strong position to advise, if not to lecture, the Europeans on their colonial administrations. Of these, the most important, in view of its size and proximity, was Dutch rule in the East Indies, which was already looking decidedly shaky.

Almost immediately after the Japanese capitulation, and before Allied forces could land at Batavia (now Jakarta), nationalists, many of whom had collaborated with the Japanese invaders, proclaimed an independent republic of Indonesia. The Japanese invasion, everywhere brutal, had different effects in different regions; Chinese and Koreans, with long and bitter experience of the Greater East Asia Co-prosperity Sphere, were left with a hatred of Japan and the Japanese. Singaporeans, Malays and Hong Kong Chinese had equally rejected Japanese claims to be anti-colonialist and looked to Britain for security; much of French Indo-China was on the whole prepared to accept French rule, if somewhat reluctantly. France, Britain and China were, however, permanent members of the United Nations Security

Council and what passed for major powers; Holland, while having been a loyal ally, was not.

Just as post-war Japan had been made an American responsibility, so the future of Indonesia – to adopt what became the name of those territories formerly known as the Netherlands East Indies (plus the small, but not unimportant, Portuguese colony of East Timor) – fell to Britain. Restoring Dutch rule was not a first priority of Lord Louis Mountbatten, the British Supreme Commander, who was later entrusted with the delicate task of bringing India and Pakistan to statehood. Faced with the certainty of nationalist resistance, Mountbatten attempted to negotiate between Dutch and nationalists to restore Dutch sovereignty while conceding an element of self-rule.[39]

Australia had a good claim to be represented in those negotiations. Australian forces had liberated much of Borneo, and by the end of the war there were more than 50,000 Australian troops in the region, who were asked to take control of the whole of Eastern Indonesia, a task they carried out well. Evatt wanted some of these troops to hold the ring in Java and superintend negotiations between Dutch and nationalists, but Chifley realized that any delay in repatriating the army would be politically disastrous. In the event, the British did enough to bring the two sides to an interim formal agreement in March 1947. This enabled Britain and Australia to withdraw their forces from Indonesia with some credit (and some Australian disappointment at having missed potential mandates in Borneo and Labuan), but neither Dutch nor nationalists were satisfied. America, while making conciliatory noises, continued to supply money and arms to the Netherlands, allowing the Dutch to maintain a huge force, more than 130,000 well-equipped men, in Indonesia.

The March agreement speedily disintegrated; within a few months a Dutch 'police action' had occupied the most important areas. Neither the United States nor Britain were inclined to intervene and it was left to Australia and India to take action by requesting the Security Council (of which Australia was at the time a member) to order an immediate ceasefire. Another agreement was fashioned under United Nations auspices, and concluded in January 1948, one considerably more to the advantage of the Dutch than had been that of the previous year. Chifley's government felt the unfairness of the decision, and with an eye also to the potential importance of trade, took action by sending a goodwill mission to the republican capital and writing stiffly to the Dutch government:

The time has come when, in justice to the Republic, we must consider taking direct steps on our own account to help the Republic economically. We propose to send post-war relief supplies to the Republic as well as to several other countries in South East Asia, and if the Dutch continue their present tactics we are contemplating making arrangements to carry on trade direct with the Republic, even at risk of conflict with Dutch blockade measures.[40]

Once again, mainly owing to Dutch intransigence, the agreement fell apart, with Dutch forces occupying Jakarta and arresting the principal Republican ministers. Despairing of the Security Council's weak response, India attempted a solution by calling a conference of Asian and Middle Eastern countries to discuss 'Ways and Means of dealing with the Indonesian issue', and Australia was among those invited.

It was a moment of decision for the Australian government. Her proven allies and only potential protectors, the United States and Britain, were absenting themselves. Britain did not want to risk a clash with her old ally, the Dutch, who were judged to be 'in a mood to resist a challenge'. Ernest Bevin, the Foreign Secretary, feared 'a direct clash with them may lead either to our having to face a rebuff or to a course which will raise the question of sanctions', while Dean Rusk at the State Department in Washington candidly explained in a telegram: 'We are pursuing our own interests and policies, as they appear both outside and inside framework UN. Today pursuit of our policy may make us critical of Dutch; tomorrow pursuit of same policy in different circumstances may make us equally critical of Indonesians.[41] On the other hand, Australia was 'a country with Western ties and traditions but located in Asia' and should be prepared to take an independent line. A compromise was therefore arrived at, putting an exploratory toe in the Asian water by sending, not ministers, but two officials of the Department of External Affairs. One of these, Dr John Burton, made a favourable impression in a speech which asked:

Is Australia to set itself against Asia and rely upon Western powers to assist it when an un-cooperative policy has antagonised Asia? The map answers the question. There is no alternative to encouraging mutual assistance in the region, encouraging the development of genuine national aspirations, and by removing economic distress and thwarted national feelings combat infiltration of foreign, unwelcome, disruptive elements in Asia. Accompanying this, and compatible with it, is close British Commonwealth co-operation and special relations with the United States insofar as the United States is prepared to enter into special relations with Australia.[42]

It earned Australia a place on a United Nations committee (the others, significantly were all Commonwealth members, India, Pakistan and Ceylon, hardly comprising a representative Asian selection) which drafted a recommendation to the Security Council for a speedy transfer of sovereignty in the Dutch East Indies to a United States of Indonesia. This worked, and after some vigorous arm twisting, the Dutch agreed. On 27 November 1949 the new Republic was internationally recognized. Australia had, it seemed, proved that it could act in Asian interests as an Asian country, and Evatt had won a personal triumph; but as regimes in Indonesia developed unpleasant characteristics, and as the Labor government was replaced by a less sympathetic opposition, Australian policies stiffened.

Australian action was also required further afield. The whole of the Malay peninsula had been overrun by the Japanese in the course of the war, and with their expulsion the traditional rulers were restored, as part of the Federated Malay States under British control. Peninsular Malaya had a racially mixed population, the majority ethnic Malays, but with a substantial Chinese minority, and a number of Indians. Their security was quickly threatened by a guerrilla campaign almost entirely composed of Chinese, intending to thrust communist rule upon the unwilling Malays. This was vigorously opposed by the British administration, which appealed in July 1948 to Australia for assistance, in the modest form of a supply of small arms. Attempting to exercise political muscle, the seamen's union threatened to prevent the shipment, but Evatt agreed with Chifley that Australia should ensure the weapons' despatch. It appeared that Evatt had been chided by the Prime Minister after Chifley had been warned by Ernest Bevin that his External Affairs minister was regarded as 'unpredictable' and 'critical merely for the sake of being critical', following which Evatt became more cooperative. Evatt's ministerial career, however, was shortly after ended.[43]

Menzies is Back

In December 1949 the Chifley government was soundly defeated by the opposition parties, the new Liberal Party led by Robert Menzies and the Country Party led by Arthur Fadden. Objections to Labor's policies had been evinced by the defeat of the referendum on widespread control in May 1948 and by the unpopularity of their effort to nationalize banks, reinforced by such tactless moves as the introduction of petrol rationing and the alienation of some voters by their repressive industrial legislation. Jack Lang contributed to his party's defeat by revealing that Chifley himself, the would-be scourge of usurers, had himself lent out money at high rates in the 1930s and 1940s – and Lang himself was a rack-renting Depression landlord. Contributory factors included a general feeling that it was time for the other team to take the field, and a well-funded and energetic opposition campaign, but it was not so much any government errors as the extent to which the opposition had regrouped that was decisive.

Under the leadership of Billy Hughes the UAP had slipped into idle ineffectiveness which resulted in the electoral defeat of 1943, after which Menzies was able to take the place he should have had two years previously. He found a state of chaos, with no fewer than nine different parties at state level supporting the UAP. Any hope of success was dependent upon forging some better degree of unity, and Menzies, affable, floridly handsome, socially acceptable, was the man to do it. With the prestige of his earlier wartime leadership, at a conference in October 1944 Menzies persuaded the state organizations to cohere into a unified whole to be known as the Liberal Party of Australia, equipped with a permanent Canberra secretariat and charged with a programme which, while breathing good intentions, was sufficiently vague to allow a wide range of specific policies to emerge. Profiting from the miseries experienced by Labor governments hampered by Caucus decisions, Menzies made it clear that the Liberal Federal Council would be restricted to general recommendations, 'but that the particular Election policy must be propounded by the Federal Leader in consultation with his Parliamentary colleagues'. Menzies explained that this choice of the new party's name was not intended to parallel that of the British Liberal Party, then reduced to a shadow of its former glory, but because 'We were determined to be a progressive party, willing to make experiments, in no sense reactionary but believing in the individual, his rights, and his enterprise, and rejecting the Socialist panacea'.[44]

It was a name and a programme calculated to attract maximum support and goodwill, but it was another four years before this could be translated into electoral success, and even then the Liberals were never able to command a majority on their own; coalitions between Liberals and the Country Party, under different guises, remained essential for any conservative Australian government.

Almost immediately, the new government was faced with an opportunity and a challenge. One of Menzies' specific undertakings was to introduce a Bill declaring the Communist Party of Australia, liberated from its earlier ban by the Labor government in December 1942, now to be 'unconstitutional and illegal'. The Bill gave powers to 'declare' individuals to have been members of the CPA who thereafter would not be able to take a post in the public service or a trade union; and it was up to the 'declared' individuals to prove that they were not communists. A shameful denial of individual rights, this was paralleled in democracies only by the McCarthyite hysteria in the United States, but it said much for the Australian people's broad tolerance that similar witch-hunts did not occur in the Commonwealth, and indeed the High Court duly found the Bill unconstitutional. Politically, however, it suited the Liberals' purpose by dividing the Labor opposition, many of whom were decidedly anti-communist, and some colour was given to the proposal by the outbreak, in June 1950, of the Korean War.

After the end of the war Japan had been ejected from Korea, together with other lands it had annexed since 1910. With prudent calculation, the Soviet Union declared war on Japan two days after the first atomic bomb was dropped on Hiroshima, but made good use of the time by sweeping into Manchuria and Korea. Although there were no American troops nearby at the time, Stalin agreed to Korea being divided at the 39th parallel between a Russian and American zone. A subsequent United Nations commission was denied permission to observe elections in the north, and the return of the communist candidate Kim Il Sung was, as usual in Peoples' Democracies, inevitable, but the administration of Syngman Rhee in the south was no advertisement for the virtues of the Western version. On 12 January 1950 the US Secretary of State Dean Acheson announced that Korea would no longer be considered as lying within that area of Asia which the United States was committed to defend, presenting the hard-line Marxist Kim Il Sung with an opportunity not to be missed. With the backing of Stalin in Russia and the consent of the Chinese leader Mao Tse-tung, the army of North Korea invaded the South on 25 June 1950.[45]

As a member of the United Nations Permanent Commission on Korea, Australia was bound to respond to the UN call, made on 27 June, to assist in repelling the invasion. The next day Australia, following Britain, placed her naval forces in the area at the disposal of the United States to act on behalf of the Security Council. On 26 July, answering an American appeal, Australia, Britain and New Zealand offered to contribute troops, which eventually became the British Commonwealth Division. Although representing only a small part of the total, mainly American, effort the Commonwealth troops formed perhaps the most effective unit of the UN forces, frequently found in the front of any advance, and acting as the rearguard in retreat, sometimes fired on by South Korean and American allies in the general confusion.[46]

Australian involvement in the Korean War was defensible to querulous Third World nations, scenting a renascent imperialism. One small Asian nation was assisted in resisting the aggression of another, and subsequently against a much more serious menace when Chinese troops were thrown into the fight, all under the authority of a Security Council mandate. It did not therefore represent an unusual foreign policy initiative; but Korea was the only Australian involvement in Asia which was to be quite so uncontroversial and one that aligned Australia irretrievably with 'American imperialism'.

The post-war world, and Asia in particular, was changing with bewildering rapidity. Once Britain had decided that independence was to be given to India (as well as Ceylon and Burma), the other European possessions in Asia were doomed whether their imperial owners accepted it or not. Towards each of the new nations that arose Australia had to evolve a policy, but overriding all these troubling questions was that of alliances. The war had proved that America was the supreme Pacific power, and an understanding with the United States was essential to Australian security. Britain, although a permanent member of the Security Council, and from 1947 an atomic power, had her work cut out to maintain her position in Europe without attempting to defend overseas interests as well (although it took twenty years for British governments to accept this unpalatable fact). Nor did Australia for long maintain its previous importance to Britain as a reliable ally. Any future European war was going to end in a very quick and very big bang, from which Australia would probably be spared. Those Asian difficulties which might emerge, in Malaya and as a result of the departure of the Dutch from the East Indies, should be easily dealt with to the advantage of all concerned through existing Commonwealth institutions.

Australia's relations with America were another matter. The wartime alliance had been transitory. Only occasionally thereafter did Australia engage more than peripheral American attention, most famously when Lyndon Johnson, searching desperately for any respectable military support during the Vietnam fiasco, welcomed Australian and New Zealand troops. Intimate relations with Britain, and the traditional family bonds, continued to be more important for a generation; and as a protector the United States was to prove itself less than reliable. Before the war direct Australian–United States relations had been few, and generally unhelpful. Australia was given a taste of her own medicine by America's insulting restrictions on admission; the 1930 Smoot–Hawley tariffs savaged Australian exports; Lyons' proposals for a compromise in 1934 were 'not entertained for a minute'. The American view of Australia was rather like the Australian view of Fiji – 'a remote British dependency in the Pacific from which some money could be made but for which no responsibility need be taken'. Frederick Eggleston, representing Australia in Washington, was right when he wrote in 1944 that history was repeating itself: 'When Great Britain secured complete industrial supremacy she went into free trade and thereby assisted in clamping her economic empire over the world in the Nineteenth Century' – and that this was going to occur again with the United States in the twentieth. Between 1951 and 1955 some 12 per cent of Australian imports came from America and 45 per cent from Britain; between 1968 and 1972 the respective figures were 24 per cent and 11 per cent, and between 1978 and 1982, 23 per cent of Australia's imports were American, while the United States bought only 11 per cent of Australian exports, 28 per cent going to Japan and a mere 4 per cent to Britain.[47]

After the war American politicians at least knew where Australia was, and appreciated that the country might have some uses – other than that of a ready market for American products – the greatest of which was its strategic position. The Australia, New Zealand and United States (ANZUS) pact, agreed in September 1951, was bought by Australia at the price of agreement to a 'soft' peace treaty with Japan. To Australians Japan was *the* enemy; the atrocious treatment of prisoners of war by their Japanese captors, with its strong elements of racialism, had seared Australian consciousness. Over 8,000 of the 22,000 Australians captured during the war had perished at the hands of their brutal captors, and the revolt by over 1,000 Japanese prisoners in Australia, in which 200 were killed, had provided another illustration of Japanese violence. Australia demanded 'radical changes' be imposed on post-war Japan, defining Cabinet views in a cable of 11 August 1945:

The roots of Japanese militarism are embedded in the totalitarian, political, economic and social system built up over the past 70 years by Japan's ruling groups. Superficial changes in governmental machinery and external trade would not suffice, and their imposition during a relatively short period of foreign control would only provoke a nationalistic reaction without removing the influences chiefly responsible for Japan's aggressive policies ... In short, we believe far-reaching occupation and Allied military government are essential to complete the work and sacrifice of countless Allied lives in the cause of final victory over Japanese militarism.

In order to ensure these radical changes it would be necessary to depose the Emperor, try him as a war criminal in the same way that German leaders were being tried at Nuremberg, and destroy the imperial tradition.[48]

Even the redoubtable Evatt could not, however, persuade America and Britain that this was a wise course, since the resentment that would be provoked among the Japanese would make their acceptance of constitutional reforms, on which all were agreed, very much more difficult. The best that could be achieved was that Australia would be represented at the surrender ceremony, which Sir Thomas Blamey signed on behalf of Australia, and that when an Allied Council for Japan be established to oversee the occupation, the British seat would be allotted to an Australian. This was duly done, and William Macmahon Ball, Professor of Political Science at the University of Melbourne, represented the British Commonwealth on the four-member Council. But since executive power remained firmly in the hands of General MacArthur as the Supreme Commander, determined to allow no interference, and since the USSR was doggedly uncooperative, poor Ball was hopelessly outgunned.

Evatt continued his activity, even after the Japanese constitution imposed by the United States was promulgated in November 1946, securing the Emperor's position, and among other things committing the Japanese people 'for ever to renounce war as a sovereign right of the nation'. That, both Australia and Britain, believed, was as far as placating Japan need go, but America viewed the question differently. Their Chinese protégé Chiang Kai-shek was failing to make headway against the communist advances in his country, and Churchill's famous Fulton speech in March 1946 had accurately defined the 'Iron Curtain' which the Soviet Union was pulling down across Europe. Securing a resurgent Japan as, once more, a reliable ally became an American priority, and Evatt trusted that in return for his cooperation (and hoping that Britain would be persuaded to agree) Australia would be able to bring the United States into a common defence agreement.

The 1948 Commonwealth Prime Ministers' meeting strengthened Evatt's hand by agreeing that defence in the ANZAM (Australia, New Zealand and Malaya) area was permanently an Australian responsibility and that Australian Chiefs of Staff would assume leadership should war occur. This modest acquisition of strategic importance was submerged in the Great Power disputes which put an end to any meaningful discussions about the future of Japan, and it was left to the Menzies government to progress the affair. Percy Spender, Menzies' Foreign Minister between December 1949 and April 1951, had the advantage of being irreproachably conservative, unsmirched with the socialist stain that the United States saw associated with a Labor government. Spender made it his business to cultivate the American ambassador in Canberra, Pete Jarman (his predecessor, Myron Cowen, had been treated 'shabbily' by Australian officials). By April 1950 a State Department policy statement acknowledged that: 'We now have in the Australian Government, in contrast with recent years, a friendly spirit and a desire for cooperation in the field of foreign policy which should be preserved, in so far as it lies within our power. This new attitude . . . should not be undervalued nor taken for granted.'[49] Spender had also gained the approval of his fellow lawyer and member of the Chevy Chase Country Club, Dean Acheson, Secretary of State in the Truman administration. Having a sympathetic ear in Washington was useful, but in 1950–1 Spender was able to negotiate from a position of some strength. When presented with what seemed a fait accompli, a draft United States/Japan peace treaty which did not include what Spender considered to be sufficient protection against the Japanese re-armament, the Australian foreign minister simply knocked it out of court: 'Australia would not subscribe to any Treaty with Japan unless there were adequate assurances that Australia would be protected against Japanese aggression', and went on to indicate what might be the price of Australian concurrence: 'a formal commitment by the United States which might go some way to allay our fear'.

That was in September 1950. By the following February the Australian position had been strengthened by the worsening situation in Korea, where the United Nations forces had been forced back by the Chinese intervention from their position on the Chinese border to south of Seoul, and the Republican success in the presidential election which had brought General Eisenhower to the White House and the hawkish John Foster Dulles to replace Acheson as Secretary of State. An enthusiast for military pacts, Dulles visited Canberra in February to discuss a 'formal commitment to joint security'. Very much the mountain coming to Mahomet, the visit was a triumph for Australian diplomacy: and it was Australian diplomacy, since Britain's attitude was, if not actually opposed, at least indifferent.

The ANZUS treaty was formally signed on 1 September 1951, when Spender had been replaced as Australian Foreign Minister by Richard Casey and appointed ambassador to Washington. The peace treaty with Japan was submitted for Parliament's approval, which was grudging. More liberal views were nurtured by the officials at the Department of External Affairs, but public opinion was still strongly in favour of punishing Japan, and the Labor Party still pursued its old policy of having nothing to do with coloured races, but the fact that an unpopular treaty was twinned with the welcome ANZUS pact ensured its success.

The ANZUS pact did not include Britain, and Clement Attlee's Labour government expressed no great concern at Britain's exclusion, rightly, perhaps, appreciating that the United States did not take the matter very seriously. Although Britain's membership would have been welcomed by Australia and New Zealand, the United States, at that time still concerned not to be seen as supporting the old colonial powers, insisted that Britain should not be a party. When Churchill came to power in 1951, his irritation, however, was palpable, demonstrated in an angry meeting with Governor Thomas Dewey and the Republican Secretary of State John Foster Dulles. Churchill recorded that 'Dewey proposed a scheme for a Pacific Treaty between all Pacific powers including the Philippines, Formosa and the like, excluding (repeat excluding) Great Britain. I said I would denounce such a plan scathingly.' After Dulles, at some length, complained that the Labour government had not objected, Churchill continued: '[Dulles,] who is thoroughly friendly, then said that if I objected so strongly, he would let his baby, i.e. the Pacific Treaty, die. In fact I could consider it dead'; but, Churchill added, 'rough weather may well lie ahead in dealing with the Republican party who have been twenty years out of office ... much patience will be needed'. In private Churchill raged that 'he would have no more to do with Dulles, whose "great slab of a face" he disliked and distrusted'. Over the Prime Minister's objections, but minus the fringe countries, the ANZUS pact went ahead.[50] While the agreement represented, or so it seemed, secure support from the United States, it did not mark any reduction on Australia's reliance on the British link, as events were to prove; but Dulles' decidedly anti-British attitudes signified a much less cordial relationship than had been possible with Democratic administrations, and the start of increasingly divergent foreign policies to be followed by Britain and the United States.

Menzies' parliamentary position had been bolstered by a successful election in April 1951 in which his Liberal Party won 52 seats, with the Country Party gaining 17 and the Labor Party 52, giving the coalition a comfortable majority, while in the Senate the Labor majority was overturned. The election had followed a double dissolution granted by the Governor General on the grounds that the Labor-controlled Senate had blocked a government Banking Act. Since the Governor General was then Sir William McKell, previously Labor Premier of New South Wales, appointed by Ben Chifley to succeed the Duke of Gloucester, the Labor Party was furious, but McKell's decision was both constitutionally correct and politically sensible, and the coalition was then set fair for another twenty-one years of power. As well as a numerical majority, Menzies had a biddable parliamentary party, accustomed to obedience and loyalty, not ready to question the leadership's decision, quite unlike any Labor Prime Minister, always bound either to obey or painfully to circumvent Caucus decisions. Labor, too, was painfully affected by Chifley's death in June 1951 and his replacement as opposition leader by Evatt, who, with all his talents, was not the man to paper over the permanent cracks within his party.

With so solid a position, Menzies felt able to recover from the defeat by the High Court of his attempt the previous year to ban the Communist Party. Quite why Menzies should have launched a referendum on the subject, the success of which would enable the government to alter the constitution and make membership of the Communist Party illegal, is by no means clear. Professor Macintyre is surely wrong to assume that a similar plebiscite in Britain would have produced 'a majority in favour of suppressing communism'. In Britain, membership was commonly regarded as a not-very endearing eccentricity, and copies of the *Daily Worker* were taken by respectable West End clubs because of its excellent racing correspondent. Certainly legislation which could reject the presumption of innocence and punish failure to end membership of a banned organization by five years' imprisonment would never have been considered even by a Conservative government – and from October 1951 Churchill was back as Prime Minister for the second time.[51]

Once more Evatt had to take a lead in fighting against a draconian law, and did so magnificently. At the beginning of the referendum campaign the opinion polls forecast a large 'yes' majority, but by the time the votes were cast (22 September 1951) the noes had it by a fraction – 50.6 per cent to 49.4 per cent. But the agitated hyperbole employed by Evatt signalled the onset of the mental agitation that was to force his retirement. His claim, that Menzies was 'following the road that led to the horrors of Belsen . . . it is the Hitler technique over again. First the Reds, then the Jews, then the trade unions, then the Socialist Democratic parties, then the Roman Catholic Centre Party, then the Roman Catholic and Lutheran Churches', was not one that even the most worried of civil libertarians could take seriously and there were many in the Labor Party with no great concern for civil liberties, as Evatt was to discover (and Evatt himself as wartime Attorney General, had a patchy record on such matters).[52]

Menzies continued in power until 1966, making, with the previous three years between 1939 and 1941 a total of twenty years in office, an unprecedented period for an Australian Prime Minister – and given that his immediate successors, four of them in five years, were so temporary, one can realistically speak of a Menzies generation. It can also be seen as the end of an era, the Australian equivalent of the last days of the Raj, and the beginning of serious decolonization. The high point of emotional attachment to the idea of Britain came with the visit of the young Queen Elizabeth II in February 1954, to be greeted by a crowd one-million strong, and to spend eight weeks visiting all parts of the country. Received with enormous enthusiasm, with perhaps two-thirds of the Australian population flocking to greet her, the royal tour seemed to demonstrate how strongly Australia adhered to the Imperial link. Menzies, himself an ardent admirer of a Britain which was rapidly disappearing, if in reality it ever had existed, revelled in honours, which were to include his appointment as Lord Warden of the Cinque Ports, which brought with it a splendid uniform and an agreeable seaside cottage in the shape of Walmer Castle, was embarrassingly and sentimentally effusive (although perhaps not far out of tune with a majority of the electorate), and was able to bask, like a morning-coated seal, in the glow of the royal presence. It was not the last royal visit by any means, but subsequent welcomes, affectionate and respectful though they were, failed to generate the same excitement. It was not so much that Australia was moving away from Britain, but that the British were extricating themselves from Imperial responsibilities; the Empire was ending, and the new Commonwealth of Nations was beginning its evolution.

Australia in Asia

Percy Spender had realized that any 'white-power' security pact such as ANZUS would be better reinforced by some 'brown-power' initiative, and that economic and technical aid given to the New Commonwealth countries could pay dividends in diplomatic support. The Colombo plan, developed at a meeting of Commonwealth Prime Ministers there in January 1950, was based on a Spender draft which required that as much aid as possible should be given in order to stabilize democratic governments and protect them against 'opportunist, disruptive and subversive elements', and to lure students away from the blandishments of free Moscow education by providing university and technical training. In origin purely a Commonwealth initiative, the Colombo plan was reinforced by America and Japan joining and, by 1956, Burma, Indonesia, Nepal, the Philippines, Thailand, Cambodia, Laos and South Vietnam. While the plan perhaps did not reap the diplomatic advantages for which Spender had hoped, it proved a not-ineffective instrument in countering Moscow communism; but its chief effect in Australia was the beginning of the end of the White Australia policy as hundreds – 2,650 by 1959 – of Asian students took up places in Australian universities.[53]

Commonwealth solidarity was also demonstrated by Australia's support for the new Federation of Malaysia, but a rift was developing between Australia on the one hand and Britain and most of the other Commonwealth countries on the other on the matter of the recognition of communist China. The British Labour government had accorded such recognition in 1950 – the suggestion, Churchill claimed, was first made by himself the previous year – but the United States still clung to their now discredited hero, Chiang Kai-shek, holed up with his Kuomintang nationalists in the island of Formosa. Spender and Menzies, both convinced that a third world war provoked by China could begin at any moment, were fervently supporting the unyielding American policies. Guided by this misconception, the Australian government tended to adopt American attitudes to China, which was to prove a grave, and for many young Australians, a literally fatal mistake.

American foreign policy in the twentieth century has rarely been clear and logical; perhaps its best period was during the Truman administrations, guided by two wise and courageous men, General George Marshall and Dean Acheson. After Eisenhower's victory and the appointment of John Foster Dulles, supported by his sinister brother Allen at the head of the CIA, American activities abroad were often at best mistaken, and sometimes unprincipled. Eisenhower's timid initial acceptance of the McCarthyite purges robbed the State Department of some of its best officers:

The emotional American support that had sustained Chiang Kai-shek's Nationalists during the civil war was reinforced by their defeat ... The rising tide of McCarthyite hysteria made it impossible for saner minds to question the Chiang myth; when the 'China hands' in and around the State Department came to the conclusion that 'Chiang Kai-shek and his evanescent, predatory and combat-resistant armies were not on the wave of the future', they were 'called severely to account by John Foster Dulles and McCarthyites on Capitol Hill'.[54]

For some time Richard Casey, in charge of External Affairs after May 1951, attempted to persuade his Cabinet colleagues to adopt a more realistic attitude towards China, but this failed when Menzies assumed personal control of the department in 1960 before passing responsibility the following year to Sir Garfield Barwick, a hard-line anti-communist, and although voices urging the contrary policy of recognizing the People's Republic were heard in the department itself and in the press, these were ignored.

The dangers inherent in obedience to the United States began to become apparent from 1954, when the French hold on Indo-China was slipping towards the final humiliation at Dien Bien Phu. Dulles then invoked the ANZUS pact, claiming that a communist success in Indo-China, which he believed to be Moscow-inspired, would lead to 'Communist control of South East Asia [which] would carry a grave threat to the Philippines, Australia and New Zealand, with whom we have treaties of mutual assistance' and should be met by 'united action', which should include Australia. This, the celebrated 'domino theory' was enthusiastically supported by Menzies' government. Dulles sought Congressional approval for armed intervention, but this would be given, he was informed, only if America's allies joined in. On 4 April Dulles held talks with British, French, Australian and the South East Asian countries' representatives, at which Britain made its opposition to intervention clear, an attitude shared by the Department of External Affairs officials. If there was to be a settlement it would be best achieved by the negotiations then about to begin in Geneva, and must be accompanied by the French grant of independence to its South East Asia colonies. This did not suit Dulles at all, who warned Spender that if the Commonwealth did not offer support 'we will find it hard to move in the matter but we may write it off'.[55]

On 25 April a formal appeal was made by the United States to the British government for joint intervention and immediately rejected by Churchill 'The British people would not be easily influenced by what happened in the distant jungles of SE Asia; but they did know that there was a powerful American base in East Anglia and that war with China, who would invoke the Sino-Russian Pact, might mean an assault by Hydrogen bombs on these islands.' Privately he added: 'I don't see why we should fight for France in Indo-China when we have given away India.' Fortunately the French garrison at Dien Bien Phu was forced to surrender, on 7 May, before any one could intervene, and the Geneva conference was left to sort things out. This it did with uncommon speed for such meetings, considerably helped by the presence of Pierre Mendès-France, the wisest French Premier for many years, before or since.[56]

The Geneva conference was followed by another, in September, held in Manila, which resulted in the formation of the South East Asia Collective Defence Treaty (SEATO). The organization's acronym was meant to reflect that of NATO, the North Atlantic Treaty Organization, the powerful Western instrument of the cold war in Europe, and the fact that the United States, Britain, France, Australia, New Zealand, Pakistan, the Philippines, and Thailand agreed on a measure of collective defence might have been significant, had not India and Indonesia been prominent absentees. An Indian diplomat, Mrs Pandit, commented that it was a 'South East Asian alliance minus South East Asia'. SEATO looked reasonably good in the international yearbooks, but without the unified command structure and authority of NATO was never effective; and Australia was now seen to be aligned with the United States. Sir Arthur Tange at the Department of External Affairs put it succinctly: 'We start our good neighbour policy with two handicaps: SEATO; which connotes intervention in the affairs of Asia and 'provocation'; ANZUS: which connotes accord with US foreign policy in Asia towards Peking, Chiang Kai-shek, the Geneva Agreement.'[57]

461

13

The Shadows of Vietnam

A Third Force

The longevity of the Menzies era can hardly be attributable to any exceptional qualities of the administrations. Menzies himself was a capable chairman and an adept politician, supported by some ministers with talents other than that of biddability, but any intellectual or ideological content was lacking. No such consistent series of policies as that which was characterized as 'Thatcherism' in Britain was developed in Australian conservatism (for which many Australians feel grateful). Menzies once confided to Paul Hasluck, himself a scholarly politician, that they were the only members of the Cabinet who ever read books – and Menzies' reading was confined to nineteenth-century English novelists and twentieth-century detective stories, with some predictable poetry; the works of John Maynard Keynes or Richard Tawney did not provoke lively debate in Canberra. The intellectually distinguished and the most experienced of civil servants, 'Nugget' Coombs, Director General of Chifley's Department of Post-War Reconstruction 1942–9, then Governor of the Commonwealth Bank, was listened to politely by the usually uncomprehending Menzies, and shunted off into worthy but politically impotent sidings at the Australian National University and the Council for Aboriginal Affairs, where he began the painstaking construction of a post-war Aboriginal policy. A historian of the party admitted:

It is certainly true that Liberals did steer clear of philosophical discussions. They were reluctant to explore the meanings and implications of concepts such as 'the freedom of the individual' which might drop off the tongue or find their way into party literature. Their best efforts generally consisted of warm, fuzzy and simplistic affirmations of the kind that found their way into the seventeen one-or-two-sentence paragraphs of We Believe. Published in 1954, We Believe managed to sound momentous in stating the unexceptional: a series of commitments to the

Crown, the nation, the rights of the individual, the rule of law, good citizenship, the protection of minorities, social justice, and to religious and racial tolerance. Disinclined to engage in systematic and close philosophical analysis, the Liberals just kept reprinting *We Believe* in the 1960s and, despite much trumpeting about changing the platform in 1960, did not seriously revisit their stance between the 1948 and 1974 versions.[1]

Pragmatism writ large was the key to Menzies' success. Legislation was designed to satisfy the most influential or vociferous sections, of whom the most consistently important were the Liberals' coalition partners, the Country Party. Given that the period, apart from a dip in 1960/61, was generally prosperous, part of a sustained boom which began during the war and continued until the early 1970s, and that the Country Party's special interests were clearly defined, this was not too difficult. Relations between the two parties were not always affectionate; the Country Party's leader, Commonwealth Treasurer Arthur Fadden, referred to Menzies as 'the Big Bastard' – but both parties needed the other too much to allow a great deal of public dissension.[2] In 1964 a house-purchase benefits scheme was begun, helping to raise the already high rate of home ownership. The ownership of a frame house, flimsy by European standards, but with a garden and secure behind its fence, became the aim of Australian workers, and, as the cities threw out sprawling suburbs, was a prospect well within reach. Families were gratified by the increase in children's allowances and special treatment for widows and their children. Pensioners – and by 1970 there were 779,000 – were accorded supplementary benefits, old people's homes were subsidized and means tests liberalized. All these were ad hoc reforms, aimed at special interests likely to be sympathetic to a conservative government – and the Queen's visit, repeated in 1958 accompanied by the Queen Mother, always a star attraction, and at decent intervals thereafter, amplified the effect – but they were also in accordance with the coalition's ethos of genuinely beneficent paternalism. Ad hoc and piecemeal, too, were the moves towards a comprehensive health care system. A 1953 Act introduced an insurance-based health service, where insurance was taken out with commercial or other companies who received government subsidies. Cover was limited according to the premiums paid and was not universal, but in time some three-quarters of the population were covered by the system. Those not covered, who included the people most at need, had to rely on what help was available through the state system; and since health insurance premiums were granted tax relief, the insurance system became even more advantageous to those in employment. Inevitably the Government reaped some credit for the successful Olympics, held in Melbourne in 1956, the first to take place in the southern hemisphere and in which Australia won thirteen gold medals.

Education was a cause dear to the heart of conservative meritocrats; universities and other institutes of tertiary education proliferated, to the extent that in 1972 Australia had, proportionate to the population, three times as many young Australians attending university as their British contemporaries. The universities were of mixed quality, and serious researchers often migrated to Britain and the United States, but it still came as a great shock when thirty years later no Australian university was found in the ranks of the world's 100 best, a list which contained a number of Asian institutions.[3] Secondary education was transformed as changed attitudes enabled the old dispute about state aid to Catholic schools to be settled. With the influx of Italian immigrants some of the old Irish Catholic intolerance had been dissipated, and the acceptance of the Second Vatican Council reforms helped in reducing sectarian animosity. A promise to provide state aid was an important, perhaps a vital factor in securing the coalition victory in the November 1963 election, and was duly implemented in the following year. In his review of Denoon's *History of Australia, New Zealand and the Pacific* (2000), Stewart Firth draws attention to the fact that sectarianism

has disappeared with astounding speed since the 1950s. Half a century ago a Labor state government in New South Wales was invariably overwhelmingly Catholic in composition, and its Liberal counterpart equally Protestant. Government departments were known to be either Catholic or Protestant, as were law firms, and there was a hint of Northern Ireland about Melbourne and Sydney . . . Australia was a country where the politics of class and party were refracted through the allegiances of religion. More could have been said about the sectarian identities that once split white Australia.[4]

The Irish Prime Minister Éamon de Valéra's visit in 1948 was 'met by indifference and even embarrassment', doubtless reinforced by the memory of his visit to the German ambassador in Dublin three years previously, to commiserate with him on the death of the Führer. In foreign policy, however, Catholic sympathies remained a potent influence, as was to be demonstrated in Australian actions in Vietnam, when support for the corrupt, but Catholic, regime of Ngo Dinh Diem was often a vital factor in government decisions.

One future Liberal Prime Minister, John Howard, then a Young Liberal, took pride in his role in breaking down 'the absolutely horrific opposition to state aid [to all schools, including denominational ones] inside the New South Wales Liberal Party in the early 1960s'. In an interview with Gerard

Henderson, Howard recalled the Liberal Premier of New South Wales, the deeply corrupt Robin Askin, threatening to close down the Young Liberals because of their support for state aid:

One of the things that you should understand is that I spent a lot of my early years, in the early part of the '60s, with John Carrick actually fighting the fight ... Because I totally wore the theory that in the early 1960s you had an extraordinary situation – particularly in New South Wales – where about half a million middle-class Catholics were still voting Labor when in reality, on all rational criteria other than tribal adherence, they should be voting Liberal. Menzies' great genius was to unlock that group of people with his policies. You may remember that in the 1963 election the swing to the Liberal Party was almost wholly confined to New South Wales, where we won seven seats. But what really happened is that we got Menzies' Catholics in 1963 for the first time in a really big way.[5]

In spite of his generally popular and tolerably competent conduct of domestic affairs, Menzies would have found it harder to retain office without the suicidal tendencies of the Labor opposition. Helped by the dramatic defection of a junior Soviet diplomat, Vladimir Petrov, whose wife, kidnapped by the KGB, was rescued at the last moment by the Australian police, Menzies was able to return to the communist threat. In the general election due in May 1954, a few weeks after Petrov's defection, the coalition won a majority of seats in the House of Representatives, although the Labor Party actually gained more votes. Evatt, who had been showing signs of increasing derangement, behaved so eccentrically before a Royal Commission on Espionage that he was banned from future hearings.[6]

Menzies quickly took advantage of Evatt's collapsing credibility and called another election, in December 1955, which he won more than comfortably. The Labor Party's split – its third – had begun that April in Victoria. Evatt had previously singled out the 'disloyal' Victorians, for their infiltration by Santamaria's 'Groupers', an accusation which was taken up at the annual ALP Congress in the March following, after which Evatt supporters expelled the Groupers from the Victorian Legislative Assembly. The discontented minority then formed themselves into the Australian Labor Party (Anti-Communist), which polled enough votes in the December election to reduce Labor's proportion of the vote from the 50 per cent it had gained the previous year to 44.6 per cent. New South Wales followed Victoria in September 1956 by forming a splinter group, the Democratic Labor Party (DLP), which allied itself with the Victorian Australian Labor Party (anti-communist); and Queensland formed its own Queensland Labor Party which later also became part of the DLP.

After that the DLP became kingmakers. In the November 1958 general election the party polled 9.4 per cent, bringing the ALP down to 42.8 per cent with the coalition at 46.5 per cent. Not that the allocation of seats reflected these figures, for the preferential voting system was working in favour of the coalition, as DLP preferences went to the government rather than to their old colleagues. And in 1961 (general elections now running predictably to the constitutional three-year pattern) the coalition majority was drastically reduced from 32 seats to 2, and that due to the Queensland Labor Party (DLP) giving 85 per cent of preference votes to the coalition, allowing the Liberal candidate, Jim Killen, to win by just over 100 votes. Nationally, Labor won 47.9 per cent of the primary vote against the coalition's 42.5 per cent.

The Labor Party division left acute personal bitterness in its wake. Some Catholics who had not joined with the Groupers in the DLP suffered 'abuse and ostracism . . . brutal violence by enforcers, despatch of dead rats to rivals through the mail, and calculated haranguing and harassment of the children of detested opponents'.[7] By that time Evatt had sunk into inactivity – he retired to the New South Wales Supreme Court Bench in 1960 and died in 1965 – and was succeeded by old Arthur Calwell, an unreconstructed Labor dinosaur. Claiming that his narrow majority made the conduct of foreign policy impossible, Menzies was able to force another general election on the voters, where, helped by the Catholic vote, he re-established a comfortable majority.

New Alliances

Nowhere was Menzies' pragmatism better illustrated than in his relations with Britain. In spite of his sentimental attachment to all things British – or, to be perhaps more exact, to those unchanging aspects of Britain he believed represented the shared heritage of all English-speaking peoples – Australian interests always came first with Menzies. The British economy had been so weakened by the prolonged war effort that the previously wealthy nation had been transformed, according to Chancellor of the Exchequer R. A. Butler, from a creditor nation to the extent of some £3,500 million, to an impoverished debtor of £2,500 million, with a deficiency in terms of trade of some £1,000 million annually. Chifley had recognized British difficulties in his offer to sell Australian food to Britain at prices significantly lower than those obtainable elsewhere. In December 1947, and in positively Menzian terms, Chifley defended his government's actions: 'Are we to ignore the plight of the United Kingdom because some temporary customer requires these goods and is prepared to pay dollars for them? Are we to deprive our greatest customer, friend and ally, of these goods?' Indeed, Menzies back in office was less generous than had been the Labor government; as soon as the Australian balance of trade was affected by the collapse of wool prices, import controls were immediately imposed, across the board, with no exception made for British manufacturers. Certainly indignant protests from the British government gave the Australians some concern – Casey asked whether 'we are dealing with a friend or a foe?' – but the controls remained.[8]

A similar stance of 'Australia comes first' was demonstrated in 1956 over the renegotiation of the 1932 Ottawa agreements. John ('Black Jack') McEwen, the energetic Country Party leader after 1958, insisted on combining the old Department of Commerce, Trade and Agriculture into a new Department of Trade, in which activity sharply increased. Protecting agriculture was a Country Party priority, and if Australian manufacturers were to be disadvantaged that was an acceptable risk – neither masters nor men were likely to vote for the Country Party. Black Jack, a Victorian small farmer of modest education, had ambitions of his own – he was Prime Minister for twenty-two days in December–January 1967–8 – and had no particular fondness for Britain. In May 1956 McEwen recommended replacing the Ottawa agreement with a new trade treaty, in order to allow Australia to negotiate tariff agreements with third countries, while perpetuating 'the principle of British preferences'. It took six months to reach agreement with Britain; Chancellor of the Exchequer Harold Macmillan found McEwen 'a very tough customer indeed . . . ruthless and unsmiling', presenting 'quite preposterous demands'. McEwen's next negotiations were equally difficult.[9]

Even in the twenty-first century, large areas of Australia remain uninvestigated by geologists. In 1958 Langley Hancock discovered immense deposits of high grade iron ore in the Pilbara hills of Western Australia, where the town of Newman now boasts the biggest open-cast mine in the world and Port Hedland loads 250,000-ton ore carriers. At that time a relic of wartime legislation prevented the export of iron ore to Japan, potentially by far the largest customer. In 1960 the ban was lifted, marking another stage in the emergence of Japan from post-war isolation, which had, in terms of trade, dragged on painfully after the conclusion of the peace treaty. This had guaranteed Australia's position in the Japanese markets for four years and as this period neared its termination Japanese ministers were beginning to lose patience with Australian equivocation. When in 1954 Australian negotiators showed a reluctant willingness to begin talks, the Japanese ambassador in Canberra remarked that trade negotiations should take place only if 'there was good prospect of a reasonable settlement'. Although Japan was still only a modest consumer of Australian exports – 8 per cent of the total in 1951–5 contrasted with 36 per cent going to Britain – the balance of trade with Japan was much to Australia's advantage and Australian exports mostly consisted of those sensitive commodities, wool and grain.

McEwen had been obliged to force on reluctant colleagues the necessity for a trade agreement, but when Japan became a full member of GATT in September 1955 the issue was unavoidable. Admitting Japan to 'most favoured nation' status implied, however many safeguards might be included, downgrading Britain's special position, which Menzies in opposition had been so anxious to protect. The trade agreement with Japan marked the slowly fraying link with Britain. While McEwen was finalizing the agreement Menzies was in London for a Commonwealth conference, and attempted somewhat half-heartedly to influence his Trade Minister on behalf of British exporters, but to no avail; after a year of complex negotiations the agreement's signature went ahead in Menzies' absence. The Commerce Agreement between Australia and Japan, signed on 6 July 1957, was ratified without much dissent from the Labor opposition in Parliament. A visit by the Japanese Prime Minister, Kishi Nobusuke, followed in November, in which Kishi expressed 'profound regret for the war': he did not, however, apologize, and the White Australia policy remained intact, with Japanese visitors continuing to run the gauntlet of the immigration regulations. But Australia had begun to fulfil its present role as a provider of raw materials to Japan, today one of the most important trading partners (the European Union remains the largest and the biggest source of investments).[10]

The Japanese agreement was the first indication that Australia was searching for a policy towards its Asian neighbours other than that of wary apprehension; never more than semi-attached to its northern neighbours, Australia remained part of the Anglo-American informal alliance. The alliance itself, however, was subject to strains, most evidently demonstrated in the summer of 1956, when the brief Anglo-French intervention in the Suez Crisis was brought to a halt by American opposition. Menzies represented Australian opinion – which reflected the very moderate assessment of Egyptian virtues generated by the war – accurately enough in his firm support for Britain, although the revelation of how Eden and his Foreign Minister Selwyn Lloyd had lied in attempting to hide the extent of the collusion with Israel caused subsequent re-assessment of the British action.

Very much nearer than Japan or the Middle East, indeed on Australia's own doorstep was the new state of Indonesia.

'Konfrontasi'

The only shared land border of Australian territory in the twentieth century, if the Antarctic is excluded, was that with Western New Guinea. An arbitrary line, the border divided very similar Melanesian communities, which on the Dutch side had long been subjected to relatively benign neglect. They differed totally from the other inhabitants of the Dutch East Indies, themselves varied enough, and there was no particular reason why sovereignty should be transferred to Indonesia. The territory had accordingly been left out of the 1949 settlement; agreement, it was hoped, might be reached later. Indonesian intentions remained suspect, and in 1951 Australia had appealed to the United States to join with Britain in warning Indonesia off the Western New Guinea turf. In November that year the ambassador, Percy Spender, made a final plea that the United States would at least instruct its ambassador at Jakarta 'to keep a close watch over the situation and do all in his power to prevent matters getting out of hand'. But even this modest measure was not implemented.[11]

Three possibilities existed for Western New Guinea; retention by the Dutch, independence, or absorption into Indonesia. Of these the first was contrary both to the spirit of the age and the real inclinations of the Dutch, not thoroughly committed to hanging on to the last parts of their colonial empire if the expense of a defensive action was involved, while the third would provide Australia with an unpleasantly formidable neighbour. And independence, it was acknowledged, would only be possible after a perhaps prolonged period of tutelage.

Theoretically, Australia would have preferred a Western New Guinea carefully superintended by a reliable power such as the Dutch, and commitment to continuing Dutch rule had been Liberal party policy. On 8 December 1961, however, a chain of events began which ended with Western New Guinea being handed over to Indonesia almost unconditionally. Summoned to the office of President Sukarno, the American ambassador, Howard Jones, was told that an invasion of Western New Guinea was imminent, and unless he heard that America would support the Indonesian case for annexation he would order the invasion in three days' time. The United States panicked, and the British government, obediently following, and aware that if any fighting broke out it would be difficult to stand aside, assisted in pressing Australia to agree. At first Menzies resisted; the cable to London on 16 December insisted that negotiations must be 'free from threat and on a previously agreed basis of self-determination'. Sukarno should be frankly told that his actions were likely to 'drive the foreign policy of Indonesia in [a] direction dangerous for the country's future'. And so indeed it proved, but for the time being Australia's hand was forced. With both the United States and Britain refusing to be involved, Australia reluctantly conceded that 'from the past response of the United States and from our knowledge of the probability that the United States will not give military assistance to the Dutch under attack, that Dutch withdrawal largely on Indonesian terms is inevitable'. In August 1962 it was accordingly agreed that Western New Guinea should be transferred to the United Nations and thence to Indonesia, on condition that a plebiscite should be held in 1969 to determine the will of the people. Within a short space of time it became clear that such a plebiscite would be little more than a charade.[12]

The early days of Indonesian independence, when the Chifley government had been the new republic's best ally, had been succeeded by a realization that Sukarno was no democratic leader in the pattern of a Nehru, or even a Lee Kuan Yew. The realization was slow in coming, exemplified by Australian reluctance to support its fellow Commonwealth country, the emergent Malaysia. In the 1950s Australia had sent troops to help the British combat Chinese communist infiltration which threatened the independence of the Malay States. As a result of the suppression of the communists the Malay sultanates, Singapore, the two British colonies of North Borneo, Sabah and Sarawak, and the protectorate of Brunei were able to agree to unite in a federation to be known as Malaysia. For various reasons, of which fear of losing regional leadership was probably the most influential, coupled with the fact that the British Borneo states bordered the Indonesian province of Kalimantan, Indonesia emphatically rejected Malaysia and announced a policy of confrontation; *Konfrontasi*.

The 1950–55 campaign in Malaya had been a military success, when young conscript troops were sent on long-range jungle patrols to meet, and outclass, the opposing guerrilla forces (the accompanying imperial repression did cause some raised eyebrows, but the people of Malaya were grateful). Requests for help in the defence of Malaysia were now sent to both the United States and Australia. The United States was quick to refuse, claiming that Malaysia was purely a Commonwealth concern. Australia, through Foreign Minister Barwick, while agreeing that she should continue to support the creation of Malaysia, pointed out that this would entail acceptance of the risk that thereby 'we may cause tension in our relations with Indonesia', but that an 'attempt should be made to persuade Sukarno to accept the emergence of Malaysia'. Barwick was too successful in his endeavours to please his Cabinet colleagues and when an understanding was reached by Malaya, Indonesia and the Philippines, which included an agreement 'to abstain from the use of arrangements of collective defence to serve the particular interests only of the big powers', Menzies objected. Maintaining British and American bases in Singapore and the Philippines was an essential element in Australian defence, and any sort of non-aggression pact gave Indonesia the opportunity of agitating against just such a provision. At a meeting with Barwick in Jakarta on 12 September 1963, Sukarno showed his true colours, referring to Indonesia's huge population, banging on the table and claiming to be ready to take on not only Britain and Australia, but the United States as well – this in spite of the fact that the United Nations had ascertained that the people of the British Borneo states were willing to join with Malaysia, thus undercutting an major Indonesian objection.[13]

When the chips were down Australia rallied round to the Commonwealth cause, and on 27 September Menzies announced: 'we shall to the best of our powers and by such means as shall be agreed upon with the government of Malaysia, add our military assistance to the efforts of Malaysia and the United Kingdom in the defence of Malaysia's territorial integrity and political independence'. Sukarno snapped back that he would 'gobble Malaysia raw' and 'confrontation' began.

Australia learnt just how reliable a friend was the United States. Averell Harriman, the Under-Secretary of State, had assured the Australian Cabinet on 7 June that 'if there should be an overt attack on Malaysia and if Australian forces should become involved, the ANZUS Treaty would, according to the advice given to the United States Administration by its lawyers, come into operation'. But once trouble loomed on the horizon American policies were reversed. A flurry of diplomatic activity took place in early October between Australia and America in Washington, with New Zealand and Britain – the latter now perhaps grateful at not being a party to ANZUS – intermittently participating. President Kennedy observed that the American public had forgotten about the existence of the treaty, and that he was very reluctant to get involved in any way with action against Indonesia. Malaysia was a British and Dominions responsibility, but if Australian troops engaged in defending Malaysia were openly attacked on a large scale, then the United States would respond, but such support would be limited at most to air and sea forces, together with logistic support, and would not under any circumstances include ground troops; moreover, this might well involve delay while the President sought Congressional approval. Harriman, it was clear, had gone too far, and must be sent back to the region to explain himself. Altogether it was a poor return for the Australian and British support in Korea, and a demonstration of how undependable the ANZUS treaty was.[14]

'Confrontation' continued for three years until August 1966, with 30,000 British troops engaged in the defence of Malaysia. Indonesian troops made landings in small numbers on the Malayan coast and British troops riposted with more effective raids on Indonesian Borneo. Amid reports of Indonesian aggressive intentions, including a full-scale assault on Malaysia, Sukarno announced that he was withdrawing from the United Nations. In January 1965 the Malaysian government appealed for Australian aid, and an infantry battalion was duly despatched to Sabah and Sarawak.

The subsequent fighting was very much like that earlier in Malaya, with small groups of Indonesian troops, usually of platoon size, crossing the border being met by ambushes and fighting patrols. The Australian troops were well-trained regulars, reinforced by the SAS squadrons, the first time this regiment was used on active service. Publicly, the Australian government maintained that all the action was purely defensive, and only taking place on the Malaysian side of the border. Classified as 'low-intensity' warfare, the jungle fighting was extremely unpleasant; there were only seven deaths in action, but sixteen from accident and illness.

The situation had been complicated by the fact that Singapore had decided to withdraw from Malaysia, and declare itself an independent city-state (on 7 August 1965). The British government, led by Harold Wilson since October 1964, was faced with the need for a re-appraisal. Wilson had already decided that British responsibilities east of Suez must be terminated, and the confrontation represented an embarrassing piece of unfinished business. The boot was now, as far as the United States and Australia were concerned, on the other foot, as the two countries endeavoured to persuade Wilson not to abandon Britain's obligation to defend Sabah–Sarawak, where Australia would be left with its forces exposed. Faces were saved when in September 1965 the Indonesian Communist Party attempted an insurrection, bloodily suppressed at the cost of hundreds of thousands of lives, as Indonesian army units and civilian gangs murdered anyone who could be considered remotely sympathetic to communism, or who had merely had the misfortune to be in the way. The British government prepared plans, with Australian agreement, to counter possible Indonesian escalation, which involved bombing raids from Australian bases, and agreed not to bother the United States with possibly embarrassing knowledge of their plans: but by mid-1966 *Konfrontasi* was abandoned.[15]

Menzies' Big Mistake

The decision made by the Australian government towards the end of Robert Menzies' long career, to join with the United States in the disastrous Vietnam War, must rank as his greatest error of judgement. After much hesitation Australia finally abandoned its alignment with Britain and the Commonwealth to become a military ally of America – and not, as in Korea, under a United Nations mandate. The cause was doubtful, and its conduct frequently dishonourable, while the hoped-for benefit, American recognition of Australian interests even when these were not acceptable to American voters, never transpired.

Behind American and Australian actions lurked an erroneous view of the world. Both countries still fully believed in the existence of a malignant communist plot designed to subvert the 'free' world. Since Korea and Stalin's death it was admitted that the Soviet Union and China were not working together, but both pursuing their individual agendas, which might well be contradictory. But China was still seen as the predatory villain, and any Asian communist as a tool of the Chinese government.[16] This was a misrepresentation of the historic relations between China and Indo-China, and displayed an alarming ignorance of recent events. Some reasons might be advanced for failures in Australian intelligence. The Department of External Affairs had few officers with the necessary linguistic skills, and throughout the whole of the period had no desk officer responsible for North Vietnam. Yet such diplomats as David Anderson, ambassador to South Vietnam, produced accurate assessments which were ignored at ministerial level. Sir Garfield Barwick, Minister for External Affairs between December 1961 and April 1964, was judged by the British Foreign Office to be, after Menzies, the ablest and best-informed member of the Australian Cabinet; his successor, Paul Hasluck, was a distinguished historian, with considerable diplomatic experience. It should certainly have been more generally realized that the ancient Kingdom of Annam had been formed from centuries of resistance to the Chinese empire, and that although Buddhist and Confucian traditions and methods of government continued, resentment of China was an integral part of Annamese consciousness, not to be overcome by a new attachment to communism. Ho Chi Minh was as unlikely to take orders from Beijing as his Yugoslavian counterpart Tito was to pay too much attention to Moscow diktats.

Since 1954, when it was hoped that the French withdrawal from Indo-China had been settled by the Geneva accords, the United States had nursed suspicious reservations. America had not been a signatory to the accords, but had noted a subsequent agreement. As might have been expected from an agreement which was signed neither by the United States nor South Vietnam, the Geneva accords unravelled. The undertaking that Vietnam was to be divided at the 17th parallel between a communist north – the Democratic Republic of Vietnam North (DVR) centred on the port of Hanoi – and a putatively democratic south, the Republic of Vietnam (RVN) with its capital of Saigon, was invalidated by a failure to hold the promised elections within the specified two years. True, the result of elections in the north would have been an inevitable victory, with 99 per cent voting for the communist candidates; such was the tradition in any country which contained the words 'Popular', 'People's' or 'Democratic' in its title. An election in the south might, however, have resulted in a government with some claim to democratic authority. A million Vietnamese had moved south to escape the communist threat, but many communist sympathizers had remained in the south, tightly organized, and with weapons left over from the fighting, soon supplemented by arms coming from the north, to form a guerrilla force, the Vietminh.

The failure to hold elections in the south has been blamed on the United States, with a good deal of justification. When charged with this, the normally fluent and precise Dean Rusk took refuge in embarrassed verbiage:

Well you know, remember the same time the Soviets were utterly opposed to free elections in Germany, utterly opposed to free elections in Korea. So the question must have arisen that why should we accommodate them in one spot if they wouldn't accommodate us in these other places. In other words, did we give them what they wanted, and just say 'too bad chaps' if they refused to give us what we wanted in areas of equal or more importance to us?[17]

Before the collapse of French rule, the Emperor Bao Dai, as Vietnamese head of state, had appointed Ngo Dinh Diem as Prime Minister. On the surface Diem had all the necessary qualifications: he had been a well-known figure in the first national government allowed to Annam by the French in the 1930s, and had subsequently refused several offers of the prime ministership. Prudently, he had elected to spend the war years in the United States, where he favourably impressed the young Senator Kennedy as a man of independence and integrity who had a single goal, his country's independence. His northern counterpart, Ho Chi Minh, was a resistance hero, who had lived in France, and subsequently fought French and Japanese as determinedly as he was to resist Americans. Diem was, however, also corrupt in the traditional Chinese manner, allotting posts to friends and relations, and maintaining a mandarin aloofness from the populace. His brother, Ngo Dinh Nhu, was, together with his wife, seen by many to be the real ruler. The family were also Catholic in a country with a strong Buddhist minority, a fact that had much to do with Kennedy's support and, as it turned out, with Australian participation.

It was Laos rather than Vietnam that led to the first post-Geneva disputes. Eisenhower's last advice to the incoming President had been to tell Kennedy to send troops to Laos. As part of the Geneva settlement Laos, like Vietnam, had been arbitrarily divided between the royal government, funded by the United States, and the communist movement Pathet Lao, acting as proxies for Hanoi, so making Laos, when the predictable war broke out, the only country 'where the armed forces on both sides of a civil conflict were entirely financed by foreign powers'. In March 1961 the suave Harold Macmillan, now Prime Minister, succeeded in persuading Kennedy that an intervention by SEATO would be unwise. If there were to be intervention it should be limited to a small force of British and American troops rather than a large-scale participation in what was essentially a civil war. Macmillan went on to add that 'whatever happened there must never appear to be a war between Europeans and Asiatics'; wise words, and ignored at a terrible price. Menzies, on the other hand, pressed for action, citing once again the communist advance, and in April 1961 insisting 'It is of vital importance that any operations which either now or hereafter may be undertaken should be operations employing Asian forces as well as those of White powers. The psychological effect of what would be regarded as an American incursion could easily be disastrous.'[18] The Australian Prime Minister, as would appear, was wrong on both points: Thailand and the Philippines, together with Burma and India, would probably have supported intervention, but the practical difficulties of co-ordinating 'Asian forces' with a sophisticated Western command structure would have been horrifying. Wiser counsels prevailed; Russia undertook to obtain a ceasefire and the second Geneva convention, 1961–2, succeeded in reaching a consensus on the neutralization of Laos.

Vietnam, however, was not going to be so easily settled. Diem's rule was predictably repressive, enforcing near-martial law. W. D. Forsyth, the Australian ambassador to Saigon in 1960, reported that there was no habeas corpus, freedom of association or free press, that arbitrary arrests were common, and that 'the people [were] too frightened to have anything to do with politics'. The Australian government chose not to listen, Barwick insisting that he detected 'an anti-communist nationalism' developing in the south, which would supplant the previous anti-colonialism in both the north and south, but what was in fact occurring was distaste for Diem's oppression consolidating into support for communist insurgents. This view was not shared by the American CIA, to whom Kennedy paid much attention (to his own detriment, as proved in 1961 by the Bay of Pigs fiasco). William Colby, the CIA chief in Saigon had been impressed by the British success in Malaya, and recommended a similar system be tried in South Vietnam to suppress the increasingly active Vietminh guerrillas; while in theory this had much to commend it, post-war American forces did not have the experience or training to mount such an operation.[19]

When in November 1961 the United States asked the Australian government to lend a hand to the RVN by supplying small arms and some counter-insurgency officers to pass on the methods learnt in Malaya, it cannot have seemed an unduly onerous request. Britain and France had already joined with the United States and Australia in stationing forces in Thailand, as a warning to any disturbers of the peace in that kingdom. Nothing was, however, done until an ANZUS meeting the following May, where Menzies agreed that the pact could indeed be invoked, since the unrest in the south was a consequence of external aggression from the north – a very doubtful thesis. Australia would therefore send thirty military advisers to South Vietnam.

The flimsiness of the pretext that southern disturbances were due to outside influences was manifested in 1963 when, provoked by the Diem regime's repression, riots in Saigon culminated in the astonishing pictures of a Buddhist monk burning himself to death, which swept around the world. Roger Hillsman, Director of Intelligence and Research at the State Department, described the crisis: 'a Frenchified Catholic Vietnamese President began to beat up the Pagodas and kill Buddhist priests and Buddhist nuns. This horrified us and we said: "Look if you go on like this we are going to have to disavow you." '[20] George Ball, Rusk's second in command, then became 'finally disillusioned' with the Diem family, feeling that the United States could not stay close to an ally who was behaving in such a thoroughly detestable manner. The decision was accordingly made in August 1963 to agree to a *coup d'état* which would remove Diem and replace the President with General Duong Van Minh. Two telegrams were sent from the State Department to the ambassador, Henry Cabot Lodge, in Saigon agreeing that the 'US would support a coup which has a good chance of succeeding', and that 'immediate action must be taken'. It was to be the first of twelve coups in the next two years, none of which succeeded in producing a stable regime.[21]

These events were nervously received by the Australian government, depending as it did upon the preference votes given to the Liberals by the dissident Democratic Labor Party. Barwick had touted Diem as a 'true patriot whose policies had cost him popular support', a statement which a former Secretary of the Department, Alan Watt, accurately described as: 'staggering . . . evidence of the failure of the Australian government, either to understand the clear signs of the disintegration of South Vietnam, especially between 1961 and 1963, or to explain to Australian public opinion the developing risk involved with policy the government was pursuing.'[22] A true assessment might, however, have jeopardized the Catholic anti-communist vote, which would account for the government's reluctance to explain the developing risks to the public.

Menzies restored his parliamentary position in November 1963 by convincing the Governor General that his fragile majority made stable government impossible, and secured a general election for the House of Representatives which gave the coalition another 10 seats. One result of the election was the appointment of Paul Hasluck as Minister for External Affairs. Until Malcolm Fraser gained office, Hasluck was the lone conservative intellectual in government, an upright and honourable man but like many intellectuals ill at ease with political realities and, after a long stint of domestic responsibilities, inexperienced in foreign relations. A preliminary tour through South East Asia convinced Hasluck that Australia was in imminent peril from an aggressive China and North Vietnam and that it was essential for the United States immediately to quell the troubles in the south and extend the war into the north. It was in vain that the Australian ambassador in Saigon, David Anderson, reported on the chaotic situation; General Duong had lasted only two months before being replaced by General Nguyen Khanh, and there was little likelihood of South Vietnamese forces alone making any headway against the militants, now supplemented by northern volunteers. Hasluck did not want to hear 'that our efforts are likely to fail, but [rather] that we are shown the possibilities, if there are any, of taking action to ensure that our efforts succeed' – still clinging to the illusion that a united and stable anti-communist government was possible. The United States must be pushed forward, and Australia should 'remove any reservation on the part of the Americans'.[23]

According to General Maxwell Taylor, American ambassador to Saigon from 1964, the removal of Diem was welcomed in the north: 'the best news Hanoi ever got . . . so there the leaders immediately said "Well, this is fine," let's get going to exploit this', and began moving larger units south. After the second coup American diplomats warned that the countryside was 'exhausted and sick of 20 years of civil conflict' and that the aims of the

Vietcong – communist guerrillas – were 'easily identifiable with the desires of the peasantry'. There was, David Nes, the deputy chief of mission at Saigon, warned, little choice between escalation and neutralization. General de Gaulle, who had bitter experience of Vietnam, and would not have been entirely displeased to see what would be interpreted as an American climb-down, was equally quite correct in striving for a diplomatic solution; but Lyndon Johnson, who after Kennedy's assassination had become American President, would have none of it. America would 'expend every effort and mobilize every resource to get Viet Nam strong enough to be independent and feared by any aggressor'. With its echoes of the Kennedy inaugural speech and its wildly impossible aim, the President's letter to the American ambassador in Saigon indicated how remote from reality Johnson had become. The Australian Department of External Affairs, however, agreed with Nes's evaluation: 'as there is no prospect of Western military victory over the Viet Cong, America's allies must find some way of enabling her to disengage militarily in South Viet Nam before the situation worsens.'[24]

But Hasluck and the Australian government continued faithful to the Johnson line. From May 1964 the American administration began strenuous efforts to muster some international support which could lend credibility to an aggressive American participation in Vietnam. Initial negative response led the President to send a personal cable on 2 July to the American ambassadors in Tokyo, Bonn, London, Rome, Brussels, Ottawa, Copenhagen, Bangkok, Taipei, Karachi and Athens – every potential ally, however unlikely (were Denmark or Greece ever really going to consider helping out in South East Asia?). The ambassadors were instructed, in a heavy-handed fashion, to ensure that the governments to which they were accredited understood that America expected them to share 'the burden of responsibility for defending that freedom' which was then being challenged in Vietnam, and the ambassadors were to prepare an 'adequate program' for each country's participation. The outstanding exceptions to the Presidential arm-twisting were Paris, a hopeless cause, Canberra, judged correctly to follow the United States obediently, and Seoul, where self-preservation dictated obedience, although a hefty price was demanded. The yield was laughably small; only Thailand was willing to accede to any despatch of troops; Japan offered medical assistance, and Britain sent £6,000 to General Khanh for the purchase of marine diesel engines.

Australia had already agreed in June to double (to sixty) the number of army instructors and to send six RAAF transports; not much, but as the only non-American forces in Vietnam of enormous political assistance. Hasluck would willingly have had the Americans go further, telling Menzies

(17 June) that it was 'essential for the US to step fully into the fray, inflict military reverses on the Viet Cong and cut off their supplies and links to Hanoi' – which he still believed to be under the control of China. What was not known by Canberra at the time was that the United States had already planned for an escalation, for which some excuse had to be found. Two American destroyers were sent on coat-trailing exercises off the North Vietnamese coast at the same time that South Vietnamese forces attacked two nearby islands. Claiming an attack on the warships which almost certainly never took place (President Johnson himself said 'Hell, those dumb stupid sailors were just shooting at flying fish'), Congress was immediately convened to approve what was generally thereafter known as the Gulf of Tonkin resolution, which gave the President powers that he interpreted as being able to commit the country to war as, when and how he pleased. By pure coincidence, doubtless, a draft resolution, part of perhaps prudent forward planning, lay ready to hand in the State Department. General Khanh had been informed, ten days previously, that he might expect some increased action in the next week or so; bombing raids on North Vietnam immediately commenced.[25]

On the same day – 5 August – Hasluck sprang into action to defend the air strikes as an appropriate response to a 'deliberate' attack (which never actually took place) on a routine patrol (which it wasn't). Not only the Cabinet, but even the opposition agreed. Gough Whitlam, the rising Labor star, then deputy leader, agreed that 'It is difficult to think that any United States President, or any other Head of State, could have reacted differently'. The other allies made polite murmurs of support, and China sent three squadrons of fighters to Hanoi – but no pilots.[26]

Going any further in supporting war in Vietnam presented Australia with a major manpower dilemma. One battalion of the regular army and a not inconsiderable part of the Royal Australian Navy and Royal Australian Air Force were already engaged in Borneo. On 14 December, having safely won his first presidential election, Johnson cabled Menzies to ask for a hundred more advisers, minesweepers and hospital ships – which the Royal Australian Navy did not possess. The Cabinet believed they could do rather better, and suggested a full infantry battalion, plus an SAS squadron and some naval support; but if this were to be possible, conscription must be introduced in Australia. This time there was no question of a referendum, and on 10 November Menzies gave one day's notice that conscription was instituted.

The method adopted was complex and unsatisfactory. Recruits were to be selected by ballot to serve for two years, anywhere in the world, with another three years in the militia. Those who chose, before the ballot, to hedge their bets, could opt for six years' militia service. Conscripts were to be integrated into the regular army and to perform exactly the same duties as the regulars. All this was totally at odds with previous policy when only volunteers were to be sent abroad, and might have been expected to provoke widespread indignation but in fact was received with only limited objections; it was, after all, believed to be a very small war. One of the regular three-yearly half-Senate elections was due in December, which the Labor Party was able to turn into a plebiscite on conscription. Somewhat surprisingly, given the previous Labor success in opposing conscription, and the aversion that might be expected to have conscripts sent overseas to a shooting war (although at that time Borneo was the only actual conflict), the challenge did not work, with the coalition scoring 45.7 per cent of the popular vote, with the support of the DLP at 8.4 per cent, and Labor 44.6 per cent.

The electoral lesson was duly digested, and in February 1965 the Federal Labor Party approved American actions in Vietnam, and voted for the despatch of troops to Borneo. Armed then with the assurance that the voters and opposition would not contest the decision, the Cabinet were confident, 'looking for a way in and not a way out' to join with the Americans in Vietnam. In Canberra, Hasluck worried that the Americans were not being aggressive enough, and cabled Keith Waller, the ambassador in Washington, to stiffen up their sinews – 'bring certainty to American policy and planning' – and confirming that Australia's intention was to 'remove any hesitation on the part of the Americans'. On 7 April President Johnson, perhaps fortified by the knowledge of Australian support, announced that the United States would commit ground troops to fight alongside the South Vietnamese, and on the same day the Australian government agreed that an infantry battalion would be sent to Vietnam. The public announcement prepared for Menzies by the Department of External Affairs was doctored by the Prime Minister in a misleading fashion. It originally read: 'The take-over of South Viet-Nam would be a direct military threat to Australia and all the countries of South and South-East Asia. It must be seen as part of a thrust by Communist China between the Indian and Pacific Oceans, exploiting weak-nesses in the multi-racial and economically underdeveloped countries of the region.' Menzies omitted the qualifying clauses after the word 'China' which the department, well understanding that the only country likely to be a threat to Australia was Indonesia, had inserted; but even the department's draft was inept, given China's attitude to Vietnam, perhaps long on rhetoric, but with no practical threat to far-off Australia.[27]

Arthur Calwell, the Labor Party leader, countered Menzies' decision on

4 May with an accurate forecast, indicating that he, at any rate, understood the true situation:

The government will try . . . to project a picture in which once the aggressive invaders from the North are halted, our men will be engaged in the exercise of picking off the Vietcong, themselves invaders from the North and stranded from their bases and isolated from their supplies. But it will not be like that at all. Our men will be fighting the largely indigenous Vietcong in their own territory . . . They will be fighting at the request of, and in support, and presumably under the direction of an unstable, inefficient, partially corrupt military regime which lacks even the semblance of being, or becoming, democratically based . . . Our present course is playing right into China's hands, and our present policy will, if not changed surely and inexorably lead to American humiliation in Asia.

The Labor leader did not, however, appreciate the lengths to which the United States was willing to go before the inevitable humiliation. Public opinion supported the government, with one noteworthy exception in the press. Keith Murdoch's son Rupert had begun his own spectacular career in July 1964 with the launch of what was intended to be a national news-paper, based in Canberra and entitled, following William Wentworth, the *Australian*. On Australian participation in Vietnam the revived *Australian* was forthright:

[the] decision is wrong, at this time, whichever way we look at it. It is wrong because Australia's contingent can have only insignificant military value, because it will be purely a political pawn in a situation for which Australia has no responsibility whatsoever . . . But Australia has lined up her generations against the hatred and contempt of resurgent Asian peoples – without adding one iota of confidence or strength to the tragically embroiled American nation. It could be that our historians will recall this day with tears.[28]

Unlike the Commonwealth intervention in Korea, when troops from Britain, Canada, New Zealand, India and Australia were formed into an integrated division, Australian battalions had to be placed under American tactical command, which presented immediate difficulties. American mili-tary doctrine depended upon supremely efficient logistics, the ability to concentrate, very quickly, masses of men and *matériel* which would enable devastating fire to be poured in the general direction of where the enemy was supposed to be, and indeed sometimes was. Australian tactics, developed with the British in Malaysia, and previously in the New Guinea fighting, emphasized small-scale stealthy patrols and a willingness to endure a long war. Matters improved somewhat as a second battalion was added to form a Task Force, with its own Logistic Support Group. Later expanded to three battalions, a total of some 8,300 men, the Australian Task Force made its mark. In one two-day battle at Long Tan in August 1966 an Australian company forestalled a Vietnamese attack, killing 245, with many other casualties, for a cost of 17 dead. Such an action was unusual, and most Australian military activity was the painstaking foot-slogging of patrol work, with occasional small-scale, hand-to-hand combat.[29]

Finding the reasons why Australia chose to side with the United States in the unwinnable and sordid war in Vietnam, the only independent country (with New Zealand unhappily tagging along behind) to do so, since even Japan declined and Thailand and South Korea were permanent United States clients, is not an easy task. Behind the assent, general at the time, loomed the universal distrust, fear and dislike of China and the Chinese bred into the Australian psyche over a century, which resulted in the mere mention of the Middle Kingdom arousing apprehension. And when linked to 'communism', a menace so carefully nurtured both by Liberal governments and by Santamaria's 'Movement', the formula was a winning one. Not, of course, only in Australia; Sinophobia was even more virulent in the United States, where the continuing support for Chiang Kai-shek and the legacy of McCarthyism nurtured the fears of the 'Yellow Peril'. The mere fact that China harboured no actively hostile intentions towards the West was ignored. The increasingly mad leadership of Mao, the Hundred Flowers campaign of 1956, the Great Leap Forward of 1958, and the Great Proletarian Cultural Revolution which began in 1966, in the course of which some 20 million people died, were reducing that unhappy country to impotent misery. Hong Kong's survival, a colonial relic on the very soil of China, ought to have stimulated some realization of Chinese tolerance – or inertia, if tolerance be judged too gracious a word. Given, too, the fact that Australian troops were fighting in Indonesia, a suspicion might have been raised that the real threat to Australia came from that immediate neighbour, which now shared a common and insecure border, the geographic line separating Australian Papua New Guinea from what had become the Indonesian province of West Irian. But Indonesia had proved its anti-communist credentials by slaughtering half a million or so of its own people, thereby proving a valuable potential ally to the forces of freedom.

Good reasons certainly existed for Australia's seeking the protection of the United States, since links with Britain were rusting. It was not so much that Australia was drifting away from Britain, a process which had been slowly developing over half a century, but that Britain was considering a decisive break with previous Imperial policies, involving a blunt disregard for all ties of sentiment and joint loyalty. Harold Wilson's government, in power between 1964 and 1970, which depended for its survival on American support for sterling, managed to resist pressure to join in Vietnam, and following the devaluation of 1967 had decided to withdraw all forces east of Suez: the succeeding Conservative government amended the timetable somewhat, but could not fault the logic of Wilson's decision. Once the last colonial obligation in the region, the defence of Malaysia, had been discharged, Britain would be in no position to offer Australia much in the way of protection. Worse, Britain seemed about to abandon the remaining commercial agreements that had sustained Australian trade for so long. Britain's first application to join the European Economic Community (EEC) had been ignominiously vetoed by General de Gaulle in 1967 as the cunning Prime Minister well knew it would be, thus postponing an awkward problem for a successor to solve; but the likelihood of Britain's accession, which occurred only in 1971, would force a re-appraisal of Australian commercial policy. The replacement of the Australian pound by the dollar in 1965 hardly seemed more than a straw in the wind; there was never any likelihood that Menzies' own preference, which was to name the new currency the 'royal', would do more than arouse mild derision.

Whether Sir Robert Menzies' sentimental attachment to British traditions, and to the person of the monarch especially, was other than a source of embarrassment to Australians is questionable. Certainly his declaration to an alarmed Queen in 1963 that 'I did but see her passing by, but I shall love her till I die' was the source of many vulgar speculations, but his resignation in December 1965 was seen as the end of a political generation for whom the attachment of Australia to the mother country had rarely been seriously in doubt.

The Second Eleven

That end, however, was some time in coming. Harold Holt, from 1956 identified as Menzies' successor at the head of the Liberals, took over both the government and Menzies' policies in January 1966, consolidating his position by a decisive victory in the November general election, in which the coalition won 50 per cent of the primary vote and 80 seats to Labor's 41, with 1 independent. Australian foreign policy continued as before. Britain had been allowed to use the central Australian desert for nuclear tests in the 1950s, thereby causing much pollution and some still unknown, but certainly dangerous, effects on health. The expected cooperation with

Britain on nuclear developments did not, however, come about, as Britain developed its own arrangements with the United States. On the surface, relations with Britain continued much as before; royal visits continued, Prince Charles was sent to spend a year at an Australian school, and the Australian National University and the Atomic Energy Authority began the construction of a seismological station in the Northern Territory. What of the alternative protector, the United States? Australia was surely doing enough to prove its loyalty. As well as that invaluable moral support, and not despicable physical support, being given in Vietnam, Australia had obediently allowed America 'facilities'. All were strictly secluded and guarded as being 'extremely critical to American military and intelligence operations' – and all of course would be high on the list of potential targets if war broke out. Their nature was described in a secret White House document of May 1986:

Australia currently facilitates projection of US power into the Indian Ocean and Southwest Asia by receiving some four–five dozen ship visits per year and by facilitating B-52 reconnaissance and training missions. In addition, Australia hosts joint defense and intelligence facilities that: (a) provide communications with our submarines and surface vessels in the Indian Ocean and the Western Pacific, (b) enhance strategic early warning in the event of Soviet ballistic missile attack, and (c) provide critical intelligence on Soviet military operations and testing, including information necessary for the verification of arms control agreements. During 1986–88 agreements on the joint facilities will revert from a long-term to a year-by-year basis.

In addition, Australia has the potential to play an important role of its own in regional security. The Australian armed forces – although small on a global scale – are one of the largest military organizations in the Southern Hemisphere. These forces can serve as stabilizing elements in the South Pacific and southeast Asia and in safeguarding passage through vital straits linking the Pacific and Indian Oceans.[30]

Not surprisingly, Menzies could summon up little enthusiasm for his successor. Holt had a wonderful win in the 1966 election but 'in his second year, he did nothing right. He disclosed what I hadn't quite realised and I should have. It was his besetting sin – he wanted everyone to love him. And the result was he made a muck of everything in his second year . . . It was a dreadful performance. Dreadful.' Hasluck was dismissive:

Holt was an affable fellow . . . I found him a good colleague but he had what I call a tangential mind. He couldn't focus. If you were having a discussion with Holt and trying to expose some problem to him, presently up would come a point which he recognised and off he would go at a tangent. And after you had about 10 minutes on that you would have to pull him back and try to get him back on the separate point again. Then another thing would arise and off he would go on another tangent.

But he agreed with Menzies: 'Another of Holt's weaknesses was the desire to be liked. He wanted to be liked.'[31]

Menzies' command of embarrassing quotations was matched by Holt's originality when, on a visit to the United States the new Prime Minister claimed that 'Australia was an admiring friend, a staunch friend, that will go all the way with LBJ', a phrase that was to haunt the Liberal Party thereafter. In a strange resemblance to Johnson's own division of policies between strongly liberal at home – the final demolition of barriers to black equality – and doggedly aggressive abroad, Holt's administration saw the first serious attempts to demolish the White Australia legacy and to address the Aborigines' justified resentment, while abroad he showed a blind obedience to the Sinophobic and anti-communist line. His comment on the Indonesian massacres to a New York audience in July 1966, that '500,000 to 1,000,000 communist sympathizers' had been 'knocked off', either ignored or gloried in the fact that a great proportion of those 'knocked off' were Chinese. In May of the same year the House of Representatives was told by Mr Holt that China was 'implacably committed to its goal of a communist-dominated world' and that Australians were fighting for 'free peoples everywhere'.[32]

The honeymoon between the Liberal hawks and the people could not be expected to survive intact the dispatch of national servicemen to the front, and a Gallup poll in March 1966 indicated that 57 per cent opposed conscription, although support for the war itself continued generally solid. Students and their sympathizers, as expected, staged noisy demonstrations, but the real threat came when respectable middle classes, led by such impeccable characters as the prolific Victorian novelist Morris West, whose *The Shoes of the Fisherman* was then a runaway success, publicized their opposition to the war, and such new organizations as the Liberal Reform Group began to constitute an electoral threat. When Lyndon Johnson himself visited Australia in October 1966, it appeared an unprecedented honour for the gratified Holt, apparently symbolizing the realization of Curtin's famous message of December 1941. In fact Australia was low on the list of the President's priorities; the State Department briefings were cursory, compared with the detailed analysis of South East Asian politics. Australians, as seen by the State Department were open, friendly, good humored people, and there seems to be a natural affinity between them and Americans. The common traditions and outlooks that bind Australia and the United States are many – both countries were developed by pioneering people who built their new nations in rugged and largely empty continents. The political, social and juridical origins in the British system were evolved and modified to suit the new situations encountered and emerging aspirations of the people. Both countries have repeatedly demonstrated their devotion to freedom by defending it in foreign lands – often together.

Australians for years have been sensitive and even defensive at being 'taken for granted' and 'patronized' (the latter particularly by the British). The former feeling has diminished considerably in the recent past because of the greatly increased communication between the United States and Australia.

These amiable natives should be put at ease by the President drawing 'on his experience during the time he spent in Australia and New Guinea at the beginning of World War II' – and 'he should not forget to convey his pleasure at meeting the Prime Minister's stepsons and their beautiful wives'. Genuine enthusiasm did exist, and the archetypical Texan Johnson responded to Australia, where could be found all the virtues that Texas once possessed and, on a much larger scale:

Here was the faithful ally being rewarded by an imperial visit, offering the spectacles of the triumphal motorcade, the imperial limousine, the imperial lectern, the imperial secret service guard, the impromptu stops, the hand shakings, baby kissings, and distributions of ball point pens, the bull roarings ('I love ya, Australia' . . . 'Hooray Australia, your way is our way'), the release of pigeons and balloons, the immense and enthusiastic crowds.

But there were also shouts of 'Ho Ho Ho Chi Minh' and 'Hey Hey, LBJ, How many kids did you kill today?' and demonstrators lying on the road in front of the motorcade; in spite of this opposition, indeed powerfully reinforced by the presidential visit, the Liberals did resoundingly well in the November elections in which the coalition won 82 seats to Labor's 41, with 1 Independent Labor.[33]

'Smoothing the pillow of a dying race'

For the first thirty years after Federation, the Australian government had placidly accepted that their responsibility for the Aboriginal population was limited to slowly 'easing them over the bumps' on the way to the graveyard.

Attempting as best he could to stem the decline, Bishop George Frodsham of North Queensland lamented: 'The Aborigines are disappearing. In the course of a generation or two, at the most, the last Australian blackfellow will have turned his face to warm mother earth ... Missionary work then may only be smoothing the pillow of a dying race.' To the mass of the population living in the great cities, this seemed self-evident; the only visible Aborigines were a few shiftless specimens hanging round in the shadows. In the countryside, and even more so in the frontier societies of the Northern Territory, Western Australia and Queensland, Aborigines appeared in a very different light.[34]

At Federation, Aboriginal affairs had been left to the states but when the Commonwealth took over the Northern Territory in 1911 numerous Aborigines became Commonwealth responsibilities, although not of course Commonwealth citizens. As a Territory the north was administered jointly with Papua, and something of William MacGregor and Hubert Murray's ideals of tutelary guidance towards a political future began to colour Australian perceptions, that 'the native inhabitant was a potential citizen with rights to be protected until he was in a position to assert these for himself'.

Some perception of Aboriginal culture was slowly developing among a very small number of anthropologists and such sympathizers as Mary Bennett, brought up in close and friendly contact with the Dalleburra people of Queensland. The central importance of ceremony to mark acceptance in the community, to revere the tutelary clan guardians, to mark the passage of the seasons and mankind's integration with the spirit world in Aboriginal communities, was beginning to be appreciated – a century after South African missionaries had begun analysing the fundamentals of Khoisan religion. In a society like that of White Australia, which was so deeply rooted in British values, customs and literature, the need to revisit the ancestral places metaphysically and actually, should perhaps have been appreciated. Pilgrimages to Scotland and Ireland made by Australian Prime Ministers were in some way paralleled by the importance Aborigines attached to visiting their own ancestral lands; in an illiterate society physical presence was essential. Such perceptions, however, rarely reached officials.[35]

To all Australian governments, state and Commonwealth, the concept of 'control' was much more influential than that of 'protection'. Little effort was expended on ensuring that Aborigines living on reserves were given tolerable employment conditions, although under Commonwealth regulations cash payments were theoretically necessary. A licence costing 5s. was needed to employ an Aboriginal, and this was often the only cash necessary; at 7s. 6d. a dog licence was more expensive. It was much easier to enforce regulations upon confused Aborigines than on disgruntled and resentful employers. The powers of control were intimidating. Under the 1911 Commonwealth Act any Aboriginal under the age of 18, including 'half-castes', defined as anyone with an Aboriginal parent or grandparent, was automatically placed under the control of the Protector, who might remove, without any reason offered, and without the parent's consent, any such child. Aboriginals were forbidden to marry non-Aboriginals without the consent of the Commonwealth Minister, so absurd a restriction that 'Protectors' – one feels that the word should be placed in inverted commas – rarely forwarded such requests.[36]

The first indications of changed attitudes were visible in the later 1920s, when the Aborigines Protection League proposed setting up a number of Aboriginal states, where Aborigines could own land, govern themselves according to their own customs, at least on a quasi-municipal level, and be represented by Aboriginal members of Parliament. Owing something to New Zealand Maori policy, the proposals also resembled the South African Nationalist Party's representation of blacks by Native Representatives in both houses of Parliament. The idea was frowned upon by the South Australian Advisory Council of Aborigines, when the government's Royal Commission was asked to consider granting 64,000 acres on the Eyre Peninsula for such a 'State or Territory'. 'Past experience', the Minister for Education claimed, 'had shown that with a few exceptions the aborigines did not inspire confidence in their ability to manage a farm without the help of a white man.' Part of the government's antipathy might have been due to the irritable advocacy of Herbert Basedow, the author of *The Australian Aboriginal*, published in 1925, the first book to provide detailed information on Aboriginal life, who had been pressing for the creation of a large Aboriginal reserve since 1914, and who in 1927 had become an awkward member of the South Australian House of Assembly.

John Bleakley, chief Protector of Aborigines in Queensland from 1914 to 1942, was particularly interested in 'half castes', who did not choose to live as tribal Aborigines but who were not accepted into white society. In February 1929 Bleakley presented a report to the Commonwealth government which poured more cold water over the idea of an Aboriginal state, stating that this would be 'to thrust upon them a social machine that they cannot understand'. Bleakley was able to pray in aid the changed opinion of David Unaipon, the best-known and most respected Aboriginal in the nation. In 1926 Unaipon had advocated a model Aboriginal state, but in 1929 Bleakley claimed that Unaipon now believed that 'his people would never voluntarily change their tribal customs and laws for any national government', and that to 'press such a system upon them would only result in chaos, for the different tribes would not agree'. A convinced paternalist, who did much to improve physical conditions for Queensland Aborigines, Bleakley was content for them to have their land – he suggested 65,000 square miles of it – but required that it be kept firmly under government control, free from white encroachment, and with the inhabitants subject to strict regulation. In 1931 Arnhem Land, 31,000 square miles of the north-western coast-lands of the Gulf of Carpentaria was created as such a reserve, well away from any centres of settlement. It was an essentially negative development, with Aborigines treated as 'zoological specimens', with no bearing on the central problem, which was that Aborigines were not classed as Australian citizens but as a minority that needed protection and control before being ushered into the precious privilege of citizenship – and the nearer an Aborigine approached this goal, the more he was conscious and resentful of the unjust and patronizing way he was being treated. When concessions were made the conditions were often humiliating. A Western Australian Act of 1944 granted certificates exempting Aborigines from some restrictions: a hopeful Aborigine was obliged to convince a magistrate that he had 'dissolved tribal and native associations' and adopted 'the manner and habits of civilised life', could speak good English and was not afflicted by leprosy, syphilis, granuloma or yaws; backsliders would have their certificates withdrawn.[37] C. D. Rowley, one of the first scholars to study twentieth-century Aboriginal society, could well regret that the 'transition from the philosophy of a Gipps or a Grey, with their worry about human equality before the law, to a situation where those in control thought mainly in categories of racial origin, had been long since completed'.[38]

Bowing to pressure from Britain and India, the Australian government reluctantly agreed that British Indians could acquire Australian citizenship with most rights appertaining thereto, and that their children, if born in Australia, would automatically become full citizens. It was an illustration of their attitude that both Queensland and Western Australia were reluctant to fulfil these obligations; it was ten years before Western Australia did, and although Queensland was a little more prompt, taking only five years, both states continued legislative discrimination against Indians and other 'Asiatics'. Aborigines, however, remained excluded. Harassed state officials attempted to define exactly what constituted an 'Aboriginal'; they were given little help from central government:

In keeping with contemporary thought and in contrast to current practice, aboriginality was seen quite literally as a question of blood rather than identity. Taking a different tack from that followed in America and South Africa, the Commonwealth bureaucracy resisted strongly moves by the political masters in 1929 to construct a complex formal caste system based on distinguishing, as was then popular, between 'full blood', 'mulatto', 'quadroon', 'octoroon' and 'half-caste'.

It was also quite possible for the same person to be treated as belonging to different races under different laws. Paul Hasluck pointed out that in Derby, Western Australia, some citizens who as Aborigines could not vote in the lower house of the state Parliament, possessed property enough to entitle them to a vote for the upper. One absolutely necessary preliminary to any reform was the transfer of powers over Aborigines from states to Commonwealth. From 1914 onwards this had been constantly urged, and after 1942 attempted four times, first in the aborted Commonwealth Powers Act of that year, then in the Powers Referendum of 1944, with two subsequent efforts in a post-war Premiers' Conference and a last-minute attempt before the Chifley government was defeated in 1949. All were unsuccessful, but helped to focus some attention on the issue.[39]

Aborigines themselves were becoming militant as their share of the population grew, from about 60,000 in the 1920s to an estimated 106,000 in 1961 and 115,953 when in 1971 they were included in the census for the first time. An Aboriginal view of history was advanced by William Cooper, founder of the Aborigines Progressive Association, proposing that the 150th anniversary of the First Fleet, in January 1938, should be observed as a 'Day of Mourning' for an epoch of 'misery and degradation'. Somewhat strangely, it was the right-winger John McEwen who, as Minister for the Interior in 1939, initiated the first really humane statement of Aboriginal policy since the end of British colonial administration. Stimulated by the advice of the anthropologist A. P. Elkin, McEwen's statement was a restatement of old colonial ideas; the aim of the administration would be 'the raising of their status so as to entitle them by right and by qualification to the ordinary rights of citizenship, and to enable them and help them to share with us the opportunities that are available in their native land'. James Stephen would have approved; admirable sentiments even if a century too late. But at least the possibility of a future for Aborigines, albeit conforming to white Australian mores, was acknowledged.

War did much to change attitudes, black and white. Army camps employed hundreds of Northern Territory Aborigines, and the more friendly atmosphere, with good rations and decent facilities, where Aboriginals were treated as valuable colleagues rather than as threats to white employment, raised the question of fair wages for blackfellows. This dangerous possibility was averted by Judge Portus's decision in February 1948, on the application to the Commonwealth Conciliation and Arbitration Commission, that any 'interference' with the administration of the Northern Territory would 'not be justified as the Administration is much better equipped than a court of arbitration to attend to the welfare of the Aboriginals living and working on Cattle Stations'.[40]

Public apathy had also been stimulated somewhat by Aboriginal servicemen – the first Aborigine to be a commissioned officer was Reginald Saunders in 1944 – and in the 1949 Commonwealth Electoral Act, Aborigines in South Australia, New South Wales, Victoria and Tasmania (those states where the local franchise was already given) were allowed to be counted as citizens, but in Queensland and Western Australia the privilege was granted only to those who had served in the forces (who had already received a temporary vote in 1940, scheduled to end six months after the end of hostilities). The Labor Party, where some twinges of conscience might have been expected, was sublimely indifferent: in David Day's lengthy biography of John Curtin, there is, if the index be trusted, not a single mention of Aborigines.

It was not a good beginning to a brave new post-war world; some Australian Aborigines could be citizens, and be allowed to vote, but their individual liberties were subject to many restrictions. The road to hell is invariably paved with good intentions, and the intentions of Sir Paul Hasluck, in charge of Aboriginal Affairs and of the Territories from 1949 for twelve years, were demonstrably excellent. In 1980 he explained the reasons for initiating the Commonwealth policy of removing children from Aboriginal families to be educated in foster homes and institutions.

In the early 1930s a policy was accepted of transferring some children – described as 'octoroons' or 'quadroons' – out of the Territory into southern denominational institutions with a view to their ultimate adoption by white parents. Several children were transferred. It seems that part of the argument was that these children were waifs and strays but to place them in government institutions for half-castes at Darwin and Alice Springs would not be suitable for their successful 'absorption'. This transfer of children out of the Territory seems to have originated with the Christian missions.

When I became Minister for Territories opinion in the Territorial administration was still divided about the policy of transfer, but in southern church circles and among those sympathetically concerned with the plight of Aborigines there was a strong continuing advocacy of giving children 'a chance in life.' Inquiries were made too from those wishing to be foster parents or to adopt light-skinned aboriginal children. Some determination of policy was needed. In a minute of 12 September 1952 I wrote that the policy of assimilation was likely to be assisted by transferring out of the Territory into suitable institutions and private homes in the southern States 'those light-coloured children who have no strong family ties in the Territory.' It was essential, however, that the transfer should be made at an early age and that each case should be treated as an individual case.

The test to be applied is simply what action is likely to be conducive to a happy future life for the child ... I do not want hard and fast rules, but rather that this possibility should always be kept in mind and used to the best advantage and that a recognized procedure for transfer, placement, inspection, after-care and eventual employment may be laid down.[41]

It is noteworthy that Sir Paul is concerned only with light-skinned children, who might not be too conspicuous in the wider community, and that no mention is made of parental consent. Sometimes this might have been given, but one officer reported on the removal of children from Wave Hill, the Vestey station in the Northern Territory during Sir Paul's period of office: 'The removal of children from Wave Hill . . . was accompanied by distressing scenes the like of which I wish never to experience again. The engines of the plane are not stopped at Wave Hill and the noise combined with the strangeness of the aircraft only accentuated the grief and fear of the children, resulting in near-hysteria in two of them.'

While there was later much justified criticism of the removal of Aboriginal children from their families, at the time it was considered the way forward to a better life, for whites as well. During the 1930s large numbers of children had been, with the best of intentions, but often with dissimulation and some deceit, removed from poor living conditions in Britain and taken to farm camps, particularly in Western Australia, thence to foster homes. The number of children removed – 'stolen' – was later a source of virulent discussion, but it is surely permissible to question its relevance; one family destroyed by enforced separation was one too many, but leaving deprived and sometimes abused children in miserable conditions was also to be deplored.[42]

What inspired Harold Holt to agree in May 1967 to a referendum on whether all Aboriginals should be given citizenship rights, allowing them to be included in the census and, quite as importantly, finally allowing the Commonwealth rather than the states to legislate on Aboriginal matters, is not clear. Six years had passed since a Senate report recommended that all Aborigines should immediately be given the right to vote at federal elections, without any action being taken, but more recently there had been some indications of progress. Guarded approval had been given to the previous year's announcement that non-Europeans need in future wait for only five years rather than fifteen before qualifying for citizenship and that 'well-qualified and useful' might be substituted for 'distinguished and highly qualified' as residential criteria. South Australia had once more led the way in 1966 by prohibiting discrimination in service industries – cafés and pubs being notoriously sensitive – and passing the first Aboriginal Lands Trust Act to allow Aboriginal communities to own their own land. Equal pay for stockmen had been granted by the Arbitration Commission, which did not prevent the Wave Hill stockmen (the station from which the children had been removed eight years before) from occupying some of the land in a protest. For the first time, Aboriginal discontent was being manifested in the cities as a new type of leader, personified by Charles Perkins, led 'Freedom Rides' on the American model to protest against discrimination; the town of Moree in northern New South Wales was the Australian equivalent of Birmingham, Alabama. The most decisive factor in Harold Holt's calculation must, however, have been a correct assessment of its electoral appeal, for the referendum received the clearest assent of any; 89 per cent voting positively for this modest but essential first step.

As it turned out, Holt was never able to show what might have been done for Aboriginal Australians beyond appointing a Federal Council under the chairmanship of the invaluable 'Nugget' Coombs, for on 17 December the Prime Minister went for a swim off Portsea, in Melbourne, and disappeared without trace. An elaborate essay, suggesting that Holt had been in the pay of the Chinese for many years and was removed in a Chinese submarine, has been made by Anthony Grey, but on the other hand the Liberal Party was also preparing to remove their leader without such assistance. Holt was given the consolation of a state funeral attended by Harold Wilson and President Johnson, which was not perhaps quite so great a tribute, since in four and a half days the President also visited Thailand, South Vietnam, Pakistan and Rome. He was met at Canberra by the former Deputy Prime Minister John McEwen during his brief period of office, who was able to assure President Johnson that Australia would 'stay steadfast with the Republic of Vietnam and the US and with other Allies . . . until a just peace is won'.[43]

Holt's disappearance left the Governor General, Richard Casey, now Lord Casey, to provide for continuity, which he did by appointing John McEwen of the Country Party until the Liberals should elect a new leader. It was abundantly clear that this should not be William McMahon, 'a treacherous liar', according to his colleague Hasluck, a 'leech' and a 'congenital liar', 'a contemptible squirt ... pathetic ... a dreadful little man', were the comments of other Liberal ministers – the last two from Menzies himself. The choice was effectively between Paul Hasluck and Senator John Gorton, who had the great merit of a low public profile which meant he had not made too many enemies. Hasluck, experienced and well regarded, was the obvious choice, but was also perhaps a shop-worn one, and younger Liberal members of Parliament preferred a fresh face, one who might promise a new future after nearly twenty years of Menzies and his ministers.[44]

Gorton was certainly different. The first Australian Prime Minister since Bruce to have attended an English university (Oxford), Gorton was no intellectual, but had a lively natural curiosity and an originality that bordered on eccentricity. A distinguished war record (again, the first Prime Minister to have seen action since Bruce) had left him with an engagingly battered countenance, and these, together with his appointment of a remarkably personable private secretary, the talented Ainsley Gotto, all recommended him to male Australian voters. In many respects Gorton was a surprisingly liberal Liberal, finding Australian immigration policies 'morally reprehensible', inviting the Indian Prime Minister, Mrs Gandhi to visit, suggesting a series of non-aggression pacts with Asian neighbours and appointing Gordon Freeth, a relative left-winger, as Minister for External Affairs. Freeth's appointment marked the start of an unsettled period in the Department of External Affairs (renamed the Department of Foreign Affairs from November 1970). Prior to Freeth's appointment there had been only four ministers in fifteen years; between 1969 and 1975 there were to be seven incumbents. The historian of Australian foreign affairs T. B. Millar commented, wryly but accurately, that 'It is not usual for Australian foreign affairs ministers to make speeches that are in any way provocative of thought. It is almost unheard of that they should introduce new ideas', but Freeth's speech on 14 August 1969 was, in the context of Australian post-war foreign policy, almost revolutionary. Reacting to a speech made the previous month by the Russian Foreign Minister Andrei Gromyko, in which Gromyko announced that 'The prerequisite and potential for an improvement of our relations with Australia exist', Freeth told the Australian Parliament that 'Australia has to be watchful, but need not panic whenever a Russian appears. It has to avoid both facile gullibility and automatic rejection of opportunities for co-operation. The Australian government at all times welcomes the opportunity of practical and constructive dealings with the Soviet Union, as with any other country.' It seemed that the spectre of a predatory communism threatening Australia was finally giving way to a more realistic appreciation of contemporary world events. The acceptance of these uncomfortable facts took some while to become general. Freeth had cleared his speech with Gorton, but other members of the government were alarmed, and the DLP, still clinging to their myth of a rampant anti-Christian monolithic Marxism, were appalled, and immediately called a conference to consider their continued support for such governmental heresies.[45]

On Vietnam, however, Australia remained not only loyal to America, but displayed greater solidarity than did the American public. The Tet offensive of February 1968 was a military defeat for the north, but inflicted fatal damage on American morale, and was, the American commander General Westmoreland admitted, 'the stroke which took America out of the war'. Only a few days before risings broke out in towns all over the south, including a brief occupation of the American embassy in Saigon, General Westmoreland had forecast that victory was in sight and spoke of being able soon to reduce troop levels. After Tet he urgently requested another 200,000 American soldiers. A discouraged President Johnson announced that he would not stand in the presidential election, leaving the poisoned chalice of the Vietnam War to be passed on, and declaring: 'I am taking the first step to de-escalate the conflict. We are reducing, substantially reducing, the present level of hostilities. We are doing so unilaterally and at once.' Johnson's retreat was enough to bring the north to the negotiating table, but not enough to end the war.[46]

The Australian government was disturbed by this news, and defiantly declared that Australian troops would not be withdrawn until fighting had ceased; John Gorton proved that the capacity for fulsome phrase-making exhibited by his predecessors had not been lost by declaring to the President that if America wanted to dance, 'We'll come a-waltzing Matilda with you'. Peter Howson, the Air Minister, feared that Johnson's action was 'the first step of the Americans moving out of South-east Asia . . . within a few years . . . there'll be no white faces on the Asian mainland . . . from now on, to a much greater extent, we shall be isolated and on our own'. Mr Howson need not have worried overmuch, since the Saigon government refused to join in the peace talks, and the war continued.[47]

Richard Nixon, succeeding Johnson in January 1969, attempted a new policy, of 'Vietnamization', allowing the South Vietnamese army to effect their own liberation, while providing American support at reduced troop levels. In July the new President amplified his policy in what became known as the Guam Doctrine; while confirming existing treaty commitments, the United States would avoid future intervention in the 'peripheral areas' and expect 'the nation directly threatened to assume the primary responsibility for providing the manpower for its defense' – and since Australia was just such a peripheral area the limitations of future American aid were made unpleasantly clear. Public opinion wavered in its previous support of the Vietnam War; an opinion poll in August 1969 showed 55 per cent in favour of an Australian withdrawal, and the Labor opposition adopted disengagement as an election policy. Public demonstrations mustering tens of thousands of supporters marched against the war, but Gorton remained staunch; there would be no Australian troops removed from the battlefields. This position was so untenable that by the end of 1970 there was no alternative but to fall in line with the American withdrawals; but by then it was too late for John Gorton. The October 1969 election had not gone well for the Liberals, with the coalition majority reduced from 41 to 7; once again the Democratic Labor Party preferences had secured a narrow coalition victory, although the popular vote was negative – 43.4 per cent for the coalition and 47 per cent for Labor.

Australian participation in Vietnam left few of the psychological scars that the American Vietnam generation suffered. The draft system was less demanding and fairer than that of the United States; the Australian forces were not so obviously made up of the poorest sections of the community, while a much greater percentage than justified of the American rankers were black. No draft-resisting students were shot down by police, and returning soldiers were neither cheered nor jeered more than reasonably. In a small cohesive force discipline was much tighter, and the sole allegation of Australian misbehaviour towards the civilian population, the 'Water Torture' case, caused a tremendous row, many investigations, and turned out to be, as it were, a damp squib. On the other hand at least two junior officers were murdered by their own men, which does not suggest the highest of military standards.[48]

A new cast of political figures was moving towards the centre of the stage. Malcolm Fraser was not only the rising star of the Liberal Party, but the only outstanding figure anywhere near the leadership. A generation removed from his predecessors, born in 1930, Fraser had been an uncommonly young undergraduate at Oxford and won his first parliamentary seat at the age of 25 – with the help of DLP preference votes. During loyal but not particularly distinguished service on the back benches, Fraser was developing a political philosophy which in many respects harked back firmly to the Deakin consensus. Individual freedom of choice was essential, but to exercise it state action was imperative. He did not believe, his successor John Howard remarked, in the prayer that 'we should be godly and quietly governed'. Fraser proved himself as committed as any Australian Labor Prime Minister to justice both internally and internationally, but also to being a tough politician, vigorous to the boundaries of propriety: indeed, very much a twentieth-century Gladstone, though without Gladstone's power to command admiration and detestation alike.[49]

His opposite number in the Labor Party was Gough Whitlam, fourteen years older, who like Gorton had served during the war in the RAAF. Whitlam was a middle-class intellectual, from an urban middle-class family, himself a barrister, with six books to his credit before 1971, a rare phenomenon in Australian Labor, who might well have appeared to be more comfortable in the Liberal ranks. Whitlam had risen speedily, unmatched by any contemporary. In October 1966 the American ambassador took a poor view of the Australian Labor leadership: Calwell was 'aging and ineffectual', strongly opposed to Australian involvement in Vietnam, but a 'firm supporter of US ties'. Accurately reckoning that Calwell would not survive the next election, Ambassador Clark thought better of his likely successor Gough (the President was told to pronounce it 'Guff') Whitlam, 'well educated, and moderate', but calculated that in view of the 'continued death wish of the Labor party' this was unlikely to be soon. As deputy leader, Whitlam had done much to transform the party from its obsolescent structure that so long a period of opposition had rusted into disuse. The hold of Caucus had been loosened, the previous insistence on centralization and diminution of states' powers reduced the commitment to nationalization of industry, which was quietly interred, and the tradition of leaders being working-class trade unionists, preferably Catholics, had been broken, but some sacred cows remained unslaughtered, including that ancient Chartist demand, the abolition of the upper house. Labor was now a truly national rather than a class party, an organization which would welcome intellectual argument, with a leader with panache and wit such as it had rarely known.[50]

It was Malcolm Fraser himself, as Defence Minister, disagreeing with the chief of the Defence Staff, General Sir Thomas Daly, and resigning when the Prime Minister sided with Sir Thomas, who precipitated a leadership election. Whitlam, sensing the opportunity, indicated he would move a no-confidence motion which, given any Liberal abstentions, might defeat the government. The subsequent Liberal leadership election led to a tie; Gorton, very properly, resigned. Donald Horne cynically wrote: 'For his own people, despite his good early run, he was soon failing great tests of statesmanship – his eyebrow movements emphasised the wrong part of his sentence and he placed stress on the wrong words; he wasn't any good on television.'[51]

When William McMahon was elected as Liberal leader and therefore as Prime Minister, it was the beginning of the end for the Liberal Party. Progressively upstaged by the more attractive performer Whitlam, clinging on to power by courtesy of the DLP, McMahon fumbled and procrastinated. Menzies' inheritance of confident authority, of the Liberal Party as the natural party of government, which had crumbled under Holt and Gorton, disintegrated in McMahon's hands.

Nothing, however, can be attributed solely to the faults or virtues of a single politician, and the Liberal Party was also suffering in the states. At the beginning of the 1970s only South Australia had a Labor government, led by the personable Don Dunstan, with the opposition, the merged Liberal and Country League, in disarray. Very much the natural party of power, the LCL had been in continuous office from 1933 to 1965, for the last twenty-seven years under the venerable Sir Thomas Playford (whose grandfather had been Premier of South Australia and one of the first members of the Commonwealth Senate), protected by a Legislative Council which retained all the original powers of veto, elected on a property-based franchise, and with representation favouring country constituencies. But even in South Australia democracy threatened, and by 1972 the LCL split between the left-ish Steele Hall and the splendidly named conservative Renfrey Curgenven DeGaris. Western Australia, where Labor won the February 1971 election, was no better. It was significant, and helps to explain McMahon's nervousness, that the DLP won 10.7 per cent of the popular vote in that election.[52] Three states continued to reject Labor; profiting from the continuing animosity between Labor and DLP supporters, and the firm leadership of Henry Bolte, Premier 1955–72, the Liberals held on in Victoria, but neither New South Wales nor Queensland were good advertisements for non-Labor governments.

Politics at Canberra, conducted in the goldfish bowl of a small town, where press and politicians shared the same bars and golf courses, well distanced from the fleshpots of the big cities, was tolerably righteous and honest. Not so in the states. Robert (Robin or Bob) Askin, Liberal Premier of New South Wales between 1965 and 1975, led a blowsy and corrupt government, plagued by scandals involving police and gambling interests, New South Wales being very much the gambling centre of Australia with an adult per capita expenditure of $1,221 p.a. (the average for Australia, still extraordinarily high by international standards, was $710). Not, it must be admitted, that the scandals did much harm to Askin in the electorate's opinion, since it seemed that 'the colourful casino bosses replaced the bushrangers as the folk heroes of their time'.[53]

Queensland was even more bizarre. The entrenched rule of successive Labor governments came to an end in August 1957 with the vote divided between four parties: on the left were the ALP, with 28.9 per cent, and the anti-communist Queensland Labour Party, which changed its name to the DLP, facing the Liberal Party and the Country Party. Although the Country Party achieved only the smallest share, 20 per cent of the popular vote, it retained, thanks to Queensland's inbuilt gerrymandering, 24 of the 75 seats, which, together with the Liberals, gave the coalition a majority, with the Liberals as junior partner. From August 1968, when Joh Bjelke-Petersen became Premier, Queensland was run as that powerful and eccentric politician's family fief, in the interests of business and those who regretted the passing of unquestioned settler dominance; as in New South Wales, the Queensland administration was fringed by corruption and more or less permanently tainted by scandal.[54]

Against this background of failing support at home, McMahon completed his downfall by fumbling abroad, especially over the issue of the recognition of Communist China. Holt, Gorton and McMahon had always followed America's lead with faithful obedience, but McMahon followed so closely as to stumble over Uncle Sam's coat-tails. Paying the now usual obeisance during his visit to Washington, the Australian Prime Minister contrived to make even President Nixon look dignified by his rendering of 'Moon River', assuring the President that Australia would follow the United States wherever she might be going. However touching Audrey Hepburn had been with the song in *Breakfast at Tiffany's*, McMahon was simply ludicrous. It might have been that he was misled by the President, as so many others had been, or that McMahon simply chose to ignore the facts, but between October 1970 when the first evidence was presented, and the following July, when the truth was out, the Prime Minister refused to acknowledge the possibility of recognition that China would be welcomed into the community of nations.

The probability should have been sufficiently clear. In November 1970 the Department of Foreign Affairs warned:

In the final analysis we must remember that the United States, as a super power, will tend to move at its own pace, and that pace will be largely dictated by the desire on the part of Washington and Peking to achieve some accommodation of interests. There is little chance that Peking's diplomacy will evolve quickly and flexibly, but should it do so we cannot expect the Americans to keep us fully briefed on every detail of change in the position.

If Australia was caught on the wrong foot, the department predicted,

We would soon then find ourselves singled out from our friends and neighbours, many of whom have difficulty now in understanding our apparently conflicting policy of economic ties combined with political hostility towards the PRC [People's Republic of China]. This would also of course affect our freedom of manoeuvre. We have already lost much freedom of manoeuvre to promote our own interests with the PRC by our long-standing policy of unswerving support for the ROC [Republic of China, i.e. Taiwan]. To continue to adhere to that policy in the face of the changes that are obviously about to occur in the international scene will mean a further narrowing of the options that are available to us. This would clearly be against our interests.[55]

Alerted too, and quite specifically, by the Australian ambassador in Burma that there 'was no time to be lost since the US was evidently anxious to achieve its own break-through and would do so in a flash if Peking gave the green light', McMahon dithered, concerned that any appearance of withdrawing support from Taiwan would antagonize the DLP – who were on track to win so large a share of the Western Australian vote. 'The political realities in Australia made it essential to support the position of the ROC', he told Winthrop Brown, on mission from the Department of State, on 26 February 1971.

McMahon paid the penalty for his procrastination in July. Reading the situation much more accurately, Gough Whitlam, as leader of the opposition, sent a telegram to the Chinese Premier Chou En-lai, proposing a visit to 'discuss terms on which your country is interested in having trade and diplomatic relations with Australia'. Coming from the leader of a party which had not been in office for twenty-three years, this was a bold initiative, but Chou was well briefed, and welcomed the proposal. In Beijing, Chou confirmed that his government well understood that they must wait until the next election, when Whitlam and Labor would doubtless be in power. Sensing, as he believed, a rare opportunity for scoring a point over the opposition, McMahon launched a bitter attack on Whitlam's 'betrayal' of Australian interests. 'Chou', the Prime Minister jibed, had 'played Whitlam as a fisherman plays a trout'.

But McMahon did not know, for Nixon had not told him, that even at that time Dr Henry Kissinger was in Beijing negotiating the normalization of relations between the United States and China. Three days after his 'trout' speech, the truth was out, and a humiliated McMahon had to acknowledge that he had been, to all intents and purposes, betrayed by his closest ally. Once again, however, McMahon refused to acknowledge inevitability. Told by the Australian ambassador in Paris that Australia had 'no choice' but to recognize the People's Republic, McMahon fell back on 'community attitudes in Australia' and the 'influence of the Democratic Labor Party' in order to justify his forlorn attempt to keep Australia pure and anti-communist.[56]

14

It's Time

Crashing Through and Out

Against such a background Gough Whitlam and the Labor Party's election victory was inevitable. Little needed to be done except to reiterate the slogan 'It's Time'. A late convert to Labor – he joined in 1945 – Whitlam was a reformer who wanted not only to improve social conditions – there was little discussion between the parties on that old Deakin consensus, believed to safeguard the working man, at the cost of international competitiveness – but to transform society. Labor's campaign was well financed, and supported by Rupert Murdoch, whose obedient newspaper, the *Australian*, and its associates rallied behind Whitlam and the Labor candidates. Much as in the British election of 1997, when the handsome and youthful Tony Blair was able to present a 'New Labour' Party to an enthralled electorate, Whitlam was able to shed some of the old encumbrances, although the Australian leader was considerably more skilled than Mr Blair in constantly evoking the loyalty of the party faithful; he had indeed all the qualities needed to succeed in politics, except that of judgement. After a generation of opposition it seemed that 'the light on the hill' had almost gone out; 'Let us set it aflame again,' was Labor's cry to arms. It struck a chord with a new generation of voters, those with no recollection of war and the Depression, brought up in the long post-war boom, with heightened expectations of what was due to them and what could be expected of political leadership. For perhaps the first time in the country's history Australia was showing its distinctive style; the young Germaine Greer, Clive James, Richard Neville and Barry Humphries were beginning their own brilliant careers; Thomas Keneally had published his influential novel *The Chant of Jimmy Blacksmith* and Patrick White was awarded the Nobel Prize for Literature; the first legal casino was opened, and that in Hobart.

Gough Whitlam had already, while leader of the opposition, secured his own position, spiking the Caucus guns by resigning in protest against their interference, and being successfully re-elected. The election in December 1972, which brought the first Labor government to power for twenty-three years produced, not a landslide, but at least a workable majority in the lower house – 67 of the 125 seats, although the Senate remained in coalition hands.[1]

The Whitlam government was much less successful than its later British counterpart in adjusting to the possible. Still hampered by the requirement that ministers be elected by their parliamentary colleagues, necessitating a delay in forming an administration, Whitlam dashed into action with a Cabinet of two, the Duumvirate, himself and his deputy, Lance Barnard. During its brief tenure of office – the 41st Commonwealth Ministry lasted from 1 to 19 December before the Labor members approved a new ministry – the new Prime Minister lived up to his slogan of 'crash through or crash'. Conscription was ended and Australian troops withdrawn from Vietnam; the People's Republic of China was recognized, and racially selected visiting teams banned (South Africa being the country targeted). At a stroke the old British system of honours was replaced by a new, no less ridiculous, set of Australian awards (although all members of the Executive Council continue to cling to their title of 'Honourable'). Having to consult with other members of the Cabinet never troubled Whitlam overmuch and his 42nd Ministry colleagues proved themselves ready to cooperate in a storm of legislation which saw much of Australian society transformed. The Northern Territory and the Australian Capital Territory were both given elected Legislative Councils and Senate representation, and the age of voting in Commonwealth elections was reduced to 18. Civil service conditions were improved by increased holidays and maternity leave; environmental impact statements were required for industrial developments; the minimum wage was increased. Education was transformed with generous financial aid being given to schools, university fees abolished and the responsibility for funding tertiary education transferred to the Commonwealth. Bill Hayden, the young Minister for Social Security, scored a notable victory when, after three years spent in often acrimonious discussion with the medical profession, he secured a comprehensive medical insurance scheme, Medibank, later Medicare.[2]

Labor's previous policy of a White Australia, epitomized by Arthur Calwell in his defence of white-only immigration, was finally abandoned. It had been disintegrating since 1958, when the dictation test was dropped, followed by the relaxation of naturalization requirements, but henceforward there was to be no discrimination as to race, colour or nationality, a decision accepted with somewhat surprising equanimity by public opinion. The

Labor Party had already, in opposition, abandoned its previous restrictive ideas, and the younger Liberals now in positions of power were no longer so firmly attached to the British interest as to promote immigration from Britain, especially when skilled Asian labour was available at lower cost. The Vietnam War had not scarred Australia as badly as it had America, even if it was the first defeat suffered by Australian forces, and there was a readiness to acknowledge some responsibility for the Vietnamese refugees, especially after the fall of Saigon in 1975. Malcolm Fraser in particular was radically anti-racist, founding the Australian Ethnic Affairs Council when in office, and in opposition sponsoring its report which recommended the preservation of ethnic cultures rather than their submergence in a bland uniformity favoured by American legislators. Such support enabled a bipartisan approach to immigration to be pursued; at least, for the time being. Australia took, proportionate to her population, more Indo-Chinese refugees than any other country, some 60,000 between 1978 and 1982. In the forty years after 1947 some five and a half million 'New Australians' arrived, from all parts of the world. The impact on Australian society was impressive. From being a colonial backwater searching for an identity, Australia has become a multi-cultural society. From meat pies and cold beer, Australia has evolved its own cuisine, which makes it one of the best places in the world to eat. Although Australia may be the only country where the main news is presented by the public broadcasting service in seven languages, and which provides a channel devoted to broadcasts in twenty languages, it might be accurate to say that the multi-culturalism became most apparent in the two great metropolises. In country towns, the familiar Anglo-Celtic customs usually hold good, and even the other capital cities are noticeably less cosmopolitan than Melbourne and, more particularly, Sydney.

It was the purest of accidents, but a valuable bonus for the Whitlam government, when, in October 1973 the second of Australia's iconic constructions, the Sydney Opera House, opened. Splendidly sited on Bennelong Point, on the other side of Circular Quay from the great bridge, the white curves of the Opera House are magnificent; one of the architectural masterpieces of the twentieth century, sealing Jørn Utzon's reputation. Its breathtaking external effect, however, conceals a massive disappointment. The project began in 1954, largely at the instigation of Sir Eugene Goossens, director of the Sydney Symphony Orchestra, with a competition to be judged by the eminent architects Sir Leslie Martin and Eero Saarinen, joined by the New South Wales Government Architect Cobden Parkes (son of Sir Henry). If the choice of Utzon was a tribute to the judges' vision, its acceptance by the New South Wales Labor government was an act of notable political courage. The Labor Premier, J. J. Cahill, a tough unionist, ex-railway fitter, was an unlikely godfather for such a project, but he and his Labor successors faithfully supported the lengthy and expensive development. In May 1965, when the Liberal coalition under Robert Askin gained power in New South Wales, the still-unfinished Opera House became a political issue. Askin personally established new records in corruption. He was a colourful personality. On election night he exclaimed with evident relish: 'We're in the tart shop now, boys.' By 'the tart shop', it should be explained, he meant the government of the Sovereign State of New South Wales, in which Askin controlled the police and, via the police, a wide range of criminal activities. Assisted by compliant Police Commissioners such as Norman Allan (1962–72), who took bribes from the criminals who ran the highly profitable illegal casinos in King's Cross, and his successor, Fred Hanson (1972–6), corruption was institutionalized from the top down. 'Askin saw to it that crime did pay in New South Wales. His legacy to the state was the systemic corruption in the police and the unprecedented expansion of crime.'

That there should have been problems in controlling so technically complex a development, with the architect resident in Denmark and a client obliged to answer to the electorate for cost overruns, might have been expected and indeed duly arose. Identified as it was with the previous Labor government, the Opera House project became a welcome target for the new administration, diverting public attention from the Askin government's dubious practices. Utzon's enforced resignation opened the door to remunerative contracts for local suppliers, and it was in vain that the world's most famous architects deluged the New South Wales government with protests. 'Malice in Blunderland' was Utzon's final verdict. The botched re-design did not unduly damage the external appearance, although it falsified both the architectural logic and the building's name; there is no opera house in the Sydney Opera, only a redesigned Minor Hall, with its complex stage machinery scrapped, the original Major Hall being relegated to the status of a concert hall. But the building stands a monument to the vision of some New South Wales governments and the ruthless philistinism of others.[3]

Whitlam personally made a real effort to implement promises previously made to Aborigines, by the appointment, shortly after the election, of the Woodward Commission, charged with establishing processes whereby Aboriginal land rights should be established. The occupation of Wave Hill land by the Gurindji tribe had aroused much public interest, and some sympathy. The Vestey family, who ran the Wave Hill Station, were notoriously tough employers, who would, a few years earlier, doubtless have summarily ejected the Gurindji, but the times they were a-changing. The

McMahon government could eject the 'Aboriginal Embassy' from its tented headquarters in Canberra, and Mr Justice Blackburn of the Northern Territory Supreme Court might decide that 'the Aborigines belong to the land more than the land belongs to the Aborigines', but Whitlam had charged Mr Justice Woodward to decide not whether the Aboriginals had rights to land, but how best these rights might be recognized – and the Gurindji had asked for 500 square miles of Wave Hill. Overcoming the diffidence natural to a young Etonian peer who had served with the Scots Guards, Lord Vestey expostulated that 'all the trouble about the Northern Territories Aborigines is stirred up by Communists and the Melbourne papers. People down here wouldn't know a Gurindji from a Walibri.' He pointed out, however, that his family did not own the land, but merely held a lease from the Australian government, who must decide what they wanted to do with it. Since Woodward recommended in April 1974 that Parliament should clarify what rights Aborigines did in fact possess, and that an Aboriginal Land Commission be established to help further such land claims, Prime Minister Whitlam personally handed over the Wave Hill titles to the Aboriginal leader, Vincent Lingiari.[4]

It was a fine gesture, well made, but in all probability most of Whitlam's voters did *not* know a Gurindji from a Walibri and cared less, although probably ready to prefer a black Australian to an English peer. The sharp increase in spending on Aborigines, from $23 million in 1971–2 to $120 million in 1974–5 and the proliferation of committees, initiatives and programmes, applauded by liberals, was greeted with general indifference. What did perturb voters was that Labor's ambitious schemes were affecting their jobs. Economic difficulties did not respond to the quick-fix Whitlam methods, and problems were pressing. In an attempt to slow the influx of foreign investment – and 1973 was a boom year for exports, giving the first current-account surplus for many years – the Australian dollar was revalued twice and tariffs slashed by 25 per cent across the board. Locally produced commodities in which Australia was nearly self-sufficient shot up to match export price levels; the cost of food rose by some 25 per cent between 1972 and 1974. More committees, departments and commissions were appointed, and average earnings, still largely controlled, allowed to rise by 35 per cent in 1974 alone. Opposition from Billie Snedden, who succeeded McMahon after the coalition's election defeat, posed little threat, but Whitlam faced hostility within Labor ranks. Farmers and countrymen were infuriated by what seemed to be an attack by 'townies' on their economic privileges; industrial workers were horrified by the reduction in protective tariffs and apprehensive about competition from immigrants. The powerful trade unions were snubbed by a Prime Minister with no industrial experience and more attracted by the television lights and international acclaim than by patient negotiation in smoke-filled rooms. When in September 1973 a restive Labor Caucus resolved to call a referendum giving Canberra the authority to regulate prices – a resolution mandatory on the government – Whitlam managed to link the question with a concurrent referendum to give similar power over wages – a proposal that was anathema to the trade unionists. As usual, the electorate rejected both. Opposition within the party was focused on the person of Bob Hawke, President both of the Australian Council of Trade Unions (ACTU) and the Australian Labor Party, an unparalleled power base. Younger than Whitlam – 43 in 1972 – Hawke was a trained economist, with an Oxford degree, who had come from the Labor Party research department rather than the shop floor. Regarded as a foul-mouthed drunken boor by his political enemies (and his friends would have quarrelled with the tone rather than the fact of such a description), Hawke was nevertheless a superb political operator, communicating with easy charm both on television and in person. He precisely noted Whitlam's failings – his obsessive vanity, his ignorance of economics, his impatience with detail and his lack of control – and determined to avoid the last three of these, which he was to do with unprecedented electoral success.[5]

When Whitlam refused to increase indirect taxation in his 1973 budget Hawke protested that the government was 'becoming removed from the realities of day-to-day politics, and are not keeping in touch with the grass roots'. Whitlam delivered a stern rebuke to his party's leader, pronouncing: 'The president of the federal executive of the Labor Party does not determine such matters; he is not consulted on such matters; he doesn't speak for the party on such matters.' Whitlam's addiction to long overseas trips was another irritation to his colleagues. Delighting in exhibiting the new Australia, with a new national anthem, 'Advance Australia Fair'[6] replacing 'God Save the Queen' (the words were no less banal, but the tune inferior; when commemorating the anniversary of the 2002 Bali bombing the mourners instinctively chose 'Waltzing Matilda'), Whitlam took great pleasure in such receptions as that afforded by Chou En-lai in Beijing on 2 November 1973, with Chou waiting on the tarmac, an honour guard and thousands of children performing elaborate dances, followed by a motorcade to Tiananmen Square which was adorned with Australian and Chinese pennants. The ironic American ambassador, David Bruce, gently noted that

Mr Whitlam's foreign policy is not entirely clear to me, but at least it is adventurous and imaginative. He seems to have concluded that essentially his Nation is a Far

Eastern power; though anxious to maintain close ties with the west, its destiny will unfurl more importantly in the Orient. This is a far cry from Sir Robert Menzies.

Coming from a diplomat of Bruce's stature, 'adventurous' is no compliment, and Whitlam's decisions were not uniformly wise.[7] That Australia, alone of the reputable countries, should choose to recognize the Soviet occupation of the Baltic republics, especially in view of the number of Australian Balts, ought to have been more of an embarrassment than it was, but the greatest error was the willingness to accommodate the Indonesian occupation of Portuguese East Timor, and this can be placed firmly at the Prime Minister's door. For the first year Whitlam had assumed personal responsibility for the Department of Foreign Affairs, and, although he relinquished this to Don Willesee in November 1973, continued to act as he thought fit.

Strategic reasons could be advanced for maintaining good relations with Indonesia, Australia's nearest neighbour. The American defeat in Vietnam and Nixon's Guam declaration spelled the end of the forward defence policy, where Australia's front line was South East Asia. The ANZUS treaty, as reinterpreted by America, offered little protection against any but a nuclear threat, and the British withdrawal to Europe marked the end of Imperial protection, for what that was worth. For the first time for many years Australian politicians began to criticize American actions. Nixon's renewed bombing of North Vietnamese cities at Christmas 1972 was particularly resented, and relations between the two countries cooled.[8] Australia's commitment to Vietnam may have ceased to matter, but Australia remained an important passive ally. The radio-communication station at North-West Cape, the Space Research facility at Pine Gap, and the satellite monitoring base at Nurrungar, together with another dozen or so smaller stations, formed a vital part of American defence programmes – all safe from espionage or dissident interference. The Australian Secret Intelligence Service (ASIO) had been working closely with the CIA, to the extent of sending agents to Chile in 1970–72.

All these useful contributions were threatened by the arrival of a Labor government, which had proclaimed its devotion to socialist and internationalist convictions, and the United States was duly alarmed; but in fact Whitlam's major foreign policy initiative was very much in accordance with American objectives. It was eminently reasonable that the Australian Prime Minister should confer with his Indonesian counterparts, but given Whitlam's voluble defence of human rights his cosying up to this unpleasant regime was distasteful, to an extent that it had eventually to be concealed from the Australian public.[9] The immediate occasion was the future of Timor Timur – East Timor, one of those few remaining relics of the Portuguese East Indies empire. It would have been in accordance with previous policy, especially bearing in mind the fact that Australian troops and Timorese guerrillas had fought together against the Japanese, that Australia would have supported the independence of this country, admittedly small, but one that had no links of language, religion or tradition with its Indonesian neighbour. Indonesia's President Sukarno had been responsible for the hundreds of thousands of murders in 1965 and retained an enormous number of political prisoners in gaol without trial. In the early 1970s, somewhere between 50 and 100 thousand were held by a regime notoriously corrupt and controlled to a high degree by the army. Indonesian disregard for the United Nations had already been evidenced by the failure to consult the people of Western New Guinea, now known as West Irian, where Indonesian officials were brusquely civilizing the natives by the usual methods. With such a record Indonesia could hardly be considered a suitable candidate to take over East Timor, but Whitlam made no bones about his support for such an outcome, telling Parliament that 'Portuguese Timor is in many ways part of the Indonesian world'.

Behind the Timor controversy, as behind so many twentieth-century contentions, lay the facts of oil. Geophysical exploration in the Timor Sea, begun in 1962, had by 1970 indicated the probable presence of considerable oil and gas reserves, which should be shared by the adjoining countries, as defined by the Geneva Convention on the Law of the Sea of 1958. What might have been a reasonably simple agreement between Indonesia and Australia concerning the waters to be shared between them was complicated by the existence of the Timor Trough, 'a huge steep cleft or declivity . . . considerably nearer to the coast of Timor than to the northern coast of Australia'. According to the Australian interpretation of the international law, this gave Australia a much more extensive seabed area in that region than Indonesia. Between 1970 and 1972 Australia and Indonesian negotiators agreed a line of demarcation; but there was one remaining snag. At the time East Timor remained Portuguese, and Portugal had not been party to the settlement; the area left uncertain was to be known as the 'Timor Gap'. When Portugal was eventually consulted Lisbon made it clear that it did not agree within the Australian–Indonesian line in so far as it affected East Timor. The ensuing polite diplomatic war intensified when both Australia and Portugal granted different companies exploration permits, which duly revealed good prospects. Then, in April 1974, the regime of Salazar's heirs was overthrown in Portugal by the 'Carnation Revolution', which brought to power a government committed to decolonization. Labor sentiment would instinctively support the right of the Timorese to decide their own future, a privilege which so signally had been denied the people of West Irian, and which while in opposition, Whitlam had established as party policy, but it would be inconvenient if an independent Timor did not decide to implement the agreement already reached with Indonesia. A plot was then hatched between Robert Furlonger, the Australian ambassador at Jakarta, and Harry Tjan, representing the Indonesian government. Tjan proposed, having told the Australians of his intention, that an undercover operation should be mounted to ensure that the East Timorese opted for the desired solution. Quite specifically, Whitlam was not told of this, but Furlonger was convinced that 'a poor, uneducated, probably unstable independent East Timor . . . should be no more attractive to us than Indonesia'.[10]

The Australian defence chiefs had important reservations on the subject, and Ambassador Furlonger's views were certainly not those of the Department of Foreign Affairs, then headed by Don Willesee. Prior to the Prime Minister's meetings with General Suharto (who had displaced President Sukarno in 1967), arranged for September 1974, Willesee had advised his chief that 'any future disposition of Portuguese Timor which was contrary to the wishes of the people would be likely, in Australia's view, to have a destabilising influence in the region'.

With his customary arrogance, and paying no attention to his colleague's briefing, Whitlam told Suharto at their meeting that, although Australian policy had not yet been officially defined, 'since coming to office in 1972 the decisions he had made about Australian foreign policy had been accepted by his party' and that two things were basic to his thinking: 'Portuguese Timor should become part of Indonesia' and 'this should happen in accordance with the properly expressed wishes of the people'. Some excuse for this attitude could be found in the fact that Richard Woolcott, who had succeeded Furlonger as ambassador in March 1975, had insisted in his reports that 'We are dealing with a settled Indonesian policy to incoporate Timor' and that Indonesia looked to Australia for 'some understanding of their attitude'.[11]

Nevertheless, when Willesee heard of Whitlam's abandonment of the agreed policy he admitted that 'You could have knocked me down with a feather'. The Australian participants have subsequently disagreed among themselves as to what exactly was said and done, but at the time Whitlam's sell-out to the Indonesians was clear. On 17 October 1974 the *Australian Financial Review* reported that 'Senator Willesee for his part is emphasising the idea of self-determination in an as yet unstated reversal of the priorities

Mr Whitlam gave to the Indonesians in which "self-determination" was only needed as some sort of "gloss" to the unflurried handover to Indonesia'. A fortnight later the *Age* quoted 'an informed source' as saying that 'It would be extremely embarrassing to the Australian government if it was ever revealed that Indonesia used Mr Whitlam's conditional endorsement to muck around as it pleased with Portuguese Timor'.

Driving the point home and letting the cat out of the bag, Richard Woolcott told the press in December 1975 that if Australia had helped to establish an independent East Timor, 'it could have become a constant source of reproach to Canberra. It would probably have held out for a less generous seabed agreement than Indonesia had given off West Timor.' The betrayal of East Timor has indeed been 'a constant source of reproach' and did not even succeed in its aim, for Indonesia refused to accede to Australia's requests.[12]

The deceits continued, as it became apparent that Indonesia had no intention of allowing the East Timorese to decide their own destiny. Covertly at first, Indonesian commandos infiltrated East Timor to attack the independence movement, Fretilin, but when Fretilin appeared to be gaining the upper hand and began to form a government Indonesia attacked openly. Warning was given to Australia that the attack was to begin, but five Australian-based journalists inconsiderately got themselves killed in the fighting, placing the government in an embarrassing situation.

The degree to which the government had allowed its hands to be tied by the possession of secret knowledge was shown by Woolcott's advice to Canberra following the deaths of the journalists. He urged Canberra not to criticise the actual intervention, either to Jakarta or in a public statement, since that would be tantamount to accusing the Indonesians of lying, as they publicly denied any of their forces were in Portuguese Timor ... When as a result of media reports in Australia about the journalists it became imperative in late October for Willesee to make a statement about events in East Timor, Woolcott insisted that direct references to Indonesian military intervention in the affairs of Portuguese Timor be deleted. This was done.

The truth about Whitlam's negotiations was concealed for some time by his Liberal successor Malcolm Fraser's government, which attempted to suppress a collection of documents, *Australian Defence and Foreign Policy*, edited by Richard Walsh and George Munster. Walsh commented: 'The US Department of State is writing the script for Australian foreign policy.' The attempt may have been due to Fraser's desire to conceal his own involvement, characterized by an energetic effort to cut Fretilin's channels of communication, and by his government's refusal to provide transport for a UN investigation.[13]

On 7 December the Indonesian army openly invaded East Timor. 'The tragedy', Alan Renouf, of the Department of Foreign Affairs, recorded, 'was, for all practical purposes, finished. It cost about 10,000 lives.' That, however, was not the end of the killing. The last foreign journalist in Dili, Roger East, was executed on 8 December, and in the next twenty-five years of Indonesian oppression and Timorese resistance thousands of others perished. Adam Malik, previously Indonesian Foreign Minister, admitted that 'perhaps 80,000 might have been killed . . . It was war . . . Then what is all the big fuss?' Among all the countries of the world, only Australia recognized the Indonesian occupation of East Timor. Twenty years later another Labor Prime Minister, Paul Keating, was to demonstrate that the lesson that should have been learnt, concerning devils and long spoons, had been neglected.

Another Whitlam slogan was 'Let's buy back the Farm', a counter to the complaint that foreign investors were buying up mineral rights over huge areas, extracting the ores, using foreign equipment, and transporting the results, on foreign ships, to foreign countries. Such sentiments were attractive, but costly. Given great good luck such an expansive policy might have worked, but 1973 saw the great oil crisis when, as a reaction to the Yom Kippur campaign by Israel, the Arab countries deployed the oil weapon, cutting supply and raising prices to throw the Western world into financial turmoil. Oil prices trebled. Combined with uncontrolled and sometimes lavish spending, the strain on finances prompted the unassuming and efficient Treasurer, Frank Crean, to characterize the Cabinet's budget deliberations as 'like a lunatic asylum'. It was not difficult for the opposition to find promising issues on which government legislation could be delayed, to the extent that, in May 1974, the Senate refused to agree a supply Bill. This, according to the written constitution (Section 53) it was entitled to do, but, if the conventions of British parliamentary life were followed, as they had always been in Australia, the will of the majority in the lower house was expected finally to prevail. To the man on the St Kilda tram, 'to whom constitutional details lurked on the fringes of political awareness', this was somewhat surprising. The remedy, however, was also in the constitution: a joint sitting of both Houses – the first attempted – having failed to solve the problem, the Prime Minister could, and did, ask for a double dissolution; Whitlam was confident that Labor would win an ensuing election, and his confidence was not misplaced. Governor General Sir Paul Hasluck, the former Liberal minister appointed by Harold Holt, demonstrated the traditional political impartiality of his office by immediately granting the necessary double dissolution, but the subsequent election did not solve Mr Whitlam's problems; his majority in the House of Representatives was actually slightly reduced, and the best that could be achieved in the Senate was parity with the coalition, the balance of power being held by two independents.[14]

The year 1975 was downhill all the way. Thrashing around for some dramatic solution to enable him to buy back the farm, and the government to escape from its financial embarrassments, the Minerals and Energy Minister, Rex Connor obtained permission, at an Executive Council meeting, to authorize a Pakistani businessman, one Tirath Khemlani, to raise a $4,000 million loan on behalf of the Australian government. It was a quite extraordinarily naive and badly advised operation, and although the operation was discussed at length with ministers and advisers Khemlani himself was seen only by Connor and Clyde Cameron, a trade unionist minister and former shearer. Mr Khemlani was one of those hundreds of 'runners' with some pretensions to sources of finance, usually in Arab countries, who attempted to peddle their often illusionary wares to unsuspecting borrowers. Hooking the Australian government in this way was a magnificent triumph for Mr Khemlani, the slightest of so-called financiers, and it would have been no surprise to any tolerably well-informed outsider that nothing positive came of his commission. In view of subsequent events it is worth noting that the decision taken by the Executive Council was communicated to the Governor General, ex officio chairman of the Council, although not present at the decisive meeting. Disillusionment soon set in; in January Connor's authority was reduced to $2,000 million and on 20 May 20 removed altogether. The affair might have blown over, but Connor was not the only culprit.

In March the flyweight Billie Snedden was replaced as Liberal leader by the heavyweight Malcolm Fraser. Lance Barnard, the former duumvir, prop and stay of the government, resigned; 'an act of lunacy', according to Hawke. The resultant by-election showed a massive swing against Labor. Sensible Frank Crean was replaced as Treasurer by the eccentric Dr Jim Cairns, who also became Deputy Prime Minister; in July Cairns, involved with one Junie Morosi, was dismissed by Whitlam after being caught in a lie over yet another financial scandal, where another runner had been offered a large commission for arranging a loan to the government. Suspicions were aroused that Khemlani was still active, and the opposition kept pressing for elucidation; Connor promised Whitlam that all contact was at an end, and the Prime Minister so assured Parliament on 9 October. Only days later the *Melbourne Herald* published proof that the Minister had been lying.

Connor was forced to resign, which he did as a man enmeshed in situations he had never understood, caught out in a mis-statement, but few governments could have hoped to survive two such scandals. Almost all Whitlam's colleagues had been offended by the Prime Minister's dictatorial habits, frequent reshuffles and persistent absences (a part-time tyrant is particularly aggravating). Fraser went for blood. 'The people of Australia no longer trust their Government. The affair arises from an appalling attempt to keep secret one of the worst scandals of Australia's history – a scandal compounded with stupefying incompetence and brazen deceit. The whole country is concerned with the ineptitude, intrigue and deception. The whole country is demanding answers.' Opposition in the Senate was strengthened when a Queensland Labor Senator died, to be replaced, not by another Labor supporter, as convention required, but by an avowed anti-Whitlamite (it should be noted that one of the first, and in the circumstances very creditable, actions of the succeeding Liberal administration was to draft a referendum, which was carried, making the convention a legal requirement).[15]

As it became clear that the Senate was going to resist approving a supply Bill, as it had the previous year, some public support was recovered and Cabinet solidarity improved. This time there was no question of Whitlam's opting for elections, which would surely result in Labor's defeat. Unemployment had doubled since the government had first come to power and inflation at 17 per cent was horrifying the electorate; the Prime Minster had tried to 'crash through' and failed. A 'crash' was inevitable and other solutions had to be investigated. Of these, the most obvious was merely to continue the delay, giving the government time to arrange temporary finance while attempting to do a deal with the opposition, persuade some wavering senators to agree – the first Aborigine to take a Senate seat, Neville Bonner, was a likely prospect – or simply to emulate Mr Micawber: such would doubtless have been the attitude of a nineteenth-century colonial Governor, who saw it as part of his job to knock a few politicians' heads together, with appropriately soothing noises. There seemed little reason to expect Governor General Sir John Kerr, himself a Whitlam appointee, not to allow this sort of leeway, rather than side with a Senate of doubtful authority after the Queensland intervention, against a government whose mandate was only twelve months old; but this is exactly what occurred.

Was the Ref. Fixed?

Australia had been well served by its Governors General since the Second World War; Sir William McKell was an experienced politician, a minister under Billy Hughes and a former Premier of New South Wales; his successor, Field Marshal Lord Slim, a veteran of Gallipoli and one of the best fighting soldiers of the next war, was immensely popular; another soldier, Lord De Lisle and Dudley, helped by his Victoria Cross and a generous portion of aristocratic tact, never put a foot wrong; and Sir Paul Hasluck behaved with impeccable propriety and wisdom. All were men of great note in the world. Why then did Gough Whitlam nominate as Sir Paul's successor John Robert Kerr, a not particularly distinguished lawyer, previously Chief Justice in New South Wales? It might have been expected that Sir John, as he became on his appointment, would at least go through the prescribed motions and avoid scandal; instead, he precipitated the most severe constitutional crisis ever known in the country. Bitterly debated and much misunderstood, the events were as follows.

When the constitution was being debated, back in the 1890s, three different principles were introduced:

1. Responsible government – the sovereignty of the lower house of Parliament, as in Britain.
2. An elected Senate, with powers and authority greater than the British House of Lords.
3. Federalism, which left many powers with the constituent states, and had resulted in all states having equal representation in the Senate, which, given the gross disproportion of population, was demonstrably un-democratic.

Since 1911 the mismatch of these three factors had become more accentuated, as in that year the powers of the British House of Lords were drastically curtailed to that of limited delay on the assent of Bills coming from the House of Commons – and no powers to interfere with 'supply'. Contrariwise, in Australia the Senate was able to refuse a supply Bill, thus potentially holding the country to ransom and exercising a power equal to that of the – much more representative – lower house.

It was not that the founding fathers were unaware of the risks, but rather that, nurtured as they were on the practice of representative government, they simply did not believe that the Senate would ever exercise its veto on supply, which would 'invite a revolution in the country'. Sir Samuel Griffith, the central figure in constitution framing, did 'not think the subject worth half an hour's discussion', while Sir Harrison Moore, author of *The Constitution of the Commonwealth of Australia*, thought a deadlock 'a contingency so remote as hardly to be within the range of practical politics'. And should such a contingency ever arise, the Governor General had the power to dissolve both Senate and House of Representatives and order a new election.

Here another complexity arises. Under responsible government the Governor General is meant to act on the advice of his ministers – who have to command confidence in only the lower house. In Britain, that presents few problems; if a government cannot secure a vote of confidence in the House of Commons the Prime Minister walks over to Buckingham Palace, and recommends a successor, but as long as a British government retains its majority it can act as an elective oligarchy. In Australia, an unresolvable confrontation between two houses of very similar authority can only be resolved by the Governor General exercising a Crown prerogative which has fallen into desuetude in England.[16]

Why, it may well be asked, should the Governor General have such powers? Again, quite unlike the practice in the United Kingdom, the Australian Governor General has an important day-to-day constitutional role as chairman of the Executive Council – no mention of either Cabinet or Prime Minister appears in the constitution; the Queen, on the other hand, relies on informal chats with the Prime Minister. To the objection that the Governor General can be seen as the representative of a monarch 12,000 miles off, the answer can be made that the position is a necessity of the present constitution, that its holder is the representative not of the person of the monarch but of that abstraction, the Crown – and that the system works, and still continues to work, although many more logical solutions could be offered.

On 11 November Whitlam was called to Government House and handed a letter of dismissal.

Dear Mr Whitlam,

In accordance with Section 4 of the Constitution I hereby determine your appointment as my chief adviser and Head of government. It follows that I also hereby determine the appointments of all the Ministers in your Government.

You have previously told me that you would never resign or advise an election of the House of Representative or a double dissolution and that the only way in which such an election could be obtained would be by my dismissal of you and your ministerial colleagues. As it appeared likely that you would today persist in this attitude I decided that if you did I would determine your commission and state my reasons for doing so. You have persisted in your attitude and I have accordingly acted as indicated. I attach a statement of my reasons which I intend to publish immediately.

It is with a great deal of regret that I have taken this step both in respect of yourself and your colleagues.

I propose to send for the Leader of the opposition and to commission him to form a new caretaker government until an election can be held.

Yours sincerely

John. R. Kerr.

Malcolm Fraser, who had been waiting in another room, having been warned by Kerr, was immediately given a commission to form a new government.[17]

This summary dismissal came as a great shock to both government and public, probably the greatest shock in Australian political history. Sir John Kerr had been appointed Governor General by Whitlam himself, and a mere eighteen months previously (11 July 1974). When Whitlam had asked for a dissolution in May of that year it had been granted by Sir Paul Hasluck, and had Sir Paul still been in office some display of party sympathy might have been expected (but political Governors General almost without exception shed their party affiliations when they take post and behave with impeccable impartiality), but for a recent Labor appointee to behave in such a fashion was unprecedented. Sir John had behaved just as old George Higinbotham would have had him act, as an Australian constitutional monarch acting to solve a political dilemma; but no British ruler would have become so enmeshed in party politics as did Sir John. King George VI gave advice when asked – the startling but successful appointment of Ernest Bevin as Foreign Secretary in 1945 was suggested by the King – and Queen Elizabeth II, in her more than fifty-year reign, has encountered governments she would much rather not have had in office, but only the most indirect hint of any personal feeling ever emerges. Had any of the previous Governors General been in office the result must have been different (Lord Slim, notoriously blunt, would have had all concerned on his viceregal carpet), but Gough Whitlam had made a poor choice when he selected John Kerr. A short person with oversized vanity, Kerr had been known as the 'Liberace of the Law' or 'Old Silver'; as Governor General he attached great importance to the viceregal aspects of the job and was assiduous in his pursuit of honours. Given his collusion with Malcolm Fraser it would appear that the ref. had indeed been fixed.

When the news was given to the House of Representatives a motion of no-confidence in what was officially now the Fraser government was passed, introducing a new complexity into the constitutional imbroglio. The Speaker was dispatched to remonstrate with the Governor General, who simply refused to see him. Philip Knightley describes the public announcement:

By now the nation had heard news flashes of what was happening in Canberra and a crowd of furious Labor supporters and journalists had gathered at Parliament House. The lasting image of the moment was captured by photographer Maurice Wilmott. It shows a young man, immaculately dressed in black suit with a silver tie, reading Kerr's proclamation while microphones hover around his face. Standing immediately behind him and towering over him is Gough Whitlam, staring grimly into the future.

Then the still image comes alive, and as the young secretary finishes reading the proclamation with the words 'God Save the Queen' Whitlam steps forward in front of the microphones and says, 'Well may we say, "God save the Queen", because nothing will save the Governor-General. The proclamation you have just heard was countersigned "Malcolm Fraser", who will undoubtedly go down in Australian history from Remembrance Day 1975 as Kerr's cur.' Then he added, 'Maintain your rage until polling day.'[18]

Perhaps the most surprising aspect of this constitutional crisis was the unanimous acceptance of what was a very dubious decision. Much local indignation was expressed in pubs and clubs, but, apart from one modest riot in Melbourne, not in the streets. Rage, although widespread, was not maintained. No attempt was made to assert Labor's economic muscle, and attention focused on the impending election.

It was no surprise, and provided some justification for the dissolution, that this was a massive victory for the erstwhile opposition. The Labor government was seen to have made a hash of the economy and to have sacrificed public trust in the two loans scandals. Coalition candidates won 91 of the 127 seats, with 53 per cent of the popular vote. Labor could do no better than 42.8 per cent and won only one seat in Queensland and in Western Australia and none at all in Tasmania. In the Senate, the coalition's position was strengthened with 35 seats to Labor's 27. Australian democracy had been well served by Kerr's decision, but spirited debate about its validity continued for many years.

Although it might have been expected that intervention by a representative of the Crown might have stimulated republicanism, this did not happen, at any rate in the short term. Kerr might have been a bastard but he was unmistakably an Australian bastard, operating in Australian politics (there was, of course, no contact with Britain on the issue). It was not a situation that could have arisen in the United Kingdom, and no constitutional precedent could have been initiated. The idea of a conspiracy, assisted by the CIA, has been floated, by Philip Knightley and John Pilger among others:

Whitlam had shown that he was not only prepared to emasculate his own intelligence and security services, but put the CIA presence in Australia at risk by identifying and naming in Parliament CIA officers working in the country. The CIA director, William Colby, later wrote that the threat posed by the Whitlam government was one of the three world crises in his career.

Mr Knightley suggests that the CIA created a climate 'bordering on hysteria in which any damaging rumour would be believed', which might be so, but was surely the work of supererogation, since the Whitlam government was doing such an excellent job of destroying confidence through its own efforts. Mr Knightley cites one piece of evidence, although without a reference:

In mid November 1975, the CIA in Langley, Virginia, sent a cable to ASIO in Canberra saying that recent behaviour of the Whitlam government was causing acute concern about the implications for Australia's future relationship with the United States. The cable was not intended to be shown to Whitlam but the sentiments of the cable did reach Kerr, either directly from ASIO or via the British intelligence liaison officer in Canberra – because Kerr was the Queen's representative. During the war Kerr had been in a specialist research unit that had some connection with the American Office of Strategic Services, the forerunner of the CIA. On 11 November Kerr sacked Whitlam. He may have sacked him anyway, but to believe that the CIA's role in the preceding months and its cable to ASIO had not the slightest influence on his decision defies logic.[19]

Britain Declares Independence

It might have been expected that controversy about the British connection and the Queen's role as head of state would have been exacerbated by the British referendum vote in June 1975 in favour of joining the European Economic Community (EEC), an act which implied the severe reduction in Commonwealth trade and the loss by Australian citizens of previous unquestioned rights to enter and live in Britain. Indignation, however, had subsided over the previous fourteen years (during which British interest in joining Europe had become increasingly obvious), to the point of being replaced by sentiments of disappointment and, among some, of betrayal.[20]

The first clear indication, after two years of uncertainty and conjecture, had been given by Prime Minister Harold Macmillan in a letter to Robert Menzies of 15 April 1961, in which he had informed the Australian Prime Minister that President Kennedy and he had agreed that 'in order to provide an element of stability' on the continent it would 'be better if the United Kingdom were to join the political association of the Six [the EEC].' There would be, Macmillan admitted, 'some economic disadvantages both for the United Kingdom itself and for other Commonwealth countries'.

A subsequent Commonwealth meeting, between finance ministers in September 1961, at which Australia was represented by Harold Holt, was indignant. It was apparent that no real thought had been given to the question of safeguarding Commonwealth interests, for whom British trade was a matter of very real significance. Exports to Britain were declining, down from 37 per cent of the total in 1951–4, to 20.5 per cent in 1960–3, but Britain was still Australia's largest customer, taking a third of Australian cheese, butter, sugar, dried fruits, and over half its tinned meat and fruit – and these included the products most likely to be displaced by European producers. Australia was at least able to join directly in the negotiations on Britain's terms of entry into the EEC, but these were not rewarding. Australian interests were vigorously defended by Jack McEwen who toured Europe in 1962, but he was battling against the intransigent French, dedicated to the preservation of their most sacred cow, the Common Agricultural Policy (CAP). Still the least appealing part of European economic policy forty years on, the CAP was promulgated in January 1962, just in time to face Britain with a fait accompli. The policy fixed uniformly high prices for European produce, with foreign imports deterred by a flexible levy which could make it impossible for any foreign producer to undercut the artificially high prices. Moreover, income derived from the levy could then be used to subsidize European food exports. European farmers were gratified, but at the very considerable expense of the domestic consumer, who continued to pay more, often much more, for food than anyone else, and other agricultural producers who found themselves cut off from European markets at the same time that their own home markets were being invaded.

There was never any hope that Australia would be able to penetrate the French resistance, but the attitude of the United States complicated the issue. Britain's entry was there regarded as essential to preserving European stability as a bulwark against communism, especially as a restraint against General de Gaulle, arrogantly unreliable, stirring up trouble in Canada, preparing to pull France out of NATO and having left a heap of trouble in Indo-China. This view was bluntly presented by George Ball when McEwen visited Washington on his way to China. Any attempt by Britain to squeeze in special conditions for Commonwealth membership would 'almost certainly assure a protracted and complex negotiation'.

Macmillan applied soft soap with his usual expertise, writing to Menzies on 17 March 1962:

You and I were born into a very different world which seems, as one now recalls it, almost as long ago as the age of George III or Queen Elizabeth I. Queen Victoria, the Jubilee, Kipling, universal pride and confidence in the successful transformation of territories won haphazardly . . . into an orderly Empire . . . And now here we are, my dear Bob, two old gentlemen, Prime Ministers of our respective countries, sixty years later, rubbing our eyes and wondering what has happened.

The message was, however, the same. What the United States and Britain wanted would be done, and if this meant the end of Commonwealth preferences, so be it. Menzies was able to resist the British Prime Minister's saponification: 'Those in Europe, and those in America', should they continue to press too hard, will 'accept a great responsibility before history, since they will face the British government with the dilemma of choosing between Europe on those terms and the Commonwealth'.[21] Put in such terms, the decision would not be difficult for British people: neither French nor Germans were popular, and the family and historic ties with Australia and New Zealand especially were well rooted. No such clear-cut decision was ever offered. After de Gaulle terminated discussions by brusquely vetoing the Anglo-Saxon plot negotiations continued until a final resolution was reached in 1972–3. New Zealand was offered some concessions, but Australia none. The British electorate understood the merits of the arguments only dimly; when finally offered the opportunity to vote, in the 1975 referendum, only 43 per cent recorded an affirmative, while 35.5 per cent did not bother to come to the polls.

By then Australia had adapted to the changed circumstances; by 1972 only 11 per cent of Australian exports went to Britain and by 1982 only 4 per cent. The British 1968 Immigration Act restricted admission to those who could claim at least a native grandparent, which many young Australians could no longer do. The whole protracted and difficult episode can justly be viewed as a great betrayal of an old comradeship or as a realistic affirmation of national interests, but it was also, as Macmillan put it in his diary for 12 September 1962, a declaration of independence: 'It is ironical to hear countries which have abused us for years now beseeching us not to abandon them. The thought that UK might declare herself independent seems so novel as to be quite alarming.'[22]

The Liberals Return

Just as Gough Whitlam won by virtue of not being William McMahon, Malcolm Fraser would have triumphed again three years later by being so obviously not Gough Whitlam. He chose instead to make a series of election promises which, given the economic climate, were not only unrealistic but downright impossible. All personal tax was to be fully indexed, wages would rise with inflation, as would social security payments: Whitlam's health-care initiative, the Medibank, would be retained intact and a 6 to 7 per cent growth-rate achieved by the Australian economy.

The clash between these undertakings and Fraser's own commitment to sound administration was severely damaging, and sat uneasily with his earlier warning that 'no responsible government can behave like Father Christmas'. Just how such a programme could be reconciled with the advice Fraser said he gave to Margaret Thatcher is difficult to imagine:

When Mrs Thatcher got into office I told her that your Treasury people will say that when you cut a bit that's enough. But you've got to get in quickly before your ministers believe your political opponent's programmes are their own programmes. And so go in with a broad axe. Don't go in with a tomahawk. And she said 'Malcolm, that sounds like good advice.' And I said: 'Look, Margaret, I don't think you'll take it; I hope you do, because I'm sure it's right.'[23]

Since Menzies' retirement the Liberal Party had produced only one notable, if idiosyncratic leader, in John Gorton. Malcolm Fraser was the first robust and effective politician to head the coalition – now with the National Party, the Country Party having changed its name, if not its spots – and was to be the last before John Howard brought the Labor government down in 1996. Brusque to the point of rudeness, he worked his colleagues hard, but they knew where they were with him. The one notable initial failure was with Don Chipp, a minister under Holt, Gorton and McMahon, who was not included in the first full ministry. Offended, Chipp, who was lively and articulate, walked out to form a party of his own, the Democrats, whose slogan was a promise 'to keep the bastards honest'.[24]

Once in office, with realism setting in, Fraser cut public expenditure, although not severely enough; John Howard, who became in 1996 the next Liberal Prime Minister, instanced Fraser's backtracking on the commitment to abolish the Price Justification Tribunal, which would have enabled manufacturers to raise prices more freely. It was not the only reversal of policy that events demanded; Medibank was scrapped, replaced by Medicare, a less comprehensive scheme, indexation was dropped when it became too expensive and 'razor gangs' were sent to cut public service posts. Apart from the need to consolidate after Whitlam's extravagances, Fraser was a liberal Liberal, and electoral rhetoric aside, maintained two pillars of the Deakin settlement, protection and arbitration, while completing the final interment of the third, White Australia.

The cuts and back-pedalling worked to an extent. Inflation, at 15 per cent under Labor, dropped to less than 10 per cent, unemployment fell, and public spending as a proportion of GDP was reduced, a difficult task for any government: but the percentage of government spending devoted to social security and welfare rose during Fraser's period of office from 21.8 per cent to 28.2 per cent. A worldwide boom in the mining industry boosted Australian exports, leading to a 50 per cent rise between 1978 and 1980; inevitably, wages and prices rose in consequence. The nature of exports was changing, with minerals increasing from some 35 per cent of the total in 1975 to over 50 per cent in 1983; over the same period the share of manufactured exports fell from 27.4 per cent to 21.4 per cent; Australia was becoming a source of raw materials for those Asian economies which were then developing sophisticated manufacturing industries. Export earnings were not enough to counterbalance the loss on 'invisible' items, chiefly remittances servicing foreign debt. The balance on current account, which stood at $900 million in 1974–5, had increased tenfold by 1981–2, representing 6 per cent of GDP, a dangerously high level.

The political honesty of the Liberal coalition was called into question by its programme for the December 1977 – the 'Fist Full of Dollars' – election, called before it was due, both to overcome any remaining doubt about the legitimacy of the 11 November manoeuvring and to take advantage of the still-staggering Labor Party. Once again an optimistic manifesto was produced which promised large tax cuts. While it doubtless helped the subsequent victory, which was the second most successful in Australian history (the best being Fraser's previous win), the promises were probably unnecessary and their subsequent inevitable withdrawal seriously damaging to Fraser's reputation.

It is always difficult for a party of the centre-right, which values principles of prudence, decency, toleration and the responsible conduct of public affairs, to advance a positive programme. Decent conservatives value principles rather than measures and distrust legislation which seems to interfere with the individual's personal liberty or the freedom of corporations to manage their own affairs; wisdom, they say, may often lie in prudent inactivity. But it was becoming painfully clear that the Australian welfare state was seizing up, and the imperative necessity for liberalization was widely accepted. Just as, in Britain, the Labour Prime Minister James Callaghan was ready to put into effect at least some of the brisk measures later introduced by Margaret Thatcher, a policy energetically pursued by his successor Tony Blair, so informed Australian opinion was moving to the economic right – and in due time was to be acknowledged by the Hawke–Keating Labor governments. In a society such as that of Australia, where the principle of an active government, legislating freely and extending its responsibilities into so many aspects of life, was accepted by both parties, it is particularly difficult to construct an acceptable moderate conservative programme. When complicated by the Federal constitution in which a state such as Joh Bjelke-Petersen's Queensland could go its own reactionary way in defiance of Commonwealth authority, the task approached near-impossibility – all of which perhaps explains Fraser's unlikely baskets of goodies offered as manifestos.

Whitlam's overseas initiatives were for the most part followed by the coalition. Foreign Affairs was entrusted first to Andrew Peacock, until November 1980, and subsequently to Tony Street, an uncommonly long period for those turbulent times; in the six years before Peacock's appointment there had been seven ministers in the Department of Foreign Affairs, an intolerable situation if continuity in policy was to be achieved. The new Prime Minister's liberalism was demonstrated when on at least one issue Fraser very pointedly differed from his predecessor's actions. Whitlam continued his pro-Indonesian stance over East Timor after his parliamentary defeat, claiming – which was conspicuously misleading – that 'We opposed any military action in Timor and insisted on the right to self-determination for the Timorese people. While Labor was in power, President Suharto's undertakings to me on these points were honoured by Indonesia.'[25] Fraser, on the other hand, was manifestly unhappy with the aftermath of the Indonesian invasion, and insisted on sticking to the initial condemnation, only, and with great reluctance, allowing de facto recognition in January 1978. Mr Fraser's eventual acquiescence was influenced by pressure from the United States, whose diplomats were 'working over-time to contain the dispute', apparently since American submarines used the deep channel off Timor, a passage which might be endangered by political instability.

Although Fraser did not follow Whitlam's ostentatious displays of Australian 'independence' he was in many ways a more aggressive defender of Australian rights abroad. The Common Agricultural policy of the EEC – or the European Community (EC), as it later became, had bitten deep into traditional Australian markets, and was being used by American apologists as an excuse for stepping up their own agricultural protectionism. A farmer himself, Fraser was sympathetic to his coalition partner's anxieties, and took an active personal part in defending Australian exporters. 'Frontal assaults, blunt criticism and uncompromising negotiations at official level', as well as brusque personal interventions, characterized Australian relations with the EC in Fraser's term of office. The Prime Minister delegated some of the negotiations to the new Minister for Special Trade Representation, John Howard, who proved less than effective; 'perfectly nice,' according to the British Cabinet minister Roy Jenkins, 'but inexperienced. He had clearly been sent by the egregious Fraser with an extremely rough but foolish negotiating brief' – but Howard was nevertheless promoted in 1977 to the vital post of Treasurer.[26]

Nor was much deference shown to the United States. Whitlam's threats to exert Australian control over the American bases were allowed to lapse, but objections to American agricultural policies continued to be pressed, with little effect; Americans had distanced themselves from South East Asia and its problems, and Australian influence was accordingly reduced. Fraser made his mark more clearly as a Commonwealth statesman, persuading Margaret Thatcher to a more moderate position over South Africa and Southern Rhodesia – and, in opposition, nominated by Prime Minister Hawke, as chairman of the 'Eminent Persons' 1986 Commonwealth Mission to South Africa in their attempt to negotiate the end of apartheid. As had Whitlam, his successors all placed emphasis on Australia's role as an Asian nation, accepting differences in tradition and its connections with the United States and Britain, but seeking to build links with Asian countries and to reject Australia's heritage of racism and colonialism. Prime Minister Fraser was successful in concluding a wide-reaching treaty with Japan, which established, in effect, equal treatment with British and American investors for Japanese businessmen. Much of the credit for this should go to the previous administration, and to Whitlam himself, who had vowed that 'apathy, cynicism, old entrenched attitudes at any level will not be allowed to stand in the way of its consummation', but it was Fraser and Peacock who brought finality to the long negotiation.

Possible reproaches of Australia's own colonial possessions were avoided by speedy grants of independence to Papua New Guinea; too speedy, indeed, for wisdom. If Australians, by contrast with some European colonial powers, had little seriously to reproach themselves for more than seventy years of generally well-intentioned administration of their colony and mandate, which included not only eastern New Guinea but the scatter of islands stretching over nearly 1,000 miles of ocean, there were also not many grounds for congratulation. An eventual transition to self-government had long been intended, but it was assumed, when the matter was considered (which was neither frequently or at a high level), that the longest of terms would be inevitable; this was not to be.

Many of the bloodiest current troubles stem from a declaration of the United Nations General Assembly (Resolution 1514 (xv 14/xii/1960)) insisting that: 'Immediate steps shall be taken, in Trust and Non-Self Governing Territories or all other Territories which have not yet attained independence, to transfer all powers to the people of these territories, without any conditions or reservations'. This could be, and too often was, taken by colonial powers as an invitation to abdicate their responsibilities in countries, often artificial creations, in which little or no preparation had been made for self-government; and those members of the United Nations who had been most active in moving the resolution contributed nothing to the resulting chaos. Papua New Guinea was just such an example, and it is a great tribute to its people that it has survived.

To outside observers it was clear that this congeries of peoples, many living in traditional fashion in unexplored territory, speaking at least 700 different languages, with only the most fleeting of exposure to the difficulties of government, needed a much longer preparation for independence. In 1972 the United States Naval Institute reviewed the status of the Pacific Trust territories, and concluded:

In Papua New Guinea the educational and economic problems alone are so overwhelming as to seem almost to defy solution. Yet, despite these problems, the United Nations continues to press Australia for a target date for independence ... It is generally conceded that the [United Nations Committee on Ending Colonization] will probably bring enough pressure to bear upon Australia to ensure that independence will be forced upon New Guinea long before the native population is prepared to cope.[27]

Paul Hasluck's long tenure of office as Minister for Territories between 1951 and 1963, when he had been left alone to run Papua New Guinea as 'virtually the Premier and the whole of the State cabinet', had developed education at primary level (in 1963 only fourteen pupils completed high school) and public health facilities, but continued the Murray tradition of paternalism, grown out of date in the post-war world, which 'banned people from drinking alcohol, playing contact sports or (for men) wearing clothes above the waist'. A population with very different cultures in the highlands and littoral was administered by district officers in the classic colonial style. Northern New Guinea expatriates regarded the Papuan administration as too soft, instead 'pinning their faith on "bashing the coons" as the only sound basis of race relations' and considering 'the "humanitarian" attitude of the Papuans as pure hypocrisy'.[28]

Modest progress was made after the United Nations received a critical report from Sir Hugh Foot (Lord Caradon), a distinguished colonial civil servant, in 1962, but the crisis came four years later. With tongues presumably in cheeks, the first Papua New Guinea Legislative Council asked if they might indeed become an Australian state; after all, this was the presumed future intended for the Northern Territory, which enjoyed the same status. The thought of what would happen if a couple of million 'fuzzy wuzzies' were entitled to cross the Torres Strait and demand all the privileges of Australian citizens filled the Australian Cabinet with horror. New Zealand had already sold the pass by negotiating a free association agreement with their own colony of the Cook Islands, which allowed islanders to hold dual citizenship and to travel and work in New Zealand, an opportunity taken up with alacrity until in 1991 nearly 5 per cent of the population were Islanders. To avoid such a frightening prospect, the Australian government decided that Papua should become independent, at some future, probably distant, date.

The Papua New Guinea Legislative Council was a Hasluck creation, mostly composed of expatriates but with some indigenous members. It was Hasluck's successor, the Queensland stud-farmer Charles Barnes – 'Kind-hearted and honest, loyal to God, Queen and Country' – who took the next step, the formation of a House of Assembly, with a majority of elected members. Its power was limited, its ordinances subject to disallowance by the Governor General, its members generally obedient to official guidance, so the official members, experienced in the ways of the government, could direct business much as they pleased; altogether a situation very much like that of New South Wales in the 1820s. In 1971 the McMahon administration announced a five-year plan for developing internal self-government, far too measured a progress to suit Gough Whitlam, who declared that Papua would become self-governing on 1 December 1973 and independent three years later. Even this was too short a time for an Australian government desperate to relinquish responsibility, and on 6 September 1975 Papua New Guinea joined the ranks of newly independent 'nations'. Malcolm Fraser's own commitment to colonial independence and the prospect of so many blacks claiming the right to citizenship made it easy for the Liberal government to agree to the Whitlam initiative, and to share responsibility for the chaos that followed.

Papuans had in fact made remarkable progress in so short a time. Two parties, the Pangu Pati, led by Michael Somare and Julius Chan's Papuan Peoples Party, were evolving, and in the first democratic elections of 1972 were able to form a coalition government with some pretensions to real power but facing some difficult issues. Of these the Bougainville mining venture was potentially explosive.[29]

The island of Bougainville, culturally and geographically part of the Solomon archipelago, had been attached to German New Guinea by the 1886 agreement with Britain, and so had remained. In 1964, CRA, an Australian subsidiary of Rio Tinto Zinc (RTZ), a vigorous mining company, sometimes accused of less than scrupulous conduct, had proved substantial reserves of copper in the island and projected an extensive open-cast mine. As eventually implemented the enterprise was enormous – thousands of acres of land were ruined as hundred of millions of tons of soil and rock were removed – 150,000 tons a day to be disposed of. Plantations, villages, fields and gardens were obliterated. There were substantial compensations, as new housing, towns, hospitals, roads and schools were built, and well-paid – by local standards – employment was offered, but the social and environmental consequences were devastating, and many Bougainvilleans remained resentfully angry. Richard West, a keen investigator, visited Bougainville in 1972 and described the scene in the capital, Kieta: 'Three "indigenes" were teasing a drunk old white man by holding a dollar in front of his face and, when he reached for it, passing it to the next man. "How can you expect the native to feel any respect for us?" said an Australian engineer ... You ask what effect the mine has had on them? It's fucked them.' A secessionist movement had begun in 1968, particularly among the south Bougainvilleans, progressively more affected by the mine, but with the northerners remaining warily cautious. West, prophetically, reported that since a secession would deprive Papua New Guinea of half its revenue, it would 'cause political uproar in the region. There might well be demands from the mainland for an invasion of Bougainville.' Which was, eventually, exactly what happened.[30]

The first independent Papua New Guinea government was able, in 1974, to renegotiate the original contract with CRA, which gave a more substantial share of the income to public funds, and a more secure future to the mine; but only, as it turned out, for a limited period. Not nearly enough time had been allowed for the country to move from classic colonialism to independence, and Papua New Guinea began its existence as a country with unresolved problems, particularly of succession and the conflicts between mining companies and landowners, the most serious of which, the struggle for Bougainvillean independence, led to a bloody civil war, settled, perhaps only temporarily, in 1997, and after New Zealand intervention. Both Australia and New Zealand sent truce monitors, but while many of the New Zealanders were Maori, which made their task easier, there were very few Aborigines among the Australians; thus was a century and more of different racial policies and attitudes in the two countries reflected. Australians trusted that independence, together with financial assistance, had 'wiped the slate clean, making Papua New Guinea just another underdeveloped country', but while Port Moresby remains a violent and disturbed community so near to Australia's coast responsibility will not be painlessly abandoned.[31]

On Aboriginal affairs, the Fraser government also continued Whitlam's policies and followed the recommendations of the Woodward report. In November 1981 a complex Bill ceded a huge tract of land, amounting to 10 per cent of South Australia's area, to the Pitjantjatjara. In the Northern Territory, the Aborigines Land Act gave the Nabarlek uranium field, and reserves comprising 20 per cent of the Territory to Aboriginal ownership; in 1982 it was the Aboriginal Northern Land Council which authorized the exploitation of a $600 million uranium mine. Although they were more than merely cosmetic, such advances did not address the problem of the position of Aborigines in Australian society. Neither the rescue of Truganini's remains from the Tasmanian museum and their cremation, nor the election of an Aboriginal member, Neville Perkins, to the Territory's Legislative Assembly in 1977, reflected much change in the realities of Aboriginal existence. In Queensland Joh Bjelke-Petersen simply defied Commonwealth legislation by insisting that states' rights be respected: 'Sly, ruthless and revelling in the reputation of a Whitlam-destroyer, he ran the Queensland cabinet in his own style – with little attention to collective decision-making or Westminister traditions of behaviour. Dealing with Queensland meant dealing with Joh.'[32] The Queensland government cared little for Aboriginal rights and a good deal for the profits of mining companies, which led to a protracted argument with the Federal government. When the going was rough Bjelke-Petersen simply declared that his ministers were too busy to meet, and told Fraser to leave Aboriginal affairs to the state government. Fraser's commitment to Aboriginal rights was hardly in doubt, but he was not prepared to force the issue with Bjelke-Petersen, and risk the loss of his political support.

A general disgust with political dishonesty had brought down the Whitlam government, and in Fraser voters got an irreproachably honest head of government; but Fraser's insistence on high standards of parliamentary probity combined with his personally abrasive style to produce a high turnover of ministers dismissed on relatively slight grounds – and sometimes reinstated when the facts or lack of substance in the accusations became apparent – or after quarrels. When Andrew Peacock resigned in April 1981 it was the fifteenth resignation, dismissal or suspension of a Fraser minister and he went in a burst of fury.

I believe the prime minister has engaged in acts of gross disloyalty to me and my office. The prime minister has allowed false and damaging reports to be published about me in my capacity as a senior minister. He has bypassed the system of government by acting with a manic determination to get his own way. I find the constant disloyalty and erratic acts of behavior intolerable and not to be endured.[33]

The electorate also expected administrative competence, and this was not being demonstrated. The regular three-year election in 1980 showed the coalition's parliamentary seats falling from 86 to 74 of a total of 125 but what finally brought about the collapse of the last Fraser administration was the Prime Minister's very public stand on tax evasion. Many doubtful schemes had been produced, and authorized, to allow large-scale tax avoidance, but illegal tax evasion was known to be widespread. John Howard, as Treasurer, and Fraser did not see eye to eye on the solution, with Fraser being much more willing to impose retrospective legislation, deeply unpopular in the business world with which the Liberal Party was closely linked. When an investigation exposed a particularly outrageous, cunning and devious evasion, in which several prominent members of the party were named, Fraser clashed publicly and frequently with supporters as the economy deteriorated and seats were lost at by-elections. The clarity that Menzies had brought about had been obscured by internal dissent. The Country Party, uncomfortable with its specifically rural image, had been born again, first as the National Country Party, and finally, in October 1982, as the National Party. In the Northern Territory the Country Liberal Party had backed to the extreme right, vocal against Aboriginal rights and 'totally Territory-nationalist' to the point of Territorial chauvinism.

Against the inclination of Howard and the Reserve Bank, the August 1982 budget combined steeply increased expenditure – up by 13.9 per cent – with substantial concessions. Within weeks the figures disintegrated, as a projected deficit was seen to rise from $1,674 million to $3,725 million – and with unemployment running at 460,000. If a conservative government could not maintain prudent economic policies and insist on decent standards, then it deserved to fail; and fail it did, dramatically. Very properly, seeing that the authority of his government was fading, Malcolm Fraser requested and was granted a double dissolution in March 1983. Until almost the last moment he believed that his opponent in the general election would be the worthy, honourable but uninspiring Queensland ex-policeman, the 'old Labor'. Bill Hayden. It was an unpleasant setback to Fraser's hopes for victory when Hayden resigned, pushed out to be replaced by Hawke on 8 February 1983, three weeks before the general election was due. The result showed Hayden was right when he said that 'even a drover's dog could lead Labor to victory', – 75 seats out of 125, reflecting the eclipse of the DLP's influence.

New Labor

Hawke's chief advantage as Prime Minister, apart from his personal appeal and neat political judgement, was the absence of Hawke as chairman of the party, continually destabilizing the government in the fashion Whitlam had been made to suffer, there being no potential Labor challenger willing to raise a head above the ramparts. It was not that Labor was short of able ministers, especially in finance – the Cabinet was described as having 'a degree of economic sophistication which puts the Whitlam government in the caveman class'. Certainly the austere Peter Walsh at Finance and John Dawkins, in that department and later at Trade, were excellent administrators, but the unquestioned second-in-command was Paul Keating, the promising young Treasurer. Even Keating, however, was slapped into place when he seemed to be deviating from the Prime Minister's line, but Keating and Hawke shared credit for the Big Idea of Hawke's four governments. 'Reconciliation, Recovery, Reconstruction' was to be the keystone of government policy, the practical expression of which was to be the Accord – the bringing together of politicians, unions and employers (the latter very much of tertiary importance) – to agree fundamental economic policy, a policy which was to include that rarest of phenomena, a voluntary wages freeze by the unions.

Britain had tried, and failed, to develop a similar understanding when Employment Minister Barbara Castle launched her proposal 'In Place of Strife' in January 1969, which was scuppered by Prime Minister Wilson's reluctance to face left-wing opposition and replaced by the infamous 'Solemn and Binding' undertaking signed by the TUC. Ultimately the failure was to be disastrous to British unions as the determined Thatcher government cut away their entrenched powers and prerogatives. By 1983 the lesson that continued intransigence and the irresponsible exercise of power could lead to eventual impotence had been well learnt by the Australian unions, but only Hawke, with his background at the highest level of union and party politics, combined with his unchallenged authority as Prime Minister, could have successfully implemented the Accord, and perhaps only Keating, with his adroitness in changing policies to suit circumstances, could have ensured its continuing success. It is also undeniable that Hawke had, in the shape of Bill Kelty, an ACTU president a great deal more amenable than he had been himself. Hawke could now be aptly described as 'a reformed arsonist selling a fire-protection policy'.

Immediate action was necessary, since the previous outgoing government had been more than usually duplicitous. The deficit, originally announced in the 1982 budget at $1,674 million and stated at the time of the handover to be $4,000 million, turned out to be $9,600 million. Although this was an immediate embarrassment, it turned out, as Hawke admitted, to be 'a stick with which we were justifiably able to beat the Liberals' for many years to come.[34]

One immediate and remarkable effect of the first Accord was the fulfilment of Hawke's electoral pledge to create 500,000 new jobs within three years; it was achieved with five months to go, but unemployment remained high. Labor was not drifting to the right, but steering purposefully in that direction; as Tony Blair and Gordon Brown demonstrated in Britain after 1997, a Labour government with a substantial majority, and with union opposition stunned, could adopt those conservative garments best suited to the national interest with impunity.

Fraser had already begun action on fulfilling conservative economic precepts by the appointment of a commission in 1979 which recommended comprehensive financial deregulation and a reliance on market forces. Treasurer John Howard enthusiastically backed Sir Keith Campbell's recommendations, but Prime Minister Fraser was less enthusiastic and the only positive decision was an agreement, too late to be effective, to allow foreign banks into the Australian market. In line with Old Labor policy the ALP had scornfully rejected both the Campbell report and foreign bank entry, but very shortly afterwards Hawke, the former party leader, who had once declared that 'free market dogma ... had no place in a Labor administration', was adopting both.

The year 1979 saw the election of Margaret Thatcher in Britain and Ronald Reagan in the United States, both exponents of the 'right-wing' economics associated with Milton Friedman, and the Hawke government proved themselves more enthusiastic for such free market policies than had their Liberal predecessors. The first and most striking illustration of this was the decision to allow the Australian dollar to float, against the firm advice of Treasury officials who wanted to cling on to the Reserve Bank control of rates. Encouraged by a currency crisis, Keating announced the abolition of exchange controls and the floating exchange rate on 9 December 1983. Keating later analysed the move:

One of the things is that the born-to-rule brigade, – the coalition – have never lived with the discipline of a floating exchange rate. They think their mere presence will affect how the world markets treat them. It won't matter a tinker's curse. The float is the decision where Australia truly made its debut into the world and said, 'O.K., we're now an international citizen.'[35]

The last part of Mr Keating's assertion was certainly true. Australia was emerging from the shell of self-imposed isolation which had followed cutting free from sterling and the Bank of England's guidance, and placing the Australian economy in the world market. Sidelined in opposition, John Howard could only applaud, and, albeit with misgivings, the Labor Caucus acquiesced.

Although essential for long-term growth, deregulation brought immediate dangers. The economy with its massive reliance on primary producers and its uncompetitive manufacturers was highly exposed to world market movements; Australian banks and credit institutions simply did not have the experienced management to cope with the new opportunities, leading to more foolish decisions than might reasonably be expected and encouraging such corporate bandits as Alan Bond, assisted by the fact that a watchdog, the Australian Securities Commission, was not established until 1990. Business lending expanded at the rate of over 25 per cent p.a., often made without adequate consideration.

Whitlam's across-the-board 25 per cent reduction in protective tariffs was followed by a steady and progressive removal of protection to manufactures. Standing at some 34 per cent in 1992, reduced the following year to about 26 per cent, by the time Labor left office in 1996 the effective rate of assistance for manufactured products had dropped to under 10 per cent. Faced with this successful adoption of their policies the Liberal opposition had a hard row to hoe. Their two leaders, Andrew Peacock, handsome, sporting and charming, and John Howard – none of the above, but a shrewd politician and able administrator – worked together tolerably well, with Howard content to allow Peacock to lead the party into what looked like inevitable defeat at the next election. As a consequence of the bewilderingly complex Australian electoral system, a half-Senate election was due in 1985. Hawke decided to advance this to December 1984 and to combine it with a House of Representatives election; it would be the eighth time since 1972 that the Australian voters had been summoned to the urns. The Prime

Minister's calculation had been correct, and defeat for the coalition duly followed, but not by any means so serious as might have been expected. Peacock personally performed well, outclassing Hawke in a television debate and the result was a modest swing to the coalition, but with Labor still holding a substantial majority of 16 seats. Bill Hayden, whose seat in Cabinet as Foreign Minister had not healed the bitterness of his leadership loss said: 'Well, the drover's dog will win again, but it looks a bit clapped-out this time.'[36]

Before the election Hawke had indicated that he would probably resign in a third term, after one more election victory, leaving Paul Keating as the obvious successor, a solution which Keating was prepared to accept. Relations between the two men worsened appreciably in 1985 when a public debate on taxation policy culminated in an extraordinary tax summit, at which over three days delegates from all sections of society discussed a detailed White Paper describing options for future taxation policy. Keating and Treasury officials were clearly in favour of introducing indirect taxation through a sales or value added tax at $12\frac{1}{2}$ per cent, to be offset, theoretically at any rate, by direct tax reductions. This policy was a central feature of what was accepted as right-wing economics and therefore an extraordinary proposal from the supposedly left-wing government.

By day three of the summit, opposition to the sales tax appeared widespread and vocal, and an opinion poll published that day showed the coalition leading. Prime Minister Hawke promptly abandoned his Treasurer as 'The Keating package fell victim to a strange alliance – business, the ACTU, the centre-left and left wing, the welfare lobby and the Joh Bjelke-Petersen and John Stone flat rate tax mania; opponents threw rocks from every vantage point.'[37] Without telling Keating, Hawke slipped out for a private meeting with his successor at the head of ACTU, Bill Kelty and his colleague Simon Crean, both of whom had been key figures in preparing the Accord. The Prime Minister did not attempt to negotiate but simply offered the ACTU what they had originally suggested – which did not, of course, include a sales tax. Keating learnt of the deal in the morning papers.

Hawke's conduct was at once an extraordinary abrogation of cabinet responsibility – a key policy decision had been taken effectively by a brace of union leaders – and a betrayal of his closest colleague. Paul Kelly, in his book *The End of Certainty*, described Hawke's speeches to the summit on the last day, and at a subsequent press conference

an effort was made to decorate the wreckage that remained after what Hawke called amid the sniggers 'an extraordinarily successful Summit'. Hawke now assembled a new tax cart from the broken pieces. It was the worst type of policy improvisation. The government was left with an odd group of ill-fitting taxation parts – like a stunned schoolboy whose prize invention has just exploded.

It was also an act of political realism; the sales tax had been a conservative bridge too far, and ironically, was eventually introduced by John Howard himself, over stiff opposition in 2000. But so public a humiliation of his Treasurer by the Prime Minister marked the end of good relations between the two men.

Hawke's quite enormous personal vanity, combined with his genuine concern for international affairs, led him to enjoy and indulge himself in numerous overseas tours, on which his ebullient style was well received as a welcome respite from other, often tedious world leaders. The first great public clash between Hawke and Keating took place during one of the Prime Minister's visits to China and Japan. Deregulation had opened Australia to international pressures, and in 1985 a dramatic downturn exposed the country's weakness, as a supplier of raw materials as prices weakened, and the failure to employ borrowings in capital investment bit home. Foreign debt as a proportion of GDP had risen from 6 per cent in 1980 to nearly 30 per cent in 1986, and been used to a great extent in financing domestic consumption. After February 1985 the Australian dollar dropped on the foreign exchange markets by as much as 40 per cent, at one time trading below 50 cents US. Stern economic pressures demanded a change of course. Amazingly, the ACTU came up with Accord Mark II, accepting actual wage cuts. The situation remained dire, however, with the current account deficit climaxing at $1,400 million when Keating made it direr by giving a radio interview by telephone, always a perilous business, on 14 May 1986 in which he told the Australian public the truth:

Keating: We are importing about $12 billion more than we are exporting on an annual basis. What it means is that we are living beyond our capacity to meet our obligations by $12 billion . . . we must let Australians know truthfully, honestly, earnestly, just what sort of international hole Australia is in. It's the prices of our commodities – they are as bad in real terms [as at anytime] since the Depression . . . and if we don't make it this time we never will make it. If this government cannot get the adjustment, get manufacturing going again and keep moderate wage outcomes and a sensible economy policy, then Australia is basically done for. We will just end up being a third-rate economy . . . If in the final analysis Australia is so undisciplined, so disinterested in its salvation and its economic well being, that it doesn't deal with these fundamental problems, then the fallback solution is inevitable because you can't fund $12 billion a year in perpetuity every year ... the only thing to do is to slow the growth down to a canter. Once you slow the growth under 3 per cent, unemployment starts to rise again.

John Laws: And then you have really induced a depression.

Keating: Then you are gone. You are a banana republic.[38]

If a 'banana republic' is taken to mean an economy which relies upon the export of primary commodities to finance its trade, the description did in fact aptly describe Australia. Industry, protected by tariffs and the Accords, had failed to develop at more than a fraction of the pace of the 'Asian tigers', notably lagging behind in such sectors as office machinery, telecommunications equipment, industrial machinery and motor vehicles. Australia produced only a fraction of the country's requirements, while two-thirds of the exports were in the form of raw materials.

In Japan, Hawke was furious at Keating's amazingly indiscreet phrase. A press conference in Beijing was followed by a conference telephone call from Hawke to the Cabinet in Canberra. One account gives a picture of the elegant exchanges of views between Cabinet colleagues.

The ministers saw Keating's temper flaring. 'Be careful, the Chinese will be listening,' they cautioned. 'Fuck the Chinese,' Keating replied. 'Just what's the point of this bullshit, Bob?' Keating demanded. 'Who's that?' Hawke asked. 'Who the fuck do you think it is?' replied Keating. 'We've got problems here and we're trying to solve them. Just what the hell do you think you're playing at?'

– and that exchange was characterized by Mr Hawke as 'amicable'![39] Two subsequent minor scandals connected with travel expenses and a failure to file income tax returns put Mr Keating in a slightly weak position; but, as the indispensable man, the wunderkind at the Treasury retained his office and his position as heir apparent.

In July 1987 the third election in the life of what could fairly be called the Hawke–Keating administration was comfortably successful. The coalition's cause had not been assisted by a clumsy manifesto, presented by John Howard, which promised impossibly generous tax cuts, and whose faulty arithmetic was mercilessly exposed by Keating. A leaked conversation between Peacock and his Victorian colleague Jeff Kennet in which they abused Howard and his supporters as 'a pile of shit' and 'fucking cunts', language which even in Australia was regarded as overstepping the bounds of inter-party familiarity, did nothing to enhance the Liberal's reputation. But the main ally of Labor was the now slightly mad figure of Sir Joh Bjelke-Petersen, who had broken with the Queensland Liberals and was running Queensland with obedient National Party colleagues. A flavour of the 'Joh for Prime Minister' campaign is given by a supporter's speech: 'Maintain your love; your love for our nation, our party, our Premier and Senator who have been a light in the darkness . . . And in that love go into the shires, the towns and cities of our State and ensure in this election that we light a fire that will never be put out . . .'[40] and the description by one well-regarded broadcaster of Sir Joh: 'The Premier of Queensland, a man who can't string together three words in the English language, a man who believes in water-powered cars and quack cancer cures, this man is stomping the country preaching voodoo economics and flat earth finance and he's being listened to.'[41] The campaign was doomed to failure but caused much harm to the coalition, and buried the political reputation of prominent Liberals; Peacock described Sir Joh's campaign as 'a God-driven and abiding duty to drive the Hawke government from power'. In this it failed, and not only failed but brought down Sir Joh and his corrupt allies.

After Labor's election victory it was time for Keating to begin calling in his markers. The coalition's self-immolation had lost them the election, but Labor's victory – the first time a Labor government had won three consecutive elections – was largely due to Keating's bold attempt to put the economy right. He took the electorate into his confidence, spelled out the gravity of Australia's plight and detailed the painful remedies needed. A refreshing change from the humbug expected of politicians, and in glaring contrast to Howard's inept manifesto, such candour encouraged the voters to put their trust in the Treasurer. Hawke, however, did not share the view that the time for him to retire was approaching, which he made publicly and offensively clear. It would be a pity if Keating resigned, but 'there are people of very considerable talent in the ministry and the position would be filled' (24 July 1988).

This was too much for the excitable Treasurer who stormed into the Prime Minister's office: ' "You've made a thoroughgoing bastard of yourself," Keating said. "You think I'm dispensable. What you're really saying is the relationship between you and me is finished. I'm telling you, you're dead right. As far as I'm concerned, you and I are finished. The relationship is over, dead and buried." '[42] For three months the situation festered until on 25 November a secret meeting was held at the Prime Minister's Sydney residence, Kirribilli House, between Hawke, Keating, Bill Kelty and Sir Peter Abeles, a trusted friend of Hawke and a colleague of Rupert Murdoch, who had maintained close relationships with the Labor government – details of which were at the time kept well away from public scrutiny.[43] What transpired at Kirribilli was subsequently glossed over and variously interpreted as it suited the protagonists, but an agreement was reached that Hawke would retire after the next election, thus giving at least a taste of office to Keating before the risk of a quite likely defeat in a fifth election – five successive wins, especially for a Labor government, being unprecedented. It was an agreement, a contemporary wit observed, between an egomaniac and a megalomaniac.

Keating continued to serve as Treasurer, promising to behave politely towards Hawke and his colleagues, but whereas his previous performance had helped to transform the Australian economy, after mid-1988 Keating's self-confidence led him badly astray. Expectations of early improvement in standards of living had been raised, and at a time when fiscal restraint was essential, huge tax cuts, which increased wages by as much as 12 per cent, injected some $6,000 million into an overheating economy. Interest rates soared to 20 per cent, and remained there. Finance Minister Peter Walsh's pleas for greater firmness were ignored, leading to that apostle of fiscal restraint's eventual resignation: 'This government has the stink of decay, and I don't want to be part of it.' Keating was forced to approach the next election with a claim that a recession would be avoided. He was not helped by the spectacular incompetence of the Labor government in Victoria, spiced by more than usual corruption, nor that in Western Australia where Hawke's friend Brian Burke and two of his ministers were under investigation; on the other hand the agitated procrastination of Bjelke-Petersen in Queensland had finally led to the collapse of his long period of personal rule and the election of a Labor government.[44]

It was Liberal incompetence rather than Labor brilliance that won Hawke's final election, in March 1990. A clumsy coalition attempt to structure a credible health service was exposed by the Labor Health Minister, Neal Blewett; his Liberal opposite, Richard Shack, admitted 'with all the frankness that I can muster, the Liberal and National parties do not have a particularly good track record in health and you don't need me to remind you of our last period in government'. Once again Peacock's coalition seemed to project a lack of ordinary competence, which, in default of a policy, should have been the signal merit of a conservative party. 'The party that cannot govern itself cannot govern Australia' was Hawke's most telling electoral cry.[45]

The old dichotomy of Australian politics, Labor versus all anti-Labor coalitions, was changing as special interest groups developed political structures. Don Chipp's Australian Democrats, 'keeping the bastards honest', shifted allegiances as they approved or not the major parties' policies. In 1990 Labor won 56.7 per cent of the preference votes which contributed substantially to their victory, since the primary vote was a miserable 39.4 per cent; and in the June election the Democrats won a convincing 11.3 per cent of the primary vote. Thus placed in a position not unlike that of the Liberal Democrats in Britain, the Australian Democrats were free to affect the results of national elections without the responsibility of advancing costed and credible proposals of their own.

Many Democrat voters shared environmental concerns with the new Green Party. There was cause enough for concern about Australian environmental issues; the most evident, if not the gravest, being the depletion of the ozone layer due to global warming. Worries about the carcinogenic properties of unfiltered solar rays led to soaring sales of intensive sun-block and hats, and the establishment of skin-cancer clinics. The disadvantages of the great irrigation and hydroelectric schemes made themselves apparent in the salination of river waters and the Murray River's drying up. In Tasmania, where the finest native trees had almost disappeared, controversy was aroused in 1990 by an application for extensive logging. The government's eventual rejection, allied to what had been almost the first decision of the 1983 administration, the cancellation of the Franklin dam, proved Labor's green credentials, but did nothing to heighten the government's popularity among Tasmanians, angry at the loss of employment opportunities. Few votes for Labor can have been gained by what was probably Hawke's most valuable personal contribution, which was to secure an amendment to the 1988 Convention in the Regulation of Antarctic Mineral Resource Activity that would have permitted mining and oil drilling to take place. With the help of the pioneer of marine exploration, Jacques Cousteau, and the support of the French Government and Senator Al Gore in the United States, the Australian government was able to secure an international agreement leaving the whole continent as an enormous nature reserve; and in 2002 the coalition Prime Minister John Howard was able to follow this up by extending the protection to the southern coasts of Australia. Admirable though these efforts were, there were few primary votes to be gained in this fashion, and this was also true of the other issue troubling liberals', if not Liberal, consciences.

Bill Bryson recounts two conversations during his trans-continental journey on the subject of Aborigines. Keith and Daphne were

Quiet middle-aged teachers from rural north Queensland.

'It's a problem,' he said, staring hard at his food.

'At the school where I teach,' Daphne went on, hesitantly, 'the Aboriginal parents, well, they get their dole payment and spend it on drink and then go walk-about. And the teachers have to . . . well, feed the children. You know, out of their own pockets. Otherwise the children wouldn't eat.'

'It's a problem,' Keith said again, still fixed on his food.

'But they're lovely people really. When they're not drinking.'

And that pretty well killed the conversation.[46]

Bryson's second conversation was with a retired Canberra solicitor:

'Ah, Aborigines,' he said, nodding solemnly. 'A great problem.'

'So I gather.'

'They want hanging, every one of them.'

I looked at him, startled, and found a face on the edge of fury.

'Every bloody one of them,' he said, jowls trembling, and without another word took his leave.

That was in 1999, and while it is likely that few would be found to echo the solicitor's judgement, that of Keith is probably still shared by very many Australian voters.

A division was developing between town and country, between south and north, those areas where Aborigines were hardly noticeable, and where concerns on job security, education, violent crime and health were more pressing, and those areas, particularly north Queensland and the Northern Territory where Aborigines formed a substantial minority. There, as Keith indicated, alcohol addiction and the resultant petty crimes were a major problem. The Northern Territory government had moved only slowly towards addressing the subject; until 1964 Aborigines had not been allowed access to alcohol, and drunkenness was decriminalized only ten years later. The resultant spectacle of helplessly intoxicated men and women in towns led to a 1982 order banning public drinking within two kilometres of a liquor store; if Aborigines must get drunk they should do so out of town. Such attitudes sat uncomfortably with metropolitan notions of human rights and dignity.[47]

The enthusiasm for Aboriginal rights evinced in the 1967 referendum was being eroded as these rights were being claimed by many whose Aboriginality was doubtful, as the Aboriginal population shot up – 200 Tasmanian Aborigines in 1971 had become 13,873 by 1996. To be Aboriginal was both modish and a pathway to local power and influence, and seemed to many Australians to provide a distinctive national identity. Qantas began decorating its aeroplanes in 'Aboriginal' patterns, but such claims were irrelevant to those five million 'New Australians' who had arrived since the war and who could advance no pretensions to Aboriginal ancestry. Their interests and energies turned on mastering the arts needed to prosper in an English-speaking society; as Robert Hughes pointed out,[48] it was hardly feasible to persuade 'the daughter of a Croatian immigrant of the mystic bond she was supposed to feel with Prince Charles or his mother' (or, for that matter, with the Aborigines), but her career would be in universities, businesses, professions and institutions which were still 'Basically British', albeit with an Australian flavour.

Aborigines themselves were becoming more vocal and ambitious. A treaty was called for by the National Aboriginal Conference in 1979, demanding, *inter alia*, that 5 per cent of GNP be applied for Aboriginal purposes. Taken up by the poet Kevin Gilbert, this was raised to 7 per cent in his draft of a treaty which protested against James Cook's 'criminal, unlawful' conduct which allowed 'the terror and invasion, the massacre and theft of our land'. Coupled with an appeal for Libyan help, such initiatives did not recommend themselves to the average Australian.

The Aboriginal issue, however, was abruptly shifted from an interesting topic of conversation to a matter of real and pressing significance. The historic turning point was the Mabo judgment of June 1992. Eddie Mabo, a groundsman at Townsville University College (now James Cook University), was a native of Murray Island in the Torres Strait, and a friend of the young lecturer Henry Reynolds, who has since become the recognized authority on Aboriginal land rights, and indeed on many aspects of Aboriginal history. Islanders were ethnically and culturally quite distinct from the mainland Aborigines, as the first encounters with Europeans had proved. Reynolds remarked that at the time

I knew enough about Murray Island to realise that it had an entirely different social structure, system of land use and tenure and different settlement patterns from those of the Aborigines on mainland Australia. The Murray Islanders were closely related to the Papuans; they were gardeners who lived in villages. Property was owned by families and not collectively. The small garden plots were clearly marked with boundaries which were known and normally recognised throughout the community.[49]

This being so, he reasoned, the Islanders had a claim to their lands which the Aborigines, as nomadic hunter-gatherers, might not possess. It was many years before Eddie Mabo, with the help of Reynolds and other sympathizers, was able to bring such a claim and Mabo himself died just before judgment was given in his favour in the High Court of Australia on 3 June 1992. The judgment established that in principle 'native title' existed where there had been 'continuous association' with the land, and where such title had not been superseded by a grant to settlers: as Lord Grey had said in 1849, the British government's intention was to allow 'only the exclusive rights of pasturage in the runs, not the exclusive occupation of the lands, as against the natives using it for ordinary purposes'. As Reynolds commented:

The evidence, then, is very clear. The Colonial Office created pastoral leases to allow for the mutual use of the same land – the pastoralist had a right to conduct his pastoral enterprise, the aborigines to use the land in their traditional manner. The pastoralist had no authority to deny access to the customary owners, who had rights which had to be respected. They were rights not granted by government but recognised to exist because they derived from the time before the arrival of the Europeans.[50]

Had the decision been applied only to the Torres Strait islands, its impact would have been limited, and indeed it took some years, and another major case, before the full consequences were appreciated. Certainly it hardly figured in Labor's March 1993 campaign, the first fought by Paul Keating as leader, who was advised that 'the decision would have only a very restricted impact' – but the Aboriginal claim to participate in that most fundamental of principles, the disposal of land, which had aroused so much indignation in the 1830s and 1840s, was firmly established.[51]

At Last

At the end of December 1991, with distinguished acrimony and mutual recrimination, after one failed attempt in June, Paul Keating succeeded in dislodging Bob Hawke from his position as leader of the Labor Party. After his first failure Keating needed to do little except wait; his replacement in June as Treasurer, the genial farmer John Kerrin, was not up to the job, especially when faced with a Liberal challenge headed by John Hewson, himself a professional economist, although, as it turned out, politically inept. Kerrin lasted for five months before a now desperate Hawke replaced him, only to be forced to resign the leadership himself on 19 December, and to be defeated in the subsequent Caucus election. After nine years of waiting in the wings, acting almost as Prime Minister to Hawke's President, Paul Keating had finally achieved his ambition. Within days a planned visit by President George Bush gave the new Prime Minister the useful benediction of Australia's powerful ally.

Although Australian Prime Ministers continued to visit American Presidents, Australian fidelity to the alliance did not seem to warrant Presidential visits to Australia, and there had been a gap of more than fourteen years between Johnson's attendance at Harold Holt's funeral, in the middle of the

Vietnam War, and George Bush's visit in December 1991. The tone of the visit differed markedly from those previous enthusiastic welcomes given to Lyndon Johnson. Bush was met not by cheering crowds but by angry farmers protesting against the President's increased subsidies to American wheat growers; his explanation that this was all the fault of the European Community's agricultural policy was not well received. Just as Australian loyalty to Britain had been insulted by Britain siding with the European Community, so Australia's value as an American ally was being dismissed as secondary to maintaining the living standards of American farmers. Surely Australia deserved better? By supporting, quickly and without question, the American-led Desert Storm action against the Iraqi occupation of Kuwait, the Labor government had once more proved its reliability; indeed, as had happened earlier with Vietnam, Australia eagerly demanded to be allowed to join the party.

From an American point of view, Australia had followed obediently, voting for a World Bank loan to Pinochet's regime in Chile and supporting the unprincipled American invasion of Grenada, a fellow Commonwealth country in 1983. It took twenty-four hours and a single telephone call from President Bush to Prime Minister Hawke to change initial Australian condemnation of the 1989 invasion of Panama to full understanding and support. When in 1987 New Zealand banned visits by American vessels that might be carrying nuclear weapons Australia, in spite of its strong anti-nuclear stance, refused to follow, and the ANZUS pact disintegrated. None of these obliging policies gained any reward; meetings between 'Bob' and 'Ron' produced amiable platitudes, but no action on the pressing question of American restraints on trade.

A secret National Security Council directive of 28 May 1986 summarized the American view.

NSDD 229. U.S. AUSTRALIAN RELATIONS; VISIT OF AUSTRALIAN PRIME MINISTER ROBERT ('BOB') HAWKE. (p.705)
(Secret) May 28, 1986. (Page 3 of this directive was deleted by the NSC.)

Australia is regarded in Washington as by far the most important U.S. ally in the southern Pacific. Due to Australia's geographic position, political stability, and cultural links to the United States, U.S. military and intelligence organisations operate scores of highly sensitive strategic missions in Australia. Australia is also an important source of strategic minerals and a major U.S. trading partner.

Prime minister Bob Hawke's election in 1983 troubled the Reagan administration, however. Hawke was seen as a potential problem because of the Australian Labor Party's (ALP's) sometimes critical views on the East–West arms race, on

U.S. military bases in Australia, and on U.S. subsidies for agricultural goods that compete with Australia's in international markets. Some ALP leaders had also publicly charged that the CIA and Australian security agencies had conspired to unseat the previous ALP prime minister, Gough Whitlam, in 1975. The Reagan administration's mistrust of Hawke was compounded when the ALP refused to denounce New Zealand's decision to bar warships with nuclear weapons from entering its ports. The United States regarded New Zealand's decision as counter to the spirit of the ANZUS military pact, to which Australia, New Zealand, and the United States were signatories.

New Zealand was, however, right to be suspicious, since the United States was even at that time secretly deploying nuclear weapons in South Korea, Taiwan and the Philippines – and probably still is. Whether Australia was given any hint of this is unknown.[52]

Hawke's April 17 visit to Washington, D.C., resulted in U.S. concessions on subsidies for U.S. wheat farmers, Hawke's support for U.S. military bases in Australia insofar as they contributed to 'verifiable arms-control agreements,' and renewed Australian commitment to the ANZUS pact. Two months later, however, the United States effectively expelled New Zealand from ANZUS. The U.S.-Australian tension over agricultural subsidies was resumed the following August when the United States announced new U.S. wheat sales to the USSR that the Australians viewed as subsidized.

The confusion within the NSC over U.S. relations with Australia's ALP government under Hawke was illustrated by the fact that this policy directive was adopted in late May 1986, more than a month after Hawke's April visit to Washington had concluded.

It was left to Kim Beazley, Minister of Defence, to embarrass Secretary of State Shultz at a press conference on 29 June 1988:

Q: Mr Shultz, Mr Hayden said that when it came to trade matters, Australia expects a good ally to be treated as a good friend and yet, clearly, many Australians feel they're not being treated as a good friend on trade matters. Is that a problem for you?

SECRETARY SHULTZ: Of course it's a problem when we see that Australia is upset about something that we're doing. Mr Hayden did raise particularly our Export Enhancement Program and the sugar quota program. We discussed those, among other trade issues, but I think those were the two that particularly troubled the Minister ... The export Enhancement Program is a necessary effort undertaken by the United States in response to the heavy subsidies of the European Community which were dislodging unfairly our farmers from their traditional markets. We had no alternative but to fight back, and that is the principal objective of that program. We make every effort to see that we don't use that in markets that are traditionally Australian markets. . . .

Q: Can I ask a supplementary on that point, sir? Can you understand that many Australians who question this relationship are concerned that Australia has to bear the responsibility of the joint defense facilities while Australian farmers feel that American actions are detrimental to their trade. I know that you might answer that trade and defense are separate matters. But can you agree that for some people they're not?

SECRETARY SHULTZ: Well, as far as trade is concerned, of course, we have a strong trading relationship with Australia. We have a problem in the agricultural field that we have different analyses of. I think we'd have to say to our friends in Australia that if they were us and saw the European subsidy program taking the markets away from their farmers, would they just sit there. I think the answer is no.[53]

Over the years the excuses changed slightly, but the harsh fact that American farmers' votes mattered more than Australian protests remained. President Clinton's claims to be an advocate of free trade were not matched by any action as the American agricultural support programme moved from merely countering EC protectionism to 'blatant market promotion'. Although the personal relations between the leaders were excellent, nothing could hide the fact that Australia was very low down on the list of American priorities.

Like Whitlam and Hawke, Keating had a style and panache lacked by his coalition counterparts. By some way the most interesting figure in Australian politics at the time, Paul Keating's enthusiasms included the works of Richard Strauss, French Empire furniture and clocks. Sensitive, even delicate in spite of his innate toughness, his emotional reactions and a passion for grand visions and sweeping ideas sometimes clouded his usually accurate sense of realpolitik. His command of personal skills, exemplified by his exchanges with Hawke, was limited; an admirer, John Edwards, noted his capacity for being 'waspish and venomous'. As Treasurer, Keating had been essentially a nuts-and-bolts man, a finance minister through and through, with little opportunity to develop the capacity to charm and influence that Hawke possessed in such abundance. Since another general election was due within fifteen months the new Prime Minister had little time to establish himself and to correct a gloomy economic position, with nearly a million unemployed and a miserable rating in the opinion polls. Seasoning the unpalatable prospect with a dose of nationalism, Keating campaigned for a new flag, which would, according to Keating's speechwriter Don Watson, help 'it to be universally understood that we were, as never before, on our own and that the future depended on our having the courage to make radically new choices. He thought that from this clearing of the national decks might come the energy that would make the whole Australian experiment exciting again.' It was not, however, clear that Australians preferred to be part of an exciting experiment to the enjoyments of security and prosperity. More practically seeking to consolidate his position and present an integrated policy, Keating produced a document entitled *One Nation* – which should not be confused with the eccentric right-wing party of that name begun in Queensland by Pauline Hanson. *One Nation*, 'choreographed' in conjunction with Kelty and the ACTU, was not unfairly (but perhaps unwisely, given the coalition's record) described by the opposition as 'pork-barrelling'; promised tax cuts offered a hostage to fortune, certainly rash in the existing state of the economy, and which led to the resignation, once its impracticability had become obvious, of Keating's Treasurer, John Dawkins, when the Prime Minister proved reluctant to face the inevitability of cancelling tax cuts.[54]

The Liberal opposition, for so long puzzled for some way of countering Labor's policies, had at last produced a coherent programme – over 700 pages of it, to be sure, not an easy item for an electorate to digest. The basis of *Fightback!*, which was finally activated in 2000 by John Howard's Liberal government, was Keating's old idea of a sales tax, to be balanced by a cut in income tax; again, although an elegant solution, not an easy one to sell to a suspicious electorate.

Success for Keating in the next election looked even less likely, with unemployment rising and the deficit ballooning, but again he was rescued by the opposition. Boldly, but perhaps foolishly, Dr Hewson had chosen to participate in two formal exchanges with the Prime Minister, in which he was voted, in a subsequent poll, to be a clear loser. The essential issues facing the electorate, in order of importance, were the sales tax, the economy, healthcare and industrial relations, issues which still, although perhaps with different priorities, preoccupy Australians. In spite of an almost universal assumption in the Australian press that Hewson would win, the March 1993 election led to another convincing Labor victory, with a net gain of two seats, the fifth successive win. The primary vote was increased, an achievement not matched by a government in office since 1966. Paul Keating was now established as Prime Minister with an unmistakeable personal mandate. The concussed opposition retained John Hewson as leader and quietly allowed *Fightback!* to retire from the ring. Disputes among the opposition continued to provide Keating with useful cover. On 23 May 1994 the unlucky Hewson was replaced by Alexander Downer, protégé of Malcolm Fraser, scion of a distinguished political dynasty (grandfather, Sir John, one of the Founding Fathers, father, Sir Alexander, a Menzies minister) and very conscious of the fact. Talented and attractive, but gaffe-prone, Alexander junior did not last long before giving place to the previously rejected John Howard, in January 1995; and it was the outwardly dull and uninspiring Howard (in cartoons resembling the Frog footman in *Alice* and nearer in age to Malcolm Fraser than to Alexander Downer) who was to defeat the brilliant young Keating.

Continuing and reinforcing Hawke's policy of engagement with Asia, Keating and Gareth Evans, the sure-footed and ironic Foreign Minister who had succeeded Hayden in 1986, developed the role of the Asia-Pacific Economic Co-operation, intended to reduce tariffs and integrate the region's markets. APEC had been established at Bob Hawke's initiative in January 1989, but it was largely due to Keating's persistence that meetings of heads of government of the member countries, which included the United States and Canada as well as China and Japan, were begun. Not always of the friendliest – there was one spectacular row between Dr Mahathir of Malaysia and Paul Keating – APEC marked a hopeful beginning to regional co-operation, without which even the hesitant return of a united, communist Vietnam to the international community would have been difficult. With the transfer of sovereignty in Hong Kong from Britain to China imminent, and very much in the news (the retrocession took place in 1997), there was much talk of 'Asian values' as being somehow distinct from those of the West. Leaving aside the interesting philosophical debate provoked by such concepts (did the Cultural Revolution or the Hundred Flowers best illustrate Confucian philosophy?), it was commonly believed that the invocation of Asian values was used as an excuse for authoritarian-minded governments to disregard those inconvenient aspects of human rights generally accepted in Europe and North America. Certainly the tens of thousands of Hong Kong Chinese who rushed to obtain foreign passports that would allow them to live in countries where 'Asian' values were not imposed indicated that such a suspicion was justified.[55]

Asian APEC countries varied from such basically democratic and respectable societies, albeit with a sometimes strong flavour of authoritarian personal control, as Malaysia, Singapore, Taiwan and South Korea, through traditional monarchies (Thailand) and that economic giant Japan, to the huge, still dormant colossus of China, twitching uneasily, only starting to show its potential for growth. Economically, APEC was also strangely assorted: it contained the five countries in the world whose economies were growing most rapidly – China, Thailand, South Korea, Singapore and Malaysia; Japan had the largest current account surplus in the world; Australia the largest (after the United States and Germany) deficit. Japan in 1997 had the biggest industrial output in the world, comfortably above that of the United States; Australia, although thirteen in world ranking, was well below South Korea. While the United Nations Human Development Index, which combines GDP with literacy, education and life expectancy, is a shaky indicator of life's pleasanter aspects (it ranked North Korea above Turkey), Australia's ranking, then a fraction in advance of New Zealand and Britain, seemed appropriate enough, ahead of all APEC countries, Japan always excepted, with Thailand and Brazil doing much less well. The jokers in the pack were the Philippines, where institutionalized corruption, revolution and counter-revolution would have threatened continuity had American protection been absent, and Indonesia, neighbours on the Human Development Index at 99 and 98 respectively.

Asian attitudes to Australia were equally mixed. The poorer countries were grateful for Australia's generous aid policies and its participation in World Bank loans; Japan, regarding itself quite as much a part of the Western alliance as an offshore archipelago of the Asian mainland, maintained close and friendly relations with Australia; Malaysia's Dr Mahathir, in contrast, opposed Australian participation at such important meetings as the biennial Asia-Europe summits (ASEM) attempting to form an inner purely Asian clique and insisting that Australia must move towards 'Asian' values (but not, presumably, to follow Dr Mahathir's example in imprisoning his political rivals on trumped-up charges). The picture was to change radically in the period after the great Asian economic crisis of 1997, but APEC was already becoming much less 'Asian' as the United States and Russia began influencing its councils, and such undoubtedly Pacific but certainly non-Asian countries as Mexico, Peru and Chile joined. The competing group, ASEAN, remained exclusively non-white.

As far as ASEAN countries were concerned, Australia was a long way from proving its Asian credentials, continuing as it did to represent an outpost of white, Anglo-Saxon values. The 'real test of Australian commitment to Asia would be when Australian troops assisted their Asian neighbours in issues of regional concern, such as fundamentalism in Sumatra, secession in Bougainville or insurgency in East Timor', and stopped fussing about human rights; after all, as the Vietnamese ambassador said: 'If you go into a family, you don't go into places where the family would not like you to go.'[56] Australian public opinion, sensitive as it was to anything that smacked of unfairness and bullying, would never allow such deference, but Keating insisted on meeting such demands as far as might be practicable.

It was Keating's error to cosy up to Indonesia just as the corrupt and unpleasant government of President Suharto was beginning to crumble. The appointment of Gareth Evans as Australian Foreign Minister and Ali Alatas as his Indonesian counterpart in 1988 improved relations. Evans was inclined to be conciliatory, claiming the 'Human rights issues, for all their importance, should not be allowed to dominate our relationship with Indonesia, but neither should they be submerged', and pointing out that 'at least thirty other countries recognised Indonesia in East Timor' – to which the rejoinder should have been 'But really, Mr Evans, is that the sort of company you want to keep?'[57] Senator Evans might nevertheless have discouraged what followed. When, at a Canberra conference on Indonesia on 23 August 1994, Keating declared that 'no country was more important to Australia than Indonesia', the Prime Minister appeared to disregard all the facts. Strategically, Australia remained dependent on her alliance with the United States. On trade, the European Union was Australia's largest partner with 20.2 per cent of Australian transactions, closely followed by Japan with 19.8 per cent and the United States at 18.4 per cent; all other Asian countries together accounted for only 11.7 per cent. Investment with European Union countries was $26,000 million, and in ASEAN only $5,200 million. From Indonesia, the view was rather different, and perhaps more realistic:

Australia will continue to be a small market viewed from the Indonesian side . . . Indonesia is more important to Australia than Australia is to Indonesia. Indonesia is a powerful neighbour who also plays an important role in ASEAN and APEC which are crucial to Australia's own objective of integration with the region. However, Australia does not as yet feature in the strategic plan of Indonesia.[58]

It was true that Australian ignorance of Indonesia was widespread. The Indonesian national philosophy of *Ekonomi Pancasila* – a compound of God, humanitarianism, democracy, nationalism and social justice – was attractive, but more often than not turned out to be the same old story of a corrupt oligarchy primarily concerned with self-preservation.

Australians, too, were impolitely critical of Indonesia, protesting against Indonesian brutalities against East Timorese dissidents. 'Asian values', as understood by their contemporary protagonists, ensured that these unruly objectors were severely repressed. The massacre of some two hundred Timorese in the churchyards of the capital, Dili, by the Indonesian army in November 1991 was justified by the commanding officer, General Herman Mantiri (a Christian, oddly enough), because the demonstrators 'even yelled

slogans against the Government. To me that is identical with rebellion.'
Such firmness was rewarded by the Indonesian government in making
General Herman ambassador to Australia, an appointment which it required
much diplomatic wrangling to revoke.[59]

Such difficulties did not deter Prime Minister Keating from pressing ahead
with his big idea, the conclusion of a defence agreement with Indonesia,
concluded in December 1995, and described by Keating's biographer John
Edwards as 'one of his best moves – conceived and carried out in secrecy
... cutting through timid and conventional concerns to change the way
Indonesia and Australia thought about each other – a wonderful production'.[60] An examination of the treaty itself hardly bears out so positive
an assessment. What was indeed surprising was the shadow of secrecy which
hung over the negotiations, carried out personally between Keating and
Suharto. The agreement itself was well described as 'lightweight, ambigu-
ously worded and of symbolic rather than practical significance'.[61] Given
the mounting proof of the unpleasantness of the Indonesian regime – Alan
Taylor, the Australian ambassador to Jakarta, investigating reports of
abuses in Irian Jaya (West New Guinea) confirmed 'at least 22 people'
had been killed by the army in the previous twelve months; the Labor
government's reluctance to allow refugee status to Timorese, together with
the Defence Minister Robert Ray's proposals to extend arms sales to Indonesia, and to make the burning of 'friendly' countries' flags illegal, seemed
to violate every principle of democratic tolerance.[62] One veteran Labor
worker, Pat Kennelly, summed up a general opinion: 'I hold the Labor
Prime Ministers more culpable than their Liberal counterparts. The right to
self-determination for the people of East Timor was Labor Party policy
completely ignored by our Labor Prime Ministers. To me it was the ultimate
in betrayal.'[63]

It is more than likely that such matters made little impact on the electorate,
more concerned with domestic affairs, and with good reason. Moreover,
some Australian voters were hardly showing a sophisticated reaction to
international issues. When France resumed nuclear testing in the Pacific a
french-polisher's store was vandalized, croissants spat upon, and an unfortunate Sunnybank couple walking their poodle were assaulted and their dog
beaten to death. 'Actes de crétinisme xénophobe,' as Libération, the left-
wing French newspaper described them. In his analysis of foreign affairs in
the Australian Journal of Politics and History, Glen St John Barclay wondered whether 'Australia in fact possesses the kind of informed public
necessary to be able to conduct a sophisticated foreign policy'.[64]

Prime Minister Keating's propensity not only to shoot from the hip, but sometimes to discharge his piece before fully withdrawing it from its holster was exemplified very soon after his appointment. The British tabloid press brooks no competition in the field of vulgarity, superficiality or malice, and its attacks on Keating were particularly spiteful. Pilloried as the 'Lizard of Oz', after having placed a hand on the Queen's back during her visit of February 1992, and by John Howard's condescending lecture on proper respect, the Prime Minister lashed out in Parliament:

'I was told I did not learn respect at school,' Keating said. 'I learned one thing: I learned about self-respect and self regard for Australia, – not about some cultural cringe to a country which decided not to defend the Malayan peninsula, not to worry about Singapore and not to give us our troops back to keep ourselves free from Japanese domination. This was the country that you people wedded yourselves to, and even as it walked out on you and joined the Common Market, you were still looking for your MBEs, and your knighthoods and all the rest of the regalia that comes with it.'[65]

The survivors of *Prince of Wales* and *Repulse*, the 100,000 British and Commonwealth troops surrendered at Singapore, and those conscripts who had fought for Malaya and Malaysia's freedom over thirty years might well have been disgusted at this vituperation from a young man who was six months old when British, American and Canadian forces landed on the Normandy beaches to begin the liberation of Europe. One result of Keating's outburst was to colour what should be a reasonable and constructive constitutional debate on Australia's future with bitterness. Keating did not further his reputation when, visiting Papua, he threw himself to the ground to kiss the earth, declaring that it was on the Kokoda Track, and not Gallipoli, that the Australian nation was born; more serious matters awaited attention on the island, which were sketchily addressed.

Whether or not Australia should decide, as Ireland, India and South Africa had previously, to adopt a republican form of government was certainly a reasonable question for the end of the twentieth century. Constitutional monarchy had served Britain well for three centuries, and continued to flourish in Norway, Denmark, Sweden, Spain, Holland and (rather less fortunately) in Belgium, but these were self-contained societies with a resident monarch, while Australia was separated by geography and, increasingly, by sometimes opposing interests (as indeed were New Zealand and Canada, but the issue in those countries remained dormant). The last formal remains of British sovereignty had been extinguished in 1986 with the Australia Acts which abolished the right of appeal to the Privy Council, and which had to be passed by both Australian and British Parliaments. With the increasing integration of Britain into the European Community, and as the last of the veterans of the First World War AIF died, and those of the Second aged, the old emotional ties dissolved. Even although Queen Elizabeth remained a welcome visitor, she appeared more and more as a visitor, and not as the Australian Head of State, progressing through her southern dominions. In October 1993 a new oath of office was approved which made no reference to the Queen; perhaps as compensation, her likeness supplanted that of Mrs Chisholm on the $5 note, to a mixed reception. Transition to a republic seemed only a matter of time, and not much time at that. Deciding what sort of republic should be preferred, however, demanded a searching debate. Prime Minister Keating was quite clear. The Governor General should be replaced by a President, appointed in the same way by the Prime Minister, and with the same very limited powers. There would be no doubt about the protocol to be observed on foreign visits, the number of guns to be fired and the correct greeting party to be assembled. (Some Governors General, including Sir John Kerr, had been embarrassed by the imperfect understanding of their status.) It would, indeed, be a very suitable post for retired Prime Ministers, with a comfortable salary, generous expenses and luxurious accommodation. The monarchy would simply disappear, and Australia would have the choice (South Africa and India opted to stay, Ireland and Zimbabwe to leave) on its future membership of the Commonwealth.

But such a decision would do nothing to solve the real constitutional difficulties that faced Australia. In his comprehensive textbook *Australian Democracy in Theory and Practice*, Professor Maddox sums up the 'incoherence of the minimalist position':

Without much more informed discussion, Australian republicanism – indeed, Australian constitutionalism – is likely also to lose its way. It is doubtful whether the 'minimalist' position can be sustained. The minimalists want to replace the Queen with an indigenous head of state, but without devising new institutional foundations and restrictions of the new office. This position is fundamentally incoherent. The present governor-generalship is an office founded squarely and essentially on the monarchy. The governor-general, for all that he or she might act on the advice of the elected Australian government, exercises royal powers. Under sensible interpretations of the constitution, this arrangement is highly democratic. But the sensible interpretation depends upon our taking on board all the history of the monarchy which has removed it from day-to-day politics and induced it to make space for democratic action. Without that history, the restraints of history are also removed. We may be able to surround the new office with new traditions, but we shall have to manufacture them pretty fast, and that is hardly how traditions are made. The alternative form of legitimacy for a head of state would be to constitute the office through popular election, but that would raise the serious difficulty of setting up competing centres of democratic authority – and arousing the spectre of political deadlock. The minimalists certainly do not want that.[66]

Certainly Mr Keating would have been appalled by such a suggestion. A Republic Advisory Commission was appointed, under the chairmanship of Malcolm Turnbull, a former Rhodes Scholar, investment banker and a committed republican. A debate was initiated, but without much real enthusiasm on either side.

Republicanism did not serve for a Labor election issue, and it is doubtful whether the praiseworthy efforts of the two Keating administrations to deal with the aftermath of the Mabo judgment did as much to assist in the 1996 election as it perhaps ought to have done. The Aboriginal Affairs ministers had consistently been regarded as rankers in the Cabinet hierarchy. Robert Tickner, whose grasp of the subject seemed firmer than that of his predecessors, Clyde Holding and the emotional left-winger Gerry Hand ('You have your heart in the right place, Gerry,' Keating once told him, 'but your head is in the wrong place and it's about bloody time you woke up to it'), but great battles in the Cabinet were needed before Tickner could secure agreement over what action should be taken. 'During the Cabinet meeting tempers frayed and emotions ran high. Some who publicly purported to be the friends of Aboriginal people consistently advocated an industry line in Cabinet. Others who were supporters of the Aboriginal cause (or were assumed to be so by the Left of the party) said little or nothing.'[67]

Genuine idealism led Keating into some difficulties. His commitment to bringing women into positions of power was intended to rectify an ancient and particularly stupid injustice. In 1978 there were only three Labor women MPs; after an affirmative action in 1990 there were still only nine; Susan Ryan was given a ministerial post by Bob Hawke, which she did not keep long. At least she remained in the party, but the most senior Labor woman, Jean Melzer, elected to the Senate in 1974, left disillusioned to join a fringe Nuclear Disarmament Party. Hawke had appointed Ros Kelly and Margaret Reynolds (wife of the Aborigines' historian Henry) to ministerial posts and Keating, prompted by electoral considerations as well as good sense, was committed to expanding opportunities for the other half of the human race. He was not well rewarded; Ros Kelly had to resign after being found to have laxly administered the department and made politically motivated grants;

her successor, Dr Carmen Lawrence, previously Premier of Western Australia, was accused by a Royal Commission of having lied to a previous inquiry. Labor men did no better. In 1992 John Bannon, the South Australian Premier, was forced to resign, as was Graham Richardson, the Transport Minister. In 1994 Alan Griffiths, the Minister of Industry and Trade, resigned amid allegations of using public monies to finance his Melbourne sandwich shop, and the Western Australian former Premier Brian Burke got two years for fraud – and another three years for theft in 1997. His successor Ray O'Connor was sent down in February 1995 with eighteen months for theft.

Nor did an interesting South Australian imbroglio assist. Anxious to show sensitivity to Aboriginal concerns, Robert Tickner, in July 1994, without much enquiry, ordered cancellation of work on a road bridge to Hindmarsh Island, the construction of which, it was claimed, would interfere with a site sacred to Aboriginal women; since the nature of the women's beliefs was secret, an explanation could not be given. Hampered by this restraint, a Royal Commission, chaired by Judge Iris Stevens, nevertheless found that the Aboriginal ladies had 'fabricated' convenient secret religious beliefs; it was the stuff of which satire is made, and did nothing to advance Aboriginal causes, Tickner's credibility or Labor's appeal to cynical voters.

Even without the air of unreality that hung around the last months of the Labor government, it would have been uncommonly difficult for the coalition to lose an election when, after thirteen years in government, inflation and unemployment continued high and the deficit was reaching unprecedented proportions. Increasingly petulant and impatient, sometimes viciously so, Keating no longer seemed a reliable leader. Such once-modish cries as unrestricted immigration and Aboriginal rights had produced a backlash, and had combined with the Prime Minister's republican initiative to alienate many electors. One thoughtful observer believed that it was 'the social dislocation and insecurity being experienced by people and communities who were reeling from the impact of economic deregulation and restructuring' that led to the 'overwhelming defeat' of the Keating government in March 1996. To such the subfusc and sober figure of John Winston Howard looked safe in comparison. Very much of a contrast to Keating, and indeed to some extent to his successor as Labor leader, Kim Beazley, an Oxford graduate and former university lecturer, Howard was sober, self-controlled, a 'plain man' from a solid working-class background, whose father and grandfather both fought in the First World War, and whose four heroes were Menzies and Bradman, Churchill and Mountbatten. Looking back on his early years at a Sydney primary school, Howard said:

I am a strong believer that one of the best things that Australia has going for it – or used to have going for it, perhaps – is its egalitarian non-class structure. The fragmentation of that is one of the less happy developments in modern Australia. We are a less equal society . . . The distinguishing thing of my years at Earlwood Primary School was the feeling that everybody was about the same.[68]

Ammunition lay to hand. In the election campaign Howard was able to point out that under Labor, the bottom 10 per cent of the taxpayers had admittedly gained a real increase of $10 a week, but that the top 10 per cent had received $100, and the vast majority, the remaining 80 per cent had actually seen their real incomes decline; and the protections once given by central control and the closed shop had been replaced by the disciplines of the market. A target was thus clearly defined for the coalition, that of Middle Australia, the 'Battlers', as Howard called them.

The election campaign was fought in a haze of unreality, since both Keating and his Treasurer, Ralph Willis, insisted on basing all their plans on a budgeted surplus which all knew to be excessively optimistic, which enabled both parties to make promises of increased spending that they, and most commentators, knew to be impossible of fulfilment. Promises to attack welfare fraud and to restrict immigration were popular with the 'Battlers', who failed to respond to Keating's attempt to promote republican enthusiasm. It should have been easier for Keating to defeat Howard, not known as a good speaker, in the television debates, but the coalition leader was generally held to have obtained a draw. Labor was losing its traditional voters and a generalized dislike of Keating personally was completing the move to the right. On 2 March 1996 the coalition won by a landslide in the House of Representatives, the Liberals winning 75 seats of 148, an absolute majority in their own right, in addition to the 18 seats of their Nationalist partners; from 80 seats in the outgoing Parliament, Labor fell to 49. In the Senate, however, the change was minimal, one seat gained by the Liberals and one lost by Labor, leaving the balance of power with the Democrats and one Tasmanian Green, a factor which was to be a grave embarrassment to the first Howard administration. Keating immediately resigned the Labor leadership, replaced by Kim Beazley with Gareth Evans as deputy, so leaving two Oxford intellectuals running the party once headed by Curtin and Chifley. Something of the excitement vanished from Australian politics when Paul Keating left, but it might be that Australia would profit from a period of rather boring government. Events proved, however, far from tedious and the first administration headed by John Howard was fraught with difficulties.

15

The Coalition Strikes Back

John Howard succeeded to a generation of larger-than-life performers; for twenty-three years the central political figures – Whitlam, Fraser, Hawke and Keating – operated on the grand scale, stimulating bitter enmities and attracting devoted admirers. By contrast, Mr Howard might seem dull and insipid, not given to flamboyant obscenities or to striking impressive poses. Certainly President Clinton's visit in November 1996 gave a useful boost to the new administration, given Mr Clinton's mastery of both prepared and impromptu speeches; but the Prime Minister inevitably appeared flat and stolid by comparison.[1] As some compensation, Mr Howard possessed two valuable assets. In the first place he had a well-prepared economic agenda, begun since his first ministerial post in 1975 and refined during his six-year stint as Malcolm Fraser's Treasurer, but the new Prime Minister's chief strength lay in his feeling for the issues that were worrying the voters, which were not necessarily the same issues that engaged commentators. Two polls taken by the *Australian* in June 2001 and February 2003 consistently judged the most important issues (of seventeen choices) to be, by a considerable margin, education and health, with unemployment, the environment and other social concerns following; at the bottom of every poll was the subject of 'Aboriginal Issues' – and constitutional questions did not appear at all. So much, it might be said, for two of the major Labor initiatives; but both Aboriginal and constitutional problems were to be forced on government attention.

Back in power, after fourteen years in opposition, the coalition had a difficult start. The ministry was, with the exception of Howard, completely inexperienced in Federal administration, and their ineptitude showed. With stringent personal standards himself, and a blameless private life, the Prime Minister expected his colleagues to be similarly irreproachable; this, partly through lack of acquaintance with parliamentary conventions, and partly through excitement at finding themselves in the 'tart shop', did not happen. Within eighteen months no fewer than five ministers and two close advisers had been forced to resign, two Senators found themselves charged with fraud and one National Party MP was committed to trial for fraudulently claiming travel expenses.

Fortunately for the coalition, the dispirited opposition was in no condition to take advantage of these lapses – and were hardly without blame in such matters themselves. The greatest danger to the Howard government came from a putative ally, the Queensland MP Pauline Hanson, originally a Liberal candidate. When the coalition's grip on the state had been prised open on the fall of Joh Bjelke-Petersen and his corrupt associates, and temporarily replaced in 1989 by a Labor government, many rural Queenslanders felt exposed to the cold winds of change. The state, covering an area somewhat greater than that of Germany, France, Spain and Great Britain combined, had a population equivalent to that of Hampshire and Sussex, and nearly half of that – 3 million plus – lived in and around Brisbane. From Cairns in the north to Mount Isa in the west, the scattered population, traditionally Nationalist, looked around for some new advocate.

In so male-dominated a society Pauline Hanson, a fish-and-chip-shop proprietor, member for the suburban constituency of Oxley, was an unlikely saviour, but she leapt into prominence with her maiden speech in which she inveighed against taxpayers' dollars being spent on Aborigines and the 'brown tide' of Asian immigration.[2] In so doing she gave a new voice to an old fear, that of Alfred Deakin, concerned that industrious and intelligent Chinese might compete only too effectively with well-paid Australian workers. Geoffrey Blainey, the distinguished historian, had raised a storm of not-too-intelligent controversy in 1984 when he had questioned the pace of Asian immigration, but in reality Australians had demonstrated their capacity for amicable tolerance in absorbing the immigrants – and profited greatly thereby, as a visit to Sydney's fish market or Melbourne's Victoria Market can prove. Mrs Hanson's views were welcomed, it appeared, by Prime Minister Howard, who subsequently told the Queensland Liberals that the coalition's election would release Australia from the grip of political correctness and 'enable them to speak a little more freely and openly about what they feel'.

Australian opinion was exposed as being deeply divided. On the one hand were those often disparagingly dismissed as the 'chardonnay socialists' – most of the professionals and urban middle-class, who were conscious of the damage the White Australia policies had done to Australia's international reputation, and the peril that any resurgence would present to Australia's relations with its Asian neighbours – and on the other, a fair proportion of

Howard's 'Battlers' – farmers and industrial workers. These last had some reason to feel threatened, since some three-quarters of a million Asians had by then arrived, and were proving their worth, advancing in their careers, and it seemed, almost monopolizing the best places in education. Such immigrants were, even if still a modest proportion of the general population, capable of exerting an economic influence well beyond their actual numbers. Asians, for the most part quiet and well conducted, were not personally resented, but other immigrants, particularly Lebanese, were seen as potentially threatening, and with some reason.[3]

Mrs Hanson's other target was what she saw as the divisive policies pursued in response to Aboriginal claims, and in particular a claim by activists that Aborigines constituted a separate nation, distinct from that of 'settler' Australia, symbolized by the invention of an Aboriginal flag, with the corollary that a 'treaty' could be negotiated as between two sovereign states. The name of her new party, 'One Nation', founded in April 1997, specifically challenged that assumption and has led, although the party itself has disintegrated, to some heated debate. The difficulties, not to say dangers, of such a concept might be shown by looking at South Africa, where the Coloureds, concentrated in the Cape, who incorporated the original Khoisan inhabitants, with their own traditions, could make the same assertion of nationality. So, with only a little stretching of credulity, might some Afrikaners, who could claim precedence over blacks in the same area in point of time, and who do in fact argue for separate recognition, as do Natal Zulus; but the success of any of these groups would be disastrous for the 'Rainbow Nation'. Many Aboriginal activists might find the comparisons uncomfortable, but it is not unreasonable. Backed by some logic, and much resentment, Hanson's initial success was worryingly rapid. Within two months One Nation had won 11 seats in the single-chamber Queensland Parliament and something like 25 per cent popular support in the state. Given the precarious balance of power within the State Legislature – in 1996 Labor and the coalition both held 44 seats, with a single independent – One Nation's success threatened that Queensland might once again embrace an eccentric administration of the sort which, it was hoped, had ended with the downfall of Sir Joh. The Queensland National Party, encouraged by Howard's reluctance to interfere, decided to back One Nation, calling for Aboriginal benefits to be cut, for restrictive gun laws to be modified, and for opposition to any Liberal policy which might afford a target for One Nation.

One Nation never attracted the same level of support in other states, but discontent on official approaches to Aboriginal complaints was widespread.

Since Whitlam's original initiative, more than 5,000 indigenous organizations had been founded, nearly all holding either title to land or benefiting from government grants to provide services to Aboriginal Australians. The opportunities for winning influence or making money were considerable. Land judged to be subject to Aboriginal title might be sold for the profit of the holders; the number of those claiming to be Aboriginal, many perhaps, like Colin Johnson, on uncertain grounds, soared from 283,000 in 1991 to 469,000 ten years later; the Aboriginal populations of Tasmania and of Queensland nearly doubled in the same period. With such a proliferation of groups, not fitting into local or state structures, control is next to impossible, and every revelation of mismanagement or worse, mostly petty enough, was seized on eagerly by those grudging 'special treatment' for Aborigines.

Fuelling this discontent was another High Court judgement, passed in December 1996, in the 'Wik case'. Whereas the Mabo judgement had indicated that native title could be legally extinguished by a Crown grant of land, whether freehold or leasehold, in the Wik judgement the High Court decided by a vote of 4 to 3 that a leasehold grant did *not* necessarily extinguish native title, and that the two rights could exist simultaneously. The claims made by the Wik and Thayorre people to two northern Queensland properties were characterized by special circumstances in that the properties were so extensive and badly managed – one without fences or buildings, with little contact existing between the Aborigines and the few stockmen that were to be found – but the precedent established led to an avalanche of others as some groups laid claim to pastoral properties all over Australia. In Western Australia one property faced 14 separate claims, and in Queensland a single claim targeted some 3,000 leases. Altogether, some 70 per cent of the land mass was suddenly placed in contention. It was no longer possible, as Nugget Coombs had suggested after the Mabo judgement, to have a moratorium for reflection.[4] In such a situation only speedy and well-judged legislation could provide clarity and security, and this was not forthcoming.

The Prime Minister had made his sympathy with those who protested against Aboriginal claims so clear that the Governor General, Sir William Deane, an international lawyer and High Court Judge, was moved to speak for constructive action in what he termed 'the most important problem facing Australia' – discrimination against Aborigines. Inflaming the situation was the controversy over the 'stolen generation', the practice justified in 1980 by Sir Paul Hasluck of removing, sometimes forcibly, part-Aboriginal children from their parents (see p. 491 above).

The report of the National Inquiry into the Separation of Indigenous

Children from Their Families, *Bringing them Home*, written by Sir Ronald Wilson and Mick Dodson and issued in May 1997 by the Human Rights and Equal Opportunities Commission (HREOC), was not without flaws. Australian Royal Commissions do not resemble their British prototypes. In Britain they are composed of a group selected from 'the good and the great', unpaid, prepared to spend sometimes many years on investigations, writing their own terms of reference, supported by a team of civil servants, with (theoretically) unlimited funds and power to command the attendance of witnesses, while Australian Royal Commissions are commonly entrusted to a single judge. Sir Ronald was not only Chairman of the HREOC but an official of the Presbyterian Church, and Mr Dodson a prominent Aboriginal activist; it would be asking much to expect them to set aside previous convictions in the interests of impartiality. It proved indeed too much to ask, and a later inquiry by Mr Justice Loughlin found grounds for criticism. The HREOC's statement that 'most, if not all of the mixed race children in the [Northern] Territory' had been placed in missions, was untrue – 'the evidence did not support an argument that there was a large scale policy of forced removals'. More importantly, there were instances of maltreatment and abuse in Aboriginal families which would have justified children being removed, and the consequences of failing so to do would doubtless have aroused much indignation. Most of the cases investigated were from the mixed descent communities in the southern states rather from those in the north where Aboriginal customs and traditions prevailed. In those areas it would have been often accurate to claim that many children were 'rescued' rather than 'stolen'; a later investigation, published in December 1999, concluded that 'The degree of violence and destruction in Aboriginal and Torres Strait Islander communities cannot be adequately described ... Appalling acts of physical brutality and sexual violence are being perpetrated within some families and across communities to a degree previously unknown in indigenous life. Sadly, many of the victims are women and children.' The consequences of not intervening in such circumstances are such that no responsible government could well contemplate, but it was stretching the evidence to conclude that the mixed-race children removed from their families had been subjected to such treatment. Yet, when all qualifications are made, what might be called the 'large truth' was right. The assumption that part-Aboriginal children in difficult circumstances were better removed into institutions or foster-homes where they could be brought up to share the habits of white Australians, and that the parent – usually singular – might not be allowed much say in the matter, was unacceptably authoritarian, to say nothing of being blandly racist.[5]

The report went well beyond the child-removal question, to all aspects of Aboriginal (or Indigenous, which was becoming an accepted alternative, following the French *indigène*, popular among readers of Frantz Fanon) life. Accusations of 'genocide' were hurled around (somewhat oddly in view of the great increase in the Aboriginal population); at the Adelaide Writers Week scriptwriter Bob Ellis compared Australian settlement with the Nazi Holocaust. 'Aboriginal Children were put on trains taking them away from their families and there were thousands of deaths through massacres, the desperate drunkenness of parents and the despairing suicides of children.' Quite rightly, the historian Inga Clendinnen dismissed such talk as 'besmirching the language', but, as inevitable, truth became the first casualty of hysteria, and the real problems of the Aboriginal communities within Australia were only partly and partially addressed.

Responses to the report were received from all states, as well as from the Commonwealth government. All administrations expressed sympathy, and pledged themselves to future good behaviour, but refused to consider establishing a compensation fund. Once again, public opinion was divided. Seizing upon a semantic point, the Aboriginal Affairs Minister, Senator John Herron denied that there had ever been a 'stolen generation' and claimed that the policy was 'essentially lawful and benign in intent'. Understandably incensed, the Aboriginal and Torres Strait Islanders Commission's deputy chairman, veteran activist Charles Perkins, claimed: 'Reconciliation is finished now . . . we are now facing major confrontation between black and white in this country.' Mick Dodson, co-author of the report, pointed out that it was not 'some mathematical formula you're talking about . . . It needs only one kid in twenty to be taken for the family to be affected. Not everyone in the generation that went through the war went to war, but every Australian was affected by that.'[6] At a time when sensitivity and generosity were called for, qualities which Malcolm Fraser, for example, would have been very capable of displaying, the Howard government's response seemed, and so continues, to be poor-spirited and mean.

Although unable to find the words which might have gone some way to healing wounds, the government made serious efforts to settle the land issue, proposing a substantial Bill after the Wik judgement (which ran to nearly 300 pages) that would have clarified the situation, at the cost of establishing the priority of pastoral leases over Native Title claims, a condition insisted on by mutinous Nationalists. Although the House of Representatives passed the Bill in October 1997, against predictable Labor opposition, and with some National Party members also opposing, for very opposite reasons, public opinion was split. Most large businesses, including the mining corporations, backed the Bill, while Aboriginal interests were vociferously opposed to it, encouraged by many Churches, and some lawyers aware that the Bill might infringe the Racial Discrimination Act.

It was for the Senate to decide, and with the numbers of coalition members exactly balanced by Labor and Democrats, the decision lay with the Independent, Brian Harradine of Tasmania. Senator Harradine, elected by some 22,000 first preference votes could hardly claim much authority to speak for nearly 20 million Australian people, but he was able to force many changes in the legislation passed by a lower house with an authoritative majority; it was the House of Lords pre-1911 writ large. Not that Senator Harradine's objections were in any way frivolous, or anything but principled and reflecting a considerable body of opinion, but Howard found himself caught between Hanson and Harradine; and the 'stolen generation' was inflaming opinion.

The Wik Bill was, with Harradine's vote, rejected by the Senate, and reintroduced in March 1998. After much discussion and many amendments, which left both Queensland Nationalist and Aboriginal leaders unhappy, the Senate passed an amended Bill which was immediately rejected in the lower house. The remedy of a double dissolution was attractive to nobody, with the possibility that One Nation might take as many as 12 Senate seats. Faced with such a prospect, Senator Harradine consented to a Bill which the government judged reasonable. As things turned out, One Nation did less well than its opponents had feared, but the legal situation remained fraught with uncertainty, and Mr Howard's personal standing with the liberals and Aboriginal activists was severely damaged.

Any attempt to repair that essential flaw in the constitution, the relative strengths of Assembly and Senate, was pushed aside by the republican debate originally initiated by Paul Keating. In February 1998 a formal Constitutional Convention met to debate the possible adoption of a republican system. Over two weeks the arguments developed, not so much over whether there should be a republic or not, but what form it should take. From the beginning, 'monarchists' – a misleading description for those conservatives who believed 'if it ain't broke, don't fix it' rather than fervent supporters of the House of Windsor – were outnumbered. A strong body of opinion favoured a full-blown presidential system, as in the United States or France, but in the end it was – by 75 to 71 votes – the minimalists who prevailed. The recommended system was one where a nominee, agreed upon by the Prime Minister and the leader of the opposition, after taking advice from a worthy committee, would be appointed by a two-thirds majority of both houses, who would have no option but to accept or reject, acceptance having presumably been previously agreed in the Canberra corridors. It was not a system calculated to stimulate public enthusiasm, nor did it. An Australian President so elected would be as unrecognizable to the rest of the world as any Governor General; who outside Germany for example, even knows the name of the President of that great country?[7] Since Bill Slim and Lord De L'Isle (both VCs, as it happened), Governors General had been either retired politicians or distinguished lawyers, distinguished in their fields but unlikely to attract international fame – nor did the appointment of an Anglican archbishop in 2001, followed two years later by another senior soldier, bring an outstanding name to act as Australia's Head of State.[8] Elizabeth Alexandra Mary Windsor, on the other hand, is Queen of five nations and a number of territories ranging between the coasts of France and the South Pole, which between them cover most of two continents and a major part of a third. She is also Supreme Governor of the Church of England and Head of a Commonwealth which includes a quarter of the world's population, and while in constitutional terms an abstraction personally commands widespread respect. There are advantages in having such a figure as a formal head of state, if the Crown's national representative has appropriate qualities.[9]

As Ian Ward of the University of Queensland observed: 'oddly, the convention marked the end rather than the beginning of the debate. When a referendum was finally held, on November 6th 1999, the result was, as expected, a negative: 55% voted to retain the existing system, fortified by their distrust of politicians.'[10] In spite of the almost unanimous support of the press – the Murdoch newspapers in Britain as well as Australia were suspiciously of one mind – republican enthusiasm was manifested more by the urban middle classes than by country folk and those on lower incomes; indeed, 'so uneven and biased was the media coverage' that Mr Justice Michael Kirby, a serving High Court judge and scholarly observer, believed that it 'became part of the problem' for republican advocates.[11] Some comic relief was given by the Prime Minister's decision that he would personally draft a preamble to a new constitution which could be incorporated in any legislation. Mr Howard was keen to include the principle of 'mateship', a suggestion criticized both for the obvious reason and because the idea perpetuated the peripheral status of women and excluded the Aboriginal population. Whether Aborigines would be recognized as the earliest 'inhabitants' – Howard's version – 'custodians' – preferred by Gareth Evans – or 'owners' – a suggestion of the writer David Malouf – was a contentious subject. On Labor's behalf Kim Beazley offered to accept 'mateship' if the Prime Minister would include 'custodianship'. Nationalists, in Queensland the Federal party, worried that any such reference would encourage land claims, and campaigned with the cry: 'Safe Way to Go, vote NO NO.'

So the electorate decided, for the constitutional preamble was rejected even more firmly that the minimalist republic, by 60.66 per cent to 39.34 per cent. Constitutionally, such a debate was not only irrelevant, but shifted attention from more important matters. Professor Kenneth Wiltshire pertinently observed:

As to the problems of the future which the Australian system of government will have to face, very few of them directly relate to the issue of republic versus monarchy. There is no reason to suppose that the reform of parliament, role of the Upper House, a more efficient federal system, clearer accountability, less politicalisation of the public services &c. would necessarily be better addressed under a republican form of government . . . but . . . slightly more messy to achieve whilst retaining a constitutional monarchy.[12]

The defeat of the referendum signified, if not quite the end, at least the postponement of the debate even though the *Sydney Morning Herald* (7 November 1999) announced that

The people have spoken. Now be prepared for the debate over exactly what they mean. Expect both sides to claim a moral victory. But don't be fooled by any of that. Last night's historic result represents a massive setback for the cause of republicanism. It really was time. And it is hard to see when it will be time again . . . Australia's elite . . . were roundly rejected in so many parts of the country, it is hard to see how they can recover. Worse, they were routed by a Coalition of battlers, supported by a Dad's Army, and a monarch living 17,000 kilometers away.

If agreement could be reached on the form a republic might take, many, probably indeed most, Australians might prefer a republican rule. If so, a structured argument would need to be advanced, but for the time being the steam has indeed gone out of the issue.

It was a stroke of luck for the Prime Minister, faced with attacks from many different quarters, that Sydney had been chosen as the site for the millennial Olympics. The organization was highly praised, in contrast to the poor administration of the previous Games in Atlanta, and Australian athletes were successful; the sight of the Aboriginal runner Cathy Freeman first lighting the Olympic cauldron and then winning the 400-metre event in spectacular fashion did more to discredit the rednecks of One Nation than any intellectual protest. Even although much of the credit was due to the New South Wales government, and the Games, to the Prime Minister's chagrin, were opened by the Governor General, the Coalition government enjoyed the reflected glory as Australia's reputation flourished.

Mr Howard's economic skills and power of political compromise were demonstrated in other fields. In July 2000 that long-discussed measure, a General Sales Tax (GST), was introduced. Essentially a levy on most non-food products, this was combined with tax concessions designed to produce, for most, a neutral effect. Accompanying the introduction of the new taxation was an overhaul of the financial relations between the Commonwealth and state governments, accepted by all states, including those with Labor administrations. Once again, the Senate Democrats and Brian Harradine had insisted on amendments to the Government's proposals, and a bundle of 'pork barrel' concessions to be introduced in the budget. With the Senate amendments included, it appeared that the greatest beneficiaries of the new measures would be low-income single-parent families, while self-funded retirees and dual-income couples with no children would gain least. For the Coalition, the Act had the added merit that the Federal Labor Party pledged itself to abolish GST, an albatross from which disengagement was bound to be difficult. By the spring of 2000 the public telecommunications network Telstra had been partly privatized, a massive increase in private healthcare had been made, a work-for-welfare scheme introduced and the closed shop's entrenchment much restricted. In March 2000 it could well be claimed that 'Every idea and policy John Howard has ever had, every promise he has ever made, has been delivered'.[13] And on the whole accepted by the voters; it did not take long for Labor to water down its commitment to abolishing GST merely on women's sanitary products and mobile homes.

On the other vexed question, that of immigration, Coalition governments moved cautiously. Family members would be allowed in only if financial guarantees were provided, and priority given to those with skills in such areas as information technology, nursing and, surprisingly, accountancy. Asylum seekers not judged suitable would be repatriated, forcibly if necessary and it was asylum seekers that won the next election for the coalition.

Professor Wiltshire might have added to his list of constitutional alterations profoundly to be desired some alteration in the disturbingly short intervals between elections. With the necessity to placate opposition in the Senate, which can lead to a dissolution even when a majority in the House of Representatives is retained, the frequency of general elections means that an Australian government is rarely out of election mode and able to construct policies without having to bow to short-term pressures. The widespread collapse in the Asian economies that began in 1997 initially spared Australia, but by the beginning of 2001 prospects were looking bleaker. Unemployment increased, investment declined, and the Australian dollar fell to an unprecedented 50 per cent of the US dollar. Even after a generous tax reward to pensioners, plus some backtracking on the duty levied on beer sold in bars (a concession reluctantly granted when, after the most successful protest ever made in Australia, one which attracted over 850,000 signatures, the government backed down, giving the revenue already collected to charity). By-elections went badly and One Nation continued to threaten. It was the events in August 2001 that saved the Howard Government. Some 500 refugees, mostly Afghan, but having embarked from Indonesia and making for Australia, were rescued by the master of a Norwegian merchantman, the *Tampa*. The ship's master, following the ancient custom of the sea, then made for the nearest port, Christmas Island. This isolated Indian Ocean peak had officially been Australian territory since Menzies had, for largely imaginary strategic reasons, lobbied for it to be transferred from Singaporian jurisdiction in 1957. In spite of proclaiming Australia's 'humanitarian obligations as a warm-hearted, decent international citizen', Howard declined to allow the refugees to land. Even after the captain appealed for emergency medical help the government refused to respond, eventually sending an SAS squad to seize the ship. Although both harsh and illegal, and bitterly criticized both at home, even by his predecessors as Liberal leader John Hewson and Malcolm Fraser, and abroad, Mr Howard's actions accurately judged the mood of his electors. A Border Protection Bill, only feebly opposed by Labor, was rushed through Parliament, and the search for a suitable refugee dumping ground begun in earnest. There was to be a 'Pacific Solution' to the refugee problem; some impoverished island would be bribed to take the undesirables. After many rejections the government of Nauru showed willing. Ruined by decades of phosphate mining, precipitated into independence with a population of some 11,000 under an incompetent and corrupt administration, Nauru was paid generously to accept the miserable Afghans, well away from intrusive television cameras. Chris Sidoti, the Australian Human Rights Ombudsman between 1995 and 2000, characterized the 'Pacific Solution' as 'the apprehension and forcible removal of people across national boundaries for profit. Desperate people are being dumped in desperately poor island states . . . paid bribes to accept people Australia does not want'.[14]

It was altogether a shameful episode, but what followed was worse. In October 2001 a boatload of Iraqi refugees was rescued by HMAS *Adelaide*. Peter Reith, the agitated Minister of Defence, insisted that the desperate survivors had demonstrated their barbarity by throwing children into the water: 'It is an absolute fact . . . If you don't accept that, you don't accept anything.' When this claim was contradicted by *Adelaide*'s officers, Reith, already in trouble for having allowed his son to spend $50,000 of public money on personal telephone calls, eventually resigned.

Perhaps the most distressing result was that some 80 per cent of the public appeared to approve the Howard government's measures; the White Australia policy was reviving. Certainly in 1999–2000, 47 per cent of new arrivals were European – including New Zealanders – and another 7 per cent were from the Commonwealth. Nor were refugees exactly pressing in on Australia; in the same year there were 5,870 'unauthorized' arrivals, immediately despatched to serve long periods in bleak and distant detention centres, judged by the United Nations to be the worst of any inspected (an attempt was made to prevent Mary Robinson, the UN Commissioner for Human Rights, from visiting the camps). Britain, by contrast, with more than 100,000 'unauthorized' arrivals, had in March 2000 only 1,000 held in detention.[15]

Defying criticism from the international press, the Government persisted, causing an aggrieved Hanson to complain that the coalition had stolen One Nation's policies. There was, however, merit in an appeal to 'fair goes'. If a hundred thousand or so immigrants were legally accepted every year, then the six thousand unauthorised entrants could be seen to be 'jumping the queue'. Mrs Hanson's case was strengthened by the government's refusal to interfere with the Northern Territory's policy of mandatory imprisonment on conviction for a third crime, even when the offence was minimal, a decision seen to target Aboriginal offenders and much criticized by all liberal opinion, including that of the Australian judiciary. Since a chorus of disapproval was also generated abroad, however, especially in the United Nations, and that from countries whose own record in such matters was deplorable, many Australians sided with the government. Immigration, which in June had been regarded as very important by only 30 per cent of those questioned in the *Australian*'s poll, worried 50 per cent of respondents in September.

Assisted by improving economic circumstances an election win for the government was practically guaranteed by the horrors of 11 September in New York, and on 10 November 2001 what might be described as a 'Khaki election' confirmed the coalition's control of the lower house, with 81 seats to Labor's 65. Once again the 8 Democrats and 2 Greens in the Senate held the balance of power, exposing the constitutional conflict between a representative lower house and a Federal Senate. Somewhat strangely, Canadian Senators (still appointed for life until 1981, when a retirement age of 75 – scarcely a revolutionary change – was introduced) were less disruptive. An unspoken self-denying policy inhibited the Canadian Senate from interfering with the Commons legislation, a practice only interrupted in 1991 when an abortion Bill was refused, but Australian Senators, driven as they were by their own electoral necessities, continue to obstruct and amend policies agreed in the House of Representatives.[16]

Kim Beazley resigned the Labor leadership after the electoral defeat, replaced by Simon Crean, son of the former Labor minister, who failed to impress voters, but who bravely committed himself to reducing the influence of the unions within the Labor Party; if the Coalition could be accused of stealing One Nation's clothes, Labor was continuing Paul Keating's policy of appropriating Liberal garments. With the potent support of Gough Whitlam, Bob Hawke and Kim Beazley behind the new leader, the Labor Party agreed to dilute union influence in the National Conference and to move to a policy of affirmative action, aimed at bringing more women – at least 40 per cent by 2012 – into winnable seats. That action was taken on 5 October and the dangers of such a move were speedily demonstrated at a by-election on the 19th at Wollongong, considered a safe Labor seat. Angered at having a woman forced on them by headquarters, local left-wingers supported an independent candidate; although Shirley Bird, the official nominee, won 38 per cent of the popular vote, it was not enough to stop the Green Party representative coming second and then, by collecting the preference votes from Liberals and disgruntled Labor supporters, win what should have been an impossible victory. Old Labor had signalled that not too many liberties could be taken with traditional customs. What might be called the 'tough' and 'tender' rather than left and right of the Labor Party also clashed over the asylum-seekers issue, and when the party conference did not go far enough in opposing the government on this issue one shadow minister, Carmen Lawrence, resigned, complaining that Labor was becoming 'increasingly conservative [and] timid'. Correctly interpreting the evidence a new leader, Mark Latham, was elected, who united most of the party behind a populist programme, tough on immigration and with no mention at all of Aboriginal policies.[17]

In spite of escalating criticism, foreign or domestic, it seemed that Australians were content with their undramatic, rather dull and uncharismatic leader. There was no questioning the country's economic success under the continuous supervision of Treasurer Peter Costello, playing Keating to Howard's Hawke (although how far economic progress can be attributed to ministerial measures is another question). In 2003 the international credit-rating agency Standard & Poor advanced Australian government securities to their highest AAA rating; the economy continued to grow at an average of 4 per cent over the previous ten years, well above the average for all major economies; after the previous flurry in 2001 the dollar strengthened substantially against the US currency and labour productivity increased steadily, and faster than that of the United States.

John Howard retained the oversight of Foreign Affairs to himself (the title was changed to Foreign Minister from that of Minister for Foreign Affairs in 1993), with former rival Alexander Downer in departmental charge, kept on the shortest of leashes. The Prime Minister struck his own attitudes on foreign policy issues, sometime visibly against the opinions of departmental officials and Downer himself. Attempts at mending fences with Indonesia fell foul of Indonesian resentment and suspicions that West Irian might follow East Timor, in spite of Australian reiteration of recognition of Indonesian sovereignty over that miserable region. Relations with ASEAN continued uneasy, as the non-white Asian communities showed little sign of moving towards recognition of Australia as properly Asian.

More important to John Howard was the relationship with the United States under the new George W. Bush administration. Having endorsed the Bush candidature, Howard welcomed the announcement by the incoming Secretary of State, Colin Powell, that Washington would 'look to Australia for leadership and guidance' on Indonesian policy. The quid pro quo, it was hoped, would be the long-sought-after bilateral trade agreement. Often promised, that particular boon only materialized, in a very diluted form, early in 2004, to widespread criticism; ironically the biggest bilateral deal ever reached by Australia was with China, $25,000 million for the supply of liquid natural gas over twenty-five years, agreed in August 2003.

All was changed and a new era of Australian foreign policy begun by the terrorist bombing in Bali on 12 October 2002 in which 88 young Australians were killed by an Islamist faction associated with Al-Qaeda. Britain had long suffered from terrorist attacks, and America was still in shock after the previous year's tragedy, but this was the first time in half a century that Australian civilians had been torn apart by bombs; the 'profound sense of shock', historian Meg Gurry wrote 'is difficult to overstate'.[18] The prompt arrest and trial of the bombers by the Indonesian authorities, and the sympathy of many Indonesians, helped to restore mutual goodwill; the fundamentalists were threatening the Indonesian government as well as Australians abroad. One indication of possible future cooperation was the formation of a new group, the South West Pacific Dialogue, by which the foreign ministers of Australia, Indonesia, the Philippines, New Zealand, East Timor and Papua New Guinea agreed to meet regularly. ASEAN leaders, however, angrily spurned Australia's new policy of unilateral anti-terrorist measures which, the Prime Minister warned, might include pre-emptive strikes in third countries. It seemed that Australian efforts to be accepted by other Asian countries were floundering; but maintaining reasonable relations with the three most important states, Indonesia, Japan and China, was much more important to the country's security and prosperity.

Events in 2003 seemed to confirm that Australia was reverting to older, Menzian values. The government rushed to support the Anglo-American invasion of Iraq, over the protests of numerous Australians (although opposition was somewhat modified after the disgusting character of the Ba'athist regime was made apparent). An impressive memorial to Australian war dead in London's Hyde Park was dedicated by the Queen and Mr Howard. General Sir Michael Jeffery, a former SAS officer (and a Commander of the Royal Victorian Order, a decoration in the personal gift of the Queen), was appointed in August 2003 to succeed Archbishop Peter Hollingworth as Governor General, the first professional soldier to hold the post since Viscount De L'Isle forty years previously. At the remembrance service for the Bali victims, Mr Howard, in tears, joined in the singing, not of the national anthem, 'Advance Australia Fair', but of 'Waltzing Matilda', instinctively chosen as the true expression of national identity.

But unquestionably the great Australian event was the Rugby Union World Cup, held in the capital cities, with the final in Sydney. Although Rugby Union is not the national winter game to the same extent that cricket dominates the summer season, it is the only truly international team game in which Australia participates at the highest level. Soccer has never developed a great following there, and cricket is confined to Commonwealth countries, but rugby offers the opportunity for the stars of the northern hemisphere, England and France, to meet the southern giants, the Australian Wallabies, New Zealand All Blacks and South African Springboks – and teams from the United States, Ireland, Fiji, Italy and Japan help to give a cosmopolitan touch. When it became clear that the final was to be between England and Australia emotions soared and during the match two nations held their breath before, in the last minutes, the game went to England. Had any other country been opposed, Australian enthusiasm would not have been so great; England was the one to beat – and besides, it was time the Pommies won something.

And Then?

In spite of the real and very great advantages enjoyed by Australians a sense of discontent persists, as noticed in the introduction to this book. I end, with some daring, in suggesting reasons and advancing possible remedies. Geographical facts are unyielding. In 1840 the cultivated, humorous and very European Charles La Trobe, Superintendent of the little Port Phillip community, regretted that, in spite of the natural beauties of the place, he could never see a building older than 1834. Something of the same deprivation continues: five hours' motoring from our home in France would bring one to Paris, Spain, the Loire châteaux, the Alps, the Mediterranean and the Atlantic coasts; the free shows available in London include all the national museums, changing the guard at Buckingham Palace and evensong in Westminster Abbey; the comparison hardly needs to be laboured. Making all allowances for the great pleasures of Australian life, anyone formed in a European tradition, as most Australians are, undergoes a sort of spiritual isolation (although they may well be happily unconscious of this) which goes some way to explain why so many talented Australians make their careers in the Old World. And why, on the other hand, Australia sits uneasily near Asian countries of different cultures.

No initiatives are likely to alter this aspect of the tyranny of distance. But all things change, and today change very rapidly as improved communications shrink global distances and as the world becomes blander and more homogenous – although this American-inspired transition provokes violent reactions (the Bali bombings illustrating both points).

Much, on the other hand, can be done to straighten out the convolutions of government. It is not just that there is an overwhelming mass of government machinery – Federal and state elections or referendums being near-annual events, in which participation is enforced, enlivened by the occasional royal commission or judicial inquiry – but that it can be brought to a halt by one or two individuals; what might be termed the Harradine effect. To governments preoccupied by the next election, subject to constant media quests for a juicy story, and therefore anxiously seeking a quick fix, studied decisions become quite extraordinarily difficult. Those serious discussions that have developed have focused on the wrong subjects. To attain a republic, within the conventions of responsible government, solves none of the entrenched constitutional problems; proliferating near-independent Aboriginal bodies does little to heal resentment (indeed, often the opposite) or to improve the still-miserable condition of too many Aborigines.

What is instead demanded is a careful study which can propose action on all these fronts. Lacking as it would simple slogans and therefore electoral appeal this is unlikely to come from government or opposition, but Australia has an ample supply of retired politicians of all parties (Fraser, Whitlam, Hawke, or Beazley come to mind), Governors General and lawyers. Such a combination of talents – which must surely include one or two Aborigines – could prepare a Green Paper, the preliminary discussion document. Among the subjects covered should be the frequency of elections, the relations of Commonwealth and states, the powers and composition of the Senate, the future of responsible government, a possible republic and the multifarious Aboriginal organizations. One of the recommendations would surely be the integration of these last into a democratic and accountable system of local government, a proposal first made by the invaluable Nugget Coombs.

Ten years elapsed between the first stir of Federation proposals and the inauguration of the Commonwealth. In the end it was the Australian people themselves – let us take the inevitable reservations about Aborigines and women as read; if imperfect the debate itself was national and popular – who decided what sort of country they wanted. Today an effort on the same scale is needed, if Australians are to reconstruct a Commonwealth, Republic or what you will that may ensure another prosperous and perhaps more equitable century for this extraordinary continental nation.

Appendix:
Australian and British Rulers

GOVERNORS OF NEW SOUTH WALES

1788–1792	Captain Arthur Phillip
1795–1800	Captain John Hunter
1800–1806	Captain Philip King
1806–1808	Captain William Bligh
1810–1821	Major-General Lachlan Macquarie
1821–1825	Major-General Sir Thomas Brisbane
1825–1831	Lieutenant-General Ralph Darling
1831–1837	Major-General Sir Richard Bourke
1838–1846	Sir George Gipps
1846–1855	Sir Charles FitzRoy
1855–1861	Sir William Denison
1861–1867	Sir John Young
1868–1872	Somerset Lowry-Corry, 4th Earl Belmore
1872–1879	Sir Hercules Robinson
1879–1885	Lord Augustus Loftus
1885–1890	Charles Wynn-Carington, 3rd Baron Carrington
1891–1893	Victor Albert George Child-Villiers, 7th Earl of Jersey
1893–1895	Sir Robert Duff
1895–1899	Henry Robert Brand, 2nd Viscount Hampden
1899–1901	William Lygon, 7th Earl Beauchamp

GOVERNORS OF QUEENSLAND

1859–1868	Sir George Bowen
1868–1871	Colonel Sir Samuel Blackall
1871–1874	George Augustus Constantine Phipps, 2nd Marquess of Normanby
1875–1877	William Cairns
1877–1883	Sir Arthur Kennedy
1883–1889	Sir Anthony Musgrave
1889–1895	General Sir Henry Norman
1896–1901	Charles Baillie, 2nd Baron Lamington

GOVERNORS OF SOUTH AUSTRALIA

1836–1838   Captain John Hindmarsh
1841–1845   Captain George Grey
1845–1848   Lieutenant-Colonel Frederick Robe
1848–1855   Sir Henry Fox Young
1855–1862   Sir Richard Macdonnell
1862–1868   Sir Dominick Daly
1869–1873   Sir James Fergusson
1873–1877   Sir Anthony Musgrave
1877–1883   Sir William Jervois
1883–1889   Sir William Robinson
1889–1895   Algernon Keith-Falconer, 9th Earl of Kintore
1895–1899   Sir Thomas Buxton
1899–1902   Hallam Tennyson, 2nd Baron Tennyson

GOVERNORS OF TASMANIA

1804–1810   Colonel David Collins*
1813–1817   Colonel Thomas Davey*
1817–1824   Colonel William Sorell*
1824–1836   Colonel George Arthur*
1837–1843   Captain Sir John Franklin*
1843–1846   Sir John Eardley-Wilmot*
1847–1855   Sir William Denison*
1855–1861   Sir Henry Young
1862–1868   Colonel Thomas Browne
1868–1874   Charles Du Cane
1875–1880   Frederick Weld
1881–1886   Major Sir George Strahan
1887–1892   Sir Robert Hamilton
1893–1900   Jenico Preston, 14th Viscount Gormanston
1901–1904   Captain Sir Arthur Havelock

*Lieutenant-Governors

GOVERNORS OF VICTORIA

1851–1854   Charles La Trobe*
1854–1855   Captain Sir Charles Hotham*
1855   Captain Sir Charles Hotham
1856–1863   Sir Henry Barkly

1863–1866	Sir Charles Darling
1866–1873	Sir John Manners-Sutton
1873–1879	Sir George Bowen
1879–1884	George Phipps, Marquess of Normanby
1884–1889	Sir Henry Loch
1889–1895	John Hope, 7th Earl of Hopetoun
1895–1900	Thomas Brassey, 1st Baron Brassey
1901–1903	Sir George Clarke

*Lieutenant-Governors

GOVERNORS OF WESTERN AUSTRALIA

1828–1832	Captain James Stirling*
1832–1839	Captain James Stirling
1839–1846	John Hutt
1846–1847	Lieutenant-Colonel Andrew Clarke
1847–1848	Lieutenant-Colonel Frederick Irwin
1848–1855	Captain Charles Fitzgerald
1855–1862	Arthur Kennedy
1862–1868	John Hampton
1869–1875	Frederick Weld
1875–1877	William Robinson
1878–1880	Major-General Sir Harry Ord
1880–1883	Sir William Robinson
1883–1889	Sir Frederick Broome
1890–1895	Sir William Robinson
1895–1900	Lieutenant-Colonel Sir Gerard Smith
1901–1902	Captain Sir Arthur Lawley

*Lieutenant-Governor

GOVERNORS GENERAL OF AUSTRALIA

1901–1902	The Earl of Hopetoun
1902–1904	Lord Tennyson
1904–1908	Lord Northcote
1908–1911	The Earl of Dudley
1911	Lord Denman
1911–1920	Sir R. C. Munro-Fergus (Earl Novar)
1920–1925	Lord Forster
1925–1930	Lord Stonehaven
1930–1931	Lord Somers

1931–1936	Sir I. A. Isaacs
1936–1945	Earl Gowrie
1945–1949	The Duke of Gloucester
1949–1953	Sir W. J. McKell
1953–1960	Viscount Slim
1960–1961	Viscount Dunrossil
1961–1965	Viscount De L'Isle
1965–1969	Lord Casey
1969–1974	Sir P. M. C. Hasluck
1974–1977	Sir J. R. Kerr
1977–1982	Sir I. Cowen
1982–1989	Sir N. Stephen
1989–1996	Sir W. G. Hayden
1996–2001	Sir W. Deane
2001–2003	Rt Revd Dr P. Hollingsworth
2003–	Major-General M. Jeffery

PRIME MINISTERS OF AUSTRALIA

1901–1903	Sir Edmund Barton
1903–1904	Alfred Deakin
1904	John Christian Watson
1904–1908	Alfred Deakin
1908–1909	Andrew Fisher
1909–1910	Alfred Deakin
1910–1913	Andrew Fisher
1913–1914	Joseph Cook
1914–1915	Andrew Fisher
1915–1923	William Morris Hughes
1923–1929	Stanley Melbourne Bruce
1929–1932	James Henry Scullin
1932–1939	Joseph Aloysius Lyons
1939	Sir Earle Christmas Grafton Page
1939–1941	Robert Gordon Menzies
1941	Arthur William Fadden
1941–1945	John Curtin
1945	Francis Michael Forde
1945–1949	Joseph Benedict Chifley
1949–1966	Robert Gordon Menzies
1966–1967	Harold Edward Holt
1967–1968	John McEwen
1968–1971	John Grey Gorton

1971–1972	William McMahon
1972–1975	Edward Gough Whitlam
1975–1983	John Malcolm Fraser
1983–1991	Robert James Lee Hawke
1991–1996	Paul John Keating
1996–	John Winston Howard

PRIME MINISTERS OF GREAT BRITAIN

1812–1827	Lord Liverpool
1827	George Canning
1827–1828	Lord Goderich
1828–1830	Duke of Wellington
1830–1834	Lord Grey
1834	Lord Melbourne
1834–1835	Sir Robert Peel
1835–1841	Lord Melbourne
1841–1846	Sir Robert Peel
1846–1852	Lord John Russell
1852	14th Lord Derby
1852–1855	Lord Aberdeen
1855–1858	Lord Palmerston
1858–1859	14th Lord Derby
1859–1865	Lord Palmerston

FOREIGN SECRETARIES OF GREAT BRITAIN

1812–1822	Lord Castlereagh
1822–1827	George Canning
1827–1828	Lord Dudley
1828–1830	Lord Aberdeen
1830–1834	Lord Palmerston
1834–1835	Duke of Wellington
1835–1841	Lord Palmerston
1841–1846	Lord Aberdeen
1846–1851	Lord Palmerston
1851–1852	Lord Granville
1852	Lord Malmesbury
1852–1853	Lord John Russell
1853–1858	Lord Clarendon
1858–1859	Lord Malmesbury
1859–1865	Lord John Russell

COLONIAL SECRETARIES OF GREAT BRITAIN

1812–1827	Lord Bathurst
1827	Lord Goderich
1827–1828	William Huskisson
1828–1830	Sir George Murray
1830–1833	Lord Goderich
1833–1834	Lord Stanley
1834	T. Spring Rice
1834–1835	Lord Aberdeen
1835–1839	C. Grant (Lord Glenelg)
1839–1840	Lord Normanby
1840–1841	Lord Russell
1841–1845	Lord Stanley
1845–1846	W. E. Gladstone
1846–1852	Lord Grey
1852	J. Pakington
1852–1854	Duke of Newcastle
1854–1855	G. Grey
1855	S. Herbert
1855	Lord Russell
1855	W. Molesworth
1855–1858	H. Labouchere
1858–1859	Lord Stanley
1859–1865	Duke of Newcastle

Notes

AAS   *Australian Aboriginal Studies*
ADB   *Australian Dictionary of Biography*
AEHR   *Australian Economic History Review*
AH   *Aboriginal History*
AHM   *Australian History Monographs*
AHS   *Australian Historical Studies*
AIAS   Australian Institute of Aboriginal Affairs
AIATSIS   Australian Institute of Aboriginal and Torres Strait Islanders Studies
AJ   *Arena Journal*
AJIA   *Australian Journal of International Affairs*
AJPH   *Australian Journal of Politics and History*
AJPS   *Australian Journal of Political Science*
APJ   *Australian Paediatric Journal*
AQ   *Australian Quarterly*
AS   *Aboriginal Studies*
AVSJ   *Australian Victorian Studies Journal*
BL   British Library
CO   Colonial Office
CPD   Commonwealth Parliamentary Debates
CUL   Cambridge University Library
DNB   *Dictionary of National Biography*
ER   *Edinburgh Review*
HJ   *Historical Journal*
HJAS   *Historical Journal of Australian Studies*
HRA   Historical Records of Australia
HRNSW   Historical Records of New South Wales
HRV   Historical Records of Victoria
HS   *Historical Studies*
HSSA   Historical Society of South Australia

HSV	Historical Society of Victoria
ICS	Institute of Commonwealth Studies
JAPS	*Journal of Australian and Pacific Studies*
JAS	*Journal of Australian Studies*
JHSSA	*Journal of the Historical Society of South Australia*
JICH	*Journal of Imperial and Commonwealth History*
JPH	*Journal of Pacific History*
JRAHS	*Journal of the Royal Australian History Society*
JRH	*Journal of Religious History*
JRHSQ	*Journal of the Royal Historical Society of Queensland*
JRWAHS	*Journal of the Royal Western Australian History Society*
JSAHS	*Journal of the South Australian History Society*
LH	*Labour History*
MJP	*Melbourne Journal of Politics*
NAUSA	National Archives of the United States
NLS	National Library of Scotland
NMM	National Maritime Museum
PP	Parliamentary Papers
PRO	Public Record Office (Kew)
RCS	Royal Commonwealth Society
SA	South Australia
SDA	State Department Archives
SDB	State Department Bulletin
SHR	*Scottish History Review*
SOAS	School of Oriental and African Studies
SRO	Scottish Record Office
THRA	*Tasmanian Historical Research Association*
VHJ	*Victorian Historical Journal*

INTRODUCTION

1. Human Development Index (UNESCO, 2001).

2. K. Windschuttle's painstaking work has proved that there has been much exaggeration of atrocities perpetrated against Aborigines, but hardly that the record of official actions over a very long period has not been deplorable. For (sometimes irate) arguments against Windschuttle see R. Manne (ed.), *Whitewash* (Melbourne, 2003). For the argument on 'genocide' see H. Reynolds, *An Indelible Stain: The Question of Genocide in Australian History* (Ringwood, Victoria, 2001). To anyone who lived through the Second World War the word 'genocide' has a quality demanding great care in its use.

3. At least one scholarly work in 3 volumes, B. Mollison and C. Everitt's *Tasmanian Aborigines* (n.p., Tasmania, 1978), was made available to me in 2003 only after

a special request and a brief interview. See also T. Flannery, *Beautiful Lies* (Melbourne, 2003) pp. 7–9. When questioned by Flannery only one academic admitted the – unquestionable – existence of cannibalism in Aboriginal society.

4. After I pointed out this remarkable omission, I was courteously informed (by Antonia Lamanna, Customer Services Manager): 'I have spoken to one of the curators for the Australian Society and Technology Department, who informs me that while self-government is not directly stated it is implied. A careful reading of the Australia Gallery does provide information about the settlement and growth of Melbourne before 1850.' *Hamlet* without the Prince?

5. The information, and that on the economic statistics, is taken chiefly from the *Economist Pocket World in Figures* (2001). It is more than likely that the comparative figures are overstated, since the efficiency of police and medical services ensure that more crimes and diseases are reported.

6. For the baffled, these are Rugby Union – the International game – Rugby League and Australian Rules; a version known as Gaelic football is also gaining recognition.

7. B. Bryson, *Down Under* (London, 2001), 16 ff. My first visit to Australia was made as a director of a London bank with many years' experience of Australian trade (now part of the ANZ group) but more particularly as chairman of some steel and engineering companies. On the second day I found myself at a pleasant party at Palm Beach, when the conversation turned to government borrowing. At the time there was vocal discontent with British policies. Britain had refused to participate in the Vietnam adventure, had shown willingness to shrug off any remaining Imperial responsibilities, by joining the European Economic Community (as it then was), and by devaluing the pound, thus slashing the value of Australian sterling investments. My suggestion that international currencies other than sterling existed, and that a country with very considerable receipts from many substantial trading partners could well diversify, was seized upon with lively interest. Telephone calls were made, and within twenty-four hours I found myself, after being vetted by the redoubtable Ainsley Gotto, talking to Prime Minister John Gorton in his Canberra office. It seemed at the time, and still does, to be a remarkable example of the openness of Australian society; but Gorton was a strikingly unconventional and enterprising politician.

CHAPTER I

1. Charles Boxer's books – *Dutch Merchants and Mariners in Asia* (London, 1988), *The Dutch Seaborne Empire* (London, 1965), *The Portuguese Seaborne Empire* (London, 1991) and *The Church Militant and Iberian Expansion* (Baltimore, 1978) – are the synoptic works; for Tordesillas, see the classic J. H. Parry, *The Spanish Seaborne Empire* (London, 1966), 43–7. K. G. McIntyre, *Secret Discovery of Australia* (London, 1977), chap. 3 has a good analysis.

2. J. C. Beaglehole, *Exploration of the Pacific* (Stanford, Calif., 1981), 9.

3. J. Needham, *Science & Civilisation in China*, 5 vols. (Cambridge, 1954–2000), vol. iv, part iii, pp. 536–40. A small (4-inch) fifteenth-century statuette found under tree roots may have been left there by Chinese or Buginese.

4. H. Yule, *Book of Ser Marco Polo*, 2 vols. (London, 1903), vol. ii, pp. 272, 284.

5. The *Australian Encylopaedia*'s article (1965) on 'Exploration by Sea' is a good introduction, with helpful maps. A. Day, *Historical Dictionary of the Discovery and Exploration of Australia* (Oxford, 2003) is an excellent guide. One of the most interesting Portuguese voyagers was the fervently religious Pedro de Quiros, whose 1605–6 expedition – or rather, musings thereon – have formed 'a national icon'. C. Kelly, 'Geographical narrative' and 'P. F. de Quiros', *HS* 9/33, 34 (1959–60), and L. Scheps 'Unkellying Quiros', *JAS* 42 (1994). R. H. Major (ed.), *Early Voyages to Terra Australis* (London, 1859), remains an excellent collection. *JAS* vols. 18, 19 and 21 record a lively controversy on the Portuguese voyages between W. A. R. Richardson and I. F. McKiggan. See also (with reservations) G. A. Wood, *Discovery of Australia* (Melbourne, 1969/1980), and O. H. K. Spate 'Terra Australis – Cognita?', *HS* 8/29 (1957).

6. A. Sharp, *Discovery of Australia* (Oxford, 1963), 14 ff. MacIntyre, *Secret Discovery*, 56–7 makes a case for an earlier Portuguese landing in Napier Broome Bay, Western Australia.

7. See H. Van Zanden *1606: Discovery of Australia* (Perth, 1997), 25–6 – a useful little book for the *Duyfken*; T. D. Mutch 'First Discovery of Australia', *JRAHS* 28/3 (1942), and G. Schilder, *Australia Unveiled* (Amsterdam, 1976).

8. Dutch names such as Janszoon and Carstenszoon are also sometimes rendered by the abbreviations 'Jansz', etc. There is a good account of Carstenszoon in Van Zanden, *1606*, chap. 7.

9. Sadly, although other replicas have safely made the voyage, the *Batavia* had to be transported to Australia, because of safety regulations. The fatal reef was on Houtman Abrolhos, a group of islands discovered earlier by VOC Commander Houtman, who warned the company of the dangers. For the possible fate of the Dutch see R. Gerritsen, *And Their Ghosts May be Heard* (Fremantle, 1994).

10. For Tasman's journal and documents, see J. E. Heeres, *Tasman: Journal & Documents* (Amsterdam, 1898), and the authoritative A. Sharp, *Voyages of A. J. Tasman* (Oxford, 1968); for background see M. Bennett 'Van Diemen, Tasman', *THRA* 39/2 (1991). Extracts in the original Dutch are in E. Duyker, *Discovery of Tasmania* (Hobart, 1992).

11. W. Dampier, *A New Voyage Round the World* (London 1927 [1697]), 312. For Dampier's brief transition to respectability, see *DNB*. 'Hottentot' for the autochthonous Khoikhoi of southern Africa is deemed pejorative; the culturally distinct San or Bushmen are often combined as Khoisan to distinguish them from the black Bantu, later arrivals in the region.

12. There is a good account of Dalrymple in Glyndwr Williams 'The Endeavour Voyage', in M. Lincoln, *Science and Exploration in the Pacific* (Woodbridge, 1998).

For his contacts with Bougainville and Charles de Brosses (President of the Parlement of Dijon), whose *Histoires des Navigations aux Terres Australes* (1756), was the main pre-Cookian source of information, see A. C. Taylor 'Charles de Brosses', in B. Greenhill, *Opening of the Pacific: Image and Reality* (London, 1970).

13. 'Whether this continent exists or not may perhaps be uncertain; but supposing it does exist, I am very certain you will never find a man fitter for discovering it': Adam Smith to Lord Shelburne, Feb. 1767 quoted in Williams, 'The Endeavour Voyage', 7. For the unknown continent, see G. A. Wood, *Discovery of Australia*, 255–7.

14. Professor Beaglehole's editions of Cook's (3 vols., Cambridge, 1955–1974) and Banks's journals (2 vols., Sydney, 1962) are not only immensely learned, but sparkle with humour. That part of the journals devoted to Australia is relatively modest, fewer than 100 pages (vol. i, pp. 298–392). The cautious Cook expressed a doubt as to whether the coast sighted by Mr Hicks was 'one land or no' with that described by Tasman (p. 299). He has been blamed for describing Botany Bay as a suitable place for settlement, but, apart from the fact that the suggestion was made by Banks, Cook was mainly struck by the absence of larger trees, the greatest challenge to hopeful farmers, and the 'deep black soil' he described was simply overlooked by the first settlers (p. 309 n. 1). Patrick O'Brian, *Joseph Banks* (London, 1981), is a good short biography but H. B. Carter, *Sir Joseph Banks* (London, 1998), is authoritative.

15. The question is discussed with authority by Henry Reynolds in *The Law of the Land* (Ringwood, 1992).

16. For prehistory and climate, see J. Dodson, *Naïve Lands* (Melbourne, 1992); for an introduction to climate, see A. Sturman and N. J. Tapper, *Weather and Climate of Australia and New Zealand* (Melbourne, 1996).

17. Few aspects of history change more rapidly than prehistory, and that of Australia has become an object of particular controversy. Any bibliography will need constant updating. T. Flannery, *The Future Eaters* (Sydney, 1984), is a popular ecological history. For archaeology, see G. Connah. *Archaeology of Australia's History* (Cambridge, 1994) and G. Irwin, *Prehistoric Exploration and Colonisation of the Pacific* (Cambridge, 1994). H. Lourandos, *Continent of Hunter Gatherers* (Cambridge, 1997), is stimulating; and for a fascinating specialist view see S. Webb, *Palaeopathology of Aboriginal Australians* (Cambridge, 1995). The most recent readable and wide-ranging survey, in P. McConvell and N. Evans (eds.), *The Prehistory of Australia* (Oxford, 1997), can supplement J. Flood, *Archaeology of the Dream Time* (Sydney, 1983), a well-illustrated introduction to the subject. Although older, D. J. Mulvaney, *Prehistory of Australia* (Melbourne, 1975), and G. Blainey, *Triumph of the Nomads* (Sydney, 1983), remain classic texts. Although McConvell and Evans comment on the 'striking cultural unity in Aboriginal Australia', climate and geography must have led to significant regional differences. Notable contrasts exist between the hunter-gatherers of the tropics and the fisherfolk of the Hunter valley, with their relatively

sophisticated marine equipment. Their canoes are described as being constructed on the same principle as the Greek trireme, with the hull held together by a hypozoma. J. Maynard, 'Muloobinbah' *JRAHS* 87/2 (2001), 250. J. Diamond, *Guns, Germs and Steel* (London, 1997), 279, suggests that, as of 4,000 years ago, Native Australian societies enjoyed a big head start over societies of Europe and other continents, possessing perhaps the earliest boats, and that subsequent regression owed much to the lack of domesticatable animals and cereals – only 2 of the world's 56 species being found in Australia (p. 30). See also R. Rudgley, *Lost Civilisations of the Stone Age* (London, 1998), for comparison with other paleolithic cultures. For ceremonial sites, see I. McBryde, *Aboriginal Prehistory in New England* (Sydney, 1974), and for the latest research of the emergence of homo sapiens see T. White and C. Stringer, in *Nature*, 12 Dec. 2003. For early skeletal remains, see Flood, *Archaeology of the Dream Time*, chaps. 3 and 4; J. Lahn, *Finders Keepers, Losers Weepers* (Brisbane 1996). C. Pardoe, 'The Pleistocene is still with us', in M. A. Smith, M. Spriggs and B. Fankhauser, *Sahul in Review* (Canberra, 1993) has a scholarly analysis.

18. See Blainey, *Triumph of the Nomads*, chap. 5, 'Burning Continent'.

19. J. R. Baker, *Race* (Oxford, 1974), is a useful if controversial guide.

20. N. Sharp, *Stars of Tagai* (Canberra, 1993), 22. See J. Beckett, *Torres Strait Islanders* (Canberra, 1987), for a description of island cultures. For George Grey see *Journals of Two Expeditions of Discovery* (London, 1841) vol. 2, pp. 19–20.

21. For the lower figure, A. Radcliffe Brown in *Commonwealth Year Book* (1930); for 3 million see B. Thorpe, 'Frontiers of Discourse', *HJAS* 46 (1995). N. G. Butlin, *AEHR* 26/2 (1986), 105, suggests about a million. 'Walbiri' is also 'Wailbri'; see the standard work N. B. Tindall, *Aboriginal Tribes of Australia* (Canberra, 1974), and K. Maddock, *The Australian Aborigines: A Portrait of their Society* (Ringwood, 1982).

22. R. L. Kirk and A. G. Thorne, *Origin of the Australians* (Canberra, 1976), 123–4. Only comparatively recently has Aboriginal religion and mythology become the object of much interest and discussion: see A. Capell, *Linguistic Survey of Australia* (Sydney, 1963), M. Walsh and C. Yallop, *Language and Culture in Aboriginal Australia* (Canberra, 1993), pp. xv and 16 ff., and B. J. Blake, *Australian Aboriginal Languages* (St Lucia, 1991), chap. 6. The best introduction to Aboriginal philosophies is perhaps still the first, by W. E. H. Stanner, in T. A. G. Hungerford, *Aboriginal Australian Signpost* (Melbourne, 1956), and reproduced, with somewhat condescending comments, by W. H. Edwards in Edwards (ed.), *Traditional Aboriginal Society* (South Yarra, 1987/1998). In 1956, writing of the Dreaming, Stanner described the Aboriginal world picture as 'many things in one. Among them, a kind of narrative of things that once happened; a kind of charter of things that still happen; and a kind of *logos* or principle of order transcending everything significant for Aboriginal man. If I am correct in saying so, it is much more complex philosophically than we have so far realised. I greatly hope that artists and men of letters who (it seems increasingly) find inspiration in Aboriginal

Australia will use all their gifts of empathy . . .' (p. 65). The Dreaming has, in fact, much in common with the African Bushman myths but has become a source of inspiration to Australian writers to a much greater extent than have the Bushmen to modern South Africans; but the Bushmen have long since been absorbed into Black societies, with their endangered remnants scattered, while Aborigines are still very much a force in modern Australia. See e.g. T. Hahn, *Tsuni-//Goam: The Superior Being of the Khoi-Khoi* (London, 1881).

23. 'Always Ask' was F. R. Myers' formula: see Edwards (ed.), *Traditional Aboriginal Society*, 39; in the same book, M. Langton on 'Grand-maternal Influence', p. 189, and L. R. Hiatt, 'Aboriginal Political Life', *passim*, are especially illuminating. Hiatt points out that although 'the disciplines imposed by Pintubi men are sustained and severe . . . tooth avulsion, nose piercing, circumcision, sub-incision, fire ordeals, and the removal of finger nails' (but thereafter all men are equal). In the same book, Stanner characterizes Aboriginal society as one in which 'the primary virtues are generosity and fair dealing . . . a notion of reciprocity as a moral obligation; a notion of generously equivalent return; and a surprisingly clear notion of fair dealing, or making things "level"' – all of which might well be said to be very much a code to which all Australians are deeply attached. But Stanner continues: 'The blacks do not fight over land. There are no wars or invasions to seize territory. They do not enslave each other. There is no master-servant relationship. There is no class-division. There is no property or income inequality. The result is a homeostasis; far-reaching and stable' (p. 238).

24. W. K. Hancock, *Discovering Monaro* (Cambridge, 1972), 21–2. Mr Robert Vyner, who ate a quart of the insects in 1865 praised their sweet nutty flavour (ibid., p. 26). 'Their deepest want, when tribal society became a wreck, was admission to the society that was supplementing[?] it'. Hancock may well have meant 'supplanting'.

25. Beaglehole, *Journals of Captain Cook*, vol. i, p. 399. Cook listed a number of commonplace Aboriginal words, described by Beaglehole as from the Koko–Yimidir languages, indicating the ability of both Aboriginals and Cook's British crew to establish friendly relations with each other. The near-contemporary French scientist François Péron compiled a similar list, but with a wider vocabulary which included the Aboriginal words for 'to urinate, defecate, belch, strangle, and to have an erection' – the French *are* different: N. J. Plomley, *Baudin Expedition and the Tasmanian Aborigines* (Hobart, 1983), 86.

26. For an egregious example of such see Simon Forrest, an Associate Professor of Edith Cowan University, in J. Hartey and A. McKee, *Indigenous Public Sphere* (Oxford, 2000), 118–21. It is extraordinary that in 1996 a reprint of a work (A. W. Howitt, *Native Tribes of Southeast Australia*) originally published in 1904 should claim that 'the book contains a great deal of information that would probably not have been included if the work were being published for the first time today'.

27. W. Hickey, *Memoirs*, 3 vols. (3rd edn., London, 1919), vol. ii, p. 233.

28. 'Australasia' was submitted as a prize poem at Cambridge in 1823; it came second.

29. Quoted in P. Langford, *A Polite and Commercial People* (Oxford, 1989), 55. For the debate on crime and punishment generally, see M. Foucault, *Discipline and Punishment*, trans. A. Sheridan (London, 1977). In an interval of discussing that much more entertaining topic, the Prince of Wales's debts, the House of Commons found time (28 April 1787) to hear Mr Minchin on the 'Bloody Spirit of the Penal Laws'.

30. Quoted in A. G. L. Shaw, *Convicts and the Colonies* (London, 1966), 47. For the Penitentiary Act see S. Devereaux, 'Making of the Penitentiary Act', *HJ* 42 (1999). E. O'Brien, *Foundation of Australia* (London, 1937), although dated, remains valuable.

31. Bentham took the liveliest interest in the question of transportation (he was against it) and corresponded with David Collins, the first law officer of the new colony; see R. V. Jackson 'Theory and Evidence', *JAPS* 39/3 (1993).

32. Historians working in Australia have written many long and often interesting speculations on the motives for selecting Botany Bay as a location for convict settlement. Some writers have attempted to argue for commercial motives behind the settlement, convincingly refuted by A. Frost in *Convicts and Empire* (Melbourne, 1980) as 'a striking example of how writers who lose sight of historical reality can be enticing and plausible, and yet quite wrong' (p. 185). See also A. Atkinson, 'First Plans for Governing New South Wales', *AHS* 24/94 (1990), G. Martin (ed.), *Founding of Australia* (Sydney, 1978), D. J. Mulvaney and J. P. White (eds.), *Australians to 1788* (Melbourne, 1985), and D. MacKay, *Place of Exile* (Melbourne, 1985). The truth is that to British governments then, or later, colonial settlements, or colonies in general, were matters of minor importance. Unless war, or major expenditure, or interesting scandals were concerned colonial debates were poorly attended, and colonial affairs remained the preserve of that small number of MPs who chose to take an interest. In the 1780s the Pitt administration's prime concern had been to make the lives of their constituents, and especially those inconveniently near the Palace of Westminster, more secure by removing dangerous, or more usually merely inconvenient, criminals.

33. Lord Auckland, 'Discourse on Punishment', reproduced in J. J. Auchmuty, *Voyage of Governor Phillip to Botany Bay* (Sydney, 1969), 339 ff. For Banks's responses, see Carter, *Sir Joseph Banks*, 164 ff. For the proposals, see HRNSW, vol. 1, pt. 2, pp. 1–19.

34. Botany Bay comments: M. Clark, *HS* 9/35 (1960). That old enemy, France, was also provoking some anxiety: in 1786 Captain John Gore reported on Laperouse's design to 'set up some establishment beyond Hudson's Bay' – and Laperouse was also planning to visit New Holland, at the other end of the Pacific (G. Williams, *Voyage of Delusion* (London, 2002), 342). Joseph Banks as an empire-builder is interestingly discussed in J. Gascoigne, *Science in the Service of Empire* (London, 1998) 166–78.

35. J. Stockdale, 'Historical Narrative', quoted in A. Malaspina, *The Secret History of the Convict Colony*, ed. R. J. King (Sydney, 1990), 15. See also G. Abbott, 'The Expected Cost of the Botany Bay Scheme', *JRAHS*, 81/2 (1995).

CHAPTER 2

1. The best source is what may be Phillip's own *Voyage of Governor Phillip to Botany Bay* (ed. J. J. Auchmuty; Sydney, 1969) supplemented by A. Frost, *Arthur Phillip; His Voyaging* (Melbourne, 1987), which has good bibliographical notes. See also J. J. Auchmuty, *Voyage of Governor Phillip to Botany Bay* (Sydney, 1969). M. Scorgie and P. Hodgson, 'Arthur Phillip's Networks', *JRAHS* 82/1 (1996), deals interestingly with his appointment.
2. 18 March 1787, Phillip to Nepean, HRNSW, vol 1, pt. 2, p. 59 (a private letter). Phillip wrote a much stiffer letter to Lord Sydney on 12 March 1790, in which he declined to accept responsibility if the Marines' rations were not improved; he gained his point (ibid., pp. 56–7).
3. White's remark, and many others, lie easily to hand in T. Flannery, *The Birth of Sydney* (Melbourne, 1999), 48. For the selection of Port Jackson, see W. Bradley, *Voyage to New South Wales* (Sydney, 1969); Worgan and Daniel, see P. Bridges, *Foundations of Identity* (Sydney, 1995), 8. The British were about to move to Port Jackson when Laperouse made an appearance in Botany Bay, without any aggressive intent and to a warm welcome, testified by the surviving memorial to Abbé Receveur, who died during their stay. See R. J. King, 'What Brought Laperouse to Botany Bay?', *JRAHS* 85/2 (1999).
4. For King's account of the meeting see Flannery, *The Birth of Sydney*, 44–7. David Collins described the scene on the beach with 'convicts everywhere straggling about, collecting animals and gum to sell to the people of the transports who at the same time were procuring spears, shields, swords, fishing lines . . . the loss of which must have been attended with many inconveniences to the owners' (*An Account of the English Colony in New South Wales*, 2 vols. (London, 1798, 1802), vol. i, p. 17). Like many early visitors, Collins mistook the throwing sticks – *woomeras* – for swords. For the biographies of the newcomers, see M. Gillen, *Founders of Australia: A Biographical Dictionary of the First Fleet* (Sydney, 1989).
5. Tench is an incomparable observer and a lively writer, see *1788*, T. Flannery's edition (Melbourne, 1996) of Tench's books *A Narrative of the Expedition to Botany Bay* (1789) and *Complete Account of the Settlement at Port Jackson* (1793). In *The Birth of Sydney*, Flannery also gives extracts from the unpublished notebooks (M686 in SOAS library) of Tench's brother-officer, William Dawes, a more serious and sober-minded young man, and of the letters and diary of the gloomy Lieutenant Ralph Clark (see *Journals and Letters*, ed. P. G. Fidlon and R. J. Ryan (Sydney, 1981)). Taken together, and with David Collins's more studied work, the different accounts provide not only an excellent description of the

colony's first years, but an intimate view of the eighteenth-century Marines. P. Bridges, *Foundations of Identity*, is a good account of the early years and Collins has a good recent biography by J. Currey (Melbourne, 2000). See also I. Clendinnen, *Dancing with Strangers* (Melbourne, 2003), a sympathetic review.

6. D. Neal, *The Rule of Law in a Penal Colony* (Cambridge, 1991), 144, for the Night Watch. A. C. V. Melbourne, *Early Constitutional Development in Australia* (St Lucia, 1963), is essential for the period.

7. Major Ross to Nepean HRNSW 14 March 1787. For the crimes, see J. Cobley, 'Crimes of the First Fleeters,' *JRAHS* 52/2 (1966); M. Clark 'Origins of the Convicts', *HS* 7/26, 27 (1956); L. L. Robson, 'Women Convicts', *HS* 2; M. Flynn, *The Second Fleet* (Sydney, 2001); A. Needham, *Women of the 1790 'Neptune'* (Dural, 1992). Flynn (pp. 27–8) suggests that administrative pressure led to an unquestioning acceptance of the lowest tender and a contract which provided financial incentives for the safe arrival of the stores, but not of the convicts; see also K. Daniels, *Convict Women* (St Leonards, 1998). Samuel Marsden's reports to London divided the female population arbitrarily into married (those whose weddings had been solemnized according to the rites of the Church of England) and 'concubines' – all the rest, including Jews and Catholics. Marsden's descriptions of sexual promiscuity sent delicious shivers down respectable English spines. Such conclusions have perhaps been accepted too readily by feminist historians, including Miriam Dixon and Anne Summers; for another view, see P. Robinson, *Hatch and Brood of Time* (Melbourne, 1985) – a lively work – chap. 3. For Ikey Solomon see J. Sackville-O'Donnell, *The First Fagin* (Melbourne, 2001).

8. Quoted in A.-M. Whitaker, 'Wedgwood, Darwin and the Sydney Harbour Bridge', *History*, 71 (2002).

9. In a demonstration of the sheer silliness of some Australian views of history, the *Sydney Morning Herald* published, in February 2003, a letter from an established academic stating as an accepted fact that Phillip had executed six Aborigines as a punitive measure.

10. Flannery, *1788*, 107–8.

11. Ibid., p. 104. The theory that smallpox was deliberately spread by means of the serum seems absurd: it is too dangerous a disease to tamper with, and respiratory diseases were the most widespread and fatal. Although General Jeffrey Amherst, a generation earlier, had attempted to infect American Indians, such a deliberate atrocity would also be completely at odds with Phillips's character. Bennelong's wife, Bangaroo, whose clan, the Cadigai, had been nearly wiped out by smallpox in 1789, was a 'proud and assertive' matriarch, dined at Government House, and announced her intention of giving birth there; she was, however, dissuaded; see P. Grimshaw *et al.* (eds.), *Creating a Nation* (Ringwood, 1994), chap. 1. See also two articles, by N. G. Butlin and J. Campbell, in *HS* 21, on Aboriginal smallpox: Campbell, in *Invisible Invaders*, points out that the first recorded outbreaks of smallpox in 1789 took place on the north coast, far away from the Sydney settlement, almost certainly brought there by traders from the Indonesian islands,

where smallpox was endemic; see also N. G. Butlin, *Our Original Aggression* (Sydney, 1983), which points out that smallpox never affected Van Diemen's Land, where venereal disease caused reduced rates of reproduction, disastrous to so small a population (p. 235). It is, Butlin concludes (p. 230), 'a sorry tale . . . of ignorance, antagonism and rejection by non-Aborigines and lack of resources, opportunity, incentive and direction by Aborigines', and he suggests that there may be merit in the 'traditional historical understanding that the blacks largely faded away before the entry of the white man'. G. Blainey, *Our Side of the Country* (Sydney, 1984), 30 ff., agrees. It was 'smallpox, influenza, measles – and despair' that were the Four Horsemen of the Aboriginal Apocalypse. Dr Henry Reynolds describes the British arrival as an 'invasion', a term I would question, proposing that 'intrusion' or 'arrival' might be better. Most of the newcomers were distinctly unwilling, and would far rather have been at home. The process, too, was gradual, and has continued over two centuries, nor was it primarily achieved by force of arms; the indigenous population was shouldered aside, sometimes fairly brutally, rather than conquered. For the arguments see H. Reynolds *An Indelible Stain* (Ringwood, Victoria, 2001) chap. 3.

12. The officer was possibly Tench: quoted in Flannery, *1788*, 98 ff. Phillip had taken great care in selecting seeds and plants, but some experience of the New South Wales climate was needed before market gardening was successful; see A. Frost 'Antipodean Exchange', in D. P. Miller and P. H. Reill (eds.), *Visions of Empire* (Cambridge, 1996), 59 ff.

13. Flannery, *1788*, 101–2. Flynn, *Second Fleet*, is an exhaustive account of the 'Grim Armada' which among others brought the founders of the Macarthur and Wentworth dynasties to Australia.

14. Phillip to Grenville, quoted in A. G. L. Shaw, *Convicts and the Colonies* (London, 1966), 64–5. Traill attempted to abscond, hiding himself in the hold. HRA, series 1, vol. 1, p. 207.

15. Elizabeth's crime was stealing two pairs of silk stockings; married in St George's Hanover Square, she was accustomed to good society, being supported while in New South Wales by her former employer, Lord Winchelsea. See G. M. Webb, 'Elizabeth Needham,' *JRAHS* 79/1–2 (1993). D. Oxley, in *Convict Maids* (Cambridge, 1996), goes a long way to vindicating the reputation of women convicts.

16. For Collins as a law officer, see J. F. Nagle, *Collins, the Courts and the Colony* (Sydney, 1966).

17. For the Kables, see D. Neal, *Rule of Law*, 143 ff. B. Kercher, *Debt, Seduction and Other Disasters* (Sydney, 1996), an important book, traces the evolution of the colonial legal system; see chap. 2, 'Military Honour', and, for Collins, chap. 3, 'Freedom for Aborigines and the Law'. G. Karskens, *The Rocks* (Melbourne, 1997), is a colourful investigation of the lively Sydney community of that name.

18. For the 'Scottish Martyrs', see P. B. Ellis and S. Mac A'Ghobhainn, *The Scottish Insurrection of 1820* (London, 1970), *passim*, and D. Hughes, 'Scottish Martyrs', *JRAHS* 82/2 (1996).

19. The amiable William Charles Wentworth, Minister for Aboriginal Affairs in the Gorton and McMahon governments (d. 2003), was the latest representative. The philoprogenitive D'Arcy also fathered at least seven other children in addition to the three he acknowledged legally.

20. For this and what follows, see F. Welsh, *Four Nations* (London, 2002), chap. 8. In marked contrast to their compatriots in the United States, the great majority of Irish Australians settled contentedly and successfully; Australia had no Tammany Hall or race riots.

21. In his impressive book, *The Fatal Shore* (London, 1996), Robert Hughes travesties eighteenth-century Irish history: 'by the end of the eighteenth century these "penal laws" reached into every cranny of the Catholic majority's life. Under them, Catholics were legislated down to helotry. Under the Popery Laws, no Catholic could sit in Parliament, on the bench or in a jury; none could vote, teach or hold an army commission . . . These laws cut across all class barriers. They beat the Catholic peasantry "into the clay," as the phrase went, but they also gagged and paralyzed the Catholic landowner, the intellectual, the entrepreneur. Thus, they unified the Irish Catholics more strongly than softer laws could ever have done and voided the question of a class struggle within the Catholic ranks' (p. 182). The cold facts are very different. By the end of the eighteenth century, Irish Catholics were able to vote in parliamentary elections on a more generous basis than the English, Protestant or Catholic; most of the 'Popery Laws' had been repealed; Irish Catholics were both barristers (Daniel O'Connell, the 'Liberator' was called to the Irish bar in 1798, and his family owned considerable Irish estates) and army officers (Colonel Christopher Bird was commissioned in 1794, spent some years in the War Office, became assistant secretary to the Commander in Chief, the Duke of York, and colonial secretary – the head of civil government – at the Cape of Good Hope). Catholics could be elected to the House of Commons; the barrier to their taking a seat was the necessity of taking an obnoxious oath, removed only in 1829. Far from 'the question of a class struggle within the Catholic ranks' being 'voided', prosperous Catholic burgesses and landlords were horrified by the rebellion; Richard Caulfeild, Catholic Archbishop of Ferns, appealing to the mob 'to relinquish their wild notions of rebellion' was at one with the Protestant James Caulfeild, Lord Charlemont; the Irish yeomanry who cut down the fleeing rebels had Catholic 'strong farmers' as well as Protestant gentry in their ranks. Dr Hughes also believes that 'When nine ships appeared from the Pacific with the condemned men and women of the 98 rebellion on board, they brought the worst load of bitterness the System had yet seen. Of the 1,067 people on board, 775 were at a conservative estimate political exiles.' In fact, only if *anyone* sentenced in *any* Irish country assizes for *any* crime is regarded as a 'political exile' can such a 'conservative estimate' (p. 186) be reached; almost all the leading United Irish rebels who chose to stay in the colony became model citizens. A better-informed account is found in P. O'Farrell, *The Irish in Australia* (Kensington, 1986): 'Rebels conformed in peace, setting up a marvellous tension between myth and reality' (p. 51).

22. Some rehabilitation to the Rum Corps officers is offered in A.-M. Whitaker, *Joseph Foveaux* (Sydney, 2000), chap. 1. See also W. Foster, 'Francis Gore', *JRAHS* 51/3 (1965), and T. McAskill, 'An Asset to the Colony', *JRAHS* 82/1 (1996). As always, A. G. I. Shaw produces concentrated quality in 'Some Aspects of the History of New South Wales', *JRAHS* 57/2 (1971). R. J. Craig and S. A. Jenkins, 'Cox and Greenwood Ledger', *JRAHS* 82/2 (1996), point out that the officers' bills were used to buy consumer goods shipped by the incoming captains more often than rum. A stimulating article by N. G. Butlin, 'Yo, ho, ho', *AEHR* 23/1 (1983), puts alcoholic consumption in perspective.

23. HRA, series 1, vol. 1, pp. 602–43, and T. G. Parson, 'Was John Boston's Pig a Political Martyr?', *JRAHS* 71/3 (1985). Trespassing animals were a constant annoyance, causing many complaints.

24. The best short account of the period is still A. G. L. Shaw's chapter in F. Crowley (ed.), *A New History of Australia* (n.p., Victoria, 1974), which has most of the relevant source notes.

25. HRA, series 1, vol. 2, pp. 169–70. John Macarthur has an uncritical biography by M. H. Ellis, *John Macarthur* (Sydney, 1955); for later family history see J. M. Ward, *James Macarthur* (Sydney, 1981); for his relations with Atkins, see chap. 9. A new biography, M. Duffy, *Man of Honour* (Sydney, 2003) was published too late to be evaluated.

26. See Collins, *Account*, vol. ii, pp. 75–7.

27. For a synopsis of all explorations see *Australian Encyclopaedia*, 'Exploration by Sea and Exploration by Land'. The excellent *History of Australia, New Zealand and the Pacific* by D. Denoon and P. Mein-Smith (Oxford, 2000) is essential. Interestingly, it has been suggested by I. Clendinnen in 'Spearing the Governor', *AHS* 33/118, that an attack on Governor Phillip was arranged by Bennelong as a ritual to 'resolve political conflicts between the races'. A. Atkinson, *Europeans in Australia* (Melbourne, 1997), comments on the 'fathomless power of Phillip's politeness' (p. 151).

28. Flinders ranks next to Cook as the great Australian navigator. Nearly fifty years younger, his lighter and more playful style is evinced in his memoir of Trim, his faithful cat. Both his Aboriginal friend and interpreter, Bongaree, and Trim accompanied Flinders on his 1799 coastal voyage. 'In an expedition made to examine the northern parts of the coast of New South Wales, Trim presented a request to be of the party, promising to take upon himself the defence of our bread bags, and his services were accepted. Bongaree, an intelligent native of port Jackson, was also on board our little sloop; and with him Trim formed an intimate acquaintance. If he had occasion to drink, he mewed to Bongaree and leaped up to the water cask; if to eat, he called him down below and went straight to his kid, where there was generally a remnant of black swan. In short, Bongaree was his great resource, and his kindness was repaid with caresses. In times of danger, Trim never showed any signs of fear; and it may truly be said that he never distrusted or was afraid of any man' (Flinders, *Biographical Tribute to the Memory of Trim*

(Sydney, 1997), 28–9). A more sedate account is found in Flinders' two-volume *Voyage to Terra Australia* (Adelaide, 1966 [1814] the introduction to which has an excellent summary, by Flinders, of the previous voyages; see also R. J. Smith, 'Mr Flinders', *JRAHS* 85/2 (1999). All his explorations were completed by his twenty-ninth birthday, and his career was cut short by his spiteful detention by the French governor of Mauritius while on his way home (typically in a 29-ton schooner). The biography is J. D. Mack, *Matthew Flinders* (Melbourne, 1966). Bass, too, died young, at 33, having disappeared with his ship *Venus* on a trading voyage. See K. M. Bowden, *George Bass* (Melbourne, 1952). A. J. Brown, *Ill Starred Captains: Flinders and Baudin* (London, 2001), is an engaging and substantial comparative study of Flinders and N.-T. Baudin (see below). The Mitchell Library, Sydney, has Bass's letters and those of Flinders have been edited by P. Brunton (Sydney, 2002). The *Lady Nelson* was the creation of the ingenious Admiral John Schank; see *DNB*.

29. L. Ryan, *Aboriginal Tasmanians* (Crow's Nest, 1996), 67. Captain Shield of the Enderby ship *Emilia* made the first Pacific whaling voyage in 1790, but the New Englanders soon became prominent: see R. C. Kugler, in B. Greenhill (ed.), *Opening of the Pacific: Image and Reality* (London, 1970).

30. C. Massy, *Australian Merino* (Ringwood, 1990), 9 – and for much of what follows.

31. P. O'Brian, *Joseph Banks* (London, 1981) 272; see also H. B. Carter, *Sheep and Wool Correspondence of Sir Joseph Banks* (London, 1979).

32. For King on Macarthur etc., see M. H. Ellis, *John Macarthur*, chap. 17. As well as turning a memorable phrase, King was notable for being the only early Governor with much of a sense of humour: see J. and J. King, *Philip Gidley King* (North Ryde, 1981), P. G. Fidlon and R. J. Ryan (eds.), *The Journal of Philip Gidley King* (Sydney, 1980), and J. P. Graham, 'Humour and Pastimes of Early Sydney', *JRAHS* 1/2 (1901).

33. For Serle, see Mitchell Library, Marsden papers A 1992: Samuel Marsden has been heartily abused as a 'flogging parson', a hypocritical profiteer, an uncaring shepherd of souls, and much else. The much more complex reality should include his dedicated missionary work in New Zealand and the Pacific and his energetic administration. There were not too many of his contemporaries who would claim (of New Zealand): 'let there be one colony, at least, in which the Aborigines shall share the intruders' prosperity' (J. B. Marsden, *Memoirs of the Reverend Samuel Marsden* (London, 1858).

34. Massy, *Australian Merino*, 44.

35. P. Carter, *Terre Napoleon* (Sydney, 1999), 22. Baudin wrote a rather sententious but entirely justified letter to Governor King on 23 December 1802: 'I have never been able to conceive that there was justice and equity on the part of Europeans in seizing, in the name of their governments, a land seen for the first time when it is inhabited by men who have not always deserved the title of savages or cannibals which has been given them whilst they were but the children of nature

and just as little civilised as are your Scotch Highlanders or our peasants in Brittany, who, if they do not eat their fellow men, are nevertheless just as objectionable. From this it appears to me that it would be infinitely more glorious for your nation, as for mine, to mould for society the inhabitants of the respective countries over which they have rights, instead of wishing to occupy themselves in improving those who are so far removed by seizing the soil which they own and which has given them birth.'

36. Serle to Marsden, Mitchell Library, Marsden papers A 1992: letter dated 9 November 1801, received 18 February 1803! Serle correctly commented that the proposal to harvest timber for naval use in the United Kingdom would not repay the trouble and expense.

37. See L. Audel, 'David Collins: Early Life', *THRA* 35/1 (1988). For John Hayes, see *DNB*.

38. Shaw, *Convicts*, 70.

39. For early Australian theatre, see P. Parsons (ed.), *Companion to Australian Theatre* (Sydney, 1995).

40. P. O'Farrell, *Documents in Australian Catholic History*, 2 vols. (London, 1969), vol. i; L. R. Silver, *Battle of Vinegar Hill* (Sydney, 2002).

41. See HRNSW, vol. 6, pp. 332 ff. G. Lemcke, *Reluctant Rebel* (Sydney, 1998), is an interesting study of the 'Rum Rebellion' from Colonel Johnston's point of view. The prominent Labor politician H. V. Evatt defended the Governor in his *Rum Rebellion* (London, 1939). See also R. Fitzgerald and M. Hearn, *Bligh, Macarthur and the Rum Rebellion* (Kenthurst, 1988). B. W. O'Dwyer, 'Michael Dwyer' *JRHAS* 69/2 (1983), suggests the old rebel was used to discredit Bligh. G. Dening, *Mr Bligh's Bad Language* (London, 2000), points out Bligh's reluctance to flog. For Marsden's views, see M. Saclier, 'Sam Marsden's Colony', *JRHAS* 52/2 (1966).

42. M. H. Ellis, *John Macarthur*, 421.

43. HRA, series 1, vol. 8, p. 134.

44. For Macquarie's instructions, see HRA, series 1, vol. 7, pp. 190 ff. Shaw, *Convicts*, chap. 4, has an excellent account of Macquarie's policies.

45. Arago was Freycinet's artist, who visited Sydney in November 1819: see Flannery, *Birth*, 221 ff. For early Sydney architecture, see Bridges, *Foundations of Identity*. Mrs Macquarie had brought with her a book of *Designs for Elegant Cottages and Small Villas*, and took an informed interest in architecture, herself designing the little fountain in Macquarie Place. Lieutenant John Watts, the Governor's *aide de camp*, a competent amateur, worked with Mrs Macquarie's encouragement on St John's, Parramatta and what became the Fort Street National School.

46. Mitchell Library, Macquarie papers A 797: 14 May 1809. The collection is used to good effect in J. H. Ritchie, *Lachlan Macquarie* (Melbourne, 1986); the Governor's journals have been published by the NSW Public Libraries. See also L. Cohen, *Elizabeth Macquarie* (Sydney, 1979). Both the Governor and his wife were prominent in attempts to encourage Aboriginal education.

47. Coinage: Macquarie to Bathurst, 28 June 1813, HRA, series 1, vol. 7, pp. 722–3.

48. T. Barker, 'Crossing of the Mountains', *JRAHS* 5/2 (1965).

49. Together with Mrs Forlong, the success of Eliza Walsh in managing her own farms is noteworthy. A spinster, landing free in 1819, she was grazing over 1,000 cattle on her own land within five years; see P. Clarke and D. Spender (eds.), *Lifelines* (North Sydney, 1992), 32–5.

50. See H. L. Hall, *Colonial Office: A History* (London, 1937), and P. Knaplund, *James Stephen and the Colonial Office* (Madison, 1953). The reorganization under Bathurst is well described in J. H. Ritchie, *Punishment and Profit* (Melbourne, 1970), chap. 1.

51. Hansard, House of Commons, 18 February 1819. See also N. D. McLachlan, 'Bathurst at the Colonial Office', *HS* 13.

52. J. J. Eddy, *Britain and the Australian Colonies 1818–1831* (Oxford, 1969), 58. For Bennett's statistics, see Hansard, House of Commons, 18 February 1819. The colony's future was threatened by Jeremy Bentham, hot to promote his Panopticon, who in his *Letters to Lord Pelham* and *Plea for the Constitution* attacked the principle and practice of transportation; see R. V. Jackson, 'Theory and Evidence', *AJPH* 39/3.

CHAPTER 3

1. T. D. A. Le Sueur, 'William Baker', *JRAHS* 74/2 (1988), 133; see also J. Elliott, 'Was there a convict dandy?', *AHS* 26/104 (1995).

2. P. Knaplund, *James Stephen and the Colonial Office* (Madison, 1953) – still invaluable – p. 39.

3. For Macquarie on Marsden, see *DAB*.

4. For Bigge in South Africa, see F. Welsh, *A History of South Africa* (London, 1999), 132. Macquarie on Loane: in a distant but civil letter to Bigge (25 December 1820), 'I beg you will accept my best thanks for your kindness' (HRA, series 4 (1922), pp. 273–4). The reports are printed in PP, 1822, vol. XX (448), and analysed in J. H. Ritchie, *Evidence to the Bigge Reports*, 2 vols. (Melbourne, 1971). A flavour of Bigge's dourness is given in his recommendations that rations for those of 'advanced age' should be reduced and that 'all employments that have a tendency to encourage a passion for dress should be avoided' – incidentally indicating the ability of the convicts to enjoy themselves. P. Bridges, *Foundations of Identity* (Sydney, 1995), 132, points out that Bigge brought 'firmness of purpose and an acute legal mind' – never popular qualities – to bear on his task.

5. M. H. Ellis, *John Macarthur* (Sydney, 1955), chap. 32 for Macarthur's demarche; for the estates, see A. Atkinson, *Camden* (Melbourne, 1988).

6. On Wentworth, see A. C. V. Melbourne, *William Charles Wentworth* (Brisbane, 1934); D. C. Fifer, *W. C. Wentworth*, 2 vols. (n.p. [Australia], 1983, 1991).

7. On J. Stephen, see Melbourne, *Early Constitutional Development*, 102: Stephen to R. W. Horton 2 August 1827, quoted Knaplund, *James Stephen*, 231.

8. T. Brisbane, *Reminiscences* (Edinburgh, 1860). For H. de Bougainville, see T. Flannery (ed.), *The Birth of Sydney* (Melbourne, 1999), 235–8. He found Sydney could not really be compared with 'even our third-rate towns'. See also PP, 1826, vol. XXVI, pt. 2 (277), which recorded the use of flogging in New South Wales to extort confessions – acts condemned as 'entirely opposed to the principles of reformation and the interests of the welfare of society'.

9. For land alienation, Brisbane's proposals, see Brisbane to Bathurst, 24 July 1824, HRA, series 1, vol. 11, pp. 331–6.

10. Australian Agricultural Co., ibid. Bathurst to Brisbane, 17 April 1825, pp. 562–8. For Oxley, see R. Johnson, *Search for the Inland Sea* (Melbourne, 2001), and H. Proudfoot, 'John Oxley', *JRAHS* 79/1–2 (1993). J. C. H. Gill, *Missing Coast* (South Brisbane, 1988), calls attention to Oxley's achievements (p. 183), derided by Ellis, *John Macarthur*, 465. Mitchell is his own best historian in the journals, but see W. C. Forster, *Sir T. L. Mitchell* (Sydney, 1985); D. W. A. Baker, 'Thomas Mitchell', *JRAHS* 80/1–2 (1994) gives due credit to the explorer.

11. Australian pastoral properties, the equivalent of American ranches, were generally known as 'stations'. For that much-criticized and often misunderstood man Samuel Marsden, see A. T. Yarwood, *Samuel Marsden: The Great Survivor* (Carlton, 1977). M. Saclier, 'Sam Marsden's Colony', *JRHAS* 52/2 (1966), 2 refers to the 'tortured strands of unconscious, idealistic and economic motivation which drove this strange man'. See also R. Border, *Church and State in Australia* (London, 1962), 25 ff.

12. The 1707 Act of Union had established the Presbyterian Church of Scotland in that country, – see K. Grose, 'Status of the Church of Scotland', *JRAHS* 74/2 (1988). *ADB* describes Lang as 'clergyman, politician, immigration organiser, historian, anthropologist, journalist, gaol bird', and, according to his wife, 'patriot and statesman'. A necessary gadfly, Lang rarely exercised a serious influence: see A. Gilchrist (ed.), *John Dunmore Lang*, 2 vols. (Melbourne, 1951). For Therry, much more of a pastor than Lang (Brisbane instanced him as a 'model of discrimination and good judgement' to the horrified Presbyterian Lang (*ADB*)), there is a good article by J. Gregory, 'State Aid to Religion', *VHJ* 70/2 (1999). Brisbane's quarrel with Frederick Goulburn was the proximate cause of both men's recall, but the Governor's support for free institutions, 'to consider the Settlement as a Colony and not as a place for Punishment' (a 'great Error', according to Lord Bathurst, in a warning letter to G. Murray BM Loan 57/64), was at the bottom of Whitehall's annoyance; see N. D. McLachlan, 'Bathurst', *HS* 5/13, 484–5. Stephen, in one of his masterly minutes, to Horton, 27 March 1825 (HRA, series 4, vol. 1, pp. 591–612), adumbrates every aspect of a revised constitution – including the warning that 'no distinction' must be made between 'the Natives and the Settlers' and that 'the same methods may lawfully be taken to repress

outrage and Riot, whether the Aggressors are of the European or Aboriginal race'. For Hall and the *Monitor*, see E. Inde, 'Monitoring the Situation', *JRAHS* 85/1 (1999).

13. J. J. Eddy, *Britain and the Australian Colonies 1818–1831* (Oxford, 1969), 24. Stephen to Arthur: Mitchell Library, Arthur papers A 2164. For Bathurst and New South Wales, see N. Thompson, *Earl Bathurst* (Barnsley, 1999), and Bathurst Papers, BL Loan 57. See also Fox Maule to Ramsay, 20 December 1830; SRO Dalhousie Muniments, Alexander Turnbull Library MicroMS437, quoted M. Francis, *Governors and Settlers* (Basingstoke, 1992), 86 ff. For a defence of Darling see B. H. Fletcher, *Ralph Darling: A Governor Maligned* (Melbourne, 1984).

14. For Baxter, see *ADB*.

15. Minute of October 1827, quoted J. W. Cell, *British Colonial Administration in the Mid Nineteenth Century* (New Haven, 1970), 75.

16. For Patten, see F. Welsh, *A History of Hong Kong* (London, 1994), 538. K. McNaught, *The Penguin History of Canada* (London, 1988), is an accessible one-volume work.

17. The authoritative works on the Victorian Colonial Office are two by W. P. Morrell, *Colonial Policy of Peel and Russell* (Oxford, 1930) and *British Colonial Policy in the Mid-Victorian Age* (Oxford, 1969). Many of the documents are reproduced in F. Madden and D. Fieldhouse, *Settler Self-Government* (Westport, Conn., 1990).

18. Lord Durham: Cell, *British Colonial Administration* 96, quoting C. P. Lucas (ed.), *Lord Durham's Report*, 3 vols. (Oxford, 1912).

19. Address to Darling: HRA, series 1, vol. 12, pp. 144–7. For Darling see L. N. Rose, 'Administration of Governor Darling', *JRAHS* 8/2–3 (1958), and Francis, *Governors and Settlers*. A. G. L. Shaw, *Heroes and Villains in History* (Sydney, 1983), compares the administrations of Darling and Bourke.

20. J. M. Ward, *Colonial Self-Government* (London, 1976), 148.

21. Young Lord Howick's advanced ideas worried his more conservative father, ambitious for his heir's success; the author of the great Reform Bill, he had spent the enormous sum of £14,000 in the first attempt to buy the young man a parliamentary seat.

22. Quoted Ward, *Colonial Self-Government*, 149.

23. HRV vol. 1, pp. 24–6, 13 April 1836.

24. Wakefield: see Morrell, *Colonial Policy*, especially chaps. I, II and XIV. For Wakefield and policies in Australia see S. H. Roberts, *History of Australian Land Settlement* (Melbourne, 1968), Part II.

25. H. P. Egerton (ed.), *Sir William Molesworth's Speeches* (London, 1903). Molesworth eventually got the opportunity to oversee policy as Colonial Secretary in July 1855, but died within weeks of his appointment.

26. See Welsh, *History of South Africa*, 160 ff.

27. Personal efforts to 'civilize' Aborigines by taking them into settlers' homes began soon after the arrival of the First Fleet, Marsden being a notable example.

Governor and Mrs Macquarie encouraged Shelley's school. Successes were temporary, the attractions of traditional culture being too strong, but were enough to prove Aboriginal talents, as when one Parramatta girl came first in the public examinations. J. Harris, *One Blood* (Sutherland, 1990), gives a clear account of missionary endeavours and has a good bibliography; see also H. M. Carey, 'Missionary Wives', *JRH* 19/2 (1995). The Reverend J. R. Orton found 'almost insuperable barriers in the way of establishing within the territory of NSW' and moved to Port Phillip.

28. For Threlkeld, see J. Harris, *One Blood*, 53 ff; N. Gunson, *Australian Reminiscences, and Papers of L. E. Threlkeld* (Canberra, 1974).

29. For missions, see PP, 1834, vol. XLIV. Macquarie wrote: 'Those natives, who dwell near Sydney and the other principal settlements, live in a State of perfect Peace, Friendliness, and Sociality with the Settlers, and even Shew a Willingness to Assist them Occasionally in their Labours; and it seems only to require the fostering Hand of Time, gentle Means and Conciliatory Manners, to bring these poor Un-enlightened People into an important Degree of Civilization, and to Instill into their Minds, as they Gradually open to Reason and Reflection, a Sense of the Duties they owe their fellow Kindred and Society in general (to Which they Will then become United), and taught to reckon upon that Sense of Duty as the first and happiest Advance to a State of Comfort and Security' (October 1814: HRA, series 1, vol. 8, pp. 367–72).

CHAPTER 4

1. For the water supply, see Evandale Hist. Soc. Pamphlet 'Convict Built Water Scheme' (n.d.).

2. Foveaux's term on Norfolk Island is described in A.-M. Whitaker, *Joseph Foveaux* (Sydney, 2000), chap. 3.

3. The standard history of Tasmania is L. Robson (Melbourne, 1983). For the Tasmanian Aborigines, see L. Ryan, *Aboriginal Tasmanians* (Crow's Nest, 1996), an influential work: Rhys Jones's appendix on Tasmania in N. B. Tindall, *Aboriginal Tribes of Australia* (Canberra, 1974), is excellent; his estimate of the Aboriginal population is between 3,000 and 4,000, in over fifty bands. For early settlement, see S. Morgan, *Land Settlement in Early Tasmania* (Cambridge, 1992). The Tasmanian Historical Research Association (THRA) publications are a rich source. T. Murray and C. Williamson 'Archaeology and History' in R. Manne (ed.), *Whitewash* (Melbourne, 2003) has a summary of the most recent research.

4. See HRA, series 3, vol. 1, pp. 337 ff., 360 ff., 369 ff.

5. Reproduced in S. Morgan, *Land Settlement*, 146; Abel and Roadknight, ibid. p. 131. One of the settlers killed was William Russell who was alleged to have murdered or tortured any Aborigines 'who unfortunately came within his reach';

his death was seen as 'a striking instance of divine agency' (ibid., p. 155). For violence generally, see D. J. Mulvaney, *Encounters in Place* (St Lucia, 1989), 49–52, and for an iconoclastic analysis, K. Windschuttle, *Fabrication of Aboriginal History* (Sydney, 2002).

6. See H. Reynolds, *Fate of a Free People* (Ringwood, 1995), 31 – an essential corrective to simplistic views.

7. For Dry, see ibid., pp. 30–31; see also *ADB*.

8. A. Alexander, *Obliged to Submit: Wives and Mistresses of Colonial Governors* (Hobart, 1999), is illuminating. For Howe, see T. E. Wells, *Michael Howe* (Hobart, 1818); Wells, a contemporary, was Sorrell's convict clerk: p. 38 for Pugh's capture. Morgan, *Land Settlement*, 129, produces evidence of 'a reign of terror' produced by bushrangers, and adds that 'At least until 1825, they were far more of a worry than Aborigines'.

9. For Macquarie Harbour (not to be confused with Port Macquarie in New South Wales, a penal settlement rather than a severe prison), see D. Munro 'From Macquarie Harbour', *THRA* 36/3 (1989); J. Backhouse, *Narrative of a Visit to the Australian Colonies* (London, 1843).

10. The Leith Company's activities were another example of that Scottish enterprise which created the Victorian Clyde Company, originally also a Tasmanian venture – see P. Brown, *Clyde Company Papers* (Oxford, 1941–68).

11. For George Arthur, see *DNB*, *ADB*, A. G. L. Shaw, *Sir George Arthur* (Melbourne, 1980). Robert Hughes is at his best in analysing Arthur: 'Few people could extract much pleasure from Arthur's company, but none could doubt that here was the most incisive and vigilantly ordered mind ever to immerse itself in the problems of running a convict colony in the antipodes' (*The Fatal Shore* (London, 1996), 381 ff.).

12. A. G. L. Shaw, *Convicts and the Colonies* (London, 1966), 227 ff. From the 1820s on, with better trial and sentencing procedures, the character of transportees became more specifically criminal, varied by some contingents, from Ireland and Canada, of 'political' offenders. See e.g. I. Donnachie, 'Convicts of 1820', *SHR* 65/1 1 (1985); I. Brand, *Penal Peninsula* (Launceston, 1989). Since Port Arthur has become a major tourist attraction many highly coloured accounts of the alleged atrocious conditions have appeared. D. Young, *Making Crime Pay: The Evolution of Convict Tourism* (Sandy Bay, 1996), provides a useful corrective, disposing of many fables. For convict resistance, see T. Dunning and H. Maxwell-Stewart, 'Mutiny at Deloraine', *LH* 82 (2002).

13. For Arthur's incompetent officials, see P. A. Howell's entertaining essay, 'Shovelling out Distressed Gentlefolk', in G. Winter (ed.), *Tasmanian Insights* (Hobart, 1992), 77 ff. The Mitchell Library has a collection of Arthur papers, 2161–2220B, D290–292.

14. M. Roe, 'Mary Leman Grimstone', *THRA* 36/1 (1989). For Grimstone, see also *DNB*. See also E. M. Miller, *Australia's First Two Novels* (Hobart, 1958). Mary's attitudes, and her varied work, surely invite a biography.

15. Mary Reibey achieved immortality on the $20 Australian banknote: see N. Irvine, *Mary Reibey: Molly Incognita* (Sydney, 2001).

16. For what follows, see particularly Reynolds, *Fate of a Free People*, and C. Turnbull, *Black War* (Melbourne, 1974). Reynolds aptly characterizes Turnbull's views, still widely shared, as 'Pity for the Poor Black', which completely crowded out respect or balanced assessment.

17. Reynolds, *Fate of a Free People*, 88–91.

18. Ibid., pp. 95–6.

19. The 'Black Line' was one of the very few occasions on which British troops were deployed in Australia. 'Vinegar Hill' and the fight at the Eureka stockade were the most prominent clashes (see pp. 67 and 209–15 respectively). Against Aboriginals a file of the 21st Regiment took part in the 'Battle' of Pinjarra in 1834, but almost all actions against the native population were carried out by the local police or the settlers themselves, much more bloodily. Very few Australian Aborigines perished at the hands of British soldiers. For an overview see J. Connor, *Australian Frontier Wars* (Sydney, 2001).

20. Colonial Secretary to Lord Goderich, 6 April 1833, CO 280/41. See Reynolds, *Fate of a Free People*, chap. V. Arthur emphasized to Robinson and John Batman on 12 November 1831 that 'hostile' Aborigines should be 'induced, if possible, to proceed to the establishment at Great Island': PP, 1834, vol. XLIV.

21. Robinson's journals are edited by N. J. B. Plomley, *Friendly Mission* (Hobart, 1966); see also V. Rae-Ellis, *Black Robinson* (Carlton, 1988).

22. Hughes, *Fatal Shore*, 423.

23. Quoted in Reynolds, *Fate of a Free People*, 142.

24. Ibid., pp. 176, 184.

25. The petition is ibid., pp. 7–9.

26. Ibid., pp. 12–15.

27. Ibid., pp. 176–7.

28. For 'Old Scott', see M. Howard, 'Barque *Rebecca*', *THRA* 34/4 (1987). Captain McTaggart did indeed look after the children. The girls were taken in by Anne Drysdale, one of the two Port Phillip women pioneers – the other was Caroline Newcomb (see p. 130 and *ADB*) – and the boy by the magistrate Robert Fenwick of Geelong. It is interesting to contrast these accounts, by reliable witnesses, with that given of the islanders by Robert Hughes: 'There they guzzled rum, which was thoughtfully provided by their keepers, they posed impassively for photographers in front of their filthy slab huts, and they waited to die. In 1855 the census of natives was three men, two boys and eleven women, one of whom was Trucanini' (*Fatal Shore*, 423).

29. K. Fitzpatrick's biography (Melbourne, 1999) is still good; *Correspondence of Sir John and Lady Franklin* has been published by G. Mackaness, 2 vols. (Hobart, 1947). The Archives Office of Tasmania and the Cambridge Scott Polar Research Institute both have extensive collections of Franklin papers.

30. A. Alexander, *Obliged to Submit*, 137–8.

31. The letter is printed in Mackaness, *Correspondence*, vol. ii, pp. 22–9. See also J. Parrott, 'Elizabeth Fry', *THRA* 43/4 (1996), and P. Russell, *This Errant Lady* (Canberra, 2002). For incarceration, see e.g. 'Ross Female Factory', a pamphlet published by the Tasmanian Parks Service, which has an account of the 'depraved and abominable habits' of the inmates. See also A. Bartlett, 'Launceston Female Factory', *THRA* 41/2 (1994). One of Arthur's reforms was to abolish the use of neck irons, which weighed 5¼ pounds.

32. Maconochie; J. Clay, *Maconochie's Experiment* (London, 2001), is unfair to Arthur, and Fitzpatrick is better on Franklin.

33. Henry Lytton Bulwer should not be confused with his brother Edward, later Bulwer-Lytton and Lord Lytton, Colonial Secretary and novelist.

34. Australian constitutional development at this period is best followed in Morrell, *Colonial Policy of Peel and Russell* (Oxford, 1930).

35. See Shaw, *Convicts*, chaps. XI and XII for the debate.

36. Evidence to Molesworth: speech in House of Commons 5 May 1840; H. E. Egerton (ed.), *Sir William Molesworth's Speeches* (London, 1903), 90. Fitzpatrick, *Sir John Franklin*, is a corrective (p. 45). Maconochie had an exaggerated sense of his own importance, and very little sense of humour: 'dogmatic . . . tactless and too ready to teach before he had learnt.' The Report of the Select Committee is published in the House of Commons papers, vol. xxii, no. 669 (1837), and extracts are reproduced in C. M. H. Clark, *Sources of Australian History* (London, 1957), 189–223.

37. For d'Urville, the authoritative work is C. Forster, *France and Botany Bay* (Melbourne, 1996). After a lifetime's adventures d'Urville was killed in a rail accident.

38. John Batman has been posthumously praised for at least attempting an agreement with the Aborigines: in reality, Batman was a tough frontiersman who can have had little hope in his arrangement holding. All colonial land was Crown property, and only the government could extinguish any rights the Aborigines had to land and transfer *some* of these – more rarely all – to individuals. B. Bridges, 'Aborigines', *JRAHS* 56/2 (1970), 95, rightly calls 'the whole business a . . . farce'. R. F. Haines, 'The Respectable Emigration', *JAS* 33 (1992); in its issue of 12 July 1828 the *Lancet* recommended the climate of Australia for consumptives. For the early settlements, see T. F. Bride (ed.), *Letters from Victorian Pioneers* (Melbourne, 1969).

39. For Mitchell, see T. L. Mitchell, *Journal of an Expedition into the Interior of Tropical Australia* (London, 1848), and *Tasmanian Journal*, 3 (1849), 165, which also contains a dissertation on skeletal remains of the Bunyip – an otherwise fabulous creature. For Mrs Walsh and the early days at Port Phillip, see P. de Serville, *Port Phillip Gentlemen* (Melbourne, 1980), and the entertaining *Georgiana's Journal* (ed. H. McCrae (Sydney, 1966), 56); Mrs McCrae records 'Paddy' Walsh's ultimate downfall and bankruptcy in 1843 (p. 186). M. Akers, 'Crinolines and Red Knickers', *VHJ* 55/4 (1984), is entertaining.

40. For La Trobe, see D. McCaughey, N. Perkins, and A. Trumble, *Victoria's Colonial Governors* (Melbourne, 1993), 13–39; L. J. Blake (ed.), *Letters of*

C. J. *La Trobe* (Melbourne, 1975), 17, and A. Gross, *Charles Joseph La Trobe* (Melbourne, 1980).

41. For the Protectorate, see P. Bridges, *Foundations of Identity* (Sydney, 1995), 102–5.

42. Robertson's letter is reproduced in Clark, *Sources*, 172 ff.

43. Ibid. pp. 180–81. Critchett, *A Distant Field of Murder* (Melbourne, 1990), appendices 2 & 3; Windschuttle, *Fabrication of Aboriginal History*, chap. 1.

44. This section is based on M. H. Fels, *Good Men and True* (Carlton, 1988).

45. Ibid., p. 65.

46. See A. G. L. Shaw, 'Separation and Federation', *VHJ* 68/1 (1997).

47. R. D. Murray, *A Summer at Port Phillip* (Edinburgh, 1843), 37; Westgarth, *Australia Felix* (Edinburgh, 1848), 204 ff.

48. HRA series 1, vol. 12, pp. 700 ff.

49. J. M. R. Cameron, 'Foundation of Western Australia Reconsidered', *JRWAHS* 12/2 (1996), is an intriguing account of the negotiations behind the start of the Swan River settlement.

50. For a review of Aboriginal historiography, see P. Biskop, in G. Osborne and W. F. Mandle (eds.), *New History: Studying Australia Today* (Sydney, 1982). For Aboriginal resistance, see C. T. Stannage *et al.* (eds.), *New History of Western Australia* (Nedlands, 1981), 82 ff., and for a revisionary account (to be taken with a pinch of salt), Windschuttle, *Fabrication of Aboriginal History*. Much ink has been expended on the violent encounters between Aborigines and settlers, to very little point. Any uninvited occupation of land and homes by an alien people is highly likely to lead to bloodshed (searching for exceptions, the joint occupation of the 'barren island' of Hong Kong by British and Chinese, or the southward spread of the African Bantu tribes might call for consideration). As long as the Australian colonies continued to be a British responsibility some efforts were made to insist on Aboriginal rights. When, in the 1850s, elected colonial governments took over, Aboriginal rights were, largely, ignored and Aboriginal freedoms restricted, albeit often with benevolent intentions. On the frontiers, violence continued. Freedom and rights have since been restored, against vocal opposition, and more recently than might have been expected. Current problems require current solutions, and the use of history to inject passions into politics is, as many examples instance, rarely without dangers. The 'Battle' of Pinjarra, and other more recent clashes should be recorded, regretted, remembered, and accorded only their proper place in the complex history of Australia. The clearest view is that of J. Connor, *Australian Frontier Wars* (Sydney, 2001).

51. On theatres, see P. Parsons (ed.), *Companion to Australian Theatre* (Sydney, 1995); the Theatre Royal in Hobart and the Victoria in Adelaide were both opened in Queen Victoria's Coronation year. The Hobart theatre was later the only one in the Empire to boast a saloon licence: see G. Winter, 'A Colonial Theatrical Experience', *THRA* 32/4 (1989). In 1848 W. H. Wells, in his *Geographical Dictionary of the Australian Colonies* (Sydney, 1970 [1848]), described Adelaide's

public buildings as 'not to be surpassed by any erections of a similar kind in any part of the more modern colonies of the British Empire'; Perth was merely noted as 'a town of Western Australia'.

52. For Lochee, see *ADB*.

53. For New Norcia, see E. J. Stormon (ed.), *The Salvado Memoirs* (Perth, 1977).

54. Printed in full in Clark, *Sources*, 161–4.

55. For South Australia, see D. Pike, *Paradise of Dissent* (London, 1957); PP, 1841, vol. XVII and B. Dickey and P. Howell, *South Australia's Foundation* (Netley, SA, 1986).

56. Comment by Robert Hay, parliamentary under-secretary at the Colonial Office, February 1813, quoted in J. J. Eddy, *Britain and the Australian Colonies 1818–1831* (Oxford, 1969), 254. The South Australia Act (4 & 5 Will. IV, c. 95), clause xxii, ensured that 'no person convicted in any court of justice . . . shall at any time, or under any circumstance . . . be transported to the new colony'.

57. K. N. Bell and W. P. Morrell, *Select Documents on British Colonial Policy, 1830–1860* (London, 1928), 199–204.

58. J. Bentham MSS, University College London, Box 8; quoted D. Pike, *Paradise of Dissent*, 57.

59. Napier (always known as Charles and confusingly referred to in Pike, *Paradise of Dissent*, as *James* Napier) wrote an indignant book, *Colonization: Particularly in South Australia* (London, 1835), in which he attacked the Western Australians and Tasmanians for their treatment of the Aborigines, 'equal to all other men', who displayed 'nobleness and courage' in the face of 'aggression and horrid cruelties' (p. 94). The Colonel insisted that the colonists must be held 'in subjection' by '*hanging them* (I hate indeterminate expressions)'. Napier, who went on to subjugate a large part of India, was an imperialist quite unlike those characterized by hostile writers.

60. C. D. Rowley, *The Destruction of Aboriginal Society* (Canberra, 1970), 74.

61. SA Archives D73327(T).

62. For Hindmarsh, see F. S. Hindmarsh, *From Powder Monkey to Governor* (Northbridge, WA, 1995).

63. Fidelia Hill; see P. Butterss, 'Fidelia Hill', *JSAS* 23 (1995).

64. For Cobb & Co., see G. Blainey, *Tyranny of Distance* (Melbourne, 1966), 143 ff.

65. Religious persecution, by the Austrian emperor, also brought the Society of Jesus to the colony, whose members tempered the largely Irish traditions of the Australian Church: R. Schumann, 'In the Hands of the Lord', *JHSSA* 14 (1986). For a thoroughly biased account of South Australian missionary work, C. Stevens, *White Man's Dreaming* (Melbourne, 1994), is a fine example.

66. See T. K. Hardy, *Pictorial Atlas of Australian Wines* (Melbourne, 1986).

67. Grey has a sympathetic biographer in J. Rutherford (London, 1961); for a more critical view see NLS, Minto MS 1423.

68. For Zonnenbloem, see A. Odendal, 'South Africa's Black Victorians', ICS

paper no. 4 (1996); the school's cricket team was the best in the Cape Peninsula. For Grey's views on 'civilizing' Aborigines see G. Grey, *Journals* (London, 1841) vol. 2, pp. 373–88.

69. For Brisbane's views, see Shaw, *Convicts*, 190.

70. Quoted in Hughes, *Fatal Shore*. 443.

71. See Forster, *France and Botany Bay*, chap. 8.

72. For the Scots, see J. MacKenzie-Smith, 'Moreton Bay Scots', *JRHSQ* 16/11. Lang envisaged three new 'provinces' to the north of New South Wales: 'Flindersland, Cooksland and Leichhardtsland'.

CHAPTER 5

1. See C. P. Lucas (ed.), *Lord Durham's Report*, 3 vols. (Oxford, 1912); see also K. McNaught, *Penguin History of Canada* (London, 1988), 92–6; P. A. Buckner, *Transition to Responsible Government* (Westport, Conn., 1985); J. W. Cell, *British Colonial Administration in the Mid Nineteenth Century* (New Haven, 1970).

2. G. Martin, in A. Porter (ed.), *The Nineteenth Century* (Oxford History of the British Empire, Oxford, 1999), 539, having skated over the Durham Report, concludes that the defining moment was the House of Commons refusal in 1849 to challenge the Rebellion Losses Act. For New South Wales, see A. C. V. Melbourne, *Early Constitutional Development in Australia* (St Lucia, 1963); T. H. Irving, 'The idea of Responsible Governments', *HS* 11; the published Elgin–Grey correspondence, ed. A. Doughty (Ottawa, 1937) is less revealing than the unpublished letters and journal GRE/V/1/C3/13 in the Grey collection at Durham University.

3. J. Gipps, *Every Inch a Governor* (Port Melbourne, 1996), is a dutiful biography. For the changing character of governors in the period, see R. V. Kubicek's classic *Administration of Imperialism* (Durham, NC, 1969). M. Francis's apt analysis, in *Governors and Settlers* (Basingstoke, 1992), 157, is that Gipps 'possessed tightly structured and internalized political ideas which resulted in persistent attempts to change the constitutional structure and the behaviour of the colony'.

4. Russell's extraordinary industry is illustrated by the fact that in the twelve months after October 1840 he sent 147 dispatches to Gipps, recorded in HRA series 1, vol. 21, plus another 27 mentioned by heading only.

5. See D. Denoon and P. Mein-Smith, *A History of Australia, New Zealand and the Pacific* (Oxford, 2000), 124 ff.

6. See J. M. Ward, *James Macarthur* (Sydney, 1981), 114 ff. Lowe's Australian activities are well covered in R. Knight, *Illiberal Liberal* (Carlton, 1966). For 'higgling and bargaining', see CO 201/356, Gipps to Stanley, 13 February1845, quoted in W. P. Morrell, *Colonial Policy of Peel and Russell* (Oxford, 1930), 98.

7. Legislative Council's protest: Votes and Proceedings, 9 August 1844.

8. F. Madden and D. Fieldhouse, *Settler Self-Government* (Westport, Conn., 1990), 288 ff.

9. For 'The Squatter who Failed', see C. M. H. Clark, *Sources of Australian History* (London, 1957), 276–8. *The Times* reported from Sydney (11 July 1844) with a tinge of *schadenfreude* that 'Doctors, lawyers and tutors wish they had been bred carpenters, shoemakers or some other trade that people cannot dispense with'.

10. Gipps to Russell, 19 December 1840, HRA, series 1, vol. 21, p. 122.

11. For the effects of the Order in Council, see E. Scott (ed.), *Australia* (Cambridge History of the British Empire, Cambridge, 1988 [1933]), 205.

12. CO 881/1 no. 1 quoted J. M. Ward, *Colonial Self-Government* (London, 1976), 171.

13. *Encyclopaedia Britannica*, 8th edn.: 'Prisons'.

14. See J. Clay, *Maconochie's Experiment* (London, 2001). For Gipps's relations with Maconochie, see S. McCulloch, 'Sir George Gipps and Captain Alexander Maconochie', *HS* 7.

15. The truly horrible conditions of Norfolk Island under Childs are described in R. Hughes, *The Fatal Shore* (London, 1996), 533–42. When the reports reached London Lord Grey was horrified, and had them published in the parliamentary papers. Childs was dismissed by the Tasmanian Legislative Council (against the opposition of Eardley-Wilmot) but ended his career as a major general. His successor, the well-connected civilian John Price, was possibly worse: see Hughes, *Fatal Shore*, 543–51 for the curious details. Price's conduct was exposed by the admirable Catholic bishop Robert Willson, and the penal settlement finally closed; Price, transferred to Victoria, continued his sadistic conduct and was eventually murdered by the convicts. See also J. V. W. Barry (himself a judge criminologist), *Life and Death of John Price* (Melbourne, 1964), and A. G. L. Shaw, *Convicts and the Colonies* (London, 1966), 339–40 and 352–3.

16. Lord Grey, clearly unsure as to exactly what constituted the British Empire, wrote to old James Stephen to ask whether the islands 'are claimed as British possession, and if so would there be any objection to a grant being made . . . to Mr. Enderby for a whaling station'. For the miserable colonists, see J. F. Hogan, *The Gladstone Colony* (London, 1898), 63 ff., and G. Barney, 'Settlement of North Australia', in R. Cilento, *Triumph in the Tropics* (Brisbane, 1959), 130–35; Col. Barney reported favourably and forecast 'the speedy formation of a settlement under private enterprise' (p. 5). Boys who had benefited from Parkhurst prison, being trained under probation at Point Puer in the Port Arthur complex, had previously been termed exiles; they were stigmatized as 'troublesome, deceitful, liars and drunken' and the experiment was abandoned; Shaw, *Convicts*, 286.

17. Stanley's description of Eardley-Wilmot as a 'muddle-brained blockhead' is from a letter to Sir Robert Peel, December 1842, quoted in Morrell, *Colonial Policy*, 389.

18. See R. M. Hartwell, *The Economic Development of Van Diemen's Land 1820–1850* (Melbourne, 1994). For the Council, see V. Korobacz, 'Legislative

Council', *THRA* 21/1 (1974). For Stephen on Eardley-Wilmot, see one of the most revealing documents of the period, a candid memorandum by James Stephen in the Cambridge University Library, Add. MSS 7511, discussed by T. Barron and K. J. Cable in *HS* 13. Sodomy is judged by R. Hyam, *Empire and Sexuality* (Manchester, 1990), 101, to have 'flourished' and was 'treated as less serious than pipe-smoking'. 'Shall Tasman's isle so fam'd,/So lovely and so fair,/From other nations be estranged/The name of Sodom bear?': so lamented a Scots visitor; J. Syme, *Nine Years in Van Diemen's Land* (Dundee, 1848), 200–1.

19. See Grey's apologia: *Colonial Policy of Lord John Russell's Administration* (London, 1853); see also J. M. Ward, *Earl Grey and the Australian Colonies* (Carlton, 1958), and Grey's journal (see n. 2 above). C. C. F. Greville, *Memoirs*, 3 vols. (London, 1875), vol. iii, pp. 312–13. 15 February 1847, CO 280/196, Stephen to Treasury.

20. Grey to Stephen, Grey papers, Durham, Add. 7888/II/10. The self-contained and distant Grey was not given to unburdening himself, and this letter is a rare example of an unconstrained disclosure.

21. Proceedings of the Legislative Council for 1846, 2nd Session, quoted in Clark, *Sources*, 226, 231. See also I. Wynd, *Pentonvillains* (Geelong, 1996).

22. Lowe and Grey, quoted Knight, *Illiberal Liberal*, 216. Grey's minute on Fitzroy despatch, 21 March 1849, CO 201/412.

23. *Sydney Morning Herald*, 12 June 1849, quoted in Clark, *Sources*, 249.

24. For Captain Henderson, see Morrell, *Colonial Policy*, 408 ff., and *ADB*; for Hampton, see Shaw, *Convicts*, 356.

25. CO 201/375 no. 203, quoted F. Madden and D. Fieldhouse, *Settler Self-Government* (Westport, Conn., 1990), 296 ff.

26. Grey to Fitzroy, 31 July 1842, PP, 1847–8, vol. XLII (715), p. 6.

27. PP, 1848, vol. XXV (Cmd. 1074), pp. 33 ff.

28. See P. Knaplund, *James Stephen and the Colonial Office* (Madison, 1953), 244; see also P. Knaplund, 'Sir James Stephen', *Victorian History Magazine*, 12 (1928).

29. For Clergy and School Lands Corporation, see K. Grose, 'Educational Experiment of the 1820s', Ph. D. thesis (Sydney, 1974); and idem, *AHS* 25/99 (1992).

30. On the Protector William Thomas, see A. G. L. Shaw, 'British Policy towards the Australian Aborigines', *AHS* 25/99 (1992); for Protectors' duties as defined by the Colonial Office, see p. 272. For Thomas, see also T. F. Bride (ed.), *Letters from Victorian Pioneers* (Melbourne, 1969), 65–100.

31. That perceptive and entertaining traveller Bill Bryson, in *Down Under* (London, 2001), 253–8, writes of a visit to Myall Creek and Bingara, where he found no memorial, but a journalist who told him that most people had never heard of the massacre. 'All that was different . . . was that white people were punished for it.' Since Bryson wrote, a tribute to the 'Wirrayaraay people . . . murdered . . . in an unprovoked but premeditated attack' has been constructed. See H. Goodall in *AHS* 118 (2002). An extensive report of Nunn's actions was

submitted to Lord Glenelg on 22 July 1839 (HRA, series 1, vol. 20). Plunkett confessed: 'I see the whole case surrounded by so many embarrassing circumstances that it is very difficult for me to determine what course should now be taken.' See also R. H. W. Reece, *Aborigines and Colonists* (Sydney, 1974), chap. 1 'Blacks and Whites' and chap. 4 'Myall Creek Trials'. I. McBryde, *Records of Times Past* (Canberra, 1978), 38, notes that Plunkett accused prosperous squatters, led by Robert Scott, of attempting 'to protect the stock-keepers and shepherds in their extermination of the blacks'; Gipps removed Scott from the bench as a result of his actions.

32. For Myall Creek and Threlkeld, see N. Gunson, *Australian Reminiscences and Papers of L. E. Threlkeld* (Canberra, 1974), 274 ff. Keith Windschuttle (*Quadrant*, December 2000) queries with some justification the reliability of Threlkeld's evidence; but the incident at Myall Creek *was* at the time investigated and the accused sentenced. What is perhaps remarkable, and supports Threlkeld, is the perpetrators' lack of awareness that they had done anything particularly wrong, and the general public shock at their execution.

33. See J. N. Molony, *An Architect of Freedom: John Hubert Plunkett* (Canberra, 1973).

34. Quoted in 'Legend of the Good Fella Missus,' *Aboriginal History*, 142 (1990) – a condescending essay. Henry Parkes, later New South Wales Prime Minister, also wrote: 'Loud talk ye of the savages/As they were beasts of prey! – /But men of English birth have done/More savage things than they.'

35. Another variation of the arsenic story is reported by E. Lloyd, *Visit to the Antipodes* (London, 1846), 124 ff., in which arsenic was mixed with flour, marked 'Arsenic – Poison!' and left where Aborigines might, without too much difficulty, steal it. For the evidence against Coutts, see C. D. Rowley, *The Destruction of Aboriginal Society* (Canberra, 1970), 192–3.

36. HRA, series 1, vol. 20, 21 December 1839.

CHAPTER 6

1. For events in Canada see K. McNaught, *Penguin History of Canada* (London, 1988), 102 ff. For the Grey committee report and subsequent Bill see W. P. Morrell, *Colonial Policy of Peel and Russell* (Oxford, 1930), 365–70.

2. It was to a great extent the colonial lobbyists in London, objecting to the federal tariff proposals, who delayed the Bill's passage, John Jackson of Van Diemen's Land being notably influential: *ADB* and Morrell, *Colonial Policy*, 369–70. For an extended view, see J. M. Ward, *Earl Grey and the Australian Colonies* (Carlton, 1958), chap. 7.

3. Hansard, House of Commons, 8 February 1850. Lord John's reference was to William Russell, executed in 1683 for his resistance to the Stuart monarchy; his father was created Duke of Bedford after the 1688 Revolution as a result.

4. Hansard, House of Lords, 31 May 1850 and 14 June 1850.

5. Russell's speech, Hansard, House of Commons, 28 June 1850. Stephen to J. W. Cunningham, 20 March 1850, quoted C. E. Stephen, *Sir James Stephen* (London, 1906), 143–4.

6. Fitzroy stayed in office for eight years, an unusually long time, and very sensibly attempted not to exercise any of his powers as Governor General outside New South Wales. See J. M. Ward, *Australia's First Governor-General* (Sydney, 1963). J. Badger, 'Lamentable Death of Lady Mary Fitzroy', *JRAHS* 87/2 (2001) is an entertaining account of Sir Charles's unfortunate carriage accident, in which Lady Mary was killed, while her husband was at the reins. For the constitutionalists, see J. A. Ellis, 'Benevolent Society', *JRAHS* 77/4 (1991).

7. On 1 May 1851; New South Wales Legislative Council Proceedings, 1851, vol. 1, quoted in C. M. H. Clark, *Select Documents in Australian History*, 2 vols. (Sydney, 1955), vol. ii, pp. 322–5; ibid., 10 August 1852.

8. G. Cecil, *Life of Robert, Marquess of Salisbury*, 4 vols. (London, 1921, 1931, 1932), vol. i, pp. 33–4. For Hawes, see Hansard, House of Commons, 8 February 1850.

9. For Pakington, see W. F. Monypenny and G. E. Buckle, *The Life of Benjamin Disraeli*, 6 vols. (London, 1910–14), vol. iii, p. 348.

10. Pakington to Fitzroy, 15 December 1852, New South Wales Legislative Council Proceedings, 1853, vol. 1, extract in Clark, *Select Documents*, vol. ii, p. 328.

11. Almost immediately after his appointment (18 January 1853), Newcastle wrote to Fitzroy to say that 'nobody was more competent than the Legislative Council to decide the future New South Wales constitutions' and withdrawing Pakington's restriction (CO 201/453, no. 13).

12. A. C. V. Melbourne, *Early Constitutional Development in Australia* (St Lucia, 1963), 373.

13. CO 201/445, no. 10070; see W. P. Morrell, *British Colonial Policy in the Mid-Victorian Age* (Oxford, 1969), 420–21.

14. PP, 1852/3, vol. LXVI (12636), pp. 24–6, quoted Morrell, *British Colonial Policy*, 48. It was more than a hundred years before full-blood Australian Aborigines gained the political rights – and therefore the experience in political organization – of South African Coloureds and blacks. Nelson Mandela and the present South African constitution are the heirs of Newcastle's initiative.

15. Ward, *Australia's First Governor-General*, 321.

16. On 16 August 1853, quoted in Clark, *Select Documents*, vol. ii, 334–40.

17. Ibid., pp. 341 ff. For Deniehy, see also E. A. Martin, *Life and Speeches of Daniel Henry Deniehy* (Melbourne, 1884), and D. Headon and E. Perkins, *Our First Republicans* (n.p. [Australia], 1998).

18. 'A person named Rogers' is a remark by George Higinbotham (see below). For Rogers's correspondence with Gladstone, see e.g. BL. Add. MSS 44107 WEG/ 236. For Higinbotham and Newcastle's views, see K. H. Bailey in E. Scott (ed.),

Australia (Cambridge History of the British Empire, Cambridge, 1988 [1933]), 395–8.

19. On reserved Bills, see ibid., p. 411.

20. For Victoria, see especially G. Serle, *The Golden Age* (Melbourne, 1963), and *Rush to be Rich* (Melbourne, 1974).

21. Gipps to Russell 19 December 1840, 'Memo on Land Policies', HRA, series I, vol. 21, p. 122; see S. H. Roberts in Scott, *Australia*, 200–20.

22. Foster, 16 December 1853, quoted Serle, *Golden Age*, 147. For a comparative view, see P. Knaplund in *HS* 7/28 (1957).

23. G. Davison, *Marvellous Melbourne* (Melbourne, 1998), 167.

24. Quoted by J. B. McMaster in *The Cambridge Modern History*, vol. vii, chap. XII, pp. 401 ff.

25. On gold, see B. Hodge, 'Gold and Mrs Silver', *JRAHS* 78/1–2 (1992). J. N. Molony, *Penguin History of Australia* (Ringwood, 1987), 103. For Charlotte Godley, see J. R. Godley, *Letters from Early New Zealand* (Christchurch, 1951), 355 ff.

26. 'A Retired Officer', *Australia a Mistake* (London, 1855); see also *Australia and her Treasures* (London, 1852) by a more optimistic 'Nugget', H. Capper, *Australian Colonies: Where They Are and How to Get to Them* (London, 1852); J. Fairfax, *Colonies of Australia* (London, 1852), G. C. Mundy, *Our Antipodes* (London, 1857), and W. H. Hall, *Practical Experience at the Diggings* (London, 1852).

27. For Cecil's journey, see A. Roberts, *Salisbury: Victorian Titan* (London, 2000), 17–20.

28. W. Howitt, *Two Years in Victoria* (London, 1856), 61; Davison, *Marvellous Melbourne*, 63.

29. Howitt, *Two Years in Victoria*, 427. For Wright, see *ADB*.

30. For Bull, See *ADB*. Sandhurst-educated, like Wright, the Irish Bull described the licence fee as 'an unfortunate tax'. For Hotham and Malmesbury, see D. McCaughey, N. Perkins and A. Trumble, *Victoria's Colonial Governors* (Melbourne, 1993), 44.

31. Headon and Perkins, *Our First Republicans*, has a good selection from Lang.

32. See, *inter alia*, Serle, *Golden Age*, chap. 6; W. Bate, *Lucky City* (Carlton, 1978), chap. 4; J. N. Molony, *Eureka* (Melbourne, 1984); and idem, *History of Australia*, chap. 6. Molony points out that although the Eureka flag was subsequently seized by restless elements of the political and industrial left, the 'British Freedoms of religion, press and association were upheld and treasured by many. Law and order on the English model was accepted' (*History of Australia*, 108 ff.). P. O'Farrell, *The Irish in Australia* (Kensington, 1986), 92, describes Eureka 'in its Irish context' as an historical re-enactment (of the 1798 rebellion), 'just as much a mixture of the glorious, the farcical and the stupid' – but, he might have added, very much less sanguinary and brutal; 30,000 were killed in the atrocities

of 1798 – see F. Welsh, *Four Nations* (London, 2002), chap. 8; see also J. Ireland, 'Eureka Politics or Self Defence?', *VHJ* 68/1 (1997), and the Victorian parliamentary papers, ed. H. Anderson. P. Pickering, 'Ripe for a Republic', *AHS* 34/121 (2003), analyses British working-class radical responses to Eureka; see also A. B. Sunter, 'Celebrating the Nation and Empire in Ballarat', *AVSJ* 7 (2001) and M. McKenna, *Reluctant Republic*.

33. Hotham, see McCaughey *et al.*, *Victoria's Colonial Governors*, 56, and *Ballarat Times*, 2 September 1854, quoted ibid., p. 57.

34. The Ballarat Reform League, 2 February 1854, quoted Clark, *Select Documents*, vol. ii, pp. 58–60.

35. See Bate, *Lucky City*, 33. When elected to the Victoria Legislative Assembly in 1856 Lalor voted against manhood suffrage, and for a nominated upper house. R. W. Birrell, 'Guided Democracy', *VHJ* 68/1 (1997), describes the contribution to reduced tension afforded by the miners' courts established after Eureka, underlining the essential commitment of Australian miners to the rule of law.

36. *Argus*, 4 December and 5 December 1854: 'Fatal Collision at Ballaarat' (*sic*), reproduced in C. M. H. Clark, *Sources of Australian History* (London, 1957), 300–307. For the deficiencies in the administration of justice, see D. Palmer, 'Magistrates', in D. Philips and S. Davies, *A Nation of Rogues?* (Melbourne, 1994).

37. W. Bate, *Lucky City*, 170, 173, 174.

CHAPTER 7

1. Sir George Grey to General R. H. Wynard, 8 December 1854: see W. P. Morrell, *British Colonial Policy in the Mid-Victorian Age* (Oxford, 1969), chap. VIII.

2. Denison's autobiography, *Varieties of Vice-Regal Life*, 2 vols. (London, 1870), is entertaining, as is A. Alexander, *Obliged to Submit: Wives and Mistresses of Colonial Governors* (Hobart, 1999), chap. 11, on Lady Denison. For the initial problems, see A. C. V. Melbourne, *Early Constitutional Development in Australia* (St Lucia, 1963), chap. VI.

3. F. Madden and D. Fieldhouse, *Settler Self-Government* (Westport, Conn., 1990), 328.

4. Parker was John Macarthur's son-in-law, and all things considered did well to hold on for a year and to get four Bills through the House.

5. Parkes has a good biography, A. W. Martin, *Henry Parkes* (Melbourne, 1980), and *Letters from Menie* (Melbourne, 1983); see also R. Travers, *Grand Old Man*, (Kenthurst, 1992); N. B. Nairn, 'Political Mastery of Sir Henry Parkes', *JRAHS* 53 (1967); and Parkes' own work, *Fifty Years in the Making of Australian History* (Hobart, 1892).

6. Cowper and Robertson: see *ADB*. Robertson is described as having a natural gift for profanity; still something of an asset in Australian political life. Forster,

liberal minded and acute, 'offended society with his bushman's clothes', quarrelled with Parkes over his poetry and wrote a verse play (among a prolific output) the *Weirwolf* (sic).

7. Madden and Fieldhouse, *Settler Self-Government*, 328.

8. Land League of New South Wales Manifesto, 26 April 1859, quoted C. M. H. Clark, *Select Documents in Australian History*, 2 vols. (Sydney, 1955), vol. ii, pp. 99–103.

9. Journal of the Legislative Council New South Wales, 1883, vol. 34, pt. 12, pp. 28–35, quoted in Clark, *Select Documents*, vol. ii, pp. 126–35. The authoritative work is S. H. Roberts, *History* part IV.

10. Legislative Assembly speech in June 1869, quoted ibid., pp. 115–16.

11. The admirable Caroline Chisholm made it her business to create a system for welcoming and settling immigrants. 'It is only those who have been in the Colony that can understand the sacrifice': PP, 1847, vol. VI (737). See also M. Kiddle, *Caroline Chisholm* (Carlton, 1996). For the Highland family see I. L. Bird, 'Australia Felix', *Leisure Hours* (1877), 251.

12. For O'Shanassy, see PP, 1856, vol. xliii, no. 1; Hotham to Russell, 27 June 1855 quoted in Clark, *Select Documents*, vol. ii, pp. 329–31.

13. See G. Serle, *The Golden Age* (Melbourne, 1963), 279.

14. Barkly has an enthusiastic biography: M. Macmillan, *Sir Henry Barkly* (Cape Town, 1970); see also D. McCaughey, N. Perkins and A. Trumble, *Victoria's Colonial Governors* (Melbourne, 1993).

15. For the 1858 crisis, see Serle, *Golden Age*, 273–82.

16. C. Dilke, *Greater Britain*, 2 vols. (London, 1869), vol. ii. Temptations to restless demagoguery were heightened by the institution of triennial Parliaments, beginning in South Australia in 1856, followed by the other states ending with Tasmania in 1935.

17. S. J. Butlin, *Australia and New Zealand Bank* (London, 1961) chap. 10, is in excellent source of statistics. One mark of Melbourne's status was the visit of the scandalous Lola Montez in 1855, severely condemned by the Reverend A. Cairns: 'We know of no instance of good effected by stage playing' – an early example of what became known as 'wowserism'.

18. See C. Nance in *JHSSA* 5 (1978), *South Australia Register*, 28 June 1855.

19. Dilke, *Greater Britain*, 121.

20. J. Gregory, 'State Aid to religion', *VHJ* 70/2 (1999).

21. MacDonnell was described by one disgruntled colonial servant as 'coarse, bumptious, and exceptionally inconsiderate and uncourteous', and 'habitually addressed the grandees of the Colonial Office in terms not ordinarily used by colonial governors'; he was an excellent man for South Australia; see F. Welsh, *A History of Hong Kong* (London, 1994), 238. For Henry Young, see *DAB*. For Mints, see *Australian Encyclopaedia*, vol. vi, p. 102, and the Royal Australian Mint's publication *Making Money*. PP, 1852, vol. xxxiv, p. 1508. Young to Grey 6 January 1682, quoted in Clark, *Select Documents*, vol. ii, pp. 86–8.

22. MacDonnell to Russell, 22 August 1855, PP, 1856, vol. XLIII. I, quoted Clark, *Select Documents*, vol. ii, p. 342.

23. Hansard, House of Lords, 4 March 1851.

24. Lady Denison's diary, 10 August 1851, quoted W. P. Morrell, *Colonial Policy of Peel and Russell* (Oxford, 1930), 418.

25. For the Hampton case, see W. A. Townsley, *Struggle for Self-Government in Tasmania* (Hobart, 1977), (hardly an aptly named book), chap. VII.

26. See M. French, *A Pastoral Romance* (Toowoomba, 1990), 125.

27. CO 234/1 no. 19, 6 February 1860. Bowen complacently went on to claim that in Queensland 'distress and pauperism were unknown; all classes were devoted to law and order'.

28. Welsh, *History of Hong Kong*, 292–3.

29. T. Sykes, *Two Centuries of Panic* (Sydney, 1988), chap. 5 for the railway crises; the reaction of the unemployed to the crisis (pp. 102–5) contradicted Bowen's optimism. For the constitutional implications, see Lord Carnarvon's letters to Bowen published in Queensland Legislative Assembly Votes and Proceedings, 1867, pp. 83 ff., in which Carnarvon emphasizes the need for 'a frank and confidential relationship between the Governor and his advisers'.

30. Dilke, *Greater Britain*, 124–5.

CHAPTER 8

1. G. Serle, *Rush to be Rich* (Melbourne, 1974), 235.

2. For a summary of Australian exploration, see the two articles in *Australian Encyclopaedia*: 'Exploration by Sea' and 'Exploration by Land'. The best general survey, being extracts from the expedition diaries, is T. Flannery, *The Explorers* (Melbourne, 1998), plus K. Fitzpatrick, *Australian Explorers: A Selection from Their Writings* (London, 1958), and R. D. Haynes, *Seeking the Centre* (Cambridge, 1998). For Leichhardt, see E. M. Webster, *Whirlwinds on the Plains* (Melbourne, 1986), and idem, *An Explorer at Rest* (Melbourne, 1986). Patrick White's novel *Voss* is based on Leichhardt.

3. T. H. Huxley, the great geologist and palaeontologist, as a young man had hoped to join Kennedy's expedition during his tour of duty in HMS *Rattlesnake*; he judged Kennedy a 'fine noble fellow'. See A. Desmond, *Huxley: Devil's Disciple* (London, 1994). During the visit Huxley witnessed an operation with ether as an anaesthetic, and married an Australian girl.

4. Eyre went on to become Governor of Jamaica, and infamous for his needlessly bloody suppression of a rebellion; Huxley was one of his bitterest critics. When George Goyder investigated reports of water in the lake bed in 1857 he 'returned with words of rapture on his lips', reporting 'babbling brooks and succulent grasses and everything the pastoralist could desire': E. Scott, in Scott (ed.), *Australia* (Cambridge History of the British Empire, Cambridge, 1988 [1933]), 140.

5. A. C. and F. T. Gregory, *Journals of Australian Explorations* (Brisbane, 1884).

6. S. Murgatroyd, *Dig Tree* (London, 2002), a lively account of the Burke and Wills expedition, also covers Stuart's parallel expedition. T. Bonyhady, *Burke and Wills* (Balmain, 1991), is fuller and deals with the iconography.

7. Quoted, with a reproduction of the original, in an astonishingly clear and firm hand, in Murgatroyd, *Dig Tree*, 267–71.

8. For the explorations, see Forrest's four volumes of exploration journals; the biography is G. C. Bolton, *Alexander Forrest* (Melbourne, 1958). His later career indicates that the qualities needed for success in colonial politics did not necessarily translate into national affairs.

9. *South Australian Advertiser*, 6 November 1874.

10. Quoted in H. Reynolds, *The Law of the Land* (Ringwood, 1992) – an historic book – p. 149.

11. Ibid., p. 151. The Waste Lands Occupation Act is 9 & 10 Vict., c. 104.

12. In 1877 another shoot killed some 20,000 wallaby and kangaroo which would otherwise have nourished the Aborigines; B. Thorne, 'Fauna War', *JAS* 19 (1986). The most comprehensive account is E. Rolls, *They All Ran Wild* (Sydney, 1977), part 1.

13. See T. Flannery, *1788* (Melbourne, 1996) chap. 14.

14. Quoted in D. W. A. Baker, *John Piper* (Aboriginal History, Canberra, 1993).

15. Not only Aboriginal men, but women too, were appreciated for their skills. The *Queenslander* in 1883 reported 'gins, who are employed as stockmen nearly everywhere out here, strutting about in moleskins and flannel shirts': quoted in H. Reynolds, *With the White People* (Ringwood, 1990), 204 ff. Like Reynolds's other books, this is well researched, briskly written, and has done much to change Australian attitudes. For settlement and Aboriginal societies see the same author's *North of Capricorn* (Crows Nest, 2003). For Western Australia see K. Forrest, *The Challenge and the Chance* (Victoria Park, 1996).

16. Reynolds, *With the White People*, pp. 166, 171.

17. Ibid., p. 184.

18. For an early assessment of refrigerated meat, see the *Field*, 60 (1 May 1880). For Mort, see A. Barnard, *Visions and Profits: Studies in the Business Career of Thomas Mort* (Melbourne, 1961).

19. C. Dilke, *Greater Britain*, 2 vols. (London, 1869), vol. i, and A. Trollope, *Australia and New Zealand* (London, 1872), 586 ff. Much more diffuse than Dilke, Trollope displays those flashes of insight that at times distinguish his novels. He comments: 'the records speak of [the West Australian Aborigines] as horrible savages. They were probably brave patriots, defending their country and their rights' (p. 564).

20. For Western Australian gold, see A. F. Calvert, *Western Australia and its Gold-fields* (London, 1893). For camels, see P. E. Warburton, *Journey Across the Western Interior of Australia* (London, 1875), and Rolls, *They All Ran Wild*, chap. 12.

21. See P. F. Donovan, *At the Other End of Australia* (St Lucia, 1994). R. Duncan,

'Annexation of the Northern Territory', HS 6, is a good synopsis: but still see – eighty years later – D. Howard, *English Activities on the North Coast of Australia* (London, 1924).

22. For the period, see M. Kerr, *The Surveyors* (London, 1972). For Finnis, see J. Booth, *B. T. Finnis* (Adelaide, 2001).

23. For blackbirding, see E. W. Docker, *Blackbirders* (Sydney, 1970), F. Clune, *Captain Bully Hayes* (Carlisle, 1997), D. Shineberg, *The People Trade* (Honolulu, 1999). At the time, and for much longer, the islanders were called Kanakas or Polynesians. The geographical term 'Pacific Islanders' is now more usual. *JRAHS* 88/1 (2002) has an interesting article by J. Hopkins-Weise on 'Pacific Islanders in the Gulf of Carpentaria', with a useful bibliography.

24. For Patrick Murray, see G. S. Searle, *Mount and Morris Exonerated* (Melbourne, 1875).

25. A. G. Austin (ed.), *The Webbs' Australian Diary* (Carlton, 1965), 44 ff. Needless to say, a select committee of the Queensland Legislative Assembly (Proceedings, 1876, vol. 3) found that the islanders were 'cheerful and contented' and that 'many false reports' had been circulated: quoted C. M. H. Clark, *Select Documents in Australian History*, 2 vols. (Sydney, 1955), vol. ii; pp. 211 ff.

26. J. Chandler, *Forty Years in the Wilderness* (Hartwell, 1893), 70–71.

27. A. Markus, *Fear and Hatred* (Sydney, 1979), contrasts the experience of Chinese in America and Australia; see also P. Jacobs and S. Landau, *To Serve the Devil*, vol. ii: *Colonials and Sojourners* (New York, 1971), a collection of documents, pp. 66–166. For the *Republican*, see Markus, p. 7; 'this barbarian': ibid., p. 37. As in Hong Kong, the Chinese appreciated the protection afforded by British law, which was much greater than that ever expected in China. The racism shown in immigration restrictions was not – at least, generally – reflected in judicial matters; see A. Dwight, 'Chinese in New South Wales Law Courts', *JRAHS* 73/2 (1988).

28. The first restrictions in 1855 imposed an entrance tax and a limit on the number of passengers that a ship might carry; in 1857 a small residence tax was added; from 1859 to 1862 penal clauses were added.

29. For Victorian anti-Chinese incidents, see B. C. Hodge, 'Goldrush Australia', *JRAHS* 69/3 (1984). For Lambing Flats, see Markus, *Fear and Hatred*, 29–34.

30. C. Connolly, 'Miners' Rights', in A. Curthoys and A. Markus (eds.), *Who are Our Enemies?* (Sydney, 1979), concludes the riots were 'a monument to fear; the dread of economic competition, to cultural chauvinism, to racial prejudice, and to government neglect'. All these formed the basis for later White Australia policy – but there was no government neglect. For repugnancy, see K. H. Bailey, in Scott, *Australia*, 411 ff.

31. For the Queensland fields, see R. Cilento (ed.), *Triumph in the Tropics* (Brisbane, 1959) – an unrelenting apologia for the worst aspects of the state – chap. 18. For Kearney and O'Donnell, see Markus, *Fear and Hatred*, 52–4, 114–17.

32. For Higinbotham, see A. Davidson, *Invisible State* (Cambridge, 1991) – a stimulating book – pp. 169–76.

33. For Darling, see D. McCaughey, N. Perkins, and A. Trumble, *Victoria's Colonial Governors* (Melbourne, 1993). For the Legislative Council, see G. Serle, 'Victorian Legislative Council', *HS* 6/53–4, in which it is noted that the ability of the Council to hang on to power illustrates 'the limited extent of democratic convictions and . . . the popular lack of understanding of the participation in political life in Australia'.

34. For the critical despatch and response, see McCaughey, *et al.*, *Victoria's Colonial Governors*, 116 ff.

35. For the *Shenandoah*, see ibid., pp. 106–8 and Bailey in Scott (ed.), *Australia*, 408–10; A. Davidson, *Invisible State*, 174–6.

36. For Black Wednesday, see McCaughey *et al.*, *Victoria's Colonial Governors*, 76 ff. Bowen was much criticized in London for his adherence to the doctrine of 'responsibility', especially by the new, inexperienced and dogmatic Tory Colonial Secretary, Michael Hicks-Beach. G. Serle, 'A New Light on the Victorian Constitutional Crisis', *HS* 13, is properly severe on Bowen, as 'evasive and deceitful . . . quite improperly involved with the government in its detailed planning of political warfare' and 'quite properly disqualified as Governor of Victoria'.

37. B. Nairn, 'The Governor, the Bushranger and the Premier', *JRAHS* 86/2 (2000).

38. Hansard, House of Lords, 16 April 1875.

CHAPTER 9

1. For Smith O'Brien, see J. Brownrigg, 'Early Proposal for Federal Constitution', *New Federalist* 4 (1999); see also J. M. Ward, 'Germ of Federation', *HS* 4/49 (1955).

2. Quoted by John Fletcher, 'Karl Scherzer', *JRAHS* 71/3 (1985).

3. For the Garden Palace, see P. Proudfoot, 'John Young, James Barnet and the 1879 Exhibition', *JRAHS* 86/1 (2000).

4. See J. Parris and A. G. L. Shaw, 'Melbourne International Exhibition', *VHJ* 51/4 (1980). After little Nellie's debut in Melbourne, one of her friends hissed: 'Nellie Mitchell, I could see your knickers.'

5. For Reibey, see L. Ryan, *Aboriginal Tasmanians* (Crows Nest, 1996), 225–6.

6. For Montgomery, see ibid., pp. 230–40.

7. The Roth Royal Commission report of 1905 is summarized in C. Rowley, *The Destruction of Aboriginal Society* (Canberra, 1970), 190–95. The author, W. E. Roth, was the younger of two brilliant English-educated Hungarian-descended medical brothers; see *ADB*.

8. For inter-colonial trade disputes, see J. Hirst, *Sentimental Nation* (Melbourne, 2000), an essential book, pp. 47–51. For the causes of the negotiations' collapse, see the *Argus*, 6 June 1863, in C. M. H. Clark, *Select Documents in Australian History*, 2 vols. (Sydney, 1995), vol. ii, pp. 283–6.

9. It was symptomatic that the *Age* (9 April 1887), comparing New South Wales (unfavourably) with Victoria, spoke of 'the two countries'.

10. See *Sydney Morning Herald*, 24 August 1870. Some Victorian patriots wanted their warship to join in the 1860 Maori War (*Age*, 13 April 1860); see also B. Knox, 'Earl of Carnarvon', *JICH* 26/2 (1998).

11. For Bismarck's colonial policy as seen by the Foreign Secretary, see E. Fitzmaurice, *The Life of Granville George Leveson Gower, Second Earl Granville K.G. 1815–1891*, 2 vols. (London, 1905), vol. ii, chaps. X and XII

12. Queen Victoria, *Letters*, series II, ed. G. H. Buckle (London, 1928), vol. iii, 29 June 1883. R. C. Thompson, *Australian Imperialism in the Pacific* (Melbourne, 1980), is a key book; see pp. 45, 57. Chester arrived only hours before a German warship turned up with similar intentions.

13. See chap. 1 of T. B. Millar, *Australia in Peace and War* (Botany, 1991), and J. M. Ward, *British Policy in the South Pacific 1786–1893* (Sydney, 1948). Thompson, *Australian Imperialism*, 66, 71 The conference also resolved that a committee should be formed to consider the foundation of a Federal council.

14. Fitzmaurice, *Granville*, vol. ii, p. 374.

15. For the first meeting of the Federal Convention, see Hirst, *Sentimental Nation*, 72 ff.

16. For the Imperial Federation League, see E. H. H. Green, 'Political Economy of Empire', A. Porter (ed.), *The Nineteenth Century* (Oxford History of the British Empire, Oxford, 1999), chap. 16.

17. See M. Saunders, 'Public Opinion and the NSW Contingent', *JRAHS* 69 (1983). For the expedition see R. Inglis, *The Rehearsal* (Adelaide, 1985).

18. Deakin's own published writings, although valuable sources, have to be taken with a pinch of salt. The long correspondence with Charles Dilke (BL 43877 ff. 70–191) is more candid.

19. For the New Hebrides, see Hirst, *Sentimental Nation*, 75 ff., and A. Deakin, *The Federal Story* (Melbourne, 1944), 22: he continues that the plot 'remained not only unexecuted but even unsuspected till this day' (p. 23). Conferences of Colonial Prime Ministers have continued, in slightly different forms, to become the current meetings of Commonwealth Prime Ministers. For the Conference, see J. E. Kendle, *Colonial and Imperial Conferences 1887–1911* (London, 1967), 10 ff., and editorial in *British Australasian*, 4/140 (1887), 17.

20. General Edwards' report is given in Clark, *Select Documents*, vol. ii. Continuing its policy of defiant dissent, the Queensland Assembly refused to ratify the naval agreement.

21. The Parkes–Carrington correspondence is printed in the New South Wales Records 2/8095.B2

22. Deakin (*Federal Story*, pp. 26–7) compares Parkes rather with Disraeli: 'it was always a problem with Parkes as with Disraeli where the actor posture-maker and would-be sphinx ended and where the actual man underneath began.' For the Melbourne speech, and reactions to it, see Hirst, *Sentimental Nation*, chap. 5. The

often decidedly cross background discussions are recorded in the New South Wales State Archives, 4/902.1, 'Correspondence Respecting the Federation of the Australian Colonies', 19 December 1889.

23. The Tenterfield speech is reproduced in Clark, *Select Documents*, vol. ii, pp. 467–70.

24. The Australian diaries of Sidney and Beatrice Webb (ed. A. G. Austin (Carlton, 1965)) have some pithy comments on Australian politicians. Barton is described (p. 52) as 'an amateur uncertain of the worthwhileness of his hobby . . . he looks as though he chronically over-ate himself', and Deakin as a 'thoughtful pessimist'. (p. 63).

25. For the influence of Canada and America, see H. Irving (ed.), *To Constitute a Nation* (Cambridge, 1999), an essential work, p. 69. For Clark, see ibid., p. 71, and Hirst, *Sentimental Nation*, 11–14. H. Evans, in *New Federalist*, 2 (1999), points out that the then current developments in the United States (particularly the move to direct election of Senators) were closely followed in Australia.

26. See L. F. Crisp, *Parliamentary Government of the Commonwealth of Australia* (London, 1961), chap. 1.

27. For the banking crisis, see S. J. Butlin, *Australia and New Zealand Bank* (London, 1961), chap. 12, 'Riding the Whirlwind'. M. Edelstein, *Overseas Investment in the Age of High Imperialism* (London, 1982), 250, describes the period 1861–91 as 'a major accumulation boom' and the 1880s as 'reflecting the lumpiness of the social overhead or urban development needs' (p. 40). The *Economist* had sagely warned of difficulties ahead in May 1891, that the colonies 'should not count as part of their inheritance that their credit . . . should constantly improve' (quoted in D. Kynaston, *Golden Years* (London, 1996) – a remarkable book – p. 48). But the 1893 crisis had its origins, at least in part, in the Baring crisis, the first time in which that bank involved itself in badly managed business. See also Edelstein, *Overseas Investment*, chap. 11.

28. Letter of 25 December 1892, in P. Lewsen (ed.), *Selections from the Correspondence of J. X. Merriman* (Cape Town, 1963).

29. R. McMullin, *Light on the Hill* (Oxford, 1991), an essential, if too-uncritical history of the Australian Labor Party, p. 7.

30. J. D. Fitzgerald, *Rise of the New South Wales Labor Party* (Sydney, 1925), 14 ff. Writing in 1909, Spence reflected that 'the industrial war . . . had at last brought home to the worker the fact that he had a weapon in his grasp stronger than Governments or capitalists': quoted in Clark, *Select Documents*, vol. ii, pp. 575–6.

31. P. de Serville, *The Australian Club* (Melbourne, 1998), 54.

32. For Deakin and Parkes on Dibbs, see Deakin, *Federal Story*, 11–12. For the emergency measures, see E. O. G. Shann, in E. Scott (ed.), *Australia* (Cambridge History of the British Empire, Cambridge, 1988 [1933]), 37, Butlin, *Australia and New Zealand Bank*, 286, and *Victorian Year Book*, 2 (1893), quoted in Clark, *Select Documents*, vol. ii, pp. 295–300.

33. See McMullin, *Light on the Hill*, chap. 2; J. Faulkner and S. Macintyre, *True Believers* (Sydney, 2001).

34. On the ANA, see Hirst, *Sentimental Nation*, 36–44; for the 1894 election, B. Nairn, *Civilising Capitalism* (Melbourne, 1989), 118–29.

35. For Corowa, see Irving, *To Constitute a Nation*, 135, and Hirst, *Sentimental Nation*, 121–3. The resolutions are printed in Clark, *Select Documents*, vol. ii, pp. 497 ff. A useful move was made in September 1894 in adopting common time zones for the continent, in place of the multitude of local times – five in Queensland alone.

36. Forrest's difficulties are exposed in F. Crowley, 'Forrest and the Federal Constitution', *JR WAHS* 2/3 (1997), and summarized as 'a very difficult situation. Not only was a majority in the Legislative Council opposed to Federation, but also most of his ministers, his rural electors and his relatives and friends' (p. 299). See B. de Garis, 'Western Australia', in H. Irving (ed.), *The Centenary Companion to Australian Federation* (Cambridge, 1999), chap. 6. Western Australian goldfield agitation had been reinforced by the 'Westralian' boom on the London stock exchange, fired by the notorious Horatio Bottomley, yet to be exposed as a fraudster. Bottomley's near-failure in 1899 contributed to weakening the goldfield's case. The downfall of the other Western Australian speculator, Whitaker Wright, was more precipitous, ending in his conviction and suicide in 1904; see Kynaston, *Golden Years*.

37. For the elections, see Hirst, *Sentimental Nation*, chap. 8.

38. For the discussion, see ibid., p.23, Irving, *To Constitute a Nation*, 76–9, and J. A. La Nauze, 'Name of the Commonwealth of Australia', *HS* 15/57 (1971), 158–72. Winston Churchill, with minimal tact, also kept pressing the King to name a ship *Pitt*; the experienced monarch pointed out the inevitable ribaldries to be expected from the lower deck.

39. For Dibbs's views, see Irving, *To Constitute a Nation*, 51 ff., Hirst, *Sentimental Nation*, 112 ff. Dibbs himself was bankrupted in 1893, albeit temporarily. See T. W. Campbell, 'My Dear Lord Jersey', *JRAHS* 88/3 (2002).

40. *Official Report of the National Australasian Convention Debates* (Adelaide, 1897).

41. Republicanism featured very rarely in any serious programme: the Associated Riverina Workers harked back to the Peasants' Revolt in wanting to abolish 'all lawyers' along with 'black and yellow labour', and demanded 'the complete political independence of the United Australian Commonwealth on a basis of pure democratic republicanism': *Hummer*, 26 March 1892, quoted in Clark, *Select Documents*, vol. ii, pp. 586 ff. M. McKenna, *Captive Republic* (Cambridge, 1997), notes that 'only rarely did republicanism slide into separatism . . . For the most part Irish settlers kept any republican sentiments focussed on their homeland' (p. 6).

42. *Bulletin*, 2 July 1887.

43. For B. O'Dowd, see F. Bongiorno, 'From Republican to Anti-Billite – Bernard O'Dowd', *New Federalist*, 4 (1999).

44. Quoted by Irving, *To Constitute a Nation*, 48.

45. For the *Bulletin*, see R. B. Walker, *Newspaper Press in New South Wales* (Sydney, 1976), chap. 9; G. Partington, *Australian Nation* (New Brunswick, NJ, 1997), 208–25.

46. Population statistics from D. H. Akenson, *Small Difference* (Montreal, 1991), which combines philosophy and statistics with great felicity: pp. 59–85 for Australia.

47. P. O'Farrell, *The Irish in Australia* (Kensington, 1986), 31.

48. M. Davitt, *Life and Progress in Australia* (London, 1898), 130. 'We are free, I hope,' Davitt concluded, 'to be loyal if we like, which we do.'

49. See J. B. Hirst, *Strange Birth of Colonial Democracy* (Sydney, 1989), chap. 13; M. Finnane, *Police and Government* (Melbourne, 1994), 133–4.

50. The first recorded bushranger was a black American, liberated, along with many thousand others, by the British during the American revolution, an act described by C. Pybus, in *Arena*, 57 (2002), as 'one of the better kept secrets' of that time. One such, John Caesar, was transported in 1788, and thereafter took to the bush before being killed in 1796. 'How much better', Pybus comments, 'Caesar's act of rebellion fits the archetype of one who would "scorn to live in slavery bound down by iron chains" than a murderous horse rustler like Ned Kelly.' Over a century later (see G. Roberts, *Sydney Morning Herald*, 30 March 2000), descendants of the Queensland Native Police trackers, who had finally discovered the gang, were still awaiting their promised reward, paid to the state government but never passed on. For a cool appreciation of the myth, see R. B. Hall, 'Bushranging in Fact and Legend', *HS* 11 which points out that not only bushrangers, but criminals in general were more often native Irish than was warranted by the proportion of the population – 21 out of 27 of those convicted or in gaol for armed robbery and foreign-born in 1871 were from Ireland (p. 207).

51. B. Bryson, *Down Under* (London, 2001), 219 ff.

52. In an article on larrikins (8 January 1881), the *Bulletin* characterized larrikins as 'undergrown, meagre, and angular. There were no *manly* youths': quoted in Clark, *Select Documents*, vol. ii, pp. 686–8. Stone's novel *Jonah* (1911) is the story of a typical Sydney Push.

53. The Mount Rennie case was notable for several aspects: rape was not then a capital offence in Britain; did the prerogative of pardon rest with Governor or Executive Council? There had been two previous gang rapes, in Waterloo and Woolloomooloo, in which both the victims had died; and the executions were horribly botched. See D. Walker, 'Youth on Trial', *Labour History*, 50 (1986), For the rape of the Aboriginal woman, Jenny Green, see chap. 4 in D. Philips and S. Davies, *A Nation of Rogues?* (Melbourne, 1994), and M. Finnane, *Punishment in Australian Society* (Melbourne, 1997), 133 ff.

54. For Métin, see Clark, *Select Documents*, vol. ii. p. 676. Davitt believed Australians were 'the best-fed people in the world', spending much more per head than Americans or British (£43+, £32+ and £29+ respectively). B. Gandevia, in

the *Australian Paediatric Journal* (1977), comparing the height of boys transported to Australia found those from London 'considerably shorter at all ages' than those from the rest of the United Kingdom and remarked that 'Contrary to most predictions the first generation of Australians was remarkable for its good behaviour. It is interesting to observe that its other striking and well-attested characteristics – its brashness, its independence, its self-reliance, its awkwardness and its capacity for heavy work at an early age – would all be enhanced and facilitated by an increase in height' – but the larrikins need to be taken into account.

55. Austin (ed.), *Webbs' Australian Diary*, 75.

56. From H. Lawson, *Poetical Works* (c 1895), quoted in Clark, *Select Documents*, vol. ii, pp. 797 ff. Of Paterson's work, 'Clancy of the Overflow', with its rollicking rhythms and internal rhymes, and the immortal 'Waltzing Matilda' are good examples. J. Ramm has a perceptive article, 'Learning the Australian Myth', *JAS* (1987); see also Partington, *Australian Nation*, chaps. 9 and 10: 'During the 20th century anti-British and republican sentiments in Australia flourished in inverse proportion to the dangers Australia faced from external enemies.' *Geoffrey Hamlyn* has the first, and one of the best, decriptions of a bushfire. G. Serle, *From Deserts the Prophets Come* (Melbourne, 1973), 67, describes Furphy's work as 'full of the bog-philosophy of the uneducated man'.

57. Again, Serle, *From Deserts*, is an excellent review of later Australian writers.

58. Quoted in J. N. Molony, *Native Born* (Melbourne, 2000), 30.

59. For Aboriginal cricket, see B. Harris, *The Proud Champions: Australia's Aboriginal Sporting Heroes* (Crows Nest, 1989), and J. Pollard, *Formative Years of Australian Cricket* (London, 1987).

60. See ibid., chap. 5 and Harris, *Proud Champions*, chap. 1. For Gilbert's treatment, see Harris, p. 19.

61. Rules *v.* Rugby divides the continent between Victoria, South Australia, Western Australia and Tasmania, who are all Rules states, and the rest, faithful to the older game; see also article in R. Cashman *et al.* (eds.), *The Oxford Companion to Australian Cricket* (Melbourne, 1996).

62. For New Zealand attitudes, see Irving, *To Constitute a Nation*, 112 ff., and Hirst, *Sentimental Nation*, 22 ff. See also M. Moore, 'New Zealand,' *New Federalist* (No. 1, 1998), who identified New Zealand's own expansionist ambitions, race and economic competition as factors leading to New Zealand's decision not to join. For an overview see G. Martin, *Australia, New Zealand and Federation* (London, 2001).

63. Quoted in R. McMullin, *Light on the Hill*, 22.

64. Captain Russell's views are given in Clark, *Select Documents*, vol. ii, pp. 477–9.

65. Reid's portly frame and walrus moustache hid what Beatrice Webb rightly described as 'amazing cleverness … pugnacity, humour, cunning', but without 'perceiving as yet any sign of statesmanship' (Austin (ed.), *Webbs' Australian Diary*, 45).

66. Crisp, *Parliamentary Government*, 174. Crisp is a good guide to the constitution, itself reproduced as appendix C in his book.

67. *Scribner's Magazine*, October 1891.

68. The Webbs found 'an evil odour of past financial frauds' (Austin (ed.), *Webbs' Australian Diary*, 45–6). For Queensland's abstention, see D. Waterson, 'Absentees from North of the Tweed', *New Federalist* (No. 1, 1998), which instances the crisis in the Queensland National Bank, the vested interests in retaining coloured labour and separatist pressures among the reasons.

69. Hirst, *Sentimental Nation*, 238 ff.

70. For the negotiations, see ibid., chap. 12; P. A. Howell, 'Joseph Chamberlain', *New Federalist*, 7 (2001). They were not helped by the fact that the Governor of Western Australia, Sir Gerard Smith, had been recalled after some questionable business dealings. The British government's case is outlined in a memo on the draft Bill, published as Cd. 188, 1900.

71. Bongiorno, 'From Republican to Anti-Billite', 51.

72. *South Australian Register*, 1 November 1899.

73. H. Lawson, *Bulletin*, 21 October 1899.

74. A. M. Davey, *Breaker Morant* (Cape Town, 1987), is authoritative; see also B. Bridges 'Lord Kitchener', *JRAHS* 73/1 (1988), which suggests the implication of the Commander in Chief Lord Kitchener – and that unscrupulous character's motives are always questionable. A good article in the *Australian* by C. Wilcox (11 October 1999) points out that 'the murder of Boer prisoners was no rare thing, but now it was being conducted by officers and the army's intelligence staff were determined to stamp it out'. See also C. Wilcox, *Australia's Boer War* (South Melbourne, 2002) p. 368.

75. An interesting light on colonial jealousies is cast by a holograph letter in the South African Library (Milner collection), MSB351, 1(10), from B. R. Wise, New South Wales Attorney General, to Lord Milner, High Commissioner at the Cape and old (Balliol) college friend, complaining of the conduct of Colonel J. C. Hoad, officer commanding the Australian regiment, who had been favouring officers from his own state, Victoria, although 'it was certain that the New South Wales infantry troops, both in officers, men and equipment, are superior in a marked degree to the contingent from Victoria'.

CHAPTER 10

1. The question of precedence was arguable, but Moran's seniority – nearly thirty years in the episcopate – and his personal distinction should have prevailed. Everyone blamed everyone else for the muddle, and in ecumenical support many Nonconformist leaders followed the Cardinal's boycott of the procession.

2. See Queensland Official Yearbook, 1901, p. 417 and D. B. Waterston, 'Above and Beyond the Arches', *New Federalist*, 6 (2000). Meston, paternalistic but a

strong supporter of Aboriginal rights, had previously attempted to gain their rightful reward for the Kelly gang's Aboriginal trackers: see also D. May, *Aboriginal Labour and the Cattle Industry* (Cambridge, 1994); for Miss Bethell, see *Town and Country Journal*, 19 January 1901.

3. H. McQueen, *Tom Roberts* (Sydney, 1966), 474, quoted in J. B. Hirst, *Sentimental Nation* (Melbourne, 2000), 318. For the description of the opening see the first volume of the Commonwealth Hansard. The first Parliament had a Scottish flavour; 16 members had been born there, compared with 25 in England, 8 in Ireland and 1 Welshman; quoted in W. K. Anderson, 'Andrew Fisher', *JRAHS* 87/2 (2001), 195.

4. For Hopetoun, see Hirst, *Sentimental Nation*, 278–83, 304 ff., and J. Waugh, 'First Governor-General', *New Federalist*, 6 (2000). For the offer to Lyne, see J. A. La Nauze, *Hopetoun Blunder* (Melbourne, 1957), and the same author's important work *Making of the Australian Constitution* (Melbourne, 1972). D. McCaughey, N. Perkins and A. Trumble, *Victoria's Colonial Governors* (Melbourne, 1993), chap. 1, reveals Hopetoun as a successful Governor of Victoria, somewhat surprisingly considering his youth (29) and complete inexperience. Queen Victoria needed some persuasion to allow Hopetoun to go, dismissing the suggestion at first as 'Quite impossible', but was persuaded by Prime Minister Balfour; 'still, it would be a great loss to me': *Letters*, series III, ed. G. E. Buckle (London, 1932), 518 ff.

5. B. Nairn, *Civilising Capitalism* (Melbourne, 1989), 226, aptly describes Watson's 'natural understanding of people and . . . innate generosity'. See also A. J. Grassby and S. Ordoñez, *John Watson* (Melbourne, 2001).

6. *Worker*, 30 March 1901, p.13. See E. Sullivan, 'Revealing a Preference', *JICH* 29 1(2001).

7. For the Queensland *Patriot*, see A. Markus, *Governing Savages* (Sydney, 1990), 20. Chamberlain appealed to the traditions of the Empire 'which make no distinction in favour of or against race or colour'. Sweeping and unjustified though the statement was, as Gandhi could have confirmed, it was still something more than a pious aspiration.

8. See W. K. Hancock, in E. Scott (ed.), *Australia* (Cambridge History of the British Empire, Cambridge, 1988 [1933]), 502 ff.

9. Quoted in D. Dutton, 'British Outpost', in D. Goldsworthy (ed.), *Facing North* (Melbourne, 2001), an essential work; chap. 1.

10. Commonwealth Hansard (House of Representatives), 26 September 1901.

11. Caucus control was not set in stone, and the more influential Prime Ministers contrived to retain a good measure of freedom. For the records see P. M. Weller, *Caucus Minutes*, 3 vols. (Carlton, 1975).

12. For Watson's resignation, R. McMullin, *Light on the Hill* (Oxford, 1991), 62.

13. For Deakin as Prime Minister, the account by W. Murdoch (Melbourne, 1999) is a useful addition to the standard biography, and the articles submitted to the London *Morning Post* during his period of office are a major curiosity – journalist

Alfred anonymously commenting on the doings of Deakin Prime Minister! See J. A. La Nauze, 'Arthur Deakin and the *Morning Post*', HS 6/24 (1955).

14. The judgement on Harvester is quoted in C. M. H. Clark, *Sources of Australian History* (London, 1957), 501–7. The Harvester Company was paying unskilled labourers 6s. a day, while Higgins considered that 7s. should be a reasonable minimum.

15. For Mrs Dugdale see A. Oldfield, *Woman Suffrage in Australia: A Gift or a Struggle?* (Cambridge, 1992), an authoritative book, pp. 134–5; and S. Margarey, *Passions of the First Wave Feminists* (Sydney, 2001). For an overview see M. Lake, *Getting Equal* (St Leonards, 1999), M. Sawer and M. Simms, *A Woman's Place: Woman and Politics in Australia* (St Leonards, 1993).

16. See Oldfield, *Woman Suffrage*, 84–5: the Governor's wife, Lady Jersey, thought Mrs Ashton's sentiments 'atrocious'; they also caused the Women's Christian Temperance Union to decide on separation. Eliza was married to a painter, Julian Rossi Ashton: see also Margarey, *Passions*, 24 ff. M. Lake, 'Hour of Womanhood', *New Federalist*, 7 (2001), draws attention to the close links between Australian and British feminists.

17. For the Bill's passage, see Oldfield, *Woman Suffrage*, 63 ff.

18. Commonwealth Hansard (House of Representatives), 23 April 1902.

19. Sir Edward Braddon, ibid., 24 April 1902.

20. Exactly what constituted an 'Aboriginal Native' was to be the cause of much later discussion: see T. Clarke and B. Galligan, 'Aboriginal Native', *AHS* 26/105 (1995), and P. Stretton and C. Finnimore, 'Black Fellow Citizens', *AHS* 25/101 (1993). Most of those who now classify themselves as Aboriginals would not have been so termed in 1901, and would have been entitled to the vote; see Clarke and Galligan, p. 525. For a full discussion, see J. Chesterman and B. Galligan, *Citizens without Rights* (Cambridge, 1997). The major work on parliamentary history is G. Souter, *Acts of Parliament* (Carlton, 1998): see particularly p. 394, Franchise Act 1902, which notes that subsequently qualifying for a state vote did not give Aborigines a Federal vote, and that only in South Australia and Tasmania were Aborigines allowed a vote on the same terms as whites.

21. The *Bulletin* was scornful about the flag; it was 'vulgar and ill-fitting, a stale rechauffé of the British flag, with no artistic value, no national significance . . . With the New Leaders will come a New Flag' (28 September 1901). More than a century later the flag remains, but see F. Kwan, 'Australian Flag', *AHS* 24/103 (1965). For the selection of capital site, see L. F. Fitzhardinge, 'W. M. Hughes in Search of a Federal Capital', *JRAHS* 51/1 (1965), G. F. Sherington, 'The Selection of Canberra', *JRAHS* 56/2 (1970), and *New Federalist* 37 (1999), 'Heart of a Nation'. For the choice of name, see Anderson, 'Andrew Fisher'.

22. For Fisher, see ibid. and J. Murdoch, *A Million to One Against* (London, 1998).

23. For the Commonwealth Bank, see S. J. Butlin, *Australia and New Zealand Bank* (London, 1961), 349–51

24. The suggestion that referendums be used to decide future constitutional issues was almost implicit in the decision to hold a referendum on the constitution itself.

25. *North Territories Times*, 6 January 1911.

26. Quoted in T. B. Millar, *Australia in Peace and War* (Botany, 1991), 48.

27. W. G. Beasley, *The Rise of Japan* (London, 1995), is a good short history of modern Japan.

28. The Anglo-Japanese Treaty had been renewed in August 1905.

29. March 1902, quoted in Millar, *Australia in Peace and War*, 24 n. 1.

30. Australians had generally welcomed the American success in the war with Spain that established the United States as a Pacific imperial power. With Hawaii and the Philippines, Anglo-Saxon influence of that ocean seemed surely established.

31. For Churchill and Elgin at the Colonial Conference, see R. S. Churchill, *Winston S. Churchill*, vol. ii: *The Young Statesman* (New York, 1966), 202–9, and N. Meaney, *Search for Security in the Pacific 1901–14* (Sydney, 1976), 182 ff. Sir John Young at the Colonial Office, considering the apportionment of honours, compared the Prime Ministers of large colonies to English Lord Mayors. See B. Knox, 'Colonial Honours', *AHJ* 25/99 (1992).

32. Although only five years separated the visit of the American fleet from the arrival of HMAS *Australia*, the new ship was instantly visible as impressively more powerful, representing the latest generation of warships. The sixteen American ships were for the most part cruisers and, as pre-dreadnoughts, survivors of a previous era.

33. For the 1911 Imperial Conference, see J. E. Kendle, *Colonial and Imperial Conferences 1887–1911* (London, 1967), and M. Ollivier (ed.), *Colonial and Imperial Conferences 1887–1937* (Ottawa, 1954); for Fisher's reluctance to sport the lace, see Anderson, 'Andrew Fisher', 204 ff.

34. For military preparations, see J. Grey, *Military History of Australia* (Cambridge, 1999), chap. 4; and BL Add. MSS 50084 ff. 132, 148, 150 for Fisher's correspondence. For the history of the Militia see C. Wilcox, *For Hearths and Homes: Citizen Soldiering in Australia 1854–1945* (St Leonards, 1998).

35. F. K. Crowley, in Crowley (ed.), *New History of Australia* (n.p., Victoria, 1974), 309.

CHAPTER 11

1. The 2-vol. biography is by L. F. Fitzhardinge (Melbourne, 1973); vol. ii is *The Little Digger*. Hughes's role as the first Australian politician to make an international reputation is well covered in P. Spartalis, *Diplomatic Battles of Billy Hughes* (Sydney, 1983).

2. Letter to Asquith, 5 December 1915, quoted Spartalis, *Diplomatic Battles*, 1.

3. Quoted in R. McMullin, *Light on the Hill* (Oxford, 1991), 92

4. The impressive Australian War Memorial in Canberra houses an extensive

library and museum. J. Grey, *Military History of Australia* (Cambridge, 1999), is a sound short history, with a good bibliography, dedicated to T. B. Millar, whose *Australia in Peace and War* (Botany, 1991) has been much used here. The view quoted here is from Grey, *Military History*, 84: on the other hand, as E. M. Andrews points out (*Anzac Illusion* (Cambridge, 1994), chap. II), the great majority of Australians saw themselves as British, carried British passports if they went abroad, and perhaps 40 per cent of the first volunteers were British-born. Overall, the recruitment figures in Australia, New Zealand and Britain were similar; Britain was still 'home' to the Antipodeans. The official history of the war is in 12 volumes, the first six by C. E. W. Bean, covering the Gallipoli campaign and the fighting in France.

5. For Rabaul, see S. S. Mackenzie, *The Australians at Rabaul* (Sydney, 1927). Able Seaman W. G. V. Williams became the first Australian fatality of the war on 11 September. Works on Gallipoli are innumerable; F. McLeod, *Gallipoli Campaign: Select Bibliography* (Canberra, 1990), is already out of date. J. Robertson, *Anzac and Empire: The Tragedy and Glory of Gallipoli* (Melbourne, 1990), and L. Carlyon, *Gallipoli* (Sydney, 2001), are the standards by which others can be judged, but A. Moorehead, *Gallipoli* (Ware, 1997), remains worthwhile.

6. For Keith (and Rupert) Murdoch, see W. Shawcross, *Murdoch* (London, 1992); B. Page, *Murdoch Archipelago* (London, 2003); for the letter to Fisher and relations with Northcliffe, see BL Add. MS 62179.

7. *Freeman's Journal*, 27 April 1916.

8. For the riots, see *Daily Telegraph* (Sydney), 16 February 1916. The Returned Soldiers Association developed into the Returned Services League, an influential pressure group.

9. For the Middle East, see H. S. Gullett, *The AIF in Sinai and Palestine 1914–1918* (Sydney, 1923).

10. For the Western Front, see C. E. W. Bean, *The AIF in France*, 4 vols. (Sydney, 1929, 1933, 1937, 1942). P. Charlton, *Pozières* (London, 1982), 263–8, details Australians' disciplinary problems: in December 1916, 130 of 182 convictions for desertion were Australians; 9 per 1,000 Australians were in prison, 1.6 per 1,000 other Dominions and 1 per 1,000 British. But the culprits were usually from rear units, since in the line discipline was rarely criticized.

11. Montagu to Asquith, April 1915, Asquith papers MS 27/93–95, quoted Spartalis, *Diplomatic Battles*, 12. Montagu went on: 'I would far rather cede Australia to the Japanese than to cede to Australia anything that the Japanese want.' While not meant to be taken seriously, Montagu's comment indicates the difficulties Hughes faced in being given due weight in the Allied councils.

12. *Age*, 15 April 1916. For the visit to London, see Fitzhardinge, *Little Digger*, chaps. 4–6, and for Hughes and Lloyd George in the push against Asquith, see E. M. Andrews, 'For Australia's Wartime Interests', *AJPH* 41/2 (1995).

13. For the conference, see Spartalis, *Diplomatic Battles*, 28–34, and W. J. Hudson, *Billy Hughes in Paris* (Melbourne, 1978) passim.

14. Hughes to Murdoch, quoted ibid., p. 36. Hughes used the immigration bogey

as a useful weapon, with the suggestion that the victorious Japanese would insist on free entrance to Australia after the war. It was noteworthy that the majority of those men on active service voted against conscription, although the total vote was narrowly affirmative. For the debate see Spartalis, pp. 35–43, Andrews, *Anzac Illusion*, 120–26, Grey, *Military History*, 10–12, and J. B. Hirst, 'Australian Defence and Conscription', *AHS* 25/101 (1993). For the Maltese, see D. Day, *Claiming a Continent* (Sydney, 1997), 244.

15. For Ferguson's remarks, see Spartalis, *Diplomatic Battles*, 41–2.

16. Lloyd George to Carson: A. J. P. Taylor, *Lloyd George* (London, 1971), 155. The Labor parliamentary Caucus voted on 4 December to expel all those who had supported conscription, which apparently anti-patriotic action damaged the party's electoral prospects, as evidenced in the next year's general election. Caucus Minutes Appendix 2, and Melbourne *Argus*, 15 November 1916. The sympathetic Governor General wrote: 'The fact is that the poor little man [Hughes] was in a position of such extraordinary difficulty himself that one can hardly blame him for any device he might adopt to carry the Referendum in which he disbelieved but which he was forced into' (Fitzhardinge, *Little Digger*, 213). His opinion of the Cabinet was that its ability was limited to the 'hurricane force of the prime minister, and the good character of Senator Pearce, and the trained mind of Mr. Garran' (ibid., p. 28). Garran being the industrious and liberal senior civil servant. For Pearce, see P. Heydon, *Quiet Decision (G. F. Pearce)* (Melbourne, 1965). On conscription see also R. C. Thompson, *Religion in Australia* (Melbourne, 2002).

17. See a thoughtful article on the conscription debate, J. Kildea, 'Australian Catholics and Conscription', *JRH* 26/3 (2002). Kildea considers that revived sectarianism destroyed hope of 'increased amity for a generation' (p. 312); see also J. Brett, 'Class, Religion etc.', *AJPS* 37/1 (2002).

18. The 1917 Imperial War Conference was a significant step, a series of meetings at which Dominion Prime Ministers could sit as meetings of the War Cabinet. After Lloyd George's accession the Colonial Secretary had not been included in the War Cabinet (indeed, not even Lord Balfour as Foreign Secretary was a member), so this invitation to Australia to be represented in the direction of the war was a great opportunity.

19. Monash has a good biography by G. Serle (Melbourne, 1980); see also A. D. Spaull, 'Sir John Monash', *JRAHS* 56/3 (1970), which emphasizes Monash's distinguished civilian career. Andrews, *Anzac Illusion*, *passim*, describes the Murdoch/Bean anti-Monash campaign (see below), which Monash himself likened to a 'pogrom'.

20. For war-weariness, see Grey, *Military History*, 112. The conscription debate was equally lively in Canada, with many French Canadians deeply opposed (see K. McNaught, *Penguin History of Canada* (London, 1988), 215–18), but the December 1917 general election was won by the pro-conscription Unionists. For Hughes in the United States, see Spartalis, *Diplomatic Battles*, 55–65 and Fitzhardinge, *Little Digger*, 313–19. Hughes met a kindred spirit in Teddy Roosevelt,

who delighted Hughes by describing Wilson as a member of 'the only family where white men didn't fight on either side in the Civil War – and has done no fighting since!' (ibid., vol. ii, p. 315).

21. See R. Reid, *Beaucoup Australians Ici* (Canberra, 1998), 24 ff. One British officer reported the Australians to be 'the first really cheerful stubborn people we had met during the retreat'. One rifleman told a villager: 'Fini retreat, Madame – beaucoup Australians ici.'

22. Andrews, *Anzac Illusion*, 199.

23. Henry Braddon was that rare bird, an intellectual business man, acknowledged by Ferguson to have been successful in the few months he was allowed in New York.

24. In a cable, quoted Spartalis, *Diplomatic Battles*, 86, to the apprehensive William Watt, holding the fort in Melbourne. Hughes paid attention to his Cabinet colleagues only occasionally and his frequent cable interchanges with Watt were often acerbic. See *ADB* for a good article on Watt. For the casualties, see Grey, *Military History*, 115–16.

25. Spartalis, *Diplomatic Battles*, 87.

26. Ibid. pp. 114, 116.

27. Ibid., p. 120.

28. See D. Lloyd George, *The Truth about the Peace Treaties*, 2 vols. (London, 1938), vol. i, p. 542, quoted Spartalis, *Diplomatic Battles*; 139. Hughes was less successful in obtaining British control over the New Hebrides, a cause earnestly pressed by Australian Presbyterians, anxious for their missions, but one which did not much concern Hughes, although he continued to push the issue. See R. C. Thompson, *Australian Imperialism in the Pacific* (Melbourne, 1980), 208–10 and 220–1. The status quo was preserved until 1980, when the New Hebrides became independent as Vanuatu. See Spartalis, p. 180.

29. Piesse had been the director of Military Intelligence – Australia's 'M', during the war, particularly interesting himself in Japanese affairs. Appointed director of the new Pacific Branch of the Prime Minister's Department in May 1919, his was the best-informed and most realistic voice on Australian foreign policy between the wars.

30. For Makino Nobukai, see W. G. Beasley, *The Rise of Japan* (London, 1995), 182–3, and Spartalis, *Diplomatic Battles*, 178–9.

31. See D. Goldsworthy (ed.), *Facing North* (Melbourne, 2001): Piesse bitterly commented in May 1919 that 'the whole business in Paris seems to have gone badly for us, from our apparent lack of cordiality towards the United States to the barren victory over racial discrimination . . . We have been perhaps the chief factor in consolidating the Japanese nation behind the imperialists – and it needs little imagination to see how serious that may be' (p. 56). Although Piesse was eventually proved right, there was still to be a fierce struggle in Japan between imperialists and liberals. Like Hughes, Meighen was a lawyer with a gift of invective, but an extreme anti-labour conservative and a committed supporter of the United States.

See Spartalis, *Diplomatic Battles*, 226; McNaught, *Penguin History of Canada*, 228–9, 233–4. For a detailed account see S. Brawley, *The White Peril* (Sydney, 1995), chaps. 2 and 3; Brawley points out that Hughes's success was very convenient for the American and British who were privately sympathetic and who spoke with 'forked tongues' (p. 27). For the 1921 Imperial Conference, see ibid., chap. 10.

32. The Washington treaties were central to subsequent history: as Hughes said in the House of Representatives on 26 July 1922, they would 'profoundly [affect] the destiny of mankind'. The size of capital ships was limited to 35,000 tons, a restriction German naval architects would ingeniously overcome. As Hughes pointed out, however, in the same debate, 'these Treaties are not in the nature of an alliance. They do not guarantee to us material support if we are attacked. They assure merely moral support and the public opinion of the people of the contracting countries. The policy of the United States government is opposed to interference in the differences of other States, and that, in itself, has precluded anything in the nature of an alliance ... as far as material support is concerned, we are as dependent as ever on the Navy of the Empire.' Professor Max Beloff accurately described the outcome: 'Instead of the Anglo-Japanese alliance, based on a nice calculation of mutual interests and relative capacities, Britain was to enter into a new system whose functioning would principally depend upon the incalculable shifts and whims of the American democracy': *Britain's Liberal Empire*, vol. i: *Imperial Sunset* (London, 1969), 342, quoted P. Kennedy, *The Rise and Fall of British Naval Mastery* (London, 1991), 326.

33. For Hughes's secret telegram see Spartalis, *Diplomatic Battles*, 238–40; see also M. Gilbert, *Winston Churchill*, vol. iv: *1917–1921* (London, 1975), 833, which omits the telegram.

34. Commonwealth Parliamentary Papers: Report of Royal Commission on Basic Wages 1920–1921, vol. 4.

35. See B. Dyster and D. Meredith, *Australia in the International Economy in the Twentieth Century* (Cambridge, 1990), table 5.3, p. 93.

36. In October 1921 (Queensland Parliamentary Debates Legislative Assembly, 25 October), Theodore had confidently claimed that 'If it is thought that the members of the Legislative Assembly, then being in absolute and supreme control ... are likely to do something to the detriment of the people, they can be called to book by the people of Queensland'. He found the reality different. For the appalling Wren, millionaire, bookmaker, racecourse owner and boxing promoter, who extended his influence, lavishly purchased, far beyond his native Victoria, see McMullin, *Light on the Hill*.

37. For the Country Party, see B. D. Graham, *Formation of the Australian Country Party* (Canberra, 1966). For the 'bushies', see U. Ellis, *History of the Australian Country Party* (Parkville, 1963), 10.

38. See D. J. Murphy, writing of the period in *Labor in Power* (St Lucia, 1980): 'Ill-defined ideological differences were often formed about particular personalities.

Solidarity and conformity became intermixed and it was often unclear which was which' (p. 18).

39. Mrs Edith Cowan was elected to the Western Australia Assembly in July 1921 as a Nationalist, but claimed to 'belong to no party in this House' (Assembly Debate, 28 July 1921). It was only after the war, between 1918 and 1923, that women became eligible to sit in state Parliaments outside South Australia; they had of course been able to sit in the Commonwealth Parliament, but had not done so. For Payne, see Commonwealth Parliamentary Debates (Senate) 17 July 1924.

40. For the manifesto, see the Sydney *International Socialist*, 2 October 1920. Full of sound and fury, 'Let the ruling classes tremble', the Communist Party's non-industrial base was risible. The Crimes Act was amended in March 1926, the Immigration Act in September 1925. The September 1926 referendum was in two parts, the first concerning company law, employment and cartels, the second limiting the effects of strikes. James Scullin, the Labor leader, enthusiastically supported the proposals: 'almost all that is required for practical purposes, and one would have to be traitor to all that he has fought for in the past to oppose them' (Melbourne *Argus*, 7 June 1926). Such was by no means a unanimous Labor view.

41. For Australia and the gold standard, see Dyster and Meredith, *Australia in the International Economy*, chap. 4. Also W. H. Richmond, 'S. M. Bruce and Australian Economic Policy', *AEHR* 23 (1983).

42. D. T. Merrett, *ANZ Bank* (Sydney, 1985), 106.

43. See *ADB* entry for Hughes.

44. *Labor Daily*, 27 August 1930; C. M. H. Clark, *A History of Australia*, 6 vols. (Melbourne, 1962–88), vol. vi, p. 345.

45. For Niemeyer's visit, see Dyster and Meredith, *Australia in the International Economy*, 132–9, K. Tsokhas, 'Sir Otto Niemeyer', *AJPS* 30 (1995), B. Attard, 'Bank of England and the Origin of the Niemeyer Mission', *AEHR* 32 (1992); for Theodore, see *ADB*.

46. The episode is well describe in McMullin, *Light on the Hill*, 166–7.

47. The Treasurers of New South Wales, Victoria and South Africa were joined with the Commonwealth Treasurer as a watchdog, a measure of very doubtful worth. For Anstey and the unhappy Labor members, see ibid., pp. 175–6.

48. *Labor Daily*, 14 May 1932, called the dismissal a foul blow: 'The most appalling tragedy in the constitutional history of Australia since the white race superseded the black', and Lang continued to argue the point for the rest of his long life. There is a good biography of Lang by B. Nairn, *The Big Fella: Jack Lang and the Australian Labor Party, 1891–1949* (Melbourne, 1986); Nairn is in no doubt that Game was right, acting with 'persistent fairness' in the face of a 'sham financial proposal' (p. 258), betraying the 'derangement of the government' (p. 259); 'He could not allow New South Wales to cease to function as a stable society, with a solution being effected by blood in the streets of Sydney and by dissolution in the country. He had tolerated Lang, even sustained him to a significant extent, for seventeen months: from January 1931 when the premier's

erratic behaviour had begun to provoke conservative reaction which added to the great pressure on the governor. Inexorably, Lang had reached the limit of ineptitude' (p. 260). See also B. Foott, *Dismissal of a Premier* (Sydney, 1968), and T. Sykes, *Two Centuries of Panic* (Sydney, 1988), chap. 12.

49. For the New Guard, see K. Amos, *New Guard Movement* (Melbourne, 1976), and B. Alder, 'Ideology of the N.G.M.', *JRAHS* 82/2(1996). Nairn describes de Groot in 'an over-sized, second-hand military uniform on a decrepit horse' (*Big Fella*, 256), an episode which, although with a comic side, betrayed a 'Fascist contempt for democracy'.

50. Philip Knightley, in his lively book *Australia: Biography of a Nation* (London, 2001), devotes a whole chapter to the Bodyline controversy. Bradman has an excellent biography by Charles Williams (London, 1997), who comments 'It was perhaps impossible for anybody to survive the rigours of a Winchester education during the First World War without developing some abnormal character traits' (p. 85). While sport is surely as important in Britain as Australia, it has not become such a nationalist preoccupation. Popular heroes are as likely to be pop singers as politicians, and often as evanescent; and sportsmen may be admired even from opposing teams; Leary Constantine springs to mind. Were there an English Bradman it would perhaps be Stanley Matthews. As an example of 'Bradmanism' the Australian Broadcasting Commission chose the great batsman's test average (99.4) as its PO box number. For Mason, see Knightley, pp. 159–60.

51. G. Shirely and B. Adams, *Australian Cinema* (n.p. [Australia], 1989), is a comprehensive history; see A. Moran and T. O'Regan, *Australian Screen* (Ringwood, 1989), and B. McFarlane *et al.* (eds.), *Oxford Companion to Australian Film* (South Melbourne, 1999).

52. Melbourne *Argus*, 18 November 1937. The train was called *Spirit of Progress*. Until 1962 passengers to Sydney still had to change at Albury because of the change of gauge.

53. Casey's letters to Bruce, *My Dear Prime Minister*, ed. W. J. Hudson and J. North (Canberra, 1980), are an entertaining source. For trade figures, see Goldsworthy, *Facing North*, appendix VII.

54. In a Senate speech: CPD (S) 27 July 1922.

55. L. F. Crisp. 'J. H. Scullin's account of the Buckingham Palace Interviews', *HSV* 11.

56. Beasley, *Rise of Japan*, chap. X

57. Goldsworthy, *Facing North*, appendix VII.

58. S. L. Smith, ibid, pp. 72–4.

59. Ibid., pp. 82–5.

60. Hughes told Parliament that Australia was 'in a position to administer these islands . . . as integral portions of her territory'. The League of Nations could rely upon the mandate being 'faithfully carried out, in accordance with the traditions of the British government of native races', but commercial considerations were emphasized. 'New Guinea is potentially, a very rich country . . . We hope that we

shall provide opportunities for our enterprising young men who came back from the war . . . The possibilities of trade, and what that trade will mean to Australia in wealth and opportunity, can hardly be exaggerated.' There is a good summary by H. Nelson, in G. Osborne and W. F. Mandle, *New History* (Sydney, 1982), chap. 8. As Nelson points out, the Australian government 'was responsible for the administration of more peoples north of Torres Strait than in that two-thirds of the continent made up of Western Australia, South Australia and the Northern Territory' – which makes the summary treatment given in such recent histories as those of Macintyre and Day (two paragraphs in 470 pages) the more surprising. See also J. Griffin, H. Nelson and S. Firth, *Papua New Guinea: A Political History* (Richmond, 1976): 'Papuans . . . Remember Murray as a man they could talk to; he seemed to care about them' (p. 30). For Pearce, see Heydon, *Quiet Decision*, chap. 10. If Western Australians had their way Pearce's duties would have been reduced, since in April 1933 a substantial majority voted – unsuccessfully – to secede from the Commonwealth.

61. For the unhappy status of Namatjira, see C. Macleod, *Patrol in the Dream Time* (Sydney, 1987), 1–5, a sensible and lively book, especially on the 'Stolen Children'. See also J. T. Wells and M. F. Christie, 'Namatjira', *AHS* 31/114 (2000). For Robert Love, and the Apostolic Church, see R. Broome, *Aboriginal Australians: Black Response to White Domination* (Crows Nest, 2002), chap. 7 – an essential text.

62. J. Turnbull and P. Y. Navaretti (eds.), *Griffin in Australia and India* (Melbourne, 1998). Many Griffin buildings have been demolished including the notable Australia Café in Melbourne.

63. The standard biography of Mawson is P. Ayres (Melbourne, 1999); see also B. Hains, *The Ice and the Inland* (Sydney, 2002).

64. Fitzhardinge, *Little Digger*, 619.

65. For Mannix on Mussolini, see *ADB*, which has the statement quoted here as having been made in 1943, surely an error; Mannix was ostracized by the Irish hierarchy during a visit to the country in 1926 as a supporter of the IRA against the Free State government, an episode his biographer, M. Gilchrist, *Daniel Mannix: Priest and Patriot* (Melbourne, 1982), wisely ignores, and lived to honour the corrupt Vietnamese President Ngo Dinh Diem. Even his colleague, Archbishop Sir James Duhig of Brisbane, a more liberal character, believed that 'There are very few Fascists in Spain' (*Freeman's Journal*, 10 October 1936). For Forde on Abyssinia, see McMullin, *Light on the Hill*, 196–7.

66. Ibid, pp. 186 ff; but it was not a good time for Australian intellectuals. 'By common consent,' G. Serle wrote in *From Deserts the Prophets Come* (Melbourne, 1973), 'the 20s are seen in retrospect as a scurvy period, when Australians seemed content to accept second-rateness' (p. 148). There does not seem to have been much improvement in the 1930s. Curtin has a fine biography by D. Day (Sydney, 1999).

67. For Lyons' resignation, see A. W. Martin, *Robert Menzies*, 2 vols. (Melbourne, 1999), vol. i, p. 189.

CHAPTER 12

1. L. F. Fitzhardinge, *William Morris Hughes*, vol. ii: *The Little Digger* (Melbourne, 1973), 647. The British Labour Party, similarly worried about the Catholic vote, also dithered about Spain, but the reality of the Spanish Civil War had, by 1937, forced the parliamentary Labour Party to swing in favour of re-armament. See A. Thorpe, *A History of the British Labour Party* (Basingstoke, 1997), 91.

2. Curtin (D. Day, Sydney, 1999), Scullin (J. Robertson, Perth, 1974) and Menzies (A. W. Martin, Melbourne, 1999) have biographies; P. G. Edwards, *Prime Ministers* (Melbourne, 1983), is a good synoptic guide. For Curtin and revolution, see Day, p. 199 and chap. 23. See also Paul Hasluck, *The Government and the People, 1939–1941* (Canberra, 1965). The two volumes of the official history of the war written by Hasluck are especially useful since Hasluck was himself an active politician, and a scholarly writer, isolated to an extent by his independent views. Another work from the centre of national life is H. C. Coombs, *From Curtin to Keating* (Darwin, 1994).

3. M. Gilbert, *Finest Hour* (London, 1988), 436.

4. For Page's attack and Menzies' reply, see CPD (R) 20 April 1939 and Martin, *Menzies*, vol. i, pp. 274–9.

5. For Menzies on Munich, see ibid., chap. 10, *passim*, but Menzies' assessment of Hitler 'a dreamer, a man of ideas, many of them good ones' (p. 235) was surpassed by Page, demonstrating purblind parochialism: 'what Australia desired . . . was a politically satisfied Germany which would be ready to take her share in the peaceful developments of the world.'

6. D. Denoon and P. Mein-Smith, *History of Australia, New Zealand and the Pacific* (Oxford, 2000), 318 ff. For the declaration of war, see N. Mansergh (ed.), *Documents and Speeches on British Commonwealth Affairs* (London, 1953), 479–84. Curtin's support was equivocal, in marked contrast to his predecessor Andrew Fisher's pledge of the 'last man and the last shilling'; ibid., pp. 482–4. The September 1940 election produced 36 seats each for the UAP/Country Party and for Labor, although the Labor members included four semi-detached Langites, with the Independents Coles and Wilson supporting the coalition. Two powerful Labor figures were introduced into Parliament, Ben Chifley and Herbert Evatt, whose restless ambition, unable to brook staying in opposition, and finding Curtin 'woefully timid' and 'afraid to press for power', led him to attempt personal discussions with Menzies. Curtin's position was strengthened in February 1941 when the Langites returned to the official fold.

7. J. Grey, *Military History of Australia* (Cambridge, 1999), 143 ff. For the militia figures, see ibid., p. 134. F. Johnson, *R.A.A.F over Europe* (London, 1946), complements the four volumes of the official history.

8. Particularly by D. Day in *Claiming a Continent* (Sydney, 1997), *Great Betrayal* (Melbourne, 1988), and *Reluctant Nation: Australia and the Allied Defeat of*

Japan 1942–45 (Oxford, 1992). Curtin and the Labor Party had refused to accept the principle of collective security, had opposed increases in defence spending, had claimed, in April 1938, that events in neither Europe nor Asia could justify a war, had refused to join a coalition government and had opposed the banning of iron ore exports to fuel Japanese industry. British undertakings to commit land and sea forces to Singapore, which were to lead to the loss of two capital ships and tens of thousands of Commonwealth soldiers are dismissed by Day as 'blithe' (*Claiming a Continent*, 352) and 'bland' (ibid., p. 374). Again, on the same page, it is stated that Britain 'retained the great bulk of its army and air force at home' rather than commit forces to France in 1939–40, 'a wise presentation in the circumstances but one which Australia did not emulate'. This is blatantly false, for the quarter of a million soldiers snatched from the Dunkirk beaches constituted almost the only major combatant force available – to say nothing of the casualties previously incurred. For a corrective see 'Poland to Pearl Harbor', in C. Bridge (ed.), *Munich to Vietnam* (Carlton, 1991).

9. Gilbert, *Finest Hour*, 725. C. Barnett, *Engage the Enemy More Closely* (London, 2001), is invaluable for the Royal Navy's war.

10. Gilbert, *Finest Hour*, 822.

11. Hasluck, *Government and People*, 335. For Australian agreement, see L. Woodward, *British Foreign Policy in the Second World War*, 2 vols. (London, 1970), vol. i, pp. 536–7: 'The consent of the Australian and New Zealand Governments was the most striking because at this time it seemed that the Japanese might decide to enter the war' but Woodward also points out (ibid., n. 1) that Australia protested against the grant of discretionary powers to Anthony Eden, who had used the power without prior consultation. Sir Alexander Cadogan, head of the Foreign Office thought that Menzies had been poorly treated: '[Eden] has rather jumped us into this' (Martin, *Menzies*, vol. i, p. 326).

12. Hasluck, *Government and People*, 504.

13. Ibid., pp. 381–3. Elkin was a significant figure in Aboriginal policy; see below, note 28; see also Martin, *Menzies*, vol. i, chap. 16.

14. Day, *Reluctant Nation*, 98 ff.

15. For what follows, see W. G. Beasley, *The Rise of Japan* (London, 1995), chap. 11; the best account of Singapore is A. Warren, *Singapore* (London, 2002).

16. For the *Prince of Wales* and *Repulse*, see Barnett, *Engage the Enemy*, chap. 13.

17. A. J. P. Taylor, *English History 1914–1945* (Oxford, 1965), 541.

18. For the reaction to Darwin attacks, see R. McMullin, *Light on the Hill* (Oxford, 1991), 217. Sir Frederick Shedden, secretary of the War Cabinet, described the ministers as running about 'like a lot of startled chooks': Day, *Curtin*, 450. For Johnson's views (12 October 1942), see P. G. Edwards (ed.), *Australia through American Eyes 1935–45* (Melbourne, 1994), 79. The Japanese imperial headquarters had agreed on the Papua and Solomons invasion, after which the naval staff wanted to press on and isolate Australia from the United States, while the navy wanted to confront the US fleet in the central Pacific; there was no thought

then of an invasion of Australia, and the Coral Sea battle 'more or less ended any likelihood of Australia facing serious hostile landings': Warren, *Singapore*, 283.

19. The cable is reproduced in T. B. Millar (ed.), *Australia in Peace and War* (Botany, 1991), 103–4 – and is not mentioned by Day. Millar describes Curtin's attitude as 'uncharacteristic . . . double talk', but, caught as he was between his former fuzzy idealism and the cool facts of political life, Curtin only gradually became an effective leader. For Curtin's 1944 revision, see M. Gilbert, *Road to Victory* (London, 1986), 755–6

20. For the genesis of Curtin's message, see Day, *Curtin*, 438–40.

21. For the naval actions, see Barnett, *Engage the Enemy*. The battle of the Java Sea, with Dutch, British, Australian and American ships involved (p. 426) demonstrated the dangers of divided command; for Somerville's Ceylon action, see pp. 863 ff. G. H. Gill, *Australia in the War of 1939–1945*, 2 vols. (Canberra, 1957, 1968), deals with the actions in detail. Although the British naval base was temporarily moved to East Africa, and the capital ships withdrawn, Ceylon was preserved until the allied sea offensive began in April 1944.

22. For the High Command disputes, see Grey, *Military History*, 175 ff., and J. Gallaway, *Odd Couple* (St Lucia, 2000). For the Papua fighting, see Grey, *Military History*, 174–7; D. McCarthy, *South West Pacific Area* (Canberra, 1959).

23. For the attacks on Curtin, see Day, *Curtin*, 491 ff. Curtin wanted a more extensive geographical range of militia service, but was opposed by his party colleagues. See J. B. Hirst, 'Australia's Defence', pt. II, *AHS* 102.

24. Grey, *Military History*, 184–6.

25. At first, Australia was not prepared to admit any 'coloured' troops, although ships carrying such dangerous passengers would be allowed to stop at Australian ports, if they were bound elsewhere, and permission to land was refused. Most blacks were sent to New Guinea: see Day, *Claiming a Continent*, 326 ff.; P. and R. Bell, *Implicated: The United States in Australia* (Oxford, 1993), 100 ff.

26. For the referendum, see Day, *Curtin*, 549 ff.

27. Chifley has a sympathetic biography by D. Day (n.p. [Australia], 1944), but one which gives only a minor part (86 pages of 534) to the Premiership.

28. Herbert Cole 'Nugget' Coombs was, over a career spanning more than half a century, Australia's most liberal and dedicated public servant, as an economist, administrator and friend of the Aborigines. For an assessment, see T. Rowse, *Obliged to Submit* (Cambridge, 2000).

29. McMullin, *Light on the Hill*, 251 ff.

30. A number of books about the Movement and its founder have been written, the latest being B. Duncan, *Crusade or Conspiracy?* (Sydney, 2001), which concentrates on the division that developed within the Church leading to a Vatican reprimand for Cardinal Mannix. G. Henderson, *Mr Santamaria and the Bishops* (Sydney, 1982), has a less reverential approach.

31. Nationalizing banks had indeed been a plank of Labor policy since 1921, and the post-war Labor government had implemented other promises in telecommuni-

cations and airlines; but Chifley lacked Attlee's judgement of the politically possible and economically desirable. One fine example of Chifley's illogicality was his statement that 'since private banks [by which was meant all trading banks] are conducted primarily for profit, and therefore follow policies which in important respects run counter to the public interest, their business should be transferred to public ownership' – which ignores the whole battery of controls that any government and central bank can exercise to harass trading banks. Menzies was afforded a splendid opening, which he took every advantage of, claiming that this was 'the most far-reaching, revolutionary, unwarranted and un-Australian measure' which would create 'a money monopoly' able to exercise 'dictatorial controls over all production and business'. CPD (R) 15, 23 October 1947.

32. See Day, *Claiming a Continent*, 349–53; D. Goldsworthy (ed.), *Facing North* (Melbourne, 2001), 128–33; P. Knightley, *Australia: Biography of a Nation* (London, 2001), 216–19. Knightley also points out that no attempt was made to exclude Nazis, and that 'Australia is the only major Western country which admitted large numbers of Nazi war criminals and has failed to successfully convict a single one' (p. 219). Calwell has an autobiography *Be Just and Fear Not* (Hawthorn, 1972).

33. Knightley, *Australia*, 221 ff. For refugees admitted see A. Calwell, *Be Just and Fear Not* (Hawthorn, 1972).

34. For Evatt, see P. Crockett, *Evatt: A Life* (Melbourne, 1993); K. Buckley *et al.*, '*Doc Evatt*' (Melbourne, 1994); Millar, *Australia in Peace and War*; C. Waters in Goldsworthy, *Facing North*, chap. 3 *passim*. W. J. Hudson, *Australia and the New World Order* (Canberra, 1993), while acknowledging Evatt's achievements, believes Evatt 'was a problem even for his own Labor Party. He lacked utterly the panache of a Whitlam, but neither did he project the earthy decency of a Curtin or Chifley.' For Bevin's views (see below), see C. Waters, *The Empire Fractures* (Melbourne, 1995), 195.

35. See R. J. Bell, *Unequal Allies* (Melbourne, 1977), 60.

36. The Anzac pact was a milestone in being the first treaty Australia made without consultation (indeed, with some clauses contrary to Britain's wishes); see Waters, in Goldsworthy, *Facing North*, 111. The US State Department believed the pact 'aimed all too obviously at the US' (Bell and Bell, *Implicated*, 96): see also Bell, *Unequal Allies*, 146–9. Australia's arguments were advanced with the help of a professional foreign affairs team. The original Department of External Affairs had been amalgamated with the Department of Home Affairs in 1916, with many of its responsibilities already lost to the Prime Minister's Department in 1911, and from 1919 to 1935 remained subordinate to that office. Even after regaining its independence in 1935, the Department had a minuscule staff with patchy experience. In 1934 a recruitment and training scheme was begun, and with the appointment of the brilliant young (31-year-old) John Burton as secretary in March 1947, Evatt's department became a professional institution for the first time (Burton's predecessors, Sir William Dunk and Colonel Hodgson, were totally

unqualified). The long period of control exercised by Evatt and Casey between 1941 and 1961, with an 18-month break under Percy Spender, gave the department real political status.

37. Waters, in Goldsworthy, *Facing North*, 129 ff.

38. For Ward, see McMullin, *Light on the Hill*, 243. For Menzies on GATT, see R. Pitty, in Goldsworthy, *Facing North*, 222.

39. For what follows, see D. Lee, in D. Goldsworthy, *Facing North*, chap. 4: 'Indonesia's Independence', *passim*.

40. Lee, ibid., p. 160.

41. Ibid., p. 135.

42. Ibid., p. 136.

43. For Malaya, see S. L. Smith, chap. 2: 'Towards Diplomatic Representation', ibid., p. 126.

44. G. Henderson, *Menzies' Child: The Liberal Party of Australia* (Sydney, 1998), 88 ff. For the history of the Liberal Party, see I. Hancock, '*National and Permanent? The Federal Organisation of the Liberal Party* (Melbourne, 2000).

45. The defensive perimeter as defined by Acheson would be from the Aleutian Islands to Japan, thence through the Ryukyu Islands to the Philippines, thereby excluding Korea.

46. For the war see J. Grey, op.cit., 204–10 and R. O'Neill's official history *Australia in the Korean War*. Conscription into the militia began in March 1951, but with an initial three months training, and no liability to serve abroad, it had no effect on Australian participation in Korea.

47. For the trade figures, see R. Pitty, in Goldsworthy, *Facing North*, appendix VII.

48. For ANZUS, see J. A. Camilleri, *The Australia, New Zealand and US Alliance* (Boulder, Colo., 1987), which points out that although the Treaty provided for joint planning, in practice the US command succeeded in amending the agreement 'to remove any obligation for combined military planning in peace time' thus substantially weakening the pact (p. 9). See also Millar, *Australia in Peace and War*, 166 ff.; Bell and Bell, *Implicated*, chap. 5, *passim*. In his diaries (ed. T. B. Millar, *Australian Foreign Minister: Diaries of R. G. Casey* (London, 1972)), Casey identifies the exclusion of the Philippines as the main British point p. 20. See also D. Lowe, 'Percy Spender's Quest', *AJIA* 55/2 (2001). This *AJIA* special issue covers the fiftieth anniversary of the pact in detail.

49. P. Gifford, in Goldsworthy, *Facing North*, 180 ff.

50. M. Gilbert, *Never Despair* (London, 1988), 791.

51. S. Macintyre, *A Concise History of Australia* (Cambridge, 1999), 210.

52. One of Evatt's achievements was his contribution to a solution of the problem presented by Commonwealth countries, especially India and Ireland, becoming republics. Although Ireland left the Commonwealth, Irish citizens retained all existing dual-citizenship privileges, which mollified traditionally Anglophobic tendencies among Irish Australians, and did much to secure the future of the

multi-racial Commonwealth; see R. J. Moore, *Making the New Commonwealth* (Oxford, 1987), *passim*, J. O'Brien, 'Australia and the Repeal of the External Relations Act', and B. Murphy, 'Ireland, Australia and the Commonwealth', both in C. Kiernan (ed.), *Australia and Ireland* (Dublin, 1986).

53. See P. Gifford, chap. 5: 'Cold War', in Goldsworthy, *Facing North*. Spender's own account in *Exercises in Diplomacy* (Sydney, 1969) should be read with D. Lowe (ed.), *Australia and the End of Empire* (Geelong, 1996).

54. F. Welsh, *A History of Hong Kong* (London, 1994), 442.

55. For Dulles, see Gifford, in Goldsworthy, *Facing North*, 199 ff. The experienced Richard Casey, then Minister for External Affairs, was concerned by American attitudes. 'I do not believe that the Americans have thought it through . . . they seem intent on inserting themselves, physically, into the area, which might well bring communist China in and lead us all into a third World War. Apart from a couple of voices . . . my colleagues appear to support my views': Millar (ed.), *Australian Foreign Minister*. But Menzies' government paid little attention to official advice.

56. Gilbert, *Never Despair*, 973.

57. Gifford, in Goldsworthy, *Facing North*, 206 ff.

CHAPTER 13

1. I. Hancock, *National and Permanent? The Federal Organisation of the Liberal Party* (Melbourne, 2000), 5.

2. 'Affable Artie' Fadden, from a Queensland elementary school, was a very different character from the suave Menzies.

3. In 2001; such assessments are subject to dispute and the Group of Eight leading universities can claim some outstanding achievements, but it does seem that many Australian universities are more noted for undergraduate teaching than for advanced research – as is increasingly the case in Britain.

4. *JPH* 36/2 (2001).

5. G. Henderson, *Menzies' Child: The Liberal Party of Australia* (Sydney, 1998), 137.

6. See J. Waterford, 'A Labor Myth', in A. Curthoys and J. Merritt, *Australia's First Cold War*, 2 vols. (Sydney, 1984, 1986), vol. ii, chap. 6, for an investigation.

7. For Groupers in Victoria, see R. McMullin, *Light on the Hill* (Oxford, 1991), 262.

8. S. Ward, *Australia and the British Embrace* (Melbourne, 2001), is a penetrating study of the effects on Australia of the British entry into the European Economic Community, an event which decisively broke the economic nexus and forced Australia to a radical reconsideration of the country's place in the world. Chifley's remarks were made in Parliament on 4 December 1947 and are quoted in Ward, p. 17.

9. With nearly thirteen years' service as Minister, first of Commerce and Agriculture, then of Trade, McEwen was a major force in restructuring Australian overseas trade. For his renegotiation of Ottawa, see Ward, *Australia and the British Embrace*, 33–8; R. Pitty, 'Post War Expansion', in D. Goldsworthy (ed.), *Facing North* (Melbourne, 2001), 239.

10. Pitty, ibid., pp. 232–50.

11. Foreign Relations of the USA, 1951, vol. vi, p. 737. Earlier that year Secretary of State Dean Acheson had emphasized to Menzies (ibid. pp. 593 ff.) that Indonesia and the Netherlands must be left to sort out the dispute – with the bias towards Indonesia – but there was no hint that the population of New Guinea should have a vote.

12. P. Gifford, in Goldsworthy, *Facing North*, 210–19; P. G. Edwards and G. Pemberton, *Crises and Commitments* (Sydney, 1992), chaps. 14 and 15. See also S. Doran, 'Toeing the Line', *JPH* 36/1 (2001), for a definitive view.

13. D. Lee and M. Dee, in Goldsworthy, *Facing North*, 270. G. Woodard, 'Best Practice', *AJPS* 33/1 (1998), praises Australian policy. For Australian action in Malaya, see Edwards and Pemberton, *Crises*, chap. 10.

14. Ibid., pp. 270 ff. Foreign Relations of the USA, 1961–3, vol. xxiii, pp. 731–57; for Kennedy's remark that 'People have forgotten ANZUS', see p. 752.

15. For the British plan see PRO PREM 13/428. Two phases, 'Mason' and 'Addington', which involved not only using the Darwin airbase, but Australian bomber and fighter aircraft for strikes on Indonesian targets, were agreed; Addington, the most drastic option, was not to be disclosed to the Americans.

16. CPD (R) 29 April 1965.

17. In a conversation with M. Charlton, recorded between December 1976 and May 1977, published in M. Charlton and A. Moncrieff, *Many Reasons Why* (London, 1978), an invaluable source book.

18. Menzies on 2 May 1961, quoted Gifford, in Goldsworthy, *Facing North*, 209. For Macmillan and Kennedy, see PRO PREM 13/429 30 March 1961; also for Anglo-Australian discussions. C. Waters, 'Macmillan, Menzies, History and Empire', *AHS* 119 (2002), describes their correspondence.

19. For Forsyth, see Lee and Dee, in Goldsworthy, *Facing North*, 286; for Colby, see Charlton and Moncrieff, *Many Reasons Why*, 76 ff.

20. Ibid., p. 84.

21. State Department, CAS 265; TAB E State 316; 320 and 329 TAB B. See also F. Logevall, *Choosing War* (Berkeley, 2001), chaps. 3 and 4.

22. A. Watt, *Vietnam* (Melbourne, 1968), 112.

23. Hasluck to the DEA Secretary, A. Tange, quoted Lee and Dee, in Goldsworthy, *Facing North*, 289. The extent to which Hasluck was out of his depth is exposed by G. Clark, an official of the Department of External Affairs, in chap. 2 of P. King (ed.), *Australia's Vietnam* (Sydney, 1983), which describes a meeting with the Russian Premier Kosygin and Foreign Minister Gromyko (pp. 18–21).

24. General Taylor, quoted Charlton and Moncrieff, *Many Reasons Why*, 102.

25. For Hasluck's remarks, see Lee and Dee, in Goldsworthy, *Facing North*, 288 ff; see also Edwards and Pemberton, *Crises*, 344 ff.

26. For Whitlam, see Lee and Dee, in Goldsworthy, *Facing North*, 290. Whitlam's enthusiasm for American actions is queried by G. Clark, in King (ed.), *Australia's Vietnam*: 'On several occasions I found that Whitlam did not read the material essential for his foreign affairs brief. He particularly feared any course of action which might strengthen the position of his ALP rival. Had Cairns not dominated intellectual left-wing opposition to the Vietnam War, Whitlam might have moved to a more progressive position more quickly' (p. 29). A more detailed explanation is offered by Kim Beazley, later himself Labor leader, in chap. 3 of the same work.

27. Waller is quoted in Dee and Lee, in Goldsworthy, *Facing North*, 291. For Menzies' statement, see Edwards and Pemberton, *Crises*, 372. For Australian eagerness to join the war, see M. Sexton, *War for the Asking: How Australia Invited Itself to Vietnam* (French's Forest, 2002).

28. Calwell: CPD (R) 4 May 1965; *Australian*, 30 April 1965.

29. For the fighting, see J. Grey, *Military History of Australia* (Cambridge, 1999), 229–43.

30. National Security Directive, no. 229, 28 May 1986.

31. See Henderson, *Menzies' Child*, 186, 197 ff.

32. Holt, reported in the *New York Times*, 6 July 1966. Holt's enthusiasm for killing communists was appreciated by his hosts: 'America should not be apologetic over the civilian casualty problem "involved in bombing N. Vietnamese cities". He did not foresee any opposition to such strikes in his government which he could not overcome and he would support the US regardless of the unfavourable British reaction'. He wondered how Britain could 'expect to be a major power without being involved in the business of South Vietnam': Memorandum of Conversation, 29 June 1966, SDA I.24673/66 SE Asia Region; for the advice on dealing with Australians see National Archives NND 979506.

33. The documents concerning President Johnson's visit are in *SDB* 28 November 1966. For the Australian reaction, see D. Horne, *Time of Hope* (Sydney, 1980), chap. 3. See also P. D. Williams, 'Holt, Johnson', *AJPH* 47/3 (2001), and G. Langley, *Decade of Dissent* (North Sydney, 1992).

34. For Frodsham, see R. Broome, *Aboriginal Australians: Black Response to White Domination* (Crows Nest, 2002), 104.

35. See M. M. Bennett, *Australian Aboriginal* (London, 1930), Bennett had insisted: 'On land ownership alone can a just settlement be based . . . It is not our problem only. It has been termed the most important business of the century' (p. 135). But it was another forty years before any attention was paid to it. See also Bennett's 'Condition of Aborigines under the Federal government', British Commonwealth League, 5 June 1929, and *ADB*. Violence had not ceased in the border region, either; an account of one 'massacre' in the Kimberleys, in the 1930s, is given by J. Bohemia and W. McGregor, *JAS* 33 (1992).

36. For what follows, see C. D. Rowley, *The Destruction of Aboriginal Society*

(Canberra, 1970), chap. 13. For a different flavour, the scholarly *White Flour, White Power* (Cambridge, 1998) by T. Rowse is an essential record of twentieth-century Aboriginal policies. See also R. McGregor, *Imagined Destinies: Australia and the Doomed Race Theory 1880–1939* (Carlton, 1997). For the protectors see A. Haebich, *For Their Own Good: Aborigines and Government in the South West of Western Australia 1900–1940* (Nedlands, 1988), the factual basis for the film *Rabbit-proof Fence.*

37. For Basedow and Bleakley, *ADB*; see also K. Blackburn, 'White Agitation', *AJPH* 45/2 (1999). Queensland's view was well expressed in the *North Queensland Register* of October 1983: 'one of the troubles of a colonising nation is the decent disposal of the native inhabitants of the country, of which the latter have been dispossessed'; quoted in N. Loos, *Invasion and Resistance* (Canberra, 1982), 160. Unaipon was the first and most prominent of the early Aboriginal activists, but William Ferguson of New South Wales, who helped to launch the 'Day of Mourning' in 1938, was perhaps more competent and aggressive; see *ADB* and A. Markus, *Governing Savages* (Sydney, 1990).

38. Rowley, *Destruction of Aboriginal Society*, 238. For the definition of 'Aboriginal', see P. Hasluck's valuable book, *Shades of Darkness* (Melbourne, 1988), written in 1987 after an unequalled experience of Aboriginal affairs at all levels.

39. Ibid., chap. 3.

40. Rowley, *Destruction of Aboriginal Society*, 33. See also D. May, *Aboriginal Labour and the Cattle Industry* (Cambridge, 1994), and D. S. Trigger, *Whitefella Comin'* (Cambridge, 1992).

41. Hasluck, *Shades of Darkness*, 121 (my italics).

42. D. Day, *Claiming a Continent* (Sydney, 1997), 366; C. Macleod, *Patrol in the Dream Time* (Sydney, 1987), G. Wagner, *Children of the Empire* (London, 1982); A. Haebich, *Broken Circles* (Fremantle, 2000). For Freedom Riders see A. Curthoys, *Freedom Ride* (Crows Nest, 2002).

43. One reason for Holt's Bill was increasing criticism from the United Nations, where comparisons, exaggerated but wounding, were being made with apartheid South Africa, where Nelson Mandela had been sentenced to life imprisonment in 1964; in September 1966 the Aboriginal Rights Council made an appeal directly to the United Nations. The comparison with Queensland was perhaps more telling, where the official celebration of the state's centenary, *Triumph in the Tropics*, published in 1959, was aptly described by R. Fitzgerald, *History of Queensland: From 1915 to the Early 1980s* (St Lucia, 1984), 551 ff. as containing 'racist attitudes unequalled almost anywhere in the world'. Hasluck was scathing: 'In sixteen years with him in Cabinet I had never known him to show any interest in Aborigines': *Shades of Darkness*, 124.

44. For comments on McMahon, see Henderson, *Menzies' Child*, 201; see also A. W. Martin, *Robert Menzies*, 2 vols. (Melbourne, 1999), vol. ii, p. 556.

45. T. B. Millar, *Australia in Peace and War* (Botany, 1991), 313, 312.

46. See Charlton and Moncrieff, *Many Reasons Why*, chap 6.

47. Horne, *Time of Hope*, 58; Lee and Dee, in Goldsworthy, *Facing North*, 298. Gorton's relations with Johnson were truly cordial, both tough-minded men with experience of war; Mrs Gorton was herself American. During the visit Gorton claimed that 'we, who for two centuries were shielded by the British Navy, have as our major shield the ANZUS pact'. To an objective observer, it might seem that in both instances Australia was paying a heavy price for such protection, itself of very doubtful value.

48. In *Australia's Vietnam* (ed. P. King) Jane Ross concludes: 'Australian servicemen were more fairly treated than their American counterparts; the ballot resulted in a more representative section of the age group being sent to the front, while American troops were disproportionately black and working class', but nevertheless notes: 'There were *only* [my italics] two instances in Vietnam of a soldier deliberately causing the death of his officer (in 1968 and 1969) both times by the use of grenades' (pp. 76, 88).

49. For Fraser, see P. Ayres, *Malcolm Fraser* (Richmond, 1987), B. D'Alpuget, *Malcolm Fraser* (Melbourne, 1982), P. M. Weller, *Malcolm Fraser Prime Minister* (Ringwood, 1989), and B. W. Head and A. Patience, *From Fraser to Hawke* (Melbourne, 1989).

50. For Whitlam, see G. Freudenberg, *A Certain Grandeur* (Ringwood, 1987), and G. Whitlam, *The Whitlam Government* (Ringwood, 1985). For American views, see National Archives PAT/BUN – 27, QG 19 CF 91/56, CF 89/109: 14 October 1966.

51. Horne, *Time of Hope*, 159 ff.

52. For the Liberal Party, see Henderson, *Menzies' Child*, chap. 8.

53. For Askin, see D. Hickie, *The Prince and the Premier* (London, 1985).

54. See H. Lunn, *Johannes Bjelke-Petersen* (St Lucia, 1984).

55. Quoted in D. Goldsworthy *et al.*, chap. 8, 'Re-orientation', in Goldsworthy, *Facing North*, 332 ff.

56. Ibid., pp. 331–8.

CHAPTER 14

1. Whitlam has left his own, highly approving account in *The Whitlam Government* (Ringwood, 1985); see also J. H. Walter, *The Leader* (n.p., Queenland, 1980). For Rupert Murdoch and the *Australian*'s role, see B. Page, *Murdoch Archipelago* (London, 2003), chap. 6. For the younger generation, see R. Neville, *Hippie, Hippie, Shake* (London, 1995).

2. Walter, *Leader*, is revealing. See also G. Freudenberg, *A Certain Grandeur* (Ringwood, 1987). For the Duumvirate, see M. Powell, 'The Whitlam Labor Government', *AJPH* 43/2 (1997).

3. For Utzon, see P. Drew, *The Masterpiece* (n.p., Victoria, 2001), and F. Fromonot, *Jørn Utzon* (Corte Madera, CA, 1998); for Askin's corruption, see Drew,

p. 304, and D. Hickie, *The Prince and the Premier* (London, 1985). Sydneysiders do not perhaps miss the opera stage too much; the 2002 season of some 60-plus performances was hardly innovative or risky, including 11 performances of *Iolanthe* and 13 of *Cav.* and *Pag.* With the exception of *Ariadne auf Naxos* and *Lady Macbeth of Mtsensk* the rest were all well-loved favourites.

4. For Wave Hill, see P. Knightley, *Australia: Biography of a Nation* (London, 2001), 265–8. Earlier efforts by W. C. Wentworth as Minister for Aboriginal Affairs in 1968 to persuade the Vesteys to accommodate the Gurindji demands led to his replacement; see G. F. Gale and A. Brookman, *Race Relations in Australia and the Aborigines* (Sydney, 1975), 95–8. For a similar case, see G. Macdonald, 'Struggle for Recognition', *AAS* 1 (2002), 87–90.

5. It is symptomatic that all but one of the illustrations in Hawke's autobiography (London, 1994) are of the man himself, in varied company; the exception is a picture of his mother.

6. 'Advance Australia Fair' was written by Peter McCormick in 1878; the first verse gives a taste of its quality: 'Australia's sons let us rejoice/For we are young and free./We've golden soil and wealth for toil/Our home is girt by sea.' The choice was 'largely spurious' according to T. B. Millar (*Australia in Peace and War* (Botany, 1991), 331). Another gesture was made by removing the 'E II' from postboxes.

7. For David Bruce, see P. M. Roberts (ed.), *Window on the Forbidden City* (Hong Kong, 2001), 337. Australia's ambassador at Beijing was Stephen Fitzgerald, well regarded by Bruce.

8. For the Hanoi bombing, see D. Goldsworthy *et al.*, 'Reorientation', in D. Goldsworthy (ed.) *Facing North* (Melbourne, 2001).

9. For Whitlam in East Timor, see R. Tiffen, *Diplomatic Deceits* (Sydney, 2001), *passim*; M. B. Salla, 'East Timor', in D. Lee and C. Waters (eds.), *Evatt to Evans* (St Lucia, 1997); C. Brown (ed.), *Indonesia* (St Leonards, 1996).

10. On oil, see particularly R. J. King, 'Timor Gap', *JRAHS* 88/1 (2002). For Furlonger and Tjan, see Goldsworthy *et al.*, in Goldsworthy, *Facing North*, 361.

11. For Willesee brief and Whitlam–Suharto meeting, see ibid., pp. 361 ff. The records have been published in W. Way (ed.), *Australia and the Indonesian Incorporation of East Timor* (Carlton, 2000), which quotes a despatch from Ambassador Woolcott to Secretary Renouf that 'We are dealing with a settled Indonesian policy to incorporate Timor' and that 'our policy should be based as far as possible on disengaging ourselves as far as possible from East Timor'. See also J. R. Walsh and G. J. Munster (eds.), *Documents on Australian Defence and Foreign Policy* (Hong Kong, 1980), 197–200.

12. For Willesee, see King, 'Timor Gap', 93; newspaper reports, ibid., p. 94; Woolcott, ibid., p. 96. See also Walsh and Munster, *Documents*. Recent negotiations have been more productive.

13. Goldsworthy *et al.*, in Goldsworthy, *Facing North*, 368. See J. Birmingham, 'Appeasing Jakarta', *Quarterly Essay*, 2 (2001) and correspondence 3 (2001). Salla, 'East Timor', in Lee and Waters (eds.), *Evatt to Evans*, reveals that Whitlam

smugly believed that he knew better than the East Timorese themselves, for whom 'four hundred years of Portuguese domination may have obscured for them their ethnic kinship with west Timor' (p. 226) and who refused to listen to representations that the Timorese themselves wanted independence (p. 229).

14. Labor won 49.3 per cent of the vote, almost the same as in 1972 (49.6), but Democratic Labor votes slid to the Liberals.

15. For Khemlani, see Knightley, *Australia*, 269–71; McMullin, *Light on the Hill* (Oxford, 1991), 356–62; for the Morosi scandal, see ibid., pp. 357–61. For the *Melbourne Herald* exposure, see Page, *Murdoch Archipelago*, 178–81.

16. For a discussion of the Governor General's role, see L. F. Crisp, *Parliamentary Government of the Commonwealth of Australia* (London, 1961), chap. 8.

17. Many books and articles, often partisan, have been written on this subject, among them P. Kelly, *November 1975* (St Leonards, 1995). For a balanced view see H. V. Emy and O. E. Hughes, *Australian Politics* (Melbourne, 1991), 366–72. For Fraser in the next room see G. Henderson, *Menzies' Child: The Liberal Party of Australia* (Sydney, 1998), 236 ff. Whitlam's own account, in *The Truth of the Matter* (London, 1979), is a bitingly brilliant apologia. An opposite view is expressed by Garfield Barwick, then Chief Justice, in *Sir John Did his Duty* (Wahroonga, 1983).

18. Knightley, *Australia*, 274.

19. Ibid., p. 279. See also J. Pilger, *A Secret Country* (London, 1989), chap. 5.

20. For what follows, see the authoritative S. Ward, *Australia and the British Embrace* (Melbourne, 2001).

21. Ibid., pp. 152, 167.

22. Ibid., pp. 208 ff.

23. Henderson, *Menzies' Child*, 255; Fraser to Thatcher, quoted P. Ayres, *Malcolm Fraser* (Richmond, 1987), 306 ff.

24. Chipp, quoted ibid., pp. 259 ff. For the Democrats, see J. Warhurst (ed.), *Keeping the Bastards Honest* (St Leonards, 1997).

25. For Whitlam's apologia, see Tiffen, *Diplomatic Deceits*, 35.

26. See A. Benvenuti, 'Australian's Battle', *AJPH* 45/2 (1999).

27. J. L. Butts, in W. R. Louis (ed.), *National Security and International Trusteeship in the Pacific* (Annapolis, Md., 1972), chap. IV, and D. G. Wilson, ibid., p. 32.

28. R. West, quoting Dr L. O. Mair, in his *River of Tears* (London, 1972), 110. For Papua New Guinea, see J. Griffin, *PNG-Australia Relationship* (Canberra, 1990); J. Griffin, H. Nelson and S. Firth, *Papua New Guinea: A Political History* (Richmond, 1976); S. Dorney, *Papua New Guinea* (Sydney, 2000). P. Hasluck has left his own account, *A Time for Building* (Melbourne, 1976); see also H. Wright, 'Economic or Political Development', *AJPH* 48/2 (2002) and 'Political Chronicle', *AJPH* 35/2 (1989).

29. For Papua New Guinea Independence, see D. Denoon and P. Mein-Smith, *History of Australia, New Zealand and the Pacific* (Oxford, 2000), 400; Dorney, *Papua New Guinea*, chap. 2.

30. West, *River of Tears*, 124, 13.

31. Denoon and Mein-Smith, *History of Australia*, 454–7; M. L. O'Callaghan, *Enemies Within* (Sydney, 1999); S. Dorney, *Sandline Affair* (Sydney, 1998).

32. See A. Patience, *The Bjelke-Petersen Premiership* (Melbourne, 1985).

33. See Henderson, *Menzies' Child*, 262 ff.

34. For the Accords, see P. Kelly, *The End of Certainty* (St Leonards, 1992), chap. 3. In addition to Hawke's autobiography, see the (uncritical) B. d'Alpuget (Melbourne, 1982), who later married Hawke. For Keating, see his own accounts and J. Edwards, *Keating: The Inside Story* (Ringwood, 1996). For the 'arsonist' comment, see Kelly, p. 64. For the stick to beat the opposition, see Hawke, *Hawke Memoirs*, 148.

35. Quoted in Kelly, *End of Certainty*, 186–7.

36. See Henderson, *Menzies' Child*, 151; and see A. Leigh, 'Trade Liberalisation and the A.L.P.', *AJPH* 48/4 (2002).

37. Kelly, *End of Certainty*, 171.

38. Ibid., p. 212. For Labor's reforms, see A. Leigh, 'Trade Liberalisation and the Australian Labor Party', *AJPH* 48/4 (2002).

39. Kelly, *End of Certainty*, 216.

40. David Russell, quoted ibid., p. 295. For the Peacock–Kennet conversation see the *Melbourne Sun*, 23 March 1987, quoted ibid., p. 319. One of the more surprising aspects of the affair was the support given by the influential Ian McLachlan, later Minister for Health and Defence Minister in the Howard Liberal government; see Henderson, *Menzies' Child*, 288.

41. Richard Carlton, of ABC, quoted Kelly, *End of Certainty*, 302. Bjelke-Petersen's career was terminally wounded by the results of the Fitzgerald inquiry, which in 1988–90 exposed the essential shabbiness of Queensland's political life and which led to the chief constable being given fourteen years for corruption. See P. Reynolds, '1989 Queensland Election', *AJPH* 36/1 (1990).

42. Kelly, *End of Certainty*, 444.

43. For the relations between Abeles, Murdoch and the Hawke government, see Page, *Murdoch Archipelago*, 408–11.

44. For Walsh's resignation, see ibid., pp. 494 ff., and his autobiography, *Confessions of a Failed Finance Minister* (Milsons Point, 1995). Burke was involved in WA Inc., an dubious attempt to gather funds for the Labor Party.

45. Shack on health is quoted in Kelly, *End of Certainty*, 555.

46. B. Bryson, *Down Under* (London, 2001), 41 ff. For the Murray River see M. Sexton, *Silent Flood: Australia's Salinity Crisis* (Sydney, 2003).

47. F. Merlan, *Caging the Rainbow* (Honolulu, 1998), 196 ff.

48. R. Hughes, *Culture of Complaint* (New York, 1997), 88. B. Attwood and A. Markus, *The Struggle for Aboriginal Rights* (St Leonards, 1999), part 4. For non-Aboriginal Aborigines see J. Docker and G. Fischer (eds.), *Race, Colour and Identity* (Sydney, 2000).

49. Henry Reynolds has not only chronicled, but done much to bring about

progress in establishing Aboriginal rights to land. See particularly *The Law of the Land* (Ringwood, 1992), esp. p. 189.

50. Ibid., p. 211.

51. Edwards, *Keating*, 519. For an analysis of the Mabo case, see H. Patapan, *Judging Democracy* (Cambridge, 2000), 114 ff. and R. Broome, *Aboriginal Australians: Black Response to White Domination* (Crows Nest, 2002), 235–240. M. Goot and T. Rowse (eds.), *Make a Better Offer: The Politics of Mabo* (Leich- hardt, 1994), is a useful overview with many documents.

52. See S. W. Hook and J. Spanier, *American Foreign Policy since World War II* (Washington, DC, 2000), p. 86.

53. For Beazley and Schultz, see American Foreign Policy Documents 1988, no. 306, pp. 518 ff.

54. For the phrase 'waspish and venomous', see Edwards, *Keating*, 504.

55. For APEC, see T. B. Millar (ed.), *Australia in Peace and War* (Botany, 1991), 367 ff. and A. Gyngell and M. Wesley, *Making Australian Foreign Policy* (Cambridge, 2003) pp. 116–19.

56. G. St. J. Barclay, 'Problems in Australian Foreign Policy', *AJPH* 41/2 (1995), 177. For contemporary issues I have relied considerably on the *AJPH*.

57. G. Evans and B. Grant, *Australia's Foreign Relations* (Melbourne, 1992), 187.

58. Ibid., p. 176; see also P. Dibb (ed.), *Australia's External Relations in the 1980s* (Canberra, 1983).

59. Barclay, 'Australian Foreign Policy', *AJPH* 42/1 (1996), 351. (*AJPH* dropped the 'Problems' in 1995.)

60. Edwards, *Keating*, 533.

61. C. Brown, 'Australian Foreign Policy', *AJPH* 42/1 (1996), 159.

62. Ibid., pp. 147–9.

63. P. Kennelly, *Hummer*, 3/6.

64. Barclay, 'Problems in Australian Foreign Policy', *AJPH* 41/5 (1995).

65. Edwards, *Keating*. G. Bolton, 'Beating up Keating', in D. Grant and G. Seal (eds.), *Australia in the World* (Perth, 1994), speculates that if the Afro-Asian part of the British Empire was lost by the British landlady it may be that the last remnant of the British Commonwealth will be lost by the British sub-editor.

66. G. Maddox, *Australian Democracy in Theory and Practice* (Melbourne, 1996), 516 ff. Keating's 'somewhat crude, absolute nationalism' is discussed by J. Curra, 'Thin Dividing Line', *AJPH* 48/4 (2002).

67. R. Tickner, *Taking a Stand* (Sydney, 2001), 111, 147. The initial government reaction to the Mabo judgment, made in June 1993, was a White Paper proposing a complex method of identifying 'native right' which 'appeared to set the stage for prolonged disagreement between Commonwealth and state governments, Aborigines and mining and other economic interests': C.L., 'Political Chronicle', *AJPH* 39/2 (1993), 387 ff.

68. Henderson, *Menzies' Child*, 5.

CHAPTER 15

1. US Library of Congress, Administration of William J. Clinton, 20–21 November 1996. Howard has an unconvincing biography, D. Barnett, *John Howard, Prime Minister* (Ringwood, 1997).

2. B. Catley, 'Rise and Fall of Pauline Hanson's One Nation', *AS* 15/1 (2000); S. Jackman, 'Pauline Hanson', *AJPS* 33/2 (1998). For a considered analysis of Mrs Hanson's views, see S. Jackman, 'Pauline Hanson, the Mainstream, and Political Elites', *AJPS* 33/2 (1998).

3. For Lebanese criminals see T. Priest, 'The Rise of Middle Eastern Crime in Australia', *Quadrant*, 403, 2004.

4. For the Aboriginal Population, see *Year Book Australia* (2001), 76 ff. On the Wik ruling, see H. Patapan, *Judging Democracy* (Cambridge, 2000), 126; R. Broome, *Aboriginal Australians: Black Response to White Domination* (Crows Nest, 2002), chap. 13.

5. R. Brunton, 'Justice O'Loughlin and *Bringing them Home*', *Quadrant*, December 2000, for the qualifications.

6. For Dodson, see *Sydney Morning Herald*, 3 April 2000. Both Sir Ronald and Mr Dodson might well have been included in a British-style Royal Commission, but some care would have been taken to select other members known to have different views, and others uncommitted. See also P. Read, 'Historians and the Stolen Generations', *AHS* 118/54, and P. Grimshaw, 'Federation as a Turning Point', ibid., for the 'great silence' during the Federation centenary celebrations, in which 'the picture of the peaceful birth of the Australian nation blatantly ignores the past tragic aggression against Aborigines, the murders, starvation and forced dislocation that shaped their lives'.

7. It is Johannes Rau.

8. Until June 2001 when Archbishop Peter Hollingworth was appointed, followed in August 2003 by General Sir Michael Jeffery, M.C., C.V.O.

9. The nations are England, Scotland, Canada, Australia and New Zealand; the territories include the Channel Islands and the British, Australian and New Zealand Antarctic Territories.

10. *AJPH* 46/4 (2000).

11. M. Kirby, 'The Australian Referendum on a Republic', *AJPH* 46/4 (2000). See also A. J. Ward, 'Trapped in a Constitution', *AJPS* 35/1 (2000), H. Irving, 'The Republic Referendum', ibid., and I. McAllister, 'Elections without Cues', *AJPS* 36/2 (2001).

12. Professor Wiltshire's proposals are advanced in his *Tenterfield Revisited* (St Lucia, 1991).

13. Dennis Shanahan, *Weekend Australian*, 4–5 March 2000.

14. C. Mason, 'Issues in Australian Foreign Policy', *AJPH* 48/4 (2002). See also M. MacCallum, *Girt by the Sea* (Melbourne, 2002), 49–60, P. Mores, *Borderline*

(Sydney, 2001) and G. Rundle, *The Opportunist: John Howard and the Triumph of Reaction* (Melbourne, 2001).

15. For the statistics, see *Year Book Australia* (2002); for the camps, see P. D. Williams, 'Political Chronicle', *AJPH* 48/4 (2002), and A. Bashford and C. Strange, 'Asylum Seekers', *AJPH* 48/4 (2002). Former Governor General Sir Zelman Cowen wrote of a new 'Colour Bar' in *AHS* 32/116.

16. See J. Warhurst, 'Australian Federal Election 2001', *AJPS* 37/1 (2002).

17. See P. D. Williams, 'Political Chronicles', *AJPH* 49/2 (2002).

18. M. Gurry, 'Issues in Australian Foreign Policy', *AJPH* 49/4 (2003).

Bibliography

ARCHIVES AND DOCUMENTS

The principal Australian printed sources are the Historical Records of Australia, the Historical Records of New South Wales and of Victoria, and the Historical Manuscripts of Tasmania. The State Libraries at Brisbane (Oxley Library), Hobart, Melbourne (La Trobe Library), Adelaide (Mortlock Library), Perth (Battye Library) all hold extensive collections and publish the relevant State Archives. These are supplemented by the collections of documents made by C. M. H. Clark and by F. K. Crowley, together with P. O. Farrell's Catholic History collection and W. R. Johnston on Queensland. Sydney's Mitchell Library and the National Library in Canberra are the great repositories of private papers. A. G. L. Shaw's *Convicts and the Colonies*, the classic book on the subject, has an excellent analysis of published documents, which includes the relevant British Parliamentary Papers. American printed sources include the Foreign Relations of the United States (FRUS), the State Department Bulletin and the various Presidential Papers, including those of Lyndon Johnson and Bill Clinton.

BOOKS

Abbott, T., *How to Win the Constitutional War* (Adelaide, 1997).

Akenson, D. H., *Small Difference* (Montreal, 1991).

Aldrich, R., *French Presence in the South Pacific* (London, 1990).

—— *France and the South Pacific Since 1940* (London, 1993).

—— *Hidden Hand* (Woodstock, NY, 2002).

Alexander, A., *Obliged to Submit: Wives and Mistresses of Colonial Governors* (Hobart, 1999).

Alexander, F., *Australia Since Federation* (Sydney, 1967).

Ambrose, S. E., *Eisenhowever, the President* (London, 1984).

Amos, K., *New Guard Movement* (Melbourne, 1976).

—— *Fenians in Australia* (Kensington, NSW, 1988).

Anderson, E. M., *History of Australian Foreign Policy* (Melbourne, 1988).

Anderson, W., *The Cultivation of Whiteness* (Carlton South, 2002).

Andrews, E. M., *Anzac Illusion* (Cambridge, 1994).

Anon. (A Bushman), *A Voice from the Far Interior of Australia* (London, 1847).

Arnold, J., *et al.* (eds.), *Out of Empire* (Port Melbourne, 1993).

—— *et al.* (eds.), *Australia: A Reader's Guide* (Port Melbourne, 1996).

Atkinson, A., *Camden* (Melbourne, 1988).

—— *Europeans in Australia* (Melbourne, 1997).

Attwood, B., *Making of the Aborigines* (Sydney, 1989).

—— and Markus, A., *The 1967 Referendum* (Canberra, 1997).

—— *The Struggle for Aboriginal Rights* (St Leonards, 1999).

—— *Rights for Aborigines* (Crows Nest, 2003)

Auchmuty, J. J., *Voyage of Governor Phillip to Botany Bay* (Sydney, 1969).

Auckland, Lord (Wm. Eden), *Discourse on Banishment* (London, 1771).

Austin, A. G. (ed.), *The Webbs' Australian Diary* (Carlton, 1965).

Ayres, P., *Malcolm Fraser* (Richmond, 1987).

—— *Mawson* (Melbourne, 1999).

Bach, J., *Australia Station* (Kensington, 1986).

Backhouse, J., *Narrative of a Visit to the Australian Colonies* (London, 1843).

Baker, D. W., *A Civilised Surveyor: Thomas Mitchell* (Melbourne, 1997).

—— *John Piper* (Aboriginal History, Canberra, 1993).

Baker, J. R., *Race* (Oxford, 1974).

Bambrick, S. (ed.), *Cambridge Encyclopedia of Australia* (Cambridge, 1994).

Banks, Joseph, *The Endeavour Journal*, ed. J. C. Beaglehole, 2 vols. (Sydney, 1962).

Barclay, G. St. J., *Friends in High Places* (Melbourne, 1985).

Barnard, A., *Visions and Profits: Studies in the Business Career of Thomas Mort* (Melbourne, 1961).

Barnett, C., *Engage the Enemy More Closely* (London, 2001).

Barnett, D., *John Howard, Prime Minister* (Ringwood, 1997)

Barry, J. V., *Life and Death of John Price* (Melbourne, 1964).

Barwick, G., *Sir John Did his Duty* (Wahroonga, 1983).

Basedow, H., *The Australian Aboriginal* (Adelaide, 1925)

Bastock, J., *Australia's Ships of War* (Sydney, 1975).

Bate, W., *Lucky City* (Carlton, 1978).

Bateman, S., and Sherwood, D. (eds.), *Australia's Maritime Bridge into Asia* (St Leonards, 1995).

Beaglehole, J. C. (ed.), *Journals of Captain Cook*, 3 vols. (Cambridge, 1955–74).

—— *The Life of Captain James Cook* (London, 1974).

—— *Exploration of the Pacific* (Stanford, Calif., 1981).

Bean, C. E. W., *The AIF in France*, 4 vols. (Sydney, 1929, 1933, 1937, 1942).

—— *The Story of Anzac* (Sydney, 1934)

Beasley, W. G., *The Rise of Japan* (London, 1995).

Beckett, J., *Torres Strait Islanders* (Canberra, 1987).

Bell, K. N., and Morrell, W. P., *Select Documents on British Colonial Policy, 1830–1860* (London, 1928).

Bell, P., and Bell, R. J., *Implicated: The United States in Australia* (Oxford, 1993).

Bell, R. J., *Unequal Allies* (Melbourne, 1977).

Bell, S., *Ungoverning the Economy* (Melbourne, 1997).

Bennett, M. M., *Australian Aboriginal* (London, 1930).

Bennett, S., *Affairs of State* (North Sydney, 1992).

Bennett, T., *et al.* (eds.), *Celebrating a Nation* (St Leonards, 1992).

Bevan, I. (ed.), *Sunburnt Country* (London, 1953).

Bird, I. L., *Australia Felix* (London, 1877).

Birman, W., *Gregory of Rainworth* (Nedlands, 1979).

Birmingham, J., *Appeasing Jakarta* (Sydney, 2001).

Black, D., *Women Parliamentarians in Australia 1921–1996* (Perth, 1996)

Blaikie, G., *Remember Smith's Weekly* (Adelaide, 1975).

Blainey, G., *Tyranny of Distance* (Melbourne, 1966).

—— *Land Half-Won* (South Melbourne, 1980).

—— *Triumph of the Nomads* (Sydney, 1983).

—— *Our Side of the Country* (Sydney, 1984).

—— (ed.), *J. A. Froude 'Oceana'* (North Ryde, 1985).

—— *A Short History of Australia* (Melbourne, 1994).

Blake, B. J., *Australian Aboriginal Languages* (St Lucia, 1991).

Blake, L. J. (ed.), *Letters of C. J. La Trobe* (Melbourne, 1975).

Blankfield A., and Corfield, R. S., *Never Forget Australia: Australia and Villers Bretonneux 1918–1993* (Melbourne, 1994).

Blewett, N. A., *Cabinet Diary* (Kent Town, 1999).

Blomfield, G., *Baal Belbora* (Armidale, 1992).

Bohemia, J., and McGregor, B., *Nyibayarri* (Canberra, 1995).

Bolton, G. C., *Alexander Forrest* (Melbourne, 1958).

—— *Richard Daintree* (Brisbane, 1965).

—— *Oxford History of Australia: Volume 5 1942–1995: The Middle Way* (Melbourne, 1996)

—— *Edmund Barton* (St Leonards, 2000).

Bongiorno, F., *The People's Party* (Melbourne, 1996).

Bonyhady, T., *Burke and Wills* (Balmain, 1991)

—— *Colonial Earth* (Melbourne, 2000).

—— and Griffiths, T., *Words for Country* (St Lucia, 2002).

Booth, J., and Borrow, K. T., *B. T. Finnis* (Adelaide, 2001).

Border, R., *Church and State in Australia* (London, 1962).

Borrie, W. D., *European Peopling of Australia* (Canberra, 1994).

Bosworth, R., and Ugolino, R., *War, Internment and Mass Migration* (Rome, 1992).

Bowden, K. M., *George Bass* (Melbourne, 1952).

Boxer, C. R., *The Dutch Seaborne Empire* (London, 1965).

—— *The Church Militant and Iberian Expansion* (Baltimore, 1978).

—— *Dutch Merchants and Mariners in Asia* (London, 1988).

—— *The Portuguese Seaborne Empire* (London, 1991).

Bradley, W. *Voyage to New South Wales* (Sydney, 1969).

Brand, I., *Penal Peninsula* (Launceston, 1989).

Brawley, S., *The White Peril* (Sydney, 1995).

Brett, J., *Robert Menzies' Forgotten People* (Sydney, 1992).

Bride, T. F. (ed.), *Letters from Victorian Pioneers* (Melbourne, 1969).

Bridge, C. (ed.), *Munich to Vietnam* (Carlton, 1991).

—— and Attard B., (eds.), *Between Empire and Nation: Australia's External Relations from Federation to the Second World War* (Melbourne, 2000)

Bridges, P., *Foundations of Identity* (Sydney, 1995).

Brisbane, T., *Reminiscences* (Edinburgh, 1860).

Brock, P., *Outback Ghettos* (Cambridge, 1993).

Broeze, F., *Mr Brookes and the Australian Trade* (Carlton, 1993).

—— *Island Nation* (St Leonards, 1997).

Brookes, J. E., *International Rivalry in the Pacific Islands* (Berkeley, 1941).

Broome, R., *Aboriginal Australians: Black Response to White Dominance* (Crows Nest, 2002).

Brown, A. J., *Ill-Starred Captains: Flinders and Baudin* (London, 2001).

Brown C. (ed.), *Indonesia* (St Leonards, 1996).

Brown, P., *Clyde Company Papers* (Oxford, 1941–68).

Browning, H. O., *1975 Crisis* (Sydney, 1985).

Brunton, P. (ed.), *Matthew Flinders* (Sydney, 2002).

Bryson, B., *Down Under* (London, 2001).

Buckley, K., *et al.*, *Doc Evatt* (Melbourne, 1994).

Buckner, P. A., *Transition to Responsible Government* (Westport, Conn., 1985).

Bunbury, B., *Unfinished Business* (Sydney, 1998) (sound recording).

—— *It's Not the Money It's the Land* (Fremantle, 2001).

Burchardt, D. H., *Australian Bibliography* (Sydney, 1963).

Burger, A., *Neville Bonner* (Melbourne, 1979)

Burgmann, V., *Power and Protest* (St Leonards, 1993).

Burnett, A., *Australia and the European Communities* (Canberra, 1983).

Burns, P., *The Brisbane Line Controversy: Political Opportunism v National Security* (St Leonards, 1998)

Butler, A. G., *The Digger* (Sydney, 1945).

Butler, L. J., *Britain and Empire* (New York, 2002).

Butlin, N. G., *Our Original Aggression* (Sydney, 1983).

—— *Economics and the Dreamtime* (Cambridge, 1993).

—— *Forming a Colonial Economy* (Cambridge, 1994).

Butlin, S. J., *Foundations of the Australian Monetary System* (Melbourne, 1953).

—— *Australia and New Zealand Bank* (London, 1961).

Cairns, A., *Dangers and Duties of the Young Men of Victoria* (Melbourne, 1856).

Calvert, A. F., *Western Australia and its Goldfields* (London, 1893).

Calwell, A., *Be Just and Fear Not* (Hawthorn, 1972)

Camilleri, J. A., *Australian–American Relations* (South Melbourne, 1980).

——*The Australia, New Zealand and US Alliance* (Boulder, Colo., 1987).

Campbell, J., *Invisible Invaders* (Melbourne, 2002)

Campion, E., *Australian Catholics* (Ringwood, 1987)

Cannon, M., *That Damned Democrat* (Melbourne, 1981).

—— *Who Killed the Koories?* (Port Melbourne, 1990).

Capell, A., *Linguistic Survey of Australia* (Canberra, 1963).

Capper, H., *The Australian Colonies: Where They Are and How to Get to Them* (London, 1852).

Carew, E., *Keating* (Sydney, 1988).

Carlyon, I., *Gallipoli* (Sydney, 2001).

Carrington, Lord, *Reflect on Things Past* (London, 1989).

Carroll-Burke, P., *Colonial Discipline: The Making of the Irish Convict System* (Dublin, 2000).

Carroll, J. (ed.), *Intruders in the Bush* (Melbourne, 1992).

Carter, H. B., *Sir Joseph Banks* (London, 1998).

—— (ed.), *Sheep and Wool Correspondence of Sir Joseph Banks* (London, 1979).

Carter, P., *The Road to Botany Bay* (London, 1987).

—— and Hunt, S., *Terre Napoleon* (Sydney, 1999).

Casey, R. G., *My Dear Prime Minister*, ed. W. J. Hudson and J. North (Canberra, 1980).

Cashman, R., *Paradise of Sport* (Oxford, 1995).

—— *et al.* (eds.), *The Oxford Companion to Australian Cricket* (Melbourne, 1986).

Castles, F. G. (ed.), *Australia Compared* (Sydney, 1991).

Castles, S. *et al.*, *Mistaken Identity* (Leichhardt, 1990).

Cecil, G., *Life of Robert, Marquess of Salisbury*, 4 vols. (London, 1921, 1931, 1932).

Cell, J. W., *British Colonial Administration in the Mid Nineteenth Century* (New Haven, 1970).

Chambers, J. H., *Australia – A Traveller's History* (Moreton-in-Marsh, 1999).

Chandler, J., *Forty Years in the Wilderness* (Hartwell, 1893).

Chapman, P. (ed.), *Historical Records of Australia* (Canberra, 1996).

Charlton, M., and Moncrieff, A., *Many Reasons Why* (London, 1978).

Charlton, P., *Pozières* (London, 1982).

Chaturvedi, S., *Dawning of Antarctica* (New Delhi, 1990).

Chesterman, J., and Galligan, B., *Citizens Without Rights* (Cambridge, 1997).

Childs, D., *Britain Since 1945* (London, 1979).

Churchill, R. S., *Winston S. Churchill*, vol. ii: *The Young Statesman* (New York, 1966).

Cilento, R. (ed.), *Triumph in the Tropics* (Brisbane, 1959).

Clark, C. M. H., *Select Documents in Australian History*, 2 vols. (Sydney, 1955).

—— *Sources of Australian History* (London, 1957).

——*A History of Australia*, 6 vols. (Melbourne, 1962–88).

Clark, D. (ed.), *New Holland Journal of Baron Ch. v. Hugel* (Melbourne, 1994).

Clark, I. D., *Scars in the Landscape* (Canberra, 1995).

—— (ed.), *Journals of G. A. Robinson*, 4 vols. (Melbourne, 1998).

Clarke, C. (ed.), *Australian Foreign Policy* (Melbourne, 1973).

Clarke, F. G., *Australia: A Concise History* (Melbourne, 1992).

Clarke, P., and Spender, D. (eds.), *Lifelines* (North Sydney, 1996).

Clay, J., *Maconochie's Experiment* (London, 2001).

Clendinnen, I., *Dancing with Strangers* (Melbourne, 2003)

Clune, F., *Search for the Golden Fleece* (Sydney, 1965).

—— *Captain Bully Hayes* (Carlisle, 1997).

Cochrane, P., *Simpson and the Donkey* (Melbourne, 1992).

Cohen, K., and Wiltshire, K., *People, Places and Policies* (St Lucia, 1995).

Cohen, L., *Elizabeth Macquarie* (Sydney, 1979).

Coleman, P., *Obscenity, Blasphemy, Sedition* (Sydney, 1974).

Colley, L., *Captives: Britain, Empire & the World 1600–1850* (London, 2002).

Collins, D., *An Account of the English Colony in New South Wales*, 2 vols. (London, 1798, 1802).

Connah, G., *Archaeology of Australia's History* (Cambridge, 1994).

Connell, R. W., and Irving, T. H., *Class Structure in Australian History* (Melbourne, 1980).

Connor, J., *Australian Frontier Wars 1788–1838* (Sydney, 2001).

Connor, X. et al., *Santamaria: The Politics of Fear* (Richmond, 2000).

Constantine, S., *Dominions Diary* (Halifax, 1992).

Coombs, H. C., *Trial Balance* (London, 1981).

—— *Aboriginal Autonomy* (Cambridge, 1994).

—— *From Curtin to Keating* (Darwin, 1994).

—— et al. (eds.), *Land of Promises* (Canberra, 1989).

Cornell, C., *Voyage of Discovery* (Adelaide, 2003).

Costar, B., and Economou, N., *The Kennett Revolution* (Sydney, 1999).

Cowen, Z., *Isaac Isaacs* (Melbourne, 1967).

Craven, I. (ed.), *Australian Popular Culture* (Cambridge, 1994).

Crisp, L. F., *Ben Chifley* (London, 1960).

—— *Parliamentary Government of the Commonwealth of Australia* (London, 1961).

—— *Australian National Government* (Melbourne, 1983).

Critchett, J., *A Distant Field of Murder* (Melbourne, 1990).

Crockett, P., *Evatt: A Life* (Melbourne, 1993).

Crowley, F. K. (ed.), *New History of Australia* (Melbourne, 1974).

—— *A Documentary History of Australia*, 5 vols. (Melbourne, 1973–1980).

Cumpston, I. M., *History of Australian Foreign Policy* (Canberra, 1995).

Currey, J., *David Collins* (Melbourne, 2000).

Curthoys, A., and Markus, A. (eds.), *Who are Our Enemies?* (Sydney, 1979).

—— and Merritt, J., *Australia's First Cold War*, 2 vols. (Sydney, 1984, 1986).

—— *Freedom Ride* (Crows Nest, 2002)

Dale, R. W., *Impressions of Australia* (London, 1889).

D'Alpuget, B., *Robert J. Hawke* (Melbourne, 1982).

Dalrymple, A., *Account of the Discoveries Made in the South Pacifick Ocean* (Potts Point, 1996).

Dampier, W., *A New Voyage Round the World* (London, 1927 [1697]).

Daniels, K., *Convict Women* (St Leonards, 1998).

Davey, A. M., *Breaker Morant* (Cape Town, 1987).

Davidson, A., *Invisible State* (Cambridge, 1991).

Davis, G., *A Government of Routines* (South Melbourne, 1995).

Davison, G., *Marvellous Melbourne* (Melbourne, 1978).

Davitt, M., *Life and Progress in Australia* (London, 1898).

Dawson, J., *Australian Aborigines* (Canberra 1981 [1881])

Day, A., *Historical Dictionary of the Discovery and Exploration of Australia* (Oxford, 2003)

Day, D., *Great Betrayal* (Melbourne, 1988).

—— *Reluctant Nation: Australia and the Allied Defeat of Japan 1942–45* (Oxford, 1992).

—— *Claiming a Continent* (Sydney, 1997).

—— *John Curtin – a Life* (Sydney, 1999).

—— *Chifley* (n.p. [Australia], 2001).

Deakin, A., *The Federal Story* (Melbourne, 1944).

Dening, G., *Mr Bligh's Bad Language* (Melbourne, 1993).

Denison, W., *Varieties of Vice-Regal Life*, 2 vols. (London, 1870).

—— and Grey, Earl, *Appeal against the Continuance of Transportation* (London, 1851).

Dennis, P., and Grey, J., *Emergency and Confrontation* (St Leonards, 1996).

Denoon, D., *Settler Capitalism* (Oxford, 1983).

—— *Getting under the Skin* (Melbourne, 2000).

—— and Mein-Smith, P., *A History of Australia, New Zealand and the Pacific* (Oxford, 2000).

Denton, K., *The Breaker* (North Ryde, 1973).

de Serville, P., *Port Phillip Gentlemen* (Melbourne, 1980).

—— *The Australian Club* (Melbourne, 1998).

Desmond, A., *Huxley: Devil's Disciple* (London, 1994).

Detmold, M. J., *Australian Commonwealth* (North Ryde, 1985).

Diamond, J., *Guns, Germs and Steel* (London, 1997).

Dibb, P. (ed.), *Australia's External Relations in the 1980s* (Canberra, 1983).

Dickey, B. and Howell, P., *South Australia's Foundation: Select Documents* (Netley, 1986)

Dickie, P., *The Road to Fitzgerald and Beyond* (St Lucia, 1988).

Dilke, C., *Greater Britain*, 2 vols. (London, 1869).

Dixon, R., *Course of Empire* (Melbourne, 1986).

Dixson, M., *Real Matilda* (Melbourne, 1976).

—— *The Imaginary Australian: Anglo-Celts & Identity* (Sydney, 1999).

Dobrez, L. (ed.), *Identifying Australia* (Canberra, 1994).

Docker, E. W., *Blackbirders* (Sydney, 1970).

Docker, J., and Fischer, G. (eds.), *Race, Colour and Identity* (Sydney, 2000).

Dodson, J., *Naïve Lands* (Melbourne, 1992).

Donovan, P. F., *At the Other End of Australia* (St Lucia, 1994).

Dorney, S., *Sandline Affair* (Sydney, 1998).

—— *Papua New Guinea* (Sydney, 2000).

Doughty, A. G. (ed.), *Elgin–Grey Papers 1846–1852* (Ottawa, 1937).

Dow, G. M., *Samuel Terry* (Sydney, 1974).

Downer, A., *Six Prime Ministers* (Melbourne, 1982).

Drew, P., *The Masterpiece* (n.p., Victoria, 2001).

Duffy, M., *Man of Honour* (Sydney, 2003)

Duncan, B., *Crusade or Conspiracy?* (Sydney, 2001).

Dutton, D., *One of Us?* (Sydney, 2002).

Dutton, G., and Harris, M., *Australia's Censorship Crisis* (Melbourne, 1970).

Duyker, E., *Discovery of Tasmania* (Hobart, 1992).

—— (ed.), *Voyage to Australia* (Melbourne, 2001).

Dyster, B., and Meredith, D., *Australia in the International Economy in the Twentieth Century* (Cambridge, 1990).

Ebury, S., *Weary: Life of Sir Edward Dunlop* (Melbourne, 1991).

Eccleston, G. C., *Major Mitchell's 1836 Australia Felix Expedition* (Melbourne, 1992).

Eddy, J. J., *Britain and the Australian Colonies 1818–1831* (Oxford, 1969).

Edelstein, M., *Overseas Investment in the Age of High Imperialism* (London, 1982).

Eden, W. (Lord Auckland), *Discourse on Punishment* (n.p., n.d.).

—— *Principles of Penal Law* (London, 1771).

Edmond, R., *Representing the South Pacific* (Canberra, 1997).

Edwards, J., *Keating: The Inside Story* (Ringwood, 1996).

Edwards, P. G., *Prime Ministers* (Melbourne, 1983).

—— (ed.), *Australia through American Eyes 1935–45* (Melbourne, 1994).

—— *A Nation at War* (St Leonards, 1997).

—— and Pemberton, G., *Crises and Commitments* (Sydney, 1992).

Edwards, W. H. (ed.), *Traditional Aboriginal Society* (South Yarra, 1987/1998).

Egerton, H. E. (ed.), *Sir William Molesworth's Speeches* (London, 1903).

Eggleston, E., *Fear, Favour or Affection* (Canberra, 1974).

Elder, B., *Blood on the Wattle* (Sydney, 2000).

Ellis, J. A., *Australia's Aboriginal Heritage* (North Blackburn, 1994).

Ellis, M. H., *John Macarthur* (Sydney, 1955).

Ellis, U., *History of the Australian Country Party* (Parkville, 1963).

Ellis, P. B., and Mac A'Ghobhainn, S., *The Scottish Insurrection of 1820* (London, 1970).

Emy, H. V., and Hughes, O. E., *Australian Politics* (Melbourne, 1991).

Encel, S., *Equality and Authority* (London, 1970).

Evans, G., and Grant, B., *Australia's Foreign Relations* (Melbourne, 1992).

Evatt, H. V., *Rum Rebellion* (London, 1939).

Ewers, J. K., '*Western Gateway*' (Fremantle, 1971).

Eyre, E. J., *Autobiographical Narrative 1832–9*, ed. J. Waterhouse (London, 1984).

Fairfax, J., *Colonies of Australia* (London, 1852).

Farrell, F., *Themes in Australian History* (Kensington, 1990).

Faulkner, J., and Macintyre, S., *True Believers* (Sydney, 2001).

Fels, M. H., *Good Men & True* (Carlton, 1988).

Fidlon, P. G., and Ryan, R. J. (eds.), *The Journal of Philip Gidley King* (Sydney, 1980).

—— —— (eds.), *The Journals and Letters of Lt. Ralph Clark* (Sydney, 1981).

Fifer, D. E., *W. C. Wentworth*, 2 vols. (n.p. [Australia], 1983, 1991).

Finnane, M., *Police and Government* (Melbourne, 1994).

—— *Punishment in Australian Society* (Melbourne, 1997).

Fitzgerald, B., *Australian People* (Melbourne, 1946).

Fitzgerald, J. D., *Rise of the New South Wales Labor Party* (Sydney, 1925).

Fitzgerald, R. *History of Queensland: From the Dreaming to 1915* (St Lucia, 1982).

—— *History of Queensland: From 1915 to the Early 1980s* (St Lucia, 1984).

—— and Hearn, M., *Bligh, Macarthur and the Rum Rebellion* (Kenthurst, 1988).

—— *The Pope's Battalions* (St Lucia, 2003)

Fitzgerald, S., *Sydney* (Sydney, 1992).

Fitzhardinge, L. F., *William Morris Hughes*, vol. ii: *The Little Digger 1914–1952* (Melbourne, 1973).

—— *Old Canberra and the Search for a Capital* (Canberra, 1975).

Fitzmaurice, E., *The Life of Granville George Leveson Gower, Second Earl Granville K.G. 1815–1891*, 2 vols. (London, 1905).

Fitzpatrick, D., *Oceans of Consolation* (Cork, 1994).

Fitzpatrick, K., *Sir John Franklin* (Melbourne, 1949).

—— *Australian Explorers: A Selection From Their Writings* (London, 1958).

Flanagan, R., *History of New South Wales* (London, 1862).

Flannery, T., *The Future Eaters* (Sydney, 1984).

—— *1788* (Melbourne, 1996).

—— *The Explorers* (Melbourne, 1998).

—— (ed.), *The Birth of Sydney* (Melbourne, 1999).

—— *Beautiful Lies* (Melbourne, 2003).

Fletcher, B. H., *Ralph Darling: A Governor Maligned* (Melbourne, 1984)

Flinders, M., *Voyage to Terra Australis*, 2 vols. (Adelaide, 1966 [1814]).

—— *Biographical Tribute to the Memory of Trim* (Sydney, 1997).

Flood, J., *Archaeology of the Dream Time* (Sydney, 1983).

Flynn, M., *The Second Fleet* (Sydney, 2001).

Foott, B., *Dismissal of a Premier* (Sydney, 1968).

Forrest, K., *The Challenge and the Chance: The Colonisation of North West Australia* (Victoria Park, 1996)

Forster, C., *France and Botany Bay* (Melbourne, 1996).

Forster, W. C., *Sir T. L. Mitchell* (Sydney, 1985).

Foucault, M., *Discipline and Punishment*, trans A. Sheridan (London, 1977).

Frame, T. R., *Pacific Partners* (Sydney, 1992).

Francis, M., *Governors and Settlers* (Basingstoke, 1992).

Frei, H. P., *Japan's Southward Advance to Australia* (Carlton, 1991)

French, M., *A Pastoral Romance* (Toowoomba, 1990).

—— *Pubs Ploughs and Peculiar People* (Toowoomba, 1992).

Freudenberg, G., *A Certain Grandeur* (Ringwood, 1987).

Fromonot, F., *Jørn Utzon* (Corte Madera, CA, 1998).

Frost, A., *Convicts and Empire: A Naval Question* (Melbourne, 1980)

—— *Arthur Phillip: His Voyaging* (Melbourne, 1987).

—— *Botany Bay Mirages* (Carlton, 1994).

—— and Samson, J. (eds.), *Pacific Empires* (Vancouver, 1999).

Gale, G. F., and Brookman, A., *Race Relations in Australia and the Aborigines* (Sydney, 1975).

Gallaway, J., *Odd Couple* (St Lucia, 2000).

Gascoigne, J., *Science in the Service of Empire* (London, 1998).

Gerritsen, R., *And Their Ghosts May be Heard* (Fremantle, 1994)

Gervas, F., *Pipe Dream to Pipeline* (Marylands, 2001).

Gibbs, R. M., *History of South Australia* (Mitcham, 1999).

Gilbert, M., *Winston Churchill*, vol. iv: *1917–1921* (London, 1975).

—— *Road to Victory* (London, 1986).

—— *Finest Hour* (London, 1988).

—— *Never Despair* (London, 1988).

Gilchrist, A. (ed.), *John Dunmore Lang*, 2 vols. (Melbourne, 1951).

Gilchrist, M., *Daniel Mannix: Priest and Patriot* (Melbourne, 1982).

Gill, G. H., *Australia in the War of 1939–1945*, 2 vols. (Canberra, 1957, 1968).

Gill, J. C. H., *Missing Coast* (South Brisbane, 1988).

Gillen, M., *Founders of Australia: A Biographical Dictionary of the First Fleet* (Sydney, 1989).

Gilmour, D., *Curzon* (London, 1994).

Gipps, J., *Every Inch a Governor* (Port Melbourne, 1996).

Gistitin, C., *Quite a Colony* (Brisbane, 1995).

Godley, J. R., *Letters from Early New Zealand* (Christchurch, 1951).

Goldsworthy, D. (ed.), *Facing North* (Melbourne, 2001).

—— *Losing the Blanket: Australia and the End of Britain's Empire* (Carlton, 2002)

Goot, M., and Rowse, T. (eds.), *Make a Better Offer: The Politics of Mabo* (Leichhardt, 1994).

Gordon, M., *A True Believer* (St Lucia, 1996).

Gore, J. (ed.), *The Creevey Papers* (London, 1963).

Govor, E., *Australia in the Russian Mirror* (Carlton, 1997).

Graetz, B., and McAllister, I., *Dimensions of Australian Society* (South Melbourne, 1984).

Graham, B. D., *Formation of the Australian Country Parties* (Canberra, 1966).

Grant, B., *Gods and Politicians* (London, 1982).

—— *The Australian Dilemma* (Rushcutters Bay, 1993).

Grant, D., and Seal, G. (eds.), *Australia in the World* (Perth, 1994).

Grassby, A. J., and Hill, M., *Six Australian Battlefields* (North Ryde, 1988).

—— and Ordoñez, S., *John Watson* (Melbourne, 2001).

Grattan, M. (ed.), *Australian Prime Ministers* (London, 2000).

Graves, A., *Cane and Labour* (Edinburgh, 1993).

Greenhill, B. (ed.), *Opening of the Pacific: Image and Reality* (London, 1970).

Greenway, J., *Bibliography of the Australian Aborigines* (Sydney, 1963).

Greenwood, G. (ed.), *Australia* (Sydney, 1974).

Gregory, A. C., and Gregory, F. T., *Journals of Australian Explorations* (Brisbane, 1884).

Greville, C. C. F., *Memoirs*, 3 vols. (London, 1875).

Grey, Earl, *Colonial Policy of Lord John Russell's Administration* (London, 1853).

Grey, G., *Journals of Two Expeditions of Discovery in North-West and Western Australia &c.*, 2 vols. (London, 1841).

Grey, J., *Military History of Australia* (Cambridge, 1999).

—— and Doyle, J. (eds.), *Vietnam: War, Myth and Memory* (St Leonards, 1992).

Griffin, J., *PNG–Australia Relationship* (Canberra, 1990).

—— Nelson, H., and Firth, S., *Papua New Guinea: A Political History* (Richmond, 1976).

Griffin-Foley, B., *House of Packer* (St Leonards, 2000).

Griffiths, T., *Hunters and Collectors* (Cambridge, 1996).

Grimes, S., and G. O. Tuathaigh (eds.), *The Irish–Australian Connection* (Galway, 1988).

Grimshaw, P., *et al.* (eds.), *Creating a Nation* (Ringwood, 1994).

Grocott, A. M., *Convicts, Clergymen and Churches* (Sydney, 1980).

Grose, K., 'Educational Experiment of the 1820s', Ph.D. thesis (Sydney, 1974).

Gross, A., *Charles Joseph La Trobe* (Melbourne, 1980).

Gullett, H. S., *The AIF in Sinai and Palestine 1914–1918* (Sydney, 1923).

Gunson, N., *Australian Reminiscences and Papers of L. E. Threlkeld* (Canberra, 1974).

Gunter, J., *Inside Australia* (London, 1972).

Gyngell, A. and Wesley, M., *Making Australian Foreign Policy* (Cambridge, 2003)
Haebich, A., *For Their Own Good* (Nedlands, 1988).
—— *Broken Circles* (Fremantle, 2000).
Hahn, H., *Tsuni-//Goam: The Superior Being of the Khoi-Khoi* (London, 1881).
Haines, R. F., *Emigration and the Labouring Poor* (London, 1997).
Hains, B., *The Ice and the Inland* (Sydney, 2002).
Hall, H. L. *Colonial Office: A History* (London, 1937).
Hall, R., *Empires of the Monsoon* (London, 1996).
Hall, W. H., *Practical Experience at the Diggings* (London, 1852).
Hancock, I., *National and Permanent? The Federal Organisation of the Liberal Party* (Melbourne, 2000).
—— *John Gorton: He did it His Way* (Sydney, 2002).
Hancock, W. K., *Discovering Monaro* (Cambridge, 1972).
Harding, R. W., *Police Killings in Australia* (Harmondsworth, 1970).
Hardy, J., and Frost, A., *European Voyaging Towards Australia* (Canberra, 1990).
Hardy, T. K., *Pictorial Atlas of Australian Wines* (Melbourne, 1986).
Harper, N., *A Great and Powerful Friend* (St Lucia, 1987).
Harris, B., *The Proud Champion: Australia's Aboriginal Sporting Heroes* (Crows Nest, 1989).
Harris, J., *One Blood* (Sutherland, 1990).
Harrison, P., *Walter Burley Griffin, Landscape Architect* (Canberra, 1995).
Hartley, J., and McKee, A., *Indigenous Public Sphere* (Oxford, 2000).
Hartwell, R. M., *The Economic Development of Van Diemen's Land 1820–1850* (Melbourne, 1954).
Hasluck, P., *The Government and the People, 1939–41* (Canberra, 1965).
—— *A Time for Building* (Melbourne, 1976).
—— *Shades of Darkness* (Melbourne, 1988).
Hawke, B., *The Hawke Memoirs* (London, 1994).
Haynes, R. D., *Seeking the Centre* (Cambridge, 1998).
Head, B. W., and Patience, A., *From Fraser to Hawke* (Melbourne, 1989).
Head, L., *Second Nature: The History and Implications of Australia as Aboriginal Landscape* (New York, 2000).
Headon, D., *et al.* (eds.), *The Abundant Culture* (St Lucia, 1995).
—— and Perkins, E., *Our First Republicans* (n.p. [Australia], 1998).
Healy, C., *From the Ruins of Colonisation* (Cambridge, 1997).
Heard, D. (ed.), *Journals of Chas O'Hara Booth* (Tasmania, 1981).
Heeres, J. E., *Tasman: Journal and Documents* (Amsterdam, 1898).
Henderson, G., *Mr Santamaria and the Bishops* (Sydney, 1982).
—— *Menzies' Child: The Liberal Party of Australia* (Sydney, 1998).
Henningham, J., *Institutions in Australian Society* (Melbourne, 1993).
Herman, A., *How the Scots Invented the Modern World* (New York, 2001).
Herring, G. C., *America's Longest War* (New York, 1996).
Heydon, P., *Quiet Decision (G. F. Pearce)* (Melbourne, 1965).

Hickey, W., *Memoirs*, 3 vols. (3rd edn., London, 1919).

Hickie, D., *The Prince and the Premier* (London, 1985).

Hindmarsh, F. S., *From Powder Monkey to Governor* (Northbridge, WA, 1995).

Hirst, J. B., *Convict Society and its Enemies* (Sydney, 1983).

—— *Strange Birth of Colonial Democracy* (Sydney, 1989).

—— *Sentimental Nation* (Melbourne, 2000).

Hitchens, C., *Trial of Henry Kissinger* (Melbourne, 2001).

Hogan, J. F., *The Gladstone Colony* (London, 1898).

Holthouse, H., *River of Gold* (Sydney, 1967).

Hook, S. W., and Spanier, J., *American Foreign Policy since World War II* (Washington, DC, 2000).

Hooton, J. (ed.), *Australian Lives* (Melbourne, 1998).

Horne D., *The Lucky Country* (Sydney, 1968).

—— *Time of Hope* (Sydney, 1980).

Houston, T., *Five Pound Look* (London, 1956).

Howard, D., *English Activities on the North Coast of Australia* (London, 1924).

Howitt, A. W., *Native Tribes of Southeast Australia* (Canberra, 1996 [1904]).

Howitt, W., *Land, Labour and Gold* (London, 1855).

—— *Two Years in Victoria* (London, 1856).

Hudson, W. and Carter, D., *Republicanism Debate* (Kensington, 1993).

—— and Bolton, G. (eds.), *Creating Australia* (St Leonards, 1997).

Hudson W. J., *Billy Hughes in Paris* (Melbourne, 1978).

—— and Sharp, M. P., *Australian Independence* (Melbourne, 1988).

—— *Blind Loyalty: Australia and the Suez Crisis* (Carlton, 1989)

—— *Australia and the New World Order* (Canberra, 1993).

—— and Way, W., (eds.), *Australia and the Post War World: Documents 1947* (Canberra, 1995)

Hughes, C. A., *Handbook of Australian Government and Politics 1965–1974* (Canberra, 1977).

—— and Graham, B. D., *Handbook of Australian Government and Politics 1890–1964* (Canberra, 1965).

Hughes, O. E., *Australian Politics* (South Yarra, 1998).

Hughes, R., *The Fatal Shore* (London, 1996).

—— *Culture of Complaint* (New York, 1997).

Hughes, W. H., *Price of Peace* (Sydney, 1934).

Hungerford, T. A. G., *Australian Signpost* (Melbourne, 1956).

Hunter, E., *Aboriginal Health and History* (Cambridge, 1993).

Hurst, J., *Hawke PM* (Sydney, 1983).

Hutton, H., *Flotsam and Jetsam* (Launceston, 1909).

Hyam, R., *Empire and Sexuality* (Manchester, 1990).

Inglis, R., *The Rehearsal* (Adelaide, 1985)

Ingram, E., *British Empire as a World Power* (London, 2001).

Irvine, N. (ed.), *Dear Cousin: The Reibey Letters* (Sydney, 1995).

—— *Mary Reibey: Molly Incognita* (Sydney, 2001).

Irving, H. (ed.), *The Centenary Companion to Australian Federation* (Cambridge, 1999).

—— (ed.), *To Constitute a Nation* (Cambridge, 1999).

—— and Macintyre, S. (eds.), *No Ordinary Act* (Melbourne, 2001).

Irwin, G., *Prehistoric Exploration and Colonisation of the Pacific* (Cambridge, 1994).

Jacka, F., and Jacka, E., (eds.), *Mawson's Antartic Diaries* (Sydney, 1998)

Jackson, R., *The Malayan Emergency* (London, 1991).

Jacobs, P., and Landau, S., *To Serve the Devil*, vol. ii: *Colonials and Sojourners* (New York, 1971).

Jaensch, D., *Power Politics* (St Leonards, 1991).

Jennett, C., and Stewart, R. G., *Hawke and Australian Public Policy* (Melbourne, 1990).

Johns, G., *Waking up to Dreamtime* (Singapore, 2000).

Johnson, F., *R.A.A.F. over Europe* (London, 1946).

Johnson, L. W., *Colonial Sunset: Australia & Papua New Guinea 1970–4* (St Lucia, 1987).

Johnson, R., *Search for the Inland Sea* (Melbourne, 2001).

Johnston, M., *Fighting the Enemy* (Cambridge, 2000).

Johnston, W. R., *Documentary History of Queensland* (St Lucia, 1988).

Jordens, A. M., *Redefining Australians* (Sydney, 1995).

—— *Alien to Citizen: Settling Migrants* (St Leonards, 1997).

Joy, W., *Liberators* (Sydney, 1963).

Jupp, J., *Immigration* (Oxford, 1991).

—— *The Australian People: An Encyclopaedia* (Cambridge, 2001).

Jurgensen, M. and Cookhill, A. (eds.), *German Presence in Queensland* (St Lucia, 1988).

Karskens, G., *The Rocks* (Melbourne, 1997).

Keating, P., *Engagement: Australia Faces the Asia-Pacific* (Sydney, 2000).

Kercher, B., *Debt, Seduction and Other Disasters* (Sydney, 1996).

Kelly, M., *Nineteenth Century Sydney* (Sydney, 1978).

Kelly, P., *Hawke Ascendancy* (Sydney, 1984).

—— *The End of Certainty* (St Leonards, 1992).

—— *The Unmaking of Gough* (St Leonards, 1994).

—— *November 1975* (St Leonards, 1995).

Kendle, J. E., *Colonial and Imperial Conferences 1887–1911* (London, 1967).

Kennedy, P., *The Rise and Fall of British Naval Mastery* (London, 1991).

Kerr, M. G., *The Surveyors* (London, 1972).

Kiddle, M., *Caroline Chisholm* (Carlton, 1996)

Kiernan, C. (ed.), *Australia and Ireland* (Dublin, 1986).

Kiernan, T. J., *Transportation from Ireland to Sydney 1791–1816* (Canberra, 1954).

King, J., *Ten Decades* (London, 1895).

King, J., and King, J., *Philip Gidley King* (North Ryde, 1981).

King, P. (ed.), *Australia's Vietnam* (Sydney, 1983).

King, R. J., *Secret History of the Convict Colony* (Sydney, 1990).

Kirk, R. L., and Thorne, A. G., *Origin of the Australians* (Canberra, 1976).

Knaplund, P., *James Stephen and the Colonial Office* (Madison, 1953).

Knight, R., *Illiberal Liberal* (Carlton, 1966).

Knightley, P., *Australia: Biography of a Nation* (London, 2001).

Kolko, G., *Vietnam* (London, 1986).

Kubicek, R. V., *Administration of Imperialism* (Durham, NC, 1969).

Kuna, F. (ed.), *Studying Australian Culture* (Hamburg, 1994).

Kynaston, D., *Golden Years* (London, 1996).

Lack, J., and Templeton J., *Bold Experiment: A Documentary History of Australian Immigration since 1945* (Melbourne, 1995).

Lahn, J., *Finders Keepers, Losers Weepers* (Brisbane, 1996).

Lake, M., *Getting Equal: The History of Australian Feminism* (St Leonards, 1999)

La Nauze, J. A., *Hopetoun Blunder* (Melbourne, 1957).

—— *Making of the Australian Constitution* (Melbourne, 1972).

Lane, J., *Fairbridge Kid* (Fremantle, 1980).

Lang, J. D., *Repeal or Revolution* (London, 1845).

—— *Cooksland in the North East Australia* (London, 1847).

—— *Phillipsland* (London, 1847).

—— *The Coming Event* (Sydney, 1850).

Langford, P., *A Polite and Commercial People* (Oxford, 1989).

Langley, G., *Decade of Dissent* (North Sydney, 1992).

Larkins, J., *Dictionary of Australian History* (Sydney, 1980).

Latukefu, S. (ed.), *Papua New Guinea: A Century of Colonial Impact* (Port Moresby, 1989).

Lawson, S., *Archibald Paradox* (Kingswood, 1987).

Leaver R., and Cox, D., *Middling, Meddling, Muddling* (St Lucia, 1997).

Lee, D. and Waters, C. (eds.) *Evatt to Evans* (St Lucia, 1997).

Legg, J. D., *Australian Colonial Policy* (Sydney, 1956).

Lemcke, G., *Reluctant Rebel* (Sydney, 1998).

Lett, L., *Sir Herbert Murray* (Sydney, 1949).

Levy, M. C. I., *Governor George Arthur* (Melbourne, 1953).

Lewsen, P. (ed.), *Selections from the Correspondence of J. X. Merriman* (Cape Town, 1963).

Lincoln, M., *Science and Exploration in the Pacific* (Woodbridge, 1998).

Lines, W. J., *An All-Consuming Passion* (St Leonards, 1994).

Little, G., *Strong Leadership* (Oxford, 1988).

Lloyd, E., *Visit to the Antipodes* (London, 1846).

Lloyd George, D., *The Truth about the Peace Treaties*, 2 vols. (London, 1938).

Logevall, F., *Choosing War* (Berkeley, 2001).

Loos, N., *Invasion and Resistance* (Canberra, 1982).

Louis, W. R. (ed.), *National Security and International Trusteeship in the Pacific* (Annapolis, Md., 1972).

Lourandos, H., *Continent of Hunter Gatherers* (Cambridge, 1997).

Lovell, D. W., et al., *The Australian Political System* (Melbourne, 1995).

Lowe, D. (ed.), *Australia and the End of Empires* (Geelong, 1996).

—— *Menzies and the 'Great World Struggle'* (Sydney, 1999).

Lucas, C. P. (ed.), *Lord Durham's Report*, 3 vols. (Oxford, 1912).

Lunn, H., *Johannes Bjelke-Petersen* (St Lucia, 1984).

McBryde, I., *Aboriginal Prehistory in New England* (Sydney, 1974).

—— *Records of Times Past* (Canberra, 1978).

MacCallum, M., *Girt by the Sea* (Melbourne, 2002).

McCarthy, D., *South West Pacific Area* (Canberra, 1959).

McCaughey, D., Perkins, N., and Trumble, A., *Victoria's Colonial Governors* (Melbourne, 1993).

McConvell, P., and Evans, N. (eds.), *Archaeology and Linguistics* (Oxford, 1997).

McConville, C., *Croppies, Celts and Catholics: The Irish in Australia* (London, 1987).

McCormack, G., *Cold War/Hot War* (Sydney, 1983).

MacCrae, H., *Georgiana's Journal* (Sydney, 1966).

MacDonagh, O., et al. *Nationalism and Irish Culture* (London, 1983).

—— and Mandel, W. F. (eds.), *Irish Australian Studies* (Canberra, 1989).

McFarlane, B., et al. (eds.), *Oxford Companion to Australian Film* (South Melbourne, 1999).

MacGregor, C., *Class in Australia* (Ringwood, Victoria, 2002).

McGregor, R., *Imagined Destinies: Australia and the Doomed Race Theory 1880–1939* (Carlton, 1997)

Macgregor, W., 'British New Guinea', *Proceedings of Royal Colonial Institute*, 26 (1894–5), 293–325.

McIntyre, K. G., *Secret Discovery of Australia* (London, 1977).

Macintyre, S., *Oxford History of Australia*, vol. 4: 1901–42 (Melbourne, 1986).

—— *Colonial Liberalism* (Melbourne, 1991).

—— *A Concise History of Australia* (Cambridge, 1999).

—— and Thomas, J. (eds.), *Discovery of Australian History* (Carlton, 1995).

Mack, J. D., *W. C. Wentworth* (Brisbane, 1934).

—— *Matthew Flinders* (Melbourne, 1966).

Mackaness, G., *Correspondence of Sir John and Lady Franklin*, 2 vols. (Hobart, 1947).

MacKay, D., *Place of Exile* (Melbourne, 1985).

McKenna, M., *Reluctant Republic: A History of Republicanism in Australia* (Cambridge, 1997).

Mackenzie, S. S., *The Australians at Rabaul* (Sydney, 1927).

McLachlan, N., *Waiting for the Revolution* (Ringwood, 1989).

Macleod, C., *Patrol in the Dream Time* (Sydney, 1987).

McLeod, D. W., *How the West was Lost* (Port Hedland, 1985)

McLeod, F., *Gallipoli Campaign: Select Bibliography* (Canberra, 1990).

Macmillan, M., *Sir Henry Barkly* (Cape Town, 1970).

McMinn, W. G., *George Reid* (Carlton, 1899).

McMullin, R., *Light on the Hill* (Oxford, 1991).

McNaught, K., *Penguin History of Canada* (London, 1988).

McQueen, H., *Tom Roberts* (Sydney, 1966).

Madden, F., and Fieldhouse, D., *Settler Self-Government* (Westport, Conn., 1990).

Maddock, K., *The Australian Aborigines: A Portrait of their Society* (Ringwood, 1982).

Maddox, G., *Australian Democracy in Theory and Practice* (Melbourne, 1996).

Mair, L. D., *Australia in New Guinea* (London, 1948).

Major, R. H. (ed.), *Early Voyages to Terra Australis* (London, 1859).

Malaspina, A., *The Secret History of the Convict Colony*, ed. R. J. King (Sydney, 1990).

Manne, R., (ed.), *Whitewash* (Melbourne, 2003).

Mansergh, N. (ed.), *Documents and Speeches on British Commonwealth Affairs* (London, 1953).

Marchant, L. R., *An Island Unto Itself* (Carlisle, WA, 1988).

Margarey, S., *Passions of the First Wave Feminists* (Sydney, 2001).

Markus, A., *Fear and Hatred* (Sydney, 1979).

—— *Governing Savages* (Sydney, 1990).

Marsden, J. B. (ed.), *Memoirs of the Rev. Samuel Marsden* (London, 1858).

Marsland, L. W., *Charters Towers Gold Mines* (London, 1892).

Martin, A. W., *Henry Parkes* (Melbourne, 1980).

—— *Letters from Menie* (Melbourne, 1983).

—— *Robert Menzies*, 2 vols. (Melbourne, 1999).

Martin, E. A., *Life and Speeches of Daniel Henry Deniehy* (Melbourne, 1884).

Martin, G. (ed.), *Founding of Australia* (Sydney, 1978).

—— *Australia, New Zealand and Federation 1883–1901* (London, 2001)

Martin-Allanic, J.-E., *Bougainville* (Paris, 1964).

Massy, C., *Australian Merino* (Ringwood, 1990).

Mathews, R., *Australia's First Fabians* (Cambridge, 1994).

Matthews, B., *Federation* (Melbourne, 1999).

Matthews, R. L. (ed.), *Intergovernmental Relations in Australia* (Sydney, 1974).

May, D., *Aboriginal Labour and the Cattle Industry* (Cambridge, 1994).

Mayne, T., *Aborigines and the Issues* (Sydney, 1986).

Mayo, M. P., *Life and Letters of Col. Wm. Light* (Adelaide, 1937).

Meaney, N., *Search for Security in the Pacific 1901–14* (Sydney, 1976).

—— *Fears and Phobias: E. L. Piesse and the Problem of Japan* (Canberra, 1996).

—— *Towards a New Vision: Australia and Japan* (Sydney, 1999).

Melbourne, A. C. V., *William Charles Wentworth* (Brisbane, 1934).

—— *Early Constitutional Development in Australia* (St Lucia, 1963).

Menzies, R. G., *Afternoon Light* (London, 1967).

Merlan, F., *Caging the Rainbow* (Honolulu, 1998).

Merrett, D. T., *ANZ Bank* (Sydney, 1985).

Midgely, C. (ed.), *Gender and Imperialism* (Manchester, 1998).

Millar, A., *Trust the Women* (Canberra, 1994).

Millar, E. K., *Reminiscences of 47 Years Clerical Life* (Adelaide, 1985).

Millar, T. B. (ed.), *Australian Foreign Minister: Diaries of R. G. Casey* (London, 1972).

—— *Australia in Peace and War* (Botany, 1991).

Miller, D. P., and Reill, P. H. (eds.), *Visions of Empire* (Cambridge, 1996).

Miller, E. M., *Australia's First Two Novels* (Hobart, 1958).

Mitchell, T. L., *Three Expeditions into the Interior of Eastern Australia*, 2 vols. (London, 1839).

—— *Journal of an Expedition into the Interior of Tropical Australia* (London, 1848).

Mollison, B., and Everitt, C. (eds.), *Tasmanian Aborigines*, 3 vols. (n.p., Tasmania, 1978).

Molony, J. N., *An Architect of Freedom: John Hubert Plunkett in New South Wales, 1832–1869* (Canberra, 1973).

—— *Eureka* (Melbourne, 1984).

—— *Penguin History of Australia* (Ringwood, 1987).

—— *Native Born* (Melbourne, 2000).

Monypenny, W. F., and Buckle, G. F., *The Life of Benjamin Disraeli*, 6 vols. (London, 1910–14).

Moore, A., *Growing up with Barnados* (Sydney, 1990).

Moore R. J., *Making the New Commonwealth* (Oxford, 1987).

Moorehead, A., *Gallipoli* (Ware, 1997).

Moran, A., and O'Regan, T., *Australian Screen* (Ringwood, 1989).

Mordike, J., *Army for a Nation* (Sydney, 1992).

Mores, P., *Borderline* (Sydney, 2001).

Morgan, S., *Land Settlement in Early Tasmania* (Cambridge, 1992).

Morrell, W. P., *Colonial Policy of Peel and Russell* (Oxford, 1930).

—— *British Colonial Policy in the Mid-Victorian Age* (Oxford, 1969).

Morris, M., *Ecstasy and Economics* (Rose Bay, 1992).

Mulvaney, D. J., *Prehistory of Australia* (Melbourne, 1975).

—— *Encounters in Place* (St Lucia, 1989).

—— and White, J. P. (eds.), *Australians to 1788* (Melbourne, 1985).

Mundy, G. C., *Our Antipodes* (London, 1857).

Murdoch, J., *Expediency or Principle: Liberalism in Commonwealth Politics* (London, 1997).

—— *A Million to One Against* (London, 1998).

Murdoch, W., *Alfred Deakin* (Melbourne, 1999).

Murgatroyd, S., *Dig Tree* (London, 2002).

Murphy, B., *The Other Australia* (Cambridge, 1993).

Murphy, D. J., *et al* (eds.), *Labor in Power* (St Lucia, 1980).

Murray, H., *Papua of Today* (London, 1925).

Murray, R., *The Split* (Melbourne, 1970).

Murray, R. D., *A Summer at Port Phillip* (Edinburgh, 1843).

Murray, T., *Archaeology of Aboriginal Australia* (St Leonards, 1998).

Nadely, G., *Australia's Colonial Culture* (Melbourne, 1957).

Nagle, J. E., *Collins, the Courts and the Colony* (Sydney, 1996).

Nairn, B., *The Big Fella: Jack Lang and the Australian Labor Party, 1891–1949* (Melbourne, 1986).

—— *Civilising Capitalism* (Melbourne, 1989).

Napier, C. J., *Colonization: Particularly in South Australia* (London, 1835).

Neal, D., *The Rule of Law in a Penal Colony* (Cambridge, 1991).

Neale, R. G. (ed.), *Documents on Australian Foreign Policy* (Canberra, 1975–88).

Needham, A., *The Women of the 1790 'Neptune'* (Dural, 1992).

Needham, J., *Science & Civilisation in China*, 5 vols. (Cambridge, 1954–2000)

Neville, R., *Hippie, Hippie, Shake* (London, 1995).

Niall, B., *Georgiana* (Melbourne, 1994).

Nicholas, F. W., and Nicholas, J. M., *Charles Darwin in Australia* (Cambridge, 2002).

Norris, R., *Emergent Commonwealth* (Melbourne, 1975).

'Nugget', *Australia and her Treasures* (London, 1852).

O'Brian, P., *Joseph Banks*, (London, 1981).

O'Brien, E., *Foundation of Australia* (London, 1937).

O'Brien, P., *The People's Case* (Perth, 1995).

O'Callaghan, M.-L., *Enemies Within* (Sydney, 1999).

O'Donoghue, F., *Bishop of Botany Bay* (London, 1982).

O'Farrell, P. (ed.), *Documents in Australian Catholic History*, 2 vols. (London, 1969).

—— *The Irish in Australia* (Kensington, 1986).

—— *Letters from Irish Australia* (Sydney, 1987).

Oldfield, A., *Woman Suffrage in Australia: A Gift or a Struggle?* (Cambridge, 1992).

Ollivier, I. (ed.), *Journals of Mascarin and Marquis de Castries* (Wellington, 1985).

Ollivier, M. (ed.), *Colonial and Imperial Conferences 1887–1937* (Ottawa, 1954).

O'Neill, R., *Australia and the Korean War*, 2 vols. (Canberra 1981, 1985).

Onslow, S. M., *Early Records of the Macarthurs of Camden* (Adelaide 1914/17).

Osborne, G., and Mandle, W. F. (eds.), *New History: Studying Australia Today* (Sydney, 1982).

O'Sullivan, P. (ed.), *Religion and Identity* (London, 1996).

Overholt, W. H., and Kahn, H., *US and Pacific Asia in the 1970s* (Groton, 1974).

Oxley, D., *Convict Maids* (Cambridge, 1996).

Oxley, H. G., *Mateship in Local Organisation* (St Lucia, 1974).

Page, B., *Murdoch Archipelago* (London, 2003).

Palmer, A., *Colonial Genocide* (Adelaide, 2002).

Parkes, H., *Fifty Years in the Making of Australian History* (Hobart, 1892).

Parry, J. H., *The Spanish Seaborne Empire* (London, 1966).

Parsons, P. (ed.), *Companion to Australian Theatre* (Sydney, 1995).

Partington, G., *Australian Nation* (New Brunswick, NJ, 1997).

Patapan, H., *Judging Democracy* (Cambridge, 2000).

Patience, A., *The Bjelke-Petersen Premiership* (Melbourne, 1985).

Paull, R., *Retreat from Kokoda* (Melbourne, 1958).

Pemberton, G., *All the Way: Australia's Road to Vietnam* (Sydney, 1987).

Perry, T. M., and Prescott, D. F., *A Guide to Maps of Australia* (Canberra, 1990).

Petrow, S., *Sanatorium of the South?* (Hobart, 1996).

Philips, D., and Davies, S., *A Nation of Rogues?* (Melbourne, 1994).

Phillips, D. H., *Cold War Two and Australia* (North Sydney, 1983).

Pike, D., *Paradise of Dissent* (London, 1957).

Pike, G., *Golden Days* (Mareeba, 1981).

Pilger, J., *A Secret Country* (London, 1989).

Pink, K., *Through Hell's Gates* (n.p., Tasmania, 1984).

Plomley, N. J. B., *Friendly Mission* (Hobart, 1966).

—— *Baudin Expedition & the Tasmanian Aborigines* (Hobart, 1983).

—— *Weep in Silence* (Hobart, 1987).

Pollard, J., *Formative Years of Australian Cricket* (London, 1987).

Porter, A. (ed.), *The Nineteenth Century* (Oxford History of the British Empire, Oxford, 1999).

Porter, P. (ed.), *Oxford Book of Modern Australian Verse* (Melbourne, 1998).

Powell, A., *Far Country: A Short History of the Northern Territory* (Carlton, 2000).

Prentis, M. D., *Scots in Australia* (Sydney, 1983).

Protos, A. (ed.), *The Road to Botany Bay* (Randwick, 1988).

Pybus, C. J., *Community of Thieves* (Port Melbourne, 1991).

Rae-Ellis, V., *Black Robinson* (Carlton, 1988).

Reece, R. H. W., *Aborigines and Colonists* (Sydney, 1974).

Rees, S., *Floating Brothel* (Sydney, 2001).

Reid, G., *A Nest of Hornets* (Melbourne, 1982).

Reid, R., *Beaucoup Australians Ici* (Canberra, 1998).

'A Retired Officer', *Australia a Mistake* (London, 1855).

Reynolds, H., *Breaking of the Great Australian Silence* (London, 1984).

—— *Aboriginal Land Rights in Colonial Australia* (Canberra, 1988).

—— *With the White People* (Ringwood, 1990).

—— *The Law of the Land* (Ringwood, 1992).

—— *Fate of a Free People* (Ringwood, 1995).

—— *Aboriginal Sovereignty* (St Leonards, 1996).

—— *Frontier* (St Leonards, 1996).

—— *Why Weren't We Told?* (Ringwood, 1999).

—— *An Indelible Stain: The Question of Genocide in Australian History* (Ringwood, 2001).

Reynolds, J., *Edmund Barton* (Melbourne, 1999).

Reynolds, M., *HERstory: Australian Labor Women in Federal, State and Territory Parliaments* (Townsville, 1994)

—— *The Last Bastion* (Sydney, 1995).

Reynolds, W., *Australia's Bid for the Atomic Bomb* (Carlton, 2000).

Richardson, G., *Whatever it Takes* (Moorebank, NSW, 1994).

Richelson, J. T., and Ball, D., *Ties that Bind* (Sydney, 1990).

Rintoul, S., *The Wailing Port* (Melbourne, 1993).

Ritchie, J. H., *Punishment and Profit* (Melbourne, 1970).

—— *Evidence to the Bigge Reports*, 2 vols. (Melbourne, 1971).

—— *Lachlan Macquarie* (Melbourne, 1986).

—— *The Wentworths* (Melbourne, 1997).

Roberts, A., *Salisbury: Victorian Titan* (London, 2000).

Roberts, A. (ed.), *Writing Aboriginal History* (Canberra, 1991).

Roberts, P. M. (ed.), *Sino-American Relations Since 1900* (Hong Kong, 1991).

—— (ed.), *Window on the Forbidden City* (Hong Kong, 2001).

Roberts, S. H., *History of Australian Land Settlement* (Melbourne, 1968).

Robertson, J., *J. H. Scullin* (Perth, 1974).

—— *Anzac and Empire: The Tragedy and Glory of Gallipoli* (Melbourne, 1990).

Robinson, G., *Dark Side of Paradise* (Ithaca, NY, 1995).

Robinson, P., *Hatch and Brood of Time* (Melbourne, 1985).

Robson, L. L., *History of Tasmania* (Melbourne, 1983).

—— and Roe, M., *Short History of Tasmania* (Melbourne, 1997).

Roe, M., *Australia, Britain and Migration* (Cambridge, 1995).

Rolls, E., *They All Ran Wild* (Sydney, 1977).

—— *Sojourners* (St Lucia, 1992).

Rose, J., *Intellectual Life of the British Working Classes* (New Haven, 2001).

Rowley, C. D., *The Destruction of Aboriginal Society* (Canberra, 1970).

—— *Outcasts in White Australia* (Canberra, 1971).

Rowse, T., *After Mabo* (Carlton, 1993).

—— *White Flour, White Power* (Cambridge, 1998).

—— *Obliged to Submit* (Cambridge, 2000).

—— *Nugget Coombs* (Canberra, 2002).

Royal Australian Mint, *Making Money* (Musgrave, 2002).

Rudgley, R., *Lost Civilisations of the Stone Age* (London, 1998).

Rundle, G., *The Opportunist: John Howard and the Triumph of Reaction* (Melbourne, 2001).

Russell, P. (ed.), *This Errant Lady: Jane Franklin's Overland Journey to Port Phillip and Sydney* (Canberra, 2002).

Rutherford, J., *Sir George Grey* (London, 1961).

Ryan, L., *Aboriginal Tasmanians* (Crows Nest, 1996).

Sackville-O'Donnell, J., *The First Fagin: The True Story of Ikey Solomon* (Melbourne, 2001)

Samson, J., *Imperial Benevolence* (Honolulu, 1998).

Sawer, M. and Simms, M., *A Woman's Place: Women and Politics in Australia* (St Leonards, 1993)

Scates, B., *A New Australia* (Canberra, 1997).

Schilder, A., *Australia Unveiled* (Amsterdam, 1976).

Schlesinger, A. M. (ed.), *Dynamics of World Power*, 5 vols. (New York, 1973).

Schneider, R., *War without Blood* (London, 1980).

Schwarz, B. (ed.), *Expansion of England* (London, 1996).

Scott, E., *Life of Capt. Matthew Flinders* (Sydney, 1914).

—— (ed.), *Australia* (Cambridge History of the British Empire, Cambridge, 1988 [1933]).

Searle, G. S., *Mount and Morris Exonerated* (Melbourne, 1875).

Serle, G., *The Golden Age* (Melbourne, 1963).

—— *From Deserts the Prophets Come* (Melbourne, 1973).

—— *Rush to be Rich* (Melbourne, 1974).

—— *John Monash* (Melbourne, 1980).

Sexton, M., *Illusions of Power: Fate of a Reform Government* (Sydney, 1979).

—— *War for the Asking: How Australia Invited Itself to Vietnam* (French's Forest, 2002)

—— *Silent Flood: Australia's Salinity Crisis* (Sydney, 2003).

Sharman, C. (ed.), *Parties and Federation in Australia and Canada* (Canberra, 1994).

Sharp, A., *Discovery of Australia* (Oxford, 1963).

—— *Voyages of A. J. Tasman* (Oxford, 1968).

Sharp, N., *Stars of Tagai* (Canberra, 1993).

Shaw, A. G. L., *Economic Development of Australia* (London, 1960).

—— *Convicts and the Colonies* (London, 1966).

—— *Sir George Arthur* (Melbourne, 1980).

—— *Heroes and Villains in History* (Sydney, 1983).

Shawcross, W., *Murdoch* (London, 1992).

Shineberg D., *The People Trade* (Honolulu, 1999).

Shirely, G., and Adams, B., *Australian Cinema* (n.p. [Australia], 1989).

Silver, L. R., *Battle of Vinegar Hill* (Sydney, 2002).

Simms, M. (ed.), *The Forgotten Election* (St Lucia, 2001).

Simson, C., *National Security Directives of the Reagan and Bush Administrations* (Oxford, 1995).

Singleton, G. (ed.), *Second Keating Government* (Canberra, 1997).

—— *et al.*, *Australian Political Institutions* (South Melbourne, 1996).

Smith, A., *Something to Declare* (London, 1980).

Smith, M. A., Spriggs, M., and Fankhauser, B., *Sahul in Review: Pleistocene Archaeology in Australia, New Guinea and Island Melanesia* (Canberra, 1993).

Smythe, Mrs James, *The Booanndik Tribe of South Australian Aborigines* (Adelaide, 1880).

Souter, G., *Lion and Kangaroo* (Sydney, 1976).

—— *Acts of Parliament: A Narrative History of the Senate and the House of Representatives* (Carlton, 1988)

Spartalis, P., *Diplomatic Battles of Billy Hughes* (Sydney, 1983).

Spender, P., *Exercises in Diplomacy* (Sydney, 1969).

Stanley, P., *Remote Garrison: The British Army in Australia* (Kenthurst, 1986).

Stannage, C. T., *et al.* (eds.), *Paul Hasluck in Australian History* (St Lucia, 1998).

—— *et al.* (eds.), *New History of Western Australia* (Nedlands, 1981).

Steele, J. G., *Explorers of the Moreton Bay District 1770–1830* (St Lucia, 1972).

Stephen, C. E., *Sir James Stephen* (London, 1906).

Stephens, A., *Going Solo* (Canberra, 1995).

Stephenson, M. A., and Turner, C., *Australian Republic or Monarchy* (St Lucia, 1994).

Stevens, C., *White Man's Dreaming* (Melbourne, 1994).

Stevens, H. N., and Barwick, G. F., *New Light on the Discovery of Australia* (London, 1930).

Stokes, G. (ed.), *Politics of Identity in Australia* (Canberra, 1977).

Stormon, E. J. (ed.), *The Salvado Memoirs* (Perth, 1977).

Strachan, H., *The First World War* (Oxford, 2001).

Sturma, M., *Vice in a Vicious Society* (St Lucia, 1983).

Sturman, A., and Tapper, N. J., *Weather and Climate of Australia and New Zealand* (Melbourne, 1996).

Summers, A., *Damned Whores and God's Police* (Ringwood, 1975).

Suttor, T. L., *Hierarchy and Democracy in Australia 1788–1870* (Melbourne, 1965).

Sykes, T., *Two Centuries of Panic* (Sydney, 1988).

Syme, J., *Nine Years in Van Diemen's Land* (Dundee, 1848).

Tardif, P., *Notorious Strumpets and Dangerous Girls* (London, 1998).

Taylor, A. J. P., *English History 1914–1945* (Oxford, 1965).

—— *Lloyd George* (London, 1971).

Taylor, L., *Seeing the Inside: Bark Painting in Arnhem Land* (Oxford, 1990).

Taylor, P., *Australia: The First Twelve Years* (Sydney, 1982).

Tench, W., *1788: Narrative of the Expedition to Botany Bay*, ed. T. Flannery (Melbourne, 1996).

Terry, S., *History of S.Terry of Botany Bay* (London, 1838).

Theophanous, A. C., *Australian Democracy in Crisis* (Melbourne, 1980).

Thompson, N., *Earl Bathurst* (London, 1999).

Thompson, R. C., *Australian Imperialism in the Pacific: The Expansionist Era 1820–1920* (Melbourne, 1980).

—— *Australia and the Pacific Islands in the Twentieth Century* (Melbourne, 1998).

—— *Religion in Australia* (Melbourne, 2002).

Thomson, A., *Anzac Memories* (Melbourne, 1994).

—— *The Singing Line* (London, 1999).

Thomson, R., *Australian Nationalism* (Sydney, 1888).

Thorpe, A., *A History of the British Labour Party* (Basingstoke, 1997).

Tickner, R., *Taking a Stand* (Sydney, 2001).

Tiffen, R., *Diplomatic Deceits* (Sydney, 2001).

Tindall, N. B., *Aboriginal Tribes of Australia* (Canberra, 1974).

Tingle, I., *Chasing the Future* (Port Melbourne, 1994).

Tooley, R. V., *Mapping of Australia and Antarctica* (London, 1985).

Torrence, R., and Clarke, A., *The Archaeology of Difference* (London, 2000).

Tow, W. T. (ed.), *Australian–American Relations* (New York, 1998).

Townsley, W. A., *Struggle for Self-Government in Tasmania* (Hobart, 1977).

—— *Tasmania: From Colony to Statehood* (Hobart, 1991).

Trainor, L., *British Imperialism and Australian Nationalism* (Cambridge, 1994).

Travers, R., *Grand Old Man* (Kenthurst, 1992).

Trigger, D. S., *Whitefella Comin'* (Cambridge, 1992).

Trollope, A., *Australia and New Zealand* (London, 1872).

Truman, T., *Catholic Actions and Politics* (London, 1960).

Turnbull, C., *Black War* (Melbourne, 1974).

Turnbull, J., and Navaretti, P. Y. (eds.), *Griffin in Australia and India* (Melbourne, 1998).

Turnbull, M., *Fighting for the Republic* (South Yarra, 1999).

Turner, G., *Making it National* (St Leonards, 1994).

Vamplew, W., *et al.* (eds.), *Oxford Companion to Australian Sport* (Melbourne, 1993).

Van Veldhuisen, R., and McIlvena, B., *Pipe Dreams* (Horsham, Victoria, 2001).

Van Zanden, H., *1606: Discovery of Australia* (Perth, 1997).

Vatikiotis, M. R. J., *Indonesian Politics under Suharto* (London, 1993).

Victoria, Queen, *Letters*, series II, ed. G. E. Buckle (London, 1928); series III, ed. G. E. Buckle (London, 1932).

Wagner, G., *Children of the Empire* (London, 1982).

Waiko, J. D., *History of Papua New Guinea* (Oxford, 1993).

Walker, R. B., *Newspaper Press in New South Wales* (Sydney, 1976).

Wallace, L., *Nomads of the 19th Century Queensland Goldfields* (Rockhampton, 2000).

Walsh, J. R., and Munster, G. J. (eds.), *Documents on Australian Defence and Foreign Policy* (Hong Kong, 1980).

Walsh, M., and Yallop, C., *Language and Culture in Aboriginal Australia* (Canberra, 1993).

Walsh, P., *Confessions of a Failed Finance Minister* (Milsons Point, 1995).

Walter, J., *The Leader: A Political Biography of Gough Whitlam* (St Lucia, 1980).

—— *Minister's Minders* (Oxford, 1986).

—— *Australian Nation* (Oxford, 1989).

—— *Tunnel Vision* (St Leonards, 1996).

Walton, P., *A Celebration of Empire: A Centenary Souvenir of the Diamond Jubilee of Queen Victoria 1897–1997* (Staplehurst, 1997).

Warburton, E., *Old Stradbroke* (Adelaide, 1976).

—— *Martindale Hall* (Adelaide, 1979).

—— *Speaking of the Past* (Adelaide, 1986).

—— *For Love of the Arts* (Adelaide, 1992).

Warburton, P. E., *Journey Across the Western Interior of Australia* (London, 1875).

Ward, J. M., *British Policy in the South Pacific 1786–1893* (Sydney, 1948).

—— *Earl Grey and the Australian Colonies* (Carlton, 1958).

—— *Australia's First Governor-General* (Sydney, 1963).

—— *Colonial Self-Government* (London, 1976).

—— *James Macarthur* (Sydney, 1981).

—— *The State and the People* (Sydney, 2001).

Ward, R., *Australian Legend* (Melbourne, 1966).

—— *Concise History of Australia* (Brisbane, 1992).

—— *A Nation for a Continent: The History of Australia 1901–1975* (Richmond, 1988).

Ward, S., *Australia and the British Embrace* (Melbourne, 2001).

Warhurst, J. (ed.), *Keeping the Bastards Honest* (St Leonards, 1997).

Warren, A., *Singapore* (London, 2002).

Waters, C., *The Empire Fractures* (Melbourne, 1995).

Waterstone, D. B., *Personality, Profit and Politics* (St Lucia, 1984).

Watt, A. S., *Evolution of Australian Foreign Policy* (Cambridge, 1968).

—— *Vietnam* (Melbourne, 1968).

Way, W. (ed.), *Australia and the Indonesian Incorporation of Portuguese Timor* (Carlton, 2000).

Webb, S., *Palaeopathology of Aboriginal Australians* (Cambridge, 1995).

Webster, E. M., *Whirlwinds on the Plains* (Melbourne, 1980).

—— *An Explorer at Rest* (Melbourne, 1986).

Webster, M. S., *J. McD. Stuart* (Carlton, 1958).

Weidenhofer, M., *Port Arthur* (Melbourne, 1981).

Weller, P. M., *Caucus Minutes*, 3 vols. (Carlton, 1975).

—— *Malcolm Fraser Prime Minister* (Ringwood, 1989).

—— and Lloyd, B., *Federal Executive Minutes 1915–55* (Melbourne, 1978).

Wells, T. E., *Michael Howe* (Hobart, 1818).

Wells, W. H., *Geographical Dictionary of the Australian Colonies* (Sydney, 1970 [1848]).

Welsh, F., *A History of Hong Kong* (London, 1994).

—— *A History of South Africa* (London, 1999).

—— *Four Nations* (London, 2002).

Welsh, L. P., *Geordie: Orphan of the Empire* (Perth, 1990).

West, F. J., *Hubert Murray* (Melbourne, 1968).

—— (ed.), *Selected Letters of Hubert Murray* (London, 1970).

West, R., *River of Tears* (London, 1972).

Westgarth, W., *Australia Felix* (Edinburgh, 1848).

Whitaker, A.-M., *Joseph Foveaux* (Sydney, 2000).

White, D. M., *Philosophy of the Australian Liberal Party* (Richmond, Victoria, 1978).

White, R., *Inventing Australia: Images and Identity 1688–1980* (Sydney, 1981).

Whitlam, G., *The Truth of the Matter* (London, 1979).

—— *The Whitlam Government* (Ringwood, 1985).

Wilcox, C., *For Hearths and Homes: Citizen Soldiering in Australia 1854–1945* (St Leonards, 1998)

—— *Australia's Boer War* (Melbourne, 2002)

Wilde, W. H., *Courage and Grace* (Carlton, 1988).

Wilkes, J. (ed.), *New Guinea and Australia* (Sydney, 1958).

Williams, C., *Bradman: An Australian Hero* (London, 1997).

Williams, G., *Voyage of Delusion* (London, 2002).

—— and Frost, A., *Terra Australis to Australia* (Melbourne, 1998).

Wiltshire, K., *Tenterfield Revisited* (St Lucia, 1991).

Winchester, S., *The Pacific* (London, 1991).

Windschuttle, K., *Fabrication of Aboriginal History* (Sydney, 2002).

Winter, D., *25 April 1915: Inevitable Tragedy* (Brisbane, 1994).

Winter, G. (ed.), *Tasmanian Insights* (Hobart, 1992).

Winterton, G., *Monarchy and Republic* (Melbourne, 1986).

—— *Parliament: The Executive and the Governor General* (Carlton, 1998).

Wiseman, J., *Global Nation?* (Cambridge, 1998).

Wood, G. A., *Discovery of Australia* (Melbourne 1969/1980).

Woodward, L., *British Foreign Policy in the Second World War*, 2 vols. (London, 1970).

Wynd, I., *Pentonvillains* (Geelong, 1996).

Yarwood, A. T., *Samuel Marsden: The Great Survivor* (Carlton, 1977).

Young, D., *Making Crime Pay: The Evolution of Convict Tourism* (Sandy Bay, 1996).

Yule, H., *Book of Ser Marco Polo*, 2 vols. (London, 1903).

Yunupingu, G. (ed.), *Our Land is Our Life* (St Lucia, 1997).

Index

Grey, Jeffrey 422, 423, 435
Griffin, Walter Burley, architect
  415–16
Griffith, Sir Samuel, Premier of Qld
  256, 289, 291, 294, 336; and draft
  federal constitution 291, 302, 320,
  328, 515–16
Griffiths, Alan 554
Grimstone, Mary Leman 113
Gromyko, Andrei 494
Groom, Littleton, Attorney General
  345
Grose, Major Francis 42, 53–5, 56,
  105
Grueber, Captain 255–6
Guardian, HMS, Second Fleet 46
Guildford, WA, schools 138
Guilfoyle, Dame Margaret 349
Gulden Zeepard 6
Gulf War (1991) Operation Desert
  Storm 543
Gullett, Sir Henry 412, 427
Gurry, Meg 569

Hackett, Sir John Winthrop 290–91
Hahndorf, SA 145
Haig, Earl 377
Haines, William, Premier of Victoria
  224–5
Hall, Ben 311
Hall, Edward 88, 93, 148
Hall, Ken 405
Hall, Steele 498
Hampton, Dr John 173, 232
Hand, Gerry 553
Hankey, Sir Maurice 380
Hanlon, Ned, Premier of Qld 441
Hanson, Fred 505
Hanson, Pauline 349, 567; One
  Nation Party 546, 557–8, 562
Hanway, Jonas 30
Harcourt, Lewis, Colonial Secretary
  371

Harding, Warren Gamaliel 384, 386
Hardy, Thomas 316
Hare, Inspector, Victoria police 273
hares, imported 245
Hargrave, Edward 203
Harington, General Sir Charles 386
Harradine, Brian, Independent
  Senator 562, 565
Harriman, Averell, US Under-
  Secretary 471
Harrison, H. C. A. 319
Harrison, John 11
Harrold, Father 67
Hartog, Captain Dirck 6, 10
Harvester company 346, 354
Hashemy, 'exile' ship 172
Hasluck, Paul 427, 462, 484–5, 494;
  and Aborigines 491–2, 559; as
  Governor General 512–13, 515,
  517; as Minister for External Affairs
  473, 477, 478–9, 480; as Minister
  for Territories 526, 527
Hawaii, annexed by USA 275
Hawdon, Joseph 144
Hawes, Ben 193
Hawke, Bob, Prime Minister 353,
  402, 507, 531–9, 542; relations
  with Keating 534, 535–6, 537–8;
  US view of 543–4
Hawkesbury River 55–6
Hay, R. W. 90
Hayden, Bill 503, 531, 534, 544
Haydock, Mary 113–14
Hayes, Sir Henry Brown 50, 52, 55
Hayes, John 64
health: physical development 314, *see
  also* disease
healthcare 439, 463; Medicare
  insurance scheme 503, 522–3
Helpmann, Robert 405
Henderson, Arthur 373
Henderson, Edmund 173
Henrietta Villa 55